Applied Demography Series

Volume 8

Series editor

David A. Swanson

The field of applied demography is largely driven by the quest for the knowledge required by clients, both in public and private sectors, to make good decisions within time and costs constraints. The book series, Applied Demography, provides a forum for illustrating and discussing the use of demographic methods, concepts, and perspectives in a wide range of settings—business, government, education, law, and public policy—as well as the influence of these settings on demographic methods, concepts, and perspectives. The books within the series can be used as resources for practitioners and as materials serving as case studies for pedagogical uses.

More information about this series at http://www.springer.com/series/8838

M. Nazrul Hoque · Beverly Pecotte
Mary A. McGehee
Editors

Applied Demography and Public Health in the 21st Century

Springer

Editors
M. Nazrul Hoque
Hobby Center for Public Policy
University of Houston
Houston, TX
USA

Mary A. McGehee
Health Statistics Branch, Center for Public Health Practice
Arkansas Department of Health
Little Rock, AR
USA

Beverly Pecotte
Institute for Demographic and Socioeconomic Research
University of Texas at San Antonio
San Antonio, TX
USA

ISSN 2352-376X   ISSN 2352-3778 (electronic)
Applied Demography Series
ISBN 978-3-319-43686-9   ISBN 978-3-319-43688-3 (eBook)
DOI 10.1007/978-3-319-43688-3

Library of Congress Control Number: 2016947922

© Springer International Publishing Switzerland 2017
This work is subject to copyright. All rights are reserved by the Publisher, whether the whole or part of the material is concerned, specifically the rights of translation, reprinting, reuse of illustrations, recitation, broadcasting, reproduction on microfilms or in any other physical way, and transmission or information storage and retrieval, electronic adaptation, computer software, or by similar or dissimilar methodology now known or hereafter developed.
The use of general descriptive names, registered names, trademarks, service marks, etc. in this publication does not imply, even in the absence of a specific statement, that such names are exempt from the relevant protective laws and regulations and therefore free for general use.
The publisher, the authors and the editors are safe to assume that the advice and information in this book are believed to be true and accurate at the date of publication. Neither the publisher nor the authors or the editors give a warranty, express or implied, with respect to the material contained herein or for any errors or omissions that may have been made.

Printed on acid-free paper

This Springer imprint is published by Springer Nature
The registered company is Springer International Publishing AG Switzerland

Foreword

We are living in an extraordinary political, economic, social, and demographic context in the twenty-first century United States. And that context is having and will continue to have tremendous implications for the country's health and longevity.

Politically, Donald J. Trump has acquired the necessary support to become the nominee of the Republican Party for the 2016 presidential election. Trump's boastful claims of business success and wealth, disparaging sound bites regarding his rivals, bizarre views on foreign policy, and xenophobic and misogynic comments about racial/ethnic minority groups and women, respectively, have seemingly helped him gain momentum throughout the political primary season and brought him to the precipice of becoming perhaps the most powerful person on the planet. His support seems to be especially strong among US white men. It is truly an extraordinary development that one of the two major political parties in the country is poised to nominate such a candidate for perhaps the most important political position in the world. On the Democratic side, the first-ever African American President of the country Barack Obama is winding down his second term in office while the party is poised to nominate its first-ever woman, Hillary Rodham Clinton, as its candidate for the fall election. Together, the Obama presidency and the Clinton candidacy have helped bring about and signaled a culture of greater inclusiveness in the United States, while their political efforts—particularly on the domestic front—have focused on increased educational and economic opportunities and greater access to health care for the American public, particularly among those who have long been marginalized.

Economically, the country is still emerging from the Great Recession of the late 2000s. The economy remains fragile, but is recovering. At the same time, income and wealth inequality continue to grow and have reached staggering levels when compared to the 1950s and 1960s. Such inequality has resulted in far too many adults and children living in precarious contexts on a day-to-day basis. As any student of social science can attest to (either by using the best possible data or simply by driving around any American city, town, or rural area), the country is characterized by a lot of "haves" and even more "have nots." Due to the long-term social and economic policy decisions the country has made, markers of inequality are rampant and show few signs of abatement.

Socially, the United States is far more educated, more religiously diverse while less religious, more environmentally conscious, and far more technologically and bureaucratically complex than it ever has been. Some of these social changes are undoubtedly great; for example, communicating with my two kids who live in faraway places is possible (and relatively easy) on a daily basis! And despite many examples to the contrary, I think we are generally far more religiously tolerant, accepting of people different than we are, and knowledgeable about national and international affairs than we have ever been. Social change may be challenging and sometimes difficult. But our increasing level of education is also giving us the tools to adapt to such change. On the other hand, those without an adequate level of education are really struggling in modern society.

Demographically, the United States is a far more diverse, interesting, and dynamic country than ever before. Since the mid-1960s, immigration has particularly fueled the growth of the Latino and Asian American subpopulations; in the 1990s and 2000s, immigration from Africa and the Middle East also brought new talent, cultures, and energy to the country. While diversifying, the country is also aging. Indeed, the US has a rapidly growing senior population that is much less racially diverse than the younger population and is economically better off than the youngest segment of the population; at the same time, the growing elderly segment of the population faces clear health, economic, and social challenges associated with aging in a rapidly changing, technologically complex world.

Why do I raise these extraordinary political, economic, social, and demographic contexts in the Foreword of this book? In the process of dedicating my career to the better understanding of health and mortality patterns and trends in the United States (predominantly) and other countries (to a lesser degree), I have become increasingly convinced that such patterns and trends are inextricably tied to the larger political, economic, social, and demographic forces that are unfolding in society—whether those forces are happening in the US, Mexico, Canada, or anywhere. At the individual level, health and longevity are not simply biologically determined. Individuals do not just get dealt good or bad genes and live long/short or healthy/unhealthy lives accordingly. Moreover, societies do not simply have relatively good or poor health profiles because they have populations who are born to be healthy/unhealthy or to live long/short lives. Clearly, political decisions, economic factors, social changes, and demographic transformations matter in profound ways for the health and longevity patterns of societies.

The beauty of this book is twofold. First, the editors have assembled a fabulous group of scholars who understand that health patterns and trends in the modern world are fundamentally linked to political decisions, economic factors, social changes, and demographic transformations that are unfolding in US society and around the world. The examination of public health patterns and trends must be informed by students of political science, economics, sociology, and demography and this book does just that. While the authors of the chapters of this book do not necessarily have the political, economic, social, or demographic answers to the patterns and trends they describe, the chapters are written with such contexts in mind and it shows. Second, the editors have also assembled a group of scholars who bring demographic tools to the table in trying to get the facts right. Indeed, demographers have an obsession with getting the facts right. Moreover, in my humble opinion, accurate description is the foundation of good science. Thus, for example, Richard Thomas's analysis in Chap. 2 aims to accurately describe the changing health profile of Americans while Sally Curtin and Donna Hoyert bring the best data and methods to bear in Chap. 7 to best understand racial and ethnic disparities in US maternal morbidity and mortality. The accurate descriptions that the authors of these chapters offer are not necessarily good news; but they are believable descriptions because they are based on the best available data and the best tools that demography offers.

I was honored when M. Nazrul Hoque, on behalf of the editorial team, asked me to write this Foreword. I first met Nazrul about 25 years ago at a meeting of the Southern Demographic Association and his work has always exemplified how demographic tools can be used to carefully describe and help explain social phenomena, including health and longevity patterns and trends. Nazrul and his editorial colleagues have brought together an outstanding group of scholars to examine health patterns and trends in the United States and around the world. And in doing so, the book will help all of its readers understand that health and longevity patterns and trends are tied to crucial political, economic, social, and demographic contexts unfolding in our world. As someone who cares deeply about our nation's and world's health and longevity patterns, I hope that our future political, economic, social, and demographic contexts will help facilitate, and not deteriorate, the health and longevity of the US and countries all over the world.

Robert A. Hummer
Department of Sociology, Carolina Population Center
University of North Carolina
Chapel Hill
NC, USA

Acknowledgments

This book is the product of more than 2 years of collaborative effort involving the authors, reviewers, and editors of the book. This collaboration was led by Dr. M. Nazrul Hoque, the lead editor of the book. The completion of this book would not have been possible without the help of a number of individuals, and the editors would like to acknowledge their help.

We would like to thank the authors of the individual chapters for submitting their work for publication in *Applied Demography and Public Health in the 21st Century*. All the chapters are peer-reviewed. We would like to thank the reviewers for their timely reviews and comments for the authors, which helped to improve the individual chapters in this volume. Our appreciation is also extended to the authors for their timely response to our requests for revisions.

We would like to thank Dr. Jim Granato, Director of the Hobby Center for Public Policy at the University of Houston, for his support of this book. We especially appreciate the support of Evelien Bakker and Bernadette Deelen-Mans, the editors of Springer, and their staff, as well as the staff members at the production office. This work would not have been possible without the help of Evelien and Bernadette.

We thank Robert Hummer for contributing the foreword for the book. He is one of the most respected experts in the field of health and mortality disparities by race/ethnicity/nativity and socioeconomic status in the United States. We are thankful for his insightful words.

Finally, we would like to thank our respective family members for their unending support and encouragement throughout their work. We hope that this book would be helpful for further research in the field of applied demography and public health.

Contents

1 Introduction 1
  M. Nazrul Hoque, Beverly Pecotte and Mary A. McGehee

Part I Mortality and Morbidity Trends in Developed Countries

2 Are Americans Getting Sicker? An Analysis of Emerging
  Morbidity Trends 13
  Richard K. Thomas

3 Reproductive Health Policy Variability Among the States
  Over Time: Implications of the Affordable Care Act of 2010
  for Health Researchers 37
  Monica Gaughan and Georgia J. Michlig

4 The Impact of Personality Change on Health Among a Diverse
  Sample of Older Americans: Findings from the Health
  and Retirement Study 51
  Latrica E. Best

5 Does Social Engagement Predict Frailty and Mortality
  in the Older Population? 69
  Yumiko Kamiya and Rose Anne Kenny

6 Predictors of Exceptional Longevity: Gender Differences
  in Effects of Early-Life and Midlife Conditions 81
  Leonid A. Gavrilov and Natalia S. Gavrilova

7 Maternal Morbidity and Mortality: Exploring Racial/Ethnic
  Differences Using New Data from Birth and Death Certificates . . . 95
  Sally C. Curtin and Donna L. Hoyert

8 Racial and Ethnic Disparities in Infant Mortality, 1990–2004:
  Low Birth Weight, Maternal Complications and Other Causes 115
  Ginny Garcia and Hyeyoung Woo

9   Black-White Mortality Differentials at Old-Age: New Evidence
    from the National Longitudinal Mortality Study*............... 141
    Duygu Başaran Şahin and Frank W. Heiland

10 Healthcare Utilization as a Source of Health Disparities
    Among U.S. Male Immigrants 163
    Jen'nan Ghazal Read and E. Paige Borelli

11 Activity Limitation Disparities by Sexual Minority Status,
    Gender, and Union Status 183
    Russell Spiker, Corinne Reczek and Hui Liu

12 The Relationship Between Maternal Pre-pregnancy BMI
    and Preschool Obesity... 201
    Susan L. Averett and Erin K. Fletcher

13 Prevalence and Elimination of Childhood Lead Poisoning
    in Illinois, 1996–2012... 221
    Frida D. Fokum, Mohammed Shahidullah, Emile Jorgensen
    and Helen Binns

14 A Demographic Analysis of Healthcare Satisfaction and
    Utilization Among Children from Same-Sex Households 237
    Zelma Tuthill

Part II Mortality and Morbidity in Developing Countries

15 Implications of Age Structural Transition and Longevity
    Improvement on Healthcare Spending in India 251
    Preeti Dhillon and Laishram Ladusingh

16 Impact of Scale-up of Maternal and Delivery Care
    on Reductions in Neonatal Mortality in USAID MCH
    Priority Countries, 2000–2010 269
    Rebecca Winter, Thomas Pullum, Lia Florey and Steve Hodgins

17 HIV/AIDS: A Survey of Beliefs, Attitudes, and Behavior
    in Post War Liberia 307
    Komanduri S. Murty

18 Effects of Childhood and Current Socioeconomic Status on
    Health of Older Adults in India, China, Ghana, Mexico,
    Russia and South Africa: An Analysis of WHO-SAGE Data...... 329
    Y. Selvamani, P. Arokiasamy and Uttamacharya

19 Effects of Selected Socio-Demographic Variables on Fertility
    Among Diabetic Patients in Bangladesh 349
    Md. Obaidur Rahman, Md. Rafiqul Islam, Clyde McNeil
    and M. Korban Ali

20	**Behavioral or Biological: Taking a Closer Look at the Relationship Between HIV and Fertility** .... Ayesha Mahmud	361
21	**Global Patterns of Multimorbidity: A Comparison of 28 Countries Using the World Health Surveys** .... Sara Afshar, Paul J. Roderick, Paul Kowal, Borislav D. Dimitrov and Allan G. Hill	381
22	**Does Father's Education Make a Difference on Child Mortality? Result from Benin DHS Data Using Conditional Logit Discrete-Time Model** .... Fortuné Sossa, Mira Johri and Thomas LeGrand	403

Index 417

Chapter 1
Introduction

M. Nazrul Hoque, Beverly Pecotte and Mary A. McGehee

Introduction

Applied Demography and Public Health in the 21st Century builds on the strengths, limitations, and recommendations of an earlier book, *Applied Demography and Public Health,* published by Springer (2013). This book is designed to address the research questions detailed by the earlier study. It bridges the gap between theory and research by providing several examples of cutting edge research by distinguished applied demographers and public health specialists. Each chapter provides methods and materials that can be used to conduct further research with the goal of promoting public health issues. It also presents information on a variety of health-related issues from the developed and developing world. This book is intended for public health professionals, health policy makers, social epidemiologists, administrators, researchers, and students in the fields of applied demography and public health who are interested in exploring the potential of ground-breaking research or who want to further develop their existing research techniques. Those who have read the earlier volume will find this collection illuminating as well, and will benefit from the most recent research in the fields of applied demography and public health.

M.N. Hoque (✉)
Hobby Center for Public Policy, University of Houston, Houston, TX, USA
e-mail: mnhoque@uh.edu

B. Pecotte
Institute for Demographic and Socioeconomic Research, University of Texas at San Antonio, San Antonio, TX, USA
e-mail: beverly.pecotte@utsa.edu

M.A. McGehee
Arkansas Department of Health, Health Statistics Branch, Center for Public Health Practice, Little Rock, AR, USA
e-mail: mary.mcgehee@arkansas.gov

© Springer International Publishing Switzerland 2017
M.N. Hoque et al. (eds.), *Applied Demography and Public Health in the 21st Century,* Applied Demography Series 8,
DOI 10.1007/978-3-319-43688-3_1

Overview of the Sections and Chapters

This volume is organized into two parts. The first part (Chaps. 2–14) examines mortality and morbidity trends and differentials by race/ethnicity or gender in developed countries, particularly in the U.S. The second part (Chaps. 15–22) examines mortality and morbidity status and use of mortality data in developing countries.

Part I: Mortality and Morbidity Trends in Developed Countries

The improvement in the health status of the U.S. population during the 20th century is well documented. Over that century, dramatic reductions were recorded for mortality rates (most notably for infant mortality and maternal mortality), life expectancy markedly increased, and many killer diseases were eliminated as health threats. Americans became healthier as a result of higher standards of living, expanded public health functions, and better diets. By the 1980s, however, observers began noting anomalies in the available data that suggested the improved health was moderating and the occasional piece of evidence that the trend was actually being reversed. By the dawn of the 21st century, a growing body of evidence suggested that, in fact, Americans may be getting sicker. It would be a noteworthy development if this adverse trend could be verified. However, a number of factors make it very difficult to determine if a reversal of America's health fortunes are taking place. In Chap. 2, Dr. Thomas addresses the challenges involved in definitively measuring trends in health status, reviews the evidence for declining health status, and considers the possible conclusions that can be drawn. This information will be instrumental in directing future research and informing health policy makers.

In Chap. 3, Drs. Gaughan and Michlig examine the reproductive health policies in the United States which constitute a complicated mix of determinants that vary geographically, politically, economically, and institutionally. The recent Affordable Care Act of 2010 (ACA) included a set of reproductive health policies that increase the complexity of the existing reproductive health policy system. A series of policy briefs have been issued over the past five years that, when taken together as we do here, paint a complicated picture of reproductive health access in the United States. Many scholars have demonstrated the effects of specific policies on diverse reproductive health outcomes, but empirical research on the effects of ACA implementation on reproductive health outcomes is still in its infancy, in large part owing to a lack of suitable data sources. Drs. Gaughan and Michlig compile six state-level indicators of reproductive health access that health researchers can employ to model contextual effects on reproductive health outcomes in the ACA era. They develop this historical and policy overview to assist health researchers in thinking through the policy and analytic complexity that has been introduced by this health care reform. Drs. Gaughan and Michlig present a conceptual framework of state-level policy factors that should be evaluated prior to undertaking research related to ACA implementation at the state level.

Research analyzing racial/ethnic variation in personality from a population-level is limited, yet serves as an important component in researchers' understanding of the links between psychosocial well-being and health outcomes. In Chap. 4, Dr. Best examines racial/ethnic variation in the reports of personality, as measured by the Big Five personality model, in a sample of whites, blacks and Hispanics, ages 50 and older using data from the 2006 to 2010 waves of the Health and Retirement Study. Dr. Best also evaluates changes in the mean score of personality traits by race/ethnicity between 2006 and 2010. Personality at the trait level and the change in the mean score of personality are used as predictors of hypertension in 2010. Results show that variation exists on mean personality scores, with Hispanics having higher scores on neuroticism and lower scores on openness to experience. Whites score higher on conscientiousness than both blacks and Hispanics. Small mean changes are evident in the sample, with extraversion showing a slight decline over time in all groups. Neuroticism, conscientiousness, and agreeableness are associated with the prevalence and management of hypertension. Blacks have higher rates of prevalence, yet lower rates of undiagnosed hypertension, a finding which remains significant after accounting for socio-demographic and personality related characteristics.

Several studies have shown that social engagement is associated with health outcomes, but its relationship with frailty has been less explored. In Chap. 5, Drs. Kamiya and Kenny explore the relationship between social engagement (namely, social participation, social ties, marital status, and emotional support), and frailty and their relationship to mortality. Two hypotheses are tested. The first addresses whether social engagement and frailty are independently associated with mortality. The second hypothesis looks at whether frailty mediates the relationship between social engagement and mortality. Drs. Kamiya and Kenny analyzed data from the English Longitudinal Study on Ageing (ELSA) for their research. They divided the respondents into three groups: not frail, pre-frail and frail. Multinomial logit model (MNL) was used to assess the independent contribution of baseline social engagement in predicting frailty at wave 2, adjusting for baseline demographic characteristics, health behavior, disability, cognitive function and co-morbid conditions. Drs. Kamiya and Kenny used Cox proportional hazards models to assess the independent contribution of baseline social engagement and frailty at wave 2 in predicting incidence of death. Results of the MNL model suggest that baseline emotional support lowers the risk of becoming pre-frail for those who are not frail. However, once individuals become pre-frail, emotional support is not protective against frailty. Social ties, social participation and marital status are not significantly associated with frailty. They concluded that social engagement is not directly associated with mortality and frailty might mediate the relationship between social engagement and mortality.

Knowledge of strong longevity predictors is important for improving population health. In Chap. 6, Drs. Gavrilov and Gavrilova compared over 700 American centenarians born in 1890–1891 with their short-lived peers (living 65 years) born in the same time period. The records are taken from computerized family histories, which were then validated and linked to 1900 and 1930 U.S. censuses. Parental longevity was the only common longevity predictor for both men and women. Some early-life characteristics (birth in North East region and birth in the second half of year) turned out to be significant predictors of exceptional longevity for men but not women. Drs. Gavrilov and Gavrilova found strong positive effect of farmer occupation at middle age on exceptional longevity for men. Only two factors were related to exceptional longevity of women: parental longevity and availability of radio in household in 1930. Their study suggests that men are more sensitive to the effects of early-life conditions on longevity.

Persistent racial/ethnic disparities in maternal morbidity and mortality in the United States have been documented and are complex and multifaceted. Furthering the understanding of the origins of these differences is a public health priority. In Chap. 7, Drs. Curtin and Hoyert explores racial/ethnic differences in maternal morbidity (maternal transfusion, ruptured uterus, unplanned hysterectomy, and ICU admission) using new data from birth certificates for 47 states and the District of Columbia that have adopted the 2003 U.S. Standard Certificate of Live Birth. Racial/ethnic differences in maternal mortality are examined using new data from death certificates on the three periods of maternal death relative to the pregnancy–pregnant at the time of death, died within 42 days of an ended pregnancy, or died 43 days to 1 year after an ended pregnancy. Data for the 39 states and the District of Columbia that have adopted the 2003 U.S. Standard Certificate of Death were used to analyze differences in maternal mortality. Dr. Curtin estimated maternal morbidity and mortality rates (per 100,000 live births) for non-Hispanic white, non-Hispanic black, non-Hispanic Asian, and Hispanic women. According to Dr. Curtin, racial/ethnic differences were evident for all four morbidities and in all three periods of maternal mortality but were larger for maternal mortality than morbidity. Non-Hispanic black women had among the highest rates for both morbidity and mortality, whereas Hispanic women had among the lowest rates for mortality. These new data will be an important resource for further research in tracking trends and differentials in maternal morbidity and mortality.

Demographers have long been interested in understanding persistent racial and ethnic gaps in infant mortality, which are likely a reflection of disproportionately distributed resources across groups. In Chap. 8, Drs. Garcia and Woo uses micro-level cohort linked birth-death files from the National Center for Health Statistics (NCHS) for the years 1990, 2000, and 2004 to examine race- and ethnicity-specific trends in the risk of infant death due to low birthweight, maternal complications, and other causes over time. Dr. Garcia further investigates whether or not a survival advantage by gestational age and birthweight varies across racial and ethnic groups. Findings of this chapter suggest that the risk of death has increased for non-Hispanic black infants, and that the beneficial effect of Hispanic ethnicity is reduced over time. Findings also suggest that both race and ethnicity interact with preterm and/or low birthweight delivery to magnify risk of death due to several causes in later years. Overall, this research confirms the presence of an increasing black-white infant mortality gap, lends support to findings of a survival disadvantage in Black infants, and calls attention to a survival disadvantage in Hispanic infants. Additional attention to the mechanisms that generate magnified risk of infant death among racial and ethnic minorities who experience compromised births, i.e. preterm or low birthweight, is needed.

In Chap. 9, Drs. Sahin and Heiland investigated the old-age mortality experience by race and sex of selected cohorts born between 1898 and 1913. Using large samples from the 2013 release of the National Longitudinal Mortality Survey (NLMS) and single-year age and cohort grouping, they provided new evidence on the black advantage in old-age survival. Findings of their study suggest that non-Hispanic blacks born in 1908 have greater survival probabilities between ages 75 and 85 than non-Hispanic whites. Similarly, blacks born in 1898 have greater survival probabilities between ages 85 and 95. In the 1903 birth cohort, blacks have a survival advantage from age 80 to 85 but not from age 85 to 90. The black advantage is generally more pronounced for men. Overall, the evidence points to a mortality crossover around age 80. This chapter would be very helpful for future research on cohort and gender specific analysis of black/white mortality differences.

Healthcare utilization has important implications for immigrant health. However, the concept of "utilization" remains under-conceptualized, particularly as it relates to men's health. In Chap. 10, Drs. Read and Borelli uses nationally-representative data from the 2003 New Immigrant Survey (NIS) to compare utilization behaviors and health outcomes among male immigrants (n = 3901), focusing on those from Mexico, India, and China. Dr. Read's findings suggest that Indian males are more likely than their Mexican and Chinese counterparts to interact with the healthcare system and to report good health, findings largely explained by their privileged social position and access to care. Mexican and Chinese males are hindered by their lack of English language proficiency and are more likely to rate their health as poor. In contrast to the results for self-rated health, they find no significant difference in the likelihood of being diagnosed with a medical condition across national-origin groups. These similarities and differences have research and policy implications, which we discuss in the conclusion.

In Chap. 11, Drs. Spiker, Reczek, and Liu examined whether sexual minorities have greater risk of activity limitations than the straight population and whether the association between activity limitations and sexual minority status differs by gender and union status before and after controlling for key health variables of body mass index (BMI) and psychological distress. They used nationally representative data from the 2013–2014 National Health Interview Surveys. Results of their study suggest that sexual minority status is associated with activity limitations risk, with important differences by union status and gender. Gay single men's heightened risk relative to straight married men is explained by psychological distress and BMI, while lesbian/gay single women experience no heightened risk relative to straight married women. Straight cohabiting and partnered gay men do not differ from straight married men regarding risk, while lesbian/gay partnered women experience heightened risk relative to straight married women even after controlling for psychological distress and BMI. Lesbian/gay previously married women do not differ from the straight married of either gender. Their findings suggest that activity limitations risk varies across the intersections of sexual minority status with union status and gender. Drs. Spike et al. identify several groups within sexual minorities that are at greatest risk of health disparity, demonstrating that sexual minority health is not a monolith.

The increasing prevalence of obesity during pregnancy raises concerns over the intergenerational transmission of obesity and its potential to exacerbate the current obesity epidemic. The fetal origins hypothesis posits that the intrauterine environment might have lasting effects on children's outcomes. A large literature establishes that the mother's pre-pregnancy obesity is correlated with obesity in her children. However, previous research is largely based on comparing individuals across families and, hence, cannot control for unobservable factors associated with both maternal and child obesity. In Chap. 12, Drs. Alvertt and Fletcher used both within-family comparisons and an instrumental variable approach on a sample of 4435 children to identify the effect of maternal pre-pregnancy obesity on obesity in preschool-aged children. Consistent with extant research, OLS models that rely on across-family comparisons indicate a significant correlation between maternal pre-pregnancy obesity and preschool obesity. However, maternal fixed effects render those associations insignificant. Instrumenting for mother's BMI with her sisters' BMI values confirms the null result indicating that the in utero transmission of obesity is likely not driving the increase in childhood obesity.

Lead is neurotoxic and particularly harmful to the developing nervous system of young children. Lead exposure can affect a child's ability to think, learn, or behave. Illinois ranks second nationally in number and percentage of lead poisoned children in the U.S. In Chap. 13, Drs. Fokum et al. analyzed the child blood lead data reported to the Illinois Department of Public Health (IDPH) over the period 1996 to 2012. The findings of their study suggests that sustained efforts in Illinois to identify lead-exposed children and sources of exposure, and enforced remediation or control of lead hazard sources have resulted in a 93% reduction in the number of children tested with blood lead levels of 10 µg/dL or greater.

According to a report by the Williams Institute, an estimated 3 million LGBT Americans have had a child and as many as 6 million American children and adults have an LGBT parent (Gates 2013). These children and their parents face various obstacles in obtaining adequate healthcare due to federal and state family policies that dictate what types of families are legally recognized. In Chap. 14, Dr. Tuthill analyzed secondary data from the 2011 Medical Expenditure Panel Survey Household Component (MEPS HC) on the reported health care satisfaction and utilization to examine whether there are significant differences between heterosexual and same-sex households. The results reflect minimal differences in the rating of healthcare among same-sex and heterosexual households, with same-sex households reporting higher rates of satisfaction. There appeared a notable difference in the ease of obtaining medical care and the frequency of dental visits among same-sex and heterosexual households. Although further research is needed, this study addresses the lacking data of same-sex family healthcare disparities and needs.

Part II: Mortality and Morbidity in Developing Countries

In Chap. 15, Dhillon and Ladusing link data from the National Sample Survey with healthcare expenditures (HCE) data from the National Account Statistics and projected population from the United Nations to produce health care expenditure costs that predict the possible effects of age composition changes on future healthcare costs in India. Findings reveal that the growth of age-compositional effects on HCE increase from 0.5% in 2005 to 0.8% in 2025 and are expected to remain stable afterwards. However, the age-compositional effect on GDP may drop from 0.6 to 0.4% during the same period. The findings of the study are crucial for evolving a sustainable healthcare support system in view of the impending population ageing in India.

Impressive global gains in under-five mortality between 2000 and 2010 have been accompanied by more modest reductions in neonatal mortality. Of the 18 USAID priority countries for maternal and child health with two Demographic and Health Surveys (DHS) available around the years 2000 and 2010, only six have shown statistically significant reductions in neonatal mortality within the study population of most recent children born in the five years preceding the survey. In Chap. 16, Drs. Winter, Pullum, Florey and Hodgins investigates the extent to which scale-up of maternal and delivery care is associated with reductions in neonatal mortality in the six countries. There is surprisingly little evidence that changes in coverage of measurable indicators of maternal and delivery care contributed to the improvements in neonatal survival. In the three malarious countries with complete mosquito bednet data for both surveys, household ownership of a mosquito bednet stands out as a driver of the observed reductions. This finding highlights the importance of malaria control in the arsenal of maternal and child health interventions. Overall, weak associations between other indicators of maternal and delivery care and neonatal survival were observed. This may be the result of limitations of population-based surveys to measure accurately the protective aspects of the interventions. The weak findings may also point to an issue of quality of care, highlighting the need for newborn survival strategies to emphasize strengthening health systems and improve quality of care alongside efforts to increase use of delivery health services.

In Chap. 17, Dr. Murty analyzes the association between levels of awareness of HIV/AIDS, knowledge of its origins, and knowledge of preventive behaviors and their effect on protective behaviors for safe sex. A survey of 170 Liberians was conducted through a partnership between Rust College in Mississippi, USA and Cuttington University, Liberia. The survey was funded by the United Negro College Fund Special Programs (UNCFSP) in 2006. Data were gathered on respondents' socio-economic characteristics, alcohol use, and sex life; awareness of

HIV/AIDS; knowledge of HIV/AIDS; sources of information about HIV/AIDS; beliefs, attitudes and behavior; opinions related to sexual practices; awareness of condom; and, access to media and acceptance of message on safe sex. Results of analysis suggests that, on the whole, the levels of awareness of HIV/AIDS, knowledge of its origins and knowledge of preventive behaviors appeared to be considerably higher than their level of protective behaviors for safe sex—i.e., their knowledge and awareness did not change significantly their risky behavior. Findings of his study also suggest that there is a critical need for capacity building and implementation of effective HIV/AIDS prevention strategies to overcome negative health related consequences, including dissemination, intervention and evaluation associated with the risk of contracting and spreading HIV/AIDS in Liberia.

Socioeconomic status (SES) has occupied a central stage in predicting the health of the population, even into old age; however, the role of childhood SES remains unclear in developing countries. Using the data of persons aged 50 and above drawn from WHO-SAGE-20070-10 wave 1, Drs. Selvamani, Arokiasamy, and Uttamacharya assess the effect of childhood SES and current SES on subjective health measures in six Low and Middle Income Countries (LMICs) : India, China, Ghana, Mexico, Russia and South Africa in Chap. 18. Parental education is used as the indicator of childhood SES, and household wealth and individual education are used as the measures of current SES. Poor self-rated health (SRH) and limitations in activities of daily living (ADLs) are used as the measure of subjective health. Results show considerable variations across nations in the prevalence of poor health status. The poor SRH was high in Russia and India. Higher socioeconomic status is associated with less poor health and ADL limitations. Further, their results suggest that the mother's education had a significant and independent effect on self-rated health and ADL limitations. Their findings confirm the association of education, wealth and mother's education with subjective health measures, moreover the association with self-rated health stronger than the 1 + ADL limitation. The results reiterate the importance of childhood and current SES on health, thus suggesting the importance of life course intervention to improve the health of the older population in LMICs.

Bangladesh, one of the most densely populated countries in the world, suffers from many population related problems, particularly high fertility. In Chap. 19, Rahman et al. assess fertility levels by selected socio-demographic variables and the impact of these variables on fertility among diabetic patients in Bangladesh. This study uses the multiple classification analysis (MCA) technique to examine the data of 160 female diabetic patients taken from the Rajshahi Diabetes Association, Bangladesh. Results of their study indicate that the numbers of children ever born (CEB) increase with increasing age of mother, duration of marriage and duration of suffering from diabetes, while CEB decrease with increasing household education, age at first marriage, body mass index (BMI) and duration of sleeping. Also, diabetic females 25–34 years of age are more fertile than other ages. It is also identified that the first through tenth strongest influential factors for explaining the variation on CEB are respondent's education, duration of marriage, age, living house, duration of sleeping, blood pressure, current living place, age at first marriage, duration of suffering from diabetics and BMI respectively.

Chapter 20 examines the relationship between HIV infection and fertility among women in eight countries in Sub-Saharan Africa. Dr. Mahmud used the two most recent rounds of the Demographic and Health Surveys data, which links women to their HIV test results, to distinguish between potential mechanisms linking HIV and fertility. HIV positive women had significantly lower fertility. The magnitude of the association between HIV status and fertility was consistent for women over the entire childbearing age and with different years of education. While HIV positive women desired fewer children compared to HIV negative women, the preference for smaller family sizes was not driving the relationship between HIV status and fertility. The relationship between HIV status and fertility held even after controlling for several indicators of risky sexual behavior, suggesting that changes in these indicators were not driving the observed relationship. HIV positive women had significantly lower fertility even after restricting the sample to respondents who had never been tested for HIV prior to the survey, i.e., were presumed to be unaware of their HIV status and, thus, unlikely to be changing their behavior in response to their HIV infection. The results provide evidence for a direct physiological effect of HIV infection on fertility.

Chapter 21, by Afshar et al. compares the prevalence of multimorbidity from 27 Low and Middle Income Countries (LMICs) and 1 High Income Country (HIC) by age, sex, socio-economic status (SES), and regions. Results of her research suggest that multimorbidity was positively associated with the female sex and with age, although it was common among younger adults in LMICs. A positive but non-linear relationship was found between country GDP and multimorbidity prevalence. Multimorbidity was inversely associated with SES in countries with the highest GDP; this gradient was flatter, and sometimes reversed, in countries with lower GDP. Higher SES was significantly associated with a decreased risk of multimorbidity in the all-region analyses. Multimorbidity is a global phenomenon not just affecting older adults in HICs. Policy makers worldwide need to address this combination of chronic diseases in the individual—which is contributing to health inequalities—and to support the complex health care service needs of a growing multimorbid population. This chapter would be very helpful for public health policy makers.

For various reasons, parents' education is thought to contribute to their children's health and survival. Evidence from most studies in developing countries suggests that the mother's education is more strongly associated with child mortality than the father's education. In Chap. 22, Dr. Sossa et al. examine the effect of the father's education on child mortality by taking into account the mother's education and explores whether there is an alteration of this effect when community-level factors are controlled. Using a standard logit discrete-time model and a conditional logit discrete-time model which controls for community-level factors on data from the demographic and health survey of 2006 in Benin, Dr. Sossa et al. found that children with both an educated father and mother have a low probability of dying before age five compared to children with uneducated parents.

However, the advantage of child survival with educated parents has disappeared in urban areas, while it remains strongly significant in rural areas, suggesting that characteristics of the community of residence are not to be ignored in this relation. This chapter would be helpful to researchers interested in analyzing the effects of community on health.

Public health research is and will remain a critical issue in both developed and developing countries for years to come. The applied demographic research techniques illustrated in this volume provide valuable insight into diverse questions related to both morbidity and mortality concerns. Each of the contributing authors have provided insight into specific issues and demonstrate methods applicable beyond their own research.

An ongoing problem for investigators is the lack of quality data sources which include the variables needed to thoroughly investigate heath related topics. As demonstrated by the included research, insight can still be gained by creative use of surveys and administrative data collected for other purposes. Contributing authors have shown that the analysis of data for a limited number of states can prove valuable and focus on a single gender or household type can inform health care policy. However, the research limitations discussed by contributing authors include the lack of data for larger populations, scarcity of characteristic details for subjects, limitations of time series data and inconsistencies in data from different sources. These chapters demonstrate the need for better detail in data collection including specific variables for demographic, social, economic, environmental and even political policy differentials. In addition to informing future research in health care policies, we hope to direct attention to the need of better data collection by health care providers, public agencies, and funding for additional surveys to assist in future research.

References

Gates, G. J. (2013). *LGBT parenting in the United States*. The William Institue, University of California Los Angels (UCLA).

Hoque, N., McGehee, M., & Bradshaw, B. (Eds.). (2013). *Applied demography and public health*. Springer: Netherlands.

Part I
Mortality and Morbidity Trends in Developed Countries

Chapter 2
Are Americans Getting Sicker? An Analysis of Emerging Morbidity Trends

Richard K. Thomas

Background: A Century of Health Status Improvement

One of the undisputed trends over the past century has been the steady improvement in the health status of the U.S. population. Using the year 1900 as a convenient starting point, it is possible based on a variety of indicators to trace a continuous decline in mortality, an increase in life expectancy, the reduction or elimination of many of the major killers at the beginning of the 20th century, and an overall improvement in health status based on both objective and subjective measures. Over the course of the century, it is agreed, Americans became bigger, stronger and generally healthier.

This improvement in the health status of the U.S. population can be confirmed by a number of indicators. A basic measure of health status (although somewhat of a proxy) is mortality rates. At the beginning of the 20th century, the crude mortality rate was over 17 deaths per 1000 population. By the end of the century it had dropped to less than 8 per 1000. The age-adjusted death rate was over 25 per 1000 in 1900, dropping to less than 8 by 2000 (Martin et al. 2002) (see Fig. 2.1). During the early years of the century both crude and age-adjusted death rates dropped by as much as 10 % per year.

Even more dramatic reductions were recorded for infant mortality, with the 1900 rate of around 80 infant deaths per 1000 live births dropping to around 10 per 1000 by 2000. A similar pattern was recorded for maternal mortality, with the rate declining from 80 deaths per 10,000 live births to around 2 per 10,000 over the

---

R.K. Thomas (✉)
Department of Sociology and Anthropology, University of Mississippi,
University, Oxford, MS 38677, USA
e-mail: richardkthomas@att.net

© Springer International Publishing Switzerland 2017
M.N. Hoque et al. (eds.), *Applied Demography and Public Health in the 21st Century*, Applied Demography Series 8,
DOI 10.1007/978-3-319-43688-3_2

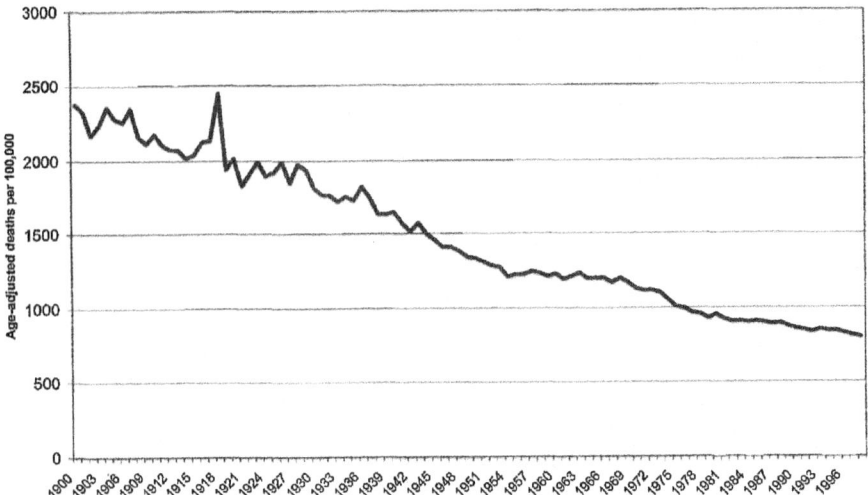

Fig. 2.1 All cause mortality. *Source* United States vital statistics data. *Note* Death rates shown are adjusted to the standard population of the United States in 1940

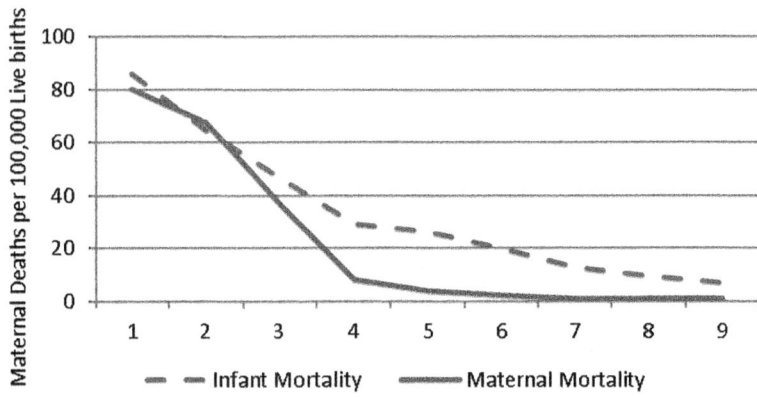

Fig. 2.2 Trends in infant and maternal mortality, U.S.: 1900–2000. *Source* United States vital statistics data

century (see Fig. 2.2). This reduction in mortality rates, particularly infant mortality, resulted in increased longevity, with life expectancy at birth increasing from less than 50 years in 1900 to nearly 80 years in 2000 (see Fig. 2.3).

More directly related to the morbidity of the population is the constellation of diseases that determine the population's health status. During the course of the 20th century, remarkable progress was made in eliminating the diseases that accounted

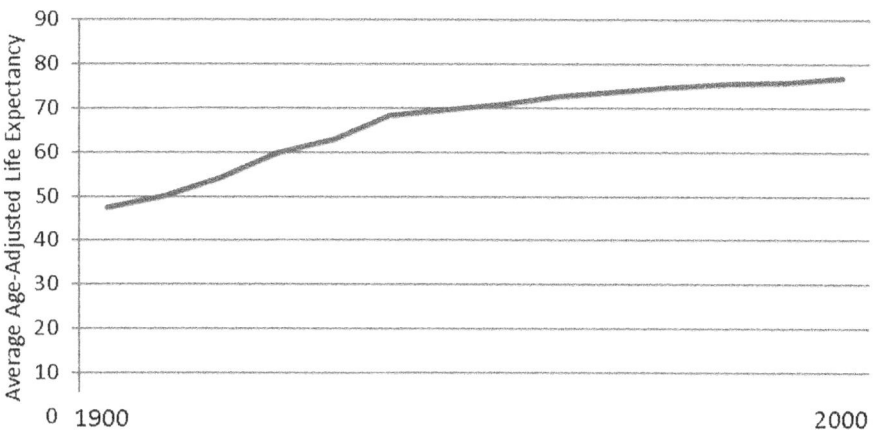

Fig. 2.3 Trends in life expectancy, U.S.: 1900–2000. *Source* United States vital statistics data

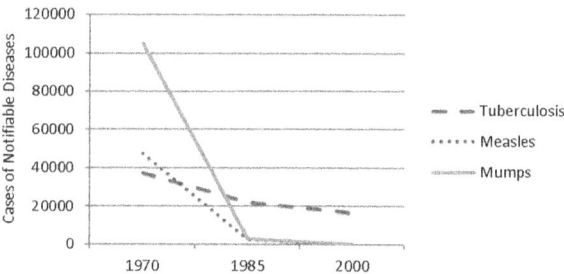

Fig. 2.4 Trends in selected notifiable diseases, U.S.: 1970–2000. *Source* United States vital statistics data

for high rates of both morbidity and mortality. The communicable and infectious diseases ("notifiable diseases" in CDC parlance) that were the scourge of the population at the beginning of the 20th century were reduced in importance if not eliminated by the end of the century. Yellow fever, cholera, malaria and other communicable diseases were virtually eliminated, and everyday conditions that posed serious health threats like mumps, measles and whooping cough were relegated to bit roles in the overall morbidity scheme (Schlipköter and Flahault 2010). The major killers of 1900—like tuberculosis, diphtheria, and diarrhea—were supplanted by heart disease, cancer and stroke during the course of the century (see Fig. 2.4). Although most of the improvement in health status was recorded during the first half of the 20th century, many communicable diseases remained common well into the post-WWII period. It is only in the last quarter of the century that some diseases were effectively eliminated.

Growing Evidence of Declining Health Status

This author's own journey to this point reflects the typical pattern involved in the discovery of a paradigm shift. In compiling statistics on the morbidity characteristics of the U.S. population and developing trend lines for that analysis, the author began to note occasional statistics that did not appear to be in keeping with the notion of steadily improving health status. Some of the figures on chronic disease, for example, from as early as the 1980s and 1990s suggested that the assumed improvement in health status was not consistent across the board. There appeared to be certain conditions for which the prevalence rate was increasing over time rather than decreasing. Given the conditions in question this fragmentary evidence was not necessarily reason for concern; it was well documented that the chronic conditions associated with an aging population were displacing acute conditions as the primary health problems. Indeed, the CDC reports that today chronic diseases are responsible for 70% of the deaths and 75% of the healthcare costs (National Center for Health Statistics 2013). It was entirely possible that, within the context of overall improving health status, one or more specific conditions might be increasing in prevalence.

Other evidence that emerged from statistics from the end of the 20th century suggested that although health status indicators like life expectancy and mortality rates continued to improve, the rate of improvement appeared to be slowing or even leveling off (Crimmins and Beltrán-Sánchez 2011). The declines in both the crude death rate and the age-adjusted death rate had slowed dramatically by the end of the century (Hoyert 2012), and as far back as the early 1990s upticks in mortality were actually being observed (Matthews et al. 1994). Again, this was not a major reason for concern given the dramatic improvement recorded in life expectancy during the 20th century (particularly the first half) and the dramatic reduction in mortality (particularly infant and maternal mortality) during that period. Obviously, the rate of improvement experienced in the early 20th century could not be maintained indefinitely, so the slowing and even leveling off of rates was not totally unexpected. Nevertheless, these trends did raise a red flag, especially since the data for comparable countries indicated continued increases improvement in life expectancy and continued reductions in mortality rates over the same time period (Woolf and Laudan 2013).

What was cause for concern, however, was the fact that, for certain subsets of the U.S. population, the mortality rate was found to be increasing and life expectancy decreasing (Kindig and Cheng 2013). The most adverse trends in morbidity patterns were admittedly limited to a small segment of the population with characteristics detrimental to good health, but the Kindig and Cheng study found declining longevity to be relatively widespread among females. The fact that any segment of the U.S. population was demonstrating negative trends in mortality was worthy of note. While the negative mortality trend noted above could be rationalized away to a certain extent, it was harder to smooth over the increase in maternal mortality reported by Kassenbaum (2014).

In the past it was easy to rationalize increases in prevalence rates for chronic diseases; the epidemiological transition was thought to explain this phenomenon. As the epidemiological transition unfolds, it is argued, the acute conditions characteristic of pre-modern populations are supplanted by the chronic diseases—the "diseases of civilization"—characterizing modern populations. One should expect an increase in the prevalence of chronic conditions as the incidence of acute conditions declines. However, according to Crimmins and Beltrán-Sánchez (2011) the prevalence of disease has actually increased more than would be anticipated in recent years. Some negative indicators related to morbidity can actually be traced as far back as the 1980s but until recently had gone essentially unnoticed, while accompanied by continued high or resurging rates for certain acute conditions. Additional evidence of adverse trends has been identified by others based on statistics from the 1990s (Murray et al. 2013).

Challenges in Assessing Morbidity Trends

The question—are Americans getting sicker?—is much easier to ask than to answer. Our inability to conclusively say whether or not Americans are getting sicker is primarily due to the difficulty in measuring health status with any degree of confidence. There is no easy way to determine the health status of the population, and the sections that follow will review the challenges involved in determining the morbidity level of this or any other population. Each of the challenges will be addressed in turn, after which the available data will be reviewed.

Population Base

The first consideration in assessing the health status of the U.S. population is: what "population"? Normally, for an analysis such as this one would routinely assess the entire population—that is, all Americans. When we say "Americans" to whom are we referring? Ideally, we would want to generate a comprehensive measure—that one number that would take into account all residents of the U.S. However, the U.S. population is obviously large and highly differentiated. In reality, there are no doubt a number of different patterns of morbidity (and morbidity change) affecting different segments of the population at any point in time. Given that fact, does it make sense to look at the total population as the baseline for assessing health status or does that approach mask too much difference? Would we be generating an "average" that may not mean anything? Even if one insisted upon "scoring" the entire population, should temporary U.S. residents be included? U.S. citizens living abroad? If not the entire population, than who?

Perhaps examining the health status of some subset of the population might give a clearer picture. Does it make sense to look at adults (excluding children and the elderly) as the most meaningful population? Or does the health of seniors [which has changed dramatically over time (Robinson 2007; Crescioni et al. 2010)] provide a more meaningful framework? Others may argue for a focus on children because they may be more susceptible to the effects of various etiological factors and certainly represent a foretaste of the future health status of the population. Given the large number of immigrants within the U.S. population, is it reasonable to include them in the mix? Or should the analysis focus on the native-born only? It is well documented that immigrants have different health status from the native born (and, even then, not all in the same way) (Jasso et al. 2004). Does excluding recent immigrants or even all foreign-born residents create a more relevant population for assessing health status?

Measuring Morbidity

Assuming the population base can be agreed upon, a second issue relates to the type of measures to be used to determine the level of morbidity within the population. Unfortunately, there is no one accepted indicator for measuring the level of morbidity (however defined). The closest that we come to a "global" indicator is self-reported health status as collected by the National Center for Health Statistics (NCHS). This subjective measure generates a global estimate of the population's health status on a scale ranging from poor to excellent. While this is useful information, obviously there are issues with self-reports of health status (Kuhn et al. 2006). Despite reservations about the validity of this measure, some—as seen below—have used changes in reported health status as evidence of changing morbidity status (Wilson et al. 2007).

In the past, although less so today, mortality rates have been used as a proxy for morbidity. This indicator does have the advantage of being that one number that presumably reflects the combined impact of various aspects of morbidity. Historically, there was a fairly close correlation between common maladies and common causes of death. The immediate cause of death was typically the primary cause of death, with few complicating factors. Further, mortality data have long been relatively complete and easily attainable. The connection between mortality and morbidity can still be made today to a certain extent, in that the leading causes of death reflect common maladies within the U.S. population (National Center for Health Statistics 2010).

There are, however, two major drawbacks to the use of mortality measures as proxies for health status today. Over time the mortality rate has become a less meaningful proxy for morbidity. In the U.S. the mortality rate has dropped to the point that death is a relatively rare event. Further, the correspondence between mortality and morbidity has become diminished. Because of the preponderance of chronic disease within the U.S. population, data extracted from death certificates may not always indicate the underlying causes. Chronic diseases typically do not kill people, but affected individuals die instead from some complication (of diabetes, AIDS or cancer, for example). This is not to say that mortality analysis cannot provide insights into morbidity patterns, but that the situation is much more complicated than in the past. Contemporary analyses of mortality data require a better understanding of disease processes (and the vagaries of death certificate preparation).

A more objective approach commonly used is to determine the symptoms characterizing a sample of individuals in a population and combine the scores from a symptom checklist into an index that presumably represents the level of morbidity within a population. This information can be obtained either from self-reports—raising again the question of validity—or from on-site physical examinations. This approach has the advantage of gathering data directly from members of the population. However, in addition to the reliance in most cases on subjects' perceptions, this method does not collect data on diseases per se, only symptoms. The only data collection effort that comes anywhere close to generating the data for such an approach is the National Health Interview Survey (NHIS) conducted annually by NCHS. Although data on symptoms is collected the data are not tied to geography and are linked to demographic traits in only a limited sense.

Another objective option would be an aggregate measure of health status based on the combined scores for all morbidity indicators—that is, a morbidity rate based on the combined incidence/prevalence of conditions affecting a population that are deemed to be relevant and, importantly, for which the necessary data are available. Thus, the totality of identified diseases within the population could be combined to determine the level of morbidity. While this approach seems intuitively useful it raises questions about the indicators to be included in the aggregate figure. Calculating the "totality" of disease, of course, is impossibly ambitious and would create an unwieldy measure even if the relevant data were available.

Given the impracticality of generating a total morbidity rate, a fallback approach might be to create an index that combines the rates for conditions that might be thought of as "sentinel" indicators for overall morbidity. Are there certain conditions that could be considered emblematic and particularly reflective of overall health status? If this approach were to be used, the standard calculations for the morbidity rate could be employed—that is, the ratio of diseased (with any disease) to healthy individuals in the population could be calculated. The logistics of this approach require considerable thought. Should this measure include a summation of rates for acute conditions, chronic conditions, reproductive health conditions, or even indicators of disability? How does one determine what conditions should be considered as sentinel?

One other option is to focus on specific diseases or health conditions and track them individually over time. The argument here would be that an individual indicator could be monitored without dealing with the challenges of aggregating indicators. This makes sense from a practical perspective, but raises questions as to the indicator or indicators to be employed. Any approach that attempts to combine rates for a number of diseases raises questions about the relative importance of candidates for inclusion. Given that there are a wide range of indicators that might be examined, do some indicators carry more weight than others? For example, a case could be made for continued improvement in health status based on the dwindling number of "notifiable diseases" that are reported to the CDC. Does the century-long decline in the incidence of diphtheria, measles, mumps and tuberculosis carry as much weight as the increase in the prevalence of heart disease, diabetes and arthritis within the population?

Even if one or several specific conditions might be chosen as indicators to track, another issue surfaces: the fact that definitions of various conditions may change over time or the criteria used may change. The constellation of diseases listed in the International Classification of Diseases (ICD) system is fluid, and conditions are added, deleted and renamed over time. New conditions may be identified (e.g., AIDS, Legionnaire's disease), common syndromes may be reclassified as morbid conditions (e.g., pre-menstrual syndrome, attention deficient disorder, irritable bowel syndrome), and even the disease status of certain conditions may change over time (e.g., homosexuality).

Data Availability

One problem inherent in longitudinal analyses such as this is having access to the necessary data for the time period under study. Certainly in recent years efforts have been made (primarily by the National Center for Health Statistics) to generate data that are comparable year to year to allow for tracking changes over time. Data on mortality can be traced back for decades with relative confidence in the quality of the data. However, morbidity data is not as well documented, and 50 years ago much more emphasis was placed on collecting data on acute conditions than chronic conditions; today, the emphasis has been reversed with data on chronic conditions receiving most of the attention.

Even if there was a central repository and all relevant parties had access to efficient means of reporting morbid cases, the actual recording of cases would still be limited. While the reporting of certain conditions (e.g., HIV/AIDS, tuberculosis) is required by law, there is no mechanism for enforcing these requirements on the hundreds of thousands of healthcare providers and healthcare organizations that might encounter these cases. For certain types of health conditions it is felt that the reporting is fairly complete—that is, most cases are actually reported to the appropriate authorities. However, for the majority of conditions a significant—and often unknown—level of underreporting exists. This means that for many if not most conditions being tracked, there will be inevitable undercounts.

Without a central repository, the researcher must access data wherever it is available. This typically means having to address a variety of issues related to the nature of the data. These include issues of case-finding, coverage, and timeliness, among others.

Case-Finding

Beyond limitations in the reporting of data on morbidity, the usefulness of data on cases that are actually identified is affected by a number of factors. A major consideration is what constitutes a "case" for calculation of morbidity rates. While the medical profession establishes agreed-upon guidelines for when a condition constitutes a case, issues remain with regard to the establishment of a diagnosis. Thresholds for the specification of a disease are established based on the best available evidence supported by professional consensus (although this may be difficult to reach for some conditions). These are not absolute indicators but represent best estimates of when a non-case becomes redefined as a case. Because of their somewhat arbitrary nature, such standards are prone to change over time and sometimes in response to factors other than advances in medical science.

Even if complete agreement could be reached with regard to the definition of a case for each of the thousands of diseases catalogued, measurement issues would still remain. To a certain extent, the diagnosis of disease is as much an art as a science, and this often leads to wide variations in the diagnosis of conditions from one practitioner to another or from one community to another, especially when being tracked over a long period of time (in this case for a century or more). In addition to the fluid nature of thresholds for the identification of some conditions there is also the issue of inaccurate diagnoses. In some cases this may involve a truly egregious misdiagnosis, the type of error that results in adverse events and malpractice suits. A much more common incident, however, relates to tests that yield false positives or false negatives. In the case of the former, the test result indicates the presence of pathology when in fact it is not present; in the case of the latter, the test result fails to detect the presence of pathology when in fact it is present. The point, for our purposes, is that any figures that are used are likely to reflect a certain amount of "slippage" in terms of accuracy of diagnosis (Kistler et al. 2010).

Another confounding factor involves changes in our ability to diagnosis a condition. Clearly, methods of detection are much improved today and the healthcare system is much more aggressive in ferreting out health conditions of various types. Thus, the reported increase in the prevalence of certain types of cancer may reflect better detection rather than an actual change in prevalence. Adjusting prevalence rates to account for improved diagnosis is difficult since it is almost impossible to determine the impact of this development for most conditions.

Coverage

Given the fact that there is no central repository of data on morbidity, the extent of coverage for any indicator is an issue. What we know about the level of sickness and disability is a function of data reported to health authorities (e.g., notifiable disease reporting to the Centers for Disease Control and Prevention) and data collected through national sample surveys (e.g., the National Health Information Survey conducted by the NCHS). The reporting of data on notifiable diseases is mandated but effectively voluntary. This means that the completeness of reporting varies from disease to disease.

The ability to track morbidity trends depends on all cases being counted, yet numerous analyses have demonstrated that the true prevalence of many conditions is much greater than that reported based on the available data. This shortfall in identified cases reflects the facts that: (1) a large number of cases go undiagnosed for certain conditions; (2) conditions may have been diagnosed yet no treatment has been obtained (thereby keeping them out of "official" records); and (3) the lack of a mechanism to assure that all identified cases are counted in determining the level of morbidity.

This situation exists to a greater or lesser extent for any number of health conditions and would apply to, for example, most behavioral health conditions for which underreporting is substantial. While data extracted from "reported cases" drawn from physicians' records is a valuable source of information on morbidity patterns, the data are limited to reported cases.

A related issue is that data may have been collected for certain subgroups within the population at various points in time. This means that, in tracking morbidity patterns over time, we may end up mixing apples and oranges. For example, some morbidity studies focus on seniors, others on children, and still others are restricted to certain segments of the population. Despite the rigor generally displayed by the NCHS, for various reasons the target subjects for data collection may change over time or vary from survey to survey. Thus, for some studies "children" may mean anyone under 19 years of age while in others it may mean anyone under 16. Some studies may carve out an age group (say, children 5–8 years) or limit the subjects to preschoolers for example.

Questionnaire Content

Another challenge is related to the fact that the topics addressed through sample surveys sometimes change over time. For example, information on high cholesterol and body mass has only been collected in recent years and this information is, thus, not available for the distant past. There also may be issues of wording changes or revisions of the measures used. What appears to be a simple wording change can have important implications for the data collected. For example, "Have you ever been told by a physician that you have diabetes?" generates different results from "Have you ever been treated for diabetes?".

Although the NCHS administers surveys to the general population (the National Health Information Survey being the most relevant here), these national surveys are limited in terms of their ability to track the thousands of diseases that would affect a population. NCHS interviewers as a practical matter can only elicit information from respondents for a limited number of diseases, and, to make matters worse, the list for which data are collected is prone to change over time. Changes in the methods of reporting health conditions and, indeed, in the definitions of the conditions themselves are mitigating factors.

Timeframe

Perhaps the most critical issue for an analysis of trends is the fact that certain data are not available for the timeframes under study. Certainly, there is limited morbidity data available for the early decades of the 20th century, before organizations like the CDC and NCHS started systematically collecting morbidity data. Even mortality data cannot be assigned the same level of confidence prior to the institution of universal coverage and standardized forms mid-century. "Hard data" from pre-WWII 20th century are not likely to exist for many health conditions—and certainly not in formats compatible with more recent attempts at data capture.

This situation is further complicated by the fact that various data-collection entities may collect data on a certain health condition for a specified time period and subsequently discontinue data collection on that topic, perhaps to resume data collection years later. After decades of reporting an aggregate rate for acute conditions, the NCHS not only discontinued the calculation of the aggregate rate but ceased collecting data in a manner that would allow others to calculate an aggregate rate going forward. Unfortunately, this situation is likely to be common for health conditions for which no alternative sources of data are available.

Determining Trend Direction

A final issue relates to the question of what constitutes a reversal of the trend. What evidence would cause us to conclude that the health status of the U.S. population is getting worse? Would it have to involve a reversal of past trends—e.g., a decline in life expectancy or an increase in death rates? Would even a slowing of rates of improvement suggest a downturn in health status under certain conditions? Or should we examine changes in the prevalence rates for chronic conditions or some aggregate measure of chronicity and identify patterns where conditions that were in decline in the past are now showing increased prevalence? Should the real test involve a comparison of U.S. morbidity trends with those of similar countries?

The most obvious indicator would be an indisputable decline in measures of health status that represents a reversal of past trends. Thus, if survey research had indicated a steady increase in perceived health status historically, a downturn in average self-reported health status could be thought to represent a reversal. Similarly, a decline in life expectancy might also be considered a reversal of previous trends. If we are using life expectancy as our indicator, do we need to see an overall decline in life expectancy for a reversal of fortunes to be verified, or should we consider a decline in life expectancy for any segment of the population as evidence of a reversal. Similarly, an increase in the death rate—not common but certainly not impossible (see post-Soviet Russia)—may signal a decline in health status.

While documented reversals in certain traits may be considered clear evidence of a reversal in morbidity trends, there may be other considerations. In some cases, a failure to improve or a slowing of rates of improvement for certain conditions may be thought to signal a reversal. Admittedly, there are limits to the extent to which some indicators of health status can improve. Life expectancy cannot be expected to increase indefinitely, for example. The question becomes: To what extent does a leveling off of improvement in life expectancy or any other measure represent a reversal of health status fortunes?

Another approach would involve an observed increase in certain measures of morbidity—an increase in the prevalence of chronic disease or a higher proportion of the population being classified as disabled, for example. An increase in some aggregate measure of chronicity may suggest a decline in health status, depending on the circumstances. Thus, continued or newly identified increases in the prevalence of key chronic conditions might signal a sickening of the population.

Even here, however, first-order relationships may be misleading. For example, an increase in the total prevalence of chronic diseases within the U.S. population would not necessarily indicate declining health status. Given the extent to which the population has aged over the past three decades, one would expect an increase in chronicity. The key is how today's level of chronic disease compares to a demographically standardized population from 20, 50 or 100 years ago.

An even thornier question relates to the interpretation of the continued high incidence of certain acute conditions in the light of the epidemiological transition. Does the re-emergence of long-eliminated communicable diseases by itself indicate a reversal of morbidity trends? The fact that some epidemiologists and public health officials use terms like "shocking" to describe the situation certainly suggests a worsening of health status. Is our failure to fully eradicate certain communicable diseases an indicator of faltering health status? Do the high—and increasing—incidence rates for sexually transmitted infections indicate a disruption of the trend toward improving health status?

One final consideration in adjudging the direction of morbidity trends is the use of comparative data from similar populations. Is it meaningful to compare U.S. morbidity trends to those exhibited by other countries? Given the fluidity of the U.S. healthcare environment and the variety of factors that could influence health status indicators, is the best measure of U.S. health status against some standard—in this case the experiences of similar countries? There could be circumstances in which it appears that an indicator of U.S. health status is improving but, in actuality, the U.S. is improving at a much slower rate than similar countries. Cross-national statistics that indicate that the U.S. population has fallen behind other countries in terms of improvement in life expectancy and reduction of overall mortality, infant mortality and maternal mortality could be interpreted as indicators of declining health status.

Research Plan

At the end of the day, there is no easy solution to the challenge of tracking health status. As is often the case in healthcare, analyses are limited by the data that are available. That is, we have to do the analysis with the data we have rather than the data we would like to have. Using primarily data generated by the National Center for Health Statistics, supplemented by data from a variety of other sources, it is possible to piece together an admittedly fragmented view of recent trends in morbidity. Few of the available data cover the entire century-plus time period, making definitive conclusions concerning long-term trends problematic. Nevertheless, it is possible to draw some tentative conclusions based on the data that are available.

While the initial intent of this analysis was to compare data for the 20th century with data from the years 2000 and beyond, the patterns of morbidity observed required a modification of this approach. Some of the changes being tracked actually started appearing in the 1980s and 1990s. Further, while some developments clearly unfolded 20 or more years ago, some of the changes in trends actually do relate to 2000 or later. This situation tended to further muddy the waters in that not only was the point in time when the reversal began not clear cut but any observed reversals varied from diagnosis to diagnosis in terms of their timeline. While it was appropriate to use pre-2000 and post-2000 figures for some measures, there were cases in which the observed "reversal" occurred in the 1980s or 1990s in which case an earlier cut point was used. For this initial review of the available data the intent was not to analyze the trends identified or to explain the patterns that were observed. Where possible data have been obtained from previously published reports, although in some cases the author compiled raw data and produced the time series. Because of the need to draw data from such disparate sources, as a practical matter not all relevant tables can be included in this paper.

The goal was to highlight statistics drawn from disparate sources that suggest a reversal of the past trend toward improved health status. The data are presented at face value without drawing conclusions with regard to what they say about the changing health status of the U.S. population. While changes—especially those that represent a negative trend—are noted, no attempt is made here to interpret the meaning of these changes. However, many of the figures presented represent actual data rather than data based on a sample, eliminating the any concern over sampling error. Figures that are based on a sample survey (e.g., certain NCHS statistics) should of course be interpreted with caution and no effort was made to test the significance of the observed changes. As noted above, there is no established barometer for determining whether the population is getting sicker or not. It is hoped that the data presented will stimulate more intensive investigation of indicators of morbidity.

The Findings

The following section summarizes the available data on trends in morbidity for the U.S. population. Each indicator or set of indicators has important limitations, and the best that can be hoped for is a fragmentary view of the population's changing morbidity patterns. A discussion of any identified trends in morbidity based on the available evidence from disparate sources will be presented as a conclusion to these findings. An important question to be considered relates to the feasibility of actually assessing whether or not Americans are getting sicker.

Global Indicators

Self-reported health status is essentially the only "global" indicator available for this analysis. Survey respondents were asked to rate their health status on some type of scale, with the most common response categories being "poor," "fair," "good," "very good," and "excellent". Data are available annually for 1997–2013 with additional data available from selected prior years. Based on data collected by the National Center for Health Statistics, self-reported health status for Americans has gradually declined over the past 15 years. The proportion reporting excellent or very good health declined from an age-adjusted 68.5% in 1997 to 61.1% in 2011. The proportion reporting only fair or poor health status increased from an age-adjusted 9.2 to 12.8% between 1997 and 2011 (National Center for Health Statistics 2013). While the youngest age cohort (under 18 years) reported little change (from 2.1 to 2.0%), all other age cohorts except seniors (65 years and older) reported decreases in health status. In contrast, the proportion of seniors reporting fair or poor health status decreased from 26.7 to 24.4%, reinforcing the notion that seniors have in fact experienced improved health status over time [Note that not all surveys have reported declining health status (Salomon et al. 2009)].

The decline in self-reported health status after 1997 indicates a reversal of the previous trend. Throughout the 1980s and into the 1990s self-reported health status steadily improved, only to be followed by a decline for the post-1997 period. This evidence suggesting a leveling off or even a decline in health status among Americans clearly requires further investigation.

Evidence that emerged from statistics from the end of the 20th century suggested that, although health status indicators like life expectancy and mortality rates continued to improve, the rate of improvement appeared to be slowing or even leveling off (Crimmins and Beltrán-Sánchez 2011). Using mortality as a proxy for health status, data collected by the National Center for Health Statistics indicate that overall mortality rates for Americans, while continuing to improve, were improving at a declining rate. Rates of decrease equaling as much as 10% per year for crude birth rates prior to WWII dropped to 0.5% per year for the 1970–2000 period and to 0.2% for the 2000–2010 period. Age-adjusted death rates averaging more than 10%

per year in the pre-war decades dropped to 0.16% per year for the 1970–2000 period and to 0.07% for 2000–2010 (Hoyert 2012).

While a slowing of the improvement in mortality rates was not unexpected, an actual increase in mortality rates was. In nearly half of U.S. counties, female mortality rates actually increased between 1992 and 2006, compared to 3% of counties that saw male mortality increase over the same period (Kindig and Cheng 2013).

The most dramatic improvement in mortality rates, of course, had been for infant mortality, with most of the decline occurring within the first half of the 20th century. As with overall mortality, the rate of improvement slowed notably after WWII. Between 1970 and 2000 the rate per 1000 live births dropped by an average of 0.4 per year. Between 2000 and 2010 the rate of improvement declined to half that or 0.2 per year. The fact that the infant mortality rate continues to improve is encouraging but, as shown below, the rate of improvement has fallen off world standards.

The figures for trends in maternal mortality display perhaps the most disturbing pattern and, in fact, offer some solid evidence of a reversal of health status in recent years. As with other mortality rates, the maternal mortality rate declined rapidly during the first half of the 20th century, with the rate of improvement slowing after WWII up until the 1980s. Death during childbirth in the U.S. it seemed had been relegated, as they say, to the dustpan of history. However, unlike other mortality rates, the trend eventually began to reverse itself, hitting its lowest mark around 1980, stagnating during the 80s and 90s and actually increasing moving into the 21st century. The rate of less than 1.2 maternal deaths per 10,000 live births in the 1980s increased to a modern high of nearly 2.5 deaths per 10,000 live births in 2010. The rate has dropped slightly (to 1.85 in 2013) but the fact that the U.S. is the only developed country for which the maternal mortality rate is increasing is certainly noteworthy (Kassenbaum 2014).

While the negative mortality trends noted above could be rationalized away to a certain extent, it is harder to smooth over the increase in maternal mortality. Admittedly, the numbers are still small but nearly double the rate of 20 years ago. This raises the question of why this is occurring in a system that has "medicalized" childbirth to an extent exceeding any other nation. Despite the micro-management of the childbearing process, all comparable countries continue to report declines in maternal mortality at a time when that for the U.S. in increasing.

While the mortality rates for many conditions have declined in recent years, there are a number of diseases for which death rates have increased over the past decade or so. These include: influenza/pneumonia, diabetes, chronic lower respiratory disease, liver disease and cirrhosis, and pneumonitis (National Center for Health Statistics 2010). While the aging of the population could explain higher rates of death for certain diseases, there is evidence that the rates are still higher when age is held constant.

As noted previously, life expectancy at birth increased from less than 50 years in 1900 to nearly 80 years in 2000. As with other indicators, however, much of the decline was recorded during the first half of the 20th century when life expectancy was increasing by nearly 0.4 years annually. While life expectancy increased nearly as fast between 1970 and 1990 (0.35 years annually), the increase between 1990 and 2006 was only 0.11 years annually. While life expectancy cannot be expected to increase indefinitely, the slowing of the rate of increase is certainly noteworthy.

For some segments of the U.S. population, there is evidence of declining life expectancy—a phenomenon not experienced within demographic memory. Recent mortality data indicates a sharp drop in life expectancy for the least-educated white Americans (Olshansky et al. 2012). The drop is greatest for those without a high school diploma, with poorly educated white women actually "losing" five years of life between 1990 and 2008. White men without a high school diploma saw a three-year decrease in life expectancy over this time period. Thus, the life expectancy for white women without a high school diploma was 73.5 years in 2008 (compared to 83.9 years for women with a college degree) and for white men it was 67.5 years (compared to 80.4 years for those with a college degree). The fact that any segment of the U.S. population was demonstrating negative trends in mortality is worthy of note. Another study found that inequality in women's health outcomes steadily increased between 1985 and 2010, with female life expectancy stagnating or declining in 45% of U.S. counties (Wang et al. 2013). Recent research, thus, suggests that women in some parts of the country are dying younger than they were a generation ago.

Aggregate Indicators

As noted, there is no acceptable aggregate measure of morbidity, although the NCHS has periodically considered the totality of acute conditions and chronic conditions for reporting purposes. The Center no longer compiles an aggregate rate for acute conditions but does present data on the prevalence of multiple chronic conditions. In the United States, almost 125 million persons (45% of the population) have at least one chronic condition, and this proportion has steadily increased over time. The proportion of Americans with a chronic condition was projected to increase from 44.7% in 1995 to 47.0% in 2010 with the proportion expected to continue to increase in subsequent years (Wu and Green 2000). Subsequent studies based on NCHS data have found, for adults 45–46 years, noteworthy increases between 2001 and 2010 in the proportions reporting 2–3 chronic diseases or 4 or more chronic diseases. For adults 65 years or older substantial increases were also reported in the proportions reporting 2–3 chronic diseases or 4 or more chronic diseases (National Center for Health Statistics 2013). What is telling is the fact that contemporary cohorts report higher aggregate rates of chronic diseases than comparable cohorts a generation ago.

The National Longitudinal Survey of Youth (ages 2–8) found the prevalence of any chronic health condition to increase from 12.8% in 1988 to 25.1% in 2000 and then again to 26.6% in 2006. There is growing evidence that American children are experiencing increasing levels of a number of chronic conditions typically attributed to older adults (Halfon and Newacheck 2010).

Another aggregate measure of a sort is the disability rate for the population. Based on data from the National Center for Health Statistics, the proportion of the U.S. population reporting activity limitation increased from 11.8% in 1970 to 28.7% in 2010, although the rate of increase has slowed since the 1990s. The proportion of respondents reporting any disability did increase from 27.0 to 30.3% between 1997 and 2009. It has been suggested that a higher proportion of the U.S. population and a greater absolute number is disabled than at any time in the past. This trend is thought to reflect the facts that a higher proportion of the population is elderly and our ability thanks to medical technology to preserve the lives of many who would have died prematurely in previous generations. This has also meant that a higher proportion of seniors report disabilities than in the past, suggesting that more people are living longer but not necessarily with the same quality of life as their forebears.

Over the last few decades, the rise in the rates of potentially disabling childhood conditions deserves special consideration in the analysis of activity limitation trends in children. During the early 1970s, when the rates of severe limitations grew from 2.7 to 3.7%, Halfon and Newacheck (2010) found increasing rates of several health conditions, especially mental health conditions, asthma, orthopedic conditions, and hearing loss. Unfortunately, changes in the questions as part of the redesign of the National Health Interview Survey in 1997 make comparisons over the entire time period impossible.

Disease-Specific Indicators

In the absence of adequate global or aggregate measures, we are left with an examination of trends in specific diseases. An examination of morbidity trends based on specific diseases requires us to revisit the notifiable diseases noted earlier. Although the effect of the epidemiological transition has been to replace acute conditions with chronic conditions as the predominant health problems, we see that certain acute conditions continue to be reported at high rates and some, in fact, at rates that are unprecedented in the modern age. These include increased rates for a variety of communicable diseases—including Legionnaire's disease, malaria, pertussis, and valley fever (Centers for Disease Control and Prevention 2014) (see Fig. 2.5). Many conditions that are associated with less healthy populations continue to generate a disturbing number of cases annually (e.g., tuberculosis, chicken pox and salmonella). In addition, sexually transmitted infections remain at epidemic levels with a recent resurgence of syphilis noted. While chronic conditions comprise the preponderance of health problems, the persistence exhibited by a number of acute conditions is noteworthy.

Understandably, much of the emphasis is on chronic disease since these types of conditions have become the predominant health threats in contemporary America.

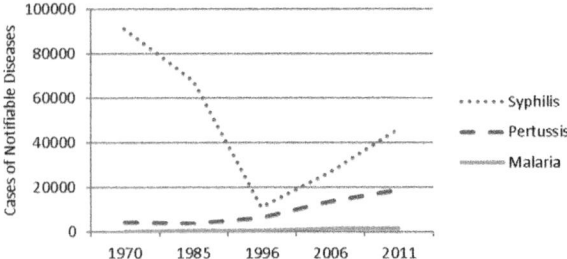

Fig. 2.5 Trends in selected notifiable diseases, United States: 1970–2011. *Source* Centers for disease control and prevention

The rise in the overall prevalence rate for chronic disease was noted above. A more nuanced view is provided when the rates for specific diseases are examined. For adults the prevalence rates for a number of conditions have increased in recent years. These include: high blood pressure (from 25.8% in 1988–1994 to 30.7% in 2007–2009); coronary heart disease from 6.0% in 1997–1999 to 6.4% in 2009–2011); stroke from 2.2% in 1997–1999 to 2.6% in 2009–2011; and cancer (all sites) (from 6.5% in 1997–1999 to 8.0% in 2009–2011) among others (e.g., asthma and depression). A good case in point is diabetes for which the prevalence rate has increased substantially over the past two decades even when aging is taken into consideration. During 2003–2006 more than a quarter of older men (65 + years) suffered from diabetes, up 5 percentage points from the 1994–1998 period. The increase in diabetes prevalence has been even more dramatic for older African-American men, with rates for this group rising three times faster than those for white males. As another example, the prevalence rate for emphysema increased from 14.0 per 1000 in 2000 to 19.8 in 2010. The rate increased for all racial and ethnic groups and rose particularly fast for blacks and other non-white groups, women and older adults. Here is one case where we can examine apples and apples—that is, prevalence rates for the same age groups over time (American Lung Association 2013). For those 45–64 in 2000 the rate was 18.9 per 1000, a figure that increased to 21.2 in 2010 (with a major jump for 2011 [26.6]).

The prevalence rate for stroke has increased dramatically for the U.S. population. The rate per 1000 population increased from 9.8 in 1990 to 15.7 in 2010 (Feigin et al. 2013). Younger Americans are increasingly being affected by stroke, with obesity, diabetes and high blood pressure all contributing to an increase in the number of strokes reported for younger age cohorts. Worldwide, the incidence of stroke increased by a quarter for those 20–64, with similar figures reported for the U.S. population.

Most of the available data point to increasing health status among elderly Americans. However, there are some counter trends to note. The rate of diabetes for both older men and older women increased between 1988–1994 and 2003–2006—from 19.6% of the older male population to 24.4% and 23.0 % for women.

Hypertension rates also increased during this period, from 57.3% for males 65 and older to 64.6% and from 64.5 to 75.3% for women.

In assessing morbidity trends for the U.S. population one further health condition that should be considered is obesity. Obesity rates for men and women 65 and older also increased substantially from 1988–1994 to 2003–2006—for men from 18.9 to 28.7% and for women from 23.2 to 30.6%. The increasing obesity level of the U.S. population is well documented, and this factor by itself could be presented as evidence of declining health status. But the real measure of the impact of obesity on health status is prospective. A wide range of health conditions—some of them potentially fatal—is associated with obesity (National Heart, Lung and Blood Institute 2013). Some of this is already taken into consideration when the health status of adults is analyzed. The prevalence of persons who are overweight and obese, characteristics that have been associated with increased prevalence of and morbidity from type 2 diabetes, hypertension, arthritis, and some cancers, has more than doubled during the last 40 years. The high rate of heart disease reflects the obesity level of the population (among other factors).

Thinking in terms of trends, however, it could be argued that the high rate of obesity among youth is more of a concern than adult obesity since childhood obesity is a harbinger of serious health problems in later life. A study by the Institute of Medicine has described the increasing prevalence of childhood obesity as a "startling setback" for child health (Institute of Medicine 2006). Americans, particularly women, are becoming obese at increasingly early ages (Trust for America's Health 2012). The full impact of the obesity "epidemic" is only likely to be felt within a decade or two.

A major consideration in evaluating the changing health status of the U.S. population is the apparent declining health status of American children (Delaney and Smith 2012). The available data, in fact, suggests sharp increases in the prevalence of most childhood physical and mental health problems. Further, there appears to be a proportionate shift away from acute health conditions to chronic health conditions. From the beginning of the twentieth century to the end of that century, the available data indicate a decline in childhood diseases such as measles and mumps and a subsequent decline in chicken pox by the end of the twentieth century. At the same time, these same data indicate an increase in many other acute and chronic conditions over the course of that century.

Major increases are identified in the incidence or prevalence of asthma, other respiratory illnesses, allergies and depression. In fact, some chronic conditions that were unknown among children in the past (e.g., diabetes, heart disease) are becoming increasingly common and at increasingly younger ages. The National Longitudinal Survey of Youth (ages 2–8) found the prevalence of any chronic health condition to increase from 12.8% in 1988 to 25.1% in 2000 and then again to 26.6% in 2006. Less dramatic but still important increases were noted for speech impediments, heart trouble, headaches/migraines, stomach problems, diabetes, epilepsy, and hypertension. Other research has found that the number of children with asthma has more than doubled since 1980 and with an increase in incidence of nearly 10% between 2001 and 2010 (Akinbami et al. 2012). Research has uncovered increases in levels of autism and ADHD, with a reported increase in the prevalence of ADHD for those 5–17 years from 6.5% in 1998–1999 to 9.6% in 2009–2011 (National Center for Health Statistics 2013). For children under 18 years, an increase in food allergies was reported from 3.4% (1997–1998) to 5.1% (2009–2011) and for skin allergies from 7.4 to 12.5%.

Cross-National Comparisons

Comparing the health status of Americans with that of citizens of other countries is instructive and generally reveals a drop in the health status of Americans relative to those of comparable societies. In terms of overall mortality rates, the U.S. dropped from 24th to 49th (or dead last) among similar countries between 1999 and 2010, a noteworthy decline for barely a decade. This relative decline is being driven by American women—a startling finding considering that white women have historically displayed the best health status of any age-sex category in the U.S. In 2010 American women ranked 41st in life expectancy among the world's countries, down from 14th in 1985. Among developed countries, American woman sank from the middle of the life expectancy range to dead last in 2010 (Hausmann et al. 2012).

In terms of mortality rates, the U.S. rate continued to decline between 1998 and 2010 as did rates for other developed countries but, as illustrated by Fig. 2.6 the rate of decline for the U.S. has slowed relative to that of other countries. In this comparison the U.S. reports a higher overall mortality rate and is the only country that exhibits a leveling off in the rate of decline.

A similar pattern is displayed for infant mortality, with the U.S. dropping off the pace of comparable countries. While the U.S. initially had an advantage in infant mortality over most other countries, that advantage has been eliminated for the most part, with the U.S. currently ranking worse than other developed countries in terms of infant mortality (see Fig. 2.7).

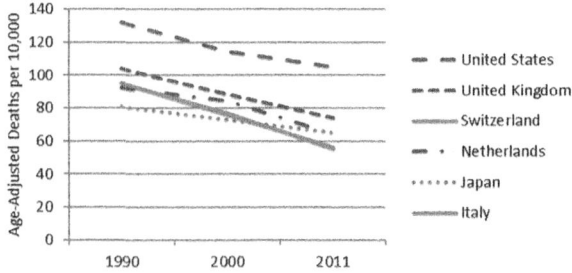

Fig. 2.6 International adult mortality (ages 15–60) 1990–2011. *Source* World health organization

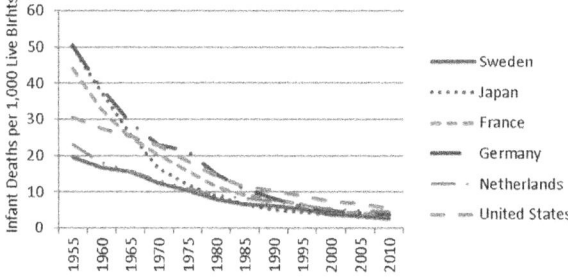

Fig. 2.7 International trends in infant mortality 1955–2010. *Source* World health organization

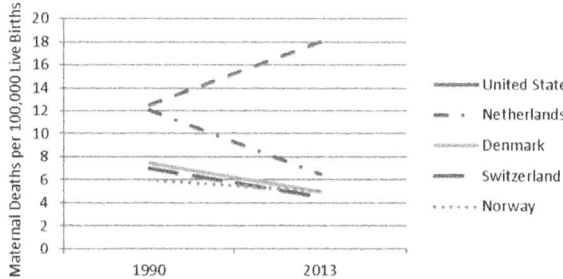

Fig. 2.8 International trends in maternal mortality 1990 and 2013. *Source* Institute for health metrics and evaluation

The most noteworthy cross-cultural comparison related to mortality, however, involves maternal mortality. As noted above, the U.S. maternal mortality rate has actually increased over the past 20 years. This increase in maternal mortality stands in stark contrast to the on-going improvement in the rates for other developed countries and the worldwide decline in maternal mortality (Kassenbaum 2014). Although it has been suggested that the methodology for calculating maternal mortality may produce misleading statistics, the international statistics displayed in Fig. 2.8 certainly suggest a negative trend (Maron 2015).

Discussion

Clearly, any attempt to identify overall trends in morbidity for the U.S. population faces a number of challenges. The first critical challenge involves developing agreement as to what measure or measures are appropriate for use in assessing the health status of the population. The lack of any global measure of morbidity leaves the door open for debate over what indicator(s) best depicts health status. Beyond this major conceptual hurdle, there are additional challenges related to data availability. Some potential indicators may have to be discarded in the absence of relevant data. Even for indicators for which data are available over an extensive period of time, there are issues related to definitions, data coverage (e.g., population, timeframe), and changes in the manner of data collection and the wording of survey items. Even if these challenges could be addressed, there remains the issue of interpretation as to what constitutes a negative trend or a reversal of health status fortunes.

Although all indicators of morbidity do not carry equal weight, this review attempted to cast a wide net in order to develop as comprehensive a view of morbidity trends as possible. While a number of observers have argued that Americans are getting sicker based on a specific indicator (e.g., mortality rates, self-reported health status, disease prevalence), there does not yet appear to be professional consensus regarding a reversal of health fortunes for the U.S. population. Based on this comprehensive compilation of indicators on morbidity, what can we conclude about emerging morbidity trends? Unquestionably, observed trends in overall mortality, infant mortality and maternal mortality—to the extent that mortality is representative of morbidity—suggest stagnation with regard to improvement in health status, a phenomenon not exhibited by the populations of other comparable countries. Prevalence rates for certain chronic conditions, while expected to increase with an aging population, appear to be increasing at a rate beyond that warranted by demographic changes. While there is no overarching indicator that allows us to definitively conclude that Americans are getting sicker, there are enough specific indicators to lead one to think that this is in fact the case.

These findings could be interpreted as anomalies within the context of continuous improvement in the health of the population, or, alternatively, as further evidence that Americans as a whole are getting sicker. It is too early in the assessment process to consider the possibility of a paradigm shift, but emerging morbidity patterns suggest a need to reconsider our morbidity model and the assumptions that support it. Conventional wisdom holds that the U.S. is on a path of continuous health status improvement. However, enough anomalies have been noted that the conventional wisdom requires reconsideration. Clearly, more evidence of a potential paradigm shift is required before the conventional wisdom can be abandoned.

At this point in time the most appropriate answer to the question—are Americans getting sicker—is probably "it depends". It depends on the segment of the U.S. population being analyzed and the indicators that are being employed. It remains to be seen if a clear change in direction for the health status of the U.S. population is occurring. Any conclusive answer to this question will require consensus on how to best measure health status and the ability to access the necessary data to support a definitive assessment.

References

Akinbami, L. J., Moorman, J. E., Bailey, C., et al. (2012). Trends in Asthma prevalence, health care use, and mortality in the United States, 2001–2010. *NCHS Data Brief, 94,* 1–8.

American Lung Association. (2013). *Trends in COPD (Chronic Bronchitis and Emphysema): Morbidity and mortality.* Washington, DC: American Lung Association.

Centers for Disease Control and Prevention. (2014). Summary of notifiable disease—United States, 2011. Downloaded from URL: http://www.cdc.gov/mmwr/preview/mmwrhtml/mm6053a1.htm

Crescioni, M., Gorina, Y., Bilheimer, L., et al. (2010). Trends in health status and health care use among older men. Hyattsville, MD: National Center for Health Statistics. Downloaded from URL: http://www.cdc.gov/nchs/data/nhsr/nhsr024.pdf

Crimmins, E. M., & Beltrán-Sánchez, H. (2011). Mortality and morbidity trends: Is there compression of morbidity? *Journal of Gerontology and Psychological Social Sciences, 66B*(1), 75–86.

Delaney, L., & Smith, J. P. (2012). Childhood health: Trends and consequences over the life course. *The Future of Children, 22*(1), 43–63.

Feigin, V. L., Forouzanfar, M. H., Krishnamurthi, R., et al. (2013). Global and regional burden of stroke during 1990–2010: Findings from the global burden of disease study 2010. *The Lancet.* Online. Downloaded from URL: http://www.thelancet.com/journals/lancet/article/PIIS0140-6736(13)61953-4/fulltext

Halfon, L., & Newacheck, P. W. (2010). Evolving notions of childhood chronic illness. *JAMA, 303*(7), 665–666.

Hausmann, R., Tyson, L. D., & Zahidi, S. (2012). *The global gender gap report 2012.* Geneva: World Economic Forum.

Hoyert, D. (2012). 75 Years of mortality in the United States: 1935–2010. *NCHS Brief, 88,* 1–8.

Institute of Medicine. (2006). *Preventing childhood obesity: How do we measure up?* Washington, DC: National Academies Press.

Jasso, G., Massey, D. S., Rosenzweig, M. R., et al. (2004). Immigrant health: Selectivity and acculturation. In N. B. Anderson, R. A. Bulatao & B. Cohen (Eds.), *Critical perspectives on racial and ethnic differences in health in late life.* Washington: National Academies Press.

Kassenbaum, N. J. (Ed.). (2014). Global, regional, and national levels and causes of maternal mortality during 1990–2013: A systematic analysis for the global burden of disease study 2013. *The Lancet* (May 2). Downloaded from URL: http://download.thelancet.com/flatcontentassets/pdfs/S0140673614604979.pdf

Kindig, D. A., & Cheng, E. R. (2013). Even as mortality fell in most US counties, female mortality nonetheless rose in 42.8 percent of counties from 1992 to 2006. *Health Affairs, 31*(3), 451–458.

Kistler, C. E., Walter, L. C., Mitchell, C. M., & Sloane, P. D. (2010). Patient perceptions of mistakes in ambulatory care. *Archives of Internal Medicine, 170*(16), 1480–1487.

Kuhn, R., Rahman, O., & Menken, J. (2006). Survey measures of health: How well do self-reported and observed indicators measure health and predict mortality. In B. Cohen & J. Menken (Eds.), *Aging in sub-Saharan Africa.* Washington, DC: National Academies Press.

Maron, D. F. (2015). Has maternal mortality really doubled in the U.S.? *Scientific American* (June 6). Downloaded from URL: http://www.scientificamerican.com/article/has-maternal-mortality-really-doubled-in-the-u-s/

Martin, J. A., Hamilton, B. E., Ventura, S. V., et al. (2002). *Vital statistics of the United States, 1971–2001.* Hyattsville, MD: National Center for Health Statistics.

Matthews, T. J., Clarke, S., & Singh, G. (1994). Annual summary of births, marriages, divorces, and deaths: United States, 1993. *Monthly Vital Statistics Report, 42*(13), 1–36.

Murray, C. J. L., Abraham, J., Ali, M. K., et al. (2013). The state of US health: 1990–2010: Burden of diseases, injuries and risk factors. *Journal of the American Medical Association.* Downloaded from URL: http://jama.jamanetwork.com/article.aspx?articleid=1710486&utm_source

National Center for Health Statistics. (2010). Death rates for 358 selected causes, by 10-year age groups, race, and sex: United States, 1999–2007. Bethesda, MD: National Center for Health Statistics. Downloaded from URL: http://www.cdc.gov/nchs/data/dvs/MortFinal2007_Worktable12.pdf

National Center for Health Statistics. (2013). *Health, United States: 2012*. Hyattsville, MD: National Center for Health Statistics.

National Heart, Lung and Blood Institute. (2013). What are the health risks of overweight and obesity? Downloaded from URL: http://www.nhlbi.nih.gov/health/health-topics/topics/obe/risks.html

Olshanky, S. J., Antonucci, T., Berkman, L., et al. (2012). Differences in life expectancy due to race and educational differences are widening, and many may not catch up. *Health Affairs, 2012*(31), 1803–1813.

Robinson, K. (2007). Trends in health status and health care use among older women. Hyattsville, MD: National Center for Health Statistics. Downloaded from URL: http://www.cdc.gov/nchs/data/ahcd/agingtrends/07olderwomen.pdf

Saloman, J. A., Nordhagen, S., Oza, S., & Murray, C. J. L. (2009). Are Americans feeling less healthy? The puzzle of trends in self-rated health. *American Journal of Epidemiology, 170*(3), 343–351.

Schlipköter, U., & Flahault, A. (2010). Communicable diseases: Achievements and challenges for public health. *Public Health Reviews, 32*(1), 90–119.

Trust for America's Health. (2012). *Bending the obesity cost curve: Reducing obesity rates by five percent could lead to more than $29 billion in health care savings in five years*. Washington, DC: Trust for America's Health.

Wang, H., Schumacher, A. E., Levitz, C. E., et al. (2013). Left behind: Widening disparities for males and females in US county life expectancy, 1985–2010. *Population Health Metrics, 11*, 8.

Wilson, K., Elliott, S. J., Eyles, J. D., et al. (2007). Factors affecting change over time in self-reported health. *Canadian Journal of Public Health, 98*(2), 154–158.

Woolf, S. H., & Laudan, A. (Eds.). (2013). *U.S. health in international perspective: Shorter lives, poorer health*. Washington: National Academies Press.

Wu, S., & Green, A. (2000). *Projection of chronic illness prevalence and cost inflation*. Santa Monica, CA: Rand Corporation.

Chapter 3
Reproductive Health Policy Variability Among the States Over Time: Implications of the Affordable Care Act of 2010 for Health Researchers

Monica Gaughan and Georgia J. Michlig

Introduction

US population policy is a complicated mix of macro and meso level determinants that vary geographically, politically, institutionally, and economically. These "population policies" are not the result of intentional policy design, in part due to American exceptionalism related to not guaranteeing universal health care (Quadagno 2005). The recent Affordable Care Act of 2010 (ACA) included a set of reproductive health related policies that affect the extant complexity of the American reproductive health policy "system" (USDHHS 2015).

State-level variability in policy promulgation and implementation creates ideal scenarios for employing natural experiments to evaluate policy effects (Brindis and Moore 2014). Policy researchers have used state-level indicators to study a variety of reproductive health outcomes, such as unintended pregnancy among adolescents (Crosby and Holtgrave 2006), adolescent childbearing (Lundberg and Plotnick 1990; Yang and Gaydos 2010), demographic characteristics of populations (Finer and Kost 2011), access to health insurance (Kost et al. 2012), and access to family planning (Matthews et al. 1997). State-level policies have also been shown to affect smoking cessation programs in pregnant women (Jarlenski et al. 2014), positive WIC impacts (Bitler and Currie 2005), and mixed alcohol policy effects (Drabble et al. 2014). With respect to abortion outcomes, state-level policy analyses have evaluated the effect of parental involvement laws (Bitler and Zavodny 2001;

M. Gaughan (✉)
School of Human Evolution and Social Change, Arizona State University, Tempe, AZ 85287-2402, USA
e-mail: Monica.gaughan@asu.edu

G.J. Michlig
Department of International Health, Bloomberg School of Public Health, Johns Hopkins University, Baltimore, MD 21205, USA
e-mail: gjmichlig@jhu.edu

© Springer International Publishing Switzerland 2017
M.N. Hoque et al. (eds.), *Applied Demography and Public Health in the 21st Century*, Applied Demography Series 8,
DOI 10.1007/978-3-319-43688-3_3

Jackson 2005), Medicaid financing restrictions (Blank et al. 1996; Joyce and Kaestner 1996; Levine et al. 1996), abortion provider ratios (Gius 2007; Jones and Jerman 2014; Meier et al. 1996), and cost (Medoff 2008).

In its attempt to develop a comprehensive, universal package of reproductive health benefits for women, the ACA touched on multiple fault lines in the nation's sensibilities (Bailey et al. 2013). These political fault lines—all of which existed long before Obama was elected—created fissures in the original policy design. During implementation, the fissures developed into fractures that continue to ripple through the system. The result is that even this ostensibly comprehensive federal health care reform is being implemented in a fragmented fashion, particularly as it relates to reproductive health policy. Our conceptual approach owes much to a recent review by Brindis and Moore (2014) in which they develop a policy framework for theorizing about state-level policy factors affecting adolescent health. In this work, we study contraceptive insurance coverage and abortion access. Each of these indicators is affected by a mix of federal, state, and private policies, including: Medicaid, Title IX and private insurance. Although these policy mechanisms pre-date the ACA, provisions of the ACA affect Medicaid and private insurance in particular. In addition, recent state-level legislative action to regulate abortion is having negative impact on the administration of the decades old Title IX program. The result is a patchwork of state-level approaches that health researchers should consider when developing explanatory models to study reproductive health outcomes. We conclude with a data table presenting six state-level indicators of reproductive health access that researchers can use to model contextual effects of the ACA on reproductive health outcomes.

Contraception in the United States

We begin with a brief historical overview of reproductive health policy to demonstrate: (1) it does not have a long history; (2) the US federal government has always played an unusually strong role in it relative to other public health issues; and (3) the federal interplay of national and state concerns is one that extends throughout this history.

19th to 20th Century

By the end of the nineteenth century, the concept of intentional control of fertility, as well as improved means to do so, was widely understood in the United States. The ideas and the means were sufficiently developed that control of fertility passed from the private domain of "women's business" to the public domain of commerce and public policy (Tone 2001). Nationally the effort to protect the public from indecent materials culminated in the federal Comstock Act of 1873, which

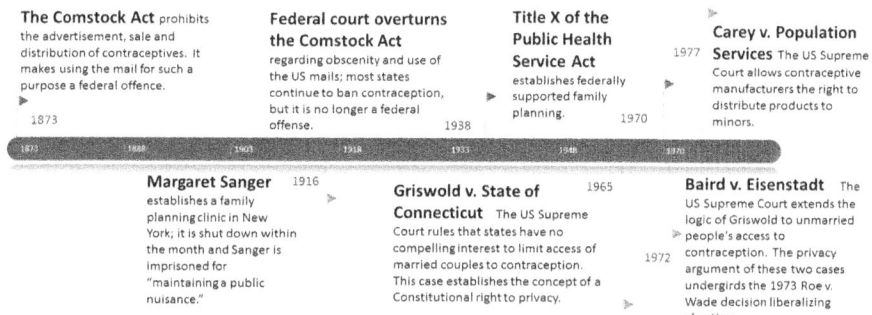

Fig. 3.1 Timeline of twentieth century contraceptive policy in the United States

prohibited advertising, selling, and distributing contraceptive information or devices. It made the use of the US Mail for this purpose a federal offense, and created an underlying federal authority to support state-level efforts to suppress information and knowledge about human reproduction. Figure 3.1 presents a timeline of earlier contraceptive history beginning with the Comstock Act.

With the 50th anniversary of "The Pill" just celebrated, it is easy to forget that a civil right to access to contraception was not recognized until after the debut of hormonal contraception. In a series of landmark cases related to human sexuality, the US Supreme Court found a previously unrecognized penumbra of the US Constitution to establish a right to privacy. In Griswold v. State of Connecticut (1965), the right to privacy was found to supersede a state's interest in controlling the access of married couples to contraceptives. In the 1972 case of Baird v. Eisenstadt, this principle was further extended to unmarried individuals' access to contraception. Without these two crucial contraception cases, the legal precedent for liberalization of state abortion laws in the 1973 Roe v. Wade would not have been established. Finally, in 1977 the Court found in Carey v. Population Services that states could not limit minors' access to contraception. In short, it was only within the lifetime of most readers of this chapter that the basic right to contraceptive access was established.

By 1970, the need to control population growth was widely recognized by world leaders, including the Americans. In 1970, the US Congress passed Title X of the Public Health Service Act of the public health service act, which established the continuing basis for federal support of family planning services in the United States. By the end of the century, the bulk of financial access to contraception was assured through a combination of Title X, Medicaid, private insurance, state appropriations, and self-payment. Although contraceptive coverage and access increased over this period, financial barriers remained, particularly for low income women (Sonfield et al. 2014).

The Third Millennium

Against this backdrop of legislative history about contraception in the United States, we can now focus more specifically on the ongoing struggle for contraceptive access, a struggle which the Affordable Care Act of 2010 has served to inflame. This section owes much to the policy analytic efforts of policy groups such as Guttmacher Institute and Kaiser Family Foundation, which have thoroughly evaluated specific components of the bill; our intent here is to consolidate this body of work into one place. The passage of the Affordable Care Act of 2010 promised significant expansions of health insurance coverage for American citizens. A particularly attractive feature of the bill is the provision that all new health insurance plans cover FDA-approved contraceptives without a cost share. In addition, the expansion of Medicaid coverage through exclusive means-tested eligibility meant that millions of women would gain access to contraceptives (USDHHS 2015). It is important to note that from its inception, the ACA excluded men from reproductive coverage (Sonfield 2015), as well as undocumented immigrants (Andrapalliyal 2013), decisions with far-reaching consequences that are outside the scope of this review.

It did not take long for the fault lines in American culture war politics to break. Because contraceptives are considered wrong by members of some religious groups, legal challenges to the private insurance essential benefits mandate started immediately. In 2012, the Obama Administration issued regulations exempting religious employers from the contraceptive mandate; the exemptions did not extend to not-for-profit religious organizations. In 2013, the Obama Administration issued regulations exempting not-for profit religious employers from the contraceptive mandate, but continues to require that the employer's insurance company cover the cost. Figure 3.2 presents reproductive health related provisions, beginning with the passage of the bill in 2010.

Meanwhile, general provisions of the Affordable Care Act have been challenged in federal courts. The three cases already decided by the US Supreme Court have

Fig. 3.2 Timeline of millennial contraceptive policy in the United States

direct and indirect implications for contraceptive coverage, placing contraception at the center of federal lawsuits about the law. In the first case decided in 2012, the Court ruled in National Federation of Independent Business v. Sebelius that the individual mandate to purchase insurance is Constitutional, but that states can choose whether or not to expand Medicaid as mandated in the Affordable Care Act. On the one hand, the affirmation of the individual mandate meant that new insurance policies would continue to provide birth control coverage, and early evidence suggests increases in access and decreases in costs for women in private plans (Finer et al. 2014; Sonfield 2013; Sonfield et al. 2014). By contrast, the finding that the Medicaid expansion was optional to states meant that the access of millions of poor women to contraception was jeopardized. The crucial aspect of that decision affecting reproductive health policy was the finding that the federal government could not compel states to expand Medicaid, one of the backbones of reproductive health services provision in the country. Currently, the country is divided evenly between Medicaid expansion states and those that did not, resulting in de facto state policy experiments (Kaiser Family Foundation 2015a). Many states' failure to expand Medicaid has left an estimated 1.7 million uninsured women below the federal poverty level without coverage. The Supreme Court's 2012 decision on the constitutionality of health care reform continues to affect implementation of the ACA, including effects of differential insurance expansion at the state level (Kenney et al. 2012).

In the second case, the Supreme Court ruled in Burwell v. Hobby Lobby (2014) that closely held corporations are exempt from ACA requirements to cover contraceptives. This added private firms to religious institutions that were already allowed to exclude contraceptive coverage through executive powers. This ruling means that women working for privately held corporations could be denied insurance coverage by their religiously motivated employers. In lieu of the employer providing such coverage, the insurance company is required to provide it. At this point, it is unclear whether this compromise leads to problems at the level of the patient in getting contraception covered (Sobel and Salganicoff 2013, 2015).

In June 2014, the US Supreme Court ruled in King v. Burwell that individuals living in states with a federally-administered insurance marketplace are eligible for federal subsidies to purchase health insurance. This is the first of the Supreme Court cases related to the Affordable Care Act—by its decision—not to affect reproductive health rights further. It is noteworthy, however, that coverage remains extremely complicated in any case.

Meanwhile, in 2015, the Supreme Court asked the 7th US Circuit Court of appeals to re-evaluate the constitutionality of the Administration's birth control accommodation for religious employers (after the Circuit Court had ruled that it was constitutional). If this regulation is over-turned, then women working for religious employers will not have access to contraceptive insurance through their regular health insurance, even under the compromise provided by the administration. It is highly likely, then, that such logic would be extended to the women working for closely-held corporations as well (Sobel and Salganicoff 2015).

In summary, the US Supreme Court is the most active battle ground regarding implementation of the Affordable Care Act, and provisions for reproductive health care are particularly at risk. In some decisions, access has been rolled back, and in others, it has been reaffirmed. Cases continue to make their way through the federal court system, and it is unlikely that there will not be another reproductive health related ACA decision in the future.

Abortion in the United States

No consideration of reproductive health in the United States would be complete without some mention of abortion. Since the Supreme Court legalized abortion in 1973 there has been a surfeit of restrictions on access enacted at both the federal and state level (Fig. 3.3). While the Hyde Amendment restricts federal funds, states may enact further restrictions to abortion coverage within their borders and enforce additional regulations on both abortion providers and those seeking care (Guttmacher Institute 2015c, d).

Since the passage of the ACA a rash of new restrictions both in funding and antiabortion measures has taken place (Boonstra and Nash 2014; Gold and Nash 2013). Previous researchers have hypothesized that the contentious political coverage surrounding events such as the passage of the ACA may create a "coat-tail effect" in which more restrictive legislation is enacted and media accounts may distort women's apparent rights to services (Trussell 1980; Roh and Haider-Markel 2003). Potential consequences include increasing the monetary cost of abortion, declining access due to clinic closures as well as increases in the time and emotional burden of abortion procedures due to restrictions such as waiting periods. While the ACA was drafted with the intent of increasing healthcare access it appears to have had the opposite effect in this instance.

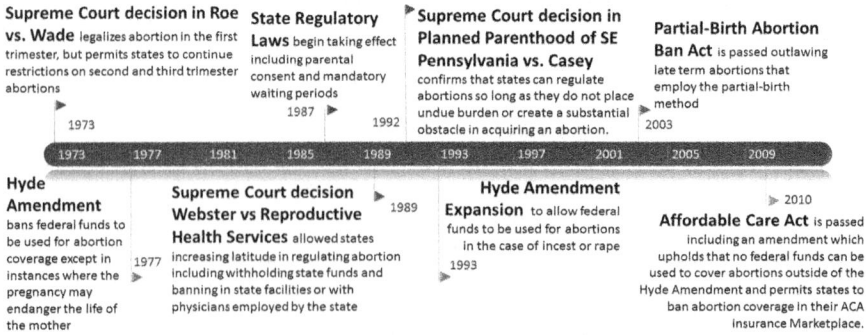

Fig. 3.3 Timeline of abortion policy in the United States

The Democratic legislators developing the ACA excluded abortion coverage from the final bill, a compromise made for Democrats opposed to abortion. This continued longstanding federal policy: Prior to the ACA, no federal financing of abortion had been allowed since the Hyde Amendment of 1977. A state-level contextual factor that introduces variation, however, is that individual states may choose to pay for abortion from non-federal funds, and they may require private insurance to cover the procedure. Therefore, abortion is publicly subsidized in some states and not others, and required by some state insurance regulators and not others. The ACA Medicaid expansion described above also results in the populations of some states obtaining improved access to abortion coverage through the state part of the funds.

In general, the US Supreme Court has prevented states from eliminating abortion, but since the Webster v. Reproductive Health Services case of 1989, it has allowed states increasing latitude in regulating abortion. This adds an additional layer of complexity at the state level, with some states engaged in minimal regulation of publicly financed abortion, while others have successfully defended increasing restrictions before the Supreme Court. In the meantime, recent years have been characterized by a proliferation of state-level legislation further restricting abortion. This state-level variation is currently working its way through the federal courts, and will surely result in another Supreme Court case. Finally, a late-breaking story is the allegation that the separate abortion riders on private insurance are not in fact being implemented uniformly, leading to allegations that the Obama Administration is failing to enforce that part of the law (Hasstedt 2015).

Moving forward, adequate surveillance of the blowback from the ACA on abortion access and usage will be vital. Most important will be to gauge not just the abortion rate as it is calculated now out of total pregnancies, but rather to capture the rate of unwanted pregnancies ending in abortion. Previous research has shown that abortion rates as a function of unwanted pregnancies is more sensitive to changes in funding options and state restrictions (Medoff 2012). Currently, mapping the status of pregnancy intention state-by-state is a complex process drawing from an abundance of disparate surveillance mechanisms (Kost et al. 2012). A unified system of intention surveillance alongside outcome data would be beneficial. Other measurements to be analyzed should include emergency room admits due to fetal loss by suspected self-induced abortions (Trussell 1980), total number of providers geographically, continuing state abortion policy changes, types of abortion being favored (surgical vs. medication), timing of abortions (weeks gestation), abortion costs and method of payment as short term indicators.

To summarize, a researcher interested in understanding policy factors that may affect US abortion rates would need to consider the status of federal abortion law in any year, whether or not abortion can be publicly funded, whether or not it must be included in private insurance plans, and the details of state-level abortion law. With respect to this latter point—the details of state-level abortion law—there are many different legal ways to restrict abortion; some states are comprehensive in their limitations, employing all policy levers while others employ none; still others choose some levers but not others. Note that this complexity existed at the time the ACA was signed into law. What, then, are the implications of the ACA for researchers interested in evaluating the effects of policy instruments on abortion rates? The news is not good: The ACA policy introduces new aspects of complexity, and its implementation is leading to still further levels of complexity related to abortion access.

Methodology to Develop Tools for Researchers

Accounting for state-level complexity is an essential feature of policy analysis and research focused on these indicators even before the ACA was passed. In Fig. 3.4, we present a contingency table to assist researchers in thinking through how specific sub-populations of women may be conceptualized with respect to the law.

On the left side of the figure are undocumented women, a subpopulation excluded from the scope of the Affordable Care Act: Undocumented women must get their care outside of the framework of ACA, so therefore reproductive health coverage limitations affecting them remain similar to those documented elsewhere. The next group of women are those insured through private insurance companies.

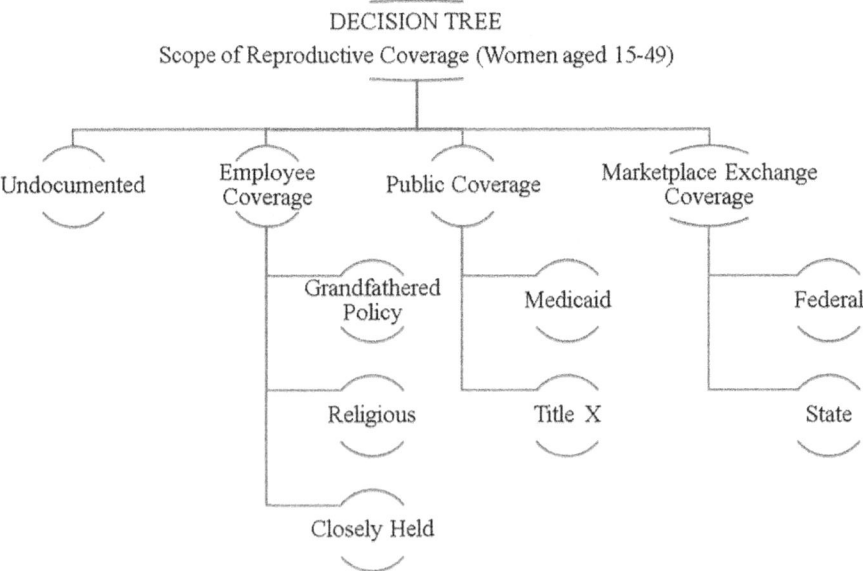

Fig. 3.4 Contingencies of contraception coverage in the ACA

Here, it is critically important that state-level variations are accounted for, as different states have different mixes of grandfathered policies, religious employers, and closely held companies—each of which potentially will affect an insured woman's access to contraceptive coverage in particular. The third branch of the figure addresses women obtaining services through public means. Here, it is particularly important that the researcher account for whether or not a state is a Medicaid expansion state, or if the state is one whose legislature has attacked Title X family planning clinics. In those contexts, reproductive access continues to shrink. Women in state-run exchanges will continue to be eligible for federal subsidies under the recent Supreme Court decision.

In Table 3.1, we provide state-specific characteristics related to the specific sub-populations identified in Fig. 3.4. The "Insurance" column indicates the 30 states that would have been affected by King v. Burwell federal subsidy decision. We retain it here as a way to identify those states that rely on the federal government (which is particularly vulnerable to Supreme Court challenges regarding ACA). In the next column are the 21 states are affected by the National Federation of Independent Business v. Sebelius decision related to Medicaid expansion. The "Family Planning" column identifies the 10 states that restrict funds for family planning if such services are related to an abortion provider (Guttmacher Institute 2015a), and the 14 states that allow professionals or institutions to refuse to treat on moral grounds (Guttmacher Institute 2015b). The "Abortion" column identifies 19 states that restrict access to abortion through insurance, and the 6 states for which a separate abortion rider is required. The last column shows the percentage of each state that is estimated to be undocumented. The national average of undocumented persons is 3.5. The failure to cover undocumented people under ACA is having a disproportionate impact on about one-fifth of states.

In Table 3.1, the states are ranked in terms of level of reproductive access threat to the state's population from exceptions to the ACA's implementation, exclusive of the percentage undocumented in a state shown in the last column. For example, the first 13 states listed have state marketplace exchanges, have expanded Medicaid, do not allow restrictions on family planning funds or abortion restrictions on the exchange, and do not have professional conscience clauses. By contrast, one state—Kansas—has in place provisions that have the potential to have maximum negative impact in terms of the policies we studied: It uses the federal exchange, did not expand Medicaid, restricts family planning funds, allows providers to refuse treatment, and restricts abortion access in health insurance. The majority of states range from one to five such limitations; within each restriction block, states are listed alphabetically, but the pattern of restrictions indicates dozens of possible combinations. In short, researchers seeking to explain state-level indicators such as contraceptive coverage, pregnancy, abortion, and other reproductive health indicators should take care to assess how the state's ACA provisions may affect outcomes.

Table 3.1 State-level variation in reproductive health policy access

State	Insurance[a]		Family planning		Abortion[b]	Undoc.
	Exchange	Medicaid	Funds[c]	Refusal[d]	Exchange	(%)[e]
California	State	Expansion	OK	OK	OK	6.3
Connecticut	State	Expansion	OK	OK	OK	3.5
Delaware	State	Expansion	OK	OK	OK	2.4
DC	State	Expansion	OK	OK	OK	3.1
Hawaii	State	Expansion	OK	OK	OK	2.4
Iowa	State	Expansion	OK	OK	OK	1.4
Maryland	State	Expansion	OK	OK	OK	4.3
Minnesota	State	Expansion	OK	OK	OK	1.8
New Hampshire	State	Expansion	OK	OK	OK	0.9
New York	State	Expansion	OK	OK	OK	3.8
Rhode Island	State	Expansion	OK	OK	OK	3.3
Vermont	State	Expansion	OK	OK	OK	0.4
West Virginia	State	Expansion	OK	OK	OK	0.2
Illinois	State	Expansion	OK	**Refusal**	OK	3.7
Kentucky	State	Expansion	OK	OK	**Restricted**	0.8
Massachusetts	State	Expansion	OK	**Refusal**	OK	2.3
Montana	**Federal**	Expansion	OK	OK	OK	0.3
Nevada	**Federal**	Expansion	OK	OK	OK	7.6
New Jersey	**Federal**	Expansion	OK	OK	OK	5.8
New Mexico	**Federal**	Expansion	OK	OK	OK	3.4
Oregon	**Federal**	Expansion	OK	OK	OK	3.1
Washington	State	Expansion	OK	**Refusal**	OK	3.3
Alaska	**Federal**	**Status Quo**	OK	OK	OK	1.8
Arkansas	State	Expansion	OK	**Refusal**	**Rider**	2.1
Colorado	State	Expansion	**Restricted**	**Refusal**	OK	3.5
Michigan	State	Expansion	**Restricted**	OK	**Rider**	1.2
North Dakota	**Federal**	Expansion	OK	OK	**Restricted**	0.3
Pennsylvania	**Federal**	Expansion	OK	OK	**Rider**	1.3
Wyoming	**Federal**	**Status Quo**	OK	OK	OK	1.0
Arizona	**Federal**	Expansion	OK	**Refusal**	**Rider**	4.6
Idaho	State	**Status Quo**	OK	**Refusal**	**Restricted**	3.0
Indiana	**Federal**	Expansion	**Restricted**	OK	**Restricted**	1.3
Louisiana	**Federal**	**Status Quo**	OK	OK	**Restricted**	1.2
Maine	**Federal**	**Status Quo**	OK	**Refusal**	OK	0.2
Missouri	**Federal**	**Status Quo**	OK	OK	**Restricted**	1.1
Nebraska	**Federal**	**Status Quo**	OK	OK	**Restricted**	2.8
Ohio	**Federal**	Expansion	**Restricted**	OK	**Restricted**	0.8
South Carolina	**Federal**	**Status Quo**	OK	OK	**Restricted**	2.0
Texas	**Federal**	**Status Quo**	**Restricted**	OK	OK	6.3

(continued)

Table 3.1 (continued)

State	Insurance[a]		Family planning		Abortion[b]	Undoc.
	Exchange	Medicaid	Funds[c]	Refusal[d]	Exchange	(%)[e]
Utah	**Federal**	**Status Quo**	OK	OK	**Restricted**	3.6
Virginia	**Federal**	**Status Quo**	OK	OK	**Restricted**	3.5
Alabama	**Federal**	**Status Quo**	**Restricted**	OK	**Restricted**	1.4
Florida	**Federal**	**Status Quo**	OK	**Refusal**	**Rider**	4.8
Georgia	**Federal**	**Status Quo**	OK	**Refusal**	**Restricted**	3.9
Mississippi	**Federal**	**Status Quo**	OK	**Refusal**	**Restricted**	0.9
North Carolina	**Federal**	**Status Quo**	**Restricted**	OK	**Restricted**	3.6
Oklahoma	**Federal**	**Status Quo**	**Restricted**	OK	**Rider**	2.6
South Dakota	**Federal**	**Status Quo**	OK	**Refusal**	**Restricted**	0.4
Tennessee	**Federal**	**Status Quo**	OK	**Refusal**	**Restricted**	2.0
Wisconsin	**Federal**	**Status Quo**	**Restricted**	OK	**Restricted**	1.5
Kansas	**Federal**	**Status Quo**	**Restricted**	**Refusal**	**Restricted**	2.6

[a]*Exchange and Medicaid* Kaiser Family Foundation (2015a)
[b]*Abortion* Kaiser Family Foundation (2015b)
[c]*Funds* Guttmacher Institute (2015a)
[d]*Refusal* Guttmacher Institute (2015b)
[e]*Undocumented* Pew Research Center, http://pewhispanic.org/interactives/unauthorized-immigrants-2012/map/population-share/

Conclusion

The Affordable Care Act constitutes a significant reform of the American health care system, but it is not an overhaul. Indeed, with respect to reproductive health care delivery and financing, the ACA adds complexity to an already bewildering situation. Although the contraceptive mandate was originally viewed as something that would simplify access to reproductive health care, the reality is that continuing action at the state and federal levels complicate even this. The purpose of this paper is to create an analytic policy primer targeted to demographic researchers, combined with a state-level data set that will enable researchers to develop and test rigorous models adjusting for potential state-level effects.

In summary, although the Affordable Care Act at first seems to provide an opportunity for tens of millions of women to obtain a federal entitlement to contraceptive coverage, the reality of implementation and state-level politics make that goal elusive. For researchers, particularly those who are interested in studying reproductive health outcome impacts of the legislation, the analytic situation is extremely complicated. Because the US population is segmented in numerous ways with respect to the contraceptive mandate, how that segmentation occurs is an important structural determinant of coverage, and its outcomes. Our purpose is to lay out the federal and state-level contextual factors that should be controlled in evaluating meso and micro level effects of the health care reform law. A researcher interested in understanding determinants of contraception coverage needs to know a variety of factors at the state level, including the state-level insurance requirements, its Medicaid expansion status, legislative actions against Title IX providers in the state, and the prevalence of employers with the potential to refuse coverage on religious grounds. The purpose of the case is to provide the legislative and policy history that demographic researchers need to sort through the complexity theoretically and empirically.

Acknowledgments An earlier version of this paper was presented as a poster at Population Association of America Meetings, San Diego, CA, April 29–May 2, 2015. The authors are grateful to the School of Human Evolution and Social Change, Arizona State University, for its support of this work.

References

Andrapalliyal, V. (2013). Healthcare for all? The gap between rhetoric and reality in the Affordable Care Act. *UCLA Law Review Discourse, 61*, 58–77.
Bailey, M. J., Guldi, M., & Hershbein, B. J. (2013). Recent evidence on the broad benefits of reproductive health policy. *Journal of Policy Analysis and Management, 32*, 888–896.
Bitler, M., & Currie, J. (2005). Does WIC work? The effects of WIC on pregnancy and birth outcomes. *Journal of Policy Analysis and Management, 42*(1), 73–91.
Bitler, M., & Zavodny, M. (2001). The effect of abortion restrictions on the timing of abortions. *Journal of Health Economics, 20*(6), 1011–1032.
Blank, R. M., George, C. C., & London, R. A. (1996). State abortion rates the impact of policies, providers, politics, demographics, and economic environment. *Journal of Health Economics, 15*(5), 513–553.
Boonstra, H. D., & Nash, E. (2014). A surge of state abortion restrictions puts providers- and the women they serve- in the crosshairs. *Guttmacher Policy Review, 17*(1), 9–15.
Brindis, C. D., & Moore, K. (2014). Improving adolescent health policy: Incorporating a framework for assessing state-level polices. *Annual Review of Public Health, 35*, 343–361.
Crosby, R. A., & Holtgrave, D. R. (2006). The protective value of social capital against teen pregnancy: A state-level analysis. *Journal of Adolescent Health, 38*(5), 556–559.
Drabble, L., Thomas, S., O'Connor, L., & Roberts, S. C. (2014). State responses to alcohol use and pregnancy: Findings from the alcohol policy information system. *Journal of social work practice in the addictions, 14*(2), 191–206.
Finer, L. B., & Kost, K. (2011). Unintended pregnancy rates at the state level. *Perspectives on Sexual and Reproductive Health, 43*(2), 78–87.
Finer, L. B., Sonfield, A., & Jones, R. K. (2014). Changes in out-of-pocket payments for contraception by privately insured women during implementation of the federal contraceptive coverage requirement. *Contraception, 89*(2), 97–102.
Gius, M. P. (2007). The impact of provider availability and legal restrictions on the demand for abortions by young women. *The Social Science Journal, 44*(3), 495–506.
Gold, R. B., & Nash, E. (2013). TRAP laws gain political traction while abortion clinics—and the women they serve—pay the price. *Guttmacher Policy Review, 16*(2), 7–12.
Guttmacher Institute. (2015a). State family planning funding restrictions, State Policies in Brief, June 1, 2015.
Guttmacher Institute. (2015b). Refusing to provide health services, State Policies in Brief, June 1, 2015.

Guttmacher Institute. (2015c). Targeted regulation of abortion providers, State Policies in Brief (as of March 1, 2015), 2015. http://www.guttmacher.org/statecenter/spibs/spib_TRAP.pdf. Accessed March 24, 2015.

Guttmacher Institute. (2015d). An overview of abortion laws, State Policies in Brief (as of March 1, 2015), 2015. http://www.guttmacher.org/statecenter/spibs/spib_OAL.pdf. Accessed March 24, 2015.

Hasstedt, K. (2015). Abortion coverage under the Affordable Care Act: Advancing transparency, ensuring choice, and facilitating access. *Guttmacher Policy Review, 18*(1), 14–20.

Jackson, D. L. (2005). A multi-year study of policies that affect the abortion rate at the state level, Electronic Theses, Treatises and Dissertations, Paper 3822.

Jarlenski, M., Bleich, S. N., Bennett, W. L., Stuart, E. A., & Barry, C. L. (2014). Medicaid enrollment policy increased smoking cessation among pregnant women but had no impact on birth outcomes. *Health Affairs, 33*(6), 997–1005.

Jones, R. K., & Jerman, J. (2014). Abortion incidence and service availability in the United States, 2011. *Perspectives on Sexual and Reproductive Health, 46*(1), 3–14.

Joyce, T., & Kaestner, R. (1996). The effect of expansions in Medicaid income eligibility on abortion. *Demography, 33*(2), 181–192.

Kaiser Family Foundation. (2015a). State decisions on health insurance marketplaces and the Medicaid expansion, April 20, 2015. http://kff.org/health-reform/state-indicator/state-decisions-for-creating-health-insurance-exchanges-and-expanding-medicaid/

Kaiser Family Foundation. (2015b). State restriction of health insurance coverage of abortion, April 1, 2015. http://kff.org/womens-health-policy/state-indicator/abortion-restriction/

Kenney, G. M., McMorrow, S., Zuckerman, S., & Goin, D. E. (2012). A decade of health care access declines for adults holds implications for changes in the Affordable Care Act. *Health Affairs, 31*, 899–908.

Kost, K., Finer, L. B., & Singh, S. (2012). Variation in state unintended pregnancy rates in the United States. *Perspectives on Sexual and Reproductive Health, 44*(1), 57–64.

Levine, P. B., Trainor, A. B., & Zimmerman, D. J. (1996). The effect of Medicaid abortion funding restrictions on abortions, pregnancies and births. *Journal of Health Economics, 15*(5), 555–578.

Lundberg, S., & Plotnick, R. D. (1990). Effects of state welfare, abortion and family planning policies on premarital childbearing among white adolescents. *Family Planning Perspectives, 22*(6), 246–275.

Matthews, S., Ribar, D., & Wilhelm, M. (1997). The effects of economic conditions and access to reproductive health services on state abortion rates and birthrates. *Family Planning Perspectives, 29*(2), 52–60.

Medoff, M. H. (2008). Abortion costs, sexual behavior, and pregnancy rates. *The Social Science Journal, 45*(1), 156–172.

Medoff, M. H. (2012). Unintended pregnancies, restrictive abortion laws, and abortion demand, International Scholarly Research Notices.

Meier, K. J., Haider-Markel, D. P., Stanislawski, A. J., & McFarlane, D. R. (1996). The impact of state-level restrictions on abortion. *Demography, 33*(3), 307–312.

Pew Research Center, http://pewhispanic.org/interactives/unauthorized-immigrants-2012/map/population-share/

Quadagno, J. (2005). *One nation uninsured: Why the US has no national health insurance.* Cambridge: Oxford University Press.

Roh, J., & Haider-Markel, D. P. (2003). All politics is not local: National forces in state abortion initiatives. *Social Science Quarterly, 84*(1), 15–31.

Sobel, L. & Salganicoff, A. (2013). A guide to the supreme court's review of the contraceptive coverage requirement, Kaiser Family Foundation Issue Brief, December 2013.

Sobel, L. & Salganicoff, A. (2015). Round 2 on the legal challenges to contraceptive coverage: Are nonprofits substantially burdened by the accommodation? Kaiser Family Foundation Issue Brief, May 2015.

Sonfield, A. (2013). Implementing the federal contraceptive coverage guarantee: Progress and prospects. *Guttmacher Policy Review, 16*(4), 8–12.

Sonfield, A. (2015). Rounding out the contraceptive coverage guarantee: Why 'male' contraceptive methods matter for everyone. *Guttmacher Policy Review, 18*(2), 34–39.

Sonfield, A., Tapales, A., Jones, R. K., & Finer, L. B. (2014). Impact of the federal contraceptive coverage guarantee on out-of-pocket payments for contraceptives: 2014 update. *Contraception, 91*, 44–48.

Tone, A. (2001). *Devices and desires: A history of contraception in America*. New York: Hill and Wang.

Trussell, J. (1980). The impact of restricting Medicaid financing for abortion. *Family Planning Perspectives, 12*(3), 120–130.

United States Department of Health and Human Services. (2015). www.healthcare.gov

Yang, Z., & Gaydos, L. M. (2010). Reasons for and challenges of recent increases in teen birth rates: A study of family planning service policies and demographic changes at the state level. *Journal of Adolescent Health, 46*(6), 517–524.

Chapter 4
The Impact of Personality Change on Health Among a Diverse Sample of Older Americans: Findings from the Health and Retirement Study

Latrica E. Best

Introduction

The relationship between personality and a wide array of health outcomes is well documented (Jokela et al. 2014; Lahey 2009; Smith et al. 2004; Turiano et al. 2011). Personality has been linked to self-rated health (Aiken-Morgan et al. 2014; Letzring et al. 2014; Turiano et al. 2011), depression (Klein et al. 2011; Mulder 2002), chronic health conditions such as diabetes (Bogg and Roberts 2004) and hypertension (Terracciano et al. 2014), and premature mortality (Jokela et al. 2013). Research examining the association between personality constructs, such as neuroticism and conscientiousness, and health outcomes has been particularly important in public health efforts to manage and prevent adverse health conditions (Bogg and Roberts 2004; Lahey 2009).

Examining differences in personality among populations can be beneficial in detecting the susceptibility, incidence, and prevalence of debilitating and modifiable health conditions such as hypertension. Hypertension, or high blood pressure, continues to be a significant public health concern. In the United States, approximately a third of adults are hypertensive, and only half of those who experience high blood pressure have the condition under control (Nwankwo et al. 2013). Racial and ethnic minorities are disproportionately burdened with the disease, with blacks having a higher incidence and prevalence, while also experiencing an earlier age of onset (Mozaffarian et al. 2015). Non-Hispanic blacks and Hispanics are also more likely than non-Hispanic whites to have uncontrolled hypertension (Egan et al. 2011; Yoon et al. 2015). Personality-related factors have been linked to hypertension in minority groups. Much of this work has focused on trait-level characteristics such as anxiety (Pointer et al. 2012), anger, and hostility as byproducts of

L.E. Best (✉)
Pan-African Studies and Sociology, University of Louisville, Louisville, KY, USA
e-mail: latrica.best@louisville.edu

© Springer International Publishing Switzerland 2017
M.N. Hoque et al. (eds.), *Applied Demography and Public Health in the 21st Century*, Applied Demography Series 8,
DOI 10.1007/978-3-319-43688-3_4

perceived racial discrimination (Dolezsar et al. 2014; Krieger and Sidney 1996; Williams and Neighbors 2001).

The ability to explore the personality-hypertension relationship is greatly aided by the inclusion of personality constructs in large, nationally representative surveys. Until fairly recently, most nationally representative datasets used by social scientists did not include constructs of personality, an important aspect of psychosocial well being. Because of past exclusions of personality at the population level, we know very little in the way of whether race/ethnic variations in personality exist and whether personality changes over time among diverse groups. Additionally, research examining whether any potential change in personality affects health conditions such as hypertension is limited.

The current study initially examines race/ethnic variation in personality at two different time periods (2006 and 2010) and the subsequent differences in the mean personality change. Next, this study seeks to uncover whether changes in personality, as measured by the Big Five personality construct (measures of extraversion, agreeableness, conscientiousness, neuroticism, and openness to experience) (Digman 1990; McCrae and Costa 1987), can predict hypertension, defined by both measured blood pressure and self reports, in an national sample of older non-Hispanic whites, non-Hispanic blacks, and Hispanics. With the inclusion of self-reported hypertension and measured blood pressure, this study attempts to distinguish between those who are controlling their condition and those who have yet to manage their hypertension. Of particular importance to this study is whether the relationship between personality change and hypertension varies by race and ethnicity.

Personality and Health

As mentioned earlier, although the link between personality and health is well established, the nature and magnitude of the relationship varies, depending on the manner in which personality is operationalized. Type A personality, a specific personality construct characterized by angry, competitive, impatient, and irritable behavior, is associated with an increased risk of coronary heart disease (Cooper et al. 2007), of which hypertension is a known modifiable risk factor. Specifically, low scores for agreeableness has also been linked to coronary heart disease (Myrtek 2001). Type D personality, which reflects tendencies to restrain self-expression and exhibit negative affectivity, is also linked to coronary heart disease (Denollet 2000). Although little research exists in examining openness to experience and health conditions such as hypertension, recent work has shown that high scores on the dimension can serve as a protective mechanism against premature mortality (Hampson and Friedman 2008; Turiano et al. 2012).

In regards to the Big Five personality construct, much of the research assessing the association between personality and health has heavily focused on the impact of neuroticism and conscientiousness (Bogg and Roberts 2013; Hagger-Johnson et al. 2012; Hill et al. 2011; Lahey 2009; Turiano et al. 2013). In a sample of older men,

Spiro and colleagues found that respondents who scored high on neuroticism were more likely to develop hypertension over time (1995). Previous research has also shown that individuals who score low on conscientiousness are more likely to have negative health outcomes, such as hypertension (Bogg and Roberts 2004). Additionally, public health researchers have increasingly become interested in the nature in which high (or low) scores on conscientiousness and neuroticism affect one's ability to manage chronic conditions (Goodwin and Friedman 2006; Lahey 2009).

Changes in Personality

Much debate has been generated over whether personality traits change across the life course. Previous research on the topic is mixed. Some researchers have argued that there are negligible differences in mean-level change in most personality traits after age 30 (Costa et al 2000; McCrae and Costa 1996). In contrast, other researchers analyzing personality change over time have utilized a more contextual perspective to describe personality throughout the life course. These researchers argue that people can experience personality changes beyond age 30 and throughout the later stages of life (Helson et al. 2002; Srivastava et al. 2003). From this viewpoint, personality is an artifact of the different life events one experiences at various life stages (Srivastava et al. 2003). Major life transitions, changes in social roles and responsibilities, as well as a culmination of life stressors are just a few of many social/environmental factors that have a significant impact on changes in personality throughout adulthood. Many of these events and transitions occur after early adulthood, therefore making significant changes in personality patterns probable.

To the author's knowledge, little research exists in examining mean-level personality changes and high blood pressure in population-based data. In a recently published article, Weston and colleagues use the 2006 and 2010 waves of the Health and Retirement Study to look at the nature upon which baseline reports of personality predict the onset of a host of health conditions in the follow-up wave (2015). The authors found that reports of conscientiousness, neuroticism, and openness to experience in 2006 predicted the onset of hypertension in 2010 (Weston et al. 2015). Changes in personality, however, have shown to be strong predictors for social factors, such as life satisfaction (Boyce et al. 2013), and other health-related outcomes, such as substance abuse (Hampson et al. 2010), obesity (Siegler et al. 2003), and mortality (Mroczek and Spiro 2007).

Does Race Matter?

To date, there is no research examining racial variation on the Big Five personality construct in a large, nationally representative sample. Prior studies have illustrated the difficulty in examining whether race/ethnic variation in personality characteristics exist (Foldes et al 2008; Johnson 2001; Ones and Anderson 2002). Many of these studies have fairly low sample sizes or restrict their samples to specific groups (Aiken-Morgan et al. 2014; Collins and Gleaves 1998; Johnson 2001; Jones 1991; Day and Bedeian 1995). Although the Big Five personality construct is one of the most utilized measures of personality, many psychological studies addressing race or cultural differences in personality use different scales, thus, making it extremely difficult to extrapolate their findings to a broader perspective (Foldes et al. 2008). Much of the research on race differences in personality are found in meta-analyses conducted in personnel and industrial/organizational psychology (Foldes et al. 2008; Goldberg et al. 1998; Hough et al. 2001). Typically, in these meta-analyses, researchers evaluate the effect sizes, or magnitude, of race/ethnic differences in personality based on variations of the Big Five.

In general, most research on race differences in personality suggests that any variation by racial group is, for the most part, negligible (Foldes et al. 2008). However, small differences were found across different studies, with some of the variation occurring across a specific item associated with a personality construct, as opposed to the aggregate of items typically utilized to measure the five constructs of personality. For example, in a meta-analysis comparing five U.S. racial groups, researchers found that whites scored slightly lower on the trait characteristics of self-esteem and even temperament. Whites, on average, also scored slightly higher than blacks on measures of emotional stability and low anxiety (Foldes et al. 2008). This finding is somewhat contradictory to another recent meta-analysis that examined black-white differences in personality in over 500 effect sizes (Tate and McDaniel 2008). In this study, the authors found that blacks, not whites, scored higher on emotional stability. Additionally, blacks were slightly more extroverted whereas whites appeared slightly more agreeable (Tate and McDaniel 2008). In general, Foldes and colleagues found very few differences in personality characteristics between Hispanics and other race groups. Hispanics scored slightly higher than whites on measures of self-esteem and low anxiety and slightly higher on sociability, but not on any of the five-factor level personality measures (Foldes et al. 2008).

There is a limited amount of research assessing race/ethnic differences in the reporting of the Big Five personality factors, especially as it relates to health issues. In a sample of 150 black and white cancer patients, researchers Krok-Schoen and Baker (2014) examine race differences on the Big Five personality factor model. The authors did not find any significant differences in the reporting of personality (Krok-Schoen and Baker 2014). Although little research evaluating the relationship between the Big Five personality factor model and hypertension exists among minority groups, research analyzing the link between hypertension and other psychosocial factors such as anxiety (Pointer et al. 2012; Spruill et al. 2007), psychological distress (Krieger et al. 2008), and racial discrimination (Cuffee et al. 2013; Dolezsar et al. 2014) can provide some insight into possible mechanisms in which specific personality facets may lead to high blood pressure. For instance, in a study of African-American hypertensive adults, Cuffee and colleagues found that those who experienced racial discrimination were less likely to adhere to their medicine regimen (2013). Experiencing discrimination can possibly lead to distrust of medical professionals, therefore leading to adverse scores on facets such as neuroticism, which is known to affect the likelihood of one utilizing health services (Lahey 2009).

In this study, I first evaluate whether any significant patterns in personality exist in a nationally representative sample of whites, blacks, and Hispanics, ages 50 and older, at baseline and, subsequently, whether changes in personality occur over a four-year time period.

Are there significant, population-level differences in personality by race? Based upon previous literature (Lincoln et al. 2003), I hypothesize that whites would score lower than blacks and Hispanics on extraversion, yet higher on neuroticism. In a paper examining the role of social support, personal control, and negative interaction among blacks and whites in The National Comorbidity Survey, Lincoln and colleagues found that whites had higher scores on neuroticism and reported lower scores on outgoing and lively, two indicators of extraversion (Lincoln et al. 2003). Similar patterns may prevail when examining this sample.

Potential Differences in Item Responses by Race/Ethnicity

Potential race/ethnic differences in personality may very well be a result of differences in responding to survey items. This difference can be exhibited two ways. First, race/ethnic differences in item responses can be an artifact of the varying social experiences unique to each group over the life course. Researchers who advocate real differences by race/ethnicity look toward literature on racial identity and personality development in order to explain variation. This line of research suggests that sustained racial discrimination and social injustice over substantial periods of time leads to a strong racial self-identity and distinct personality in minority groups (Gaines 1995; Mitchelson et al. 2009). Given that racial discrimination is linked to psychological distress, higher depressive symptomatology, and adverse physical health outcomes as early as adolescence, race differences in personality characteristics may be evident at every stage of the life course.

Second, living in potentially socially undesirable conditions could result in different reporting patterns on surveys for minority populations. In a study examining race differences in Likert scale responses, McIntyre found that blacks had a greater tendency to select midpoint responses to psychological questions, which was attributed to a more agreeable nature (1997). In turn, whites were more likely to report either of the extremes, whereas blacks and Asian-Pacific Islanders reported the highest mean number of midpoint and lowest mean number of either extreme among five race groups (McIntyre 1997). Others have also observed the positive nature of blacks' responses in surveys (Bachman and O'Malley 1984; Collins and Gleaves 1998; Johnson 2001). Drawing upon research in Black Psychology, Johnson (2001) suggests that a more agreeable nature among blacks can be a result of survival mechanisms reinforced through slavery and subsequent segregation as well as an artifact of the notion of kinship and collectivism widely prevalent within the African-American community. Given their minority status, similar patterns of collectivism that is often found among blacks and those of East Asian decent may also be evident among Hispanics.

Measurement issues arise when studying race/ethnic group variation in personality characteristics. Research on race/ethnic differences in differential item functioning (DIF) as it specifically relates to personality suggests measurement group differences do exist at the trait/item level. Mitchelson et al. (2009) found that race/ethnic variation on DIF was more significant than gender differences. Specifically, African American's greater likelihood for endorsing questions related to privacy ("I am a very private person", "privacy is important") suggests potential item bias (Mitchelson et al. 2009). This particular bias may be an artifact of the minorities' long-held suspicions regarding groups in power.

This study seeks to evaluate whether any significant race/ethnic patterns in personality exist in a nationally representative sample of older whites, blacks, and Hispanics at baseline and whether changes occur. Also, this study examines whether personality, both at the trait level and over time, can predict hypertension, as measured by a combination of measured blood pressure and self-reports of the condition. Socio-demographic factors, such as race/ethnicity, socioeconomic status, age, and gender, are utilized to control for potential relationships between personality and hypertension. Of the few studies that examine race differences in personality in the U.S. population, few have evaluated Big Five personality differences between Whites, Blacks, and Hispanics within a nationally representative sample.

Based upon previous literature, I propose the following relationships.

(1) *Given past personality research on response styles by race presented elsewhere in the paper, both Hispanics and African Americans would exhibit higher scores, on average, on agreeableness.*
(2) *Whites score lower than blacks and Hispanics on extraversion, yet higher on neuroticism.* In a study examining the role of social support, personal control, and negative interaction among blacks and whites in The National Comorbidity Survey, Lincoln et al. (2003) found that whites had higher scores on neuroticism and reported lower scores on outgoing and lively, two indicators of extraversion (Lincoln et al. 2003).
(3) *Socioeconomic Status (SES) plays an important role in the relationship between personality and hypertension.* SES has been independently associated with personality traits as well as hypertension. Specifically, negative personality traits, such as higher hostility (Barefoot et al. 1991; Kubzansky et al. 1999), poor coping behaviors (Krueger and Chang 2008; Tsenkova et al. 2008), and low openness to experience (Körner et al. 2003) are exhibited among low SES groups (Jonassaint et al. 2011) Likewise, the evidence of an SES gradient in health, where SES is positively correlated with health, has been extensively noted (Adler and Ostrove 1999; Smith 2004; Seeman et al. 2004). Research has shown that low SES is associated with high blood pressure (Grotto et al. 2008).

Given this information, the link between personality and hypertension may be more pronounced for those with lower SES.
(4) Neuroticism and conscientiousness are significantly related not only to the prevalence of hypertension but also to the undiagnosed and poorly treated cases in the study. Those who score high on conscientiousness will be less likely to have undiagnosed or poorly treated hypertension. Similarly, individuals scoring high on neuroticism will be more likely to have hypertension.

Data and Methodology

The 2006 and 2010 waves of the Health and Retirement Study (HRS) were used for this research. Sponsored by the National Institute on Aging (grant number NIA U01AG009740) and conducted by the University of Michigan, the HRS is a nationally representative, longitudinal survey of approximately 25,000 Americans 50 years of age and older (2006). While the HRS began in 1992, detailed psychosocial measures, including personality, were just added within the last 10 years. Specifically, the initial set of personality-related measures was implemented in 2004, when a pilot module to collect psychosocial information was first conducted. One half of the HRS sample completed the personality and psychosocial measures in 2006, with the remaining half of the study completing the measures in 2008. In 2010, the first half of respondents (2006 wave) was re-interviewed on the personality items. Similarly, the participants providing responses on personality characteristics in 2008 were interviewed again in 2012.

Personality. The Psychosocial and Lifestyle module represents the first comprehensive set of psychosocial indicators, including the 5 dimensions of personality, available in the dataset (HRS Psychosocial Working Group 2013). The HRS utilizes 26 items, based on the Midlife Development Inventory (MIDI) personality scales, to construct indices of the Big Five dimensions. Respondents were asked to note whether a given item described their personality (1) a lot, (2) some, (3) a little, or (4) not at all. Responses for each item were averaged and scored, creating the five dimensions of personality (Table 4.1). The reliability of the scales has been proven in past research (Lachman and Weaver 1997), and the alpha coefficients provided are acceptable. In addition to examining the mean scores of the five traits for personality in 2006, personality change scores were created to evaluate whether respondents' scores changed between 2006 and 2010. To create these change scores, the trait-level scores from 2006 were subtracted from the scores in 2010.

Hypertension. The inclusion of measurements for blood pressure, in addition to self-reports of hypertension, provides a robust amount of information for determining the severity of the condition. For the self-assessments of hypertension, respondents were asked if a doctor or health professional ever told them that they had high blood pressure or diabetes. If a person stated that he or she had been diagnosed with hypertension, a follow-up question on medication use was asked as

Table 4.1 Items used in measuring the 'big five' personality construct, health and retirement study[a]

Personality construct	Items
Extraversion (alpha = 0.75)	Outgoing, friendly, lively, active, talkative
Agreeableness (alpha = 0.78)	Helpful, warm, caring, soft-hearted, sympathetic
Conscientiousness (alpha = 0.67)	Organized, responsible, hardworking, careless,[b] thorough
Neuroticism (alpha = 0.70)	Moody, worrying, nervous, calm[b]
Openness to experience (alpha = 0.79)	Creative, imaginative, intelligent, curious, broad-minded, sophisticated, adventurous

[a]For each item, respondents answer 1 = a lot, 2 = some, 3 = a little, 4 = not at all
[b]Item is reverse coded

well. Additionally, blood pressure was measured three times via an automated inflatable cuff in order to obtain an average blood pressure reading for the analysis. Respondents were classified as hypertensive if they had an average systolic blood pressure greater than or equal to 140 mm Hg or an average diastolic blood pressure reading of greater than or equal to 90 mm Hg. These guidelines are widely accepted within the medical and public health communities (Chobanian et al. 2003).

The array of hypertension-related questions provided in the HRS provides a comprehensive set of measures in which to analyze respondents' hypertension-associated experiences. Although self-reports of hypertension are helpful, these assessments cannot capture those who have yet to be diagnosed by a health professional. The implementation of blood pressure readings allows one to incorporate undiagnosed disease. The use of biomarker measurements can also reaffirm the presence of hypertension in individuals and alert researchers to segments of the population who may not, for whatever reason, be receiving adequate care for their condition.

In this study, four outcome measures were created to capture the prevalence and management of hypertension. First, individuals are deemed *healthy* if they do not self-report a hypertension diagnosis and their blood pressure falls below the threshold discussed above. Respondents are classified as *undiagnosed* if they measure high on the average blood pressure reading and have not been diagnosed by a health professional, based on their response on the self-reported hypertension question. Respondents who report a diagnosis but measure low on the average blood pressure reading are classified as having *good control* of their condition. Finally, respondents are described as having *uncontrolled* hypertension in this study if they have been diagnosed, yet still has high blood pressure.

Covariates. Select socio-demographic variables were included in the analyses. Age is is included as a continuous variable. Race/ethnicity is classified as non-Hispanic white (referred to as whites), non-Hispanic black (black), and Hispanic. Blacks and Hispanics comprise approximately 16% of the sample, whereas women represented over half of the sample (58%) studied for the analyses.

Socio-economic measures such as education (less than high school, high school, more than high school), total household income, and insurance coverage (no health insurance, private insurance, Medicare, Medicaid) where examined in the data as well. After taking into account the number of respondents who answered personality questions in 2006, 5390 individuals were selected for the final analyses.

T-tests were used to examine the variation between the means and the change in means by race/ethnic group. Cross tabulations of the hypertension prevalence and management classifications were also assessed by race/ethnicity. Next, a series of logistic regression models were used to examine the relationship between personality and hypertension. Specifically, the mean scores of the personality traits as well as the changes in these scores from 2006 to 2010 were used as predictors of 2010 reports of (1) the presence of hypertension (self-reported or measured), (2) the occurrence of undiagnosed hypertension, and (3) the presence of poorly managed hypertension, while controlling for socio-demographic characteristics.

Results

Table 4.2 displays race/ethnic variations of the mean scores for personality for both 2006 and 2010. On average, blacks report a higher mean score on extraversion than both whites and Hispanics in 2006 and in 2010, although the gap between blacks and whites is not statistically significant in 2010. Contrary to the proposed hypothesis, agreeableness does not vary much by race/ethnicity at each point in time. Whites report a higher mean score for conscientiousness in both waves. Hispanics exhibit the highest scores for neuroticism, whereas blacks report the lowest scores on neuroticism in 2006 and 2010. Hispanics also score significantly lower than their counterparts on openness to experience.

The mean change scores also provide some insight into whether group-level changes in personality occur over a four-year time span (Table 4.3). Negative changes in personality scores were evident only for extraversion, suggesting that, regardless of race/ethnicity, respondents in this sample experienced declines on characteristics signifying extraversion. Whites, however, experienced a slightly

Table 4.2 Race/ethnic variation of mean big five personality scores, HRS 2006 and 2010[c]

Trait	2006 mean scores			2010 mean scores		
	White	Black	Hispanic	White	Black	Hispanic
Extraversion	3.20	3.27[a]	3.18[b]	3.27	3.29	3.21[b]
Agreeableness	3.51	3.55	3.46[b]	3.51	3.51	3.45
Conscientiousness	3.40	3.32[a]	3.31[a]	3.40	3.33[a]	3.29[a]
Neuroticism	2.07	1.98[a]	2.26[a,b]	2.00	1.87[a]	2.11[a,b]
Openness	2.98	3.00	2.85[a,b]	2.92	2.95	2.79[a,b]

[a]Statistically different from whites (p < 0.05)
[b]Statistically different from blacks (p < 0.05)
[c]Scale: 1–4

Table 4.3 Changes in the mean big five personality scores, HRS 2006 and 2010

Trait	Mean Change Score (SD)			Range of Score Changes		
	White	Black	Hispanic	White	Black	Hispanic
Extraversion	−0.07 (0.42)	−0.02 (0.51)	−0.03 (0.55)	−2.40 to 2.60	−1.80 to 2.00	−2.00 to 1.80
Agreeableness	0.01 (0.39)	0.05 (0.47)	0.01 (0.49)	−2.40 to 2.40	−1.60 to 1.80	−1.80 to 2.20
Conscientiousness	0.02 (0.38)	0.01 (0.49)	0.00 (0.47)	−1.80 to 3.00	−2.00 to 2.00	−1.20 to 2.55
Neuroticism	0.06 (0.50)	0.08 (0.59)	0.14 (0.58)	−2.25 to 2.00	−2.00 to 2.25	−2.25 to 2.00
Openness	0.07 (0.43)	0.04 (0.55)	0.03 (0.55)	−2.20 to 2.71	−2.25 to 1.60	−1.71 to 2.14

larger mean score change on extraversion (−0.07). Conversely, positive changes in personality scores indicate increases in traits over time. Positive mean score changes were exhibited for all race/ethnic groups on agreeableness, conscientiousness, neuroticism, and openness to experience. Blacks and Hispanics experienced the largest, positive changes on neuroticism during this time period. In fact, the largest mean score change is for neuroticism among Hispanics. This mean score also has the largest standard deviation, therefore suggesting that there are greater individual differences occurring within this group.

Table 4.4 provides a visual analysis of four hypertension categories as well as the percentages of respondents experiencing each outcome by race/ethnicity. Approximately a third of the sample is healthy, meaning they do not self-report a hypertension diagnosis nor do they measure high on the blood pressure readings. About 36% of the sample is successfully managing their hypertension. The remaining third of the population are either undiagnosed (11%) or experiencing uncontrolled hypertension (20.2%). A much smaller percentage of blacks (15.4%) as compared to both Hispanics (30.3%) and whites (34.2) are living without hypertension. A larger percentage of blacks, however, are managing their hypertension. Although the relatively smaller percentages across all groups for the

Table 4.4 Self-reported diagnosis and measurement of hypertension, by race and ethnicity, HRS 2010, weighted data

	Healthy	Undiagnosed	Good control	Sick-uncontrolled
Self-report of hypertension	No	No	Yes	Yes
Measured SBP $\geq$ 140 or DBP $\geq$ 90	No	Yes	No	Yes
All (%)	32.7	11.0	36.1	20.2
Blacks (%)	15.4	8.7	45.4	30.4
Hispanics (%)	30.3	11.4	31.9	26.5
Whites (%)	34.2	11.1	35.5	19.3

undiagnosed category may suggest that efforts to detect hypertension have been successful, higher percentages for uncontrolled hypertension also indicates that additional work is needed to reduce the burden of hypertension, particularly in communities of color.

In an effort to examine what covariates, in addition to personality, can explain potential racial differences in prevalence and management of hypertension, Table 4.5 displays a series of models assessing three main outcomes: disease prevalence (vs. no disease), undiagnosed (vs. diagnosed) condition, and poorly managed (vs. good/adequate control) disease. For each outcome, three models are specified, where demographic characteristics, personality (mean of personality in 2006 and 2010), and mean change score of personality are included as predictors. Next, demographic characteristics and SES-related variables only are added to the model, with the third and final model taking into consideration all demographic, SES, and personality-related factors.

The first set of models examines the prevalence of hypertension (self-reported or measured). The black-white disparity in hypertension prevalence is large; the odds of having hypertension for blacks are more than double the odds of their white counterparts. This disparity does not diminish when other factors are considered. As expected, the likelihood of experiencing hypertension increases with age. In regards to personality, agreeableness, conscientiousness, and neuroticism are all significantly associated with the prevalence of hypertension, when controlling for age, race, and gender. Those with higher mean scores on agreeableness and neuroticism have greater odds of having hypertension, whereas those who score high on conscientiousness are less likely to have hypertension. Once SES-related factors are considered, however, the relationships between agreeableness and conscientiousness are no longer significant; the link between neuroticism and hypertension remains.

The second set of models analyzes the association between personality, race, and undiagnosed hypertension. Compared to whites, blacks have lower odds of being undiagnosed, a finding that remains consistent across this set of models. With increasing age comes a lower likelihood of being undiagnosed, which, similar to the finding for blacks, could signal the success of targeted public health efforts to particular groups. The link between age and undiagnosed hypertension operates through SES. Those without a high school diploma are more likely to be undiagnosed, whereas those who are on Medicare are less likely to be diagnosed. Those who score high on neuroticism are less likely to be undiagnosed. For those who are more oriented towards worrying about issues, it is conceivable that these individuals may seek out help when needed. In turn, openness to experience is associated with undiagnosed hypertension.

The final set of models assesses the predictors of poorly controlled hypertension. Hispanics have greater odds of having poorly controlled hypertension, although the significance of the association diminishes once SES-related factors and personality are taken into account. Respondents possessing higher education are less likely to have uncontrolled hypertension. Medicare patients are also less likely to have

Table 4.5 Logistic regression models of personality as predictors of hypertension (prevalence, undiagnosed, and poorly managed disease), HRS 2010, weighted data

	Disease (self-report or measured)			Undiagnosed			Poor Control		
	Model 1	Model 2	Model 3	Model 1	Model 2	Model 3	Model 1	Model 2	Model 3
Demographic									
Age	**1.052*****	**1.038*****	**1.040*****	**0.980*****	1.007	1.004	**1.017*****	**1.025*****	**1.024*****
Black	**2.992*****	**2.348*****	**2.453*****	**0.536****	**0.616***	**0.545****	1.257	1.134	1.143
Hispanic	1.220	1.018	1.018	1.015	0.925	0.979	**1.534***	1.331	1.338
Female	**0.773*****	**0.777*****	**0.759*****	0.843	0.839	0.863	**0.781****	**0.769*****	**0.770****
SES									
Less than HS		1.237	1.217		**1.821*****	**1.908*****		1.251	1.237
More than HS		**0.805****	**0.823****		1.237	1.145		**0.778****	**0.770****
No Insurance		1.131	1.128		0.930	0.908		1.080	1.075
Medicaid		1.147	1.095		0.882	0.936		1.332	1.331
Medicare		1.116	1.107		**0.576*****	**0.567*****		**0.754***	**0.748***
Log Income		**0.877*****	**0.890****		**1.241*****	**1.176****		1.040	1.038
Personality									
Extraversion	0.957		0.933	1.216		1.227	1.143		1.159
Agreeableness	**1.206***		1.139	0.808		0.841	0.989		0.932
Conscientiousness	**0.777*****		0.850	1.189		1.141	0.955		0.982
Neuroticism	**1.196*****		**1.165***	**0.690*****		**0.694*****	1.056		1.044
Openness	0.915		1.004	**1.342***		**1.316***	0.960		1.032
Personality change									
Extraversion	0.910		0.893	1.123		1.139	1.043		1.024
Agreeableness	0.999		1.002	0.918		0.904	1.023		1.017
Conscientiousness	1.134		1.101	0.874		0.886	1.396		1.342

(continued)

Table 4.5 (continued)

	Disease (self-report or measured)			Undiagnosed			Poor Control		
	Model 1	Model 2	Model 3	Model 1	Model 2	Model 3	Model 1	Model 2	Model 3
Neuroticism	1.019		1.016	0.913		0.913	0.934		0.925
Openness	1.056		1.061	1.063		1.039	0.959		0.973
N	5145			3827			2793		

Notes Odds ratios are shown. Statistically significant coefficients in bold. $*p < 0.05$; $**p < 0.01$; $***p < 0.001$
Whites, males, high school graduates, and respondents with private insurance are the reference groups for the demographic variables

poorly managed hypertension, which, again, could be an artifact of greater awareness for specific groups.

Discussion

This study explores the racial/ethnic variation of personality in a nationally representative population, and attempts to explore the potential ways in which race/ethnicity and personality merge to impact health outcomes. Several noticeable patterns emerged. Hispanics score higher on neuroticism and lower on openness to experience than blacks and whites. Also, blacks have a lower average score on neuroticism than whites and Hispanics. These mean scores show only slight changes across a four-year period. The most noticeable change in mean scores was for neuroticism among Hispanics, where a slight increase in the facet occurs. Future research will examine socio-environmental factors that could potentially explain these differences.

There are several reasons why changes in mean scores for personality in this study were negligible. Longer periods of time may be needed to see noticeable differences in personality at the population level. An ideal analysis of change would incorporate more than two waves of data; future plans will include additional waves of data as they become available in the HRS. With additional data, other statistical procedures, such as growth curve modeling (Mroczek and Spiro 2007), for example, could be employed to further examine these questions and to evaluate individual-level variation. Change scores, however, are used to analyze change in personality in this study as well as in others, with promising results (Turiano et al. 2012).

The models used to predict hypertension prevalence and management show the utility of employing personality into research on health disparities. Conscientiousness, neuroticism, and opening to experience were all linked to the disease process. These findings are similar to a recent study that utilizes the HRS data, which found that conscientiousness, neuroticism, openness to experience, and agreeableness played roles in predicting health outcomes (Weston et al. 2015). How might one use personality to study race/ethnic disparities in health? Research linking other social mechanisms to work on personality and health are key to understanding how socio-behavioral processes interact with biological and environmental processes to impact health. For minority and disadvantaged populations, understanding social factors such as stress and discrimination can be extremely helpful in facilitating and fostering efforts regarding disease prevention and management. Moreover, this study also highlights both the importance of assessing the interplay between personality and other socio-demographic factors across the life course and the complexity of the link between personality and health outcomes such as hypertension. Understanding how neuroticism, for instance, operates at different points in one's life, at various stages of the disease experience, could provide researchers and clinicians with greater insight into how health disparities manifest and persist over time.

References

Adler, N. E., & Ostrove, J. M. (1999). Socioeconomic status and health: What we know and what we don't. *Annals of the New York Academy of Sciences, 896*(1), 3–15.

Aiken-Morgan, A. T., Bichsel, J., Savla, J., Edwards, C. L., & Whitfield, K. E. (2014). Associations between self-rated health and personality. *Ethnicity and Disease, 24*(4), 418–422.

Bachman, J. G., & O'Mallley, P. M. (1984). Yea-saying, nay-saying, and going to extremes: Black-white differences in response styles. *Public Opinion Quarterly, 48*(2), 491–509.

Barefoot, J. C., Peterson, B. L., Dahlstrom, W. G., Siegler, I. C., Anderson, N. B., & Williams, R. B. (1991). Hostility patterns and health implications: Correlates of Cook-Medley Hostility scale scores in a national survey. *Health Psychology, 10*(1), 18–24.

Bogg, T., & Roberts, B. W. (2004). Conscientiousness and health-related behaviors: A meta-analysis of the leading behavioral contributors to mortality. *Psychological Bulletin, 130*(6), 887–919.

Bogg, T., & Roberts, B. (2013). The case for conscientiousness: Evidence and implications for a personality trait marker of health and longevity. *Annals of Behavioral Medicine, 45*(3), 278–288.

Boyce, C., Wood, A., & Powdthavee, N. (2013). Is personality fixed? Personality changes as much as "variable" economic factors and more strongly predicts changes to life satisfaction. *Social Indicators Research, 111*(1), 287–305.

Chobanian, A. V., Bakris, G. L., Black, H. R., Cushman, W. C., Green, L. A., Izzo, J. L., et al. (2003). Seventh report of the joint national committee on prevention, detection, evaluation, and treatment of high blood pressure. *Hypertension, 42*, 1206–1252.

Collins, J. M., & Gleaves, D. H. (1998). Race, job applicants, and the five-factor model of personality: Implications for black psychology, industrial/organizational psychology, and the five-factor theory. *Journal of Applied Sociology, 83*, 531–544.

Cooper, D. C., Katzel, L. I., & Waldstein, S. R. (2007). Cardiovascular reactivity in older adults. In C. M. Aldwin, C. L. Park, & A. Spiro (Eds.), *Handbook of health psychology and aging* (pp. 142–164). New York: Guilford Press.

Costa, P. T., Herbst, J. H., McCrae, R. R., & Siegler, I. C. (2000). Personality at midlife: Stability, intrinsic maturation, and response to life events. *Assessment, 7*(4), 365–378.

Cuffee, Y. L., Hargraves, J. L., Rosal, M., Briesacher, B. A., Schoenthaler, A., Person, S., et al. (2013). Reported racial discrimination, trust in physicians, and medication adherence among inner-city African Americans with hypertension. *American Journal of Public Health, 103*(11), e55–e62.

Day, D. V., & Bedeian, A. G. (1995). Personality similarity and work-related outcomes among African-American nursing personnel: A test of the supplementary model of person-environment congruence. *Journal of Vocational Behavior, 46*(1), 55–70.

Denollet, J. (2000). Type D personality: A potential risk factor refined. *Journal of Psychosomatic Research, 49*(4), 255–266.

Digman, J. M. (1990). Personality structure: Emergence of the five-factor model. *Annual Review of Psychology, 41*, 417–440.

Dolezsar, C. M., McGrath, J. J., Herzig, A. J., & Miller, S. B. (2014). Perceived racial discrimination and hypertension: A comprehensive systematic review. *Health Psychology, 33*(1), 20–34.

Egan, B. M., Zhao, Y., Axon, R. N., Brzezinski, W. A., & Ferdinand, K. C. (2011). Uncontrolled and apparent treatment resistant hypertension in the United States, 1988 to 2008. *Circulation, 124*(9), 1046–1058.

Foldes, H. J., Duehr, E. E., & Ones, D. S. (2008). Group differences in personality: Meta-analyses comparing five U.S. racial groups. *Personnel Psychology, 61*(3), 579–616.

Gaines S. (1995). Relationships between members of cultural minorities. In J. T. Wood & S. Duck (Eds.), *Understudied relationships: Off the beaten track. Understanding relationship processes series* (pp. 51–88). Thousand Oaks, CA: Sage.

Goldberg, L. R., Sweeney, D., Merenda, P. F., & Hughes, J. E, Jr. (1998). Demographic variables and personality: The effects of gender, age, education, and ethnic/racial status on self-descriptions of personality attributes. *Personality and Individual Differences, 24*(3), 393–403.

Goodwin, R. D., & Friedman, H. S. (2006). Health status and the five-factor personality traits in a nationally representative sample. *Journal of Health Psychology, 11*(5), 643–654.

Grotto, I., Huerta, M., & Sharabi, Y. (2008). Hypertension and socioeconomic status. *Current Opinion in Cardiology, 23*(4), 335–339.

Hagger-Johnson, G., Sabia, S., Nabi, H., Brunner, E., Kivimaki, M., Shipley, M., et al. (2012). Low conscientiousness and risk of all-cause, cardiovascular and cancer mortality over 17 years: Whitehall II cohort study. *Journal of Psychosomatic Research, 73*(2), 98–103.

Hampson, S. E., & Friedman, H. S. (2008). Personality and health: A lifespan perspective. In O. P. John, R. Robins & L. Pervin (Eds.), *The handbook of personality*, 3rd edn (pp. 770–794). New York: Guilford Press.

Hampson, S. E., Tildesley, E., Andrews, J. A., Luyckx, K., & Mroczek, D. K. (2010). The relation of change in hostility and sociability during childhood to substance use in mid adolescence. *Journal of Research in Personality, 44*(1), 103–114.

Health and Retirement Study (Core, Biomarker) public use dataset. (2006). Produced and distributed by the University of Michigan with funding from the National Institute on Aging (grant number NIA U01AG009740). Ann Arbor, MI.

Helson, R., Jones, C., & Kwan, V. S. (2002). Personality change over 40 years of adulthood: Hierarchical linear modeling analyses of two longitudinal samples. *Journal of personality and social psychology, 83*(3), 752–766.

Hill, P. L., Turiano, N. A., Hurd, M. D., Mroczek, D. K., & Roberts, B. W. (2011). Conscientiousness and longevity: An examination of possible mediators. *Health Psychology, 30*(5), 536–541.

HRS Psychosocial Working Group. (2013). Psychosocial and lifestyle questionnaire: 2006–2010. Available at: http://hrsonline.isr.umich.edu/sitedocs/userg/HRS2006-2010SAQdoc.pdf

Hough, L. M., Oswald, F. L., & Ployhart, R. E. (2001). Determinants, detection and amelioration of adverse impact in personnel selection procedures: Issues, evidence and lessons learned. *International Journal of Selection and Assessment, 9*, 152–194.

Johnson, J. L. (2001). *Racial and gender differences in the five factors of personality within military samples* (No. DEOMI-RSP-00-7). Defense Equal Opportunity Management Institute. PATRICK AFB FL.

Jokela, M., Batty, G. D., Nyberg, S. T., Virtanen, M., Nabi, H., Singh-Manoux, A., et al. (2013). Personality and all-cause mortality: Individual-participant meta-analysis of 3,947 deaths in 76,150 adults. *American Journal of Epidemiology, 178*(5), 667–675.

Jokela, M., Hakulinen, C., Singh-Manoux, A., & Kivimäki, M. (2014). Personality change associated with chronic diseases: Pooled analysis of four prospective cohort studies. *Psychological Medicine, 44*(12), 2629–2640.

Jonassaint, C. R., Siegler, I. C., Barefoot, J. C., Edwards, C. L., & Williams, R. B. (2011). Low life course socioeconomic status (SES) is associated with negative NEO PI-R personality patterns. *International Journal of Behavioral Medicine, 18*(1), 13–21.

Jones, R. L. (1991). *Black psychology*. Berkeley, CA: Cobb & Henry.

Klein, D. N., Kotov, R., & Bufferd, S. J. (2011). Personality and depression: Explanatory models and review of the evidence. *Annual Review of Clinical Psychology, 7*, 269–295.

Körner, A., Geyer, M., Gunzelmann, T., & Brähler, E. (2003). The influence of socio-demographic factors on personality dimensions in the elderly. *Zeitschrift für Gerontologie und Geriatrie, 36* (2), 130–137.

Krieger, N., Chen, J. T., Waterman, P. D., Hartman, C., Stoddard, A. M., Quinn, M. M., et al. (2008). The inverse hazard law: Blood pressure, sexual harassment, racial discrimination, workplace abuse and occupational exposures in US low-income black, white and Latino workers. *Social Science and Medicine, 67*(12), 1970–1981.

Krieger, N., & Sidney, S. (1996). Racial discrimination and blood pressure: The CARDIA study of young black and white adults. *American Journal of Public Health, 86*, 1370–1378.

Krok-Schoen, J. L., & Baker, T. A. (2014). Race differences in personality and affect between older white and black patients: An exploratory study. *Journal of Racial and Ethnic Health Disparities, 1*(4), 283–290.

Krueger, P. M., & Chang, V. W. (2008). Being poor and coping with stress: Health behaviors and the risk of death. *American Journal of Public Health, 98*(5), 889–896.

Kubzansky, L., Kawachi, I., & Sparrow, D. (1999). Socioeconomic status, hostility, and risk factor clustering in the normative aging study: Any help from the concept of allostatic load? *Annals of Behavioral Medicine, 21*(4), 330–338.

Lachman, M. E., & Weaver, L. S. (1997). *Midlife develompent inventory (MIDI) personality scales: Scale construction and scoring.* Technical report. Brandeis University, Waltham, MA.

Lahey, B. B. (2009). Public health significance of neuroticism. *American Psychologist, 64*(4), 241.

Letzring, T. D., Edmonds, G. W., & Hampson, S. E. (2014). Personality change at mid-life is associated with changes in self-rated health: Evidence from the Hawaii Personality and Health Cohort. *Personality and Individual Differences, 58*, 60–64.

Lincoln, K. D., Chatters, L. M., & Taylor, R. J. (2003). Psychological distress among black and white Americans: Differential effects of social support, negative interaction and personal control. *Journal of Health and Social Behavior, 44*, 390–407.

McCrae, R. R., & Costa, P. T. (1987). Validation of the five-factor model of personality across instruments and observers. *Journal of Personality and Social Psychology, 52*, 81–90.

McCrae, R. R., & Costa, P. T. (1996). Toward a new generation of personality theories: Theoretical contexts for the five-factor model. In J. S. Wiggins (Ed.), *The five-factor model of personality: Theoretical perspectives* (pp. 51–86). New York: Guilford Press.

McIntyre, R. M. (1997). Response styles and differences in variation of responses between demographic groups in the MEOCS database. *Defense Equal Opportunity Management Institute Research Series Pamphlet* (pp. 97–98). Patrick Air Force Base, FL: Directorate of Research.

Mitchelson, J. K., Wicher, E. W., LeBreton, J. M., & Craig, S. B. (2009). Gender and ethnicity differences on the abridged big five circumplex (AB5C) of personality traits: A differential item functioning analysis. *Educational and Psychological Measurement, 69*, 613–636.

Mozaffarian, D., Benjamin, E. J., Go, A. S., Arnett, D. K., Blaha, M. J., Cushman, M., et al. (2015). American heart association statistics committee and stroke statistics subcommittee. *Circulation, 131*(4), e29–e322.

Mroczek, D. K., & Spiro, A. (2007). Personality change influences mortality in older men. *Psychological Science, 18*(5), 371–376.

Mulder, R. T. (2002). Personality pathology and treatment outcome in major depression: A review. *American Journal of Psychiatry, 159*, 359–371.

Myrtek, M. (2001). Meta-analyses of prospective studies on coronary heart disease, type A personality, and hostility. *International Journal of Cardiology, 79*(2), 245–251.

Nwankwo, T., Yoon, S. S., Burt, V., & Gu, Q. (2013). Hypertension among adults in the United States: National health and nutrition examination survey, 2011–2012. In *NCHS data brief*, Vol. 133. Hyattsville, MD: National Center for Health Statistics.

Ones, D. S., & Anderson, N. (2002). Gender and ethnic group differences on personality scales in selection: Some British data. *Journal of Occupational and Organizational Psychology, 75*, 255–276.

Pointer, M. A., Yancey, S., Abou-Chacra, R., Petrusi, P., Waters, S. J., & McClelland, M. K. (2012). State anxiety is associated with cardiovascular reactivity in young, healthy African Americans. *International Journal of Hypertension, 2*, 1–7.

Seeman, T. E., Crimmins, E., Huang, M. H., Singer, B., Bucur, A., Gruenewald, T., et al. (2004). Cumulative biological risk and socioeconomic differences in mortality: MacArthur studies of successful aging. *Social Science and Medicine, 58*(10), 1985–1997.

Siegler, I. C., Costa, P. T., Brummett, B. H., Helms, M. J., Barefoot, J. C., Williams, R. B., et al. (2003). Patterns of change in hostility from college to midlife in the UNC alumni heart study predict high-risk status. *Psychosomatic Medicine, 65*(5), 738–745.

Smith, J. P. (2004). Unraveling the ses: Health connection. *Population and Development Review, 30*, 108–132.

Smith, T. W., Glazer, K., Ruiz, J. M., & Gallo, L. C. (2004). Hostility, anger, aggressiveness, and coronary heart disease: An interpersonal perspective on personality, emotion, and health. *Journal of Personality, 72*(6), 1217–1270.

Spiro, A., Aldwin, C. M., Ward, K. D., & Mroczek, D. K. (1995). Personality and the incidence of hypertension among older men: Longitudinal findings from the normative aging study. *Health Psychology, 14*(6), 563–569.

Spruill, T. M., Pickering, T. G., Schwartz, J. E., Mostofsky, E., Ogedegbe, G., Clemow, L., et al. (2007). The impact of perceived hypertension status on anxiety and the white coat effect. *Annals of Behavioral Medicine, 34*, 1–9.

Srivastava, S., John, O. P., Goslin, S. D., & Potter, J. (2003). Development of personality in early and middle adulthood: Set like plaster or persistent change? *Journal of Personality and Social Psychology, 84*, 1041–1053.

Tate, B. W., & McDaniel, M. A. (2008). *Race differences in personality: An evaluation of moderators and publication bias*. Anaheim, CA: Annual Meeting of the Academy of Management.

Terracciano, A., Scuteri, A., Strait, J., Sutin, A. R., Meirelles, O., Marongiu, M., et al. (2014). Are personality traits associated with white coat and masked hypertension? *Journal of Hypertension, 32*(10), 1987–1992.

Tsenkova, V. K., Love, G., Singer, B. H., & Ryff, C. D. (2008). Coping and positive affect predict longitudinal change in glycosylated hemoglobin. *Health Psychology, 27*(2 Suppl), S163–S171.

Turiano, N. A., Mroczek, D. K., Moynihan, J., & Chapman, B. P. (2013). Big 5 personality traits and interleukin-6: Evidence for "healthy neuroticism" in a U.S. population sample. *Brain, Behavior, and Immunity, 28*, 83–89.

Turiano, N. A., Pitzer, L., Armour, C., Karlamangla, A., Ryff, C. D., & Mroczek, D. K. (2011). Personality trait level and change as predictors of health outcomes: Findings from a national study of Americans (MIDUS). *The Journals of Gerontology Series B: Psychological Sciences and Social Sciences, 67*(10), 4–12.

Turiano, N. A., Spiro, A., & Mroczek, D. K. (2012). Openness to experience and mortality in men: Analysis of trait and facets. *Journal of Aging and Health, 24*(4), 654–672.

Weston, S. J., Hill, P. L., & Jackson, J. J. (2015). Personality traits predict the onset of disease. *Social Psychological and Personality Science, 6*(3), 309–317.

Williams, D. R., & Neighbors, H. (2001). Racism, discrimination and hypertension: Evidence and needed research. *Ethnicity and Disease, 11*(4), 800–816.

Yoon, S. S., Gu, Q., Nwankwo, T., Wright, J. D., Hong, Y., & Burt, V. (2015). Trends in blood pressure among adults with hypertension United States, 2003 to 2012. *Hypertension, 65*(1), 54–61.

Chapter 5
Does Social Engagement Predict Frailty and Mortality in the Older Population?

Yumiko Kamiya and Rose Anne Kenny

Introduction

Several epidemiological studies have shown that social engagement is associated with health outcomes. The operationalization of social engagement was originally proposed by Berkman and Syme (1979) as four different sources of social contacts, namely, marital status, number of close friends and relatives, church attendance and participation in informal and formal group associations. Later House et al. (1982) defined social network in a similar way as composed of intimate social relationships (marital status, visits with friends and relatives), formal organizational involvement outside of work (going to church or membership of voluntary associations), active social leisure (going to classes or lectures, movies) and passive or solitary activity (watching TV, reading). These measures have been used either as a composite index or separate items and have been shown to predict a variety of health outcomes.

In this article, "social engagement" refers to a combination of objective and subjective measures of the salient aspects of people's "social" existence. The objective measures are also referred as 'structural support' in the literature (Barth et al. 2010; Holt-Lunstad et al. 2010). They are defined by connectedness to other individuals (the number of children, friends and relatives whom the respondent feels are close to him/her) participation in social groups (affiliation to or membership in religious, voluntary, political, and social associations or activities), and marital status (Holt-Lunstad et al. 2010).

Y. Kamiya (✉)
Department of Economic and Social Affairs, United Nations, New York, USA
e-mail: kamiya@un.org

Y. Kamiya · R.A. Kenny
Department of Medical Gerontology, Trinity College Dublin, Dublin, Ireland

The subjective measures comprise perceptions of available emotional support from spouse, children, relatives and friends and are also referred to as 'functional support' in the literature (Holt-Lunstad et al. 2010).

The objective and subjective measures of social engagement are not mutually exclusive; rather, they may help to explain "the influence of specific aspects of social relationships on health" (Kawachi and Berkman 2001). While all four components have been shown to be associated with morbidity and mortality (Cohen 2004; Lakey and Cohen 2000), it is hypothesized that they may act via different mechanisms: objective measures influence health behaviors and adherence to medical regimens, whereas subjective measures (e.g., perceived support) operate through a stress-buffering mechanism (Cohen 1988, 2004). Thus, each component might influence health in different ways (Holt-Lunstad et al. 2010; Kamiya et al. 2010; Lakey and Cohen 2000).

Frailty is a geriatric syndrome which is associated with disability, falls, morbidity and mortality (Ahmed et al. 2007; Bergman et al. 2007). Numerous definitions have been developed and two major approaches to frailty have emerged. One involves the accumulation of "deficits" across many systems and the other identifies frailty as a clinical syndrome or phenotype characterized by a specific set of symptoms (Hubbard et al. 2010). The best known and most frequently used is the Fried frailty phenotype, characterized by "an excess vulnerability to stressors, with reduced ability to maintain or regain homeostasis after a destabilizing event" (Walsto et al. 2006). Health behaviors such as alcohol consumption, obesity, smoking, physical inactivity, depression, and psychosocial factors such as lower social participation in productive activities and lower contact with friends and relatives have also been identified as risk factors for frailty (Jung et al. 2010; Strawbridge et al. 1998). However, the relationship between frailty and social engagement has been less explored and remains unclear.

The aim of the present study is to examine the association between each component of social engagement and frailty and the relationship to each to mortality. We test two hypotheses about these relationships. First, whether social engagement and frailty are independently associated with mortality. Second, whether frailty mediates the relationship between social engagement and mortality.

Methods

Study Design

The English Longitudinal Study of Ageing (ELSA) is an ongoing panel study of a nationally representative sample of the English population living in households. The original ELSA cohort consists of men and women born on or before 29 February 1952. The sample was drawn from households that had participated in the Health Survey for England (HSE) in 1998, 1999, and 2001. For the present analyses, data from the first two waves were used (baseline 2002–2003, second wave 2004–2005 and the mortality records related to the period between wave 2 and the end of wave 3. The two waves included a face-to-face interview. The second wave also included a clinical assessment by a nurse. This is the only wave containing objective health assessment and blood analysis data that is currently available for public use. Overall, 10,770 people participated in wave 1 (response rate 65.7%). Of these, 8688 people participated in wave 2 (82%) and 7648 participants were willing to have a nurse visit. For the current analysis we only included participants who were 60 years old and over at wave 1 (n = 7248 in wave 1), n = 6246 in wave 2, n = 5377 for nursing visit in wave 2, and n = 5905 in wave 3. Consent to link to mortality record was given by 10,769 participants in wave 1. Between wave 2 and wave 3, about 444 deaths occurred.

The weights used incorporate adjustment for three levels of attrition/non-response: (1) from initial sample (HSE) to wave 1; (2) from wave 1 to wave 2; and (3) from wave 2 to the nurse visit. These weights attenuate the potential selection biases due to attrition at different stages and should ensure that weighted data will be representative of the English population living in the community over 50 years (Cheshire et al. 2000). Details on the calculations of weights are presented in the ELSA technical report (Scholes et al. 2009).

Measurement of Frailty

Frailty status was measured within the definition developed by Fried et al. (2001), using standard criteria relating to weight loss/underweight, slow walking speed, weakness, self-reported exhaustion and low physical activity. Weight loss/underweight was determined by body mass index <18.5 kg/m^2. The lowest quintile of customary pace walking speed was measured in m/s over 8 feet (2.44 m), adjusted by sex and height. Grip strength was measured using a Smedley's hand Dynamometer. The lowest quintile of grip strength was recorded for the dominant hand, and the mean of two attempts was used. Scoring was according to quintile, adjusted by sex. Exhaustion was measured by whether a participant had a positive answer to the following item from CES-D: "Much of the time during the past week, could you not get going?" Physical activity was assessed by means of a detailed set of questions assessing frequency and duration of walking and mild, moderate, and strenuous activities. Participants were considered "frail" if they were positive for three or more of the above criteria, "intermediately frail" or "pre-frail" if they had 1–2 of the same criteria and non-frail if they had none.

Measures of Social Engagement

Four different dimensions of social engagement were examined. Social participation was measured as a count of seven activities in which the respondent reported current membership or participation. There were divided into: (1) political, trade union or environmental group; (2) tenants' groups, residents' groups or neighbourhood watches; (3) churches or other religious organizations; (4) charitable associations; (5) an education, arts or music group or evening class; (6) social clubs (e.g. Rotary Club, elderly lunch groups, women's groups); and (7) any other organisations, clubs or societies. The social participation raw score therefore ranges from 0 to 7. This was standardized as a Z-score. Scores range from −0.899 to 4.202 with weighted mean of −0.087 (SD = 0.953). Higher scores indicate greater social participation. Social ties were measured by a count of the number of children, relatives and friends felt to be close ("How many of your children/relatives/friends would you say you have a close relationship with?"). The final score was standardized and its value was averaged across the ties that were relevant for a given respondent. Scores range from −1.256 to 1.533 with weighted mean of −0.090 (SD = 0.301). Emotional support from spouse, children, relatives and friends was measured by the following three questions: (a) How much respondents feel their spouse/partner (children/relatives/friends) understand(s) their feelings; (b) How much respondents can rely on spouse/partner (children/relatives/friends) if they have a serious problem; and (c) How much respondents can open up to their spouse/partner (children/relatives/friends) if they need to talk. The responses for each item range from 0 (not at all) to 3 (a lot). Responses to all twelve questions were added up to a summary score (Cronbach's alpha was 0.88). The emotional support scale was standardized and its value was averaged across the ties that were relevant for a given respondent. Standardized scores range from −2.409 to 0.1838 with a weighted mean of −0.174 (SD = 0.554). As these variables are measured in different units, standardized coefficients were used to facilitate interpretation and comparison. Marital status was dichotomized as married (or cohabiting) and not married (never married, separated or divorced, and widowed).

Covariates

The following variables were included as control variables because they can be potential confounders of frailty and social engagement. These variables are well established covariates in the literature. Demographic and socio-economic variables included age (in years), age squared, sex (male as reference category), and education measured as the highest qualification participants obtained. Educational attainment was categorized into four groups (no education, primary, secondary and tertiary level). Interaction terms between sex and age were included.

Health behavior: Smoking was coded as never smoked and ever smoked (ex-smoker or current smoker).

Co-morbidity: Physical function was assessed by dichotomizing the Activities and Instrumental Activities of Daily Living into "0 (I)ADL", reporting no (I)ADL difficulties and "≥ 1 (I)ADL", reporting one or more (I)ADL difficulties. Known disease was assessed by self-reported angina, diabetes, myocardial infarction, stroke, heart failure, heart murmur, abnormal heart rhythm, and ischaemic heart disease. Other major chronic diseases include self-reported chronic lung disease, asthma, arthritis, osteoporosis, cancer, and Parkinson's disease. These variables are dichotomized into "0 conditions" and "≥ 1 conditions". Depression was measured by the 8-item Center for Epidemiologic Studies Depression Scale (CES-D) minus the exhaustion item. Cognitive functioning was measured by word recall, and executive function.

Statistical Analysis

We used Spearman's rho to test for independence among social engagement variables. The correlations between social participation and social ties ($r = 0.15$, $p < 0.001$), and social participation and emotional support ($r = 0.19$, $p < 0.001$) were weak in strength. Correlation between social ties and emotional support was moderate in strength ($r = 0.32$, $p < 0.001$). The correlation between marital status and emotional support was moderate in strength ($r = 0.29$, $p < 0.001$), while the correlation between marital status and social participation ($r = 0.04$, $p < 0.001$) and marital status and social ties was weak in strength ($r = 0.05$, $p < 0.001$). Therefore, these measurements were not strongly correlated and, since they are conceptually distinct, we expect that these four dimensions would have independent associations with frailty and mortality.

The following variables used in this study came from ELSA wave 1: marital status, number of close children, relatives and friends, social participation and emotional support, age, sex, education, smoking, and co-mordibity. Frailty variables were from wave 2 and mortality is recorded from the beginning of wave 2 to the end of wave 3.

Multinomial logistic regression was used to assess the independent contribution of baseline social engagement in predicting frailty status at wave 2. For this analysis, frailty was coded as three levels (not frail, pre-frail, and frail) with pre-frail used as the base category. Social engagement variables (social participation, social ties, marital status and emotional support) were adjusted by age, sex, education, comorbidity (i.e., physical disability, cognitive functioning, depression and chronic disease) and smoking. Cox proportional hazards models were used to assess the independent contribution of baseline social engagement and frailty status at wave 2 in predicting the incidence of death. Multinomial logit model and Cox proportional hazard model were both weighted for panel attrition.

Results

Table 5.1 presents characteristics of the sample at baseline. The sample was composed of 55.6% women and 44.4% men. The median age was 70.79 years (69.9 and 71.5 years for women and men, respectively). Sixty three percent were

Table 5.1 Descriptive characteristics of the sample at baseline and frailty at wave 2

Variable	Percent/mean (SD)
Social engagement	
Social participation	1.26 (1.40)
Social ties	1.93 (0.85)
Emotional support	1.93 (0.85)
Demographic and socio-economic variables	
Age (%)	
60–70	51.47
70–80	35.06
80+	13.46
Mean age	70.79 (7.79)
Currently married (%)	62.94
Female (%)	55.63
Education: levels of education attained	
Tertiary	17.88
Secondary	22.3
Primary	50.86
No education	8.96
Co-morbidity (%)	
Have depression (3 or more symptoms on the 8 items CES-D)	24.29
No Chronic disease[a]	53.4
No CVD[b]	74.83
No limitations with ADLs	68.21
Cognitive functioning	
Word recall	5.18 (1.66)
Animal fluency	18.51 (5.79)
Health Behaviors (%)	
Never smoked	82.5
Physical activity	
None	10.91
Light	18.25
Moderate	48.97
Vigorous	21.88
Fried frailty index	
None	42.3
Intermediate or prefrail	50.69
Frail	7.01

[a]Chronic lung disease, arthritis, osteoporosis, cancer, Parkinson's disease
[b]Angina, diabetes, myocardial infection, stroke, heart failure, heart murmur, abnormal heart rhythm, valvular heart disease, ischaemic heart disease

married, and 50.9% had a primary education. Thirty eight percent reported no social participation, and 9.7% of the respondents reported that they did not have children, relatives or friends that they felt close to. Twenty-five percent reported having cardiovascular morbidity, 53.4% reported having non-cardiovascular chronic conditions, 31.7% reported difficulties with at least one ADL, and 24.2% reported depressive symptoms. Approximately 10.9% were relatively sedentary, reporting no physical activity and 13.9% were smokers.

Prevalence of frailty increased with each five years age group, for example, only 2.8% of respondents in the 60–65 age group were frail compared with 30.62% for those aged 85 years and over. Frailty was slightly more prevalent among women than men by 7.51–6.16% ($p < 0.01$), respectively.

Table 5.2 presents the results from multinomial logistic regression. The results of the analyses examining the various components of social engagement and frailty level indicate that only emotional support was significant; that is, an increase in one standard deviation in emotional support decreases the odds of being pre-frail versus not frail by 26%. However, emotional support was not significant for those who already were pre-frail vs. the frail. Results from the MNL model show that baseline emotional support lowers the risk of becoming pre-frail for those who are not frail. However, once individuals become pre-frail, emotional support is not protective against frailty. The effects of other components of social engagement such as

Table 5.2 Multinomial logistic regression predicting frailty status at wave 2 (n = 4432)

	Non-frail/pre-frail		Frail/pre frail	
	Coefficient	95% CI	Coefficient	95% CI
Age	1.423**	1.170, 1730	1.047	0.828–1.325
Age squared	0.997**	0.996, 0.999	1.000	0.999, 1.002
Sex (=1 female)	1.433	0.370, 5.549	0.450	0.030, 6.774
Age * sex	0.997	0.978, 1.017	1.008	0.972, 1.044
Education	0.925*	0.856, 1.000	0.973	0.795, 1.190
Being married	1.121	0.964, 1.304	1.020	0.739, 1.406
Social participation	0.976	0.911, 1.046	0.841	0.698, 1.013
Social ties	1.034	0.967, 1.105	1.047	0.900, 1.220
Emotional support	1.349**	1.103, 1.651	1.148	0.875, 1.507
Never smoke	1.035	0.849, 1.261	0.781	0.525, 1.161
Physical limitations	0.5946**	0.501, 0.702	4.918**	3.418, 7.075
Word recall	1.027	0.982, 1.075	0.924	0.845, 1.010
Verbal fluency	1.010	0.998, 1.023	0.959*	0.930, 0.989
Depression	0.588**	0.495–0.699	2.352**	1.737, 3.186
At least one CVD	0.882	0.753–1.034	1.951**	1.463, 2.602
At least one chronic disease	0.782**	0.708–0.864	1.370**	1.147, 1.636

*$p < 0.05$; **$p < 0.01$
Base category is pre-frailty

Table 5.3 Cox proportional hazard model (n = 4432)

	Model 1	
	OR	95% CI
Age	1.223*	(1.026–1.457)
Age squared	0.999	(0.998–1.000)
Sex (=1 female)	0.458*	(0.360–0.579)
Education	0.931	(0.810–1.069)
Being married	0.829	(0.6502–1.056)
Social participation	0.925	(0.817–1.045)
Social ties	0.945	(0.843–1.060)
Emotional support	0.963	(0.778–1.192)
Never smoke	0.595**	(0.443–0.801)
Physical limitations	1.298**	(1.005–1.676)
Word recall	0.962	(0.896–1.033)
Verbal fluency	0.996	(0.975–1.017)
Depression	1.141	(0.887–1.467)
At least one CVD	1.296*	(1.041–1.628)
At least one chronic disease	1.135	(0.978–1.316)
Frailty	1.186**	(1.074–1.307)

$*p < 0.05; **p < 0.01$

marital status and social participation indicated are mediated by comorbidity and health behavioral factors.

Table 5.3 shows the findings for Cox proportional hazard models. Adjusted for demographic factors, comorbidity and health behavior, participants who are frail have death hazards 1.2 times higher than those with no frailty or intermediate frailty. Logistic regression was also performed but yielded to similar results. None of the social engagement measures were associated with mortality.

Discussion

By separately incorporating comprehensive measures of the salient aspects of people's "social" existence, indicators of marital status, number of close children, relatives and friends, social participation and emotional support we were able to examine how these distinct aspects of social engagement would affect frailty and mortality. This paper aimed to examine the complex relationship between social engagement and frailty and mortality. Notably, these different aspects of social engagement are only weakly correlated, typically ranging from $r = 0.15$ to 0.30. In a recent meta-analysis published, Holt-Lunstad et al. (2010) stated that subconstruct of structural and functional measures were only moderately correlated ranging from $r = 0.20$ to $r = 0.30$ (Holt-Lunstad et al. 2010). Therefore, it is thought that each might influence health in different ways (Holt-Lunstad et al. 2010; Kamiya et al.

2010; Lakey and Cohen 2000). Uchino and Cohen have also stated that structural and functional measures of support may ultimately influence morbidity and mortality through two distinct but not necessarily independent pathways (Cohen 2004; Uchino 2006). The findings from our paper are in line with the literature, as these subdomains or subconstructs of structural and functional support are only weakly correlated and each of them may influence health through different, but not necessarily independent pathways (Uchino 2006)

In this longitudinal cohort of English older persons, only emotional support was associated with frailty; i.e., participants who had higher levels of emotional support had lower cumulative odds of frailty 2 years later. Examining the relationship between frailty and mortality 2 years later, frailty was an independent predictor of mortality but none of the social engagement measures were associated with mortality. Results indicate that emotional support protects non-frail individuals against becoming pre-frail. However, once individuals become pre-frail, emotional support does not protect against frailty or death.

The research evidence on the relationship between social engagement and mortality is somewhat mixed. For example, in the Alameda County, California (Berkman and Syme 1979), men and women who lacked ties to others were 1.9–3.1 times more likely to die than those who had many contacts. A 1982 study in Tecumseh, Michigan, showed a similar association for men, but not for women, between social connectedness and participation and mortality risk (House et al. 1982). In contrast, some studies failed to find such an associations (Frasure-Smith et al. 2000; Turner et al. 2010). For example, Frasure-Smith et al. did not find any association between social support and cardiac mortality. Kroenke et al. (2006) did not find any association between participation in religious or community activities and being married with mortality among women. Other studies have found one or more components of social engagement related to mortality but not all of them. In our study, none of the social engagement variables was associated with mortality. Two things that may have affected these findings should be considered. First, the effect of marital status, number of close children, friends and relatives, social participation and emotional support might be mediated by other factors such as frailty and smoking. Second, although mortality ascertainment was very high, this is still a short timeframe and a relatively small number of deaths were observed. Future analyses of forthcoming panel data will allow us to explore the possible impact of this limitation.

This study has both strengths and limitations. Strengths include a large representative sample of the non-institutionalized older population from which the findings can be generalized, the use of four separate indicators of social engagement, and the careful measurement of a previously validated frailty index. The limitations are, firstly, that although the Fried Frailty criteria is widely used and validated, the inclusion of criteria such as weight loss can be questioned (Bergman et al. 2007), as some studies show that a subset of frail population can also be obese. Thus, taking into account weight loss as a measure may underestimate the prevalence of frailty in the obese population. Secondly, causality cannot be inferred from cross-sectional data analysis (necessitated by the fact that availability of health measurement is currently limited to wave 2 of the study). Therefore, future analyses of forthcoming panel data will allow us to explore this and draw stronger causal inferences from future waves. Third, because ELSA does not have baseline frailty data, it was not possible to determine the dynamics of the process of frailty (i.e., changes over time). One study comparing dynamic and static measures of frailty found that static frailty is more predictive of functional decline (Puts et al. 2005). However, another study demonstrated that older persons with a small increase in gait speed (e.g., 0.1 m/s) display a substantial reduction in mortality compared with those whose gait speed remained stable or slowed down. This study suggests that older individuals may still have considerable "physiological reserve" or resilience to improve and recover from adverse health events. Finally, although we adjusted for an extensive range of health factors and mortality ascertainment was very high (at 98% through the six years), this is still a short timeframe to observe a sufficiently large enough number of deaths. Future analyses of forthcoming panel data will allow us to explore this limitation.

This article has explored the relationships between different aspects of social engagement, frailty and mortality. Examination of different dimensions of social engagement suggests that we can identify more precise pathways through which social engagement influences frailty and whether social engagement and frailty are independent predictors of mortality. The analysis advanced here, it is hoped, will be of relevance to scholars working at the intersection of the social and biomedical sciences and seeking to understand the complex interactions between social engagement and health.

References

Ahmed, N., Mandel, R., & Fain, M. J. (2007). Frailty: An emerging geriatric syndrome. *The American Journal of Medicine, 120*(9), 748–753.
Barth, J., Scheneider, S., & Känel, R. V. (2010). Lack of social support in the aetiology and prognosis of coronary heart disease: A systematic review and meta-analysis. *Psychosomatic Medicine, 72*, 229–238.
Bergman, H., Ferrucci, L., Guralnik, J., Hogan, D., Hummel, S., Karunananthan, S., et al. (2007). Frailty: An emerging research and clinical paradigm–issues and controversies. *Journal of Gerontology: Medical Sciences, 62*, 731–737.
Berkman, L. F., & Syme, S. L. (1979). Social networks, host resistance, and mortality: A nine-year follow-up study of Alameda County residents. *American Journal of Epidemiology, 109*(2), 186–204.
Cheshire, H., Cox, K., Lessof, C., & Taylor, R. (2000). Methodology. In J. Banks, E. Breeze, C. Lessof, & J. Nazroo (Eds.), *Retirement, health and relationships of the older population in England: The 2004 english longitudinal study of ageing*. London: The Institute for Fiscal Studies.
Cohen, S. (1988). Psychosocial models of the role of social support in the etiology of physical disease. *Health Psychology, 7*(3), 269–297.
Cohen, S. (2004). Social relationships and health. *American Psychologist, 59*(8), 676–684. doi:10.1037/0003-066X.59.8.676 (2004-20395-002 [pii]).

Frasure-Smith, N., Lespérance, F., Gravel, G., Masson, A., Juneau, M., Talajic, M., et al. (2000). Social support, depression, and mortality during the first year after myocardial infarction. *Circulation, 101*, 1919–1924.

Fried, L., Tangen, C. M., Walston, J., Newman, A. , Hirsh, C., Gottdiener, J., et al. (2001). Frailty in older adults evidence for a phenotype. *Journal of Gerontolgy: A Biological Science Med Science, 56*(3), M146–M157.doi:10.1093/gerona/56.3.M146

Holt-Lunstad, J., Smith, T. B., & Layton, J. B. (2010). Social relationships and mortality risk: A meta-analytic review. *Plos Medicine, 7*(7).

House, J. S., Robbins, C., & Metzner, H. L. (1982). The association of social relationships and activities with mortality: Prospective evidence from the tecumseh community health study. *American Journal of Epidemiology, 116*(1), 123–140.

Hubbard, R., Lang, I. A., Llewellyn, D. J., & Rockwood, K. (2010). Frailty, body mass index, and abdominal obesity in older people. *Journal of Gerontoly A Medical Science, 65*(4), 377–381.

Jung, Y., Gruenewald, T. L., Seeman, T. E., & Sarkisian, C. A. (2010). Productive activities and development of frailty in older adults. *Journal of Gerontology: Social Sciences, 65B*(2), 256–261.

Kamiya, Y., Whelan, B., Timonen, V., & Kenny, R. A. (2010). The differential impact of subjective and objective aspects of social engagement on cardiovascular risk factors. *BMC Geriatrics, 10*.

Kawachi, I., & Berkman, L. F. (2001). Social ties and mental health. *Journal of Urban Health: Bulletin of the New York Academy of Medicine, 78*(3), 458–469.

Kroenke, C. H., Kubzansky, L. D., Schernhammer, E. S., Holmes, M. D., & Kawachi, I. (2006). Social networks, social support, and survival after breast cancer diagnosis. *Journal of Clinical Oncology, 24*(7), 1105–1111.

Lakey, B., & Cohen, S. (2000). Social support theory and measurement. In S. Cohen, L. Underwood, & B. H. Gottlieb (Eds.), *Social support measurement and intervention: A guide for health and social scientists* (pp. 29–52). New York: Oxford University Press.

Puts, M., Lips, P., & Deeg, D. J. (2005). Static and dynamic measures of frailty predict decline in a performance-based and self-reported measure of physical functioning. *Journal of Clinical Epidemiology, 58*, 1188–1198.

Scholes, S., Medina, J., Cheshire, H., Cox, K., Hacker, E., & Lessof, C. (2009). Technical report (wave 3): Living in the 21st century: Older people in England: The 2006 english longitudinal study of ageing.

Strawbridge, W. J., Shema, S. J., Balfour, J. L., Higby, H. R., & Kaplan, G. A. (1998). Antecedents of frailty over three decades in an older cohort. *Journal of Gerontology: Social Sciences, 53B*, S9–S16.

Turner, A., Phillips, L., Hambridge, J. A., Baker, A. L., Bowman J., & Colyvas, K. (2010). Clinical outcomes associated with depression, anxiety and social support among cardiac rehabilitation attendees. *Australian N Z Psychiatry, 44*(7), 658–666.

Uchino, B. N. (2006). Social support and health: A review of physiological processes potentially underlying links to disease outcomes. *Journal of Behavioral Medicine, 29*(4), 377–387. doi:10.1007/s10865-006-9056-5

Walsto, J., Hadley, E. C., Ferrucci, L., Guralnik, J. M., Newman, A. B., Studenski, S. A., et al. (2006). Research agenda for frailty in older adults: Toward a better understanding of physiology and etiology: Summary from the American Geriatrics Society/National Institute on aging research conference on frailty in older adults. *Jounal of American Geriatrics Society, 54*, 991–1001.

Chapter 6
Predictors of Exceptional Longevity: Gender Differences in Effects of Early-Life and Midlife Conditions

Leonid A. Gavrilov and Natalia S. Gavrilova

Introduction

Studies of centenarians (people living to 100 and older) could be useful in identifying factors leading to long life and avoidance of fatal diseases. Even if some individual characteristics have a moderate protective effect on risk of death, people with this trait/condition should be accumulated among long-lived individuals because of cumulative survival advantage. Thus, study of centenarians may be a sensitive way to find genetic, familial, environmental and life-course factors associated with lower mortality and better survival.

Most studies of centenarians in the United States are focused on either genetic (Hadley et al. 2000; Murabito et al. 2012; Perls and Terry 2003; Sebastiani et al. 2012; Zeng et al. 2010) or psychological (Adkins et al. 1996; Hagberg et al. 2001; Margrett et al. 2010; Martin et al. 2010; Murabito et al. 2012) aspects of survival to advanced ages. On the other hand, several theoretical concepts suggest that early-life events and conditions may have significant long-lasting effect on survival to advanced ages. These concepts include (but are not limited to) the reliability theory of aging and the high initial damage load (HIDL) hypothesis in particular (Gavrilov and Gavrilova 2001, 2003a, 2006); the theory of technophysio evolution (Fogel 2004; Fogel and Costa 1997); the idea of fetal origin of adult diseases (Barker 1998; Kuh and Ben-Shlomo 1997); and a related idea of early-life programming of aging and longevity (Gavrilov and Gavrilova 2004). These ideas are

---

L.A. Gavrilov (✉) · N.S. Gavrilova
Academic Research Centers (ARC), NORC at the University of Chicago,
1155 E. 60th St., Chicago, IL 60637, USA
e-mail: gavrilov@longevity-science.org

L.A. Gavrilov · N.S. Gavrilova
Department of Statistical Analysis of Population Health, WHO Collaborating Centre,
Federal Research Institute for Health Organization and Informatics,
Ministry of Health of the Russian Federation, Moscow, Russia

supported by studies suggesting significant effects of early-life conditions on late-life mortality (Barker and Costa 1997; Elo and Preston 1992;Gavrilov and Gavrilova 2003b; Hayward and Gorman 2004; Kuh and Ben-Shlomo 1997; Smith et al. 2009). The role of early-life conditions in shaping late-life mortality is now well recognized and studies of centenarians can contribute to this area of research.

Our search for appropriate data resources for centenarian studies revealed an enormous amount of life span data that could be made readily available for subsequent full-scale studies (Gavrilov et al. 2002; Gavrilova and Gavrilov 1999). Millions of genealogical records are already computerized and, after their strict validation, could be used for the study of familial and other predictors of human longevity. Computerized genealogies provide the most complete information on the life span of centenarians' relatives when compared to other sources such as death certificates or census data.

Studies of centenarians require serious work on age validation (Jeune and Vaupel 1999; Poulain 2010, 2011) and careful design including the choice of an appropriate control group. Taking general population as a control group is one of the most popular approaches in centenarian studies. Preston et al. (1998) suggested an original methodology to study longevity in the United States. The researchers collected individual death certificates for people who died at ages 85+ during Jan. 1–14, 1985. Death certificate data were then linked to the 1900 U.S. census. Individual data from the 1900 U.S. census were used as a control group. Population-based census data are available as a part of the Integrated Public Use Microdata Series (IPUMS) project at the University of Minnesota (Ruggles et al. 2004). We applied method suggested in Preston Hill et al. (1998) in our earlier study of centenarians taken from computerized family histories and compared to U.S. 1900 census data from the IPUMS dataset (Gavrilova and Gavrilov 2007). The results of this earlier study demonstrated that the region of childhood residence and the household property status were the two most significant variables that affect the chances of a household producing a future centenarian (for both sons and daughters). Spending a childhood in the Mountain Pacific and West Pacific regions in the United States were found to increase chances of long life (by a factor of three) compared to the Northeastern part of the country (Gavrilova and Gavrilov 2007). Also a farm (particularly an owned farm) residence in childhood was associated with better survival to advanced ages. These findings were consistent with the hypothesis that lower burden of infectious diseases during childhood, expressed as lower child mortality in families of farm owners and families living in the West (Preston and Haines 1991), might have far-reaching consequences for survival to extreme old ages. Some of these results are consistent with other studies of childhood conditions and survival to age 85+ (Hill et al. 2000; Preston et al. 1998). These studies, also based on linkage to early censuses, demonstrated a significant advantage in survival to age 85 for children living on farms for both African Americans (Preston et al. 1998) and native-born Caucasians (Hill et al. 2000). On the other hand, the Northeast and Midwest were found to be the best regions of childhood residence for subsequent survival to age 85+ (Hill et al. 2000). The main limitation of our earlier study was selection of population-based sample as control group that was compared with centenarians taken from computerized genealogies (Gavrilova and Gavrilov 2007).

In this article, we consider more correct approaches to choosing a control population in centenarian studies: (1) selection of centenarians and controls from the same population universe and (2) use of nonbiological relatives as a control group. These approaches are illustrated using data on American centenarians, their relatives and unrelated shorter-lived controls obtained from the same online genealogies.

Data Collection

In this study, we compare centenarians born in the United States to their peers in the same birth cohort who were also born in the United States but died at age 65. Both cases and controls were randomly sampled from the same population universe (computerized family histories) and had the same birth year window (1890–91). These records were then linked to historical U.S. censuses (1900, 1910, 1930). The main focus of the study is on the 1900 and 1930 censuses that correspond to the childhood and adulthood periods of their individual lives. The age at death for controls is selected assuming that the majority of deaths at age 65 occur due to chronic age-related diseases rather than injuries or infectious diseases (Gavrilov and Gavrilova 2015).

Sample sizes of male centenarians are small in the majority of longevity studies and to resolve this problem and have a sample balanced in regard to gender, males are oversampled in this study. This oversampling does not affect the analyses because male and female data are studied separately, taking into account that men and women may respond differently to the same set of risk factors. To obtain a more homogeneous birth cohort regarding the secular changes in mortality and life course events, a narrow birth-date window was used: 1890–91.

Prevalence of centenarians in modern populations is very low: about 1 per 10,000 population (Hadley et al. 2000), and therefore traditional methods of population sampling are difficult and not feasible for obtaining large samples of centenarians. Case-control design proved to be the most appropriate and cost-effective approach for studies of rare conditions (Breslow and Day 1993; Woodward 2005) and hence is extremely useful for centenarian studies. Breslow and Day (1993) suggested the classic case-control design can be expanded in a variety of ways. One such expansion is a design suggested in (Preston et al. 1998). According to this design, a survival to advanced ages (rather than disease or death) is considered to be a case and relative survival probabilities are used instead of odds ratios. In this study, we draw centenarians and controls randomly from the same universe of online family histories to ensure comparability and avoid possible selection bias when centenarians and controls are drawn from different populations. Also, we used data from historical sources collected when centenarians and controls were children or young adults, thereby avoiding a limitation related to self-report or recall bias.

Only records from genealogies of presumably good quality with available information on exact (day, month, year) birth dates and death dates (for centenarians) as well as information on birth and death dates of both parents are used in the sampling procedure for both cases and controls.

Individuals born in 1890–91 represent an interesting birth cohort to study. These people experienced high exposure to infections during childhood and decreasing infectious disease load later in life. It is important to note that nonagenarians and centenarians living now in the United States have very similar experiences as those born at the end of the 19th century. Therefore, more detailed analysis of past history and life course of this birth cohort may be important for understanding the underlying factors and causes of mortality among the currently living old age cohorts.

Centenarians represent a group with really rare condition of successful survival (only two men and 14 women out of 1000 from the 1900 U.S. birth cohort survived to age 100) but common enough for obtaining samples of sufficient size. In this study, we analyzed early-life and adulthood effects that operate throughout life by comparing centenarians of each gender to the respective control groups.

Data quality control procedure in this study included: (1) preliminary quality control of computerized family histories (data consistency checks), (2) verification of the centenarian's death date, (3) verification of the birth date (for centenarians and controls), and (4) verification of family information (parents, spouses and siblings). These methods of age validation were based on the approaches proposed by the experts in this area (Jeune and Vaupel 1999; Poulain 2010) and our own research experience. All records (for centenarians and controls) were subjected to verification and quality control using several independent data sources. Our primary concern was the possibility of incorrect dates reported in family histories. Previous studies demonstrated that age misreporting and age exaggeration in particular are more common among long-lived individuals (Elo et al. 1996; Hill et al. 2000; Rosenwaike and Stone 2003; Shrestha and Rosenwaike 1996). Therefore, the primary focus in this study was on the age verification for long-lived individuals, which involved death-date verification using the U.S. Social Security Administration Death Master File (DMF) and birth-date verification using early U.S. censuses.

According to our experience, the linkage to DMF selects out the majority of incorrect records for alleged centenarians (Gavrilova and Gavrilov 2007). A definite match was established when information on first and last names (spouse's last name for women); day, month and year of birth matches in DMF; and family history (Sesso et al. 2000) was verified. In the case of disagreement in day, month or year of birth, the validity of the match is verified on the basis of additional agreement between place of the last residence and place of death.

The procedure of death-date verification using DMF is not feasible for validating death dates of controls because data completeness of DMF is not very high for deaths before the 1970s. We found that approximately 30% of deaths in the control group could be confirmed through the U.S. state death indexes, cemetery records and obituaries, which cover longer periods of time. Taking into account that exact ages of death for controls are not particularly important for the study design, it is possible to rely on death-date information recorded in family histories for controls not found in external sources, as it was done in the Utah Population Database for individuals who died before 1932 (Kerber et al. 2001).

Verification of birth dates was accomplished through a linkage to the 1900 U.S. census data recorded when the person was a child (when age exaggeration is less common compared to claims of exceptional longevity made at old age). The preference is given to the 1900 census because it is more complete and detailed in regard to birth-date verification (it contains information on month and year of birth) compared to the 1910 and 1920 censuses. If a person cannot be found in the 1900 census, then he/she was searched in the 1910 census. We obtained a good linkage success rate (92–95%) in our study because of the availability of powerful online indexes provided by the Ancestry.com service and supplemental information in family histories (Gavrilova and Gavrilov 2007). These indexes allowed us to conduct searches on the following variables: first and last names (including Soundex), state, county, township, birthplace, birth year (estimated from census), immigration year and relation to head-of-household. Data on birth dates, birth places and names of siblings produced unambiguous matches in an overwhelming majority of cases.

Ancestry.com has a powerful search engine, which helps researchers find a person in multiple historical sources simultaneously (including all historical U.S. censuses up to 1940) based on all information available in computerized genealogies. Use of this service greatly facilitates the linkage procedure and helps to obtain unambiguous links in practically all studied cases. After the linkage to early censuses, the final database on centenarians and controls combined information on family characteristics (taken from family histories), data on the early-life conditions taken from the 1900–10 U.S. censuses and adult socio-economic status taken from the 1930 census. Early U.S. censuses contain a rich set of variables, which can be used to study the effects of both childhood and adulthood living conditions on human longevity (see Table 6.1).

Below we summarize the core topical domains of the variables analyzed in this study.

Childhood living conditions at household level. This information was obtained from the 1900 and 1910 censuses. Selection of variables was guided by the results obtained in previous studies on child mortality at the turn of the 20th century (Preston and Haines 1991). These studies demonstrated that child mortality is affected by household structure (including presence of a boarder in household), paternal occupation, mother's work, the occupation of household head, maternal and paternal literacy, and family structure (whether the proband lived with both parents, his/her father and stepmother, a stepfather and mother, his/her father only, mother only or on his/her own—for example, in an orphanage) (Preston and Haines 1991). An important factor of survival to advanced age is childhood farm residence —a result found in our earlier study (Gavrilova and 2007) as well as in other studies (Hill et al. 2000; Preston et al. 1998).

Table 6.1 Information available in early U.S. censuses for the search of longevity predictors

Variables	Early U.S. census						
	1860	1870	1880	1900	1910	1920	1930
Age, sex, color/race	+	+	+	+	+	+	+
Month and year of birth				+			
Marital status			+	+	+	+	+
Marriage duration (for married)				+	+		+
Literacy	+	+	+	+	+	+	+
School attendance (for children)	+	+	+	+	+	+	+
Place of birth	+	+	+	+	+	+	+
Places of birth for parents			+	+	+	+	+
Parental nativity		+	+	+	+	+	+
Mother tongue						+	+
Home ownership				+	+	+	+
Farm status				+	+		+
Value of real and personal estate	+	+					+
Number of children born and surviving (for women)				+	+		
Whether deaf and/or dumb					+		
Radio in household							+
Occupation	+	+	+	+	+	+	+
Employment			+	+	+	+	+
Citizenship		+		+	+	+	+
Year of immigration				+	+	+	+
Veteran status					+		+

Infectious burden. The main hypothesis we studied here is that early exposure to infections decreases chances of survival to advanced ages, affecting mortality later in life. Infectious burden is estimated as the within-family infectious burden. Information on all children born and children surviving allowed us to estimate proportion of surviving children for each family where the biological mother is present. Child mortality served as a proxy of infectious disease burden in the family, characterizing the living environment, as suggested by other researchers (Bengtsson and Lindstrom 2000, 2003; Finch and Crimmins 2004; Preston and Haines 1991). We based our estimates of child mortality on information available in the 1910 census whenever possible because by this time the majority of studied mothers had finished their reproductive period.

Seasonal early-life conditions. Effects of seasonal conditions on survival to extreme ages are studied using month of birth as an integral proxy for environmental seasonal conditions (e.g., seasonal infections) before and shortly after the birth. Existing literature on U.S. mortality and our own results based on the within-family approach show that month of birth may be a significant predictor of mortality not only during childhood but also in later life (Costa and Lahey 2005; Doblhammer 2004; Doblhammer and Vaupel 2001; Gavrilov and Gavrilova 1999, 2001).

Adulthood social conditions. Socio-economic achievement at adult ages for men was estimated using occupation status and dwelling ownership status (measured as in the 1900 census). In particular, we tested a hypothesis that farm background is particularly favorable for male survival because sons of farmers also become farmers (Preston et al. 1998). In this case, the farm status in both 1900 and 1930 should bring a significant advantage for survival to 100. In the case of females, estimation of socio-economic achievements through their occupation is not feasible because in 1930 the proportion of women in the labor force was relatively small in the United States. A reasonable proxy variable describing social status of non-working adult women is an occupation of husband (for married women) or occupation of the head of household for single, widowed or divorced women. Urban/rural residence in 1930 is another variable used in the study. Preston and Haines (1991) found that child mortality in 1900 was significantly higher in urban areas than in rural areas. Urban adults in the contemporary United States also have higher mortality despite better infrastructure and access to health services (Hayward et al. 1997).

Familial longevity and other family characteristics. Family histories allow us to obtain information on life span of biological and nonbiological relatives. For this particular study, the most important variables are life spans of mother and father. As yet, no studies have simultaneously examined the net effects of parental longevity and early-life conditions. Studies suggest that effects of parental longevity on longevity of the offspring may be substantial (Gavrilov et al. 2002; Kerber et al. 2001; Pearl and Pearl 1934) and heritability of life span estimates increase dramatically when parents live longer than 80 years (Gavrilova et al. 1998). Therefore, we believe that parental longevity (measured as paternal and maternal life span 80 years and over) may have significant moderating influence on the effects of childhood conditions and can be used as a proxy for genetic influences on life span. Other family variables of interest are paternal and maternal ages at person's birth, sibship size and birth order.

In this ongoing study, we have identified 838 centenarians born in 1890–91 in the United States and 910 controls born in the United States in 1890–91 who died at age 65. Further linkage to the 1900 census resulted in a 98.2% success rate for centenarians and 98.6% success rate for controls. For the 1930 census, 94.9% of centenarian records and 96.4% of control records were successfully linked. Linkage to the 1900 census revealed that 95.6% of centenarians and 96.0% of controls lived with one or both biological parents. According to the 1900 census, 67% of fathers of studied individuals were farmers. Centenarians and controls had approximately equal sibship sizes (7.6 and 7.8 respectively), which are higher compared to the general population in the 1900 census (5.6), suggesting larger sizes of families presented in computerized genealogies. In further analyses, we restricted our sample with records where information was available for both the 1900 and 1930 census. To study effects of marriage history on survival to age 100, only records for individuals married in 1930 were taken into account. Finally, data for 765 centenarians and 783 shorter-lived controls were used in our analyses. Multivariate logistic regression model was used to study survival to age 100. Our main focus was on the following three types of variables:

Early-life conditions drawn from the 1900 census (type of parental household: farm or nonfarm, owned or rented, parental literacy, parental immigration status, paternal occupation, number of children born/survived by mother, size of parental household in 1900, places of birth for household members),

Midlife conditions drawn from the 1930 census (type of person's household, availability of radio in household, person's age at first marriage, person's occupation or husband's occupation in the case of women, industry of occupation, number of children in household, veteran status),

and Family characteristics drawn from computerized genealogies (paternal and maternal life span, paternal and maternal age at person's birth, number of siblings).

Results

In the first step, we studied familial, childhood and adulthood variables separately using univariate analyses. Study of familial characteristics taken from genealogies revealed that paternal and maternal longevity was significantly associated with survival to age 100 for both men and women. Being born in the second half of the year was significantly associated with male longevity. However, loss of parents early in life (before 1910) had no effect on the chances of becoming a centenarian. Childhood conditions recorded in the 1900 census included: paternal and maternal literacy and immigration status, paternal occupation, status of dwelling (owned or rented farm, owned or rented house), household size, grandparent or boarder in household, proportion of surviving children reported by mother and region of birth. Larger household size and having father-farmer were found to be significant predictors of male (but not female) longevity in univariate analyses. Birth in the Northeast region is also predictive for survival to advanced ages in men. This result agrees with findings by (Hill et al. 2000) for people who survived to age 85, but does not agree with the results of our earlier study, which compared centenarians drawn from computerized family histories with population-based controls

(Gavrilova and Gavrilov 2007). This contradictory finding may indicate that the earlier use of population-based control could produce biased results if the studied sample of genealogical records does not represent the general population. Female longevity revealed no significant associations with any of the 1900 census variables. Adulthood conditions in the 1930 census included: dwelling status, occupation of self (husband or head of household for females), radio in household, veteran status of self (or husband), marital status, age at first marriage, availability of children (composite variable based on information taken from the 1930 census and genealogies). Univariate analyses showed that farmer occupation in 1930 was a very strong predictor of longevity for men. In the case of women, having a husband-farmer had no effect on the chances of survival to age 100. For women, availability of a radio in the household was the strongest predictor of longevity among the studied midlife variables. The effect of radio as a proxy for household wealth might potentially explain the latter finding. However, more direct characteristics of household wealth (property ownership) demonstrated no association with exceptional longevity.

In multivariate analyses, when familial, early-life and midlife characteristics are combined, having father-farmer is no longer associated with longevity of men. Parental longevity turned out to be one of the strongest predictors of survival to age 100. Table 6.2 presents the results of multivariate analyses for men. Note that farmer occupation in 1930 is one of the strongest predictors of survival to age 100, which agrees with results of other studies, including our own study of centenarians based on a population-based sample of survivors to age 100 from the 1887 birth cohort (Gavrilov and Gavrilova 2012).

Table 6.3 presents results of multivariate analyses for women. For women, having a husband-farmer has no effect on survival to age 100. Interestingly, having a radio in the household in 1930 has a positive effect on longevity for women but not for men (Table 6.3). This finding can be explained by the fact that women in 1930 spent most of their time at home and were much more exposed to radio (as an educational and entertainment source) compared to men. Listening to radio

Table 6.2 Predictors of male survival to age 100: effects of parental longevity, early-life and midlife conditions, results of multivariate logistic regression

Variable	Odds ratio	95 % CI	p-value
Father lived 80+	1.84	1.35–2.51	<0.001
Mother lived 80+	1.70	1.25–2.32	0.001
Farmer in 1930	1.67	1.21–2.31	0.002
Born in the northeast region	2.08	1.27–3.40	0.004
Born in the second half of year	1.36	1.00–1.84	0.050
Radio in household, 1930	0.87	0.63–1.19	0.374

Note N = 723. Farm childhood in 1900 was found to be nonsignificant predictor for males. Calculated using Stata 13 statistical package (procedure logistic)

Table 6.3 Predictors of female survival to age 100: effects of parental longevity, early-life and midlife conditions, results of multivariate logistic regression

Variable	Odds ratio	95 % CI	p-value
Father lived 80+	2.19	1.61–2.98	<0.001
Mother lived 80+	2.23	1.66–2.99	<0.001
Husband (or head of household) farmer in 1930	1.15	0.84–1.56	0.383
Radio in household, 1930	1.61	1.18–2.20	0.003
Born in the second half of year	1.18	0.89–1.58	0.256
Born in the Northeast region	1.04	0.65–1.67	0.857

Note N = 815. Calculated using Stata 13 statistical package (procedure logistic)

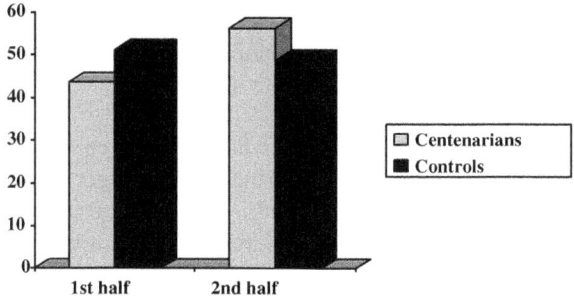

Fig. 6.1 Season of birth and survival to 100: proportion (percent) of people born in the first half and the second half of the calendar year among centenarians and controls (who died at age 65)

improves people's feelings of happiness and energy, and an electro-encephalographic (EEG) study found that listening to radio creates high levels of positive engagement in the brain, according to the findings of the "Media and the Mood of the Nation" research project conducted by Sparkler Research in spring 2011 (Redican and Barber 2012).

Finally, we tested our previous results that season of birth may be predictive for survival to long life and compared season-of-birth among centenarians and shorter-lived controls in this database. Figure 6.1 shows proportion of people born in the first and the second halves of the calendar year for centenarians and controls. Note that more centenarians than controls were born in the second half of the year and this difference is statistically significant (p = 0.008, chi-square test). This result confirms our findings obtained using the within-family analysis (Gavrilov and Gavrilova 2011), which showed that centenarians were born more often in September to November.

These findings are also consistent with our previous results as well as results of other studies, which found positive effects of farming and farm background on late-life survival (Gavrilova and Gavrilov 2007; Preston et al. 1998). Farm childhood background turned out to be particularly favorable for men who usually continue to work on a farm.

Concluding Remarks

This study demonstrated that both midlife and early-life conditions affect survival to age 100 with some gender specificity. At the same time, we found no effects of higher child mortality in the household (a proxy of infectious burden) on longevity as suggested by the inflammatory hypothesis of aging (Finch and Crimmins 2004).

Parental longevity turned out to be one of the strongest predictors of survival to age 100 for both men and women, so this variable cannot be ignored in the population health studies. Overall, parental socio-economic characteristics reported in 1900 census were not predictive for exceptional longevity for both men and women. On the other hand, some early-life characteristics (birth in North East region and birth in the second half of year) turned out to be significant predictors of exceptional longevity for men but not women. The finding of higher male sensitivity to early-life conditions may be explained in terms of reliability theory of aging and longevity (Gavrilov and Gavrilova 2006). Mortality patterns of men and women suggest that female organism is more reliable because it has higher redundancy. However, organisms with higher redundancy are able to accumulate more damage and still stay alive. Hence, women on average are able to survive with more diseases, which is a consequence of higher redundancy of female organism. At the same time men (who have fewer reserves compared to women) experiencing loss of redundancy (damage) early in life would have higher mortality risk throughout their lives due to lack of needed reserves. This may explain higher sensitivity of men to effects of early-life conditions and potential damage to their organisms during this period of life.

This study also found strong positive effect of farmer occupation at middle age on attaining exceptional longevity for men (husband's farmer occupation had no effect on longevity of women). Only limited few factors were related to exceptional longevity of women: parental longevity and availability of radio in household in 1930. This study suggests that men are more sensitive to the effects of early-life conditions on longevity compared to women.

Acknowledgments This study was supported by the U.S. National Institutes of Health (grant R01 AG028620).

References

Adkins, G., Martin, P., & Poon, L. W. (1996). Personality traits and states as predictors of subjective well-being in centenarians, octogenarians, and sexagenarians. *Psychology and Aging, 11*, 408–416.

Barker, D. J. P. (1998). *Mothers, babies, and health later in life*. London: Churchill Livingstone.

Bengtsson, T., & Lindstrom, M. (2000). Childhood misery and disease in later life: The effects on mortality in old age of hazards experienced in early life, southern Sweden, 1760–1894. *Population Studies-A Journal of Demography, 54*, 263–277.

Bengtsson, T., & Lindstrom, M. (2003). Airborne infectious diseases during infancy and mortality in later life in southern Sweden, 1766–1894. *International Journal of Epidemiology, 32*, 286–294.

Breslow, N. E., & Day, N. E. (1993). Statistical methods in cancer research. In *The analysis of case-control studies* (Vol. 1). Lyon: International Agency for Research on Cancer.

Costa, D. L., & Lahey, J. (2005). Becoming oldest old: Evidence from historical U.S. data. *Genus, 61*, 125–161.

Doblhammer, G. (2004). The late life legacy of very early life. In *Demographic research monographs*. Heidelberg: Springer.

Doblhammer, G., & Vaupel, J. W. (2001). Lifespan depends on month of birth. *Proceedings of the National Academy of Sciences of the United States of America, 98*, 2934–2939.

Elo, I. T., & Preston, S. H. (1992). Effects of early-life condition on adult mortality: A review. *Population Index, 58*, 186–222.

Elo, I. T., Preston, S. H., Rosenwaike, I., Hill, M., & Cheney, T. P. (1996). Consistency of age reporting on death certificates and social security records among elderly African Americans. *Social Science Research, 25*, 292–307.

Finch, C. E., & Crimmins, E. M. (2004). Inflammatory exposure and historical changes in human life-spans. *Science, 305*, 1736–1739.

Fogel, R. W. (2004). Technophysio evolution and the measurement of economic growth. *Journal of Evolutionary Economics, 14*, 217–221.

Fogel, R. W., & Costa, D. L. (1997). A theory of technophysio evolution, with some implications for forecasting population, health care costs, and pension costs. *Demography, 34*, 49–66.

Gavrilov, L. A., & Gavrilova, N. S. (1999). Season of birth and human longevity. *Journal of Anti-Aging Medicine, 2*, 365–366.

Gavrilov, L. A., & Gavrilova, N. S. (2001). The reliability theory of aging and longevity. *Journal of Theoretical Biology, 213*, 527–545.

Gavrilov, L. A., & Gavrilova, N. S. (2003a). The quest for a general theory of aging and longevity. *Science of Aging Knowledge Environment 28*, RE5.

Gavrilov, L. A., & Gavrilova, N. S. (2003b). Early-life factors modulating lifespan. In: S. I. S. Rattan (Ed.), *Modulating aging and longevity* (pp. 27–50). Dordrecht, The Netherlands: Kluwer Academic Publishers.

Gavrilov, L. A., & Gavrilova, N. S. (2004). Early-life programming of aging and longevity—The idea of high initial damage load (the HIDL hypothesis). *Annals of the New York Academy of Sciences, 1019*, 496–501.

Gavrilov, L. A., & Gavrilova, N. S. (2006). Reliability theory of aging and longevity. In E. J. Masoro & S. N. Austad (Eds.), *Handbook of the biology of aging* (pp. 3–42). San Diego: Academic Press.

Gavrilov, L. A., & Gavrilova, N. S. (2011). Season of birth and exceptional longevity: Comparative study of american centenarians, their siblings, and spouses. *Journal of Aging Research, 2011*, 104616.

Gavrilov, L. A., & Gavrilova, N. S. (2012). Biodemography of exceptional longevity: Early-life and mid-life predictors of human longevity. *Biodemography and Social Biology, 58*, 14–39.

Gavrilov, L. A., & Gavrilova, N. S. (2015). New developments in the biodemography of aging and longevity. *Gerontology, 61*, 364–371.

Gavrilov, L. A., Gavrilova, N. S., Olshansky, S. J., & Carnes, B. A. (2002). Genealogical data and the biodemography of human longevity. *Social Biology, 49*, 160–173.

Gavrilova, N. S., & Gavrilov, L. A. (1999). Data resources for biodemographic studies on familial clustering of human longevity. *Demographic Research, 1*, 1–48.

Gavrilova, N. S., & Gavrilov, L. A. (2007). Search for predictors of exceptional human longevity: Using computerized genealogies and internet resources for human longevity studies. *North American Actuarial Journal, 11*, 49–67.

Gavrilova, N. S., Gavrilov, L. A., Evdokushkina, G. N., Semyonova, V. G., Gavrilova, A. L., Evdokushkina, N. N., et al. (1998). Evolution, mutations, and human longevity: European royal and noble families. *Human Biology 70*, 799–804.

Hadley, E. C., Rossi, W. K., Albert, S., Bailey-Wilson, J., Baron, J., Cawthon, R., et al. (2000). Genetic epidemiologic studies on age-specified traits. *American Journal of Epidemiology, 152*, 1003–1008.

Hagberg, B., Alfredson, B. B., Poon, L. W., & Homma, A. (2001). Cognitive functioning in centenarians: A coordinated analysis of results from three countries. *Journals of Gerontology Series B-Psychological Sciences and Social Sciences, 56*, P141–P151.

Hayward, M. D., & Gorman, B. K. (2004). The long arm of childhood: The influence of early-life social conditions on men's mortality. *Demography, 41*, 87–107.

Hayward, M. D., Pienta, A. M., & McLaughlin, D. K. (1997). Inequality in men's mortality: The socioeconomic status gradient and geographic context. *Journal of Health and Social Behavior, 38*, 313–330.

Hill, M. E., Preston, S. H., Rosenwaike, I., & Dunagan, J. F. (2000). Childhood conditions predicting survival to advanced age among white Americans. Annual meeting of the Population Association of America, Los Angeles.

Jeune, B., & Vaupel, J. (1999). *Validation of exceptional longevity*. Odense: Odense University Publisher.

Kerber, R. A., O'Brien, E., Smith, K. R., & Cawthon, R. M. (2001). Familial excess longevity in Utah genealogies. *Journals of Gerontology Series A-Biological Sciences and Medical Sciences, 56*, B130–B139.

Kuh, D., & Ben-Shlomo, B. (1997). *A life course approach to chronic disease epidemiology*. Oxford: Oxford University Press.

Margrett, J., Martin, P., Woodard, J. L., Miller, L. S., MacDonald, M., Baenziger, J., et al. (2010). Depression among centenarians and the oldest old: Contributions of cognition and personalityu. *Gerontology, 56*, 93–99.

Martin, P., Cho, J., MacDonald, M., & Poon, L. (2010). Personality, functional capacity, and well-being among centenarians. *Gerontologist, 50*, 50–50.

Murabito, J. M., Yuan, R., & Lunetta, K. L. (2012). The search for longevity and healthy aging genes: Insights from epidemiological studies and samples of long-lived individuals. *Journals of Gerontology Series A-Biological Sciences and Medical Sciences, 67*, 470–479.

Pearl, R., & Pearl, R. D. W. (1934). *The ancestry of the long-lived*. Baltimore: The John Hopkins Press.

Perls, T., & Terry, D. (2003). Genetics of exceptional longevity. *Experimental Gerontology, 38*, 725–730.

Poulain, M. (2010). On the age validation of supercentenarians. *Supercentenarians* (pp. 3–30).

Poulain, M. (2011). Exceptional longevity in Okinawa: A plea for in-depth validation. *Demographic Research, 25*, 245–284.

Preston, S. H., & Haines, M. R. (1991). *Fatal years. Child mortality in late nineteenth-century America*. Princeton, NJ: Princeton University Press.

Preston, S. H., Hill, M. E., & Drevenstedt, G. L. (1998). Childhood conditions that predict survival to advanced ages among African-Americans. *Social Science and Medicine, 47*, 1231–1246.

Redican, S., & Barber, M. (2012). Radio: The Emotional multiplier, London.

Rosenwaike, I., & Stone, L. F. (2003). Verification of the ages of supercentenarians in the United States: Results of a matching study. *Demography, 40*, 727–739.

Ruggles, S., Sobek, M., Alexander, T., Fitch, C. A., Goeken, R., Hall, P. K., et al. (2001). Integrated public use microdata series (IPUMS): Version 3.0. Minneapolis, MN: Minnesota Population Center.

Sebastiani, P., Solovieff, N., DeWan, A. T., Walsh, K. M., Puca, A., Hartley, S. W., et al. (2012). Genetic signatures of exceptional longevity in humans. Plos One 7.

Sesso, H. D., Paffenbarger, R. S., & Lee, I. M. (2000). Comparison of national death index and world wide web death searches. *American Journal of Epidemiology, 152*, 107–111.

Shrestha, L. B., & Rosenwaike, I. (1996). Can data from the decennial census measure trends in mobility limitation among the aged? *Gerontologist, 36*, 106–109.

Smith, K. R., Mineau, G. R., Garibotti, G., & Kerber, R. (2009). Effects of childhood and middle-adulthood family conditions on later-life mortality: Evidence from the Utah population database, 1850–2002. *Social Science and Medicine, 68*, 1649–1658.

Woodward, M. (2005). *Epidemiology. Study design and data analysis*. Boca Raton, FL: Chapman & Hall/CRC.

Zeng, Y., Cheng, L. G., Chen, H. S. A., Cao, H. Q., Hauser, E. R., Liu, Y. Z., et al. (2010). Effects of FOXO genotypes on longevity: A biodemographic analysis. *Journals of Gerontology Series A-Biological Sciences and Medical Sciences, 65*, 1285–1299.

Chapter 7
Maternal Morbidity and Mortality: Exploring Racial/Ethnic Differences Using New Data from Birth and Death Certificates

Sally C. Curtin and Donna L. Hoyert

Introduction

Rates of maternal morbidity have increased recently as more women enter pregnancy with underlying health issues—increased obesity, diabetes, and hypertension (Campbell et al. 2013; Creanga et al. 2014a; Fridman et al. 2014). The recent definition of maternal morbidity by the World Health Organization is "Any health condition attributed to and/or aggravated by pregnancy and childbirth that has a negative impact on the woman's wellbeing" (Firoz et al. 2013). Thus maternal morbidity can be viewed as a continuum from issues such as nausea, which is common in pregnancy, to severe maternal morbidity which involves organ-system failure and "near-miss" maternal mortality (Vanderkruik et al. 2013; Centers for Disease Control and Prevention 2015a). Postpartum hemorrhage is the most common maternal morbidity worldwide that can result in maternal death (Centers for Disease Control and Prevention 2015b). In the United States, postpartum hemorrhage is also a leading cause, (Campbell et al. 2013; Berg et al. 2010). Persistent racial/ethnic disparities in both maternal morbidity and mortality are evident and involve the complex interplay of social factors, underlying maternal health, as well as differences in access and quality of healthcare (Bryant et al. 2010; Creanga et al. 2014b; Gray et al. 2012; Grobman et al. 2015). Furthering the understanding of the origins of these differences is an emerging public health priority in the United States in light of the increasing rates of maternal morbidity and mortality (Grobman et al. 2015).

With the 2003 revisions of the U.S. Standard Certificate of Live Birth and Standard Certificate of Death, new checkbox items were added to each to collect information on maternal morbidity and mortality. Four of the morbidity

---

S.C. Curtin (✉) · D.L. Hoyert
National Center for Health Statistics, Centers for Disease Control and Prevention,
Hyattsville, MD 20782, USA
e-mail: SCurtin@cdc.gov

measurements added to the birth certificate (maternal transfusion, ruptured uterus, unplanned hysterectomy, and admission to the intensive care unit (ICU)) are often associated with maternal postpartum hemorrhage, its causes and/or treatments, as well as other serious life-threatening morbidities (American College of Obstetricians and Gynecologists 2006).

For death certificates, a checkbox was added for female decedents to collect information on whether the decedent was pregnant within the past year, and the timing of her death relative to the pregnancy: still pregnant at death, death within 42 days of an ended pregnancy, or death 43 days to 1 year of an ended pregnancy. Prior to the addition of this checkbox, maternal mortality was tracked and enumerated in vital statistics according to a group of underlying cause-of-death codes and concepts, and typically confined to maternal deaths within 42 days of an ended pregnancy (Hoyert 2007). The addition of this checkbox aids in identifying maternal deaths, especially those at longer intervals after the ended pregnancy, and also allows for computation of time-specific mortality rates.

This chapter presents rates of maternal morbidity and mortality for 2013 for non-Hispanic white, non-Hispanic black, non-Hispanic Asian, and Hispanic among the states that have adopted the revised 2003 birth and death certificates. In particular, this paper explores whether the morbidity items listed on the birth certificate show evidence of racial/ethnic differences and whether these differences persist when other relevant demographic, health/clinical risk, and healthcare access factors are considered. Also examined is whether the disparity in maternal mortality rates found in total are present in all three time periods (still pregnant at death, death within 42 days of an ended pregnancy, or death 43 days to 1 year of an ended pregnancy), using both the traditional ICD-10 codes for identifying maternal mortality as well as adding in codes corresponding to late maternal deaths.

Methods

Race and Hispanic Origin

Race and Hispanic origin are reported with separate items on both birth and death certificates. Race categories are consistent with the 1997 Office of Management and Budget standards and include five mandated categories (white, black or African American, American Indian or Alaska Native (AIAN), Asian, and Native Hawaiian or Other Pacific Islander (NHOPI) as well as the option of selecting more than one race (Office of Management and Budget 1997). The Hispanic origin question asks if the woman is of Hispanic origin and then includes specific countries of origin. Hispanic women may be of any race but the vast majority classify themselves as white (National Center for Health Statistics 2014). Maternal race and Hispanic origin on the birth certificate is usually self-reported whereas race and Hispanic origin on the death certificate is typically reported by a funeral director as provided by an informant or, in the absence of an informant, on the basis of observation. Thus, there are more issues in data quality with the race and Hispanic origin data on the death certificate, discussed in detail elsewhere (Murphy et al. 2013; Arias et al. 2008). Of particular relevance to this paper is that women of Hispanic origin were shown to be underreported on the death certificate by about 6%, usually misclassified to non-Hispanic white race/ethnicity, while women of non-Hispanic Asian origin were underreported by about 4%, usually misclassified to white race. As this comparison was for maternal deaths occurring in 1991–2000, the misclassification of maternal deaths in 2013 is unknown. The implications of this misclassification on the findings in this paper are discussed.

The race and Hispanic categories in this chapter exclude women reporting multiple races (less than 3% of all US births in 2013; less than 1% of US deaths) and include groups for which there were sufficient cases to compute morbidity and mortality rates in most instances (20 cases or greater in the numerator)—non-Hispanic white, non-Hispanic black, non-Hispanic Asian, and Hispanic. Thus, other race categories as well as Hispanic subgroups are not shown separately but included in the totals. Although a total maternal mortality rate could be computed for non-Hispanic Asian women, there were too few cases to compute rates within the three maternal mortality time periods. Despite this data limitation, non-Hispanic Asian women are included in this chapter because they are the fastest growing minority in the United States (U.S. Census Bureau 2012) and had among the highest rates for some of the morbidities.

Maternal Morbidity Data from Birth Certificates

The 2003 revised U.S. Standard Certificate of Live Birth included an item on maternal morbidity for the first time (Fig. 7.1). The morbidities included on the birth certificate are those which can be reasonably ascertained during the period surrounding labor and delivery and include: maternal transfusion, 3rd or 4th degree perineal laceration, ruptured uterus, unplanned hysterectomy, ICU admission, and

Fig. 7.1 Maternal morbidity item as it appears on U.S. Standard Certificate of Live Birth, 2003 revision

47. MATERNAL MORBIDITY (Check all that apply)

(Complications associated with labor and delivery)

.. Maternal transfusion
.. Third or fourth degree perineal laceration
.. Ruptured uterus
.. Unplanned hysterectomy
.. Admission to intensive care unit
.. Unplanned operating room procedure following delivery

unplanned operating room procedure. These data were added to the birth certificate to establish a national system of data collection for these morbidities, which was previously unavailable (National Center for Health Statistics 2000).

Of these, four of the morbidities are usually associated with severe complications of labor and delivery–maternal transfusion, ruptured uterus, unplanned hysterectomy, and ICU admission. Maternal transfusions are infusions of whole blood or packed red blood cells and are most often administered to treat severe anemia and hemorrhaging (Rouse et al. 2006). Hemorrhaging is also a leading reason for unplanned hysterectomies and ICU admissions (Bateman et al. 2012; Wanderer et al. 2013). Other common reasons for ICU admissions around the time of labor and delivery are pregnancy-related hypertension, cardiac disease, and infection (Wanderer et al. 2013). These data are recommended to be obtained from the medical record (National Center for Health Statistics 2006). The most recent maternal morbidity data from birth certificates were for 2013; the reporting area includes 41 states and the District of Columbia, representing 90% of all US births. A total of 3,548,525 births were in the reporting area with the following racial/ethnic breakdown: non-Hispanic white 1,880,350 (53.0%), non-Hispanic black 511,132 (14.4%), non-Hispanic Asian 206,651 (5.8%), and Hispanic 818,006 (23.1%). The residual were births to non-Hispanic women of other or multiple races and records where race and/or Hispanic origin are not stated.

Maternal Mortality Data from Death Certificates

To identify more maternal deaths than previously, an item for female decedents was added to the 2003 U.S. Standard Certificate of Death to ascertain whether she was pregnant in the past year and then subdivided into three time periods: pregnant at the time of death, not pregnant, but within 42 days of an ended pregnancy (included in the traditional definition of maternal mortality), or not pregnant, but within 43 days to 1 year after an ended pregnancy (Fig. 7.2). Following the guidelines for coding, maternal deaths are now identified using the reported causes of death and the separate question if the information captured in the separate question was not already reported in the cause-of-death section. If the woman was pregnant at the time of death, the medical conditions on the death certificate are assigned to the one of the categories for conditions related to pregnancy. If the woman was pregnant

Fig. 7.2 Pregnancy checkbox item as it appears on U.S. Standard Certificate of Death, 2003 revision

36. IF FEMALE:
□ Not pregnant within past year

□ Pregnant at time of death

□ Not pregnant, but pregnant within 42 days of death

□ Not pregnant, but pregnant 43 days to 1 year before death

within 42 days, the medical conditions on the death certificate are assigned to one of the categories for conditions related to delivery. If the woman was pregnant between 43 days and 1 year, then the medical condition would be assigned to the late maternal death category. Guidelines specify how to assign codes when information reported in the text and question are inconsistent (National Center for Health Statistics 2013).

The latest period is not included in "maternal mortality" according the World Health Organization definition (WHO) which is limited to within 42 days of an ended pregnancy (Hoyert 2007) but is considered "late maternal mortality". Thus, ICD-10 codes O96-O97 which correspond to direct and indirect maternal causes at 43 days to 1 year after an ended pregnancy have usually been excluded from maternal cause-of-death rates. The definition included ICD-10 cause of death codes A34, O00-O95, O98-O99. The death certificate reporting area for the pregnancy checkbox in 2013 included 39 states and the District of Columbia and represented 75% of all US deaths. A total of 2,891,062 births (used as denominators for the rates) were in the death reporting area with the following racial/ethnic breakdown: non-Hispanic white 1,485,477 (51.4%), non-Hispanic black 421,098 (14.6%), non-Hispanic Asian 116,030 (4.0%), and Hispanic 586,776 (20.3%). The residual are births to non-Hispanic women of other and multiple races and records where race and/or Hispanic origin are not stated.

The reporting areas for birth and death are not nationally representative (National Center for Health Statistics 2014) and cannot be considered comparable to each other in terms of maternal characteristics. In particular, California is included in the birth reporting area but not in the death reporting area. There were 32 states and the District of Columbia that were in both reporting areas, numbering 2,625,756 or 67% of all births in 2013 The implications of this difference are discussed in the Discussion section of this paper. Reporting states for both reporting areas are listed in Table 7.1.

Computation of Rates

Rates of maternal morbidity and mortality (per 100,000 live births) are presented for non-Hispanic white, non-Hispanic black, non-Hispanic Asian, and Hispanic women. Missing cases were excluded from computation of these rates (less than 1% of records for all births in the reporting area as well as for each race/ethnic group). Rates of total maternal mortality (according to the traditional ICD-10 definition) are presented as well as rates for the three maternal mortality time periods. Missing values for the maternal mortality time period were excluded from the computations of these rates (about 6% in total, or 44 of 779 maternal deaths). Additionally, we also added deaths attributable to ICD-10 codes O96-O97 to the total rate and to the rates for each time period by race/ethnicity to ascertain how the addition of these deaths would impact the rates in total and for each race/ethnic group.

Table 7.1 Numbers of births and maternal deaths by race and ethnicity of women: Revised reporting areas, 2013

Maternal morbidity and mortality	All races[a]	Non-Hispanic White	Non-Hispanic Black	Non-Hispanic Asian	Hispanic
Maternal morbidity					
Births in birth certificate reporting area	3,548,525	1,880,350	511,132	206,651	818,006
Births with missing information on maternal morbidity	22,064	5590	3474	743	2234
Maternal transfusion	9888	5188	1687	518	2016
Ruptured uterus	922	455	199	66	166
Unplanned hysterectomy	1437	729	234	98	327
Admission to intensive care unit	5460	2252	1216	310	1485
Maternal mortality					
Births in death certificate reporting area	2,891,062	1,485,477	421,098	116,030	586,776
Including ICD-10 codes (A34, O00-O95, O98-O99)					
All maternal deaths	779	363	270	23	109
Pregnant at time of death	390	193	126	9	56
Not pregnant, but pregnant within 42 days of death	268	123	89	12	39
Not pregnant, but pregnant 43 days-1 year before death	77	34	29	2	9
Deaths missing information on timing of death relative to the pregnancy	44	5	26	0	13
Including ICD-10 codes (A34, O00-O95, O96-O97, O98-O99)					
All maternal deaths	983	477	321	30	138
Pregnant at time of death	402	202	128	9	57
Not pregnant, but pregnant within 42 days of death	290	134	97	13	41
Not pregnant, but pregnant 43 days-1 year before death	243	125	69	8	35
Deaths missing information on timing of death relative to the pregnancy	48	5	27	0	16

[a]Includes races not listed separately

Notes The revised reporting area for births in 2013 represented 90 % of all US births and included the following 41 states and the District of Columbia: Alaska, California, Colorado, Delaware, Florida, Georgia, Idaho, Illinois, Indiana, Iowa, Kansas, Kentucky, Louisiana, Maryland, Massachusetts, Michigan, Minnesota, Missouri, Montana, Mississippi, Nebraska, Nevada, New Hampshire, New Mexico, New York, North Carolina, North Dakota, Ohio, Oklahoma, Oregon, Pennsylvania, South Carolina, South Dakota, Tennessee, Texas, Utah, Vermont, Virginia, Washington, Wisconsin, and Wyoming

The revised reporting area for deaths in 2013 represented 75 % of all US deaths and included the following 39 states and the District of Columbia: Arkansas, Arizona, Connecticut, Delaware, Florida, Georgia, Idaho, Illinois, Indiana, Iowa, Kansas, Kentucky, Louisiana, Maine, Maryland, Michigan, Minnesota, Mississippi, Missouri, Montana, Nebraska, Nevada, New Jersey, New Mexico, New York, North Dakota, Ohio, Oklahoma, Oregon, Pennsylvania, Rhode Island, South Carolina, South Dakota, Tennessee, Texas, Utah, Vermont, Washington, and Wyoming

The disparity between race/ethnic groups was measured by calculating a rate ratio–the rate of the comparison group divided by that of the majority group, non-Hispanic white women. The mortality rate ratios for Hispanic and non-Hispanic Asian women could be underestimated as deaths to Hispanic and non-Hispanic Asian women have been shown to be underreported and misclassified to white (Arias et al. 2008). This is discussed more fully later in this paper.

Multivariate Analysis

Multivariate models for each morbidity were examined by race/ethnicity, both unadjusted and also adjusted for maternal sociodemographic characteristics (maternal age, marital status, plurality of the birth, parity of the birth, and maternal educational attainment), clinical/behavioral characteristics (vaginal or cesarean delivery, previous cesarean delivery, hypertension, diabetes, smoking, pre-pregnancy BMI), and healthcare coverage and access (source of payment for the delivery combined with early/not early prenatal care initiation—early care defined as care initiated in the first trimester), to determine whether racial/ethnic disparities in the morbidities persist net of these characteristics. First a bivariate analysis which shows how these covariates differ by race/ethnic group is presented for the birth certificate reporting area for a subset of 2,908,454 birth records. These were the records which had complete data for the race/Hispanic groups, the maternal morbidities, as well as all of the covariates. Then, logistic regression was used to generate unadjusted and adjusted odds ratios. First the models were adjusted for maternal demographic characteristics, then maternal health characteristics were considered as well, and then finally the models were also adjusted for healthcare access characteristics. A comparable multivariate analysis is not possible for the maternal mortality data because the death certificate is limited to a few demographic covariates.

Significance Testing

While birth and death certificate data are not a sample but based on 100-percent of records filed in the reporting areas, differences in rates and odds ratios were tested for significance based on z-tests and chi-square tests, respectively, to take into account random variation (i.e. non-sampling error) of these data. A description of this process, as well are examples, is published elsewhere (National Center for Health Statistics 2012).

Results

Maternal Morbidity and Mortality Numbers and Rates

Table 7.1 includes the numerators for the morbidity and mortality rates and the number of births in the birth certificate and death certificate reporting areas. Number of maternal deaths by time period are presented for both the traditional maternal cause-of-death codes as well as including codes corresponding to late maternal deaths (O96-O97).

In the birth certificate reporting area, non-Hispanic black women had among the highest rates for the four maternal morbidities (Table 7.2). Non-Hispanic black women had the highest rates of maternal transfusion (332.3 per 100,000 live births) and ICU admission (239.5). Non-Hispanic black along with Non-Hispanic Asian women had the highest rates of ruptured uterus (39.2 and 32.1, respectively) and unplanned hysterectomy (46.1 and 47.6, respectively). Hispanic women had the lowest rate of ruptured uterus (20.3). Rate ratios revealed that unplanned hysterectomy had the least disparity, as the only significant rate ratio was 1.2 for non-Hispanic black women relative to non-Hispanic white women. In contrast, ICU admission had the largest disparity for all groups (ratios = 2.0 for non-Hispanic black women, 1.5 for Hispanic women, and 1.3 for non-Hispanic Asian women). This was also the only morbidity where all other groups had significantly higher ratios compared with non-Hispanic white women. Non-Hispanic Asian women were less likely than non-Hispanic white women to have blood transfusions (ratio = 0.9) while Hispanic women were less likely to have transfusions (ratio = 0.9) or ruptured uterus (ratio = 0.8).

The maternal mortality rate in the reporting area for non-Hispanic black women (64.1 deaths per 100,000 live births) was 2½ times that of non-Hispanic white women (24.4) and more than 3 times that of Hispanic (18.6) and non-Hispanic Asian women (19.8). Both in total and for all race/ethnic groups, maternal mortality rates were highest for the period while the woman was pregnant at the time of death, lower for the second period (within 42 days), and lowest for the latest period of maternal mortality (43 days to 1 year). The elevated rate for non-Hispanic black relative to non-Hispanic white women was found in all time periods and was highest for the latest period, 43 days to one year after an ended pregnancy (ratio = 3.2). The maternal mortality rate ratio for Hispanic women was 0.8 compared with non-Hispanic white women overall and also significantly lower while the woman was still pregnant (ratio = 0.7). The rate for Hispanic women at the period of within 42 days of an ended pregnancy was not significantly different than that of non-Hispanic white women and there were two few cases at the latest period to compute a rate for Hispanic women. Rates for non-Hispanic Asian women by time period could not be computed due to small numbers.

Including cause-of-death codes which correspond to late maternal deaths (O96-O97), which have usually been excluded from maternal mortality rates, increased the total mortality rate by about a quarter, from 26.9 to 34.0 per 100,000

Table 7.2 Rates and rate ratios of maternal morbidity and mortality, by race and ethnicity of women: Revised reporting areas, 2013

Maternal morbidity and mortality	All races[a]	Non-Hispanic White	Non-Hispanic Black	Non-Hispanic Asian[b]	Hispanic[b]	NH black/NH white	NH Asian/NH white	Hispanic/NH white
	Rates per 100,000 live births					Rate ratio[c]		
Maternal morbidity								
Maternal transfusion	280.4	276.7	332.3	251.6	247.1	1.2***	0.9*	0.9***
Ruptured uterus	26.1	24.3	39.2	32.1	20.3	1.6***	1.3*	0.8*
Unplanned hysterectomy	40.7	38.9	46.1	47.6	40.1	1.2*	1.2	1.0
Admission to intensive care unit	154.8	120.1	239.5	150.6	182.0	2.0***	1.3***	1.5***
Maternal mortality								
Including ICD-10 codes (A34, O00-O95, O98-O99)								
All maternal deaths	26.9	24.4	64.1	19.8	18.6	2.6***	0.8	0.8*
Pregnant at time of death	14.3	13.5	33.1	–	10.0	2.5***	–	0.7*
Not pregnant, but pregnant within 42 days of death	9.8	8.6	23.4	–	7.0	2.7***	–	0.8
Not pregnant, but pregnant 43 days to 1 year before death	2.8	2.4	7.6	–	–	3.2***	–	–
Including ICD-10 codes (A34, O00-O95, O96-O97, O98-O99)								
All maternal deaths	34.0	32.1	76.2	25.9	23.5	2.4***	0.8	0.7**
Pregnant at time of death	14.6	14.1	33.2	–	10.1	2.4***	–	0.7*
Not pregnant, but pregnant within 42 days of death	10.5	9.3	25.2	–	7.3	2.7***	–	0.8
Not pregnant, but pregnant 43 days to 1 year before death	8.8	8.7	17.9	–	6.2	2.1***	–	0.7

***$p < 0.001$, **$p < 0.01$, *$p < 0.05$, two-tailed test

–Figure does not meet standards of reliability or precision; based on fewer than 20 deaths in the numerator

[a]Includes races not listed separately

[b]Deaths to Hispanic and non-Hispanic Asian women are unreported on the death certificate. See Arias et al. (2008)

[c]Rate ratio is the rate of the comparison group divided by the rate of the reference group, in this case, non-Hispanic white women

Note The revised reporting area for births in 2013 included 41 states and the District of Columbia and represented 90 % of all U.S. births. The revised reporting area for deaths in 2013 included 39 states and the District of Columbia representing 75 % of all U.S. deaths. See Table 7.1 for listings of states in the reporting areas

live births. The disparity in the reporting area between non-Hispanic black and white women was reduced slightly in total (ratio of 2.4) and by about a third for the latest period of maternal mortality, to a ratio of 2.1. Thus, non-Hispanic white women are proportionately more likely than the other groups to have codes corresponding to late maternal deaths. This also resulted in a slightly increased disparity between non-Hispanic white and Hispanic women, 0.7 in total.

Maternal Morbidity Multivariate

Table 7.3 shows the numbers and percentages of births for all of the covariates in the multivariate model in the reporting area. Non-Hispanic black and Hispanic women had a higher percentage of births to teenaged women, 10.6% each, while a quarter of births to non-Hispanic Asian women were to those 35 years of age and older (26.3%), higher than the other groups. There were large differences by group in the percent of births to unmarried mothers and in educational attainment. Non-Hispanic Asian women were the most educated, with 60.2% having a bachelor's degree or higher while Hispanic women were the least educated, with one-third (33.4%) having less than a high school education. There were also large differences in pre-pregnancy BMI by group with approximately one-third of non-Hispanic black women (34.3%) classified as obese before pregnancy. Healthcare coverage and access also varied widely among the groups with more than half of non-Hispanic white and Asian women having private insurance and early prenatal care (55.6 and 56.7%, respectively), and Hispanic women most likely of all groups to be uninsured without early prenatal care, 3.7%.

Table 7.4 shows the unadjusted and adjusted logistic regression odds ratios predicting the four maternal morbidities for the race/ethnic groups in the reporting area. While this is a reduced subset compared with the rates in Table 7.2 (due to the deletion of missing data for the covariates), the unadjusted odds ratios were only slightly different in some instances than those in Table 7.2. Controlling for confounders typically lowered the odds between non-Hispanic white women and the other groups and sometimes completely eliminated them. For example, the significant difference between non-Hispanic black and white women in transfusions was eliminated in the Model 2 which controlled for demographic characteristics. Odds ratios for transfusions for non-Hispanic Asian (OR = 0.88) and Hispanic women (OR = 0.81) were still significantly lower than non-Hispanic white women in Model 4. After adjusting for all characteristics in Model 4, non-Hispanic black women were 37% more likely to have a ruptured uterus (OR = 1.37) than non-Hispanic white women while Hispanic women were about 23% less likely (OR = 0.77). All significant differences between groups in odds ratios for unplanned hysterectomies were completely eliminated by Model 3, where both demographic and health characteristics were controlled.

Results for ICU admission were different than the other morbidities with all significant odds ratios persisting, although reduced, in the adjusted models. Even

Table 7.3 Numbers and percentages of covariates by race and ethnicity of women, Subset of revised birth certificate reporting area, 2013

	Non-Hispanic white (N = 1,576,407)		Non-Hispanic black (N = 397,232)		Non-Hispanic Asian (N = 173,021)		Hispanic (N = 685,145)	
	N	%	N	%	N	%	N	%
Demographic								
Age								
<20	78,151	5.0	42,244	10.6	2057	1.2	72,411	10.6
20–34	1,251,795	79.4	307,838	77.5	125,542	72.6	515,079	75.2
35+	246,461	15.6	47,150	11.9	45,422	26.3	97,655	14.2
Marital status								
Married	1,119,015	71.0	111,967	28.2	149,562	86.4	322,305	47.0
Unmarried	457,391	29.0	285,265	71.8	23,459	13.6	362,840	53.0
Plurality								
Singleton	1,517,554	96.3	382,036	96.2	167,440	96.8	668,722	97.6
Twins + delivery	58,853	3.7	15,196	3.8	5581	3.2	16,423	2.4
Parity								
Parity 1	654,803	41.5	149,465	37.6	80,370	46.5	236,128	34.5
Parity 2+	921,604	58.5	247,767	62.4	92,651	53.5	449,017	65.5
Education								
Less than high school	127,303	8.1	69,583	17.5	14,317	8.3	229,103	33.4
High school diploma or some college	820,732	52.1	266,883	67.2	54,487	31.5	378,330	55.2
Bachelor's degree or higher	628,372	39.9	60,766	15.3	104,217	60.2	77,712	11.3

(continued)

Table 7.3 (continued)

	Non-Hispanic white (N = 1,576,407)		Non-Hispanic black (N = 397,232)		Non-Hispanic Asian (N = 173,021)		Hispanic (N = 685,145)	
	N	%	N	%	N	%	N	%
Health/clinical								
Maternal risk factors								
Diabetic	86,826	5.5	22,073	5.6	18,035	10.4	44,618	6.5
Hypertensive	105,557	6.7	37,132	9.4	6131	3.5	32,243	4.7
Smoked during pregnancy	195,295	12.4	27,639	7.0	1318	0.8	13,726	2.0
Cesarean delivery	502,720	31.9	144,536	36.4	58,715	33.9	222,498	32.5
Previous cesarean delivery	219,271	13.9	65,139	16.4	24,952	14.4	111,867	16.3
Pre-pregnancy BMI								
Underweight BMI	59,200	3.8	13,623	3.4	14,725	8.5	19,345	2.8
Normal weight	787,686	50.0	139,734	35.2	111,984	64.7	280,102	40.9
Overweight BMI	378,229	24.0	107,517	27.1	33,752	19.5	202,617	29.6
Obese BMI	351,247	22.3	136,358	34.3	12,559	7.3	183,081	26.7
Healthcare coverage and access[a]								
Private insurance + early prenatal care	877,079	55.6	80,975	20.4	98,081	56.7	154,199	22.5
Private insurance + not early prenatal care	136,685	8.7	24,111	6.1	17,133	9.9	33,374	4.9
Medicaid + early prenatal care	346,410	22.0	168,705	42.5	31,591	18.3	296,995	43.4
Medicaid + not early prenatal care	165,420	10.5	111,068	28.0	16,640	9.6	148,401	21.7
Uninsured + early prenatal care	27,662	1.8	5180	1.3	6184	3.6	26,944	3.9
Uninsured + not early prenatal care	23,151	1.5	7193	1.8	3392	2.0	25,232	3.7

[a]Early prenatal care is care initiated in the first trimester

Table 7.4 Logistic regression odds ratios for maternal morbidity, Subset of revised birth certificate reporting area, 2013

Race/ethnicity	Transfusions	Ruptured uterus	Unplanned hysterectomy	ICU admission
Model 1. Unadjusted				
(Ref = non-Hispanic white)				
Non-Hispanic black	1.16***	1.54***	1.21*	2.00***
Non-Hispanic Asian	0.87**	1.28	1.34*	1.29***
Hispanic	0.88***	0.86	1.02	1.69***
Model 2. Adjusting for demographic variables[a]				
(Ref = non-Hispanic white)				
Non-Hispanic black	1.03	1.50***	1.23*	1.81***
Non-Hispanic Asian	0.91	1.26	1.20	1.29***
Hispanic	0.78***	0.77*	0.98	1.57***
Model 3. Adjusting for demographic and health variables[b]				
(Ref = non-Hispanic white)				
Non-Hispanic black	1.02	1.42***	1.17	1.64***
Non-Hispanic Asian	0.89*	1.20	1.16	1.29***
Hispanic	0.82***	0.79*	0.98	1.66***
Model 4. Adjusting for demographic, health and healthcare access variables[c]				
(Ref = non-Hispanic white)				
Non-Hispanic black	0.99	1.37**	1.16	1.56***
Non-Hispanic Asian	0.88*	1.18	1.15	1.20**
Hispanic	0.81***	0.77*	0.99	1.50***
Condition reported	8117	709	1153	4287
Total N	2,908,454	2,908,454	2,908,454	2,908,454

***$p < 0.001$, **$p < 0.01$, *$p < 0.05$, two-tailed test

[a]Demographic variables include: maternal age (ref = 20–34), marital status (ref = married), education (ref = high school or some college), and plurality (ref = singleton) and parity of birth (ref = first birth)

[b]Health variables include: whether diabetic, hypertensive, smoked during pregnancy, current method of delivery is cesarean, history of previous cesarean delivery, and pre-pregnancy BMI (underweight, normal weight (ref), overweight, or obese)

[c]Healthcare access variables include the following categories: private insurance and early prenatal care (care initiated in the first trimester, ref), private insurance and not early prenatal care, medicaid and early prenatal care, medicaid and not early prenatal care, uninsured and early prenatal care, uninsured and not early prenatal care)

after adjustment for all characteristics in Model 4, non-Hispanic black and Hispanic women were about 50% more likely to be admitted to the ICU (OR = 1.56 and 1.50, respectively) than non-Hispanic white women while non-Hispanic Asian women were 20% more likely (OR = 1.20).

Discussion

This chapter has presented data from new items on birth and death certificates measuring maternal morbidity and mortality for states that have adopted the 2003 revised birth and death certificates. For maternal morbidity items included in this chapter, all showed evidence of racial/ethnic disparity with non-Hispanic black women having the highest rates of transfusion and ICU admission and, along with non-Hispanic Asian women, among the highest rates of ruptured uterus and unplanned hysterectomy. ICU admission had the greatest difference in rates, twice as likely for non-Hispanic black than non-Hispanic white women while non-Hispanic Asian and Hispanic women had rates that were about 30 and 50% higher than non-Hispanic white women. ICU admission was also the only one of the four morbidities to have significantly higher odds ratios in multivariate models for all race/ethnic groups compared with non-Hispanic white women after controlling for confounders. Research has shown lower rates of postpartum hemorrhage and infection for non-Hispanic white women (Wanderer et al. 2013), two common indications for ICU admission which may account for some of the group differences in ICU admission; however, the birth certificate does not include these variables. However, racial/ethnic differences in other measures of obstetric care have been found that are not easily explained (Grobman et al. 2015). Nonetheless, ICU admission is probably the most consistent measure of severe morbidity of the morbidities on the birth certificate (Senanayake et al. 2013). While transfusions are a treatment for severe and life-threatening maternal hemorrhage, they are also used to treat anemia, especially for younger women (Rouse et al. 2006). Ruptured uterus and unplanned hysterectomy can be indicative of serious and life-threatening morbidity, but outcomes vary widely depending on its severity and treatment (Bateman et al. 2012; Yap et al. 2001). Women at the upper end of the severe maternal morbidity spectrum are almost always admitted to the ICU (Senanayake et al. 2013) and this measure has been used in scoring systems to indicate maternal morbidity of greater severity (Geller et al. 2004; Callaghan et al. 2014). Not surprisingly, recent research into the indications for obstetric-related ICU admission are consistent with the leading causes of maternal mortality—hypertension, cardiac disease, hemorrhaging, and infection (Wanderer et al. 2013).

Racial/ethnic rate ratios for the reporting area were greater for non-Hispanic black women for maternal mortality than for any of the morbidities, including ICU admission. This disparity was evident in all time periods, with non-Hispanic black women having rates at least twice those of non-Hispanic white women for both the traditional classification of maternal mortality as well as for mortality in which codes corresponding to late maternal deaths are included. This greater racial/ethnic difference for maternal mortality compared with morbidity needs further exploration. One potential contributor to the disparity for the later period is that 7 out of 10 of these women have Medicaid as the payment source for their delivery, more than any other group, and some may lose their health coverage 60 days postpartum (Center for Medicare and Medicaid Services 2015). A large, population-based study of severe maternal morbidity found that the majority of modifiable factors were not at the individual level (age, race parity, multiple birth and prior cesarean delivery), but rather at the provider and system-level (Gray et al. 2012).

Conversely, Hispanic women had higher ICU admission rates than non-Hispanic white women but their maternal mortality rates are about 20–30% lower. The lower mortality for Hispanic women compared with their non-Hispanic white counterparts was confined to the earliest period, while still pregnant, but not significantly different in the later periods of maternal mortality. More research is needed into whether the Hispanic paradox which has been well documented for infant outcomes and overall mortality (e.g. Markides and Coreil 1986; Carr et al. 2013; Arias 2010), is also present for maternal health as well. However, a recent study based on the Center for Disease Control and Prevention's Pregnancy Mortality Surveillance System comparing immigrant Hispanic women to native-born Hispanic women and non-Hispanic white women did not find evidence for this paradox with regards to maternal mortality (Creanga et al. 2012). Nonetheless, examining birth and death certificate data for Hispanic women by country of origin and nativity status might shed more light on the conflicting ICU admission morbidity and maternal mortality for this group.

While rates of maternal mortality for specific time periods could not be computed for non-Hispanic Asian women, their total maternal mortality rate was not significantly different than that of non-Hispanic white women, despite their higher rate for some of the morbidities and for ICU admission even after adjustment in the multivariate model, and their higher rates of advanced maternal age, a consistent predictor of maternal morbidity and mortality. Often times in past research, Asian women have been grouped into "other" race categories and their maternal deaths have just recently reached the threshold of computing a separate maternal mortality rate for this group. As people of Asian race are the fastest growing minority in the United States (U. S. Census Bureau 2012), it is increasingly important to understand maternal morbidity and mortality for these women.

This study is subject to several limitations. These items on the birth and death certificate are relatively new and as such, there have been limited quality assessments to date. Medical and health information have been traditionally underreported on birth certificates (Piper et al. 1993; Buescher et al. 1993) and may extend to the maternal morbidity data as well. There were too few cases of the morbidities to be included in a two-state validity study on the medical and health information from the 2003 birth certificate revision (Martin et al. 2013). In comparison with nationally-representative data from the Nationwide Inpatient Sample, transfusions and hysterectomies appear to be underreported on the birth certificate (Curtin et al. 2015). There are no large-scale, recent studies on ICU admission, but a study in

Maryland based on the Maryland Inpatient Database found a rate of 202.6 per 100,000 deliveries for ICU utilization around the time of delivery (Wanderer et al. 2013) compared with 154.8 for the birth certificate data in this study. Studies of ruptured uterus have usually included small samples and have varied in their estimates (Guise et al. 2004). While the overall levels are probably underreported, this study has been concerned with the differences among race/ethnic groups. The extent to which the underreporting is differential among the race/ethnic groups is unknown and this could potentially affect the disparity measures. While the demographic variables included in the logistic regression have been shown to be of good quality, along with method of delivery (cesarean), payment source, and month prenatal care began, some of the health items are underreported (Martin et al. 2013).

The pregnancy checkbox on the death certificate is also of uncertain data quality and has had limited quality assessments. However, a study which compared entries in the pregnancy checkbox with linked-birth and fetal death records, and medical examiner records found that pregnancy-related maternal mortality was captured 98% of the time with the checkbox (Horon and Cheng 2011). However, this study did not have any cases of maternal deaths at 43 days to 1 year after an ended pregnancy, so data quality at the latest period of maternal mortality was not assessed. Previously, maternal mortality was widely considered to be underestimated in vital statistics (MacKay et al. 2000, 2005). Adding the question to death certificates has had the effect of increasing the numbers of maternal deaths identified (Hoyert 2007; MacKay et al. 2011); however, the guidelines currently are liberal in using the recent pregnancy question. There remain many unanswered questions about how vital statistics estimates compare to other estimates and if it now may even tend to overestimate maternal deaths.

The race and ethnicity information on death certificates is of poorer quality than on birth certificates (where it is typically self-reported) as it is gathered by the funeral director by an informant and sometimes by observation alone. These issues are discussed in detail elsewhere (Murphy et al. 2013; Arias et al. 2008). The extent to which race and ethnicities are misclassified could affect the disparity measures in this paper. However, there have been no recent studies on this misclassification so the direction and extent is unknown for 2013 maternal deaths.

Another limitation of this study is that the data are not yet national and cannot be generalized to the entire United States (National Center for Health Statistics 2014). In addition, the birth and death reporting areas are not comparable and this could differentially affect the morbidity and mortality data. In particular, California is not in the death reporting area and therefore a disproportionate number of Hispanic and non-Hispanic Asian births and maternal deaths are not included in the maternal mortality rates. In addition, the countries of origin for these groups are different between the reporting areas, in particular, more Hispanic women of Mexican descent are in the birth certificate reporting area due to the inclusion of California (National Center for Health Statistics 2009). However, when only the areas that were common in both were examined (32 states and the District of Columbia), the ratio for ICU admission for Hispanic women was still elevated relative to non-Hispanic white women (ratio = 1.8), but the ratio for total maternal mortality was still lower (ratio = 0.5). It was important to include the maximum number of areas in each to obtain sufficient cases to compute some of the non-Hispanic Asian and Hispanic morbidity and mortality rates in this paper.

Despite these limitations, the new birth and death certificate data will be an important resource in examining issues surrounding the racial/ethnic disparities in maternal morbidity and mortality. A strength of birth and death certificate data is that they are based on 100% of records filed in the reporting areas and are more likely than some other data sources (e.g. sample surveys) to have sufficient cases to examine rates for smaller subgroups and rarer events (e.g. non-Hispanic Asian women, ruptured uterus, maternal deaths at 43 days to 1 year of an ended pregnancy). Although sufficient numbers are lacking even for these data for some of the rarer morbidities and time-specific mortality periods, more data will become available as more states begin to report this information. National data are expected with the 2016 data year. In addition, quality initiatives and web-based training are underway (Martin et al. 2013) and should improve the quality of these data in the coming years.

Acknowledgments The following persons provided helpful comments in the preparation of this manuscript: Elizabeth R. Arias, Ph. D., Amy M. Branum, Ph.D., William H. Callaghan, M.D., M. P.H., Jennifer H. Madans, Ph.D., Joyce A. Martin, M.P.H., and Hanyu Ni, M.P.H., Ph.D.

References

American College of Obstetricians and Gynecologists. (2006). ACOG practice bulletin no. 76: Postpartum hemorrhage. *Obstetrics and Gynecology, 108*, 1039–1047.

Arias, E. (2010). United States life tables by Hispanic origin. *Vital and Health Statistics, 2*(152), 1–33.

Arias, E., Schauman, W. S., Eschbach, K., Sorlie, P. D., & Backlund, E. (2008). The validity of race and Hispanic origin reporting on death certificates in the United States. *Vital and health statistics, 2*(148), 1–23.

Bateman, B. T., Mhyre, J. M., Callaghan, W. M., & Kuklina, E. V. (2012). Peripartum hysterectomy in the United States: nationwide 14 year experience. *American Journal of Obstetrics and Gynecology, 206*(1), 63.e1–63.e8. doi:10.1016/j.ajog.2011.07.030

Berg, C. J., Callaghan, W. M., Syverson, C., & Henderson, Z. (2010). Pregnancy-related mortality in the United States, 1998 to 2005. *Obstetrics and Gynecology, 116*(6), 1302–1309. doi:10.1097/AOG.0b013e3181fdfb11

Bryant, A. S., Worjoloh, A., Caughey, A. B., & Washington, A. E. (2010). Racial/ethnic disparities in obstetric outcomes and care: prevalence and determinants. *American Journal of Obstetrics and Gynecology, 202*(4), 335–343. doi:10.1016/j.ajog.2009.10.864

Buescher, P. A., Taylor, K. P., Davis, M. H., & Bowling, J. M. (1993). The quality of the new birth certificate data: a validation study in North Carolina. *American Journal of Public Health, 83*(8), 1163–1165.

Callaghan, W. M., Grobman, W. A., Kilpatrick, S. J., Main, E. K., & D'Alton, M. (2014). Facility-based identification of women with severe maternal morbidity: it is time to start. *Obstetrics and Gynecology, 123*(5), 978–981. doi:10.1097/AOG.0000000000000218

Campbell, K. H., Savitz, D., Werner, E. F., Pettker, C. M., Goffman, D., Chazotte, C., et al. (2013). Maternal morbidity and risk of death at delivery hospitalization. *Obstetrics and Gynecology, 122*(3), 627–633. doi:10.1097/AOG

Carr, A., Kershaw, T., Brown, H., Allen, T., & Small, M. (2013). Hypertensive disease in pregnancy: An examination of ethnic differences and the Hispanic paradox. *Journal of Neonatal-Perinatal Medicine, 6*(1), 11–15. doi:10.3233/NPM-1356111

Center for Medicare and Medicaid Services. (2015). Pregnant women. Available from: http://www.medicaid.gov/medicaid-chip-program-information/by-population/pregnant-women/pregnant-women.html

Centers for Disease Control and Prevention. (2015a). Pregnancy mortality surveillance system. Available at: http://www.cdc.gov/reproductivehealth/MaternalInfantHealth/PMSS.html

Centers for Disease Control and Prevention. (2015b). Severe maternal morbidity in the United States. Available at: http://www.cdc.gov/reproductivehealth/MaternalInfantHealth/SevereMaternalMorbidity.html

Creanga, A. A., Bateman, B. T., Kuklina, E. V., & Callaghan, W. M. (2014b). Racial and ethnic disparities in severe maternal morbidity: A multistate analysis, 2008–2010. *American Journal of Obstetrics and Gynecology, 210*(5), 435.e1–435.e8. doi:10.1016/j.ajog.2013.11.039

Creanga, A. A., Berg, C. J., Ko, J. Y., Farr, S. L., Tong, V. T., Bruce, F. C., et al. (2014a). Maternal mortality and morbidity in the United States: Where are we now? *Journal of Women's Health, 23*(1), 3–9. doi:10.1089/jwh.2013.4617

Creanga, A. A., Berg, C. J., Syverson, C., Seed, K., Bruce, F. C., & Callaghan, W. M. (2012). Race, ethnicity, and nativity differentials in pregnancy-related mortality in the United States: 1993–2006. *Obstetrics and Gynecology, 120*(2 Pt 1), 261–268. doi:10.1097/AOG.0b013e31825cb87a

Curtin, S. C., Gregory, K. D., Korst, L. M., & Uddin, S. F. (2015). Maternal morbidity for vaginal and cesarean deliveries, according to previous Cesarean History: New data from the birth certificate, 2013. *National Vital Statistics Reports, 64*(4), 1–13, back cover.

Firoz, T., Chou, D., von Dadelszen, P., Agrawal, P., Vanderkruik, R., & Tuncalp, O. (2013). Measuring maternal health: focus on maternal morbidity. *Bulletin of the World Health Organization, 91*(10), 794–796. doi:10.2471/BLT.13.117564

Fridman, M., Korst, L. M., Chow, J., Lawton, E., Mitchell, C., & Gregory, K. D. (2014). Trends in maternal morbidity before and during pregnancy in California. *American Journal of Public Health, 104*(Suppl 1), S49–S57. doi:10.2105/AJPH.2013.301583

Geller, S. E., Rosenberg, D., Cox, S. M., Brown, M. L., Simonson, L., Driscoll, C. A., et al. (2004). The continuum of maternal morbidity and mortality: Factors associated with severity. *American Journal of Obstetrics and Gynecology, 191*(3), 939–944. doi:10.1016/j.ajog.2004.05.099

Gray, K. E., Wallace, E. R., Nelson, K. R., Reed, S. D., & Schiff, M. A. (2012). Population-based study of risk factors for severe maternal morbidity. *Paediatric and Perinatal Epidemiology, 26*(6), 506–514. doi:10.1111/ppe.12011

Grobman, W. A., Bailit, J. L., Rice, M. M., Wapner, R. J., Reddy, U. M., Varner, M. W., et al. (2015). Racial and ethnic disparities in maternal morbidity and obstetric care. *Obstetrics and Gynecology, 125*(6), 1460–1467. doi:10.1097/AOG.0000000000000735

Guise, J. M., Berlin, M., McDonagh, M., Osterweil, P., Chan, B., & Helfand, M. (2004). Safety of vaginal birth after cesarean: A systematic review. *Obstetrics and Gynecology, 103*(3), 420–429. doi:10.1097/01.AOG.0000116259.41678.f1

Horon, I. L., & Cheng, D. (2011). Effectiveness of pregnancy check boxes on death certificates in identifying pregnancy-associated mortality. *Public Health Reports, 126*(2), 195–200.

Hoyert, D. L. (2007). Maternal mortality and related concepts. *Vital and Health Statistics, 3*(33), 1–13.

MacKay, A. P., Berg, C. J., Duran, C., Chang, J., & Rosenberg, H. (2005). An assessment of pregnancy-related mortality in the United States. *Paediatric and Perinatal Epidemiology, 19*(3), 206–214. doi:10.1111/j.1365-3016.2005.00653.x

MacKay, A. P., Berg, C. J., Liu, X., Duran, C., & Hoyert, D. L. (2011). Changes in pregnancy mortality ascertainment: United States, 1999–2005. *Obstetrics and Gynecology, 118*(1), 104–110. doi:10.1097/AOG.0b013e31821fd49d

MacKay, A. P., Rochat, R., Smith, J. C., & Berg, C. J. (2000). The check box: determining pregnancy status to improve maternal mortality surveillance. *American Journal of Preventive Medicine, 19*(1 Suppl), 35–39.

Markides, K. S., & Coreil, J. (1986). The health of Hispanics in the southwestern United States: An epidemiologic paradox. *Public Health Reports, 101*(3), 253–265.

Martin, J. A., Wilson, E. C., Osterman, M. J., Saadi, E. W., Sutton, S. R., & Hamilton, B. E. (2013). Assessing the quality of medical and health data from the 2003 birth certificate revision: Results from two states. *National Vital Statistics Reports, 62*(2), 1–19.

Murphy, S. L., Xu, J., & Kochanek, K. D. (2013). Deaths: Final data for 2010. *National Vital Statistics Reports, 61*(4), 1–117.

National Center for Health Statistics. (2000). *Report of the panel to evaluate the U.S. Standard Certificates and Reports.* Hyattsville, MD: USGPO.

National Center for Health Statistics. (2006). *Guide to completing the facility worksheets for the certificate of live birth and report of fetal death (2003 revision).* Hyattsville, MD: USGPO.

National Center for Health Statistics. (2009). *User guide to the 2007 natality public use file.* Hyattsville, MD: USGPO.

National Center for Health Statistics. (2012). *User guide to the 2010 natality public use file.* Hyattsville, MD: USGPO.

National Center for Health Statistics. (2013). Vital statistics, instructions for classifying multiple causes of death. NCHS instruction manual; part 2b. Hyattsville, Maryland: USGPO.

National Center for Health Statistics. (2014). *User guide to the 2013 natality public use file.* Hyattsville, MD: USGPO.

Office of Management and Budget. (1997). Revisions to the standards for the classification of federal data on Race and ethnicity. Fed Regist 62FR58781–58790.

Piper, J. M., Mitchel, E. F, Jr., Snowden, M., Hall, C., Adams, M., & Taylor, P. (1993). Validation of 1989 Tennessee birth certificates using maternal and newborn hospital records. *American Journal of Epidemiology, 137*(7), 758–768.

Rouse, D. J., MacPherson, C., Landon, M., Varner, M. W., Leveno, K. J., Moawad, A. H., et al. (2006). Blood transfusion and cesarean delivery. *Obstetrics and Gynecology, 108*(4), 891–897. doi:10.1097/01.AOG.0000236547.35234.8c

Senanayake, H., Dias, T., & Jayawardena, A. (2013). Maternal mortality and morbidity: Epidemiology of intensive care admissions in pregnancy. *Best Practice and Research Clinical Obstetrics and Gynaecology, 27*(6), 811–820. doi:10.1016/j.bpobgyn.2013.07.002

U.S. Census Bureau (2012). The Asian population: 2010. 2010 Census Briefs. C2010BR-11. Available at: http://www.census.gov/prod/cen2010/briefs/c2010br-11.pdf

Vanderkruik, R. C., Tuncalp, O., Chou, D., & Say, L. (2013). Framing maternal morbidity: WHO scoping exercise. *BMC Pregnancy Childbirth, 13*, 213. doi:10.1186/1471-2393-13-213

Wanderer, J. P., Leffert, L. R., Mhyre, J. M., Kuklina, E. V., Callaghan, W. M., & Bateman, B. T. (2013). Epidemiology of obstetric-related ICU admissions in Maryland: 1999–2008*. *Critical Care Medicine, 41*(8), 1844–1852. doi:10.1097/CCM.0b013e31828a3e24

Yap, O. W., Kim, E. S., & Laros, R. K., Jr. (2001). Maternal and neonatal outcomes after uterine rupture in labor. *American Journal of Obstetrics and Gynecology, 184*(7), 1576–1581.

Chapter 8
Racial and Ethnic Disparities in Infant Mortality, 1990–2004: Low Birth Weight, Maternal Complications and Other Causes

Ginny Garcia and Hyeyoung Woo

Introduction

Infant mortality, typically measured as the number of infant deaths per 1000 live births, is a key indicator of national well-being (MacDorman and Mathews 2008; World Bank 2011). While consistent declines in infant mortality have been observed since the 1980s, racial disparities have persisted such that infants born to black (NHB) mothers die at rates more than twice those of whites (NHW) (Frisbie et al. 2010; Mathews and MacDorman 2013). What's more, several studies have shown that a once documented survival advantage for NHB infants (those born prematurely or with low birthweight had a lower risk of death than NHW infants between 1980 and 1990 (Wilcox and Russell 1990)), appears to have eroded in more recent years (Alexander et al. 2008; Frisbie et al. 2004; Schempf et al. 2007). These studies have shown that gains earned through technological advancements have increasingly accrued to NHW infants; and for some causes, have resulted in an actual increase in the relative disparity between NHB and NHW infants (Alexander et al. 2008; Frisbie et al. 2010).

On the other hand, Hispanics (excluding Puerto Ricans) have traditionally enjoyed infant mortality rates that are similar to or slightly lower than whites (Frisbie 2005); a trend which persists for most Hispanic origin groups to the present (Mathews and MacDorman 2013). Scholars have referred to this phenomenon as the epidemiologic, or Hispanic, paradox given that their relatively lower socioeconomic background is not commensurate with such favorable outcomes (Hummer et al. 1999; Markides and Coreil 1986). Other racial and ethnic groups evidence

---

G. Garcia (✉) · H. Woo
Department of Sociology, Portland State University, 1721 SW Broadway,
PO Box 751, Portland, OR 97207, USA
e-mail: ginny.garciaalexander@pdx.edu

H. Woo
e-mail: hyeyoung@pdx.edu

varying outcomes such that Asian and Pacific Islanders have the lowest rates of infant mortality, while American Indian, Alaska Native, and Puerto Rican IMRs are elevated compared to NHW infants but lower than NHB infants (Mathews and MacDorman 2013). Less is known about the extent to which a survival advantage may be present among other racial and ethnic groups.

In our study, we aim to provide more recent evidence of a survival disadvantage in Black infants and explore the extent to which other racial and ethnic minority groups may have experienced changes in infant death outcomes over time (as compared to non-Hispanic whites). We use micro level U.S. birth cohort linked birth-death data collected at 1990, 2000, and 2004 to examine racial and ethnic differentials (racial and ethnic groups include NH white, NH black, NH other, and Hispanic) in cause-specific infant mortality rates (IMRs) over time. Several causes of death, including preterm-related and maternal complications, evidence worsening outcomes in recent years. Thus, for each racial and ethnic group we estimate the relative risk of death due to: (1) LBW or preterm delivery, (2) maternal conditions or complications, and (3) a residual other causes category; adjusting for a number of known covariates. Finally, given the contribution of preterm and LBW to infant death (MacDorman and Mathews 2009; Schempf et al. 2007), we include interaction terms to study how the effect of having a LBW/preterm birth on the odds of infant death differs by race or ethnicity. Of particular interest is the period between 2000 and 2004 in which overall improvements in rates of infant death have stagnated and preterm related deaths increased (MacDorman et al. 2010).

Racial and Ethnic Differences in Infant Mortality Rates

A large body of research has documented racial variations in infant mortality over many decades in the U.S. (David and Collins 1990; Eberstein 1989; Frisbie 2005; Geronimus 1996; Gortmaker and Wise 1997; Hummer 1993). Specifically, a black-white infant mortality gap has long been observed with several studies evidencing a widening of the gap (Alexander et al. 2008; Frisbie et al. 2010; Iyasu and Tomashek 2002; Krieger et al. 2008; MacDorman and Mathews 2009). Recent estimates indicate that black mothers continue to experience IMRs more than two times higher than white mothers (12.4 vs. 5.3) and nearly three times higher than Asian or Pacific Islanders (12.4 vs. 4.4) (Mathews and MacDorman 2013). This gap has been attributed to a complex myriad of factors including differential access to and quality of health care (Link and Phelan 1995; Phelan et al. 2010), experience of discrimination (Collins et al. 2000), and social and economic inequality (Gortmaker and Wise 1997).

On the other hand, Hispanic mothers have fared relatively well with respect to infant mortality, though some variations on the basis of origin are observable. For example, Mexican and Cuban women have rates that are similar to White women at 5.12 and 5.77, respectively; while Puerto Rican women experience slightly elevated IMRs (7.18) (Mathews and MacDorman 2013). This relative advantage is often argued to be a product of the epidemiologic paradox, which accounts for enduring evidence that the health status of Hispanics is closer to whites despite the fact that they are closer in SES to NH blacks (Markides and Coreil 1986). This is potentially explained by immigrant selectivity (healthy immigrants give birth to healthy babies) (Markides and Eschbach 2005) or pro-health behaviors that are often found among Hispanics (Abraído-Lanza et al. 2005; Franzini, et al. 2001). Alternately, the improved outcomes may simply be a product of under-registration of births due to out-migration (Palloni and Arias 2004). Some evidence supports erosion of the advantage for U.S. born Mexican infants (Frisbie et al. 2010), which account for a larger share of recent birth cohorts (Saenz 2010). Additionally, previous studies have shown that Hispanic health outcomes, including prematurity and low birth weight, worsen with acculturation (Lara et al. 2005). Because some argument as to the nature and persistence of the epidemiologic paradox continues, it is necessary to provide continued examination of infant health outcomes in this ethnic group.

Racial and Ethnic Differences in Cause-Specific Infant Mortality

Several leading causes have consistently accounted for a sizeable proportion of overall infant deaths as well as racial and ethnic disparities in infant mortality, including preterm birth, low birth weight, and maternal complications. For example, preterm-related deaths accounted for 36.5% of infant deaths in 2004 (MacDorman et al. 2010) and gestational age (along with birthweight) is considered to be the most important predictor of survival (Hummer et al. 1999; MacDorman and Mathews 2009). While some declines have been observed in recent years (2007–2009), studies documented a persistent increase in the percentage of preterm births between 1984 and 2006 (MacDorman et al. 2010; Martin et al. 2007; Mathews and MacDorman 2013). Preterm-related infant deaths evidence persistent variations by race such that NHB women experience increased IMRs while Hispanics have relatively similar IMRs as compared to NH whites (Alexander et al. 2003; Mathews and MacDorman 2013; Muhuri et al. 2004).

Birthweight is also of substantial import as low birth weight infants (<2500 g) have a much greater risk of death than those 2500 g or more (Iyasu and Tomashek 2002; Lu and Halfon 2003; Mathews and MacDorman 2013). As with gestational age, low birthweight is highly variable by race and ethnicity. Specifically, 13.7% of infants born to NHB women were low birthweight in 2009, and this group has the highest IMRs due to this cause at a rate of 68.35 per 1000 (Mathews and MacDorman 2013). This trend of increased IMRs attributable to LBW in NHB infants is a continuation of patterns observed in previous years (Alexander et al. 2003; Iyasu and Tomashek 2002; Muhuri et al. 2004). However, several scholars have argued that most of the racial disparities in infant deaths are substantially explained after accounting for preterm and low birthweight deliveries (Rosenthal and Lobel 2011), which are much more common in NHB women (Martin et al. 2007). Indeed, another study indicates that excess deaths in preterm Black infants accounted for 80% of the Black-White infant mortality gap (Schempf et al. 2007). Nonetheless, adjusting for gestational age and birthweight does not entirely explain away the discrepancy and additional attention to this relationship is needed. Accordingly, we examine how this outcome is amplified or dampened among various racial and ethnic groups via the inclusion of interaction terms.

Deaths due to maternal complications are those caused by such factors as incompetent cervix and multiple pregnancies, among others. This cause is among the top five leading causes of infant death overall and across racial and ethnic groups. Studies have shown that IMRs due to this cause are elevated in NHB women compared to NHW women (2.7 rate ratio) and Puerto Rican women (1.61) (Mathews and MacDorman 2013). Still more troubling findings indicate increases in infant mortality due to maternal complications for almost all race groups (Muhuri et al. 2004). Additionally, with the exception of a few studies such as those conducted by Frisbie et al. (2010) and Muhuri et al. (2004), examinations that consider racial and ethnic variations in this cause are sparse. Thus, this cause warrants additional consideration given that it could be argued that the social causes tied to poorer outcomes are potentially greater reflected therein.

Elevated IMRs in NHB women have long been a feature of the U.S. mortality distribution. In the 1980s, black infants experienced some survival advantage with preterm or low birthweight deliveries. But, technological advancements have led to an increased black-white infant mortality gap as gains have increasingly accrued to NHW infants in more recent decades (Alexander et al. 2008; Schempf et al. 2007). On the other hand, Hispanics have long experienced an advantage in infant mortality, though less is known about the extent to which that advantage persists in the context of low birthweight or preterm delivery. To further explicate these outcomes, we utilize National Center for Health Statistics (NCHS) birth cohort linked birth-death data (1990, 2000, and 2004) to undertake a cause-specific examination by race and ethnicity. We focus our analysis on preterm-related or low birthweight, maternal complications, and other causes of infant death, which evidence highly pronounced racial and ethnic differentials (David and Collins 2007; Muhuri et al. 2004). Additionally, we examine the role of gestational age and low birthweight more closely via the inclusion of interactions terms with race and ethnicity. Drawing on the findings in previous related research, we offer the following hypotheses:

H1: Given the persistent black-white infant mortality gap, black race is expected to amplify the risk of infant death due to multiple causes in the main effects models.

H1a: A decreased survival advantage (or a survival *disadvantage*) is expected for preterm and low birthweight black infants after 1990.

H2: Given the increasingly U.S. born share of Hispanics, Hispanic women are expected to evidence improved outcomes across causes relative to other groups in early years—with that advantage diminishing in later years.

H2a: Similarly, as technological gains have increasingly accrued to NHW infants, Hispanic mothers are not expected to experience survival advantage in the context of low birth weight/preterm deliveries in more recent cohorts.

Data and Method

Data

We use the 1990, 2000, and 2004 National Center for Health Statistics (NCHS) birth cohort linked birth/infant death dataset (restricted access files used for 1990 and 2000; public use data used for 2004). These micro-level data include statistical data from birth and death certificates provided to the NCHS under the Vital Statistics Cooperative Program, and the linkages allow for the use of variables recorded on the birth certificate. Data presented are based on births and deaths in all states but excludes data for foreign residents, Puerto Rico, Virgin Islands, and Guam. The linked files contain detailed cause of death classifications based on the underlying cause of death recorded on the death certificate, in addition to race and Hispanic origin of the mother, birth weight, prenatal care, gestation, and other characteristics detailed below. Beginning in 1989, the standard birth certificate was redesigned to include Hispanic identification along with medical risk factors, smoking, alcohol use, weight gain, obstetric procedures, labor/delivery complications, and a clinical estimate of gestation (DHHS 1995). In order to ensure the outcomes represent the most recent data available, we also include the 2004 cohort linked birth/infant death data, which represent the most recent year of data that include the necessary maternal characteristics contained in the 1990 and 2000 data files, thereby allowing us to make meaningful comparisons over time. Overall, linkage rates were very high with 97.5% of records linked in 1990, 98.7% linked in 2000, and 98.9% in 2004 (DHHS 1995, 2008, 2011). Finally, weights became available in 1995 to account for the 2–3% of cases that could not be linked. However, the values presented herein are unweighted for consistency across years.

Measures

The dependent variable, cause-specific infant death, consists of four categories: infant death due to preterm or low birth weight (1), infant death due to maternal conditions or complications (2), infant death due to other causes (3), and infant survival (base outcome = 0). Categories were constructed based on ICD-9 codes for 1990 and ICD-10 codes for 2000 and 2004. Our main predictor of interest is maternal race and ethnicity, and is based on information reported by the mother on the birth certificate as this is thought to be more accurate than information recorded on the death certificate (DHHS 2011). This variable includes non-Hispanic white (NHW), non-Hispanic black (NHB), non-Hispanic other (NHO), and Hispanic (NHW is the reference category).

We also consider several known covariates on infant mortality. Sociodemographic controls include maternal age (categorical: 10–18, 19–24, 25–34, 35+), marital status (dichotomous: married vs. non-married), foreign born status (dichotomous: US born vs. foreign born), and education (categorical: less than high school, high school, some college and beyond); and region (Northeast, Midwest, South, West) all recorded on the birth certificate. We also include several measures related to the pregnancy or birth history. Parity is based on birth order and reflects the order of the present birth based on all previous births (categorical: first birth, second-fourth birth, and fifth or higher order birth). The Adequacy of Prenatal Care Utilization Index (APNCU) reflects both early and adequate prenatal care and was included as part of the Healthy People 2010 objectives to increase the proportion of pregnant women's receipt of early/adequate care. It is categorical with inadequate reflecting little to no care, intermediate for sufficient care that originated in months five or six of pregnancy, adequate basic for sufficient care that began in the first trimester, and adequate intensive reflecting situations where more than normal care was received). Additional measures include medical risk factors such as anemia or diabetes (yes (1) = any risk factor present during pregnancy, no (0) = none); labor or delivery complications such as excessive bleeding or prolonged labor (yes = any complication, no = none); and weight gain (categorical: less than 16 lb, 16–40 lb, and 41 or more pounds). We also consider the effects of health behaviors related to tobacco use during pregnancy. This is a dichotomous variable coded 1 for any level of tobacco use during pregnancy and 0 for none. Finally, we control for the effects of preterm delivery (37 or more weeks is considered 'term' while less than 37 weeks is considered 'preterm') and low birth weight (LBW is measured as less than 2500 g vs. 2500 or more grams) as these are strongly linked to risk of infant death. Following the strategy employed by previous researchers (Frisbie et al. 2010; Muhuri et al. 2004), we assume that these controls are necessary as they should lead to a lower risk of infant death and thus more conservative analysis. We further include interactions for race by gestational age and race by low birth weight.

Analytic Models

We use multinomial logistic regression to model the risk of infant death due to preterm or low birth weight; death due to maternal complications; and death due to any other cause versus survival (alive = 0) in order to determine which outcomes are more strongly patterned by race and ethnicity. The model equation is as follows:

$$\ln \Omega m|b(x) = \ln \frac{\Pr(y=m|x)}{\Pr(y=b|x)} = x\beta m|b \text{ for } m = 1 \text{ to } J$$

Models are estimated separately by year allowing associations with the racial and ethnic categories as well as the covariates to vary by the year. Our results are reported as odds ratios.

Results

Sample Characteristics by Year

To begin, we report summary statistics for 1990, 2000, and 2004 in Table 8.1. Herein we point out several patterns observed in terms of racial and ethnic variations in IMRs by cause of death. For example, an increasingly larger proportion of infant deaths are attributable to preterm or low birthweight over time, while the proportion of infant deaths due to maternal complications or other causes has decreased slightly from 1990 to 2004. The proportion of births to NHW and NHB has decreased, while Hispanic women's share has increased markedly over time. The percentage of married women has decreased in recent years, as has the percentage of women who give birth at younger ages. The percentage of women experiencing risk factors has increased over time while the percentage experiencing complications has decreased. Tobacco use has decreased significantly over time. Finally, the percentage of preterm and low birth weight infants has increased over time.

Overall and Cause-Specific Infant Mortality Risk by Maternal Race and Ethnicity

Table 8.2 presents the absolute change in cause-specific infant mortality rates by race and ethnicity across years. Declines in overall IMRs are observed for all racial and ethnic groups. Though the largest absolute declines are observed among NHB women, their overall rates remain more than two times higher than any other group. Cause-specific outcomes reveal that all groups experienced increases in infant deaths due to preterm or low birth weight. However, deaths due to this cause among NHB women were more than four times that of any other group. Thus, the largest increase was observed among NHB women (increased from 2.67 per 1000 in 1990 to 2.95 in 2004), who were followed closely by Hispanic women (0.60 per 1000 in 1990 to 0.85 in 2004). Some variation was observed for deaths due to maternal complications. For example, NHB women experienced a minor decline in 2000 (2.31 in 1990 decreased to 2.15 in 2000) followed by an increase in 2004

Table 8.1 Selected Characteristics of 1990, 2000, and 2004 birth/death cohorts, United States

		All		1990		2000		2004	
		Frequency	Percentage	Frequency	Percentage	Frequency	Percentage	Frequency	Percentage
Infant deaths	Preterm/LBW	12,768	0.10	3864	0.09	4340	0.11	4564	0.11
	Maternal complications	12,484	0.10	4455	0.11	3839	0.09	4190	0.10
	Other causes	67,175	0.54	28,720	0.69	19,511	0.48	18,944	0.46
	Survival	12,236,974	99.25	4,121,406	99.11	4,031,213	99.32	4,084,355	99.33
Race/ethnicity	NH white	7,289,712	59.99	2,630,042	64.84	2,362,987	58.84	2,296,683	56.30
	NH black	1,844,990	15.18	661,846	16.32	604,372	15.05	578,772	14.19
	NH other	659,660	5.43	169,308	4.17	232,682	5.79	257,670	6.32
	Hispanic	2,357,409	19.40	595,173	14.67	815,887	20.32	946,349	23.30
Age categories	10–18	896,495	7.27	339,972	8.18	298,525	7.35	257,998	6.27
	19–25	4,361,187	35.37	1,537,813	36.98	1,404,976	34.61	1,418,398	34.49
	26–34	5,571,779	45.19	1,912,814	46	1,808,715	44.56	1,850,250	45.00
	35+	1,499,940	12.17	367,846	8.85	546,687	13.47	585,407	14.24
Marital status	Unmarried	3,982,770	32.30	1,165,498	28.03	1,347,082	33.19	1,470,190	35.75
	Married	8,346,631	67.70	2,992,947	71.97	2,711,821	66.81	2,641,863	64.25
Foreign born	US born	9,788,700	79.63	3,504,781	84.44	3,180,566	78.59	3,103,353	75.77
	Foreign born	2,504,062	20.37	645,616	15.56	866,219	21.41	992,227	24.23
Parity	1st birth	4,942,542	40.29	1,689,188	40.88	1,622,433	40.15	1,630,921	39.84
	2–4th birth	6,807,151	55.49	2,270,924	54.96	2,249,279	55.66	2,286,948	55.87
	5+ Birth	516,859	4.21	171,717	4.16	169,591	4.2	175,551	4.29

(continued)

Table 8.1 (continued)

		All		1990		2000		2004	
		Frequency	Percentage	Frequency	Percentage	Frequency	Percentage	Frequency	Percentage
Region	Northeast	2,162,206	17.54	793,094	19.07	692,510	17.06	677,752	16.48
	Midwest	2,728,541	22.13	945,906	22.75	898,397	22.13	888,082	21.60
	South	4,432,487	35.95	1,409,390	33.89	1,487,962	36.66	1,528,755	37.18
	West	3,006,167	24.38	1,010,055	24.29	980,034	24.15	1,017,464	24.74
Education	<HS	2,513,940	22.51	920,062	23.79	866,093	21.66	727,785	22.02
	HS	3,744,072	33.52	1,482,917	38.34	1,273,078	31.84	988,077	29.90
	college+	4,912,420	43.98	1,464,501	37.87	1,858,817	46.49	1,589,102	48.08
APNCU index	Inadequate	760,024	6.16	247,714	5.96	152,714	3.76	359,596	8.74
	Intermediate	1,045,602	8.48	360,879	8.68	241,025	5.94	443,698	10.79
	Adequate	4,517,492	36.64	1,573,326	37.83	1,562,946	38.51	1,381,220	33.59
	Adequate+	3,310,776	26.85	1,033,568	24.85	1,222,492	30.12	1,054,716	25.65
	Missing	2,695,507	21.86	942,958	22.68	879,726	21.67	872,823	21.23
Medical risk factor (any)	No	9,265,156	75.15	3,345,210	80.44	2,903,134	71.53	3,016,812	73.37
	Yes	3,064,245	24.85	813,235	19.56	1,155,769	28.47	1,095,241	26.63
Labor/deliv. complications	No	8,601,469	69.76	2,893,710	69.59	2,748,858	67.72	2,958,901	71.96
	Yes	3,727,932	30.24	1,264,735	30.41	1,310,045	32.28	1,153,152	28.04
Tobacco use	No	8,019,692	65.05	2,446,057	58.82	3,063,552	75.48	2,510,083	61.04
	Yes	1,263,424	10.25	552,925	13.3	425,108	10.47	285,391	6.94
	Missing	3,046,285	24.71	1,159,463	27.88	570,243	14.05	1,316,579	32.02
Weight gain	<16 lbs	1,091,066	8.85	277,684	6.68	376,085	9.27	437,297	10.63
	16–40 lbs	6,775,334	54.95	2,274,000	54.68	2,252,867	55.5	2,248,467	54.68
	41+ lbs	1,780,946	14.44	481,535	11.58	625,980	15.42	673,431	16.38
	Missing	2,682,055	21.75	1,125,226	27.06	803,971	19.81	752,858	18.31

(continued)

Table 8.1 (continued)

		All		1990		2000		2004	
		Frequency	Percentage	Frequency	Percentage	Frequency	Percentage	Frequency	Percentage
Gestational age (37 weeks)	Term	10,783,851	88.42	3,674,841	89.38	3,548,288	88.36	3,560,722	87.51
	Preterm	1,412,339	11.58	436,736	10.62	467,246	11.64	508,357	12.49
Low birthweight (<2500 g)	No	11,389,628	92.44	3,863,522	93.03	3,748,055	92.40	3,778,051	91.89
	Yes	931,068	7.56	289,567	6.97	308,076	7.60	333,425	8.11
N		12,329,401	100.00	4,158,445	100	4,058,903	100	4,112,053	100

Table 8.2 Overall and cause-specific infant mortality rates (IMRs) by race/ethnicity, 1990–2004[a]

IMR	Race/ethnicity	1990	2000	2004	Abs. change in rates, 1990–2004
IMR (overall)	NH white	7.133	5.649	5.651	−1.537
	NH black	16.947	13.531	13.52	−3.427
	NH other	7.314	5.445	5.101	−2.713
	Hispanic	7.500	5.437	5.433	−2.062
Preterm/low birth weight	NH white	0.531	0.704	0.766	0.135
	NH black	2.670	2.937	2.949	0.279
	NH other	0.573	0.735	0.73	0.157
	Hispanic	0.601	0.783	0.345	0.244
Maternal complication	NH white	0.788	0.719	0.752	−0.036
	NH black	2.312	2.146	2.422	0.110
	NH other	0.602	0.679	0.753	0.151
	Hispanic	0.976	0.743	0.835	−0.141
Other causes	NH white	5.319	4.226	4.133	−1.686
	NH black	11.965	3.443	3.148	−3.817
	NH other	6.639	4.031	3.617	−3.022
	Hispanic	5.924	3.911	3.777	−2.147

[a]unweighted values; weights unavailable prior to 2000

(to 2.42) to reflect a net increase in deaths due to this cause. Additionally, Hispanic women experienced a decline in 2000 (0.98 in 1990 to 0.74 in 2000) followed by an increase in 2004 (0.84) resulting in a net decrease of 0.14. Finally, all groups experienced a decrease in rates of death due to other causes. Here, it is observed that NHB women experienced the greatest decline, though their overall rate remains about twice that of other groups.

Multivariate Results

The following results depict the risk of infant death due to the listed causes for 1990, 2000, and 2004 (see Tables 8.3a, 8.3b and 8.3c). We focus on differences in these outcomes on the basis of race and ethnicity (after adjusting for controls) in our main effects models. Thus, Model 1 adjusts for maternal age, race, marital status, foreign-born status, level of education, parity, infant sex, region, APNCU index, medical risk factors, complications of labor/delivery, tobacco use, and weight gain. We further consider how race interacts with low birthweight and gestational age to produce variations in risk. Accordingly, Model 2 adjusts for all the previous covariates in addition to gestational age, birth weight, and interaction terms for race by gestational age and birthweight. Relative risk ratios are presented in the tables.

In Table 8.3a (Model 1), which depicts outcomes for 1990, racial and ethnic differences are observed for all causes of infant mortality, even after controlling for sociodemographic characteristics and other risk factors. For example, risk of infant death due to all listed causes is elevated in NHB women, as compared to NHW women. In contrast, risk of death is lower for Hispanic and NHO mothers across causes (with the exception of deaths due to other causes in NHO women), as compared to NHW women.

In Model 2, controls for preterm delivery and low birthweight are added as are interaction terms. Here, it is observed that the effects of low birthweight vary by maternal race and ethnicity. As expected, risk of infant death due to low birthweight or preterm birth is explained away upon the inclusion of gestational age and birthweight. However, the inclusion of these controls does not negate the racial and ethnic variations in risk of death due to maternal complications for Hispanic infants. Indeed, Hispanic infants have a lowered risk of death due to this cause. Interestingly, a significant interaction with low birthweight is observed such that low birthweight Hispanic infants experience increased risk of death, i.e. a survival disadvantage. While this Hispanic disadvantage is also found for infant death due to other causes, we noticed that low birthweight is somewhat protective for infants born to NHB black mothers. This suggests a survival advantage for deaths due to other causes for low birthweight NHB infants born in 1990. The effect of maternal race and ethnicity remains significant for deaths due to other causes despite the inclusion of controls for gestational age and birthweight across all groups, with NHB and NHO at increased risk and Hispanic infants at decreased risk of death.

In Table 8.3b, Model 1, results are presented for the year 2000 cohort. These outcomes reveal racial and ethnic differences similar to the ones observed in 1990. However, NHB mothers are at higher risk of experiencing infant death across causes in 2000, as the overall magnitudes of the relative risk ratios (RRR) appear to be larger than those in 1990. Indeed, non-Hispanic black mothers experience more than twice the risk of infant death due to preterm/low birthweight, compared to their non-Hispanic white counterparts.

In Model 2, the effect of maternal race and ethnicity is largely diminished with the inclusion of controls for gestational age and birthweight. However, we observe some evidence that the racial and ethnic gap in infant mortality risk due to other causes does not seem decreased at all. In fact, NHB infants have higher risk of death due to other causes while Hispanic mothers enjoy an advantage that persists even after the inclusion of all controls. Hispanic mothers also experience lower risk of death due to maternal complications despite the inclusion of additional controls (the same pattern was observed in 1990). The interactions reveal interesting patterns as NHB low birthweight infants experience greater risk of death due to maternal complications in 2000 (this relationship was not evidenced in 1990). Similarly, and in keeping with findings from 1990, low birthweight infants born to Hispanic mothers are also at increased risk of death due to this cause. Finally, the findings for the 2000 cohort also evidence a survival advantage in deaths due to other causes for low birth weight NHB infants, while low birthweight infants born to Hispanic mothers experience a survival disadvantage.

Table 8.3a Results of multinomial logit models for cause specific infant mortality risk for 1990 ($N = 4,158,445$)

Variables		Low birth weight/preterm					Maternal complication						Other cause					
		Model 1		Model 2			Model 1		Model 2				Model 1			Model		
		RRR	S.E.	RRR	S.E.		RRR	S.E.	RRR	S.E.			RRR	S.E.		RR	S.E.	
Race/ethnicity (NH White)	NH black	1.73***	0.08	1.27	0.79		1.26*	0.05	0.79	0.13			1.19***	0.02		1.16***	0.03	
	NH other	0.77*	0.09	0.00	0.00		0.59**	0.07	0.60	0.21			1.05	0.04		1.16**	0.06	
	Hispanic	0.54***	0.05	1.39	1.02		0.82**	0.05	0.44***	0.09			0.78***	0.02		0.78***	0.03	
Age of mother (19 or older)	Teen	1.06	0.06	0.99	0.06		1.01	0.05	0.97	0.05			1.23***	0.02		1.19***	0.02	
Marital status (unmarried)	Married	0.74***	0.03	0.78***	0.04		0.69***	0.03	0.75***	0.03			0.78***	0.01		0.82***	0.01	
Immigrant status (US born)	Foreign born	1.02	0.07	1.25**	0.09		0.90	0.05	1.10	0.07			0.81***	0.02		0.86***	0.02	
Parity (1st birth)	2–4th birth	0.74***	0.03	0.80***	0.03		1.02	0.04	1.04	0.04			1.23***	0.02		1.24***	0.02	
	5+ birth	0.64***	0.05	0.66***	0.06		0.98	0.07	1.05	0.08			1.46***	0.04		1.46***	0.04	
Infant sex (female)	Male	1.22***	0.04	1.28***	0.05		1.15***	0.04	1.17***	0.04			1.30***	0.02		1.36***	0.02	
Region (Northeast)	Midwest	1.46***	0.09	1.43***	0.09		1.03	0.05	0.99	0.06			1.26***	0.03		1.24***	0.03	
	South	1.21***	0.07	1.12	0.07		0.98	0.05	0.91	0.05			1.19***	0.02		1.14***	0.02	
	West	0.69***	0.05	0.74***	0.06		0.72***	0.04	0.80***	0.05			1.08***	0.03		1.12***	0.03	
Education (< high school)	High school	1.22***	0.06	1.15**	0.06		1.15***	0.05	1.10	0.06			0.94***	0.02		0.92***	0.02	
	College or higher	1.39***	0.08	1.20**	0.07		1.28***	0.07	1.11	0.06			0.86***	0.02		0.83***	0.02	
APNCU index (inadequate)	Intermediate	0.26***	0.02	0.38***	0.04		0.40***	0.03	0.53***	0.05			0.71***	0.02		0.81***	0.02	
	Adequate	0.00***	0.00	0.03***	0.02		0.07***	0.01	0.36***	0.04			0.39***	0.01		0.66***	0.02	
	Adequate+	0.00***	0.00	0.02***	0.01		0.07***	0.01	0.20***	0.02			0.41***	0.01		0.61***	0.02	
	Missing on APNCU	1.60***	0.08	0.85**	0.05		2.11***	0.11	1.14***	0.06			1.46***	0.03		1.03	0.02	

(continued)

Table 8.3a (continued)

Variables		Low birth weight/preterm				Maternal complication				Other cause			
		Model 1		Model 2		Model 1		Model 2		Model 1		Model	
		RRR	S.E.	RRR	S.E.	RRR	S.E.	RRR	S.E.	RRR	S.E.	RR	S.E.
Medical risk factor (none)	1 or More Risk Factors	1.87***	0.07	1.05	0.04	2.27***	0.08	1.24***	0.04	1.70***	0.02	1.19***	0.02
Labor/Deliv. complication (none)	1 or more complications	3.05***	0.12	1.36***	0.06	3.59***	0.13	1.71***	0.07	2.15***	0.03	1.46***	0.02
Tobacco use (none)	Yes	0.94	0.05	0.81***	0.04	0.77***	0.04	0.68***	0.04	1.22***	0.02	1.06***	0.02
	Missing	0.66***	0.04	0.70***	0.05	1.06	0.06	1.12*	0.06	0.89***	0.02	0.91***	0.02
Weight gain (<16 lbs)	16–40 lbs	0.08***	0.00	0.16***	0.01	0.15***	0.01	0.28***	0.01	0.41***	0.01	0.58***	0.01
	41+ lbs	0.01***	0.00	0.05***	0.01	0.06***	0.01	0.17***	0.02	0.32***	0.01	0.54***	0.02
	Missing	0.45***	0.02	0.61***	0.03	0.46***	0.02	0.50***	0.03	0.74***	0.02	0.87***	0.02
Gestational age (term)	Preterm			39.10***	15.13			6.04***	0.64			2.05***	0.05
Low birthweight (normal)	Low (<2500 g)			104.53***	33.80			18.30***	1.83			7.08***	0.17
Interactions	NHB × low birth weight			1.10	0.50			1.03	0.17			0.71***	0.03
	NH other × low birth weight			2.18E + 06	3.56E + 09			0.81	0.31			0.91	0.08
	Hispanic × low birth weight			0.90	0.51			1.89**	0.40			1.15**	0.06
	NHB × preterm			0.89	0.44			1.11	0.18			1.02	0.04
	NH other × preterm			1.31E + 06	2.05E + 09			1.14	0.47			0.39	0.08
	Hispanic × preterm			0.61	0.37			1.18	0.24			0.99	0.05
Constant		0.00***	0.00	0.00***	0.00	0.00***	0.00	0.00***	0.00	0.01***	0.00	0.00***	0.00
Log likelihood		−183,648.14		−156,261.96		−183,648.14		−156,261.96		−183,648.14		−156,261.96	

Note Categories in parentheses indicate reference groups

*$p \leq 0.05$; **$p \leq 0.01$; ***$p \leq 0.001$

Table 8.3b Results of multinomial logit models for cause specific infant mortality risk for 2000 ($N = 4,058,903$)

Variables		Low birth weight/preterm				Maternal complication				Other causes			
		Model 1		Model 2		Model 1		Model 2		Model 1		Model 2	
		RRR	S.E.	RRR	S.E.	RRR	S.E.	RRR	S.E.	RRR	S.E.	RRR	S.E.
Race/ethnicity (NH White)	NH Black	2.28*	0.10	0.76	0.48	1.75*	0.08	0.77	0.13	1.33***	0.03	1.32***	0.04
	NH other	1.16	0.11	0.00	0.00	0.84	0.08	0.62	0.19	1.03	0.04	0.95	0.05
	Hispanic	1.12	0.07	0.57	0.41	0.89	0.06	0.69*	0.11	0.81***	0.02	0.72***	0.03
Age of mother (19 or older) teen		1.07	0.06	1.01	0.05	0.99	0.06	0.94	0.06	1.21***	0.03	1.18***	0.03
Marital status (unmarried)	Married	0.92*	0.04	0.91*	0.04	0.96	0.04	0.97	0.04	0.85***	0.02	0.86***	0.02
Immigrant status (US born)	Foreign born	0.68***	0.04	0.87*	0.05	0.79***	0.05	0.94	0.06	0.77***	0.02	0.84***	0.02
Parity (1st birth)	2–4th birth	0.64***	0.02	0.74***	0.03	0.76***	0.03	0.82***	0.03	1.14***	0.02	1.18***	0.02
	5+ birth	0.62***	0.05	0.65***	0.05	0.72***	0.06	0.75***	0.06	1.37***	0.04	1.34***	0.05
Infant sex (female)	infsex	1.13***	0.04	1.09*	0.04	1.26***	0.04	1.26***	0.04	1.24***	0.02	1.27***	0.02
Region (northeast)	Midwest	2.08***	0.11	1.61***	0.09	1.32***	0.07	1.03	0.06	1.46***	0.04	1.31***	0.03
	South	1.61***	0.08	1.15**	0.06	1.35***	0.07	0.97	0.05	1.41***	0.03	1.20***	0.03
	West	0.92	0.07	0.88	0.07	0.95	0.07	0.88	0.06	1.20***	0.04	1.18***	0.04
Education (< high School)	High school	1.30***	0.06	1.17***	0.06	1.14**	0.06	1.04	0.05	0.93***	0.02	0.90***	0.02
	College or higher	1.41***	0.07	1.14*	0.06	1.14*	0.06	0.97	0.05	0.78***	0.02	0.73***	0.02
APNCU index (inadequate)	Intermediate	0.27	0.03	0.36***	0.04	0.50***	0.05	0.62***	0.06	0.75***	0.03	0.84***	0.03
	Adequate	0.01***	0.00	0.10***	0.03	0.08***	0.01	0.39***	0.05	0.39***	0.01	0.66***	0.02
	Adequate+	0.00***	0.00	0.02***	0.01	0.10***	0.01	0.26***	0.03	0.42***	0.01	0.50***	0.02
	Missing on APNCU	2.00***	0.11	0.91	0.06	2.21***	0.15	1.05	0.08	1.60***	0.05	1.01	0.03
Medical risk factor (none)	1 or more risk factors	1.74***	0.06	0.97	0.03	1.89***	0.07	1.09*	0.04	1.50***	0.02	1.08***	0.02

(continued)

Table 8.3b (continued)

Variables		Low birth weight/preterm				Maternal complication				Other causes			
		Model 1		Model 2		Model 1		Model 2		Model 1		Model 2	
		RRR	S.E.	RRR	S.E.	RRR	S.E.	RRR	S.E.	RRR	S.E.	RRR	S.E.
Labor/deliv. complication (none)	1 or more complications	2.61***	0.09	1.42***	0.05	2.87***	0.11	1.75***	0.07	1.88***	0.03	1.42***	0.02
Tobacco use (none)	Yes	1.16**	0.06	1.04	0.05	0.99	0.05	0.87*	0.05	1.34***	0.03	1.20***	0.03
	Missing	0.78**	0.06	0.72***	0.06	0.92	0.07	0.81*	0.07	0.80***	0.03	0.77***	0.03
Weight gain (< 16 lbs)	16–40 lbs	0.11***	0.00	0.18***	0.01	0.19***	0.01	0.28***	0.01	0.45***	0.01	0.57***	0.01
	41 + lbs	0.02***	0.00	0.05***	0.01	0.08***	0.01	0.15***	0.01	0.34***	0.01	0.49***	0.01
	Missing	0.55***	0.03	0.67***	0.03	0.61***	0.03	0.73***	0.04	0.86***	0.02	0.95	0.03
Gestational age (term)	Preterm			19.00***	5.51			5.65***	0.61			1.95***	0.06
Low birthweight (normal)	Low (<2500 g)			113.84***	35.43			13.00***	1.26			5.54***	0.19
Interactions	NHB × low birth weight			1.71	0.94			1.48*	0.26			0.73***	0.04
	NH other × low birth weight			4.50E + 05	3.00E + 08			1.42	0.49			1.08	0.10
	Hispanic × low birth weight			1.51	0.90			1.56*	0.29			1.35***	0.08
	NHB × preterm			1.31	0.54			1.23	0.21			1.02	0.05
	NH other × preterm			7.43E + 05	4.86E + 08			1.03	0.35			1.05	0.10
	Hispanic × preterm			1.43	0.77			0.95	0.18			0.98	0.06
		0.00	0.00	0.00***	0.00	0.00***	0.00	0.00***	0.00	0.01***	0.00	0.00***	0.00
Log likelihood		−152,705.39		−132,397.73		−152,705.39		−132,397.73		−152,705.39		−132,397.73	

Note: Categories in parentheses indicate reference groups
$*p \leq 0.05$; $**p \leq 0.01$; $***p \leq 0.001$

Table 8.3c Results of multinomial logit models for cause specific infant mortality risk for 2004 ($N = 4,112,053$)

Variables		Low birth weight/preterm				Maternal Complication				Other causes			
		Model 1		Model 2		Model 1		Model 2		Model 1		Model 2	
		RRR	S.E.	RRR	S.E.	RRR	S.E.	RRR	S.E.	RRR	S.E.	RRI	S.E.
Race/ethnicity (NH white)	NH black	2.44***	0.11	0.48	0.33	2.26***	0.11	0.87	0.19	1.41***	0.03	1.24***	0.05
	NH other	1.09	0.10	0.51	0.61	1.03	0.09	0.62	0.22	1.04	0.04	0.90***	0.06
	Hispanic	1.12	0.07	0.93	0.54	1.10	0.07	0.58***	0.12	0.88***	0.03	0.72***	0.03
Age of mother (19 or older)	Teen	1.23***	0.07	1.10	0.06	1.16*	0.07	1.02	0.06	1.19***	0.03	1.12***	0.03
Marital status (unmarried)	Married	0.83***	0.03	0.94	0.04	0.89**	0.04	0.99	0.04	0.80***	0.02	0.85***	0.02
Immigrant status (US born)	Foreign born	0.84***	0.05	0.94	0.05	0.90	0.05	1.00	0.06	0.77***	0.02	0.84***	0.02
Parity (1st birth)	2–4th birth	0.65***	0.03	0.73***	0.03	0.77***	0.03	0.83***	0.03	1.16***	0.02	1.17***	0.02
	5+ birth	0.81**	0.06	0.74***	0.06	0.91	0.07	0.81*	0.07	1.36***	0.05	1.20***	0.05
Infant sex (female)	infsex	1.24***	0.04	1.27***	0.05	1.30***	0.05	1.35***	0.05	1.20***	0.02	1.26***	0.02
Region (Northeast)	Midwest	1.21**	0.08	1.32***	0.09	0.87*	0.06	0.94	0.06	1.29***	0.04	1.35***	0.04
	South	1.02	0.06	1.04	0.07	0.92	0.06	0.94	0.06	1.35***	0.04	1.35***	0.04
	West	0.88	0.07	0.97	0.08	0.95	0.07	1.06	0.08	1.19***	0.05	1.27***	0.05
Education (< high school)	High school	1.16**	0.06	1.21***	0.06	1.08	0.06	1.09	0.06	0.89***	0.02	0.91***	0.02
	College or higher	1.02	0.06	1.06	0.06	1.01	0.06	1.03	0.06	0.71***	0.02	0.74***	0.02
APNCU index (inadequate)	Intermediate	0.71***	0.06	1.46***	0.13	0.66***	0.06	1.27*	0.12	0.70***	0.02	0.95	0.03
	Adequate	0.64***	0.04	1.37***	0.09	0.68***	0.05	1.33***	0.10	0.63***	0.02	0.86***	0.03
	Adequate+	2.34***	0.13	1.03	0.06	2.40***	0.14	1.07	0.07	1.39***	0.04	0.87***	0.02
	Missing on APNCU	2.26***	0.18	1.34***	0.11	2.60***	0.22	1.54***	0.13	1.47***	0.06	1.12**	0.05
Medical risk factor (none)	1 or More Risk Factors	1.57***	0.06	0.92*	0.03	1.81***	0.07	1.09*	0.04	1.45***	0.03	1.07***	0.02
Labor/deliv. complication (None)	1 or more complications	2.86***	0.10	1.42***	0.05	3.24***	0.13	1.70***	0.07	2.00***	0.03	1.41***	0.03

(continued)

Table 8.3c (continued)

Variables		Low birth weight/preterm				Maternal Complication				Other causes			
		Model 1		Model 2		Model 1		Model 2		Model 1		Model 2	
		RRR	S.E.	RRR	S.E.	RRR	S.E.	RRR	S.E.	RRR	S.E.	RRR	
Tobacco use (none)	Yes	1.11	0.06	0.92	0.05	1.10	0.07	0.90	0.06	1.44***	0.04	1.24***	0.03
Weight gain (<16 lbs)	Missing	0.39***	0.04	0.49***	0.05	0.43***	0.04	0.53***	0.05	0.68***	0.03	0.75***	0.03
	16–40 lbs	0.09***	0.00	0.17***	0.01	0.16***	0.01	0.26***	0.01	0.41***	0.01	0.53***	0.01
	41+ lbs	0.02***	0.00	0.06***	0.01	0.05***	0.01	0.11***	0.01	0.29***	0.01	0.44***	0.01
	Missing	0.62***	0.04	0.74***	0.04	0.68***	0.04	0.77***	0.05	0.82***	0.03	0.87***	0.03
Gestational age (term)	Preterm			42.58***	11.00			8.26***	0.96			2.35***	0.08
Low birthweight (normal)	Low (<2500 g)			131.31***	37.53			25.95***	3.10			7.10***	0.23
Interactions	NHB × low birth weight			0.90	0.41			0.96	0.19			0.80***	0.04
	NH other × low birth weight			1.62	1.71			1.58	0.61			0.96	0.10
	Hispanic × low birth weight			1.21	0.58			1.29	0.27			1.37***	0.08
	NHB × preterm			3.85*	2.17			1.97***	0.40			1.08	0.06
	NH other × preterm			1.21	0.93			1.02	0.32			1.24*	0.12
	Hispanic × preterm			0.99	0.42			1.52*	0.32			1.06	0.06
Constant		0.00***	0.00	0.00***	0.00	0.00***	0.00	0.00***	0.00	0.01***	0.00	0.0***	0.00
Log likelihood		−132,051.71		−108,849.32		−132,051.71		−108,849.32		−132,051.71		−108,849.32	

Note Categories in parentheses indicate reference groups

*$p \leq 0.05$; **$p \leq 0.01$; ***$p \leq 0.001$

Table 8.3c (Model 1) presents our findings for 2004. Importantly, one of our main findings from the results of the two previous years (i.e. the overall disadvantages in infant mortality risk among infants born to non-Hispanic blacks) seems more salient in 2004. For example, infant mortality risk is elevated in NHB infants across causes. For deaths due to low birthweight/preterm birth and maternal complications, the risk is more than twice as high for infants born to NHB mothers compared to their NHW counterparts. Additionally, infant mortality risk due to other causes is still more than 40% higher (i.e. RRR = 1.407) than that of infants to non-Hispanic white mothers even after controlling for all of the covariates.

In Model 2, the results of the full model for 2004 show that much of the effect of maternal race and ethnicity is removed after including gestational age and birthweight as covariates. But, as was observed in the previous two years, Hispanic mothers enjoy an advantage with respect to deaths due to maternal complications (though its effect has diminished relative to the previous years). As for deaths due to other causes, the effect of race and ethnicity is not diminished upon the inclusion of all controls, and similar to the patterns observed previously, NHB infants experience a disadvantage while Hispanic infants enjoy a reduced risk of death compared with NHW infants. However, the opposite pattern is evidenced upon inspection of the interactions. It is observed that the effects of low birthweight combine with NHB race to produce a survival advantage (low birthweight is protective) in deaths due to other causes in 2004. This extends the pattern observed in previous cohorts, though the protective effect is somewhat diminished in 2004 relative to previous years. On the other hand, low birthweight interacts with Hispanic ethnicity to produce a survival disadvantage in deaths due to other causes, and this effect is amplified in 2004. Importantly in 2004, significant racial and ethnic interactions with preterm delivery are observed that were not evidenced in previous cohorts. For example, preterm NHB infants experienced a substantial *disadvantage* in deaths due to preterm/low birthweight and maternal complications (i.e. RRRs are 3.849 and 1.973, respectively) in 2004. Preterm infants born to NHO mothers also experienced a survival disadvantage in deaths due to other causes in 2004. Finally, the significant interaction between preterm birth and Hispanic ethnicity (i.e. RRR = 1.522) indicates that preterm infants born to Hispanic mothers are more vulnerable to infant mortality due to maternal complications.

Taken together, it is observed that the harmful main effect of NHB race on deaths due to preterm delivery/LBW and maternal complications is largely diminished upon the inclusion of controls for gestational age and birthweight. On the other hand, the main effect of NHB race on risk of death due to other causes is not diminished upon the inclusion of controls for gestational age and birthweight, and the harmful effect is stronger in 2000 and 2004 than it was in 1990 (RRRs are 1.321, 1.240, and 1.158, respectively). In contrast, the main effect of Hispanic ethnicity on deaths due to maternal complications and other causes is beneficial in all three cohorts, even after controlling for gestational age and birthweight. In the case of maternal complications, the protective effect is diminished in recent years while the protective effect is slightly amplified in recent years for deaths due to other causes. Finally, no main effects of NHO race are observed.

In consideration of the race and ethnicity by low birthweight interactions, we do find some evidence of a survival advantage for low birthweight NHB infants in deaths due to other causes. As hypothesized this effect persists over time, though its effect is diminished in later cohorts. Notably, a survival disadvantage is observed for this same group in 2000 for deaths due to maternal complications. Low birthweight also interacts with Hispanic ethnicity to produce a survival *disadvantage* in several outcomes. Accordingly, LBW Hispanic infants experience increased risk of death due to other causes, an effect which is amplified over time. This harmful interaction is also observed in 1990 and 2000 for deaths due to maternal complications.

Interactions with race and ethnicity and preterm delivery were only evident in 2004 and all were harmful. Accordingly, NHB women who delivered preterm had nearly four times the risk of infant death due to preterm-related or low birthweight causes of death. A similar effect was observed for deaths due to maternal complications. These effects were not observed in previous years, and are in support of the hypothesized survival disadvantage experienced by NHB women in more recent cohorts. Furthermore, Hispanic mothers who delivered preterm experience increased risk of death due to maternal complications (i.e. survival disadvantage), relative to their NH White counterparts. A harmful interaction with preterm delivery was also observed for NHO race as risk of death due to other causes was amplified in this group relative to NHW infants.

The full models reveal some important patterns and suggest that race and ethnicity interacts with low birthweight and gestational age to produce disparate outcomes. Specifically, a survival *advantage* is observed in all years for low birthweight infants born to NH Black mothers in deaths due to other causes. But, the advantage is diminished in more recent years. In opposite fashion, LBW infants born to Hispanic mothers fare poorly in deaths due to other causes, and the magnitude of risk is amplified over time. Finally, preterm delivery interacts with all three racial and ethnic groups in a harmful way in 2004. A supplemental analysis confirms that the differences in the racial and ethnic effects observed in the models across years are also statistically significant (results not shown).

Conclusions

Our initial hypothesis (H1) predicted that the main effect of NHB race on risk of infant death due to multiple causes would be harmful. This hypothesis was fully supported as we observed that NHB women had an increased risk of infant death due to all causes, relative to NHW women. Furthermore, this risk was amplified across all causes over time. H1a additionally predicted that any survival advantage among infants born to black women would diminish in later years. Our interactions allowed us to examine this relationship and we observed partial support as NHB low birthweight infants fared better in the case of deaths due to preterm or LBW. As hypothesized, this effect was diminished in later years. However, LBW did not interact with NHB race to produce a survival advantage for the other causes of death. We also observed a survival disadvantage for NHB low birthweight infants in deaths due to maternal complications in 2000 and NHB preterm infants in 2004 (deaths due to maternal complications and other causes).

Our second hypothesis (H2) predicted a beneficial main effect of Hispanic ethnicity with lessening impact over time. Our hypothesis was fully supported with respect to deaths due to other causes. Thus, a protective effect was observed in deaths due to other causes, and its effect was lessened in later cohorts. In deaths due to maternal complications, Hispanic ethnicity resulted in decreased risk of infant death; however, the effect was only present in 1990. Similarly, a beneficial effect of Hispanic ethnicity on deaths due to preterm/low birthweight was only observed in 1990. H2a predicted that a survival advantage of infants born to Hispanic women would not be observed in later years. Again, our interactions allowed us to examine how risk of death varies by gestational age and birthweight for this group, and we observed a *survival disadvantage* that persisted across several causes. For example, Hispanic women who delivered low birthweight babies experienced increased risk of death due to maternal complications in 1990 and 2000. LBW Hispanic infants further experienced a disadvantage that was amplified over time in deaths due to other causes. Finally, in 2004, Hispanic women who delivered preterm had 1.5 times the risk of infant death as compared to NHW infants.

Discussion

Our study examines the impact of race and ethnicity on cause-specific infant mortality risk across multiple cohorts. Our findings generally confirm the previously reported pattern of persisting disparity in black-white infant mortality and add to the literature documenting evidence that the disparity has increased over time and across all causes. Additionally, our results reveal distinct and significant race-birthweight and race-gestational age interactions such that the only evidence of a survival advantage in NHB infants is present in deaths due to other causes. However, this advantage is diminished over time. Evidence of a *survival disadvantage* generates greater concern as NHB infants born preterm had increased risk of death in 2004 for multiple causes. This disadvantage was also observed in 2000 for deaths due to maternal complications. Several studies have documented an increase in preterm births (MacDorman et al. 2010; Mathews and MacDorman 2013), which may help explain such dramatic interactions with black race in 2004. In addition, studies have suggested that deaths due to maternal complications are less amenable to technological intervention and thus evidence stronger effects of race-based differentials in access to and quality of care (Frisbie et al. 2010). Overall, these findings are certainly cause for alarm and underscore the discrepancy in black-white infant health outcomes. They highlight the need for increased investments in programs to improve access to pre- and postnatal care. Furthermore, interventions designed to reduce the incidence of preterm and low birthweight deliveries in this population are of the highest necessity.

We observed varying outcomes by cause among Hispanic women that evidenced noteworthy changes over time. For example, the protective main effect of Hispanic ethnicity was dampened over time for deaths due to maternal complications while its beneficial effect was slightly increased in deaths due to other causes. These generally beneficial effects seem in line with more recent evidence of an epidemiologic paradox (Hummer et al. 2007); which may be attributable to a more favorable birthweight distribution and lower rates of smoking in this population (Muhuri et al. 2004). Because deaths due to maternal complications are potentially more closely connected to social resources, a dampened protective effect over time, i.e. erosion of the paradox, seems in line with findings that health outcomes deteriorate with acculturation (Lara et al. 2005).

Importantly, when Hispanic mothers experience compromised birth outcomes, they evidenced a survival disadvantage, which worsened over time (observed for maternal complications and other causes). This may be attributable to an increasingly U.S. born Hispanic population and/or increasing rates of preterm births in this group. Another potential explanation is changes in settlement patterns such that most of the growth has occurred in places with little infrastructure/resources to support Hispanic populations (Kandel and Cromartie 2004). This may result in poorer access to high-tech facilities and thus poorer outcomes in the context of preterm or low birthweight across causes.

Our study is not without limitations. First, we did not have access to personal characteristics, such as income, health coverage and payment information, and employment status, which potentially influence racial and ethnic differentials in birth outcomes. In addition, while the birth certificate provides many health behaviors that are relevant to birth outcomes, infant survival is more than likely a reflection of other health behaviors related to physical activity and diet, among others. Finally, we were unable to include contextual measures that are known to impact health outcomes including access to hospital/facilities and level of racial and ethnic segregation in an area. We are confident that our study is strengthened by the use of highly comprehensive and accurate data measured over multiple time points. Nonetheless, these issues should be taken into account in future research when more comprehensive data becomes available.

In summary, we observed important and noteworthy racial and ethnic variations by cause that have persisted into more recent years. The generally harmful effect of black race is likely a reflection of social inequality as medical advances and public health campaigns and interventions that have reduced the rates of certain forms of infant death have not been felt evenly across different racial groups. Additionally, our finding that the effect of being black is somewhat attenuated in the context of low birthweight, with diminishing advantage over time, suggests a need for targeted interventions for vulnerable populations to address this preventable gap. Perhaps the most noteworthy of our findings are those which evidence harmful effects among racial and ethnic minorities in compromised births, i.e. preterm or LBW delivery. The finding that preterm delivery interacts with Hispanic ethnicity in a similar way as black race in 2004 may be a reflection of similar socioeconomic status that is no longer offset by immigrant selectivity or pro-health behaviors as the Hispanic population is increasingly acculturated and/or U.S. born. Another plausible explanation is that women who qualify for Medicaid coverage due to pregnancy can utilize coverage for prenatal care and delivery but are subject to subject to a loss of coverage 60 days following the birth (MacKay et al. 2001). Thus, follow-up care, or lack thereof, may exert a measurable impact on infant deaths that occur between ages 61 to 364 days. Recent efforts to improve health coverage may begin to address these issues, and future studies should consider the impacts of health coverage. That Hispanic women are at greater risk in the context of compromised deliveries is of import and further studies of the causal mechanisms that produce these compromised outcomes are warranted. In addition, greater investments in adequate prenatal and follow-up care as well as increased efforts to reduce preterm and low birthweight deliveries in vulnerable groups are called for.

Acknowledgments A previous version of this paper was presented at the 2015 Annual Meetings of the Population Association of America in San Diego, CA. The authors would like to express their gratitude for helpful comments from the conference participants.

References

Abraído-Lanza, A. F., Chao, M. T., & Flórez, K. R. (2005). Do healthy behaviors decline with greater acculturation?: Implications for the Latino mortality paradox. *Social Science and Medicine, 61*(6), 1243–1255.

Alexander, G. R., Kogan, M., Bader, D., Carlo, W., Allen, M., & Mor, J. (2003). US birth weight/gestational age-specific neonatal mortality: 1995–1997 rates for whites, Hispanics, and blacks. *Pediatrics, 111*(1), e61–e66.

Alexander, G. R., Wingate, M. S., Bader, D., & Kogan, M. D. (2008). The increasing racial disparity in infant mortality rates: Composition and contributors to recent US trends. *American Journal of Obstetrics and Gynecology, 198*(1), 51.e1–51.e9.

Collins, J. W., David, R. J., Symons, R., Handler, A., Wall, S. N., & Dwyer, L. (2000). Low-income African American mothers' perception of exposure to racial discrimination and infant birth weight. *Epidemiology, 11*(3), 337–339.

David, R. J., & Collins, J. W, Jr. (2007). Disparities in infant mortality: What's genetics got to do with it? *American Journal of Public Health, 97*(7), 1191–1197.

David, R. J., & Collins, J. W, Jr. (1990). Bad outcomes in black babies: Race or racism? *Ethnicity and Disease, 1*(3), 236–244.

Eberstein, I. W. (1989). *Demographic research on infant mortality*. Paper presented at the Sociological Forum.

Franzini, L., Ribble, J. C., & Keddie, A. M. (2001). Understanding the Hispanic paradox. *Ethnicity and Disease, 11*(3), 496–518.

Frisbie, W. P. (2005). Infant Mortality. In D. L. Poston & M. Micklin (Eds.), *Handbook of Population* (pp. 251–282). New York: Kluwer Academic/Plenum Publishers.

Frisbie, W. P., Hummer, R. A., Powers, D. A., Song, S.-E., & Pullum, S. G. (2010). Race/Ethnicity/Nativity differentials and changes in cause-specific infant deaths in the context of declining infant mortality in the U.S.: 1989–2001. *Population Research and Policy Review, 29*, 395–422.

Frisbie, W. P., Song, S. E., Powers, D. A., & Street, J. A. (2004). The increasing racial disparity in infant mortality: Respiratory distress syndrome and other causes. *Demography, 41*(4), 773–800.

Geronimus, A. T. (1996). Black/white differences in the relationship of maternal age to birth weight: A population-based test of the weathering hypothesis. *Social Science and Medicine, 42*(4), 589–597. doi:10.1016/0277-9536(95)00159-X.

Gortmaker, S. L., & Wise, P. H. (1997). The first injustice: Socioeconomic disparities, health services technology, and infant mortality. *Annual Review of Sociology, 23,* 147–170.

Hummer, R. A. (1993). Racial differentials in infant mortality in the US: An examination of social and health determinants. *Social Forces, 72*(2), 529–554.

Hummer, R. A., Biegler, M., De Turk, P. B., Forbes, D., Frisbie, W. P., Hong, Y., et al. (1999). Race/ethnicity, nativity, and infant mortality in the United States. *Social Forces, 77*(3), 1083–1117.

Hummer, R. A., Powers, D. A., Pullum, S. G., Gossman, G. L., & Frisbie, W. P. (2007). Paradox found (again): Infant mortality among the Mexican-origin population in the United States. *Demography, 44*(3), 441–457.

Iyasu, S., & Tomashek, K. (2002). Infant mortality and low birth weight among black and white infants–United States, 1980–2000. *Morbidity and Mortality Weekly Report, 51*(27), 589–592.

Kandel, W., & Cromartie, J. (2004). *New patterns of Hispanic settlement in rural America.* Rural Development Research Report, 99. United States Department of Agriculture (USDA), Economic Research Service.

Krieger, N., Rehkopf, D. H., Chen, J. T., Waterman, P. D., Marcelli, E., & Kennedy, M. (2008). The fall and rise of us inequities in premature mortality: 1960–2002. *PLoS Med, 5*(2). doi:10.1371/journal.pmed.0050046

Lara, M., Gamboa, C., Kahramanian, M. I., Morales, L. S., & Hayes Bautista, D. E. (2005). Acculturation and Latino health in the United States: A review of the literature and its sociopolitical context. *Annual Review of Public Health, 26*(1), 367–397.

Link, B. G., & Phelan, J. (1995). Social conditions as fundamental causes of disease. *Journal of Health and Social Behavior, 35*(Extra Issue), 80–94.

Lu, M. C., & Halfon, N. (2003). Racial and ethnic disparities in birth outcomes: A life-course perspective. [Article]. *Maternal and Child Health Journal, 7*(1), 13.

MacDorman, M. F., Callaghan, W. M., Mathews, T. J., Hoyert, D. L., & Kochanek, K. D. (2010). Trends in preterm-related infant mortality by race and ethnicity: United States, 1999–2004. In *NCHS Health E-Stats.* Atlanta, GA: National Center for Health Statistics.

MacDorman, M. F., & Mathews, T. J. (2008). Recent trends in infant mortality in the United States. In *NCHS Data Brief.* Hyattsville, MD: U.S. Dept. of Health and Human Services, Centers for Disease Control and Prevention, National Center for Health Statistics.

MacDorman, M. F., & Mathews, T. (2009). The challenge of infant mortality: Have we reached a plateau? *Public Health Reports, 124*(5), 670–681.

MacKay, A. P., Kieke, B. A, Jr., Koonin, L. M., & Beattie, K. (2001). Tubal sterilization in the United States, 1994–1996. *Family Planning Perspectives, 33*(4), 161–165.

Markides, K. S., & Coreil, J. (1986). The health of Hispanics in the southwestern United States: An epidemiologic paradox. *Public Health Reports, 101*(3), 253–265.

Markides, K. S., & Eschbach, K. (2005). Aging, migration, and mortality: Current status of research on the Hispanic paradox. *The Journals of Gerontology Series B: Psychological Sciences and Social Sciences, 60*(Special Issue 2), S68–S75.

Martin J. A., Hamilton, B. E., Sutton, P. D., Ventura, S. J., Menacker, F., Kirmeyer, S., et al. (2007). Births: Final data for 2005. *National Vital Statistics Reports, 56*(6).

Mathews, T. J., & MacDorman, M. F. (2013). Infant mortality statistics from the 2009 period linked birth/infant death data set. *National Vital Statistics Reports, 61*(8), 1–27.

Muhuri, P. K., MacDorman, M. F., & Ezzati-Rice, T. M. (2004). Racial differences in leading causes of infant death in the United States. *Paediatric and Perinatal Epidemiology, 18*(1), 51–60.

Palloni, A., & Arias, E. (2004). Paradox lost: explaining the Hispanic adult mortality advantage. *Demography, 41*(3), 385–415.

Phelan, J. C., Link, B. G., & Tehranifar, P. (2010). Social conditions as fundamental causes of health inequalities theory, evidence, and policy implications. *Journal of Health and Social Behavior, 51*(1 suppl), S28–S40.

Rosenthal, L., & Lobel, M. (2011). Explaining racial disparities in adverse birth outcomes: Unique sources of stress for Black American women. *Social Science and Medicine, 72*(6), 977–983.

Saenz, R. (2010). Latinos in the United States 2010 population bulletin update: Population reference bureau.

Schempf, A. H., Branum, A. M., Lukacs, S. L., & Schoendorf, K. C. (2007). The contribution of preterm birth to the black–white infant mortality gap, 1990 and 2000. *American Journal of Public Health, 97*(7), 1255.

U.S. Department of Health and Human Services. (1995). Linked birth/infant death data set: 1990 birth cohort. In *Public Use Data File Documentation*. Hyattsville, MD: National Center for Health Statistics.

U.S. Department of Health and Human Services. (2008). Linked birth/infant death data set: 2000 birth cohort. In *Public Use Data File Documentation*. Hyattsville, MD: National Center for Health Statistics.

U.S. Department of Health and Human Services. (2011). Linked birth/infant death data set: 2004 birth cohort. In *Public Use Data File Documentation*. Hyattsville, MD: National Center for Health Statistics.

Wilcox, A., & Russell, I. (1990). Why small black infants have a lower mortality rate than small white infants: the case for population-specific standards for birth weight. *The Journal of Pediatrics, 116*(1), 7–10.

World Bank. (2011). World development indicators. http://go.worldbank.org/EROS2XNAG0

Chapter 9
Black-White Mortality Differentials at Old-Age: New Evidence from the National Longitudinal Mortality Study*

Duygu Başaran Şahin and Frank W. Heiland

Introduction

The observed mortality advantage of non-Hispanic blacks (henceforth: "blacks") over non-Hispanic whites (henceforth: "whites"), such that age-specific death rates are lower among blacks at very old ages (i.e. they "cross over") after being higher during adulthood, childhood and infancy, remains an important puzzle for demographers and health scientists. Does the phenomenon really exist or is it merely an artifact of poor data? At what age does the advantage in age-specific mortality and associated measures like remaining life expectancy occur ("crossover age")? Are the black-white differentials in old age mortality significant (e.g. from a public health perspective)? How does the pattern vary by gender and birth cohort, and what factors contribute to it?

Evidence of mortality crossovers at old age dates back to at least Pearl (1922). The first systematic analysis of black-white mortality crossovers can be found in Sibley (1930). He documented the phenomenon in 1917–27 (excluding the influenza year 1918) using vital statistics from Tennessee. Sibley observed that the age-specific death rates crossed around age 74 (see Fig. 20 in Sibley 1930, p. 35). Official national life table estimates by sex and race were first published in 1936, covering the continental U.S. in 1929–31. In these data, crossover occurs near age

---

D.B. Şahin (✉)
Program in Sociology, The Graduate Center, CUNY Institute for Demographic Research, City University of New York, 1 Bernard Baruch Way, Box D-901,
New York, NY 10010, USA
e-mail: dbasaransahin@gradcenter.cuny.edu

F.W. Heiland
School of Public Affairs, The Graduate Center of CUNY (Economics),
CUNY Institute for Demographic Research, City University of New York,
Baruch College, 1 Bernard Baruch Way, Box D-901, New York, NY 10010, USA
e-mail: frank.heiland@baruch.cuny.edu

© Springer International Publishing Switzerland 2017
M.N. Hoque et al. (eds.), *Applied Demography and Public Health in the 21st Century*, Applied Demography Series 8,
DOI 10.1007/978-3-319-43688-3_9

80 for men and 75 for women (Bureau of the Census 1936). U.S. life tables for 2010, the most recent official estimates, show a crossover near 88 for men and women (Arias 2014), an age that 16.5% of black men and 30.6% of black women reach. Life expectancy at 88 is 5.0 years for black men and 5.9 years for black women. This compares to 4.7 and 5.5 years for white men and women, respectively.

Two major explanations have been offered to elucidate the black-white mortality paradox: poor data quality and differential frailty selection. The "deficient data" hypothesis posits that the evidence of black-white mortality crossover is faulty primarily because of errors in age reporting among socio-economically disadvantaged populations, causing mortality rates at older ages to be lower for non-whites (e.g., Thornton and Nam 1968; Rosenwaike 1968, 1979; Zelnik 1969; Bayo 1972; Kitagawa and Hauser 1973; Schoen 1976; Rosenwaike and Logue 1983; Coale and Kisker 1986; Elo and Preston 1994; Preston et al. 1996, 1999; Lynch et al. 2003; Preston and Elo 2006). While there is evidence that age misstatements are much more common among blacks than whites, studies that attempt to correct for that or use data sources deemed more reliable typically still find a crossover (albeit sometimes at an older age). We review this evidence in more detail below.

The differential frailty selection hypothesis asserts that there is mortality selection and individuals in a population are heterogeneous with respect to their susceptibility of dying. Members of more frail subpopulations die earlier in the life course, resulting in a surviving population that is increasingly "robust" (Pearl 1922; Vaupel et al. 1979; Manton and Stallard 1984; Coale and Kisker 1986; Horiuchi and Wilmoth 1998). If the black population is generally disadvantaged relative to whites (e.g. as a result of socio-economic differences), it is expected to experience higher mortality at younger ages as frailer individuals die at a greater rate than their white counterparts. After some advanced ("crossover") age, blacks may display lower age-specific mortality than whites, because the black population is smaller and more selected on survival traits (e.g., Sibley 1930; Thornton and Nam 1968; Manton et al. 1979; Manton and Stallard 1981; Nam 1995; Lynch et al. 2003; Masters 2012). This is the prevailing explanation as we discuss in more detail in the background section below.

While the literature on the black mortality advantage at very old ages has paid relatively little attention to birth cohort patterns and trends, recent work by Masters (2012) suggests that cohort-specific age effects are a key driver of the phenomenon. Understanding the role of the birth cohort is of great interest: If mortality frailty is the source of the crossover between the black and the white population, in the words of Coale and Kisker (1986), then "it must have operated through the different past experience of cohorts in the two populations" (p. 392).[1] Since crossovers emerge as part of the convergence of age-specific mortality between populations

---

[1]Statements to the same effect can be found in earlier work. Sibley commented in 1930 that "the fact that in old age the Negro rates are lower than those for whites suggests the selective effect of disease of early life in eliminating the weaker members of the Negro population before they reach middle age" (p. 11).

(Nam 1995), cohort-based evidence of the phenomenon should foster our understanding of the process of black-white mortality convergence.

In the remainder of this paper we review the literature on black old-age mortality advantage and provide new evidence on black-white mortality differentials by birth cohort using data from the National Longitudinal Mortality Study (NLMS). The large samples in the NLMS allow us to look at mortality patterns by single-year of age. Analyzing non-Hispanic blacks and whites born between 1898 and 1915, we observe a black mortality disadvantage that was present at ages 70–75, then narrowed, and completely disappeared by age 85. There is some evidence that mortality is lower for blacks at ages 85–90, consistent with a black-white crossover in age-specific mortality around age 85. A distinct crossover age threshold followed by consistently lower mortality for blacks, however, was not observed.

Background

Evidence of Black-White Mortality Crossovers

The shape of mortality risk over the life course is well known to demographers and health scientists: the risk of death (from all causes combined) is highest shortly after birth then it declines, first rapidly then more gradually until early adolescence, followed by a gradual rise into old age. While the J-shape of age-specific mortality is common across populations, the level and slopes of the mortality curve can differ depending on the prevailing conditions. In turn, it is possible that age-specific curves for two populations intersect, a phenomenon known as "mortality crossover" (Nam 1995).

Systematic study of old-age mortality crossovers can be found as early as Raymond Pearl's Lowell Institute lecture series held in 1920 (Pearl 1922). He observed mortality crossovers at older ages when comparing remaining life expectancies in historic populations (Pearson's and Macdonell's tables) to the 1910 U.S. population (Glover's table). First-hand evidence of a black mortality advantage first emerged in the 1920s. Sibley (1930) documented black-white crossovers in Tennessee vital records for 1917–22 (excluding the influenza year 1918) and 1923–27. He found that the black and white mortality curves crossed near age 74 (see Fig. 20 in Sibley 1930, p. 35). In urban populations, which faced higher mortality risk at all ages at the time, he observed a crossover at age 71, compared to age 75 in rural populations. He observed the same pattern for men and women (see Fig. 21 in Sibley 1930, p. 36).

Combining death registrations and decennial census population estimates, the first national life tables by sex and race for the continental U.S. in 1929–31 became available in 1936 (Bureau of the Census 1936). The black-white crossover occurs near age 80 for men and age 75 for women in these data. Life tables for 1919–21 in the Census death registration states of 1920 show black-white crossovers near age 76 for men and 75 for women (Bureau of the Census 1936), closely matching the ages found by Sibley in Tennessee.[2] Thornton and Nam (1968) document white/non-white crossovers in all decennial years going back to 1900. Preston and Elo (2006) review official life table data going back from 2003 to 1920 and find that the probability of surviving from age 85 to age 100 is consistently greater for blacks. Overall, researchers find black-white crossovers in age-specific mortality rates between the ages of 70 and 90.

There is evidence that the age at which the mortality pattern reverses in favor of blacks has risen over time (e.g., Manton and Stallard 1984; Lynch et al. 2003). A comparison of decennial life table estimates that we conducted shows how much the black-white crossover age has increased over time in official statistics. For men the black-white crossover was near age 73 in 1939–41, 78 in 1969–71, 84 in 1979–81, 86 in 1989–91, and 89 in 1999–2001. For women the crossover age was about 74 in 1939–41, 80 in 1969–71, 85 in 1979–81, 87 in 1989–91, and 88 in 1999–2001.[3] Official life tables for 2010, the most recent figures, show crossovers at age 88 for both men and women (Arias 2014).

Life expectancy (average length of life remaining at age x, e_x) has also been used to describe mortality crossovers (e.g., Pearl 1922; Thornton and Nam 1968). Due to the summary nature of life expectancy, the crossover will occur at an earlier age when using this measure in place of age-specific mortality. For example, based on the 2010 U.S. life tables (Arias 2014), the black-white crossover in life expectancy occurs between ages 80 and 82, while the age-specific mortality curves intersect at age 88 as discussed above. At age 82 whites and blacks can expect to live another 8 years on average. At age 88, life expectancy is 5.7 years for blacks and 5.2 years for whites. Differences in the mortality advantage of blacks by sex can become more visible when looking at life expectancy: In the 2010 life tables, the crossover age based on remaining life expectancy is age 84 for men (with $e_{84}^M = 6.2$ years) and 80 for women ($e_{80}^F = 9.6$), consistent with a greater racial mortality advantage among black women than black men.[4]

---

[2]Death registration states of 1920: California, Colorado, Connecticut, Delaware, Florida, Illinois, Indiana, Kansas, Kentucky, Louisiana, Maine, Maryland, Massachusetts, Michigan, Minnesota, Mississippi, Missouri, Montana, Nebraska, New Hampshire, New Jersey, New York, North Carolina, Ohio, Oregon, Pennsylvania, Rhode Island, South Carolina, Tennessee, Utah, Vermont, Virginia, Washington, Wisconsin, and The District of Columbia.

[3]Sources: 1939-41—Greville (1947); 1969-71—National Center for Health Statistics (NCHS, 1975); 1979-81—NCHS (1985); 1989-91—NCHS (1997); 1999-2001—Arias, Curtin, Wei and Anderson (2008).

[4]Based on the 2010 life table (Arias 2014), 55.0 % of black women (64.4 % of white women) are predicted to reach the female crossover life expectancy age of 80, while 27.0 % of black men (38.3 % of white men) are expected to reach the male crossover life expectancy age of 84. Another hypothesis is greater underenumeration of the black population. Elo (2001) points to low coverage of the black population in the census. She finds that "(b)etween 1930 and 1990, census omission rates for African American men ranged from a high of 10.5 % in 1940 to a low of 7.0 % in 1980" (p.13). This is consistent with earlier evidence (e.g. Siegel 1974).

Data Quality Concerns

The evidence of lower mortality at older ages among blacks compared to whites in official life tables has been met with surprise and with questions about the quality of the underlying data (death records and population counts). The main concern is more widespread misreporting of age among blacks than whites.[5] Systematic age misreporting among the older black (or non-white) population can bias the death rates at middle ages upwards and understate (possibly increasingly) mortality at older ages, resulting in a spurious crossing of black and white mortality schedules (Thornton and Nam 1968; Rosenwaike 1968; Zelnik 1969; Kitagawa and Hauser 1973; Coale and Kisker 1986, 1990; Elo et al. 1996; Preston et al. 1996, 1999).

Research shows that age misstatement was prevalent among the black population. Mason and Cope (1987) document many discrepancies in age reporting among non-whites in the 1900 census. Elo and Preston (1994) find that only 44.7% of the non-white male (36.9% female) matched observations had consistent ages in census records and death certificates. Elo et al. (1996) compare records from death certificates to social security records and match them to 1985 census data. They find that 86% of the age records matched for black males aged 65–69 and 84% for black females. Looking at successive five-year age intervals, males had higher match percentages than females. At ages 85–89, for both sexes about 85% of the records matched across the two sources. Preston et al. (1996) compare the ages at death from death certificate of 2990 blacks who died in 1985 at reported ages 65 and older with the ages implied by their matched census records from childhood. They find that only 45% of females and 51% of males had consistent ages. They argue that death certificate ages are systematically underreported which causes an overstatement of deaths at very old age (95+). On the other hand, age reporting in the white population is generally found to be quite reliable (e.g., Mason and Cope 1987; Coale and Kisker 1990; Shrestha and Preston 1995; Hill et al. 2000).[6]

Systematic age misstatement has been linked to low death rates of blacks at the oldest ages. However, most studies find that the effect is small and does not explain away the crossover phenomenon. For example, Mason and Cope (1987) show that the

---

[5] Another hypothesis is greater underenumeration of the black population. Elo (2001) points to low coverage of the black population in the census. She finds that "(b)etween 1930 and 1990, census omission rates for African American men ranged from a high of 10.5 % in 1940 to a low of 7.0 % in 1980" (p.13). This is consistent with earlier evidence (e.g. Siegel 1974).

[6] Several explanations for why misreporting is a problem particularly for the black population have been given, even though none has emerged as a "smoking gun". Coale and Kisker (1990) suggest that "age heaping"—the tendency of people to round their age or birth dates—is more common among blacks. The authors state that "heaping on ages divisible by 5 or 10 is a generic characteristic of censuses in which age (at last birthday) is recorded when knowledge of age is imprecise" (p.30). Elo and Preston (1994) propose that poor birth registration and incentives to overstate age as a result of the introduction of Social Security retirement benefits may be at work. Most of the black population aged 60 and older in the 1980s—the period our study covers—was born before 1920 and in the rural South. Before 1920, very few southern states were members of the Birth Registration Area.

magnitudes of the errors in the reported ages are relatively small among non-whites in the 1900 census. Studies that correct for age misreporting (and other data limitations such as under-enumeration) typically find that a racial crossover persists, albeit sometimes at somewhat older ages (Thornton and Nam 1968; Kitagawa and Hauser 1973; Rosenwaike 1979; Hussey and Elo 1997; Lynch et al. 2003).[7] Some notable studies disagree with these conclusions: Coale and Kisker (1990) show that census and vital statistics errors cause mortality rates to be seriously understated above age 95, and more so for the non-white population; they argue that the crossover is spurious. Preston et al. (1996) find that the recorded ages at death among blacks tend to be too low and the crossover disappears when corrected age data are used. However, this research makes strong assumptions regarding the functional form of old-age mortality.

Studies using data from Social Security beneficiary files or Medicare enrollment and death files, sources deemed more reliable than census and vital statistics because of proof-of-age requirements, also point to underestimation of old-age mortality in official life tables but generally confirm the presence of a white/non-white mortality crossover at old age. Myers and Bayo (1965) analyze Social Security beneficiaries over the period 1941–61 and estimate that the white/non-white mortality crossover occurs near age 78 for men in 1959–61. Bayo (1972) investigates the Medicare population based on Social Security records. He reports that in 1968 mortality rates at age 85 for non-whites were 70% higher for males and 43% higher for females in the Social Security files than in the corresponding vital statistics. Mortality crossover occurs at age 80–84 in the former data compared to 75–79 in official vital statistics. Similarly, Kestenbaum (1992) finds that the old-age mortality rates based on 1987 Medicare data are substantially greater than the published rates and confirms that a black-white mortality crossover takes place before age 90.[8]

Differential Frailty Selection Hypothesis

The growing recognition that the racial crossover is not the result of poor data has put the spotlight firmly on the main alternative explanation: differential frailty selection. This hypothesis invokes two elements—mortality selection and frailty heterogeneity—to explain the crossover phenomenon (Pearl 1922; Sibley 1930; Thornton and Nam 1968; Manton et al. 1979; Vaupel et al. 1979; Manton and

---

[7]Using model life table comparisons and adjustments for major sources of error, Zelnik (1969) establishes more broadly the distinct pattern of mortality among the black population. Subsequent analysis of census mortality data by Elo and Preston (1994) affirms the unusual pattern but the authors remain very skeptical.

[8]This literature also points to problems with the age data among non-whites. For example, Kestenbaum (1992) finds that only 73 % of blacks whose age at death was 65 or over (62 % of blacks whose age at death was 85 or over) had a reported age in their Social Security files that exactly matched their death certificate. For whites this percentage was almost 95 % (92 %).

Stallard 1981, 1984; Coale and Kisker 1986; Horiuchi and Wilmoth 1998). The standard explanation for the black-white mortality crossover is as follows (see Manton and Stallard 1984; Nam 1995; Lynch et al. 2003): Since blacks are generally disadvantaged relative to whites, frail blacks are more likely to die than similarly frail whites during the early and middle stages of life, causing age-specific mortality rates to be greater in the black population. After some old age ("crossover age"), blacks may display lower mortality than whites, as the surviving black population is smaller and more heavily selected on survival traits than the surviving white population. The positive traits on which individuals are selected are constitutional endowments that capture genetics as well as early exposures, environmental factors and life experiences. As racial gaps in socio-economic conditions diminish, the frailty selection hypothesis predicts that racial mortality differentials will narrow and crossover occurs at an older age or disappears altogether (e.g. Nam 1995).

Evidence of a rising crossover age in the 20th century, as mortality conditions for blacks at younger ages improved, has been cited in support of the frailty selection explanation (see Lynch et al. 2003). Several studies test the hypothesis directly. Berkman, Singer and Manton (1989) look at mortality of subpopulations defined by functional health status as a proxy of frailty in old age. Consistent with the hypothesis, they find that the black-white mortality crossover disappears when controlling for frailty heterogeneity in a study of elderly residents from New Haven, Connecticut. Similarly, Sautter et al. (2012) investigate the role of socio-economic status on black-white mortality crossover using data from the North Carolina Established Population for Epidemiologic Studies. They find that low income is an important predictor for black-white mortality crossover, consistent with the hypothesis. Analyzing the same data set, Dupre et al. (2006) suggest that religious attendance captures an important aspect of frailty heterogeneity that contributes to the female black-white crossover.

Cause-Specific Mortality

To better understand which medical causes may explain the crossing of black-white age-specific mortality curves in late life, more precisely, the different rates at which the curves are rising (rates of mortality increase or "RMIs"), researchers have looked at cause-of-death data by race. While this literature is limited and there appear to be multiple causes that exhibit racial crossovers, studies consistently point to mortality from cardiovascular diseases as a key driver of the black-white differentials. Cardiovascular disease risk rises sharply into old age and causes about one-third of all deaths past age 50 in the U.S., with ischemic heart disease being the largest overall cause of death and strokes being the second most common cause among death from heart diseases (Fenelon 2013; Horiuchi et al. 2003).

Corti et al. (1999) analyze the differences in hazard ratios between black and white adults aged 65 years and older. They find that coronary heart disease death risk (and all-cause mortality) is lower for whites than blacks between ages 65 and 75; between 75 and 80 the crossover occurs and mortality is lower for blacks thereafter. This is consistent with earlier work by Nam et al. (1978). Hussey and Elo (1997) find that the mortality crossover is eliminated for most when more accurate age data is used. However, the crossover for ischemic heart diseases persists. Eberstein et al. (2008), using data from 2003, observe a crossover for heart disease after age 85; for deaths related to cerebrovascular diseases, influenza and pneumonia the crossover occurs between ages 75 and 84. Most recently, using data from 2000, Fenelon (2013) finds that mortality increases more rapidly with age for whites than for blacks for several causes of death, including mortality from cardiovascular disease.

Cohort Evidence and Contribution of Present Study

As apparent from the survey of the literature above, the evidence of the black old-age mortality advantage overwhelmingly stems from period data. However, racial crossovers have been observed in cohort data as well. One case with official data is a National Center for Health Statistics publication from 1973 (NCHS 1973). Looking at mortality for five-year age and birth cohort groups, white/non-white crossovers are shown to occur sometime between ages 70–74 and 75–79 for men and women born 1865–1894 (p. 18). This points to a stable cohort pattern but given the wide age and birth year ranges it is impossible to make more precise statements about the trends in the magnitude of the black advantage and the crossover age by cohort and gender.

To date the literature has paid relatively little attention to the role of birth cohorts in black-white crossover patterns and trends. This is despite a long tradition of emphasizing the importance of cohort-specific endowments and experiences over the life course in demography and public health (e.g., Ryder 1965; Finch and Crimmins 2004). Period life tables by construction do not foretell the mortality experience of actual cohorts when death rates are changing. Racial mortality patterns may differ greatly across cohorts, affecting black-white crossover ages; only careful analyses using appropriate data is able to uncover such variation.

The recent work by Masters (2012) is a notable exception in the literature. Using 1986–2008 data from the National Health Interview Surveys (NHIS) linked with death records, he performs a detailed age-period-cohort decomposition analysis, grouping the birth cohorts and the ages in 5-year intervals. He finds that the birth cohorts of 1900 and 1910 have lower mortality for black males compared to white males at ages 80, 85 and 90, but this does not hold for the cohorts 1915 and 1920. For females he observes a similar pattern, except that the 1915 birth cohort also experiences a crossover, at age 90–94.

Masters' findings suggest that cohort effects play a crucial role in the crossover phenomenon. He concludes that "the convergence and crossover of non-Hispanic black and non-Hispanic white mortality risk in the United States is chiefly a product of disparate cohort-specific age effects between the two populations" (p. 791).

Table 9.1 Birth cohorts in the study

Birth cohort	Mean age at NLMS file 11 baseline (4/1/1983)	Mean age at baseline of life table
4/2/1913–4/1/1915	69 years old	70 years old
4/2/1908–4/1/1910	74 years old	75 years old
4/2/1903–4/1/1905	79 years old	80 years old
4/2/1898–4/1/1900	84 years old	85 years old

However, he acknowledges, "there is a great deal of selection into the NHIS" (p. 794), which may bias his results.

In this paper we provide new evidence on cohort patterns in black-white mortality using data from the National Longitudinal Mortality Study (NLMS). The NLMS provides a nationally representative sample that allows us to study the mortality of specific birth cohorts in single-year age intervals. The NLMS sample is unusually large, individuals can be followed for 11 years, deaths are linked from official records, and race/ethnicity and sex information is available. Several studies have analyzed mortality differentials using data from the NLMS (e.g., Geruso 2012; Rogot et al. 1992; Sorlie et al. 1995; Elo and Preston 1996; Johnson et al. 1999). However, similar to the overall literature, these authors have given short shrift to the role of birth cohort. To our knowledge, this is the first analysis of cohort patterns in black-white mortality differentials at old age using NLMS data.

Data and Method

Data

The February 28, 2013, release of the National Longitudinal Mortality Study Public Use Microdata Sample (NLMS PUMS) is a collection of three large national longitudinal mortality data sets, each representative of the non-institutionalized population in the U.S. for a particular period. The first one, which is also called File 11 in the NLMS PUMS documentation, has the largest number of observations and follows respondents for up to 11 years. The other two files follow individuals only for six years.

To maximize sample size and period of follow-up, we are using File 11, which contains approximately 1.2 million individuals. It provides longitudinal data for the period 1983–1994. Combining data from Current Population Surveys (CPS) and a subset of the 1980 Census, the NLMS PUMS follows these individuals for up to 11 years and matches the deceased cases with information from death certificates provided by the National Center for Health Statistics.

Borrowing from studies by Census researchers involved with the NLMS, the relation between follow-up information and death status is as follows: "Mortality follow-up information was collected through a computer match to the National

Table 9.2 Sample sizes at survey baseline (April 1st, 1983)

	1913–1915 (~69 years old)	1908–1910 (~74 years old)	1903–1905 (~79 years old)	1898–1900 (~84 years old)
Non-Hispanic White	16,329	12,329	8333	4581
NHW Female	9075	7113	5120	2929
NHW Male	7254	5216	3216	1652
Non-Hispanic Black	1413	1006	635	333
NHB Female	838	590	381	218
NHB Male	575	416	254	115
Total	35,484	26,670	17,939	9828

Death Index (NDI). The NDI, a national file containing information collected from death certificates, is maintained by the National Center for Health Statistics. The matching of records to the NDI has been shown to be an effective and accurate means of ascertaining mortality information using personal identifiers including: social security number, name, date of birth, sex, race, marital status, state of birth, and state of residence" (Coady et al. 2014; Johnson et al. 1999).

The death status indicator in the NLMS is a binary variable showing whether or not the observed individual died in the follow-up period. The NLMS does not reveal the date of death, the date of birth or the age at death. However the "length of follow-up" variable, which shows the "full days between the start of follow-up and death or the full days between start of follow-up and end of follow-up for those alive at the end of the 11 years of follow-up" (NLMS PUMS File Release 4 Documentation 2013, p. 23), allows researchers to calculate how many years after the initial interview individuals have lived.

The main variables of interest are race, Hispanic origin, gender, age, death indicator and the length of follow-up. Since we are interested in black-white mortality differences, we create the common race/ethnicity categories of non-Hispanic white and non-Hispanic black. While the NLMS PUMS does not provide exact birthday information, age at last birthday is available from the File 11 baseline survey (April 1, 1983).[9] We use it to define four two-year wide birth cohort groups to be analyzed.

As shown in Table 9.1, our youngest two-year birth cohort is comprised of two groups of individuals, those who were born between April 2, 1913 and April 1, 1914, and those who were born between April 2, 1914 and April 1, 1915. On average, the former were approximately 69.5 years old at the baseline date of April 1, 1983, while the latter were approximately 68.5 (69 overall). We refer to this group as the "1913–15 birth cohort". Our second-youngest birth cohort consists of individuals who were born between April 2, 1908 and April 1, 1910 ("1908–1910

---

[9]This is the date that the NLMS PUMS assigned as a common starting point for the combined CPS records.

Table 9.3 Cohort life tables for non-hispanic whites and blacks—cohort 1913–1915

Age	Lx	lDx	lPYx	lax	1Mx	SE (1Mx)	1qx	SE (1qx)	lx	SE(lx)	ldx	1Lx	Tx	ex
Non-Hispanic blacks														
70	1373	47	1350.0	0.5	0.0348	0.0050	0.0342	0.0049	100,000	0.0	3422.0	98289.0	757266.0	7.57
71	1326	54	1298.7	0.5	0.0416	0.0055	0.0407	0.0054	96,578	490.5	3934.0	94611.0	658977.1	6.82
72	1272	53	1245.9	0.5	0.0425	0.0057	0.0417	0.0056	92,644	704.5	3859.0	90714.5	564366.1	6.09
73	1219	50	1192.9	0.5	0.0419	0.0058	0.0411	0.0057	88,785	851.5	3645.1	86962.5	473651.6	5.33
74	1169	38	1144.6	0.5	0.0332	0.0053	0.0327	0.0052	85,140	960.0	2780.5	83749.6	386689.2	4.54
75	1131	30	1116.8	0.5	0.0269	0.0048	0.0265	0.0048	82,359	1029.2	2183.0	81267.8	302939.5	3.68
76	1101	60	1066.7	0.5	0.0562	0.0071	0.0547	0.0069	80,176	1076.3	4386.5	77983.1	221671.7	2.76
77	1041	54	1015.4	0.5	0.0532	0.0070	0.0518	0.0069	75,790	1156.9	3926.2	73826.7	143688.6	1.90
78	987	55	959.8	0.5	0.0573	0.0075	0.0557	0.0073	71,864	1214.1	4003.4	69861.9	69861.9	0.97
79	932								67,860					
Non-Hispanic whites														
70	15942	427	15730.1	0.5	0.0271	0.0013	0.0268	0.0013	100,000	0.0	2678.2	98660.9	778458.4	7.78
71	15515	441	15299.5	0.5	0.0288	0.0014	0.0284	0.0013	97,322	127.9	2765.4	95939.1	679797.5	6.99
72	15074	451	14850.2	0.5	0.0304	0.0014	0.0299	0.0014	94,556	179.7	2828.7	93142.1	583858.3	6.17
73	14623	498	14375.1	0.5	0.0346	0.0015	0.0341	0.0015	91,728	218.1	3123.6	90165.9	490716.3	5.35
74	14125	514	13870.4	0.5	0.0371	0.0016	0.0364	0.0016	88,604	251.7	3223.7	86992.2	400550.4	4.52
75	13611	546	13340.1	0.5	0.0409	0.0017	0.0401	0.0017	85,380	279.8	3424.5	83668.1	313558.2	3.67
76	13065	547	12794.4	0.5	0.0428	0.0018	0.0419	0.0018	81,956	304.5	3430.5	80240.6	229890.1	2.81
77	12518	586	12221.9	0.5	0.0479	0.0019	0.0468	0.0019	78,525	325.2	3676.9	76686.9	149649.5	1.91
78	11932	602	11645.4	0.5	0.0517	0.0021	0.0504	0.0020	74,848	343.6	3771.7	72962.6	72962.6	0.97
79	11330								71,077					

birth cohort"). On average, they are approximately 74 years old at baseline. Individuals born between April 2, 1903 and April 1, 1905 make up the third birth cohort ("Cohort 1903–1905"); the last birth cohort consists of people born between April 2, 1898 and April 1, 1900 ("Cohort 1898–1900").

Table 9.2 shows the number of people alive at the beginning of the follow up (April 1, 1983) for each of the four two-year wide birth cohorts by gender and race/ethnicity. As expected, the number of cases becomes smaller for older birth cohorts and the sample sizes are much smaller for blacks. For example, at baseline there are 16,329 whites in our youngest cohort compared to 1413 blacks.

Method

We seek to determine whether there is a black mortality advantage in cohort data, how large it is, at what age it begins and whether it varies by birth cohort and gender. Standard demographic techniques—cohort age-specific mortality rates and partial cohort life tables—are used to analyze our survival data. We report death rates and survival curves by age, race and cohort. Given sample size limitations, we

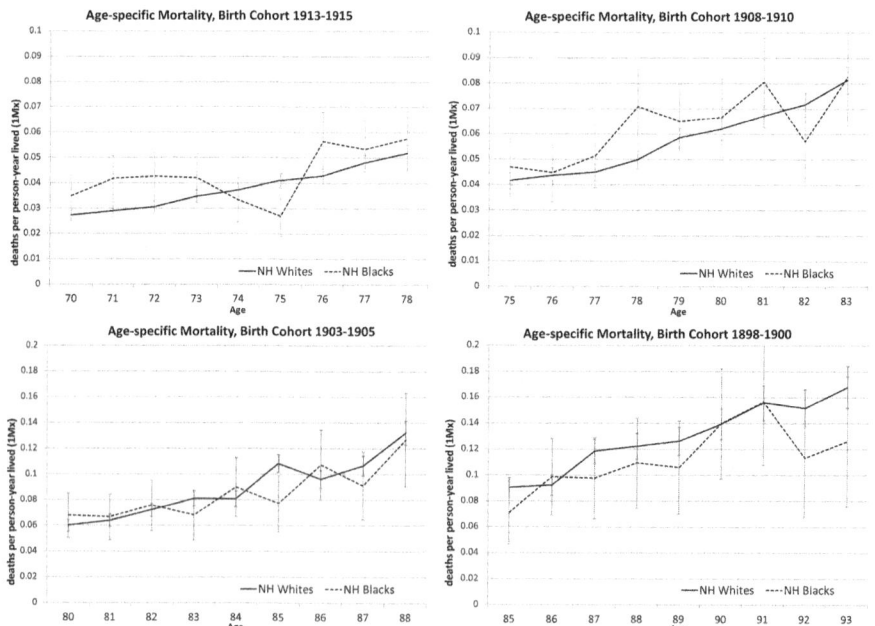

Fig. 9.1 Age-specific cohort death rates by race/ethnicity

mainly focus on results that pool the sexes, but some findings for females are also discussed. We do not show results for males as the sample sizes, especially at the oldest ages, are too small to draw reliable conclusions. We estimate age-specific cohort death rates for single-year age intervals and construct corresponding conditional (or "partial") cohort life tables (without smoothing). Individuals in the four cohorts defined above are followed either until death or until they become right-censored. Leap years are taken into account in all calculations.

To estimate cohort death rates (1Mx) for integer ages x, for each cohort, we start the death count (1Dx-numerators) at the nearest relevant integer age, which represents an average age since we only know age at last birthday on April 1, 1983. For example, for our youngest two-year cohort (1913–1915), the first age interval we report starts when the average age equals 70 years. Those born between April 2, 1913 and April 1, 1914, reach age 70 six months after survey baseline (April 1, 1983), on average; those born between April 2, 1914 and April 1, 1915, reach this age 18 months after baseline, on average (see Table 9.1). Person-years-at-risk (1PYx-denominators in death rates) are estimated over the same age intervals.

The cohort death rates are used to estimate conditional (old-age) cohort life tables. For example, for our youngest two-year cohort, we report life tables conditional on reaching an (average) age of 70 and we can follow them up to age 79. Our oldest cohort is observed from 85 to 94. Standard Errors are calculated for the estimated death rates and the number of survivors in the life table. An example of the type of life table that we prepared can be found in Table 9.3. We added a data column "Lx" that tracks the number of individuals alive in the data. All other functions are standard. Given right-censoring, remaining life expectancy (ex) refers to the subpopulation that dies within the horizon of the life table. We also note that deaths occurring during the interim period between survey baseline and the nearest relevant integer age (age 70 in Table 9.3) reduce the number of individuals entering the life table calculations (Lx) relative to the sample sizes at survey baseline shown in Table 9.2.

Main Results

Cohort Age-Specific Mortality

As we discussed in the background section, existing evidence – predominantly from period data—places the crossover in black-white mortality rates between age 70 and 90. Our analysis of populations born between 1898 and 1915, and alive in 1983, is set up to capture mortality cross-overs in that age range as we follow individuals up to age 94 in the case of our oldest cohort.

Figure 9.1 presents age-specific death rates for Non-Hispanic whites (solid lines) and Non-Hispanic blacks (dotted lines) from our four birth cohorts. 90% Confidence Intervals around the estimated rates are also shown. The top left graphs show the results for the youngest cohort, born between April 1913 and April 1915,

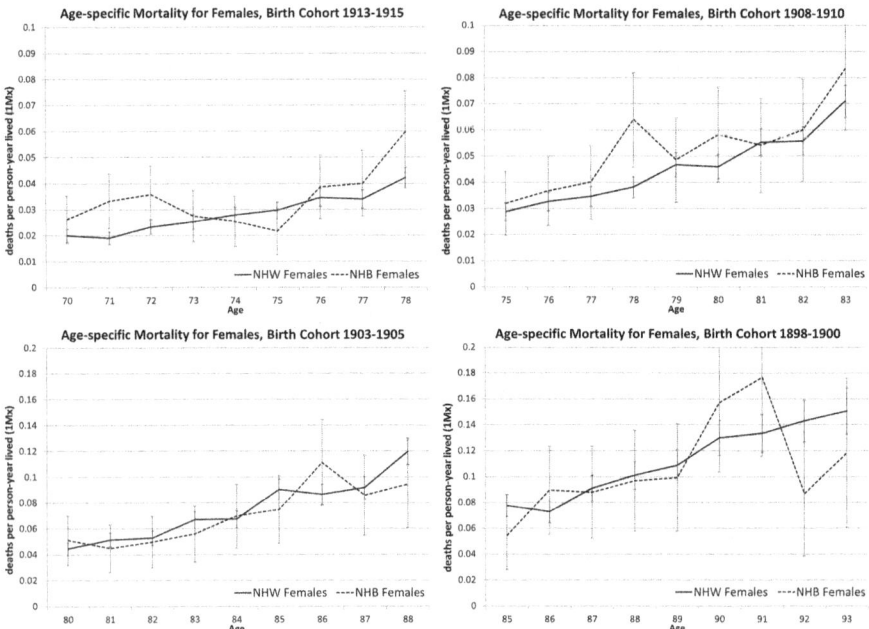

Fig. 9.2 Female age-specific cohort death rates by race/ethnicity

which we follow from age 70 to under age 79, and the graphs in the bottom right show the oldest birth cohorts studied, born between April 1898 and April 1900, which we can follow from age 85 to under age 94.

Looking at the overall patterns, as expected, we observe higher death rates at older ages within cohorts and similar rates at comparable ages across nearby cohorts. For whites in our youngest birth cohort, 1913–1915, we estimate that mortality increased from 27 deaths per 1000 at age 70 to under 71 (henceforth: "70–71") to 52 deaths per 1000 at age 78–79. For whites in our oldest cohort, 1898–1900, mortality rose from 90 deaths per 1000 at age 85–86 to 168 deaths per 1000 at age 93–94. At age 75–76, where the 1913–1915 cohort overlaps with the 1908–1910 cohort, we observe identical death rates of 41 per 1000 for whites.

Mortality is found to be increasing in age for blacks, similar to whites, but the variability in age-specific rates is much greater for blacks. Looking at the youngest cohort, the estimated death rates for blacks are above those of whites for most ages. The estimated gaps are statistically significant at ages 71–72, 72–73 and 76–77 for conventional significance levels. At ages 71–73, cohort age-specific mortality for blacks is found to be about 42 per 1000, compared to 29–30 per 1000 for whites. At ages 74–75 and 75–76 mortality dips for blacks and their death rate is significantly below that of whites at age 75–76.

For the 1908–1910 birth cohort, moving the life course window up by 5 years relative to the 1913–1915 cohort, the black mortality curve also lies above that of whites for most ages, but only the gap at age 78–79 is statistically significant. At age 82–83 the death rate for blacks dips below that of whites, but this crossover does not persist as the rates in the following age group (1M83) are identical for blacks and whites.

As shown in Fig. 9.1, the black and white mortality curves largely overlay for the 1903–1905 cohort which is observed from age 80 to under 89. Mortality for blacks falls statistically significantly below that of whites at age 85–86. While the black-mortality advantage of approximately 31 deaths per 1000 at this age is statistically significant, this age does not appear to mark a persistent black-white mortality crossover: In the following age interval (age 86–87), the point estimate for the death rate is slightly greater for blacks than whites (not statistically different).

Turning to our oldest cohort, 1898–1900, and moving up another 5 years in age, we observe that the black mortality curve is at the level or below the white mortality curve. Based on the point estimates, death rates are lower for blacks at ages 87 to under 90 and 92 to under 94. While we cannot reject that individual age-specific rates are the same for blacks and whites (given wide confidence intervals), looking at all rates jointly, there is evidence that mortality is lower, on average, for blacks than whites over this oldest age range.

Overall, the results for selected cohorts born 1898–1915 are consistent with a black mortality disadvantage that was present at ages 70–75, then narrowed, and completely disappeared by age 85. There is some evidence that mortality is lower

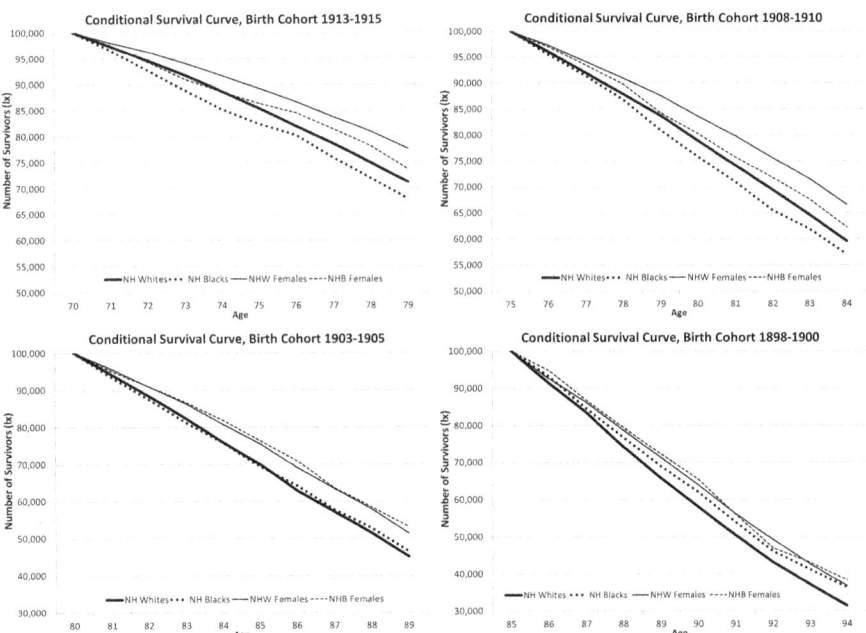

Fig. 9.3 Old-age life table survival curves by race/ethnicity

Table 9.4 Probabilities of survival by race/ethnicity

Comparison of survival probability (9 Pa) for different birth cohorts (in %)					
Survival age span	Corresponding birth cohort	Non-Hispanic white		Non-Hispanic black	
		Females	Pooled	Female	Pooled
From age 70 to 79	1913–1915	77.5	71.1	73.6	67.9
From age 75 to 84	1908–1910	66.5	59.5	62.1	56.9
From age 80 to 89	1903–1905	51.2	45.0	53.0	46.3
From age 85 to 94	1898–1900	36.6	31.2	38.1	36.2

for blacks than whites at ages 85–90, suggesting that a crossover in death rates may have occurred around age 85, but the analysis does not point to a distinct age threshold after which mortality is persistently lower for blacks. We cannot rule out that the mortality patterns by age partly reflect cohort effects, but the gradual nature of the reversal of the black mortality disadvantage and the fact that the death rates at overlapping ages are fairly consistent across cohorts does not point to important cohort effects.

Figure 9.2 shows the mortality curves by race estimated for the female subpopulations separately. Compared to the pooled results above, the female curves tend to be lower, which is consistent with lower mortality among females than males. While the precision of the estimates is diminished due to the smaller sample sizes, the differences by race are similar to those in the pooled results (Fig. 9.1).

As in the pooled data, there is evidence that mortality is significantly greater for black women than for white women at ages 71–72, 72–73, and 78–79 for the 1913–1915 cohort and at age 78–79 for cohort 1908–1910. At other ages, the point estimates for the two youngest cohorts are also mostly greater for blacks than for whites, but given the wide confidence intervals we generally cannot reject that the mortality rates are the same across racial groups. For females in the 1903–1905 cohort, spanning ages 80 to under 89, the age-specific death rates are very similar across racial groups. This suggests that any black mortality disadvantage had disappeared at those ages.

Inspecting the results for the females in our oldest cohort (1898–1900), there is little evidence that black mortality fell below whites. Only at age 92–93 is the black female death rate statistically significantly smaller than its white counterpart. The average death rates are about the same over this age span. This casts doubt at the idea that a mortality crossover occurred among females. The fact that the pattern for females differs from the pooled results in this regard suggests that the evidence of a racial mortality crossover in this cohort may mainly derive from male mortality.

Old-Age Survival Curves

To facilitate the analysis of mortality differentials by race, we look at (conditional) survival curves from cohort life tables. This enables us to capture the cumulative impact of old-age age-specific mortality by race. Figure 9.3 shows the life table survival curves for blacks and whites, both pooled and females only, for each of our four birth cohorts. The information is from the lx column of the corresponding cohort life tables; we are assuming an initial population at risk of 100,000 (radix). To illustrate how the underlying conditional life tables look like (including the relevant Standard Errors) see Table 9.3, which shows the estimated life table for the 1913–1915 cohort (pooling males and females).

The top left graph presents the curves for the youngest and the bottom right curves show the oldest of birth cohorts studied. Looking at the 1913–1915 birth cohort, we find that the survival curves (conditional on age 70) for blacks decline faster than the ones for whites up to age 73. Between age 74 and 76 the curves narrow. After that they widen again very slightly. This is consistent with our earlier findings of generally higher death rates among blacks than whites among this cohort, especially early in their 8th decade of life. The brief age span where blacks enjoy lower death rates than whites causes the temporary narrowing of the survival curves.

For the 1908–1910 birth cohort, we observe that the survival curves for blacks drop off faster than for whites and the gap tends to widen. This is the result of greater mortality among blacks than whites, especially early in this age span. The survival curves starting at age 80 for the 1903–1905 cohort tend to be very similar for blacks and whites. While, as before, the number of survivors declines (slightly) faster for blacks than whites early in the age span, that pattern reverses and the curves actually cross at age 85 in the pooled data and at age 82 among females. However, given sampling variability, we cannot reject the hypothesis that the black and the white survival curves are identical, consistent with our discussion of the age-specific mortality patterns for this cohort.

Looking at the results for the 1898–1900 birth cohort, our oldest cohort, the survival curves (conditional on age 85) for blacks are mostly above their white counterparts. Especially when pooling both sexes, a faster decline in white survivors can be observed. This reflects somewhat lower average age-specific mortality among blacks in this age range. The pattern is consistent with a mortality crossover near age 85.

Table 9.4 presents 9-year life table survival probabilities for the four birth cohorts in our analysis. For the youngest cohort, 1913–1915, whites combined (71.1% vs. 67.9% for blacks) and white females (77.5% vs. 73.6% for black females) have higher probabilities of surviving from age 70 to 79 compared to their black counterparts. Looking five years out in age and earlier in cohort, we find a similar pattern: Whites in the 1908–1910 birth cohort have higher probabilities of survival from ages 75 to 84. The mortality disadvantage of blacks appears to be greater among females than males as suggested by the contrast between the female

(62.1% for white females vs. 66.5% for black females) and the pooled results (59.5% for all whites vs. 56.9% for all blacks).

Consistent with our survival analysis above, there is evidence from the two oldest cohorts that the pattern reverses at very old-age. In the 1903–1905 birth cohort, whites combined (45% vs. 46.3% all blacks) and white females (51.2% vs. 53% black females) have slightly greater probabilities of survival from ages 80 to 89 than their black counterparts. The strongest evidence of a black survival advantage comes from the pooled data for the 1898–1900 birth cohort. The probabilities of surviving from ages 85 to 94 is 31.1% for all whites combined compared to 36.2% for all blacks. Looking at females separately, the estimated gap is much smaller (36.6% for white females vs. 38.1% for black females) and not statistically significantly different from zero.

Conclusions

This paper provides new evidence on black-white mortality differentials at old-age. We examine the survival trajectories of selected cohorts born between 1898 and 1915 in the National Longitudinal Mortality Study (NLMS). Analyzing cohort age-specific morality rates and survival curves from cohort life tables, we observe a black mortality disadvantage that was present at ages 70–75, then narrowed, and completely disappeared by age 85. There is some evidence that mortality is lower for blacks than whites at ages 85–90, consistent with a crossover in death rates around age 85. However, evidence to support a distinct crossover age threshold followed by consistently lower age-specific death rates for blacks did not emerge.

Previous evidence on the racial crossover in mortality rates—predominantly from period data—places it between age 70 and 90. Official period life table statistics show a crossover at age 73/74 in 1939–41, 84 in 1979–81 and age 88 in 2010 (Greville 1947; NCHS 1985; Arias 2014). Given our focus on populations born between 1898 and 1915, the 1979–81 data, indicating a crossover at age 84, are the most relevant to the generations studied here. A National Center for Health Statistics publication from 1973 (NCHS 1973), tabulating cohort mortality for five-year age and birth cohort groups, puts the white/non-white crossovers between ages 70–74 and 75–79 for men and women born 1865–1894. Our results are largely consistent with a crossover near age 85 for generations born around the turn of the 20th century, which is within the plausible range of crossover ages suggested by earlier studies.

There is little systematic evidence on the gender-specificity of the black mortality advantage. A notable exception is the recent study by Masters (2012). Analyzing 1986–2008 NHIS data linked with death records, he estimates that the birth cohorts of 1900 and 1910 have lower mortality for black males compared to white males at ages 80–84, 85–89 and past age 90. For male cohorts 1915 and 1920 no black-white crossover is observed. For females the pattern is similar, except that the 1915 birth cohort experiences a crossover at ages 90–94. In the NLMS, we observe black mortality advantages after age 85 in pooled data for cohorts 1898–1900. Analyzing females separately, we do not find evidence of a black advantage at older ages, suggesting that the crossover pattern holds mainly for men, which is consistent with the findings based on NHIS data by Masters (2012).

This analysis has been motivated in part by a desire to better understand the age at which the black mortality advantage begins and how pronounced the racial differences are. Examining narrow age-intervals in the NLMS was meant to facilitate more precise statements about when mortality crossovers occur and how large the differentials become. Applying the magnifying glass of the single-year age-group perspective has revealed the complexity of crossover patterns. In particular, we observe substantial variation and in some cases multiple crossings of death rates over narrow age ranges. While the precision of disaggregated mortality data at old age is a great concern, these patterns are noteworthy and are lost in studies using 5 or 10-year age groups.

While our (limited) evidence of a black mortality advantage at old age is consistent with the heterogeneity selection hypothesis, we cannot rule out that poor data quality plays a role. For example, for the 1898–1900 cohort comprehensive and consistent birth registration was almost certainly not present. It is possible that inferred gender differences reflect issues with the quality of the age data. Elo et al. (1996) compare records from death certificates to social security records and match them to census data to measure the accuracy of age reporting among older blacks by gender. They find that the information from men tended to be more consistent between the two sources. While 86% of the records matched for males for the age interval 65–69 in 1985, it was only 84% for women. Looking at successive five-year age intervals from age 70 to 84, males had higher percentages of a match than females. At ages 85–89, women appeared to have caught up with men, with both sexes having around 85% matching records. They conclude that accuracy is improving over time, which suggests that the age data for our 1913–1915 cohort should be the most accurate.

Understanding the proximate and fundamental causes behind the trends in black-white mortality differentials is important for economic, health and social reasons. Masters (2012:774) asserts that "the contexts of black and white America differed tremendously across the twentieth century, and these differences shaped life course patterns of these populations' mortality risks." Lynch et al. (2003, p. 463) suggest that blacks have been a "homogeneously frail population" due to historical discrimination. However, educational and economic opportunities, which came as a result of the Civil Rights Movement, might have increased the heterogeneity among the black population. The first half of the twentieth century saw a dramatic decline in early life course mortality from infectious diseases, which relatively benefited poorer subpopulations more. Improvements in the second half of the century were largely due to reductions in mortality from degenerative diseases at middle and older ages, more equally benefiting all demographics (Crimmins 1981; Costa 2000; Cutler et al. 2006). Further cohort and gender-specific analyses are needed to better understand the role that social, economic and technological forces have played in black-white old age morality patterns.

Acknowledgement We thank Neil Bennett for helpful comments and suggestions. We are also grateful to Charlie Nam for helpful discussion at an early stage of this project.

References

Arias, E. (2014). United States life tables, 2010. *National Vital Statistics Reports, 63*(7). Hyattsville, MD: National Center for Health Statistics.

Arias, E., Curtin, L. R., Wei, R., & Anderson, R. N. (2008). U.S. Decennial life tables for 1999–2001, United States life tables. *National Vital Statistics Reports, 57*(1). Hyattsville, MD: National Center for Health Statistics.

Bayo, F. (1972). Mortality of the aged. *Transactions of the Society of Actuaries, 24*, 1–24.

Berkman, L., Singer, B., & Manton, K. (1989). Black/white differences in health status and mortality among the elderly. *Demography, 26*(4), 661–678.

Bureau of the Census. (1936). *United States life tables: 1929 to 1931, 1920 to 1929, 1919 to 1921, 1909 to 1911, 1901 to 1910, 1900 to 1902*. Washington, DC: US Government Printing Office.

Coady, S., Johnson, N. J., Hakes, J. K., & Sorlie, P. D. (2014). Individual education, area income and mortality and recurrence of myocardial infarction in a Medicare cohort: The National longitudinal mortality study. *BMC Public Health, 14*, 705.

Coale, A. J., & Kisker, E. E. (1986). Mortality crossovers: Reality or bad data? *Population Studies, 40*(3), 389–401.

Coale, A. J., & Kisker, E. E. (1990). Defects in data on old age mortality in the United States: New procedures for calculating mortality schedules and life tables at the highest ages. *Asian and Pacific Population Forum, 4*(1), 1–31.

Corti, M. C., Guralnik, J. M., Ferrucci, L., Izmirlian, G., Leveille, S. G., Pahor, M., et al. (1999). Evidence for a black-white crossover in all-cause and coronary heart disease mortality in an older population: The North Carolina EPESE. *American Journal of Public Health, 89*(3), 308–314.

Costa, D. (2000). Causes of improving health and longevity at older ages: A review of the explanations. *Genus, LXI*(1), 21–38.

Crimmins, E. M. (1981). The changing pattern of American mortality decline, 1940–77, and its implications for the future. *Population and Development Review, 7*, 229–254.

Cutler, D., Deaton, A., & Lleras-Muney, A. (2006). The determinants of mortality. *Journal of Economic Perspectives, 20*(3), 7–120.

Dupre, M., Franzese, A., & Parrado, E. (2006). Religious attendance and mortality: Implications for the black-white mortality crossover. *Demography, 43*(1), 141–164.

Eberstein, I., Nam, C., & Heyman, K. (2008). Causes of death and mortality crossovers by race. *Biodemography and Social Biology, 54*(2), 214–228.

Elo, I. T., & Preston, S. H. (1994). Estimating African-American mortality from inaccurate data. *Demography, 31*(3), 427–458.

Elo, I. T., & Preston, S. H. (1996). Educational differentials in mortality: United States, 1979–1985. *Social Science and Medicine, 42*, 47–57.

Elo, I. T., Preston, S. H., Rosenwaike, I., Hill, M. E., & Cheney, T. P. (1996). Consistency of age reporting on death certificates and Social Security Administration records among elderly African Americans. *Social Science Research, 25*, 292–307.

Fenelon, A. (2013). An examination of black/white differences in the rate of age-related mortality increase. *Demographic Research, 29*, 441–472.

Finch, C., & Crimmins, E. (2004). Inflammatory exposure and historical changes in human life-spans. *Science, 305*, 1736–1739.

Geruso, M. (2012). Black-white disparities in life expectancy: How much can standard SES variables explain? *Demography, 49*(2), 553–574.

Greville, T. N. E. (1947). *United States life tables and actuarial tables 1939–1941*. National Office of Vital Statistics. Washington, DC: United States Government Printing Office.

Hill, M. E., Preston, S. H., & Rosenwaike, I. (2000). Age reporting among white Americans aged 85+: Results of a record linkage study. *Demography, 37*, 175–186.

Horiuchi, S., Finch, C. E., Meslé, F., & Vallin, J. (2003). Differential patterns of age-related mortality increase in middle age and old age. *The Journals of Gerontology Series A: Biological Sciences and Medical Sciences, 58*(6), B495–B507.

Horiuchi, S., & Wilmoth, J. R. (1998). Deceleration in the age pattern of mortality at older ages. *Demography, 35*(4), 391–412.

Hussey, J. M., & Elo, I. T. (1997). Cause-specific mortality among older African-Americans: correlates and consequences of age misreporting. *Social Biology, 44*(3–4), 227–246.

Johnson, N. J., Sorlie, P. D., & Backlund, E. (1999). The impact of specific occupation on mortality in the U.S. National Longitudinal Mortality Study. *Demography, 36*(3), 355–367.

Kestenbaum, E. (1992). A description of the extreme aged population based on improved Medicare enrollment data. *Demography, 29*, 565–580.

Kitagawa, E., & Hauser, P. (1973). *Differential mortality in the United States: A study in socioeconomic epidemiology*. Harvard University Press.

Lynch, S., Brown, J., & Harmsen, K. (2003). Black-White differences in mortality compression and deceleration and the mortality crossover reconsidered. *Research on Aging, 25*(5), 456–483.

Manton, K. G., Poss, S. S., & Wing, S. (1979). The black-white crossover: Investigation from the perspective of the components of aging. *Gerontologist, 19*, 291–300.

Manton, K. G., & Stallard, E. (1981). Methods for evaluating the heterogeneity of aging processes in human populations using vital statistics data: explaining the black/white mortality crossover by a model of mortality selection. *Human Biology, 53*, 47–67.

Manton, K. G., & Stallard, E. (1984). *Recent trends in mortality analysis*. New York, NY: Academic Press.

Mason, K. C., & Cope, L. G. (1987). Sources of age and date-of-birth misreporting in the 1900 U. S. census. *Demography* 24: 563–73.

Masters, R. K. (2012). Uncrossing the U.S. black-white mortality crossover: The role of cohort forces in life course mortality risk. *Demography, 49*, 773–796.

Myers, R. J., & Bayo, F. (1965). Mortality of workers entitled to old-age benefits under OASDI. *Transactions of the Society of Actuaries, 17*, 417–431.

Nam, C. (1995). Another look at mortality crossovers. *Biodemography and Social Biology, 42*(1–2), 133–142.

Nam, C. B., Weatherby, N. L., & Ockay, K. A. (1978). Causes of death which contribute to the mortality crossover effect. *Social Biology, 25*(4), 306–314.

National Center for Health Statistics. (1973). *Mortality trends: Age, color, and sex. United States 1950–69*. Series 20, No. 15. DHEW Pub. No. (HRA) 74-1852. Public Health Services. Rockville, MD: National Center for Health Statistics.

National Center for Health Statistics. (1975). *United States life tables: 1969–71*. Washington, DC: US Government Printing Office.

National Center for Health Statistics. (1985). *U.S. decennial life tables for 1979–81* (Vol. 1). No. 1. DHHS Pub. No. (PHS) 85-1150-1. Public Health Service. Washington, DC: US Government Printing Office.

National Center for Health Statistics. (1997). *U.S. decennial life tables for 1989–91* (Vol. 1). No. 1. Hyattsville, MD: National Center for Health Statistics.

National Longitudinal Mortality Study Public Use Microdata Sample (PUMS) File Release 4 Documentation. (2013, February 28). Retrieved April 22, 2016 https://biolincc.nhlbi.nih.gov/static/studies/nlms/Code_Manuals_and_Forms.pdf. Accessed on April 22, 2016.

Pearl, R. (1922). *The biology of death*. Philadelphia and London: J.B. Lippincott.

Preston, S. H., & Elo, I. T. (2006). Black mortality at very old ages in official US life tables: A skeptical appraisal. *Population and Development Review, 32*(2), 557–565.

Preston, S. H., Elo, I. T., Rosenwaike, I., & Hill, M. (1996). African-American mortality at older ages: Results of a matching study. *Demography, 33*(2), 193–209.

Preston, S. H., Elo, I. T., & Stewart, Q. (1999). Effects of age misreporting on mortality estimates at older ages. *Population Studies, 53*(2), 165–177.
Rogot, E., Sorlie, P. D., & Johnson, N. J. (1992). Life expectancy by employment status in the national longitudinal mortality study, income, and education. *Public Health Reports, 107*(4), 457–461.
Rosenwaike, I. (1968). On measuring the extreme aged in the population. *Journal of the American Statistical Association, 63*(321), 29–40.
Rosenwaike, I. (1979). A new evaluation of United States census data on the extreme aged. *Demography, 16*, 279–288.
Rosenwaike, I., & Logue, B. (1983). Accuracy of death certificate ages for the extreme aged. *Demography, 20*(4), 569–585.
Ryder, N. (1965). The cohort as a concept in the study of social change. *American Sociological Review, 52*, 1–14.
Sautter, J. M., Thomas, P. A., Dupre, M. E., & George, L. K. (2012). Socioeconomic status and the Black-White mortality crossover. *American Journal of Public Health, 102*(8), 1566–1571.
Schoen, R. (1976). Measuring mortality trends and differentials. *Social Biology, 23*, 235–243.
Shrestha, L. B., & Preston, S. H. (1995). Consistency of census and vital registration data on older Americans: 1970–1990. *Survey Methodology, 21*, 167–177.
Sibley, E. (1930). *Differential mortality in Tennessee*. Nashville, TN: The Fisk University Press.
Siegel, J. S. (1974). Estimates of coverage of the population by sex, race, and age in the 1970 Census. *Demography, 11*, 1–23.
Sorlie, P. D., Backlund, E., & Keller, J. B. (1995). US mortality by economic, demographic, and social characteristics: The National Longitudinal Mortality Study. *American Journal of Public Health, 85*(7), 949–956.
Thornton, R., & Nam, C. (1968). The lower mortality rates of nonwhites at the older ages: An enigma in demographic analysis. *Research Reports in Social Science, 11*, 1–8.
Vaupel, J. W., Manton, K. G., & Stallard, E. (1979). The impact of heterogeneity in individual frailty on the dynamics of mortality. *Demography, 16*(3), 439–454.
White, K. M., & Preston, S. H. (1996). How many Americans are alive because of twentieth century improvements in mortality? *Population and Development Review, 22*, 415–449.
Zelnik, M. (1969). Age pattern of mortality of American Negroes 1900–02 to 1959–61. *Journal of the American Statistical Association, 64*(326), 433–451.

Chapter 10
Healthcare Utilization as a Source of Health Disparities Among U.S. Male Immigrants

Jen'nan Ghazal Read and E. Paige Borelli

Introduction

A wealth of studies over the past few decades has brought research on U.S. immigrant health to a crossroads. These studies have largely focused on Hispanic immigrants and provided important theoretical and empirical insight into their health trajectories. At the same time, these frameworks have continued to guide research on newer immigrant populations whose health profiles do not fit neatly within them. For example, the well-established Hispanic paradox—immigrants arrive healthier than U.S.-born whites despite being disadvantaged socioeconomically—fails to apply to many other groups who arrive in the U.S. with higher levels of economic and social capital (Akresh and Frank 2008; Read and Emerson 2005). Likewise, the oft-noted pattern of declining health with longer duration of U.S. residence among Hispanics is inconsistent across other national-origin groups (Singh and Hiatt 2006), and explanations for the pattern among Hispanics (e.g., selectivity, health behaviors, access to healthcare) have been challenged in recent studies (Gorman et al. 2010; Read and Reynolds 2012).

These and other studies have brought us to a crossroads, one that offers a path to identify new analytic and conceptual tools to fit the increasingly heterogeneous demographic make-up of U.S. immigrant groups. The goal of this chapter is to take a step down that path, to build and extend past studies, all of which have been vital in our understanding of immigrant health and have brought us to this juncture. We take a slightly different approach from past research and examine the extent to which immigrant health varies by ethnicity within one gender: men. We use a unique, nationally-representative dataset to compare health-seeking behaviors and health outcomes of immigrant men, and we focus on males from the three largest sending countries in the U.S. today: Mexico, China, and India (Walters and

---

J.G. Read (✉) · E.P. Borelli
Department of Sociology, Duke University, Durham, NC 27708, USA
e-mail: jennan.read@duke.edu

Trevelyan 2011). The advantages of this approach are that it allows us to isolate factors that may be unique to immigrants (e.g., English language ability) and to men (e.g., health behaviors, migration processes). Similar approaches have been used to isolate and better understand the experiences of immigrant women in terms of their health outcomes (Hummer et al. 1999) and employment patterns (Read and Cohen 2007) and may be similarly beneficial for understanding those of men. Additionally, because immigrants in our sample were interviewed within the first year after receiving their green-card, studying their health provides a snap-shot of the health of the most recent cohort of male immigrants to the U.S.

This paper uses data from the 2003 wave of the New Immigrant Survey to address two related research questions: (1) to what extent do health-seeking behaviors among immigrant men vary by country of origin and duration of U.S. residence?; and (2) to what extent are these behaviors linked to health disparities between and within these groups? We focus on contact with the healthcare system because it is an under-conceptualized health behavior that is distinct from access and known to contribute to U.S. health disparities (Gorman et al. 2010). The goal in this study is not to explain the better health of immigrants vis-à-vis native-born Americans but rather to tease out health behaviors among immigrant men that may in turn shape their health outcomes. By focusing on immigrant men, we aim to make theoretical and methodological contributions to research on gendered health disparities. Theoretically, we extend the use of a "gender lens" framework, which calls for greater attention to gender as a central organizing mechanism shaping all realms of social life (Curran et al. 2006). This framework has most frequently been used to correct for a lack of attention to women's experiences but may also be useful in research on men, whose lives are also gendered, albeit in very different ways. Methodologically, this framework requires us to consider factors that may be particularly important for understanding differences among immigrant men (e.g., duration of U.S. residence) and exclude those that may be less relevant (e.g., household size).

Background

Theorizing Immigrant Health

The bulk of research on immigrant health has centered on the healthy migrant effect, whereby immigrants arrive in the U.S. healthier than native-born Americans but lose their health advantage over time (Akresh and Frank 2008; Antecol and Bedard 2006). As early as the 1970s, studies of Japanese Americans demonstrated a selective migration of healthy individuals and found deteriorating health with increased acculturation in U.S. society (Marmot and Leonard Syme 1976). Since then, there has been an explosion in the literature on immigrant health, with the majority of work focused on Mexican immigrants and the perplexing "Hispanic paradox" (good health despite low socioeconomic status). The concept has come under increasing scrutiny in recent years and its efficacy challenged by studies that find considerable variability in the health trajectories of different national-origin groups within broad racial and ethnic categories (Palloni and Arias 2004). Among Hispanics, for example, Mexicans have better health profiles than both Cubans and Puerto Ricans, the latter of which experiences health outcomes that parallel those of U.S.-born black Americans (Rogers et al. 2000). Similarly, among black immigrants, those from Africa exhibit better health outcomes than do those from the Caribbean, with black immigrants from Europe having the worst health (Read and Emerson 2005)..

Explanations for these variations have typically fallen into two camps, those that focus on health selection from the countries of origin and those that focus on factors that influence health once immigrants are in the host country. The first camp is more conceptual than empirical because health selection is hard to test due to a lack of quality data in the home country and/or a lack of access to such data (Read and Emerson 2007). In addition to health selection, immigrants are differentially selected based on education and income, which results in some groups (e.g., Indians) occupying more elite social positions than others (e.g., Mexicans) (Feliciano 2006). The second camp focuses on several complementary arguments related to a decline in positive health behaviors, increase in negative risk-taking behaviors, and the erosion of protective social and cultural factors the longer immigrants are in the United States, all of which contributes to their deteriorating health (Akresh and Frank 2008; Palloni and Arias 2004). Studies have also highlighted the unequal access of some immigrant groups to healthcare, whether it be due to socioeconomic differences that limit the availability of health insurance or to cultural differences in how individuals are socialized to think about illness (Finch et al. 2002).

As part of this second camp, recent studies have identified interaction with the healthcare system as a critical, yet under-conceptualized, health behavior contributing to U.S. health disparities (Gorman et al. 2010; Read and Reynolds 2012). Utilization is different from access because it gauges the likelihood and frequency of individuals coming into contact with the healthcare system above and beyond access. It is an important concept because much of the data used to analyze the health profiles of America's diverse sub-populations relies on self-reports and doctors' diagnoses. Doctors' diagnoses require interaction with the system, and some groups are more likely to interact than others, regardless of access. For example, in 2010, U.S.-born men were twice as likely as U.S.-born women to report that they had not seen a doctor in the past year—27% compared to 14%—and that they had no usual place for care (22% compared to 13%) despite their being more socioeconomically advantaged on average than women (Schiller et al. 2011). In analyzing these relationships, two recent studies concluded that the well-established gender gap in health (women are sicker than men) and immigrant gap in health (immigrants are healthier than the U.S.-born) is partly due to the fact that women are more likely than men and immigrants less likely than native-born Americans to interact with the U.S. healthcare system even when differences in access are taken into account (Gorman et al. 2010; Read and Reynolds 2012).

These studies have been informative and highlighted the need for a closer look at healthcare utilization patterns among immigrant women and immigrant men and not just between them. Health-seeking behaviors are gendered and shaped by the expectations and resources that accompany an individual's social position (Read and Gorman 2006, 2010). For men, pressures to conform to hegemonic ideals of masculinity can result in their reluctance to seek appropriate care—preventative or curative—even when they have access to resources needed for such care (for a review see O'Brian et al. 2005). These pressures can be exacerbated among immigrant men due to the disruption of traditional gender dynamics during migration and efforts to reestablish them in the host country (Parrado and Flippen 2005). Immigrant men are often charged with the economic security of the family, leaving immigrant women responsible for other domains of social life, including the well-being of household members. In this context, obstacles such as lack of health insurance and poor language skills constitute a greater barrier to men than women, whose status within the home and community depends, in large part, on taking care of the family (Read and Oselin 2008).

A recent study on Mexican immigrants provides evidence of the gendered nature of health-seeking behaviors. Gorman et al. (2010) found that the healthier profile of recent immigrant arrivals was due in part to lack of contact with the healthcare system, and thus lack of knowledge of their medical ailments. This was truer for immigrant men than women. On arrival, immigrant men were less likely than immigrant women to interact with the healthcare system, and over time, their likelihood of receiving medical care increased and the gender gap in health closed. Importantly, the study concluded that the declining health of immigrants with increased duration in the U.S. partly reflected limited receipt of medical care among newer immigrants. Although research that examines health disparities between men and women (controlling for national origin/nativity) or between national origin/nativity groups (controlling for gender) has been useful, it may miss important differences in health conditions and behaviors that exist at the intersection of these social locations—among immigrants of the same gender. This study examines this possibility by focusing on immigrant men from the three largest sending countries in the U.S. today: Mexico, China, and India.

A Profile of Today's Immigrants

In 2012, roughly one out of every eight Americans was foreign-born (38.2 million), up from only one out of every twenty in 1970 (9.5 million) (U.S. Bureau of the Census 2013). Over the course of the same four decades, the proportion of immigrants born in Europe plummeted from 75.4 to 13.7%, while the proportions increased for those born in Latin American (53.3%) and Asia (26.7%). The largest sending country by far is Mexico (11.7 million), followed by China (2.2 million),

India (1.9 million), and the Philippines (1.8 million) (U.S. Bureau of the Census 2012). While a great deal of immigration literature has focused on the well-being of Mexicans, much less is known about the Indian and Chinese cases (Walters and Trevelyan 2011).

We know that pre- and post-migration processes vary by gender, which in turn, contributes to different health trajectories for immigrant men and women (Antecol and Bedard 2006; Gorman et al. 2010). As such, we focus on the experiences of men and examine differences by national origin and duration of U.S. residence. Here we summarize briefly the migration histories of Indian and Chinese men to lay the foundation for a comparison to Mexican men, whose migration patterns and disadvantaged status as low-income laborers is more well-documented (Grieco and Ray 2004; Stoney and Batalova 2013). Indian immigrants began arriving in substantial numbers after the passage of 1965 Immigration Reforms, which abolished country quotas limiting the number of racially and ethnically diverse immigrants to the U.S. and created avenues for those with family or employment in the U.S. (Barringer and Kassebaum 1989). Indian men are highly selected on educational attainment and occupational skills and receive more employment visas than men of any other nationality (Pew Research Center 2012; Whatley and Batalova 2012). Dating back to British colonialism, the English language became widely used in all sectors in India, including education, government, and business sectors. As a result, 70% of Indian immigrants in the U.S. report having strong English language skills, compared to only 49% of all other immigrants (Whatley and Batalova 2012). They are also highly educated, with 75% of immigrant men over the age of 25 having attained a bachelor's degree or higher and only 2.3% having attained >12 years of education (Hao 2007; Whatley and Batalova 2012). Commensurate with these attributes, Indian males have experienced considerable occupational success and are concentrated in the IT sector (29%) and management, business, and finance (21%) (Whatley and Batalova 2012). With 72.9% between the ages of 25–44, the majority of Indian men are in their working years.

Chinese immigrants have a comparatively longer history in the U.S., beginning with the arrival of male laborers in the 19th century. The Chinese Exclusion Act in 1882 curbed this migration stream, and Chinese immigrants did not migrate to the U.S. again in significant numbers until the 1980s (Zhou 2009). Compared to Indian immigrants, Chinese are more likely to arrive on family reunification visas, contributing to a greater degree of socioeconomic diversity among Chinese immigrants. At the same time, a large number of Chinese immigrants receive employment visas, with 1 in 10 employment visas going to Chinese immigrants every year (McCabe 2012). The prevalence of employment visas among Chinese immigrants results in high educational attainment. For instance, 9.6% of Chinese immigrants have >12 years of education, and 45.4% have attained a bachelor's degree or higher (Hao 2007; McCabe 2012). Nearly two-thirds (63%) of Chinese immigrants report having limited English proficiency, which often results in blocked occupational mobility in this population (McCabe 2012; Zhou 2009). The average age of

Chinese immigrants is higher than Indians because many arrive as parents or grandparents of citizens (15% are over the age of 65) (McCabe 2012). These older adults generally have limited English language proficiency, lower rates of labor force participation, and lack knowledge about American culture, all of which can lead to isolation and depression (Kim et al. 2011; Treas 2008). Immigrant Chinese men who are in the labor force are more likely than Indian immigrant men to be concentrated in physically intensive, lower-wage service occupations, such as restaurant kitchens (Lan 2012; McCabe 2012).

Given these profiles, we might expect considerable diversity in healthcare utilization behaviors and health outcomes among male immigrants, with Indians having greater access to and utilization of health care than their Chinese and Mexican counterparts. On the other hand, one could hypothesize little variation across national-origin groups due their shared status as males and immigrants, each of which might lead to similar health-seeking behaviors and health outcomes. We examine these possibilities below.

Data and Methods

Data

Data for this study is derived from the first wave of the New Immigrant Survey (NIS) , which was collected from May 2003 to November 2003. The second wave of the survey occurred in 2007, but these data are not yet available. The New Immigrant Survey is a nationally representative, multi-cohort panel survey of recent U.S. immigrants. The NIS sampled respondents from the electronic records of the U.S. Immigration and Naturalization Services using four strata based on adult respondent visa category (Massey 2010). To create a sampling frame, the NIS randomly selected an equal number of respondents from the following four visa categories: (1) spouses of U.S. citizens, (2) employed by U.S. businesses, (3) diversity lottery winners, and (4) other visa categories. We omitted respondents with missing information on variables of interest, and we only include adult male immigrants in our analyses. Our final sample contains Mexican (N = 429), Indian (N = 410), Chinese (N = 213), and other male immigrants (N = 2849), with 3901 male respondents total. To be clear, our sample includes new arrival immigrants with legal documentation and those whose status was recently adjusted from temporary or non-legal to legal permanent residency. This excludes most foreign-born students, immigrants with temporary visas, and any immigrants without legal status due to over-staying temporary visas or not obtaining documentation prior to entering the U.S. Survey interviews were conducted in the respondents' preferred language.

Given our research goals and sample characteristics, we made several choices regarding which variables to include in the analyses and how to code them.

Specifically, the sample is all male, all immigrant, majority recent arrivals (>5 years of U.S. residence), and young (see Table 10.1). Ancillary analyses not shown here found that including too many variables (i.e., all of the "usual suspects" in health research) resulted in: (a) multicollinearity (e.g., age and duration of residence); (b) cell sizes that were too small for meaningful interpretation; or (c) both. Many of the categorical variables required we dichotomize them in the analyses due to lack of variation in responses and/or small sample sizes. We relied on theory and prior research to drive our decisions on which factors to include based on their relevance to immigrant men's health.

Dependent Measures

The dependent variables in our analysis are health conditions and healthcare utilization. Because a primary goal of the study is to tease out their interrelationships, we also treat healthcare utilization as an independent variable in various sections of the analyses. We measure health conditions with two variables that tap subjective (self-rated health) and objective (diagnosed medical conditions) dimensions of health status (Gorman et al. 2010). Self-rated health is a dichotomous variable measuring whether an immigrant reported fair or poor health in response to the question "Would you say your health is excellent, very good, fair, or poor?" Although previous research suggests that this measure accurately predicts morbidity, disability, and mortality, studies have also indicated that the correlation between self-rated health and health outcomes may vary by ethnic group (Finch et al. 2002). We measure diagnosed medical conditions with a dichotomous variable indicating whether the respondent answered yes to one of the following questions: "Has a doctor ever told you that you have diabetes or high blood sugar" and "Has a doctor ever told you that you have high blood pressure or hypertension." This measure differs from self-reported health as it is dependent on a medical diagnosis, not the respondent's self-perceived health level. The combined responses were necessary due to small sample sizes.

We measure healthcare utilization with two variables that tap interaction with doctors in the U.S. and in the home country. The first is a dichotomous variable indicating whether the respondent answered yes to the question "Aside from any hospital stays, have you seen or talked to a medical doctor about your health, including emergency room or clinic visits in the last 12 months?" As habitually seeing a doctor can impact immigrants' current healthcare usage, we measure respondents' home country healthcare utilization as a binary variable, based on the question: "Before you most recently came to the United States to live, about how often did you see a doctor? Was it more than once a year, about once a year, about once every two years, seldom, or never?" (1 = more than once a year or about once a year; 0 = about once every two years, seldom, or never).

Table 10.1 Descriptive statistics for male immigrants

	All (%)	Mexican (%)	Indian (%)	Chinese (%)	U.S. tenure ≤1 year	U.S. tenure >1 year
Health outcomes						
Fair/poor self-rated health	6.7	14.1	3.0*	11.7	5.8	7.3
Diagnosed with diabetes or hypertension	10.9	10.1	13.0	12.2	10.9	10.9
Healthcare utilization						
Seen doctor in U.S. in past year	22.8	22.3	37.8*	15.0*	3.5	35.2[+]
Seen doctor once a year or more in home country	49.8	41.0	60.0*	42.3	48.0	51.0
Need of care						
Ever confined to bed for one month or more due to health condition?	4.6	6.3	5.9	0.9*	4.3	4.7
Access to care						
Insured	51.5	51.6	73.7*	47.9	27.9	66.7[a]
Bachelor's degree[+]	41.0	6.6	82.6*	43.7*	35.8	44.3[+]
Proficient in English	59.0	43.1	89.2*	34.3*	43.8	68.9[+]
U.S. tenure ≤1 year	39.3	15.0	20.6*	53.5*	100.0	0.0
Income ≥ $44,000	49.8	34.3	67.8*	44.7*	25.1	55.1[+]
Background factors						
Married	70.0	74.5	91.4*	86.4*	62.8	74.7[+]
Obese	45.3	59.3	53.3	22.1*	33.0	53.2[+]
Smokes one + pack a day	14.4	13.8	7.9*	16.9	14.6	14.3
Drank 4 + drinks on four occasions in past 3 months	4.5	6.8	1.2*	1.4*	2.3	5.9[+]
Age in years, mean	39.2	38.3	40.0	46.5*	39.8	38.8
N	3902	428	410	214	1529	2373

NIS 2003 (n = 3902)
*Significantly different from Mexican immigrant men at $p < 0.05$
[+]Significantly different from U.S. tenure ≤1 year at $p < 0.05$

Independent Measures

The primary independent variables are ethnicity and duration of U.S. residence. We categorize respondents into one of four categories of origin: Mexico (reference), India, China, or other nationality. Duration of U.S. residence is a binary variable measuring recent immigrants (1 = U.S. tenure ≤ 1 year; 0 = U.S. >1 year). Our preliminary analyses found that immigrants living in the U.S. for a year or less are qualitatively different than their more settled counterparts. This cut-off point also allows us to gauge the relative importance of seeing a doctor in the home country for the most recent arrival. In ancillary analyses, we used unadjusted years of U.S. residence in the models, but the results did not change substantively.

The analyses also controls for other sets of factors known to influence health. *Access to healthcare* is foremost among them, and we include four variables to tap this concept, all coded to represent greater access: (1) health insurance; (2) household income; (3) education; and (4) English language proficiency. *Health insurance* measures whether the respondents reported having insurance through a private provider, Medicaid, Medicare, CHAMPUS, or CHAMPS-VA. *Household income* includes all summed wages and tips earned by the respondent and their spouse in 2003 (1 = more than $44,000; 0 = >$44,000). If the respondent reported that their spouse was more knowledgeable about household finances than themselves, their spouses were also interviewed about household earnings. Education is measured as a dichotomous variable indicating whether the respondent received a bachelor's degree or higher education (reference = less than bachelor's degree). For both income and education, we ran the models using low income and low educational attainment and found substantively similar findings. Finally, *English language proficiency* is a known obstacle to care among immigrants, thus we include a dummy variable to account for this possibility (1 = speak well or very well; 0 = all other). In the models predicting having seen a doctor in the past year, we include a measure to tap the presence of prior health conditions, or healthcare needs. It is a dichotomous variable indicating whether the respondent answered "yes" to the question "Because of a health condition, were you ever confined to bed or home one month or more?".

The analysis controls for risky health behaviors with three dichotomous measures for smoking, drinking, and body mass index. Frequent smokers is a dichotomous variable indicating that the respondent smokes more than one pack of cigarettes every day (1 = one or more pack a day; 0 = less than one pack a day). Frequent drinker is a dichotomous variable indicating that the respondent reported drinking more than four drinks on four occasions in the past three months. Obese is a dichotomous variable indicating whether the respondent's body mass index is equal to or greater than 30 (1 = BMI $\geq$ 30; 0 = BMI < 30). We also control for marital status (1 = married, 0 = unmarried), as it is known to be an important factor in promoting men's healthcare utilization (e.g., Lillard and Waite 1995). Finally, we include the respondent's age in years as a continuous variable in all models.

Results

Diversity in Immigrant Men's Health

Table 10.1 begins by examining differences in health outcomes and healthcare utilization separately by national origin and duration of U.S. residence. As seen in the table, Mexican immigrants (14.1%) are significantly more likely than Indian immigrants (3.0%) to rate their health as fair or poor but do not differ from Chinese immigrants (11.7%) in their subjective well-being. The rates for Mexican and Chinese immigrants are similar to those found for U.S.-born adult men (12%) (Schiller et al. 2011). Immigrants with more than one year of U.S. residence are more likely than newer arrivals to have poor self-rated health, though the difference is not significant (7.3% compared to 5.8% respectively). In terms of diagnosed medical conditions, there are no significant differences by ethnicity or duration of residence, with roughly 10% of each group reporting being diagnosed with either hypertension or diabetes. This is low, considering that 10% of U.S.-born males have been diagnosed with diabetes and 25% have been diagnosed with hypertension (Schiller et al. 2011).

Patterns in healthcare utilization are more variable, with Indian immigrants more likely (37.8%) and Chinese immigrants (15%) less likely than Mexican immigrants (22.3%) to have seen a U.S. doctor in the past year. Immigrants who have been in the U.S. longer are considerably more likely to have seen a doctor in the past year (35.2%) compared to those with less than one year of residence (3.5%). However, if one considers utilization practices in the home country, fewer differences exist between shorter- and longer-term immigrants (51% compared to 48% report having seen a doctor once a year or more in home country).

Our primary question aims to disentangle the relationships between health outcomes and utilization, while taking into account other factors (e.g., need, access) that might influence their connection. Looking at the need for care, there are few differences by ethnicity and duration of residence, with the exception that Chinese immigrants are significantly less likely than all other groups to have been confined to bed due to a health condition (>1% compared to roughly 6% for both Mexican and Indian immigrants). These figures are all relatively low, likely reflecting: (a) the selective nature of migration, whereby healthier individuals are more likely to immigrate; and (b) the age distribution of the sample, which is relatively young. In terms of access (or barriers) to care, Indian immigrants look the most advantaged, with higher rates of insurance coverage, educational attainment, English language proficiency, and household incomes relative to Mexican immigrants. Chinese immigrants are also more highly educated than Mexican immigrants, though they report lower levels of English language proficiency, in part because more of them are newer arrivals and older, having come as parents of citizens (Kim et al. 2011). As might be expected, longer-term U.S. residents have greater access to care than do newer arrivals. Looking lastly at background and behavioral characteristics, we see that Mexican immigrants are younger and less likely to be married than Indian and Chinese men. They also have poorer health behaviors, with higher rates of obesity (59.3%), alcohol use (6.8%), and heavy smoking (13.8% a pack or more per day). These rates are consistent with previous research on the health behaviors of foreign- and U.S.-born Hispanics (Akresh 2007, 2008). Newer immigrant arrivals look healthier than longer-term residents with respect to obesity rates and drinking behaviors but do not differ in terms of smoking.

Linking Healthcare Utilization to Health Outcomes

Because the sample is comprised entirely of immigrants—many of whom have been in the U.S. for less than one year—we compare healthcare utilization patterns in both the home country and in the U.S. and assess their relationships to self-rated health and diagnosed medical conditions (Table 10.2). Panel A focuses on immigrants with less than one year of U.S. residence and finds a significant association between healthcare utilization and diagnosed medical conditions. Men who report having seen a doctor once a year or more in their home country are significantly more likely to report being diagnosed with hypertension or diabetes (16.3% compared to 5.9%). Longer-term immigrants are also more likely to have a diagnosed condition if they saw a doctor once a year or more in their home country (12.2 and 9.6%) or if they saw a doctor at least once in the past year in the U.S. (15.1 and 8.6%). The relationship between healthcare utilization and self-rated health is weaker, with no difference in the likelihood of reporting "fair or poor" health among recent immigrants regardless of their having seen a doctor in the home country or in the U.S. Among longer-term immigrants, those who have seen a doctor in the U.S. in the past year are slightly more likely to report being in poor health (9.2% compared to 6.2%), with no significant difference based on healthcare utilization in home country (6.4% compared to 8.1%).

In Table 10.3, we use multivariate logistic regression models to explore how patterns of home country health care utilization and need and access to care are associated with U.S. healthcare utilization. Model 1 adjusts for age and shows that Indian males are twice as likely as Mexican immigrants to have seen a doctor in the U.S. in the past (OR 2.13), while Chinese immigrants do not differ from Mexican immigrants (OR 1.35). However, once we control for access and need of care (Model 2), Indian males do not differ significantly from their Mexican counterparts. The models in columns 2 and 3 indicate that the factors that explain whether or not an immigrant male see a U.S. doctor varies by duration of U.S. residence. For males who have been in the U.S. for one year or less, having health insurance is the only factor associated with increased odds of seeing a U.S. doctor, suggesting a primary barrier to healthcare utilization for newly arrived male immigrants is access. When we limit our sample to immigrants who have lived in the U.S. for more than a year, we observe a more complicated pattern. For these males, regular visits to a doctor prior to migration, being confined to bed due to a health condition, having health

Table 10.2 Percentage of immigrant men experiencing poor health outcomes by healthcare Utilization and U.S. tenure

	Panel 1: lived in US 1 year or less				Panel 2: lived in US more than 1 year			
	Seen doctor in US at least once in past year		Seen doctor once a year or more in home country		Seen doctor in US at least once in past year		Seen doctor once a year or more in home country	
	Yes	No	Yes	No	Yes	No	Yes	No
Fair/poor self-rated health	5.56	5.71	6.70	4.79	9.16**	6.22	6.41	8.13
Diagnosed with hypertension or diabetes	16.67	10.68	16.28***	5.93	15.06***	8.64	12.16*	9.60
N	450	1062	734	795	890	1427	1194	1123

NIS 2003
*$p < 0.05$, **$p < 0.01$, ***$p < 0.001$

insurance, having a bachelor's degree or higher, and a having a household income greater than or equal to $44,000 are all associated with increases of seeing a doctor in the U.S. during the past year. These findings are important, as they suggest that different factors facilitate healthcare utilization for recent arrivals compared to more established male immigrants.

In a similar vein, we use interactive models to identify which factors are related to Mexican and Indian male healthcare utilization (columns 4 and 5). The sample size for Chinese males was too small for similar analyses. When we limit the sample to Mexican males, results indicate that being insured and English language proficiency are associated with increased odds of visiting a doctor in the U.S., while living in the U.S. for one year or less is associated with decreased odds of U.S. healthcare utilization. In comparison, when we limit the sample to Indian males, our findings suggest that different factors predict U.S. healthcare utilization. Similar to Mexican males, those with insurance have significantly increased odds and recent immigrants have significantly reduced odds of seeing a doctor in the U.S. However, important differences also exist. First, Indian males who annually visited doctors prior to migration have significantly higher odds of using healthcare in the U.S. Second, having ever been confined to bed due to sickness is associated with increased odds of seeing a U.S. doctor for Indian males, which likely reflects the fact that Indian males are more likely than Mexican males to work in occupations that allow for sick days. For instance, the majority of employed Mexican immigrants work in production or transportation (29%) or the service industry (25%) (Grieco and Ray 2004), while the majority of Indian males are employed in professional occupations such as the IT sector (29%) and management, business, or finance (21%) (Whatley and Batalova 2012). English language proficiency has no significant impact on U.S. healthcare utilization patterns among Indian males, which contrasts with the findings for Mexican men. This is likely due to the fact that

Table 10.3 Odds ratios of seeing a doctor in U.S. within the past year[a]

Nationality	All	U.S. tenure ≤1 year	U.S. tenure >1 year	Mexican	Indian
Indian	1.26 (0.18)	2.36 (0.95)	1.19 (0.18)	–	–
Chinese	0.84 (0.25)	1.71 (0.93)	0.78 (0.27)	–	–
Other regions	1.20 (0.13)	2.31 (0.74)	1.15 (0.13)	–	–
Healthcare utilization					
Saw doctor once a year or more in home country	1.31** (0.09)	1.29 (0.29)	1.34** (0.09)	0.93 (0.26)	1.83* (0.25)
Need of care					
Ever confined to bed for one month or more due to a health condition?	2.08*** (0.19)	1.29 (0.62)	2.23*** (0.20)	1.04 (0.49)	5.06** (0.60)
Access to care					
Insured	2.72*** (0.11)	2.63*** (0.29)	2.73*** (0.11)	2.01* (0.27)	5.99*** (0.53)
Bachelor's degree or greater	1.19 (0.11)	0.84 (0.30)	1.26* (0.11)	0.51 (0.52)	2.22 (0.61)
English proficiency	1.17 (0.11)	1.27 (0.30)	1.14 (0.12)	2.48*** (0.27)	3.81 (1.18)
U.S. tenure ≤1 year	0.10*** (0.15)			0.08* (1.03)	0.19* (0.68)
High income (≥ $44,000)	1.24* (0.10)	1.11 (0.31)	1.24* (0.10)	1.11 (0.26)	1.47 (0.38)
Married	1.02 (0.10)	1.00 (0.30)	1.03 (0.11)	1.63 (0.31)	1.15 (0.44)
R-squared	0.20	0.01	0.09	0.11	0.25
n	3902	1529	2373	428	410

Data NIS 2003
[a]All models control for age
$*p < 0.05$, $**p < 0.01$, $***p < 0.001$

there is little variation in English ability among Indian males and most have high levels of English proficiency (Whatley and Batalova 2012).

Tables 10.4 and 10.5 next examine whether and how these healthcare utilization patterns translate into differential health outcomes among male immigrants. Table 10.4 focuses on self-rated health, and Table 10.5 looks at diagnosed medical conditions. Both tables assess adjusted and unadjusted differences among all male immigrants (columns 1–2), as well as variation by duration of U.S. residence (columns 3–4) and ethnicity (columns 5–6). Model 1 finds that all national origin groups report better self-rated health than Mexican immigrants. In the fully adjusted

Table 10.4 Odds ratios predicting fair/poor health[a]

	Model 1	Model 2	U.S. tenure ≤1 year	U.S. tenure >1 year	Mexican	Indian
Nationality (Mexican)						
Indian	0.17*** (0.34)	0.47* (0.35)	0.22* (0.71)	0.76 (0.42)		
Chinese	0.51* (0.28)	0.85 (0.29)	1.03 (0.43)	0.71 (0.46)		
Others	0.38*** (0.18)	0.60** (0.18)	0.62 (0.36)	0.65* (0.20)		
Healthcare utilization						
Saw doctor in U.S. in past year		2.00*** (0.17)	1.30 (0.68)	2.08*** (0.18)	2.55* (0.39)	1.67 (0.80)
Saw doctor at least once a year in home country		1.08 (0.14)	1.32 (0.25)	0.97 (0.17)	1.16 (0.32)	1.64 (0.68)
Need of care						
Ever confined to bed for one month or more due to health?		2.35*** (0.25)	2.92* (0.45)	2.05* (0.31)	2.23 (0.54)	8.85** (0.78)
Access to care						
Insured		1.13 (0.15)	0.84 (0.29)	1.27 (0.19)	0.81 (0.35)	3.49 (1.02)
Bachelor's degree+		0.66* (0.18)	1.14 (0.32)	0.53** (0.24)	0.41 (1.07)	0.89 (1.05)
English proficiency		0.37*** (0.17)	0.46* (0.32)	0.31*** (0.21)	0.49+ (0.40)	0.84 (1.38)
U.S. tenure ≤1 year		0.57*** (0.17)	– –	– –	0.67 (0.44)	0.46 (1.06)
Income ≥ $44,000		0.65** (0.17)	0.72 (0.34)	0.64* (0.19)	0.62 (0.39)	0.20+ (0.83)
n	3902	3902	1529	2373	428	410

NIS 2003
[a]All models control for age, marital status, and health behaviors
+$p < 0.10$, *$p < 0.05$, **$p < 0.01$, ***$p < 0.001$

model, Indian and other national-origin immigrants maintain their advantage, while Chinese immigrants look more similar to their Mexican counterparts (OR 0.84) net of controls for healthcare utilization, need and access to care, and background factors. We also find that seeing a doctor in the U.S. during the past year and need of care increase the odds of reporting poor health two-fold (OR 2.00 and 2.35, respectively). Conversely, factors related to access to care (education, language, income, duration of U.S. residence) are all associated with significantly lower odds of reporting fair/poor health. In columns 3 and 4, we use interactive models based on U.S. duration and find significant ethnic differences in self-rated health. Among

Table 10.5 Odds ratios predicting diagnosed diabetes/hypertension[a]

	Model 1	Model 2	U.S. tenure ≤1 year	U.S. tenure ≥1 year	Mexican	Indian
Nationality (Mexican)						
Indian	1.54 (0.24)	1.34 (0.24)	1.23 (0.44)	1.54 (0.30)		
Chinese	0.98 (0.29)	0.88 (0.28)	1.33 (0.41)	0.43 (0.52)		
Others	1.34 (0.19)	1.25 (0.18)	1.15 (0.34)	1.35 (0.22)		
Healthcare utilization						
Saw doctor in U.S. in past year		1.96*** (0.14)	1.96 (0.44)	2.02*** (0.15)	1.45 (0.50)	0.68 (0.41)
Saw doctor at least once a year in home country		1.69*** (0.12)	3.13*** (0.20)	1.16 (0.15)	2.99** (0.39)	2.30* (0.36)
Need of care						
Ever confined to bed for one month or more due to health?		0.92 (0.25)	1.22 (0.41)	0.69 (0.34)	0.97 (0.76)	3.29* (0.54)
Access to care						
Insured		1.06 (0.13)	0.93 (0.21)	1.16 (0.17)	0.71 (0.42)	2.15 (0.49)
Bachelor's degree[+]		0.98 (0.13)	1.04 (0.21)	1.01 (0.18)	1.38 (0.75)	0.49 (0.49)
English proficiency		0.83 (0.14)	1.14 (0.21)	0.66 (0.18)	0.60 (0.51)	1.00 (0.62)
U.S. tenure ≤1 year		1.004 (0.14)	– –	– –	0.88 (0.50)	0.85 (0.50)
Income ≥ \$44,000		0.87 (0.13)	0.91 (0.22)	0.92 (0.16)	1.02 (0.45)	0.88 (0.44)
n		3902	1529	2373	428	410

NIS 2003
[a]All models control for age, marital status, and health behaviors
*$p < 0.05$, ** $p < 0.01$, *** $p < 0.001$

newly-arrived immigrants, Indians have significantly reduced odds of reporting fair/poor health relative to Mexican immigrants, while again Chinese males do not differ from them (OR 1.03). Having been confined to bed due to a health condition is associated with higher odds of reporting poor health for both short- and long-term residents (OR 2.92 and 2.05, respectively), while being proficient in English lowers the likelihood of reporting poor health (OR 0.46 and 0.31, respectively). Among longer-term immigrants, healthcare utilization (e.g., seeing a doctor in the U.S. within the past year) is associated with a significantly increased odds of reporting fair/poor health (OR 2.08), while access to care (e.g., having a bachelor's degree or more, having high income) are both associated with significantly reduced odds of reporting fair/poor health.

Findings from our interactive models for Mexican and Indian males (columns 5–6) suggest that unique factors are related to reporting fair/poor health for each group. When we limit our sample to Mexican males, seeing a doctor in the U.S. during the past year is associated with significantly increased odds of reporting fair/poor health, and English proficiency is associated with significantly decreased odds of fair/poor health. Our findings are quite different when we limit our sample to Indians males. In contrast to Mexican immigrants, healthcare utilization is not related to reporting fair/poor health, nor is English language proficiency. But being confined to bed for a month or more is associated with a significant increase in the odds of reporting fair/poor health, while having higher income is associated with significantly decreased odds of reporting fair/poor health. Importantly, results from these two models suggest that the factors associated with poor self-rated health among male immigrants varies by ethnicity, and to a slightly lesser extent, by duration of U.S. residence.

In contrast, Table 10.5 finds fewer ethnic differences in diagnosed medical conditions and greater consistency in the association to healthcare utilization across national origin and duration of residence groups. As seen in models 1 and 2, Indian, Chinese, and other national-origin immigrants do not differ from Mexican immigrants in their likelihood of being diagnosed with diabetes or hypertension, which is particularly interesting given the differences found for self-rated health. The table also shows that healthcare utilization (in the U.S. and home country) is a primary factor linked to diagnoses. However, the strength of the relationship varies by duration of U.S. residence. For newer immigrants, what matters most is whether or not they saw a doctor annually in their home country (OR 3.13), while longer-term residents are more affected by having seen a doctor in the U.S. (OR 2.02). For both Mexican and Indian immigrants, seeing a doctor in one's home country is associated with higher odds of receiving a diagnosis (OR 2.99 and 2.30, respectively). Need of care, as defined by having ever been confined to a bed for a month or more due to illness, is also associated with a higher odds of being diagnosed with diabetes or hypertension for Indian immigrants (OR 3.29) but not Mexican (OR 0.97).

Discussion and Conclusion

Research on immigrant health disparities often focuses on the unequal access of minority groups to healthcare but less is known about the role of healthcare utilization, or the degree to which individuals interact with the healthcare system. Utilization is an important concept because many health conditions require a medical diagnosis for appropriate treatment, such as hypertension or diabetes. While utilization and access are related—access can clear the path to use—they are not the same. Indeed, recent studies indicate that some U.S. groups are more likely than others to come in contact with the healthcare system regardless of access (Read and Reynolds 2012). Thus, understanding differences in utilization behaviors is critical for addressing population health disparities.

This paper contributes to this line of inquiry by isolating a population known to have lower levels of utilization in the U.S.—immigrant men—and examining variation in their health profiles by ethnicity and duration of U.S. residence. The analysis finds that the factors shaping healthcare utilization behaviors and health outcomes among immigrant men are both similar to and different from each other across population sub-groups. They are similar in that social position matters, with the most socioeconomically advantaged having greater access to and utilization of care. Indian immigrants are highly selected on education and income and have health profiles commensurate with their status. Mexican and Chinese immigrant men are less advantaged on all fronts and report worse self-rated health than their Indian counterparts. The findings are also similar in that utilization of care (seeing a doctor in the U.S. or home country) is tied to diagnosed health conditions across groups. In other words, seeing a doctor matters for diseases that require diagnoses.

Social position also helps explain the differences that emerge across groups. Mexican and Indian immigrants are equally likely to report the need for care (bed days due to an illness), but this need is more strongly linked to Indian men's health behaviors and outcomes than Mexican men's (Tables 10.3, 10.4 and 10.5). This may be due to the fact that Mexican males are much more likely to work in service and labor industries, while Indian males are concentrated in more highly paid professional sectors where there are fewer obstacles to healthcare utilization and where paid sick leave is more common (Grieco and Ray 2004; Whatley and Batalova 2012). Differences in social class may also contribute to the conflicting patterns we find across medical conditions (self-rated health vs. diagnosed diabetes and hypertension). Specifically, Mexican immigrant men are significantly more likely than Indian men to rate their health as fair/poor but are no less likely to be diagnosed with diabetes or hypertension. A lack of economic mobility coupled with poor English language skills and work-related injuries among Mexican males may lead them to feel less healthy (and rate their health as poor), while at the same time, restricts their access to and interaction with healthcare professionals where they might be diagnosed with a medical condition.

The fact that the patterns for self-rated health differ from those for diagnosed medical conditions highlights the multi-dimensional nature of health and the unique situation of immigrant men relative to their U.S.-born counterparts. The self-rated health of certain male immigrants (i.e., Chinese and Mexican) is nearly identical to that of U.S.-born men, with around 12% of both groups reporting fair or poor health, while only 3% of Indian males report fair or poor self-rated health (Schiller et al. 2011). In stark contrast, >13% of immigrants in our sample reported having been diagnosed with *either* hypertension or diabetes compared to 25% of U.S.-born men being diagnosed with hypertension and 10% diagnosed with diabetes (Schiller et al. 2011). Medical diagnoses require interaction with healthcare professionals, and U.S.-born men are considerably more likely to have seen a doctor in the past year compared to immigrants—73% compared to only 23% of immigrants

(Table 10.1). The gap in utilization remains sizable even for longer-term residents (35% saw a doctor in the past year).

Healthcare utilization also plays a role in health disparities among immigrants in our sample but cannot explain entirely why Indian immigrant men rate their health as better than Mexican and Chinese men but do not differ from them in their likelihood of being diagnosed with a medical condition. There are several plausible explanations for these patterns. First, the gap in self-rated health may stem from their unequal social locations: Chinese immigrants in our sample are older, have low levels of English language proficiency, and the majority are new arrivals (53.5% have been in the U.S. for >1 year), all of which might drive down their perceived health. Mexican immigrants are likewise disadvantaged, with the lowest levels of education and income of any group. The gap in self-rated health could also reflect different cultural interpretations of health (Finch et al. 2002), although this is hard to verify with these data and somewhat less plausible given that the rates of reporting poor health for Mexican and Chinese men mirror those found in the general population and other immigrant groups (Read and Gorman). The lack of national-origin differences in diagnosed medical conditions could also be driven by the age distribution of our sample. The mean age is 40 years or less for all groups except Chinese immigrants (46.5), with commensurate rates of diabetes/hypertension which are quite low relative the U.S. population in general (>13% compared to at least 27.1% of U.S.-born males) (Read and Reynolds 2012).

As with all studies of this type, the findings are not without limitations. The data are based on self-reports which introduces the possibility of response bias, though there is no evidence to suggest that any potential bias would be non-randomly distributed across immigrant groups. In addition, the sample is relatively young and health conditions that afflict immigrants may be better captured in an older population. We attempted to examine this possibility by assessing older immigrants in isolation from their younger counterparts but cell sizes were too small for meaningful analyses. However, the strengths of this study balance these limitations and offer new insight into gendered health disparities by examining behaviors and outcomes among men. There is growing evidence of how migration experiences shape the differential health trajectories of immigrant women relative to men, but less attention has focused on similarities and differences among immigrant men.

Overall, our findings have broader research and policy implications for understanding and improving the health of immigrant men. The harmful effects of social disadvantage on both mental and physical health are well-established (e.g., Read and Gorman 2010), and we likewise find that social location matters for immigrant men's well-being. This is particularly true in terms of self-rated health—a measure known to be highly predictive of morbidity and mortality. As such, policy levers aimed at improving health outcomes in immigrant communities should focus on removing obstacles to healthcare that are tied to social disadvantage. Some obstacles may be harder to tackle, such as equalizing economic opportunities among immigrants, but others could be easier to address, such as removing language barriers that reduce an immigrant's ability to access and utilize care. Irrespective of national origin, immigrants need to be able to understand and communicate in their native language or in English to navigate an increasingly-complicated U.S. healthcare system. Indeed, the inclusion of a new Behavioral Section on the 2015 Medical College Admissions Test (MCAT) reflects a growing recognition that healthcare professionals need a better understanding of patient diversity when providing care. Clearing the path to effective communication will become increasingly critical as the U.S.'s immigrant population continues to grow and diversify.

References

Akresh, I. R. (2007). Dietary assimilation and health among Hispanic immigrants to the United States. *Journal of Health and Social Behavior, 48*, 404–417.
Akresh, I. R. (2008). Overweight and obesity among foreign-born and US-born Hispanics. *Biodemography and Social Biology, 54*, 183–199.
Akresh, I. R., & Frank, R. (2008). Health selection among new immigrants. *American Journal of Public Health, 98*, 1–7.
Antecol, H., & Bedard, K. (2006). Unhealthy assimilation: Why do immigrants converge to American health status levels? *Demography, 43*, 337–360.
Barringer, H., & Kassebaum, G. (1989). Asian Indians as a minority in the United States: The effect of education, occupations, and gender on income. *Sociological Perspectives, 32*, 501–520.
Curran, S. R., Shafer, S., Donato, K. M., & Garip, F. (2006). Mapping gender and migration in sociological scholarship: Is it segregation or integration? *International Migration Review, 40*, 199–223.
Feliciano, C. (2006). *Unequal origins: Immigrant selection and the education of the second generation*. New York: LFC Scholarly Publishing.
Finch, B. K., Hummer, R. A., Reindl, M., & Vega, W. A. (2002). The validity of self-rated health among Latino(a)s. *American Journal of Epidemiology, 8*, 755–759.
Gorman, B., Read, J. G., & Krueger, P. (2010). Gender, acculturation and health among Mexican American immigrants. *Journal of Health and Social Behavior, 8*, 755–759.
Grieco, E., & Ray, B. (2004). *Mexican immigrants in the U.S. labor force*. Washington, D.C.: Migration Policy Institute.
Hao, L. (2007). *Color lines, country lines: Race, immigration, and wealth stratification in America*. New York: Russell Sage Foundation.
Hummer, R. A., Biegler, M., DeTurk, P. B., Douglas Forbes, W., Frisbie, P., Hong, Y., et al. (1999). Race/ethnicity, nativity, and infant mortality in the United States. *Social Forces, 77*, 1083–1118.
Kim, G., Worley, C. B., Allen, R. S., Vinson, L., Crowther, M. R., Parmelee, P., et al. (2011). Vulnerability of older Latino and Asian immigrant with limited English proficiency. *Journal of the American Geriatrics Society, 59*, 1246–1252.
Lan, S. (2012). *Diaspora and class consciousness: Chinese immigrant workers in multiracial Chicago*. New York: Routledge.
Lillard, L. A., & Waite, L. J. (1995). 'Til death do us part': Marital disruption and mortality. *American Journal of Sociology, 100*, 1131–1156.
Marmot, M. G., & Leonard Syme, S. (1976). Acculturation and coronary heart disease in Japanese-Americans. *American Journal of Epidemiology, 104*, 225–247.
Massey, D. (2010). Immigration statistics for the twenty-first century. *The Annals of the American Academy of Political and Social Science, 631*, 124–140.

McCabe, K. (2012). *Chinese immigrants in the United States*. Washington, D.C.: Migration Information Source.

O'Brian, R., Hunt, K., & Hart, G. (2005). 'It's caveman stuff, but that is to a certain extent how guys still operate': Men's accounts of masculinity and help seeking. *Social Science and Medicine, 61*, 503–516.

Palloni, A., & Arias, E. (2004). Paradox lost: Explaining the Hispanic adult mortality advantage. *Demography, 41*, 385–415.

Parrado, E. A., & Flippen, C. A. (2005). Migration and gender among Mexican women. *American Sociological Review, 70*, 606–632.

Pew Research Center. (2012). The rise of Asian Americans. In Pew Research Center (Ed.), *Social & demographic trends*.

Read, J. G., & Cohen, P. N. (2007). One size fits all? Explaining U.S.-born and Immigrant women's employment across twelve ethnic groups. *Social Forces, 85*, 1713–1734.

Read, J. G., & Emerson, M. O. (2005). Racial context of origin, black immigration, and U.S. Black/White health disparity. *Social Forces, 84*, 183–201.

Read, J. G., & Gorman, B. (2006). Gender inequalities in U.S. adult health: The interplay of race and ethnicity. *Social Science and Medicine, 62*, 1045–1065.

Read, J. G., & Gorman, B. (2010). Gender and U.S. health inequality. *Annual Review of Sociology 36*, (371–386).

Read, J. G., & Oselin, S. (2008). Gender and the education-employment paradox in ethnic and religious contexts: The case of Arab Americans. *American Sociological Review, 73*, 296–313.

Read, J. G., & Reynolds, M. M. (2012). Gender differences in immigrant health: The case of Mexican and middle eastern immigrants. *Journal of Health and Social Behavior, 53*, 99–123.

Rogers, R. G., Hummer, R. A., & Nam, C. B. (2000). *Living and dying in the USA: Behavioral, health, and social differentials of adult mortality*. San Diego, CA: Academic Press.

Schiller, J. S., Lucas, J. W., & Peregoy, A. (2011). Summary health statistics for U.S. adults: National Health Interview Survey. In *Vital health stat*. National Center for Health Statistics.

Singh, G. K., & Hiatt, R. (2006). Trends and disparities in socioeconomic and behavioural characteristics, life expectancy, and cause-specific mortality of native-born and foreign-born populations in the United States. *International Journal of Epidemiology, 35*, 903–919.

Stoney, S., & Batalova, J. (2013). *Mexican immigrants in the United States*. Washington, D.C.: Migration Policy Institute.

Treas, J. (2008). Transnational older adults and their families. *Family Relations, 57*, 468–478.

Walters, N. P., & Trevelyan, E. N. (2011). The newly arrived foreign-born population of the United States: 2010. In *American Community Survey Briefs*. Washington, D.C.: U.S. Census.

Whatley, M., & Batalova, J. (2012). *Indian immigrants in the United States*. Washington, D.C.: Migration Policy Institute.

Zhou, M. (2009). *Contemporary Chinese America: Immigration, ethnicity, and community transformation*. Philadelphia, PA: Temple University Press.

Chapter 11
Activity Limitation Disparities by Sexual Minority Status, Gender, and Union Status

Russell Spiker, Corinne Reczek and Hui Liu

Introduction

Sexual minorities are at increased risk of worse health than their heterosexual counterparts (Meyer 2003; Institute of Medicine 2011). This has been shown for a wide range of health outcomes, but previous research has failed to examine the relationship between sexual minority status and activity limitations and disability—broadly defined as health conditions that limit a person's physical or social activities. The Centers for Disease Control (CDC 2011), Institutes of Medicine (IOM 2011), and U.S. Department of Health and Human Services (DHHS 2011) all identify issues pertaining to sexual minority health disparities as target areas for public health and social science research.

Research suggests that sexual minority status as a direct risk factor for activity limitations (Cochran and Mays 2007; Conron et al. 2010; Fredriksen-Goldsen et al. 2012), wherein sexual minorities experience a disparity that places them at higher risk of limitations than heterosexuals at the population level. Given that sexual minority and disabled populations are both underserved groups that experience health disparities relative to the general population (DHHS 2011; IOM 2011), studies need to illuminate the association between the two to encourage future research and interventions to target and reduce health inequalities.

R. Spiker (✉)
Department of Sociology, University of Cincinnati, 1011 Crosley,
Tower Cincinnati, OH 45221-0378, USA
e-mail: spikerrl@mail.uc.edu

C. Reczek
Department of Sociology, The Ohio State University, 238 Townsend Hall,
1885 Neil Avenue Mall, Columbus, OH 43210-1222, USA

H. Liu
Department of Sociology, Michigan State University, 316 Berkeley Hall,
East Lansing, MI 48824, USA

Additionally, it is important to note that sexual minorities are not a monolithic population and may experience different health risks by factors such as union status and gender, which are also associated with activity limitations risk. Relationship status (i.e., married, unmarried cohabiting, and single) appears to influence activity limitation risk in the general population (Liu and Zhang 2013; Goldman et al. 1995; Hughes and Waite 2009), yet we are aware of no sexual minority health research that explicitly investigates whether this effect extends to the sexual minority population. Moreover, gender seems to place men at a disadvantage in the general population regarding activity limitations risk (Zheng and George 2012), but studies consistently report that sexual minority women experience greater activity limitations risk than heterosexual women (Cochran and Mays 2007; Fredriksen-Goldsen et al. 2012). Additionally, gender and union status are related to health together, with men experiencing a marital health boost that women do not (Waite 1995; Kiecolt-Glaser and Newton 2001). We are aware of no study that investigates the activity limitations risk of sexual minorities by gender and union status together; the present study addresses the complex interplay of those factors in determining activity limitations risk. We do so in order to demonstrate how these three factors work together to place some minority populations at heightened disadvantage.

Background

Research reveals that sexual minority status is a direct risk for disability (Cochran and Mays 2007; Fredriksen-Goldsen et al. 2012). A handful of studies address activity limitations among sexual minorities, demonstrating that sexual minority status itself may operate as a risk factor for activity limitations. According to one study using the Washington Behavioral Risk Factor Surveillance Survey (Fredriksen-Goldsen et al. 2012) and another using the California Quality of Life Survey (Cochran and Mays 2007), sexual minority status is a direct risk factor for activity limitations. In the Massachusetts Behavioral Risk Factor Surveillance Survey, sexual minorities as a whole reported higher rates of activity limitations than heterosexuals (Conron et al. 2010). Data from the American Community Survey (ACS) suggests that same-sex partnered women are more likely than either individuals in different-sex married couples or men in same-sex couples to report a disability (Siordia 2014). These studies suggest that sexual minority status is a risk factor for activity limitations.

The most likely mechanism for this disadvantage is sexual minority stress: the unique stress experienced by sexual minority individuals in social contexts that privilege heterosexuality (Meyer 2003; Hatzenbuehler 2009). Sexual minority stress theory (Meyer 2003) proposes that the psychological consequences of sexual minority status can lead to both physical and mental health disadvantages relative to heterosexuals.

One specific mechanism through which sexual minority stress may lead to activity limitations is through psychological distress, which previous research suggests is a cause of activity limitations (Manninen et al. 1997; Strine et al. 2004). One 10-year longitudinal study from Finland reports that psychological distress predicts later disability (Manninen et al. 1997), while an American study (Strine et al. 2004) suggests that 5.1% of Americans who report a disability identify its primary cause as psychological. One study using the California Quality of Life Survey (Cochran and Mays 2007) suggests that psychological distress plays a key role in sexual minorities' experiences of activity limitations. Accordingly, we test psychological distress as a potential mechanism through which sexual minority stress may affect the risk of activity limitations.

However, although the sexual minority population experiences a shared context of stigma it is important to acknowledge that it is not monolithic, but varies across many different social statuses such as gender and union status (IOM 2011); these factors are also associated with activity limitations risk (Liu and Zhang 2013; Hughes and Waite 2009; Zheng and George 2012). Overall research on sexual minority populations has been only limited work to parse out the distribution of activity limitations risk across sexual minority status and other social factors associated with activity limitations. We are aware of no study that investigates activity limitations risk of sexual minorities by gender and union status together. This is the focus of the present study. Below, we outline how the association of sexuality on activity limitations risk is influenced by union status and gender, in tandem.

Union Status. Union status may play a key role in sexual minority inequalities. Union status appears to influence limitations in the general population (Liu and Zhang 2013; Goldman et al. 1995; Hughes and Waite 2009), but data limitations have stunted the available knowledge on how union status is associated with activity limitations risk among sexual minorities. In studies using the American Community Survey (ACS) (e.g. Siordia 2014), researchers are only able to study how same-sex couples differ from different-sex couples because single sexual minorities cannot be identified. Other studies (Cochran and Mays 2007; Conron et al. 2010; Fredriksen-Goldsen et al. 2012) include controls for whether the respondent is partnered, but union status is not the focus of the analysis and is thus not analyzed. Thus, despite evidence from the general population that union status may play a role in activity limitations, we know little about whether union status affects the distribution of activity limitations risk among sexual minorities.

Although relatively few studies address the association of union status on activity limitations, it is known that social support (Umberson 1987, 1992) and marital socioeconomic resources (Hughes and Waite 2009; Waite 1995) both affect overall health, with the straight married experiencing the largest advantage. Union status likely affects the risk of activity limitations through both of these mechanisms. For example, social support may buffer against psychological stress-related limitations and socioeconomic resources accrued through partnerships may help provide access to healthcare, thereby reducing the chance that an individual will experience limitations. According Hughes and Waite (2009), marital disruption increases the probability that an individual will face later psychological and physical problems, including activity limitations. This further suggests that union status plays a role in activity limitations risk, though the exact mechanisms and how they vary across sexuality remain unknown. Including analytical controls for socioeconomic resources will demonstrate whether potential union status advantages are due to socioeconomic advantage or whether other factors such as social support play a role.

Gender. There is also evidence that activity limitations risk for both sexual minorities and the general population varies by gender. In the general population, Census estimates suggest that women have slightly higher age-adjusted disability rates (18.3 ± 0.4) compared to men (17.6 ± 0.4) (Bruit 2012), but this difference reverses once socioeconomic resources are controlled (Zheng and George 2012). Regarding sexual minority status and gender, one study from Washington State suggests that lesbians, bisexual women, and bisexual men experience higher odds of activity limitations compared to their heterosexual counterparts even after accounting for risk factors; gay men do not differ from heterosexual men after accounting for other risk factors (Fredriksen-Goldsen et al. 2012). Population-level data from California suggests that sexual minority women are more likely than heterosexual women to receive disability income and bisexual women are more likely than heterosexual women to report a functional limitation (Cochran and Mays 2007). Data from the ACS suggests that same-sex partnered women are more likely than either individuals in different-sex married couples or men in same-sex couples to report a disability (Siordia 2014). Overall, gender appears to differentiate the activity limitation risk of sexual minority men from sexual minority women, with the population of sexual minority women experiencing a higher rate of activity limitations . In addition to the association of sexuality with union status and gender regarding activity limitations risk, research also shows that marriage and partnerships are more protective of men's health than of women's health (Kiecolt-Glaser and Newton 2001; Waite 1995). This suggests that differences across gender and union status are essential components of an investigation regarding the association of sexual minority status and activity limitations.

One gendered mechanism through which sexual minority status potentially affects the risk of activity limitations is obesity and overweight status. A large body of research suggests that lesbian and bisexual women have a higher population-level average BMI than heterosexual women (Boehmer et al. 2007; Case et al. 2004; Conron et al. 2010), suggesting obesity may play some role in sexual minority women's higher rates of activity limitations. Coupled with controls for psychological distress, which is higher among sexual minorities than among the heterosexual population (Bostwick et al. 2010; Cochran et al. 2003), BMI explains a potential pathway through which sexual minority status affects activity limitations risk.

The present study uses data available from the 2013 National Health Interview Survey to provide the first population-level look at how sexual minority status, union status, and gender interplay in the creation of activity limitations disparities. A focus on activity limitations allows us to speak to broader health inequalities in the sexual minority population, identifying those sexual minorities at greatest risk. Results from this study will contribute to identifying and targeting the social environmental risk factors associated with increased risk of activity limitations, allowing researchers and policymakers to better address the needs of disadvantaged populations.

Method

Data come from the 2013 to 2014 Integrated Health Interview Series (Minnesota Population Center 2015), which is a publicly distributed version of the NHIS that combines all NHIS survey files. The NHIS is a cross-sectional household study conducted by the National Center for Health Statistics; it is representative of the non-institutionalized US population. We include respondents aged 18 to 65 who have no missing values for all variables. The final analytic sample (N = 48,882) includes 346 lesbian/gay partnered respondents, 551 are lesbian/gay never married respondents, and 84 are lesbian and gay previously married respondents.

Measures

Relationship Status. Relationship status was constructed from the sexual orientation of the respondents combined with their union status. The 2013 wave of the NHIS was the first to include questions on sexual identity, though responses for men and women differ slightly. Men and women were asked, "Which of the following best represents how you think of yourself?" but the responses differed slightly. Women's options were: "Lesbian or gay," "Straight, that is, not lesbian or gay," "Bisexual," "Something else," and "I don't know the answer." Men's answer choices did not include "lesbian" in the responses. The NHIS also provided a marital status variable that includes "living with partner," which enabled the identification of cohabiting, married, and previously married single, and never married single individuals (i.e. "union status"). Union status and sexual minority status were combined to produce the "relationship status" categories: straight married (reference), straight cohabiting, straight never married, straight previously married, lesbian/gay partnered, lesbian/gay never married, and lesbian/gay previously married. Lesbian/gay "married" and "living with partner" groups were combined to achieve an adequate sample size.

Activity Limitations. The dependent variable measures whether the respondent has any activity limitations s, defined in the IHIS as needing assistance with getting into a bath, getting into or out of beds/chairs, dressing, eating, using the toilet, walking, getting around the home, going outside, and remembering. Activity limitation is a dichotomous variable (0 = no activity limitations, 1 = has activity limitations). The study uses activity limitations as the dependent variable for comparability with previous research on sexual minority status and disability using the NHIS (Conron et al. 2010) and because it captures a number of mental health-related questions that other variables such as functional limitations do not capture.

Socioeconomic Covariates. Three measures of SES were included in the study to account for potential confounding due to socioeconomic differences: income-to-needs (0 = less than 100% of federal poverty level, 1 = 100–199%, 2 = 200–399%, 3 = 400% and greater), insurance status (0 = uninsured during the past 12 months, 1 = covered by at least one public or private insurance plan during the past 12 months), and employment status (employed [reference]; employed, but not at work; unemployed; not in labor force). These controls are intended to account for the population-level differences in socioeconomic resources across union status, gender, and sexual orientation to account for spurious correlations with activity limitations.

Psychological Distress. To measure psychological distress, we used the Kessler-6 (K6) Psychological Distress Scale. Kessler et al. (2002) developed the scale to measure non-specific psychological distress in the general population. It is composed of six questions, which ask, "In the past 30 days, about how often did you feel..." (1) "...depressed," (2) "...hopeless," (3) "...restless or fidgety," (4) "...so depressed that nothing could cheer you up," (5) "...that everything was an effort," and (6) "...worthless." Respondents rate each question on a Likert scale (1 = None of the time; 2 = A little of the time; 3 = Some of the time; 4 = Most of the time; 5 = All of the time). To compose the scale, the answers to each question are summed up to produce a scale that ranges from 0 (respondent replies "None of the time" to all six questions) to 30 (respondent replies "All of the time" to all six questions). In our sample, K6 ranged from 0 to 24.

Body Mass Index (BMI). The NHIS provides a Body Mass Index scale, calculated as a person's weight in kilograms divided by the square of their height in meters. According to CDC guidelines, BMI can screen for population-level health problems but does not indicate a diagnosis of obese or overweight (Centers for Disease Control 2015). We used a continuous measure of BMI to capture weight variability among different gender, union status, and sexuality groups.

Other Demographic Covariates. Demographic covariates include race-ethnicity (non-Hispanic white [reference], non-Hispanic black, Hispanic white, Hispanic black, other), sex (0 = male, 1 = female), education (0 = less than high school, 1 = high school or equivalent, 2 = some college, 3 = Associate's degree, 4 = Bachelor's degree, 5 = graduate or professional degree), nativity status (0 = born in US or US territory, 1 = born outside US or US territory), and region (Northeast [reference], Midwest/North Central, South, West), and age in single years. Sex operates as a primary analytical variable in this model to test gender differences. Additionally, we include education as a demographic covariate because it is potentially endogenous to marriage and other socioeconomic variables (Ross and Mirowsky 2013). The other demographic controls are standard practice for quantitative health studies (e.g. Conron et al. 2010; Denney et al. 2013; Liu et al. 2013) to ensure that the racial, age, geographic, and nativity distributions of each population do not spuriously affect the association of interest. A control for survey year was added to account for any differences in samples or the distribution of activity limitations in the two years over which the data is pooled.

Analysis

Analyses were performed using survey-weighted nested binary logistic regression models. Model 1 included only relationship status with demographic and socioeconomic covariates. Model 2 added the interaction term to test whether the relationship status differences vary by gender. Model 3 added controls for psychological distress and BMI. Analyses were survey-weighted with the "svy" commands (StataCorp LP 2014) to account for the complex survey design of the NHIS. We performed additional tests comparing all relationship statuses by gender by predicting each group's probability of reporting activity limitations using Stata's "margins" command (StataCorp LP 2014) and using pairwise comparisons to identify significant differences.

To test gender differences, an interaction term was created using sex and relationship status. Sex (0 = male, 1 = female) was multiplied by each relationship status dummy variable (straight cohabiting, straight never married, straight previously married, lesbian/gay partnered, lesbian/gay never married, lesbian/gay previously married) to test whether gender differences accounted for a portion of the association of relationship status and activity limitations.

Results

Descriptive Results

Table 11.1 shows descriptive statistics for the analytic sample. Previously married lesbian/gay respondents are the most likely to report activity limitations (30.1; 95% CI = 19.6, 43.2), while straight married respondents are least likely (8.7; 95% CI = 8.3, 9.2). Straight never married individuals were less likely to report activity limitations (10.8, 95% CI = 10.1, 11.6) than lesbian/gay never married individuals (16.9, 95% CI = 12.8, 22.0). However, the lesbian/gay partnered and previously married do not significantly differ from their straight counterparts of similar relationship statuses in percentage reporting activity limitations. Additionally, lesbian/gay partnered respondents (12.4; 95% CI = 8.4, 17.9) do not differ from the straight married. Sociodemographic and socioeconomic factors such as race and education do differ between some groups: for example, the lesbian/gay partnered respondents show a general trend of more education, higher proportion insured, and higher proportion employed than the straight cohabiting. The straight married experience fewer activity limitations as a population than any other group, yet on several other measures (e.g., education, income-to-needs, insurance status) they most closely resemble the lesbian/gay partnered. See Table 11.1 for a complete list of descriptive statistics for all variables included in the model by relationship status. Additionally, psychological distress appears to be higher among lesbian/gay individuals than among straight individuals and higher among singles than among the partnered. BMI appears higher for singles, regardless of sexual orientation, and also among the married.

Regression Results

Table 11.2 shows the results from the binary logistic models estimating the odds of having any activity limitation. In Model 1, all relationship status groups experience heightened risk compared to the straight married. Additionally, women are less likely to report activity limitations than men (OR = 0.72; $p < 0.001$). Given that Model 1 accounts for socioeconomic and sociodemographic covariates, this suggests the association between relationship status and activity limitations is not explained by socioeconomic differences across sexuality, union status, and gender.

Adding the gender interaction in Model 2 reveals different patterns across relationship statuses for men and women. Men who identify as straight never married (OR = 1.67; $p < 0.001$), straight previously married (OR = 2.05; $p < 0.001$), gay never married (OR = 2.27; $p < 0.01$), or gay previously married (OR = 6.04; $p < 0.001$) experience higher odds of activity limitations compared to straight married men. Additional analyses from pairwise comparisons (Table 11.3) reveal that straight previously married, gay previously married, and gay never married men experience a higher probability of activity limitations than gay partnered men ($p < 0.05$). Straight previously married men and gay previously married men experience a higher probability of activity limitations than straight never married men ($p < 0.05$).

The interactions demonstrate the differences between men and women in relationship status differences in odds of activity limitations. To better illustrate the result of the significant interactions, Table 11.3 shows the predicted probabilities for men and women of all relationships statuses, with significant comparisons flagged for each group. Straight cohabiting women (pr = 0.06; $p < 0.05$), straight never married women (pr = 0.07; $p < 0.001$) previously married women (pr = 0.08; $p < 0.001$) and lesbian/gay partnered women (pr = 12; $p < 0.05$) experienced significantly higher predicted probability of activity limitations than straight married men. Straight married women (pr = 0.03; $p = 0.001$) experienced lower predicted odds of activity limitations compared straight married men (pr = 0.05); straight married women also experienced lower predicted probability of activity limitations than every group except gay partnered men, lesbian/gay never married women, and lesbian/gay previously married women, from which they did not differ.

Table 11.1 Descriptive statistics by Union Status

Variable	Straight married	Straight cohabitors	Straight never married	Straight previously married	Lesbian/Gay partnered	Lesbian/Gay never married	Lesbian/Gay previously married	Total
	N = 21,710	N = 3427	N = 13,238	N = 9466	N = 346	N = 551	N = 84	N = 48,822
Limitations (%)								
No limitations	91.3 (90.8, 91.7)	89 (87.6, 90.3)	89.2 (88.4, 89.9)	75.2 (73.9, 76.5)	87.6 (82.1, 91.6)	83.1 (78.0, 87.2)	69.9 (56.8, 80.4)	88.4 (88.0, 88.9)
Has limitations	8.7 (8.3, 9.2)	11.0 (9.7, 12.4)	10.8 (10.1, 11.6)	24.8 (23.5, 26.1)	12.4 (8.4, 17.9)	16.9 (12.8, 22.0)	30.1 (19.6, 43.2)	11.6 (11.1, 12.0)
Sex (%)								
Male	50.7 (49.9, 51.6)	51.2 (49.1, 53.4)	53.2 (51.9, 54.6)	40.3 (39.0, 41.7)	45.5 (38.7, 52.5)	65.6 (59.8, 70.9)	44.5 (33.1, 56.6)	50.1 (49.5, 50.8)
Female	49.3 (48.4, 50.1)	48.8 (46.6, 50.9)	46.8 (45.4, 48.1)	59.7 (58.3, 61.0)	54.5 (47.5, 61.3)	34.4 (29.1, 40.2)	55.5 (43.4, 66.9)	49.9 (49.2, 50.5)
Race (%)								
NH White	68.1 (67.1, 69.0)	60.3 (57.8, 62.8)	54.7 (53.1, 56.3)	64.5 (63.0, 65.9)	74.9 (68.1, 80.7)	58.2 (52.3, 63.8)	64.6 (49.9, 77.0)	63.7 (62.8, 64.5)
NH Black	7.4 (7.0, 7.9)	12.4 (10.9, 14.0)	19.5 (18.3, 20.7)	16 (14.8, 17.2)	5.4 (3.3, 8.9)	19.7 (15.2, 25.2)	9 (4.7, 16.5)	11.9 (11.4, 12.5)
Hispanic White	14.7 (14.0, 15.5)	19.5 (17.5, 21.7)	15.9 (14.9, 16.9)	12.5 (11.6, 13.5)	14.1 (9.4, 20.6)	10.1 (7.4, 13.7)	19.4 (10.2, 33.7)	15.1 (14.4, 15.7)
Hispanic Black	0.5 (0.4, 0.6)	1.1 (0.8, 1.6)	0.8 (0.7, 1.0)	0.5 (0.4, 0.7)	0.7 (0.2, 2.1)	1.0 (0.4, 2.5)	0.6 (0.1, 4.6)	0.6 (0.5, 0.7)
Other	9.3 (8.8, 9.9)	6.7 (5.8, 7.7)	9.1 (8.3, 10.0)	6.5 (5.9, 7.3)	4.9 (3.0, 7.9)	11.0 (7.8, 15.3)	6.3 (2.1, 17.8)	8.7 (8.3, 9.1)
Foreign born (%)								
No	77 (76.1, 77.9)	84.2 (82.3, 85.9)	86.5 (85.5, 87.3)	84.9 (83.9, 85.9)	88.9 (85.0, 91.8)	91.7 (88.6, 94.0)	90.7 (84.1, 94.8)	81.2 (80.5, 81.8)

(continued)

Table 11.1 (continued)

Variable	Straight married	Straight cohabitors	Straight never married	Straight previously married	Lesbian/Gay partnered	Lesbian/Gay never married	Lesbian/Gay previously married	Total
	N = 21,710	N = 3427	N = 13,238	N = 9466	N = 346	N = 551	N = 84	N = 48,822
Yes	23 (22.1, 23.9)	15.8 (14.1, 17.7)	13.5 (12.7, 14.5)	15.1 (14.1, 16.1)	11.1 (8.2, 15.0)	8.3 (6.0, 11.4)	9.3 (5.2, 15.9)	18.8 (18.2, 19.5)
Region (%)								
Northeast	16.6 (15.8, 17.3)	15.8 (14.0, 17.9)	18.4 (17.3, 19.6)	14.7 (13.5, 16.0)	20.1 (15.0, 26.4)	15.6 (11.3, 21.0)	7.6 (3.4, 16.1)	16.7 (16.1, 17.4)
North central/midwest	23.1 (22.1, 24.1)	25.2 (22.9, 27.7)	22.9 (21.4, 24.5)	21.9 (20.5, 23.3)	16.1 (12.3, 20.9)	21.2 (16.1, 27.5)	19.1 (10.2, 33.0)	23 (22.2, 23.8)
South	37.1 (35.9, 38.3)	35 (32.7, 37.4)	35 (33.3, 36.7)	42.2 (40.7, 43.8)	32.8 (27.3, 38.8)	37.1 (31.1, 43.6)	54.4 (39.3, 68.7)	37.1 (36.1, 38.0)
West	23.2 (22.3, 24.2)	23.9 (22.0, 26.0)	23.7 (22.3, 25.2)	21.2 (19.9, 22.6)	31 (26.0, 36.4)	26.1 (21.5, 31.2)	18.9 (11.1, 30.4)	23.2 (22.5, 24.0)
Year (%)								
	0.5 (0.5, 0.5)	0.5 (0.5, 0.5)	0.5 (0.5, 0.5)	0.5 (0.5, 0.5)	0.5 (0.5, 0.5)	0.5 (0.4, 0.5)	0.5 (0.4, 0.6)	0.5 (0.5, 0.5)
Insurance status (%)								
No	12.9 (12.3, 13.6)	29.5 (27.4, 31.7)	22.2 (21.1, 23.4)	20.2 (19.1, 21.5)	14.0 (10.2, 18.9)	20.1 (15.6, 25.5)	15.4 (7.7, 28.2)	17.5 (17.0, 18.1)
Yes	87.1 (86.4, 87.7)	70.5 (68.3, 72.6)	77.8 (76.6, 78.9)	79.8 (78.5, 80.9)	86.0 (81.1, 89.8)	79.9 (74.5, 84.4)	84.6 (71.8, 92.3)	82.5 (81.9, 83.0)
Employment status (%)								
Employed	71.4 (70.7, 72.2)	72.2 (70.4, 74.0)	63.5 (62.1, 64.8)	64.2 (62.8, 65.5)	76.8 (70.7, 82.0)	66.1 (59.4, 72.2)	58.2 (46.3, 69.2)	68.6 (67.9, 69.3)
Employed, not at work	3.0 (2.7, 3.3)	2.9 (2.3, 3.6)	1.7 (1.4, 2.0)	2.2 (1.8, 2.6)	3.5 (1.8, 6.7)	0.7 (0.3, 1.8)	0.5 (0.1, 3.6)	2.5 (2.3, 2.8)

(continued)

Table 11.1 (continued)

Variable	Straight married	Straight cohabitors	Straight never married	Straight previously married	Lesbian/Gay partnered	Lesbian/Gay never married	Lesbian/Gay previously married	Total
	N = 21,710	N = 3427	N = 13,238	N = 9466	N = 346	N = 551	N = 84	N = 48,822
Unemployed	3.3 (3.0, 3.7)	7.2 (6.2, 8.4)	10.6 (9.8, 11.5)	5.6 (5.0, 6.2)	5.2 (3.0, 8.7)	7.1 (4.8, 10.5)	10.0 (4.5, 20.7)	5.8 (5.5, 6.1)
Not in labor force	22.2 (21.6, 22.9)	17.7 (16.1, 19.3)	24.2 (22.9, 25.5)	28.1 (26.7, 29.5)	14.5 (9.9, 20.7)	26.1 (20.5, 32.6)	31.3 (21.5, 43.2)	23.1 (22.5, 23.7)
Age								
Mean	45.2	35.2	29.6	49.7	43.1	36.0	50.2	41.1
SE	0.1	0.3	0.2	0.2	0.8	0.8	1.5	0.1
Income-to-needs								
Mean	2.3	1.8	1.7	1.7	2.5	1.8	1.7	2.0
SE	0.0	0.0	0.0	0.0	0.1	0.1	0.2	0.0
Education								
Mean	2.6	2.0	2.1	2.1	3.0	2.5	2.6	2.3
SE	0.0	0.0	0.0	0.0	0.1	0.1	0.5	0.0
Psychological distress								
Mean	2.2	3.1	2.7	3.7	2.8	4.1	4.7	2.6
SE	0.0	0.1	0.1	0.1	0.3	0.3	0.7	0.0
BMI								
Mean	28.1	27.5	27	28.7	28.1	27.4	28.9	27.8
SE	0.1	0.1	0.1	0.1	0.4	0.5	0.9	0

Note 95% confidence intervals shown in parentheses below percentage point estimates for all percentages

Table 11.2 Select results from logistic regression of activity limitations on relationship status, demographic covariates, socioeconomic status, interaction terms, and health conditions (N = 48,822)

Variable	Model 1		Model 2		Model 3	
	OR	SE	OR	SE	OR	SE
Relationship status (Ref: straight married)						
Straight cohabiting	1.86***	0.17	1.70***	0.25	1.78**	0.30
Straight never married	1.92***	0.12	1.67***	0.15	1.99***	0.18
Straight previously married	2.23***	0.12	2.05***	0.17	2.03***	0.17
Lesbian/gay partnered	2.61***	0.59	1.11	0.36	0.96	0.34
Lesbian/gay never married	2.60***	0.57	2.27**	0.59	1.89*	0.60
Lesbian/gay previously married	3.00**	1.02	6.04***	2.68	4.22**	1.89
Gender (Ref: male)						
Female	0.74***	0.03	0.65***	0.04	0.64***	0.04
Interactions						
Straight cohabiting * female			1.20	0.25	0.95	0.22
Straight never married * female			1.32*	0.15	1.12	0.14
Different sex previously married * female			1.18	0.12	1.03	0.11
Lesbian/gay partnered * female			3.95**	1.81	4.19**	2.08
Lesbian/gay never married * female			1.40	0.65	1.47	0.72
Lesbian/gay previously married * female			0.23*	0.13	0.28*	0.17
Health conditions						
Psychological distress					1.17***	0.01
BMI					1.03***	0.00

Note $*p < (0.05)$, $**p < 0.01$, $***p < 0.001$
Regression models include controls for race, region, education, survey year, and age. Model 2 adds income-to-needs ratio, insurance status, and employment status as socioeconomic controls

Model 3 adds psychological distress and BMI as controls to test whether they explain the significant associations observed in Model 2. Table 11.2 shows that these controls had little effect on the main effects and interaction affects, with a few notable exceptions. First, the model shows reduced estimates for gay previously married men (OR = 2.27; $p < 0.01$ to OR = 1.89; $p < 0.05$) and gay never married men (OR = 6.04; $p < 0.001$ to OR = 4.22; $p < 0.01$). Additionally, the interaction of straight never married with female was reduced to nonsignificance. The predicted probabilities tell a clearer story, with several differences explained.

Among men, straight married men are no longer different from gay never married or gay previously married men; straight never married men are no longer different from straight previously married men; and gay never married and gay

Table 11.3 Predicted probability of reporting activity limitations by relationship status and gender (N = 48,822)

	Model 2 Probability		Model 3 Probability	
	Men	Women	Men	Women
Straight married	0.05†††[abce]	0.03***[abcd]	0.04†††	0.03***[abcd]
Straight cohabiting	0.08**†††	0.06*†††[c]	0.07**†††	0.05††
Straight never married	0.08***†††[c]	0.07***†††	0.08***†††[d]	0.06**†††
Straight previously married	0.10***†††[bd]	0.08***†††	0.08***†††[d]	0.06***†††
Lesbian/gay partnered	0.05[ce]	0.12*††[a]	0.04[bc]	0.10*†
Lesbian/gay never married	0.10*††[d]	0.10	0.08†	0.07
Lesbian/gay previously married	0.24*†[bd]	0.04[d]	0.16†	0.03[d]

Note Odds ratios calculated controlling for race/ethnicity, education, nativity status, geographic region, age, income-to-needs ratio, insurance status, and employment status
*Differs from straight married men ($p < 0.05$); **differs from straight married men ($p < 0.01$); ***differs from straight married men ($p < 0.001$)
†differs from straight married women ($p < 0.05$); ††differs from straight married women ($p < 0.01$); †††differs from straight married women ($p < 0.001$)
Within-gender comparisons: [a]$p < 0.05$ (ref: straight cohabiting); [b]$p < 0.05$ (ref: straight never married); [c]$p < 0.05$ (ref: straight previously married); [d]$p < 0.05$ (ref: lesbian/gay partnered); [e]$p < 0.05$ (ref: lesbian/gay never married)

previously married men are no longer different from gay partnered men. This suggests that psychological distress and BMI play a role in activity limitations disparities among single men and among gay men, and also explain the difference between gay single men and straight married men. Significant differences remain when comparing straight unmarried men to straight married men, but it appears that psychological distress and BMI measures account for most of the differences between gay men and straight married men.

Among women, straight married women are no longer different from lesbian/gay previously married women; straight cohabiting women are no longer different from straight previously married women, and lesbian/gay partnered women are no longer different from straight cohabiting women. Significant differences remain between straight unmarried women and straight married women, between lesbian/gay partnered women and straight married women, and between lesbian/gay previously married women and lesbian/gay partnered women, suggesting that psychological distress and BMI do not explain the advantage straight married women experience over unmarried straight women or over lesbian/gay partnered women. Overall, the introduction of psychological distress and BMI controls reduced seven pairwise comparisons to nonsignificance for men and reduced three pairwise comparisons to nonsignificance for women.

Discussion

This study is the first to present population-level estimates of the association between sexual minority status and activity limitations by gender and union status. Overall, we find that the straight cohabiting and lesbian/gay partnered individuals appear similar in activity limitations risk compared to the straight married. Results reveal important differences across gender and union status. For union status, the trend from the regression results reveals heightened risk of activity limitations for most relationship statuses relative to the straight married. Notably, most within-gender comparisons to the straight married regarding predicted probability of activity limitations remain significant even after controlling for psychological distress and BMI. The results suggest that the relationship between sexual minority status and activity limitations risk differs by union status, but the pattern differs by gender.

Within-gender comparisons reveal the differential impact of union status for men and women. Straight unmarried men experience higher odds of activity limitations than straight married men, but gay men do not differ significantly from straight married men after controlling for psychological distress and BMI. This suggests that the heightened risk of activity limitations experienced by gay men may be explained by the pathway of heightened psychological distress as predicted by sexual minority stress theory (Meyer 2003). Additionally, gay partnered men experience lower odds of activity risk than straight never married men, straight previously married men, or gay previously married men. These patterns reflect the findings of previous research that marriage and partnerships are protective of men's health (Kiecolt-Glaser and Newton 2001; Waite 1995), suggesting that being in a straight married partnership or a gay partnership acts to protect men from activity limitations risk. Selection may explain the disadvantage faced by straight cohabiting men; gay men do not have historical and social access to the institution of marriage to their male partner and therefore have likely institutionalized other forms of commitment (Reczek et al. 2009), whereas straight cohabiting men historically have legal access to marriage but are prevented from accessing it due to other characteristics.

The association between sexual minority status and union status for women is different from that of men. Overall, straight married women experience lower odds of activity limitations risk than all other women except for single lesbian/gay women. Unlike with men, lesbian/gay partnered women experienced a heightened probability of reporting activity limitations relative to straight married women; this difference persists after accounting for psychological distress and BMI. This suggests that the differences between lesbian/gay partnered women regarding activity limitations risk found in other studies (Cochran and Mays 2007; Conron et al. 2010; Fredriksen-Goldsen et al. 2012; Siordia 2014) are not explained by lesbian/gay women's generally higher psychological distress and BMI compared to straight women. It appears that psychological distress and BMI do account for differences between lesbian/gay partnered women and straight cohabiting women, but the mechanism through which lesbian/gay partnered women experience heightened risk relative to straight married women remains unknown.

Interestingly, lesbian/gay previously married women appear no different from straight married women, and advantaged relative to lesbian/gay partnered women. This outcome may result from the health benefits of ending an undesirable heterosexual marriage. Systematic data sources estimate between 30 and 48% of sexual minority women were previously married (Black et al. 2000). Whereas previously married status seems protective of gay/lesbian women's activity limitations risk, it may exacerbate the risk for gay men, who significantly differ from straight married men before accounting for psychological distress and BMI. Overall, our results suggest a marital advantage regarding activity limitations risk, with straight married men and women experiencing lower risk relative to most relationship statuses. Among women, marital advantage is particularly pronounced, with all groups of women except the lesbian/gay previously married experiencing higher odds of activity limitations.

Across gender, our results show that after accounting for BMI, straight married women experience lower predicted probability (a difference of 0.02) of activity limitations from straight married men, straight previously married women and straight never married women experience higher predicted probability (differences of 0.01 each) of activity limitations than straight married men, and lesbian/gay partnered women experience higher predicted probability (a difference of 0.05) of activity limitations from straight married men. Additional analyses revealed that all men except gay partnered men experience significantly higher odds of activity limitations compared to straight married women. This significant gender difference between straight married women and all men may occur because we control for SES, which has been shown to suppress men's activity limitations risk relative to women in the general population (Zheng and George 2012). Future research should investigate the role of SES in mediating and/or suppressing cross-gender differences by sexual minority status and union status. Given that cross-gender comparisons within other relationship statuses did not show significant differences, it would be interesting to see what role SES plays in cross-gender comparisons by relationship status.

Finally, the more detailed measures of union status and sexual minority status used in this study clarify the findings of other studies regarding activity limitations risk across this population. Measures that do not capture single sexual minorities (Siordia 2014) or that do not differentiate between married and cohabiting straight unions (Cochran and Mays 2007; Fredriksen-Goldsen et al. 2012) miss some variation by gender and union status. Additionally, studies that control for union status (e.g. Conron et al. 2010) may miss complex patterns such as the finding that single sexual minority women (particularly lesbian and gay previously married women) are the only group of women whose activity limitations risk is comparable to that of straight married women. This study provides further insight through the addition of psychological distress and BMI as potential mechanisms through which sexual minority stress produces activity limitations risk. We find that these mechanisms explain more differences among men than among women and that the marital advantage for both men and women generally remains even after accounting for them. Given that straight married individuals experience lower odds of activity limitations than most other groups, future research should investigate gay/lesbian married couples, which will become easier as future waves of data increase sample sizes. Additionally, research should explore potential reasons for why straight cohabiting men, gay partnered men, and lesbian/gay previously married women, do not differ from straight married counterparts of the same gender.

This study is the first population-level study to investigate the relationship between sexual minority status and activity limitations , with an in-depth look at this association across relationship status and gender. Strengths of this study include its nationally representative sample, the identity-based sexual minority status measure, and attention to the complex intertwining of sexual minority status, gender, and union status regarding a health outcome that influences quality of life. Limitations include the cross-sectional nature of the NHIS and the limited sample size. These findings cannot and should not be used to make statements of cause or effect because of the potential for unmeasured confounders that could be uncovered with longitudinal analysis; still, no such data is currently available that could answer this research question. Due to sample size and data limitations we pooled the same-sex cohabiting and married. However, given that the same-sex married should be more advantaged in terms of health, this pooling likely biased our results on the same-sex partnered toward the null hypothesis. Additionally, the sample size remains low for lesbian/gay partnered (n = 346) and lesbian/gay never married (n = 84). Finally, although we approximate it with psychological distress, we do not have a direct measure of sexual minority stress due to discrimination or stigma. Sexual minority health research would be greatly improved by the inclusion of such measure in datasets, and researchers should include and use such measures in the collection of future data.

Conclusion and Policy Implications

Our study highlights several important research and policy implications for targeting activity limitations among sexual minority communities. First, sexual minority men and women appear to have different needs regarding activity limitations support. Straight unmarried and gay single experience disadvantage compared to straight married men, with psychological distress and/or BMI working as potential pathways for gay single men's disadvantage. Straight unmarried women and lesbian/gay partnered women experience higher rates of activity limitations risk relative to straight married women. However, given that straight married women experience lower odds of activity limitations than straight married men, the higher probability of activity limitations relative to straight married men for straight never married, straight previously married, and lesbian/gay partnered women is particularly noteworthy, especially since it persists after socioeconomic controls and controls for psychological distress and BMI. While this research suggests that interventions targeting mental health and body weight may help single gay men in particular, the mechanisms through which sexual orientation, union status, and gender work to influence activity limitations remain largely unexplained.

Second, sexual minority status appears to be a direct risk for activity limitations for some groups, as seen in previous research (Cochran and Mays 2007; Fredriksen-Goldsen et al. 2012), but may buffer the health of gay partnered men. Single gay men's higher limitations relative to straight married and gay partnered men is explained through psychological distress and BMI, but lesbian/gay partnered women experience higher odds of activity limitations risk relative to the straight married of both genders even after accounting for these factors. Single lesbian/gay women do not differ from the straight married men or straight married women. For lesbian/gay previously married women, this may be explained by a protective effect from breaking off a previous heterosexual union, but for lesbian/gay never married women the reason is less clear. Overall, this study highlights the importance of attending to gender and union status when targeting health disparities among sexual minority populations.

References

Black, D., Gates, G., Sanders, S., & Taylor, L. (2000). Demographics of the gay and lesbian population in the United States: Evidence from available systematic data sources. *Demography, 37*(2), 139–154.

Boehmer, U., Bowen, D. J., & Bauer, G. R. (2007). Overweight and obesity in sexual-minority women: Evidence from population-based data. *American Journal of Public Health, 97*, 1134–1140.

Bostwick, W. B., Boyd, C. J., Hughes, T. L., & McCabe, S. E. (2010). Dimensions of sexual orientation and prevalence of mood and anxiety disorders in the United States. *American Journal of Public Health, 100*, 468–475.

Bruit, M. W. (2012). *Americans with disabilities.* U.S. Census Bureau Current Population Reports (pp. 70–131). Washington, DC: U.S. Census Bureau.

Case, P., Austin, S. B., Hunter, D. J., Manson, J. E., Malspeis, S., Willett, W. C., et al. (2004). Sexual orientation, health risk factors, and physical functioning in the Nurses' Health Study II. *Journal of Women's Health, 13*, 1033–1047.

Centers for Disease Control and Prevention. (2011). Rationale for regular reporting on health disparities and inequalities—United States. *Morbitiy and Mortality Weekly Review, 60*(suppl), 3–10.

Centers for Disease Control and Prevention. (2015). *About BMI for adults.* Retrieved from: http://www.cdc.gov/healthyweight/assessing/bmi/adult_bmi/index.html

Cochran, S. D., & Mays, V. M. (2007). Physical health complaints among lesbians, gay men, and bisexually and homosexually experienced heterosexual individuals: Results form the California Quality of Life Survey. *American Journal of Public Health, 97*, 2048–2055.

Cochran, S. D., Sullivan, J. G., & Mays, V. M. (2003). Prevalence of mental disorders, psychological distress, and mental health services use among lesbian, gay, and bisexual adults in the United States. *Journal of Clinical and Counseling Psychology, 71*, 53–61.

Conron, K. J., Mimiaga, M. J., & Landers, S. J. (2010). A population-based study of sexual orientation identity and gender differences in health. *American Journal of Public Health, 100*, 1953–1960.

Denney, J. T., Gorman, B. K., & Barrera, C. B. (2013). Families, resources, and health: Where do sexual minorities fit? *Journal of Health and Social Behavior, 54*, 46–63.

Fredriksen-Goldsen, K. I., Kim, H., & Barkan, S. E. (2012). Disability among lesbian, gay, and bisexual adults: Disparities in prevalence and risk. *American Journal of Public Health, 102*, e16–e21.

Goldman, N., Korenman, S., & Wienstein, R. (1995). Marital status and health among the elderly. *Social Science and Medicine, 40*, 1717–1730.

Hatzenbuehler, M. (2009). How does sexual minority stigma "get under the skin"? A psychological mediation framework. *Psychological Bulletin, 135*, 707–730.

Hughes, M. E., & Waite, L. J. (2009). Marital biography and health at mid-life. *Journal of Health and Social Behavior, 50*, 344–358.

Institute of Medicine. (2011). *The health of lesbian, gay, bisexual, and transgender people: Building on a foundation for better understanding.* Washington, DC: National Academies Press.

Kessler, R. C., Andrews, G., Colpe, L. J., Hiripi, E., Mroczek, D. K., Normand, S.-L. T., et al. (2002). Short screening scales to monitor population prevalences and trends in non-specific psychological distress. *Psychological Medicine, 32*, 959–976.

Kiecolt-Glaser, J. K., & Newton, T. L. (2001). Marriage and health: His and hers. *Psychological Bulletin, 127*, 472–503.

Liu, H., Reczek, C., & Brown, D. (2013). Same-sex cohabitors and health: The role of ethnicity, gender, and socioeconomic status. *Journal of Health and Social Behavior, 54*, 25–45.

Liu, H., & Zhang, Z. (2013). Disability trends by marital status among older Americans, 1997–2010: An examination by gender and race. *Population Research and Policy Review, 32*, 103–127.

Manninen, P., Heliövaara, M., Riihimäki, H., & Mäkelä, P. (1997). Does psychological distress predict disability? *International Journal of Epidemiology, 28*, 1063–1070.

Meyer, I. H. (2003). Prejudice, social stress, and mental health in lesbian, gay, and bisexual populations: conceptual issues and research evidence. *Psychological Bulletin, 129*, 674–697.

Minnesota Population Center and State Health Access Data Assistance Center. (2015). *Integrated Health Interview Series: Version 5.0.* Minneapolis: University of Minnesota, 2012. http://www.ihis.us

Reczek, C., Elliot, S., & Umberson, D. (2009). Commitment without marriage: Union formation among long-term same-sex couples. *Journal of Family Issues, 30*, 738–756.

Ross, C. E., & Mirowsky, J. (2013). Theory and modeling in the study of intimate relationships. *Journal of Health and Social Behavior, 54*, 67–71.

Siordia, C. (2014). Disability estimates between same- and different-sex couples: Microdata from the American Community Survey (2009–2011). *Sexuality and Disability,.* doi:10.1007/211195-014-9364-6.

StataCorp, L. P. (2014). *Stata 13 user's guide.* College Station, TX: StataCorp.

Strine, T. W., Chapman, D. L., Kobau, R., Ballu, L., & Mokdad, A. H. (2004). Depression, anxiety, and physical impairments in the U.S. noninstitutionalized population. *Psychiatric Services, 55*, 1408–1413.

Umberson, D. (1987). Family status and health behaviors: Social control as a dimension of social integration. *Journal of Health and Social Behavior, 28*(3), 306–319.

Umberson, D. (1992). Gender, marital status, and the social control of health behavior. *Social Science and Medicine, 34*, 907–917.

US Department of Health and Human Services. (2011). *Health people 2020 objectives.* Retrieved from http://www.healthypeople.gov/2020/topicsobjectives2020

Waite, L. J. (1995). Does marriage matter? *Demography, 32*, 483–507.

Zheng, H., & George, L. K. (2012). Rising U.S. income inequality and the changing gradient of socioeconomic status on physical functioning and activity limitations, 1984-2007. *Social Science and Medicine, 75*, 2170–2182.

Chapter 12
The Relationship Between Maternal Pre-pregnancy BMI and Preschool Obesity

Susan L. Averett and Erin K. Fletcher

Introduction and Previous Literature

Childhood obesity has more than doubled in the past 30 years (Ogden et al. 2014). While alarming on its own, recent research has also shown that obesity is persistent and associated with long-term health consequences: Obese children are more likely to be obese as adults and are at greater risk of type 2 diabetes, heart disease, stroke and certain cancers (Pan et al. 2012; Ogden et al. 2014). Authors of a recent study showed that one third of children who were overweight in kindergarten were obese by eighth grade, and almost every child who was obese remained that way as an adult (Cunningham et al. 2014). Calculations based on U.S. data indicate spending on obesity-related illnesses could be as high as 20% of annual health care expenditures (Cawley and Meyerhoefer 2012).

In addition to the well known health consequences of obesity, research has also linked childhood obesity to poor cognitive outcomes, although the evidence is mixed as to whether the effect is causal (Kaestner and Grossman 2009; Averett and Stifel 2010; Zavodny 2013). Capogrossi and You (2013) posit that the effects of childhood obesity on cognitive outcomes might be particularly acute for lower performing students. In addition, there is mounting evidence that obese children suffer emotional and behavioral problems (Griffiths et al. 2011). The consensus among experts is that it is far easier and less costly to prevent childhood obesity rather than to reverse it (Oken and Gillman 2003; Whitaker 2004). The goal of this

---

S.L. Averett (✉)
Department of Economics, Lafayette College, Quad Drive, Easton, PA 18042, USA
e-mail: averetts@lafayette.edu

S.L. Averett
Institute for Research in Labor-IZA, Bonn, Germany

E.K. Fletcher
Harvard University, 79 JFK St., Cambridge, MA 02138, USA
e-mail: erin_fletcher@hks.harvard.edu

paper is to examine a potential early determinant of obesity, whether there is a direct, observable link to childhood obesity from maternal obesity prior to pregnancy, using a large-scale, national survey.

Maternal obesity also has been significantly associated with pregnancy complications. Indeed, the research shows that obesity is fast becoming the most common complication of pregnancy in the U.S. (McDonald et al. 2010; Lu et al. 2001). Underscoring the magnitude of the problem, pre-pregnancy obesity prevalence continues to increase; in 2009 1 in 5 pregnant women were obese when they became pregnant (Fisher et al. 2013). Medical professionals have long stressed the dangers of obesity and excessive weight gain during pregnancy and highlighted how they might affect the pregnancy and the health of the fetus (Boney et al. 2005; Whitaker 2004). An increasing awareness of these links has led to repeated updating of weight gain recommendations. As recently as 2009 the Institute of Medicine (IOM) issued revised guidelines for healthy pregnancy weight gain.

The hypothesis that maternal pre-pregnancy obesity and/or excess weight gain during pregnancy might have an effect on childhood obesity has standing in the literature. Scholars from various disciplines have established that pregnancy is a critical time for children's development and that a mother's decisions and environmental exposures during pregnancy can have profound effects on birth and later life outcomes. For example, the fetal origins hypothesis posits that the uterine environment can have far-reaching and lasting impacts on adult health (Almond and Currie 2011). In this theory chronic, degenerative conditions of adult health, including heart disease and type 2 diabetes, might be triggered by circumstances occurring decades earlier, such as in utero nutrition.

The fetal origins theory posits that obesity is passed from mothers to children through high concentrations of glucose and fatty acids that pass through the placenta. Mothers with high pre-pregnancy BMI and those who gain excessive amounts of weight during pregnancy have more fat and thus deliver greater concentrations of glucose and fatty acids to the developing fetus (Catalano 2003; Lawlor et al. 2008, 2011). The resulting increase in fetal insulin accelerates fetal growth and predisposes the child to weight gain later in life (Lawlor et al. 2008, 2011).

Numerous studies using observational data have documented a correlation between maternal obesity (either pre-pregnancy or excess pregnancy weight gain) and childhood obesity (e.g. Salsberry and Reagan 2007; Whitaker 2004; Oken et al. 2007; Oken 2009; Jääskeläinen et al. 2011; Branum et al. 2011; Yu et al. 2013; Ludwig et al. 2013). Studies that focus solely on a cross-section of children generally show that maternal pre-pregnancy obesity and/or excess gestational weight gain (GWG) lead to an increased probability of childhood obesity (e.g. Oken and Gillman 2003; Oken et al. 2007; Whitaker 2004).

A primary challenge in using observational data to make cross-family comparisons of unrelated children concerning the effect of pre-pregnancy obesity on childhood obesity is that the comparisons might reflect not only the intrauterine effects of maternal pre-pregnancy obesity but also obesity-promoting or environmental factors that are shared between a mother and her child (Lau et al. 2014;

Ludwig et al. 2013). Some risk factors for childhood obesity are observable and reflect post-natal interactions between mother and child, such as time spent watching television, dietary patterns, or the general quality of the home environment (Strauss and Knight 1999; Reilly et al. 2005). Therefore, cross-section estimates could suffer from omitted variable bias. When these omitted variables are positively correlated with a woman's pre-pregnancy obesity, studies may overstate the effects of her pre-pregnancy obesity on her children's obesity. This has led researchers to compare children of the same mother (i.e. using mother fixed-effects models) to control for shared familial influences that are unobserved but do not vary across time (e.g., Averett and Fletcher 2016).

For example, Branum et al. (2011), using data on over 2700 families interviewed in the Collaborative Perinatal Project, find in OLS models that pre-pregnancy weight and GWG are statistically significantly associated with BMI z-scores in four-year old children, but this effect disappears in family fixed effects models. Using data on over 146,000 Swedish males, Lawlor et al. (2011) find no association between GWG and BMI at age 18 when comparing siblings. In contrast, Ludwig et al. (2013), using data on all school-age children in Arkansas, find evidence in a maternal fixed-effects model that high pregnancy weight gain is associated with childhood overweight status. They use this as support for the fetal origins explanation that maternal obesity might program the fetus for future weight gain and obesity, though they state that "the magnitude of the effect may be small" (Ludwig et al. 2013, p. 5).

Despite the advantages afforded by maternal fixed-effects models, they cannot control for time-varying factors that could be important. Thus, at least one previous study has turned to the method of Instrumental Variables (IV). Lawlor et al. (2008) use data on over 4000 families from the U.K. and in OLS models find a significant association between pre-pregnancy BMI and childhood BMI at ages 9–11. This effect disappears when they instrument for pre-pregnancy BMI with an obesity genotype as a predictor of pre-pregnancy BMI.

Given the health costs and potential cognitive consequences associated with childhood obesity in the literature, we seek to add to this literature and identify whether a woman's weight status before pregnancy and her weight gain during pregnancy exert a potentially causal effect on childhood obesity. If there is evidence that obesity is transmitted from mothers to children during pregnancy, policy and practice aimed at reducing maternal weight before pregnancy and controlling for weight gain during gestation might have profound health impacts for not only the women themselves, but also their children.

Like much of the existing research (e.g. Oken and Gillman 2003; Whitaker 2004), we focus on children aged 2–4 years to avoid the confounding influence of the school environment and its potential effect on obesity. Millimet and Tchernis (2015) find that transitions to kindergarten are often correlated with movements in BMI percentile, so this sample criterion is important. To preview the results, similar to previous studies that have used maternal fixed effects or IV, we find little evidence that maternal pre-pregnancy BMI exerts a causal impact on obesity among preschool-aged children. The rest of the paper is structured as follows. In the next section, we discuss our data, sample creation and the variables we use. Following that, we discuss our method and then our results. We end by drawing some conclusions.

Data, Sample Creation and Variables

We use the National Longitudinal Survey of Youth 1979 (NLSY79) cohort for our analysis (Bureau of Labor Statistics 2012). The NLSY79 sampled 12,686 individuals between the ages of 14 and 21 in 1979 with annual interviews conducted until 1994 and subsequent interviews every other year up to the year 2010 (the most recent year available at the time of this paper). The respondents report data on their labor market experience, births, and marriages every survey round. Of utmost importance to our study, children who were born to women in the NLSY79 have been surveyed biannually since 1986. In 2010, the mothers were ages 45–53. Thus, for nearly all women in the sample, complete fertility histories are observed. In fact, 99.97% of births used in this study occur by 2000 and the most recent births we observe in our sample occurred in 2004. These data do not provide a nationally representative sample of children or young adults. Rather, they are regarded appropriately as representative of the population of offspring born to U.S. women who were aged 14–22 in 1979 (Wu and Li 2005).

In our sample, observations are at the child level. Thus, mothers may appear multiple times, once for each birth. We start with a sample of all women in the NLSY and their children in the years they are sampled. We calculate each child's age- and sex-specific BMI percentile using the 2000 CDC reference data (Kuczmarski et al. 2002). Children with a BMI percentile for their age and sex over 85 are considered by health professionals to be at risk of overweight while those with BMI percentiles over 95 are described as overweight. To be consistent with the adult categories of overweight and obese we refer to children with BMI percentiles greater than 85 as overweight and those with BMI percentiles greater than 95 as obese.

The CDC growth charts were devised using survey data from three nationally representative samples of boys and girls aged 2–20 during the years 1963–1994. Thus, when a child is identified as overweight in our sample, it indicates that his BMI is higher than 85% of surveyed children of his age during the reference time period. By definition, 5% of children are obese in the reference sample, but the metric allows for variance in obesity prevalence over time and in our sample.

In addition, and crucial to this study, the NLSY collected information on the height and weight of respondents and for each pregnancy we can observe the mother's pre-pregnancy height and weight. In particular, for mothers, weight is collected every round and height was collected in four rounds: 1981, 1982, 1985 and 2006. A mother's pre-pregnancy BMI is our key explanatory variable of interest. We use the self-reported heights from 1985 and weights from each recorded year preceding a birth to create pre-pregnancy BMI. According to their BMI, mothers are each placed into one of four categories using the World Health Organization Cutoffs. Underweight corresponds to a BMI of less than or equal to 18.5; BMI in the recommended range is between 18.5 and 24.9; overweight women are those with a BMI ranging from 25 to 29.9; and obese women have a BMI greater than or equal to 30. The NLSY also asks women to self-report their GWG in pounds for each pregnancy, which we control for in all of our models (Table 12.1).

To create our analysis sample, we start with a sample of 8265 NLSY children observed from 1986 to 2010 who are 24–59 months old and for whom we have information on height and weight so that we can calculate their BMI percentile score. Because, as we noted above, the key explanatory variable of interest is mother's pre-pregnancy BMI, we drop the 1348 observations where this information is missing. In addition, because pre-term births have their own set of complications, we further limit our sample to those children who were not born preterm (eliminating an additional 845 observations), and those whose gestation length was in excess of 42 weeks (169 observations), and those born below 500 grams (6 observations) or above 7000 g (2 observations). We also drop 42 women who reported having diabetes during the year they had a birth.

Because the NLSY is longitudinal, some of the children are observed multiple times in their preschool years. When this is the case we take only their first observation (dropping an additional 1214 observations). We also drop multiple births (34 observations) and those children for whom information on breastfeeding and c-section birth were not reported (170). This leaves us with a sample of 4435 children. Of those, 1774 have no siblings in the sample. 1758 have one sibling in the sample, 672 have two siblings in the sample, 220 have three siblings in the sample, 35 have four siblings in the sample and 6 have five siblings in the sample. Of the 2691 mothers with more than one child in the sample, 1781 did not change their pre-pregnancy weight category across births. Mothers of 910 children changed their pre-pregnancy BMI category between pregnancies; of those, 213 changes were to a lower BMI category while the rest were to a higher BMI category.

Our focus in this paper is on the effect of mother's pre-pregnancy obesity on her preschool-age child's obesity status. However, as noted in the introduction, other factors such as dietary habits, genetics and the quality of the child's home environment might also affect weight outcomes. The NLSY is a particularly rich source of data and we control for many covariates to attempt to isolate the effect of mother's pre-pregnancy weight on her preschool-aged child's weight. In particular, we control for mother's age, age at first birth, parity, education, urban residence, marital status and income; these means are shown in Table 12.2.

We also control for the child's age in months, birth order, birth weight, gender, and race. In addition, we include controls for the month of the mother's first prenatal visit, whether she smoked or used alcohol during the pregnancy, whether or not the child was breastfed, and the home environment using the Home Observation for Measurement of the Environment (HOME) score. In the next section, we detail our econometric specifications.

Table 12.1 Sample means (proportions) of outcome variables by mother's pre-pregnancy BMI

	All children	Mom pre-preg, BMI < 18.5	Mom pre-preg, 18.5 ≤ BMI < 24.9	Mom pre-preg, 25 < BMI < 29.9	Mom pre-preg BMI > 30
BMI percentile >95 (obese)	0.150 (0.357)	0.115 (0.320)	0.139 (0.346)	0.171 (0.377)	0.210 (0.408)
BMI percentile >85 (obese)	0.254 (0.435)	0.224 (0.418)	0.237 (0.425)	0.291 (0.455)	0.325 (0.469)
BMI percentile	50.897 (35.481)	45.523 (35.604)	49.613 (35.252)	54.686 (35.199)	56.597 (36.300)
Observations	4435	330	2873	817	415

Standard deviations of continuous variables in parentheses

Table 12.2 Sample means (proportions) of control variables by mother's pre-pregnancy BMI

Variable	All children	Mom pre-preg, BMI < 18.5	Mom pre-preg, 18.5 ≤ BMI < 24.9	Mom pre-preg, 25 < BMI < 29.9	Mom pre-preg, BMI > 30
		Underweight	Recommended	Overweight	Obese
GWG	31.919 (13.816)	34.094 (14.422)	32.589 (12.782)	31.681 (14.859)	26.017 (16.388)
Child's age (months)	39.472 (9.375)	40.570 (9.473)	39.645 (9.443)	39.132 (9.258)	38.072 (8.890)
Hispanic	0.192	0.158	0.188	0.246	0.140
Black	0.257	0.206	0.238	0.289	0.369
Child is male	0.509	0.488	0.509	0.528	0.494
Mom's age at first birth	22.702 (4.810)	21.488 (4.073)	22.688 (4.793)	22.965 (4.854)	23.246 (5.215)
Mom's age at this birth	26.196 (4.727)	24.227 (4.468)	25.957 (4.646)	26.983 (4.670)	27.875 (4.812)
Child's birth order	2.005 (1.096)	1.812 (1.084)	1.953 (1.054)	2.143 (1.162)	2.243 (1.196)
HOME score	44.723 (30.390)	44.846 (30.878)	46.907 (30.379)	39.744 (29.692)	39.301 (29.790)
Mom's education (years)	12.728 (2.353)	12.385 (2.180)	12.777 (2.359)	12.764 (2.497)	12.591 (2.114)
Married	0.706	0.609	0.716	0.728	0.668
Sep./Div./Wid.	0.143	0.212	0.140	0.125	0.142
Income missing	0.138	0.142	0.141	0.129	0.135

(continued)

Table 12.2 (continued)

Variable	All children	Mom pre-preg, BMI < 18.5	Mom pre-preg, 18.5 ≤ BMI < 24.9	Mom pre-preg, 25 < BMI < 29.9	Mom pre-preg, BMI > 30
		Underweight	Recommended	Overweight	Obese
Low income	0.295	0.388	0.285	0.285	0.308
Middle income	0.292	0.255	0.287	0.312	0.325
Urban residence	0.748	0.718	0.7466	0.758	0.757
Month 1st prenatal visit	2.552 (1.668)	2.539 (1.623)	2.552 (1.644)	2.512 (1.677)	2.644 (1.841)
Prenatal vitamins?	0.945	0.946	0.950	0.935	0.933
Breastfed	0.527	0.473	0.551	0.499	0.468
c-section	0.223	0.146	0.200	0.286	0.318
Alcohol use during pregnancy					
Unknown	0.001	0.000	0.000	0.001	0.000
<1×/month	0.240	0.264	0.248	0.222	0.202
Monthly	0.040	0.052	0.040	0.040	0.029
Weekly	0.041	0.018	0.047	0.027	0.046
Cigarette use during pregnancy					
Unknown	0.003	0.006	0.004	0.002	0.000
Smoked at all	0.261	0.361	0.273	0.209	0.202
Observations	4435	330	2873	817	415

Standard deviations of continuous variables in parentheses

Methods

OLS Regression

Using the sample of mothers with singleton births over our sample period, we test whether pre-pregnancy obesity and GWG are correlated with obesity among two-, three-, and four-year olds using the following OLS specification:

$$y_{imt} = \alpha + O_{imt}\beta + X_{imt}\phi + Z_{imt}\xi + T_t\theta + \varepsilon_{imt} \quad (12.1)$$

where y is the ith child's BMI the first time they appear in the sample between the ages of two and four, for the mth mother in the tth year. O is a vector representing the mth mother's weight, either as a continuous measure of BMI, or a series of dichotomous variables indicating underweight, overweight or obese status and a control for GWG for each child (pregnancy) i in year t. The primary coefficient of interest is the vector β. X_{imt} is a vector of variables specific to each child as shown in Table 12.2 (e.g. child's age in months, the HOME score, mother's education, marital status, mother's age at the birth, parity, whether she smoked, used alcohol or prenatal vitamins during the pregnancy and the month of her first prenatal visit, the child's birth weight, whether the child was breastfed, and whether the child was born via c-section). The vector Z includes a mother's characteristics that do not vary with each child, which include mother's race and her age at first birth. T_t is the vector of year fixed effects.

Maternal Fixed Effects

As noted earlier, genetics and other time-invariant characteristics of the mother could affect our outcomes of interest. These characteristics might include chronic health conditions, health habits, or environmental exposure. For this reason, we add mother fixed effects to our initial OLS specification in order to account for a mother's time-invariant characteristics. This specification allows us to compare births across mothers and the effect of pre-pregnancy BMI is now identified off of mothers whose pre-pregnancy BMI status changes over pregnancies. The specification is as listed in Eq. 12.1 above but with mother fixed effects γ_m as follows:

$$y_{imt} = \alpha + O_{imt}\beta + X_{imt}\phi + \gamma_m + T_t\theta + \varepsilon_{imt} \tag{12.2}$$

Note that the Z_m vector drops out from this specification because these characteristics do not vary across children. This specification only includes those mothers who had more than one child in the sample. Identification of the parameters on the maternal pre-pregnancy BMI categories comes from discordant siblings (i.e. siblings whose mother changed pre-pregnancy BMI categories).

Instrumental Variables

Our OLS models establish a correlation between maternal obesity and preschool obesity. This association disappears when we use a maternal fixed-effects specification, which is consistent with much of the literature, as described earlier. While the maternal fixed-effects methodology is an improvement over the OLS specifications, this method cannot control for time-varying, unobservable factors that might affect both mother and child obesity. These factors include a mother's pre- and post-natal behavior that could either reinforce or compensate for a child's initial health endowments and concerns about intergenerational transmission of obesity. As a result, we cannot assert definitively that a causal relationship exists between maternal pre-pregnancy obesity and childhood obesity using either OLS or maternal fixed effects. In order to address the issue of causality, we turn to the IV method. The NLSY lacks genetic information so we cannot use the same instrument as in Lawlor et al. (2008), but we are able to exploit the large-scale nature and sampling design of the NLSY79 to secure an instrument. In particular, among the original respondents to the NLSY are a number of siblings. In the past, economists have used information on siblings and twins as controls or instruments by appealing to the argument that biological siblings and twins share many genes. Thus, using the BMI of a sibling as an instrument provides variation in obesity propensity that is independent of the outcome of interest except through its effect on obesity.

Drawing on previous work by Cawley (2004), we instrument the BMI of the mothers in our sample using the BMI of the sisters of our NLSY79 mothers, a group we expect to have similar health and obesity status as the mothers in the sample. We use BMI of sisters, but exclude that of brothers due to the lack of agreement regarding the comparability of men and women's BMI values. Identification is obtained as in Cawley (2004), who explains that on average half of any individual's genetic material is shared with siblings of the same parents. Thus, a sister's BMI should be a good predictor of an individual's BMI. This identification strategy is threatened if shared family environment is a significant predictor of obesity. We address this in a few ways. First, we include HOME score in our models to control for the quality of the home environment. In our OLS models, we found no association between HOME score and childhood obesity. Secondly, we refer to the literature, which has shown little to no observable effect of shared family environment on obesity (e.g., Grilo and Pogue-Geile 1991; Wardle et al. 2008). Finally, although previous literature cannot entirely rule out that family environment has some effect, we rely on the fact that sisters no longer live together and thus any effects of shared family environment would be less important in adulthood. Sister obesity status (or aunt obesity, from the perspective of the child) is plausibly exogenous to child obesity; as long as the aunt is not the child's primary caretaker, aunt obesity should influence the child's obesity only through the genetics that are shared between sisters and shared between mothers and children. The model we estimate is given by:

$$O_{imt} = \gamma + B_{imt}\zeta + X_{imt}\phi + Z_m\xi + T_t\theta + \mu_{imt} \qquad (12.3)$$

$$y_{imt} = \alpha + \widehat{O}_{imt}\beta + X_{imt}\phi + Z_m\xi + T_t\theta + \varepsilon_{imt} \qquad (12.4)$$

where B_{imt} is the average BMI of any sisters interviewed in the year of mth mother's birth. y is now the ith child's (child of the mth mother) obesity status in year t. The variable of interest, mother's weight status, O remains as defined in Eq. 12.1. We use the predicted values of O, $\widehat{O}$ in the second stage. As before, T_t is a vector of year fixed effects.

Using the average BMI of all sisters interviewed as an instrument is plausibly more exogenous than a mother's own BMI, which might be correlated with exercise and eating habits that are also practiced by children. Because we only have one instrument, in this specification we measure mother's pre-pregnancy BMI as a continuous variable as opposed to the categories used in earlier regressions. We note that our genetic instrument, however, is most likely to be informative about the genetic channels of inter-generational transmission of obesity.

Results

Descriptive Statistics and OLS

Table 12.2 presents descriptive statistics for the outcome variables by the mother's pre-pregnancy BMI category. The unadjusted means reveal that the average BMI percentile scores increase as a mother's BMI category increases indicating a positive correlation between a mother's BMI and her child's BMI. We also see that the proportion of children who are overweight or obese increases as a mother's BMI increases.

Tables 12.3 and 12.4 show four OLS specifications starting from the most parsimonious, and then progressively adding relevant controls. Table 12.3 shows these specifications for the dependent variable measured as overweight (BMI percentile >85) and Table 12.4 for obese (BMI percentile >95). The first column of each table presents results from a model that only includes the mother's pre-pregnancy BMI categories, her GWG and a set of binary indicators for child's age in months. These unadjusted regressions reveal that mothers who begin their pregnancies obese have preschoolers who are 9.5 percentage points more likely to be overweight and 7.3 percentage points more likely to be obese. Both effects are large with the 9.5 percentage point increase in the probability of being overweight translating to a 36.8% increase in the probability of a child falling into the overweight category ((9.5/25.41)*100 = 38.7) and the 7.3 percentage point increase in the probability of obesity translating into a 48.8% ((7.3/14.95)*100 = 48.8) increase in the probability of preschool obesity.

In column 2, we add in the child's birth weight as a covariate. Previous researchers have found that child birth weight attenuates the effect of mother's pregnancy weight gain on childhood obesity (e.g. Ludwig et al. 2013). Birth weight in pounds is positively and significantly related to both the probability of being overweight and obese as a preschooler. An additional pound at birth translates into a 2.1 percentage point (8.6%) increase in the probability of being overweight and a 1.2 percentage point (8.1%) increase in the probability of obesity. Consistent with previous literature, adding this variable only slightly attenuates the coefficients on a mother's pre-pregnancy BMI.

In column 3 we add a set of year dummy variables (coefficients not shown in the table). The coefficients on these year dummies reveal that children born in the later years of our sample are more likely to be overweight or obese which is consistent with the upward trend in childhood obesity seen in the U.S. Including these year fixed effects reduces the magnitude of the coefficients on both the pre-pregnancy overweight and obese variables, but they remain statistically significant and still exert a sizeable effect.

In column 4 we add the full set of covariates shown in Table 12.2 although due to space limitations we only show some of the coefficients. There are several notable findings. First, the addition of these covariates further attenuates the effect of maternal pre-pregnancy obesity on a preschooler's likelihood of being overweight or obese but these coefficients are still statistically significant. In particular, our findings indicate that women who begin their pregnancies obese are

Table 12.3 OLS results with full controls on overweight status (BMI percentile >85)

Variables	(1)	(2)	(3)	(4)
Mom pre-preg. BMI < 18.5	−0.014 (0.023)	−0.008 (0.023)	0.002 (0.023)	−0.001 (0.023)
Mom pre-preg. 25 < BMI < 29.9	0.055*** (0.018)	0.050*** (0.019)	0.040** (0.018)	0.033* (0.018)
Mom pre-preg. BMI > 30	0.095*** (0.024)	0.088*** (0.024)	0.064*** (0.024)	0.055** (0.024)
GWG	0.001** (0.000)	0.001* (0.001)	0.001 (0.000)	0.001 (0.000)
Birth weight, lbs		0.021*** (0.006)	0.018*** (0.006)	0.025*** (0.006)
Hispanic				0.053*** (0.020)
Black				0.007 (0.020)
Child is male				0.020 (0.013)
Mom's age at first birth				−0.004 (0.003)
Mom's age at birth of child				−0.002 (0.004)
Birth order				−0.013 (0.011)
HOME score pctile				−0.000 (0.000)
Low income				−0.019 (0.023)
Middle income				−0.002 (0.019)
Mom breastfed				−0.022 (0.015)
c section				0.039** (0.017)
Observations	4435	4435	4435	4435
R-squared	0.017	0.020	0.037	0.052

Robust standard errors in parentheses ***$p < 0.01$, **$p < 0.05$, *$p < 0.1$
All models contain full set of controls shown in Table 12.2 plus age and year FE. Coefficients on selected controls are shown

4.1 percentage points more likely to have an obese preschooler than those who begin their pregnancies in the recommended BMI range. Second, children of married mothers and those who were breastfed are less likely to be overweight or obese. However, children born via c-section are more likely to be overweight and

Table 12.4 OLS results with full controls on obese status (BMI percentile >95)

Variables	(1) Obese kid	(2) Obese kid	(3) Obese kid	(4) Obese kid
Mom pre-preg. BMI < 18.5	−0.023 (0.018)	−0.020 (0.018)	−0.011 (0.018)	−0.011 (0.018)
Mom pre-preg. 25 < BMI < 29.9	0.032** (0.015)	0.029* (0.015)	0.021 (0.015)	0.013 (0.015)
Mom pre-preg. BMI > 30	0.073*** (0.022)	0.069*** (0.022)	0.049** (0.021)	0.041* (0.022)
GWG	0.001** (0.000)	0.001 (0.000)	0.001 (0.000)	0.000 (0.000)
Birth weight, lbs		0.012** (0.005)	0.009* (0.005)	0.015*** (0.005)
Hispanic				0.058*** (0.017)
Black				0.016 (0.017)
Child is male				0.016 (0.011)
Mom's age at first birth				−0.005* (0.003)
Mom's age at birth of child				0.001 (0.003)
Birth order				−0.019** (0.009)
HOME score pctile				−0.000 (0.000)
Low income				−0.028 (0.018)
Middle income				−0.004 (0.015)
Mom breastfed				−0.020 (0.012)
c-section				0.026* (0.014)
Observations	4435	4435	4435	4435
R-squared	0.013	0.015	0.034	0.051

Robust standard errors in parentheses ***$p < 0.01$, **$p < 0.05$, *$p < 0.1$
All models contain full set of controls shown in Table 12.2 plus age and year FE. Coefficients on selected controls are shown

obese. Third, we observe mixed results on race/ethnicity: Hispanic children are more likely to be overweight and obese but we see no effect for black children relative to white children. We also find that birth order is negatively related to obesity but not to overweight status. Lastly, we find that the HOME environment is not a significant predictor of preschool obesity or overweight status.

Maternal Fixed Effects

While our OLS results establish a clear correlation between pre-pregnancy BMI and preschool overweight and obesity even after controlling for a rich set of covariates, they do not necessarily establish a causal relationship. As noted in the introduction, there are some unmeasured factors that could be correlated with mother's pre-pregnancy obesity and her child's obesity. As one example, we have no information on shared family mealtimes, some aspects of which have been linked to obesity outcomes (Fiese et al. 2012). We are also unable to observe diet and exercise habits. To move closer to potentially causal effects, we turn to the results of our maternal fixed-effects models, which are shown in Table 12.5. We show the FE results in two panels: the top panel has the overweight outcome and the bottom panel the obese outcome. All models include the full set of covariates shown in Table 12.2 and in the last column of Tables 12.3 and 12.4.

In each panel, the first column presents the OLS results to facilitate comparisons across models. The second column presents the FE model that is identical in specification to the OLS model. This model is identified off of those mothers whose pre-pregnancy BMI category changed across pregnancies, for instance, a mother who is in the recommended weight category before her first pregnancy and is in the overweight category before her second would be in this sample as would a mother who moved from the overweight to the underweight category between pregnancies. However, women who lose weight between pregnancies might be quite different than those who gain weight. Thus, in the third column of this table we present the FE model for only those who gained weight between pregnancies, a group that constitutes the majority of the changers. Finally, because mothers with more than two children might be quite different from mothers with two children (the majority of women in our sample with more than one child have two children) the last column (5) limits the sample to mothers with only two children who gained weight between their first and second pregnancy. The results from these specifications reveal that regardless of the sample, we find no effect of pre-pregnancy BMI on preschool overweight or obesity. Finally, we also performed a similar set of regressions excluding first-born children. In consideration of space, we do not show these results, but similar to the other specifications, they show no measurable relationship between pre-pregnancy BMI and preschool obesity status.

Overall, the maternal fixed-effects results indicate no statistically significant effect of pre-pregnancy BMI on our outcomes of interest. The point estimates are often smaller than the OLS estimates and occasionally switch signs. As expected, the standard errors are larger. These estimates indicate that once we have controlled for time-invariant, family-specific factors, there is no effect of maternal pre-pregnancy BMI on preschool overweight or obesity.

In order for the maternal fixed-effects approach to be valid as we noted above, any change in maternal BMI between two pregnancies should be exogenous and unrelated to all the potential confounders that might induce a spurious positive relationship between maternal and child BMI. However many of these confounders

Table 12.5 Fixed effects results on child overweight and obese status using mother's pre-pregnancy BMI

Variables	OLS	Maternal FE			
Sample	All	All	Gainers	2 kids	Gainers/2 kids
Y = 1 if child is overweight					
Mom pre-preg. BMI < 18.5	−0.001 (0.023)	0.040 (0.062)	0.040 (0.071)	0.029 (0.083)	0.066 (0.099)
Mom pre-preg. 25 < BMI < 29.9	0.033* (0.018)	−0.076* (0.042)	−0.084* (0.050)	−0.069 (0.057)	−0.096 (0.065)
Mom pre-preg. BMI > 30	0.055** (0.024)	−0.038 (0.067)	−0.049 (0.076)	0.040 (0.100)	−0.036 (0.105)
GWG	0.001 (0.000)	−0.001 (0.001)	−0.001 (0.001)	−0.001 (0.001)	−0.002 (0.002)
Table 12.2 controls	Yes	Yes	Yes	Yes	Yes
Observations	4435	2691	2478	1758	1672
R-squared	0.052	0.066	0.070	0.098	0.111
Number of CASEID		1166	1085	879	836
Y = 1 if child is obese					
Mom pre-preg. BMI < 18.5	−0.011 (0.018)	0.034 (0.047)	0.062 (0.047)	0.089 (0.069)	0.144** (0.071)
Mom pre-preg. 25 < BMI < 29.9	0.013 (0.015)	−0.059 (0.036)	−0.079** (0.040)	−0.008 (0.053)	−0.040 (0.059)
Mom pre-preg. BMI > 30	0.041* (0.022)	0.007 (0.061)	−0.018 (0.072)	0.047 (0.096)	−0.008 (0.103)
GWG	0.000 (0.000)	−0.002** (0.001)	−0.002** (0.001)	−0.002 (0.001)	−0.003* (0.001)
Table 12.2 controls	Yes	Yes	Yes	Yes	Yes
Observations	4435	2691	2478	1758	1672
R-squared	0.051	0.076	0.084	0.112	0.124
Number of CASEID		1166	1085	879	836

Robust standard errors in parentheses ***$p < 0.01$, **$p < 0.05$, *$p < 0.1$. Sample of All indicates all mothers. Gainers are those mothers who gained weight with a subsequent pregnancy and 2 kids refers to mothers with exactly two children in the sample

are precisely those that are likely to change following a pregnancy. These include health habits such as smoking, diet and exercise, stress, and the home environment more generally. These are all potentially altered by the birth of a child, especially the first child. Because of this, we also run our models on the subsample of second and later born children. For brevity, we do not show the results, but they are consistent with other models: We find no significant effect of maternal pre-pregnancy obesity on preschool obesity in the sample consisting of second born and later born children. We do caution that the sample sizes become smaller and hence our estimates are less precise.

Table 12.6 IV, OLS, and FE results using mother's BMI as a continuous variable

Variables	IV		OLS		FE	
	Overweight	Obese	Overweight	Obese	Overweight	Obese
Mom's pre-preg. BMI	−0.013 (0.010)	−0.008 (0.008)	0.003 (0.003)	0.002 (0.002)	−0.007 (0.010)	−0.004 (0.009)
Table 12.2 controls	Yes	Yes	Yes	Yes	Yes	Yes
Observations	1456	1456	1456	1456	1456	1456
R-squared	0.052	0.071	0.078	0.086	0.142	0.156
Number of CASEID					952	952

The mother's sisters' average BMI serves as the instrument for mother's BMI in the IV regressions
Robust standard errors in parentheses ***$p < 0.01$, **$p < 0.05$, *$p < 0.1$

Instrumental Variables

In Table 12.6, we present the results of our IV regressions. We also show OLS and FE models in this table to facilitate comparisons. Columns 1 and 2 are the IV model on the relevant sample. Because the IV model is estimated on a smaller sample size (only on those women who have a sister in the NLSY) we limit our OLS and FE results to that sample to facilitate comparisons. Columns 3 and 4 are the OLS model on the full sample and columns 5 and 6 are the FE models. All models include the full set of covariates (though some of these drop out in the FE models). We also do not include GWG in these models as we only have one instrument and GWG is likely endogenous. Our first stage F-statistic is 86.79 indicating a strong instrument, predictive of mother's BMI. In these models, we see no evidence of an impact of a mother's predicted pre-pregnancy BMI on the probability that her preschooler is overweight or obese. As expected, the IV standard errors are larger than the OLS standard errors although comparable to those of the FE model when using the same sample.

We have focused our attention on overweight and obese as categories since these are the conditions associated with health concerns. In appendix 1, we also examine the continuous variable of child's BMI percentile as an outcome. We show IV, OLS, and FE models. The same pattern holds in these models: our OLS results indicate a strong positive effect of mother's pre-pregnancy BMI on her child's preschool BMI percentile which disappears in FE and IV models.

Discussion and Conclusions

Evidence from numerous studies establishes a strong relationship between maternal obesity and childhood obesity. However, the extent to which such findings represent more than a correlation is unclear. Studies based solely on a single cross section of data cannot definitively address causation as a third factor that causes both the maternal obesity and the childhood obesity might be responsible for the positive correlation. Here, we examine a snapshot of obesity before the mother becomes pregnant and attempt to determine whether these correlations stand up to stricter identification strategies including one depending on within-family variation and another on an IV strategy. We consider childhood obesity before the child enters school, thus eliminating estimation problems that might arise from heterogeneous content and quality of schooling.

This paper contributes to the literature in the following ways. Our study is novel in that we use both maternal fixed-effects (FE) and instrumental variable (IV) estimation in an attempt to ascertain whether the well-established correlation between material pre-pregnancy obesity and childhood obesity is potentially causal. Our study also allows for assessment of both GWG and pre-pregnancy BMI, whereas much of the literature (e.g., Ludwig et al. 2013) can only account for GWG. Other papers have used maternal fixed-effects models to examine these questions using data from only one U.S. state (e.g. Ludwig et al. 2013), or use older national-level data (e.g. Branum et al. 2011). We use more recent, national-level, U. S. data. As far as we know, we are also the first to apply the IV method to address this research question using U.S. data.

We find, as in other studies, that there is a positive and significant relationship between a mother's obesity status before she becomes pregnant and her child's obesity during the preschool years. These correlations, however, disappear in maternal fixed-effects and IV models. These results suggest that other time-invariant, mother-specific characteristics, such as exercise habits and healthy eating, might be just as or more important than GWG or pre-pregnancy BMI for determining healthy child outcomes. A threat to our estimation strategy arises if mothers who changed weight categories from one pregnancy to the next were, for instance, aware of the dangers associated with weight gain and engaged in compensatory behavior to counteract the potential adverse effects of their pre-pregnancy weight status. In the case that these changes are correlated with lower probability of obesity, we might not see an effect on the probability of being an overweight or obese preschooler. However, our IV results reinforce the maternal fixed-effects results in that they also indicate no effect of maternal BMI on child obesity. Our results indicate that focusing too much attention on the role of maternal obesity in fostering early childhood obesity might be misguided and that physicians and policymakers should consider other factors when providing guidance to families regarding healthy weight gain for children.

Appendix 1

See Table 12.7.

Table 12.7 IV, OLS and FE results using mother's BMI as a continuous variable on o a continuous measure of child's obesity: BMI percentile

Variables	IV	OLS	FE
	Y = Child's BMI percentile		
Mom's pre-preg. BMI	−1.306 (0.881)	0.590*** (0.116)	−0.045 (0.444)
Table 12.2 controls	Yes	Yes	Yes
Observations	1456	4435	4435
R-squared	0.038	0.058	0.063
Number of CASEID			2910

The mother's sisters' average BMI serves as the instrument for mother's BMI in the IV regressions

Robust standard errors in parentheses ***$p < 0.01$, **$p < 0.05$, *$p < 0.1$

References

Abrams, B., Altman, S. L., & Pickett, K. E. (2000). Pregnancy weight gain: Still controversial. *American Journal of Clinical Nutrition, 71*(supply), 1233S–1241S.

Almond, D., & Currie, J. (2011). Killing me softly: The fetal origins hypothesis. *Journal of Economic Perspectives, 25*(3), 153–172.

Averett, S. L., & Fletcher, E. K. (2016). "Pre-pregnancy weight and gestational weight gain: The relationship between maternal weight and infant health. *Maternal and Child Health Journal, 20*(3), 655–664.

Averett, S. L., & Stifel, D. C. (2010). Race and gender differences in the cognitive effects of childhood overweight. *Applied Economics Letters, 17*(17), 1673–1679.

Boney, C. M., Verma, A., Tucker, R., & Vohr, B. R. (2005). Metabolic syndrome in childhood: Association with birth weight, maternal obesity, and gestational diabetes mellitus. *Pediatrics, 115*(290), 290–296.

Branum, A. M., Parker, J. D., Keim, S. A., & Schempf, A. H. (2011). Prepregnancy body mass index and gestational weight gain in relation to child body mass index among siblings. *American Journal of Epidemiology, 174*(10), 1159–1165.

Bureau of Labor Statistics (BLS). (2012). U.S. Department of Labor. National Longitudinal Survey of Youth 1979 cohort, 1979–2010 (rounds 1–24). Produced and distributed by the Center for Human Resource Research, The Ohio State University. Columbus, OH.

Catalano, P. M. (2003). Obesity and pregnancy—the propagation of a viscous cycle? *The Journal of Clinical Endocrinology and Metabolism, 88*(8), 3505–3506.

Capogrossi, K., & You, W. (2013). Academic performance and childhood misnourishment: A quantile approach. *Journal of Family and Economic Issues, 34*(2), 141–156.

Cawley, J., & Meyerhoefer, C. (2012). The medical care costs of obesity: An instrumental variables approach. *Journal of health economics, 31*(1), 219–230.

Cawley, J. (2004). The impact of obesity on wages. *Journal of Human Resources, 31*(2), 451–474.

Cunningham, S. A., Kramer, M. R., & Narayan, K. V. (2014). Incidence of childhood obesity in the United States. *New England Journal of Medicine, 370*(5), 403–411.

Fiese, B. H., Hammons, A., & Grigsby-Toussaint, D. (2012). Family mealtimes: A contextual approach to understanding childhood obesity. *Economics & Human Biology, 10*(4), 365–374.

Fisher, S. C., Kim, S. Y., Sharma, A. J., Rochat, R., & Morrow, B. (2013). Is obesity still increasing among pregnant women? "Prepregnancy obesity trends in 20 states, 2003–2009". *Preventive Medicine, 56*(6), 372–378.

Griffiths, L. J., Dezateux, C., & Hill, A. (2011). Is obesity associated with emotional and behavioural problems in children? Findings from the Millennium Cohort Study. *International Journal of Pediatric Obesity, 6*(2Part2), e423–e432.

Grilo, C. M., & Pogue-Geile, M. F. (1991). The nature of environmental influences on weight and obesity: A behavior genetic analysis. *Psychological Bulletin, 110*(3), 520.

Institute of Medicine (US) and National Research Council (US). (2009). Committee to reexamine IOM pregnancy weight guidelines; Rasmussen, K. M., Yaktine, A. L. (Eds), Weight gain during pregnancy: Reexamining the guidelines. Washington (DC): National Academies Press (US). Summary. Available from: http://www.ncbi.nlm.nih.gov/books/NBK32799/

Jääskeläinen, A., Pussinen, J., Nuutinen, O., Schwab, U., Pirkola, J., Kolehmainen, M., et al. (2011). Intergenerational transmission of overweight among Finnish adolescents and their parents: A 16-year follow-up study. *International Journal of Obesity, 35*(10), 1289–1294.

Kaestner, R., & Grossman, M. (2009). Effects of weight on children's educational achievement. *Economics of Education Review, 28*(6), 651–661.

Kuczmarski, R. J., Ogden, C. L., Guo, S. S., Grummer-Strawn, L. M., Flegal, K. M., Mei, Z., et al. (2002). 2000 CDC growth charts for the United States: Methods and development. *Vital and Health Statistics. Series 11. Data from the National Health Survey, 246*, 1–190.

Lau, E. Y., Liu, J., Archer, E., McDonald, S. M., & Liu, J. (2014). Maternal weight gain in pregnancy and risk of obesity among offspring: A systematic review. *Journal of Obesity*.

Lawlor, D. A., Timpson, N. J., Harbord, R. M., Leary, S., Ness, A., McCarthy, M. I., et al. (2008). Exploring the developmental overnutrition hypothesis using parental–offspring associations and FTO as an instrumental variable. *PLoS Medicine, 5*(3), e33.

Lawlor, D. A., Lichtenstein, P., Fraser, A., & Niklas Långström, N. (2011). Does maternal weight gain in pregnancy have long-term effects on offspring adiposity? A sibling study in a prospective cohort of 146,894 men from 136,050 families. *The American Journal of Clinical Nutrition, 94*(1), 142–148.

Lu, G. C., Rouse, D. J., DuBard, M., Cliver, S., Kimberlin, D., & Hauth, J. C. (2001). The effect of increasing prevalence of maternal obesity on perinatal morbidity. *American Journal of Obstetrics and Gynecology*, 845–849.

Ludwig, D. S., Rouse, H. L., & Currie, J. (2013). Pregnancy weight gain and childhood body weight: A within-family comparison. *PLoS Medicine, 10*(10), e1001521.

McDonald, S. D., Han, Z., Mulla, S., & Beyene, J. (2010). Overweight and obesity in mothers and risk of preterm birth and low birth weight infants: systematic review and meta-analyses. *BMJ: British Medical Journal, 341*–359.

Millimet, D. L., & Tchernis, R. (2015). Persistence in body mass index in a recent cohort of US children. *Economics and Human Biology, 17*(2015), 157–176.

Ogden, C. L., Carroll, M. D., Kit, B. K., & Flegal, K. M. (2014). Prevalence of childhood and adult obesity in the United States, 2011–2012. *Journal of the American Medical Association, 311*(8), 806–814.

Oken, E., & Gillman, M. W. (2003). Fetal origins of obesity. *Obesity Research, 11*(4), 496–506.

Oken, E. (2009). Maternal and child obesity: The causal link. *Obstetrics and Gynecology Clinics of North America, 36*(2), 361–377.

Oken, E., Taveras, E. M., Kleinman, K. P., Rich-Edwards, J. W., & Gillman, M. W. (2007). Gestational weight gain and child adiposity at age 3 years. *American Journal of Obstetrics and Gynecology, 196*(4), 322–e1.

Pan, L., Blanck, H. M., Sherry, B., Dalenius, K., & Grummer-Strawn, L. M. (2012). Trends in the prevalence of extreme obesity among US preschool-aged children living in low-income families, 1998–2010. *Journal of the American Medical Association, 308*(24), 2563–2565.

Reilly, J. J., Armstrong, J., Dorosty, A. R., Emmett, P. M., Ness, A., Rogers, I., et al. (2005). Early life risk factors for obesity in childhood: Cohort study. *British Medical Journal, 330*(7504), 1357–1359.

Salsberry, P. J., & Reagan, P. B. (2007). Taking the long view: The prenatal environment and early adolescent overweight. *Research in Nursing & Health, 30*(3), 297–307..

Strauss, R. S., & Knight, J. (1999). Influence of the home environment on the development of obesity in children. *Pediatrics, 103*(6), e85.

Wardle, J., Carnell, S., Haworth, C. M. A., & Plomin, R. (2008). Evidence for a strong genetic influence on childhood adiposity despite the force of the obesogenic environment. *The American Journal of Clinical Nutrition, 87*(2), 398–404.

Whitaker, R. C. (2004). Predicting child obesity at birth: The role of maternal obesity in early pregnancy. *Pediatrics, 114*(29), e29–e36.

Wu, L. L., & Allen Li, J.-C. (2005). Children of the NLSY79: A unique data resource. *Monthly Labor Review, 128*, 59–62.

Yu, Z., Han, S., Zhu, J., Sun, X., Ji, C., & Guo, X. (2013). Pre-pregnancy body mass index in relation to infant birth weight and offspring overweight/obesity: A systematic review and meta-analysis. *PLoS ONE, 8*(4), e61627. doi:10.1371/journal.pone.0061627.

Zavodny, M. (2013). Does weight affect children's test scores and teacher assessments differently? *Economics of education review, 34*, 135–145.

Chapter 13
Prevalence and Elimination of Childhood Lead Poisoning in Illinois, 1996–2012

Frida D. Fokum, Mohammed Shahidullah, Emile Jorgensen and Helen Binns

Introduction

Lead poisoning is a preventable environmental health disease. Lead can affect every organ system in children and adults, including the brain and the nervous system. It can cause neurologic damage and behavior disorders, including lower IQ, attention deficits, and reduced academic achievement (Bellinger and Needleman 2003). Common risk factors for lead exposures during childhood are older housing built before 1978, young age (two years and younger), low socioeconomic status, and African-American race (IDPH 2013).

Deteriorated lead-based paint, commonly found in older housing, is the most common source of lead in children with high blood lead levels. In a home with deteriorated lead-based paint, the dust is contaminated by lead. Children get lead on their hands by touching the floor or a painted surface and then they ingest the lead by putting their hands in their mouths. Such hand-to-mouth behavior is typical for a normally-developing young child. Other sources of lead include exterior soil, water,

---

F.D. Fokum (✉)
Illinois Department of Public Health, Office of Health Protection,
Division of Environmental Health, Springfield, IL, USA
e-mail: Frida.fokum@illinois.gov

M. Shahidullah
Illinois Department of Public Health, Office of Policy, Planning and Statistics,
Illinois Center for Health Statistics, Springfield, IL, USA

E. Jorgensen
Chicago Department of Public Health, Chicago, IL, USA

H. Binns
Ann & Robert H. Lurie Children's Hospital of Chicago, Chicago, IL, USA

© Springer International Publishing Switzerland 2017
M.N. Hoque et al. (eds.), *Applied Demography and Public Health in the 21st Century*, Applied Demography Series 8,
DOI 10.1007/978-3-319-43688-3_13

and cultural products such as cosmetics and traditional (folk) medicines, including Ayurvedic medicines (Hanna-Attisha et al. 2016; Goodman 2016; CDC 2015).

While some manufacturers voluntarily reduced lead concentration in paint after 1950, lead was banned from paint by regulation in 1978. As such, pre-1978 homes and, especially pre-1950 homes, have the highest likelihood of having deteriorating lead-based paint (U.S. Consumer Product Safety Commission 2011). In 2012, there were more than 3.5 million pre-1978 housing units in Illinois (987,000 in Chicago) and about two million of them were estimated to contain lead-based paint (IDPH 2013).

Since 1995, Illinois has required assessment for blood lead testing based on the child's age and living environment. From 1996 onward, an average of 270,000 children have been tested for blood lead annually (IDPH 2013). Based on the blood lead level (BLL), children were considered to receive nursing case management services and an environmental inspection of the children's living environment—usually their primary residence—primarily to assess the presence of lead-based paint hazards, and if warranted, order remediation of those hazards.

Data and Methods

Population estimates from the U.S. Census Bureau (U.S. Census Bureau 2013); blood lead testing data from Illinois (IDPH 2013), Chicago (IDPH 2013), and the U.S. (CDC 2014); and age of housing data from the American Housing Survey (HUD 2011) were used for this report. Medicaid data from the Illinois Department of Healthcare and Family Services (HFS) were matched to blood lead testing data following an interagency data-sharing agreement.

Illinois law requires health providers to either obtain a blood lead test or to apply a targeted blood lead testing approach. The option to apply the targeted blood lead testing approach was only applicable if the child lived in a state-assigned low risk ZIP code area. Children receiving a targeted evaluation first had the Childhood Lead Risk Assessment Questionnaire (IDPH 2015) completed by a parent/guardian to identify those at high risk for lead exposure (i.e., those with any "YES" or "I DO NOT KNOW" answer to any question on the questionnaire) and only those who were at high risk received a blood lead test. Blood lead testing and assessment were encouraged at ages one and two years (Raymond et al. 2014). All children enrolled in medical assistance programs such as Medicaid, Head Start, All Kids, or Women, Infants and Children (WIC) were required to have a blood lead test performed at ages one and two years. Illinois law also requires evidence of a blood lead test or risk assessment using the questionnaire before a child attends a licensed day care center, school, or kindergarten.

The blood lead testing data included the child's name, birth date, test date, blood lead level, race/ethnicity, and home address for blood samples drawn in 1996 through 2012, during which period, Illinois required providers to assess child risk of exposure to lead hazards and perform blood lead tests, if indicated. In Chicago, health care providers were required to test children for blood lead level. Children aged one and two years were most likely to be tested, but older children also were frequently tested. Approximately 97% of children in this report were 6 years of age or younger at time of blood lead testing.

HFS administers the Illinois Medical Assistance (Medicaid) Program. Beginning in 2011, HFS provided an incentive payment through Illinois Health Connect to health providers based on their enrollees receiving a blood lead test before age 24 months (HFS 2015). By regulation, blood lead test results of children six years of age and younger were reported directly to IDPH by health providers, hospitals, local health departments, laboratories, and medical professionals who diagnosed, performed blood lead analyses, or treated lead poisoned children in Illinois (Illinois General Assembly 2014).

Reported blood lead tests in IDPH's Lead Program Surveillance Database were used for this data analysis. Children with multiple tests matched to each other by date of test, patient last name, first name, date of birth, and testing laboratory were de-duplicated and consolidated using an established data cleaning method described here. Data reported included the highest venous blood lead test result per child. If there was no venous test, then the highest capillary test result was used. Blood lead results with incomplete addresses for the tested patient were excluded from the analyses. Note that the Centers for Disease Control and Prevention (CDC 2014) only reports blood lead data for children younger than six years of age, so comparisons of Illinois and the U.S. should be cautiously interpreted.

In this analysis, prevalence was defined as the percentage of children with a BLL of 10 µg/dL or greater among the total number of children tested in a year. The child's BLL used to compute prevalence was determined by taking all BLLs from a given year to determine the peak venous sample result for each child. If no venous blood was drawn, the highest capillary test result was used. The BLLs do not follow a normal distribution, so the geometric mean was determined based on the peak BLL for a given child in a given year (CDC 2013). Children with test results below a limit of detection were ascribed a value equal to the limit of detection. The imputation of values below the detection limit as used in this report would undoubtedly inflate the geometric mean values. As a result, caution is advised for comparing and interpreting the geometric mean values.

Results

Current Presence of Lead-Based Paint

Deteriorating lead-based paint has been identified as a primary source of lead poisoning in houses built prior to the residential lead paint ban of 1978. According to the 2012 American Community Survey) 5-year estimates (U.S. Census Bureau 2013), 66% of housing units were pre-1978 housing units in Illinois and 82% were

Table 13.1 Estimates of the number of housing units in illinois and chicago with lead hazards by year structure was built, 2008–2012

Year structure built	Estimated number of housing units[1]		Significant lead based paint hazard[2]			Prevalence of lead-based paint in the Midwest[3]		
	Illinois	Chicago	% with Lead[2]	Units with lead		% with Lead[3]	Units with lead	
				Illinois	Chicago		Illinois	Chicago
Pre-1978	3,515,998	987,240	41.1	1,446,147	514,096	59.2	2,082,053	685,553
1960–1977	1,238,000	181,171	7.7	95,326	13,950	23.8	294,644	43,119
1940–1959	1,058,626	262,684	48.7	515,551	127,927	73.7	780,207	193,598
Pre-1940	1,219,372	543,385	68.5	835,270	372,219	82.6	1,007,201	448,836
Total Units	5,293,619	1,197,248						

Sources [1]U.S. Census Bureau, 2008–2012 American Community Survey 5-year estimate
[2,3]American Health Homes Survey, Table 5-1 Midwest and Table 4-1 page 20. Available at http://portal.hud.gov/hudportal/documents/huddoc?id=AHHS_REPORT.pdf

pre-1978 housing units in Chicago. Approximately 3.5 million Illinois housing units were built pre-1978 with 28% of them in the city of Chicago. Fifty-nine percent of the pre-1978 housing units were estimated to have lead-based paint. About 1.4 million Illinois housing units were estimated to have significant lead-based paint hazards (e.g., deteriorating lead-based paint) with 36% of those units in the city of Chicago alone (Table 13.1).

IDPH designated zip codes in the state where children were at highest risk for blood lead poisoning based on age of housing, age of child, poverty level, and elevated blood lead prevalence using the U.S. Census Bureau data files tabulated by zip code areas (Fig. 13.1). Figure 13.2 displays the percent of pre-1980 housing units by county in Illinois. Out of 1.2 million housing units in Chicago, 53.3% were pre-1950 and 29 % were built from 1950 to 1979 for a total of 82.3% pre-1980.

Blood Lead Testing Rate

The blood lead testing rate was based on the percentage of all children tested using U.S. Census Bureau population data for the year the test was completed. On average, 270,000 (margin of error ± 24,000) Illinois children, of which about 41% (110,140 ± 5,726) resided in Chicago, completed a blood lead test during any one year period. Annual testing ranged from 235,290 to 304,807 children accounting for 20–30% of Illinois population of children ages six years and younger. The testing rate for blood lead in Illinois increased steadily from 19% in 1996 to 25% in 2012 (Fig. 13.3). Nationally, the Centers for Disease Control and Prevention (CDC 2014) reported a national blood lead testing rate of 10.4% for 2012 for children less than six years of age. The Illinois testing rate for the most recent year was clearly higher than that of the U.S.

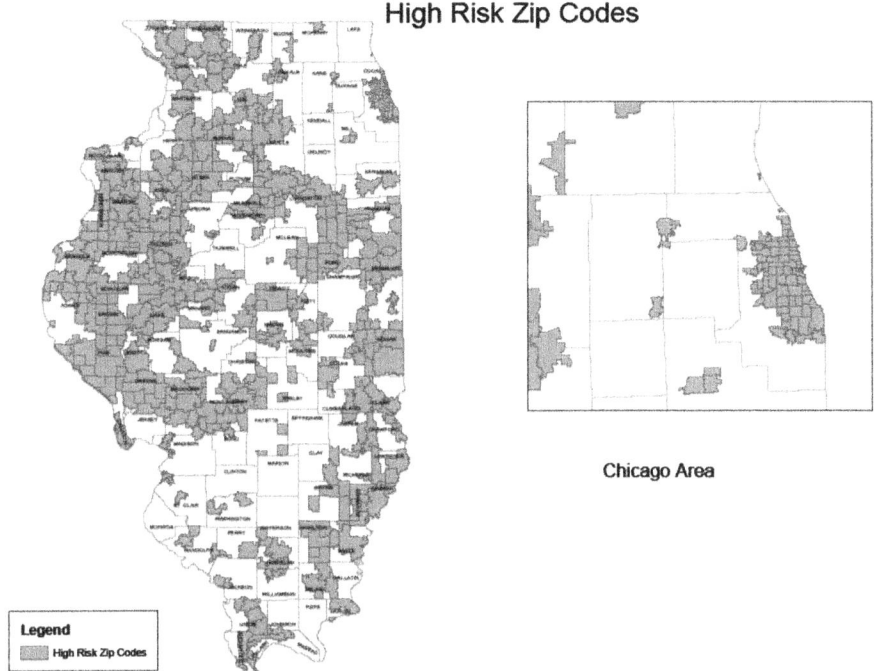

Fig. 13.1 High Risk ZIP Codes for Childhood Lead Poisoning in Illinois and the City of Chicago *Source* Illinois Department of Public Health, Lead Program Surveillance Database and U.S. CENSUS. *Note* All of the city of Chicago is designated by the Department as a high risk area for childhood lead poisoning

Blood Lead Prevalence

In 1997, approximately 19% of Illinois children were identified with a BLL of 10 μg/dL or higher; by 2012, the percentage had dropped to 1.0% (IDPH 2013). The significant decline in the number of Illinois children with lead poisoning defined as a BLL at or above 10 μg/dL is a tremendous public health success story. Prevalence of children with BLLs of 10 μg/dL or greater fell steadily across the 16 year study period (Fig. 13.4). The state of Illinois accounted for 25% of the nation's lead-poisoned children in 1997 but the Illinois share dropped to 14% in 2012 (CDC 2014).

Lead Prevalence by Race/Ethnicity

While the information about a child's race and ethnicity is requested in the mandatory BLL reporting process, much of this data is unreported, likely because

Fig. 13.2 Percent of Pre-1980 Housing Units by Illinois County and High-Risk ZIP Codes for Childhood Lead Poisoning *Note* All ZIP codes of the city of Chicago are designated by the Department as high risk areas for childhood blood lead poisoning. Out of 1.2 million housing units in Chicago, a total of 82.3% were pre-1980

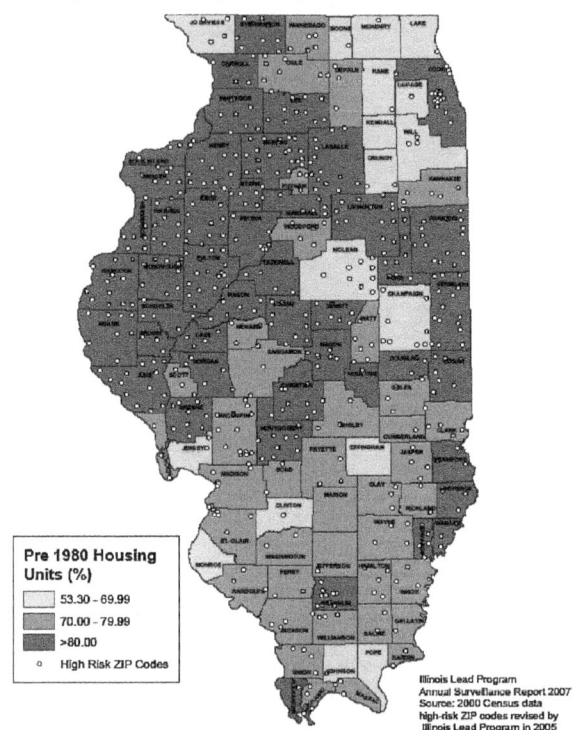

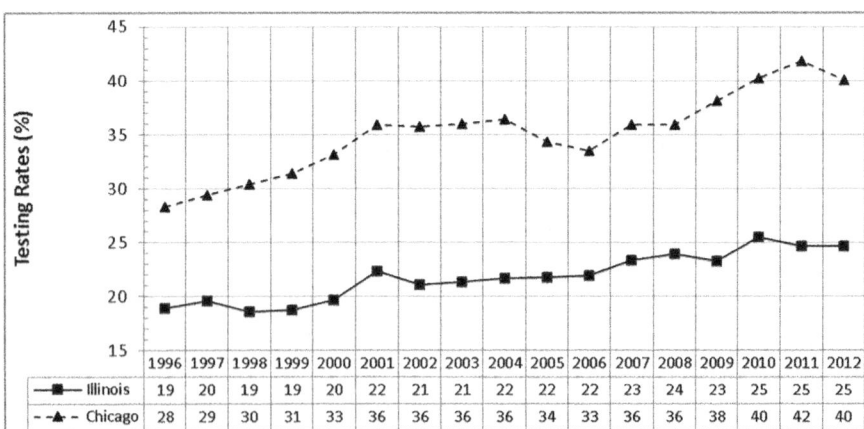

Fig. 13.3 Testing Rates for Childhood Blood Lead Prevalence in Illinois and Chicago, 1996–2012. *Source* Illinois Department of Public Health, Lead Program Surveillance Database, 1996–2012; U.S. Census Bureau; Illinois Department of Public Health, Illinois Center for Health Statistics. *Notes*: Intercensal Estimates: 1991–1999, 2001–2009; Postcensal Estimates 2011 and 2012; Census year distribution for children 0–6 was used to estimate intercensal and postcensal year estimates for 0–6 years population

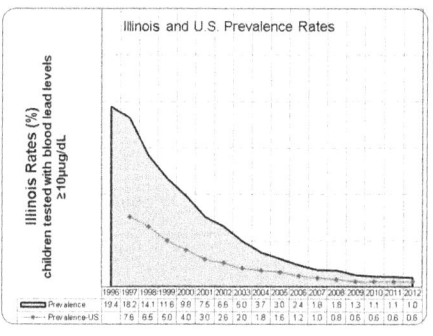 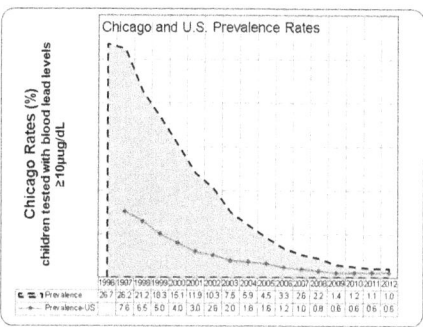

Fig. 13.4 Childhood Blood Lead Prevalence Rates for Illinois and Chicago by Year, 1996–2012. *Source* Illinois Department of Public Health, Lead Program Surveillance Database, 1996–2012. *Note* U.S. prevalence added here only to show the trend in lead poisoning decline with time based on children less than 6 years of age. Be cautious in relating the U.S. prevalence rate with the Illinois prevalence rate

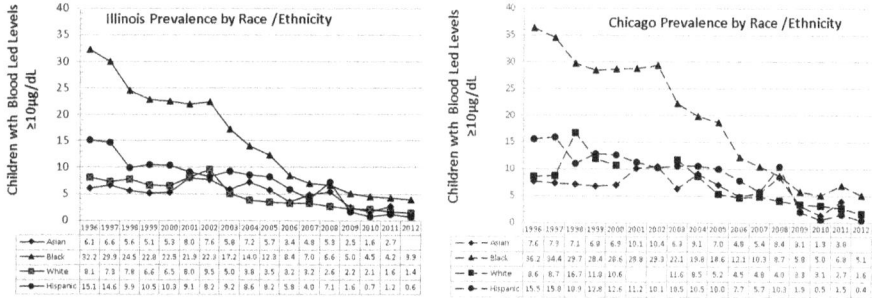

Fig. 13.5 Blood Lead Prevalence in Illinois and Chicago Children by Race/Ethnicity, 1996–2012. *Source* Illinois Department of Public Health, Lead Program Surveillance Database, 1996–2012. *Note* Other races were too few to be reported. Lead prevalence between 2001 and 2002 in Chicago was not included for White children due to very few test records

such information is not transmitted to the laboratories or is not systematically recorded in the child's medical record. Nevertheless, among those with reported race/ethnicity information Black or African American children were disproportionately burdened by lead poisoning compared to their White counterparts (Fig. 13.5).

Lead Prevalence by Gender

Male children tended to have a slightly higher lead prevalence compared to females (Fig. 13.6).

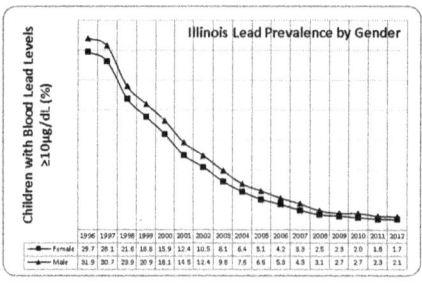 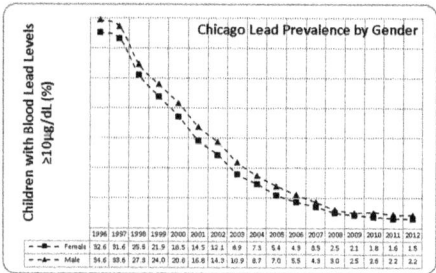

Fig. 13.6 Blood Lead Prevalence in Illinois and Chicago Children by Gender and Year, 1996–2012. *Source* Illinois Department of Public Health, Lead Program Surveillance Database, 1996–2012

Lead Prevalence by Medicaid Status

Medicaid status was used as a proxy for poverty in this report. More children enrolled in medical assistance programs including Medicaid and/or WIC had elevated blood lead levels (EBLLs) compared to other children who had other forms of medical insurance coverage (Fig. 13.7).

Lead Prevalence for Illinois Counties

Blood lead prevalence has significantly decreased across Illinois counties through the years. In 1996, all Illinois counties had at least 1.8% of children with BLLs of

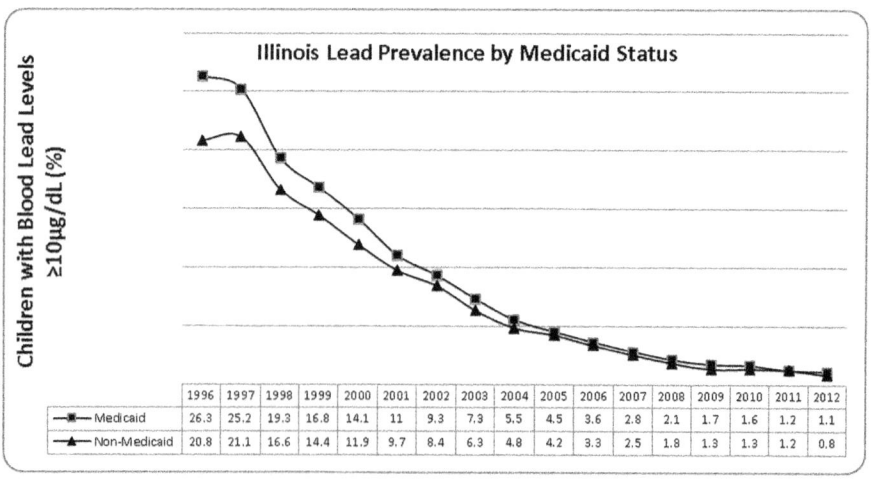

Fig. 13.7 Blood Lead Prevalence Rates by Medicaid Status and Year, 1996–2012. *Sources* Illinois Department of Public Health, Lead Program Surveillance Database, 1996–2012; the Department of Healthcare and Family Services, Enterprise Data Warehouse

10 µg/dL and greater, with the percentage ranging from 5 to 40% for counties. In 2001, six counties had less than 1.8% of children with a BLL of 10 µg/dL and greater. By 2007, a total of 53 counties had less than 1.8% of children with a BLL of 10 µg/dL and greater (median 1.6 % and maximum 7.8%). As of 2012, a total of 69 counties reported less than 1.8% of lead poisoned children (median of 1.3%) (Fig. 13.8a).

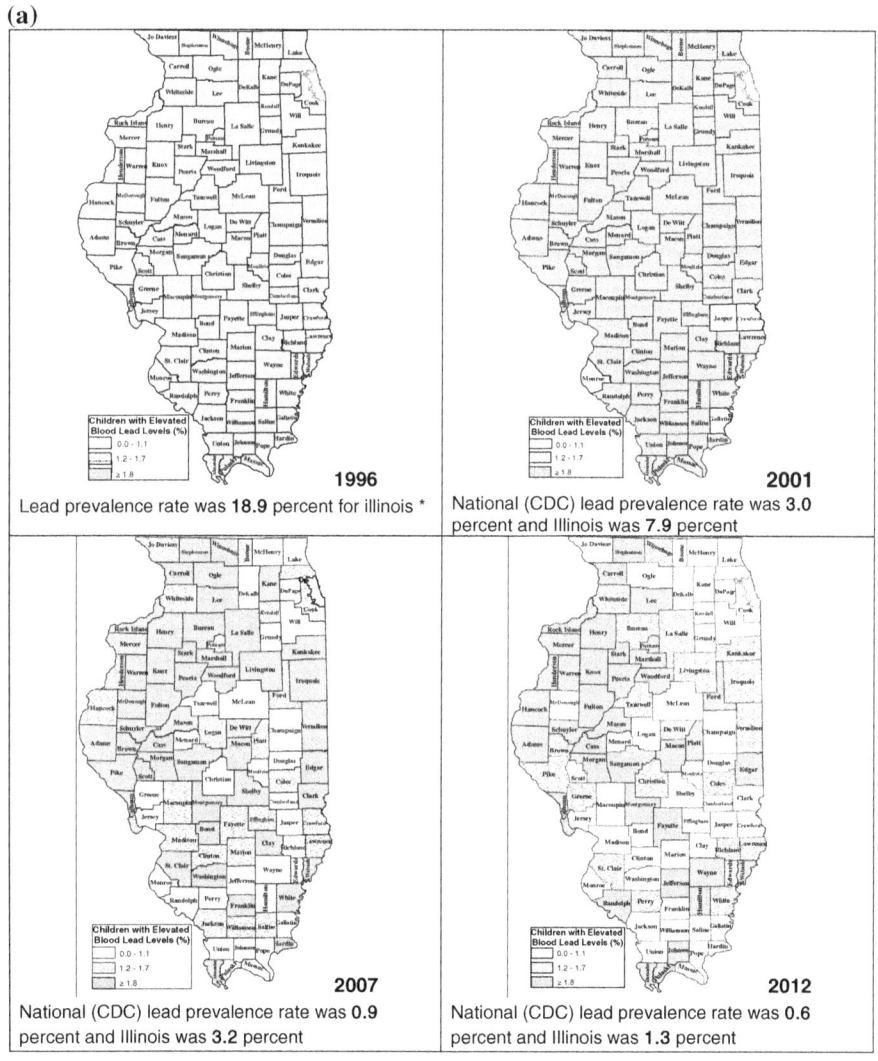

Fig. 13.8 **a** Decrease in Illinois Childhood Blood Lead Prevalence by County by Year. **b** Decrease in Chicago Childhood Blood Lead Prevalence by Community Areas by Year. *Source* Illinois Department of Public Health, Lead Program Surveillance Database, 1996-2012. *CDC not available at the time

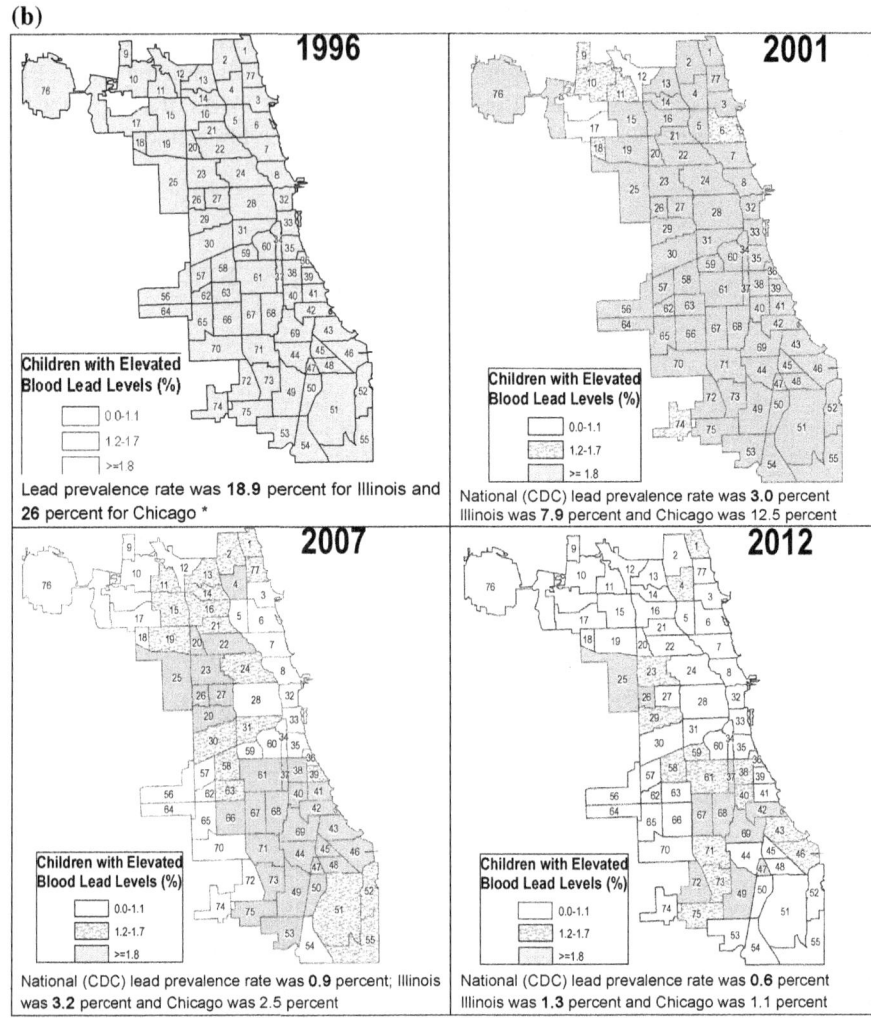

Fig. 13.8 (continued)

Similarly, blood lead prevalence in certain Chicago community areas has decreased through the years. In 1996, all 77 Chicago community areas had at least 1.8% of children with BLLs of 10 mg/dL and greater. In 2001, 69 Chicago community areas had at least 1.8% of children with a BLL of 10 mg/dL and greater with an annual prevalence of 12.5%. By 2007, only 30 Chicago community areas had at least 1.8% of children with a BLL of 10 mg/dL and greater. As of 2012, a total of 10 community areas had at least 1.8% of lead poisoned children (annual prevalence of 1.0%). Universal testing was recommended for all children living in Chicago, a designated high risk area for lead exposure. Some of the difference between

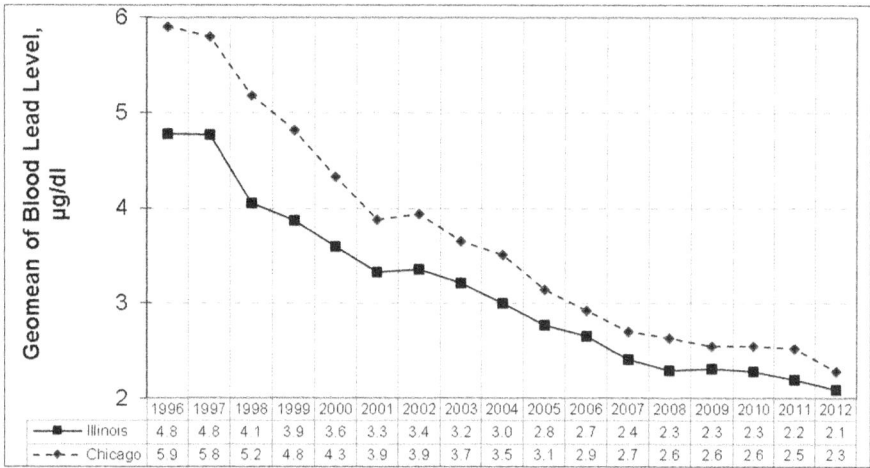

Fig. 13.9 Geometric Mean Blood Lead Levels for Illinois and Chicago Children by Year, 1996–2012. *Source* Illinois Department of Public Health, Lead Program Surveillance Database, 1996–2012

Chicago and Illinois is attributable to more wide-spread testing in Chicago that includes lower risk children (Fig. 13.8b).

Mean Blood Lead Level

The geometric mean BLL of children clearly and steadily decreased over time from 1996 to 2012 (Fig. 13.9).

Discussion

Lead poisoning is a preventable environmental health hazard that can affect any family. Although the burden of Illinois childhood lead poisoning still remains one of the highest in the nation, sustained prevention efforts have led to the dramatic decrease in the number of children with elevated blood lead levels, as the evidence has shown. Nationally and in Illinois, the large racial and ethnic disparities in lead exposure by socioeconomic status have been reduced on an absolute level (CDC 2013; IDPH 2013).

The mission of the Illinois Lead Program is to eliminate childhood lead poisoning and provide a lead safe environment for all Illinois children. The program began primarily as a blood lead registry with local programs operating from their own budgets in cities such as Chicago, East St. Louis, Kankakee, and areas of Cook

County. In 1992, IDPH realized that a coordinated, statewide effort would be more productive. A strategic plan was developed, new testing and reporting laws were adopted, and high-risk areas for childhood lead poisoning were identified. Since that time, IDPH has been spearheading the delivery of services to Illinois children with EBLLs and fostering programs and partnerships to reduce exposures to lead. The current goals of the Illinois Lead Program are (1) prevention of childhood lead poisoning through community education and public awareness campaigns; and (2) identification of lead-poisoned children and provision of prompt interventions to reduce blood lead levels and improve health and developmental outcomes (IDPH 2015).

Lead poisoning prevention activities require the development of policies, delegation, collaboration, and partnership in order to be successful.

Policy

As required by Public Act (410 ILCS 45/1) (from Ch. 111 1/2, par. 1301) (Illinois General Assembly 2014), health care providers and directors of clinical laboratories must report all blood lead analyses to IDPH. Illinois law requires children who live in high risk areas to complete a blood lead test before attending a licensed day care, school, or kindergarten. Children living in lower risk areas are required either to be assessed for risk of lead exposure using established questions or to receive a blood lead test (IDPH 2015).

Delegation

Annually, IDPH enters into grant agreements with 83–87 of Illinois' 102 counties and 5–8 municipal health departments to serve as delegate agencies. The delegate agencies provide case management for lead poisoned children in 83–95 counties. In addition, 18–23 of the delegate agencies also provide services to identify the sources of the lead poisoning. In counties where no delegate agency agreements exist, IDPH provides case management and lead investigation services.

Collaboration

The Illinois Lead Poisoning Elimination Advisory Council was formed in 2003 with the mission to develop and implement a comprehensive statewide strategic plan and has subsequently fostered partnerships in primary prevention, intervention, surveillance, and evaluation. The Advisory Council consists of professionals from governmental agencies, local health departments, and community organizations.

IDPH staff members have partnered with Advisory Council members to provide educational materials and training sessions; to develop and promote new guidelines for lead testing; and to partner with provider organizations to promote blood lead testing and risk assessment strategies.

Partnership

In order to serve lead-poisoned children enrolled in Medical Assistance Programs like Medicaid, All Kids, and WIC better, IDPH developed an interagency agreement to share data with the HFS, the Illinois Department of Human Services and the Illinois Department of Children and Family Services.

Intervention Level

An ever increasing body of research data has revealed that there is no safe level of lead in the body (CDC 2014; IDPH 2013). While this report focuses on children with BLLs of 10 µg/dL or greater, in May 2012, CDC established a new reference BLL that is used to identify children who have been exposed to lead and who require case management. The reference level, currently set at 5 µg/dL, is based on the 97.5% of the National Health and Nutritional Examination Survey (NHANES) BLLs and will be revised on a four-year cycle. Based on this new reference value, approximately 500,000 U.S. children are affected and about 30,000 of these children reside in the state of Illinois (IDPH 2013; Chicago Tribune 2015; CDC 2015). Based on the recommendation, the number of Illinois children requiring services to reduce lead exposures increased from about 3000 to more than 30,000. The Illinois Lead Poisoning Prevention Program is committed to the Healthy People 2020 goal of reducing lead exposures for all Illinois children.

Prevention Efforts

Sustained prevention efforts culminated in a significant decrease in the number of lead poisoned children. Primary prevention activities implemented included the designation of high and low risk ZIP codes for childhood lead poisoning; regional lead poisoning prevention training sessions; licensing of lead contractors in Illinois; and a comprehensive lead education, reduction, and window replacement (CLEAR-Win) program.

CLEAR-Win was the nation's first state funded window replacement program wherein original, wood-sashed windows in older homes were replaced using lead-safe work practices to prevent lead poisoning. Over the course of three years, the CLEAR-Win project assisted in the installation of nearly 8000 windows at 466 housing units. Two independent studies were performed for CLEAR-Win: one by the University of Illinois at Chicago (Jacobs et al. 2016) and the other by the University of Illinois at Urbana-Champaign. Both of these studies concluded that the project was not only successful at lowering the lead burden in the homes where window replacement was conducted, but that the return on investment was almost two dollars for every dollar spent. Furthermore, each recommended that the state should continue to fund the program and expand it throughout the state.

Secondary prevention was solely intervention through case management follow-up of children with lead in their blood and inspection of dwellings and common play areas of children to identify and remediate the sources of lead poisoning. Severe cases of lead poisoned children for chelation were rare.

Limitations

This report has some limitations. Blood lead data in this report have an inherent sampling bias. This is due to differential requirements for blood lead testing based on lead exposure risks. Illinois included areas where blood lead testing for all children is required (children living in high-risk ZIP codes and Chicago) and targeted areas where blood lead testing was based on individual child risk assessment methods. Illinois did not have state-wide representative data comparable to the National Health Nutrition and Examination Survey (NHANES) data, which is a representative sample of all U.S. children. The race and ethnic classification data were very sparse and no data on socioeconomic variables were available during this reporting period. The estimate of the annual geometric mean BLL is of limited use because of the substitution of values below a limit of detection with the detection value, and variable limits of detection due to equipment upgrades and re-certification through the years by different reference laboratories. Additionally, annually, approximately 5–13% of blood lead test results were excluded from analysis because of incomplete addresses. Research is underway to improve the quality of race and ethnicity data for children tested for lead poisoning.

Conclusion

Although the burden of Illinois childhood lead poisoning still remains one of the highest in the nation, prevention efforts, including improvements in housing and strategies focused on enhanced medical care, led to the dramatic 93% decrease in the number of children with BLLs of 10 µg/dL or greater between 1996 and 2012 (from 45,000 children in 1996 to 3000 children in 2012). In recognition of the fact that there is no safe level of lead in the body, in 2012 a new reference BLL used to identify children who have been exposed to lead was set at 5 µg/dL (CDC 2012).

The Illinois Lead Program is currently evaluating how the new reference value will affect the Program and what additional resources will be needed to implement the changes so the Program can adequately serve Illinois children. IDPH is committed to the Healthy People 2020 goal of reducing lead exposures for all children (US DHHS 2014).

Acknowledgments Thanks to Ken McCann, Environmental Health Division Chief for creating the maps and the Illinois Lead Program Team (Kert McAfee-Manager, Eddie Simpson, Kate Abitogun, Eleanor Davis, John Fee, Roxane Fleming, Jon Pressley, Tammy Pritchett, Kathy Kassing). Bill Dart, Deputy Director of the Office of Policy, Planning and Statistics provided some helpful comments. Also, thanks to the members of the Illinois Lead Poisoning Elimination Advisory Council. Funding for the Illinois Lead Program was provided by the U.S. Centers for Disease Control and Prevention (CDC), U.S. Environmental Protection Agency and Illinois State General Revenue Funds.

References

Bellinger, D. C., & Needleman, H. L. (2003). Intellectual impairment and blood lead levels. *New England Journal of Medicine, 349*, 500–502.
Chicago Tribune. (2015). Worrisome lead levels in Illinois children (data). Chicago Tribune Graphics. May 1, 2015 http://www.chicagotribune.com/news/watchdog/chi-lead-levels-in-illinois-children-data-20150430-htmlstory.html. Downloaded March 2, 2016.
Fokum, F. D., Shahidullah, M., Jorgensen, E., & Binns, H. (2015). Childhood lead exposure, testing rate, and blood lead poisoning prevalence in illinois and chicago, 1996–2012. Illinois Morbidity and Mortality Bulletin, 1(2):13–33. https://www.dph.illinois.gov/sites/default/files/publications/immb-vol1-issue2-040816.pdf
Goodman, B. (2016). Is there lead in your water. Medscape. pp. 1–3. https://www.medscape.com/viewarticle/857741. Downloaded March 2, 2016.
Hanna-Attisha, L. J., Sadler, R. C., & Schnepp, C. (2016). Elevated blood lead levels in children associated with the flint drinking water crisis: A spatial analysis of risk and public health response. *American Journal of Public Health, 106*(2), 283–290.
Illinois Department of Healthcare and Family Services (HFS). (2015). Illinois health connect bonus payment for high performance. http://www.illinoishealthconnect.com/provider/qualitytools/bonuspayment.aspx. Downloaded April, 08, 2015.
Illinois Department of Public Health. (2015). Illinois lead program 2014 annual surveillance report. http://www.dph.illinois.gov/sites/default/files/publications/publicationsohplead-surveillance-report-2014.pdf. Downloaded March 2, 2016.
Illinois Department of Public Health (IDPH). (2013). Childhood lead program surveillance report 2012. http://dph.illinois.gov/sites/default/files/publications/leadsurvrpt12_0.pdf. Downloaded on May 05, 2015.
Illinois Department of Public Health (IDPH). (2015). Childhood lead risk questionnaire. http://www.dph.illinois.gov/sites/default/files/forms/childhood-lead-risk-questionaire-and-guidelines-042116.pdf. Downloaded August 04, 2016.
Illinois General Assembly. (2014). (410 ILCS 45/) Lead poisoning prevention act. http://www.ilga.gov/legislation/ilcs/ilcs3.asp?ActID=1523&ChapterID=35. Downloaded May 05, 2015.
Jacobs, D. E., Tabin, M., Targos, L., Clarkson, D., Dixon, S. L., Breysse, J., et al. (2016). Replacing windows reduces childhood lead exposure: results from a state-funded program. *Journal of Public Health Management Practice, 00*(00), 1–10.

Raymond, J., Wheeler, W., & Brown, M. J. (2014). Lead screening and prevalence of blood lead levels in children aged 1–2 years-child blood lead surveillance system, united states, 2002-2010 and national health nutrition examination survey, MMWR/September 12 2014/ (vol. 63/No. 2).

U.S. Centers for Disease Control and Prevention (CDC). (2012). Low level lead exposure harms children: a renewed call for primary prevention. report of the advisory committee on childhood lead poisoning prevention of the centers for disease control and prevention. Atlanta, GA: US Department of Health and Human Services, CDC; 2012. http://www.cdc.gov/nceh/lead/ACCLPP/Final_Document_030712.pdf. Downloaded on May 05, 2015.

U.S. Centers for Disease Control and Prevention (CDC). (2013). Blood lead levels in children aged 1–5 Years—United States, 1999–2010 http://www.cdc.gov/mmwr/pdf/wk/mm6213.pdf April 5, 2013 (Vol. 62(13), pp. 245–248). Downloaded on May 05, 2015.

U.S. Centers for Disease Control and Prevention (CDC). (2014). Childhood Lead Poisoning Prevention Program. National surveillance data (1997–2013). Atlanta, GA: U.S. Department of Health and Human Services, CDC; 2014. http://www.cdc.gov/nceh/lead/data/Website_StateConfirmedByYear_1997_2013_10162014.htm. Downloaded on May 05, 2015.

U.S. Centers for Disease Control and Prevention (CDC). Updated 2015. Sources of lead. http://www.cdc.gov/nceh/lead/tips/sources.htm. Downloaded February 28, 2015.

U.S. Consumer Product Safety Commission (CPSC), Office of Compliance. (2011). Ban of Lead-Containing Paint and Certain Consumer Products Bearing Lead-Containing Paint, 16 C.F.R. 1303. http://www.cpsc.gov//PageFiles/111614/regsumleadpaint.pdf. Downloaded May 05, 2015.

U.S. Department of Health and Human Services (US DHHS). (2014). Healthy people 2020. Topics and objectives: Environmental health. Washington, DC: U.S. Department of Health and Human Services; 2014. http://www.healthypeople.gov/2020/topicsobjectives2020/objectiveslist.aspx?topicId=12. Downloaded May 5, 2015.

U.S. Census Bureau. (2013). 2012 American Community Survey 5-year Estimate. factfinder.census.gov.

U.S. Department of Housing and Urban Development (HUD), Office of Healthy Homes and Lead Hazard Control. (2011). American healthy homes survey- lead and arsenic findings, 2011: http://portal.hud.gov/hudportal/documents/huddoc?id=AHHS_REPORT.pdf. Downloaded May 05, 2015.

Chapter 14
A Demographic Analysis of Healthcare Satisfaction and Utilization Among Children from Same-Sex Households

Zelma Tuthill

Introduction

Same-sex parents face several obstacles in obtaining adequate resources to maintain a stable and healthy family. For children with same-sex parents, access to adequate healthcare is complicated due to family policies that limit the insurance coverage and benefits available for LGBT families. According to a report by the Williams Institute, an estimated 3 million LGBT Americans have had a child and as many as 6 million American children and adults have an LGBT parent (Gates 2013; Black et al. 2000). Although recent federal legislation has legalized same-sex marriage, variations of adherence at the state level, legal barriers in same-sex adoption and stigma continue to produce obstacles. This may impact access to adequate healthcare services for their mental and physical well-being. This study examines reported health care satisfaction and utilization of heterosexual and same-sex parents using secondary national data from the 2011 Medical Expenditure Panel Survey Household Component (MEPS HC) in order to examine any health disparities.

Prior research on the medical experiences of the LGBT community has focused on the legal obstacles and hostile healthcare environments that sexual minority individuals face when navigating the healthcare system such as homophobia, stigma and heteronormative assumptions about family structures (Ash et al. 2004; Biblarz and Savci 2010; Buffie 2011). Although the literature on the health of the LGBT community is increasing, there is currently limited research on the healthcare needs, satisfaction and healthcare utilization by children in same-sex families. Therefore, this study contributes to the lacking research on same-sex families by providing a comparison of healthcare satisfaction and utilization among children in same-sex and heterosexual households to examine potential healthcare disparities.

Z. Tuthill (✉)
Department of Sociology, Rice University, 6100 Main St., Houston, TX 77005-1892, USA
e-mail: oyarvidezl@gmail.com

Literature Review

Current research on the healthcare experience of LGBT adults document uncomfortable and negative interactions between medical providers and patients that impact their decisions to seek future services (Buchmueller and Carpenter 2010; Hughes and Evans 2003; Scherzer 2000). However, there is minimal research available on the healthcare experiences of the children of same-sex parents. If LGBT adults face uncomfortable and negative medical experiences, it is important to evaluate if this in turn affects the medical experiences of their children. Although the literature on healthcare satisfaction and utilization of same-sex families is limited, this section summarizes some of the key points that emerged from previous research about healthcare issues.

Family Policy and the Government; Unequal Healthcare for Same-Sex Families

Prior limited research on the healthcare experiences of same-sex families shows that they must confront heterosexual assumptions in the healthcare system that ignores the needs of their types of families (Shields et al. 2012). Additionally, research on the healthcare access of the LGBT community reflects an unequal opportunity in obtaining adequate and stigma-free healthcare compared to heterosexual individuals (Aaron et al. 2003; Hayman et al. 2013). Prior to the 2013 Supreme Court ruling that the Defense of Marriage Act (DOMA) which defined marriage between a man and a woman was unconstitutional, the federal government defined the family unit based on a heterosexual marriage. As a result, members in same-sex couples were unable to extend healthcare coverage to their family members, make important medical decisions and participate in various federal family-centered benefit programs (LGBT Families: Facts at a Glance 2011; Perrin and Siegel 2011; Lynch 2000). Since several government safety net programs use a narrow definition of family that is tied to marital status, non-legally recognized parents are restricted in their eligibility and participation in these federal programs (Ash 2004). Empirical research has provided evidence that link negative health effects with discriminatory policies in regards to marriage (Buffie 2011). Thus, the family policies that impede same-sex families from equal healthcare may also be creating negative health effects, which can result in greater unmet medical needs.

Research focusing on children raised by same-sex parents has found that they are twice as likely to live in poverty and are more likely to be raised by racial/ethnic minorities (Badgett et al. 2012). Since children in same-sex families may be more likely to live in poverty, non-participation in these programs is detrimental to their financial stability. Additionally, many same-sex parents are unable to provide health insurance benefits to the children in the home that are not biological, since many states have legislations that impedes second parent adoption for same-sex couples

(All Children Matter 2011). Thus, children raised by same-sex parents face limitations to their legal ties to both parents, which undermine family stability by creating an insecure economic relationship between family members.

Since certain inequalities are embedded in social structures, heterosexual assumptions and expectations embedded in family and medical policies reproduce unequal access to health care by constraining the medical choices of same-sex families. Shields et al. (2012) suggest that strategies need to be implemented to improve the quality of healthcare services for same-sex families to ensure that their needs are met. Similarly, research needs to address the healthcare experiences of same-sex families to highlight any disparities and potential mechanisms that reproduce unhealthy families. Thus, this study addresses the healthcare satisfaction and utilization of same-sex households.

Healthcare Satisfaction and Utilization

Although research on the medical experiences of same-sex families is limited, previous research has found that many same-sex parents reported being satisfied with the healthcare experiences of their children and mostly positive experiences for their children (Rawsthorne 2009; Shields et al. 2012). This is surprising, given the high number of documented negative medical experiences reported by sexual minority adults. It may be that medical experiences of same-sex parents differ from that of their child, with children experiencing more positive and satisfactory medical interaction. Although this study addresses satisfaction of healthcare services, more research is needed to address this seemingly paradoxical finding within same-sex families.

Previous research on healthcare utilization suggests that the frequency of visits to medical providers may be an indicator of health and ability to manage their condition (Litaker et al. 2005). Although recent Medicaid expansion has increased the number of children covered by health insurance, data shows that children (especially racial/ethnic minorities) experience various transitions of insurance coverage which impact their utilization of healthcare services (McCormick et al. 2000; Buchmueller and Carpenter 2010). Research on healthcare utilization of children has shown that dental care visits are problematically low, with younger children, insured children and white children more likely to have dental visits within the last year (McCormick et al. 2000). Since disparities in utilization of dental care services among children are documented, frequency of dental visits are examined in this paper.

Significance of Study

Few studies have provided detailed information on the healthcare experiences of the children of same-sex parents. This may be due to the limited number of large nationally representative samples of children in same sex households. However, additional data on the utilization and healthcare experiences of same-sex families is needed to identify any unequal healthcare experience as a family unit. This study contributes to public health research that examines health disparities of same-sex families.

Methodology

Data

This paper uses data from the 2011 Medical Expenditure Panel Survey Household Component (MEPS HC) regarding healthcare satisfaction and utilization of same-sex and heterosexual families. The MEPS is a set of large-scale surveys of families and individuals, their medical providers, and employers across the United States; it provides yearly data on the cost and use of health care as well as health insurance coverage (meps.ahrq.gov). The MEPS Household Component is a subsample of households participating in the previous year's National Health Interview Survey (NHIS). The MEPS HC provides estimates of demographic and socio-economic characteristics, employment, and family relationship information of the respondent of the survey. This data is well suited for this study given its large and nationally representative sample that emphasizes healthcare coverage of families.

Sample

The sample in this paper consists of same-sex and heterosexual parents from the 2011 MEPS HC. The 2011 MEPS HC collected data on 9386 children ages 0–17 from same-sex and heterosexual households. The MEPS has demographic variables from each reporting unit (RU) which serves as the analytical unit and consists of "group of persons in the sampled dwelling unit who are related by blood, marriage, adoption, foster care or other family association" (meps.ahrq.gov).

Since the 2011 MEPS HC did not collect information about sexual orientation, the sample size of same sex and heterosexual households was obtained by evaluating the dwelling unit (DU), FAMID, FAMSIZ, and RFREL11X variables which identify a respondent's family affiliation and family size. The FAMID and FAMISIZ variables reflect information about family size and the RFREL11X variable indicates the relationship of an individual to the reference person (RU) filling out the survey; relationship to the reference person is indicated by codes representing husband/spouse, wife, spouse, son, daughter, female partner, male partner etc. Since the 2011 MEPS HC does not identify same-sex families, spouse or partner and sex information were utilized to categorize same-sex and heterosexual parents. Since this study does not include self-identified same sex parents, this sample sixe might not capture all same sex parents. Additional research should examine differences in satisfaction and utilization with data sets that inquire about sexual orientation.

Measures

Healthcare Satisfaction: Healthcare satisfaction in this study is measured by obtaining data regarding perceived ease of getting needed medical care for their child and rating of healthcare. Ease of getting needed medical care is an indicator of satisfaction using the question that asks "In the last 12 months, how often was it easy to get the care, tests, or treatments you or a doctor believed necessary?", with response categories of "never," "sometimes" "usually" and "always." Rating of child's healthcare was also used to measure healthcare satisfaction using the question that asks "Using any number from 0 to 10 where 0 is the worst health care possible, and 10 is the best health care possible, what number would you use to rate health care in the last 12 months?" with response categories between 0 and 10.

Healthcare Utilization: Frequency of dental visits is measured as an indicator of healthcare utilization using response categories of "2x a year or more," "1x a year," "less than 1x a year" and "never." Since prior research has documented disparities in the use of oral care services among children, dental visit are examined for this paper.

Design

Due to previous research documenting the complexities to healthcare access for same-sex families, I expect that same-sex families will report lower rates of ease of obtaining healthcare, lower rating of healthcare, fewer dental visits and report higher rates of inability to obtain medical care compared to heterosexual families. Frequencies of responses to variables regarding healthcare satisfaction and utilization are presented in percentages for both the same-sex and heterosexual family sample in Table 14.1.

Results

Demographic information about the sample sizes are presented in Tables 14.1 and 14.2 and in Figs. 14.1 and 14.2. The average income for the same-sex households is $23,381 compared to the average income of $61,364 among

Table 14.1 Descriptive statistics

	%	Mean	Standard deviation
Heterosexual households (N = 12,673)			
Age		26.9	19.3
Income		61,364.3	55,053.3
Female	51.6		
Male	48.4		
White	68.9		
Black	19.9		
Other	11.1		
Same sex households (N = 195)			
Age		35.4	10.4
Income		23,381.9	24,578.8
Female	43.9		
Male	56.1		
White	72.5		
Black	21.6		
Other	5.8		

Source Medical Expenditure Panel Survey, Household Component 2011

Table 14.2 Distribution of healthcare satisfaction and utilization

	Easy getting medical care	Rating of healthcare	Frequency of dental visits
Heterosexual households			
Never	1.3		
Sometimes	4.3		
Usually	18.7		
Always	75.7		
Rating 0–5		10.3	
Rating 6–10		89.7	
2× a year or more			39.5
1× a year or more			27.1
<1× a year			17.2
Never			16.2
Same-sex households			
Never	2.5		
Sometimes	10.7		
Usually	31.6		
Always	55.3		
Rating 0–5		12.9	
Rating 6–10		87.1	

(continued)

Table 14.2 (continued)

	Easy getting medical care	Rating of healthcare	Frequency of dental visits
2× a year or more			16.9
1× a year or more			27.1
<1× a year			26.1
Never			29.9

Source Medical Expenditure Survey, 2011

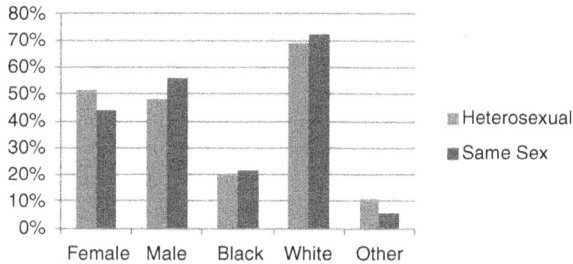

Fig. 14.1 Demographic variables of respondent: Medical Expenditure Survey, 2011

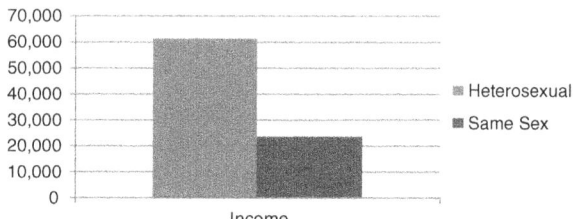

Fig. 14.2 Family Income Average: Medical Expenditure Survey, 2011

heterosexual households with great variability. The average age of respondent for the same-sex households was approximately 35 compared to 27 from heterosexual families. This reflects similar findings to previous reports by the Williams Institute, All Children Matter and LGBT Families at a Glance that document economic disparities between same-sex and heterosexual families.

There are a higher percentage of white respondents in the same-sex households compared to the heterosexual households. This does not reflect previous data that suggests that same-sex parents are most likely to be racial/ethnic minorities and tend to have lower educational attainment and income levels compared to Whites (Badgett et al. 2012). However, this could be due to the difficulty of obtaining large probabilistic data sets with same-sex parents of color. Additional research should examine how healthcare satisfaction and utilization differs by racial/ethnic identity.

Healthcare Satisfaction

There are differences in the "easy getting needed medical care" responses between same-sex and heterosexual households. In heterosexual households 1.3% reported never, 4.3% reported sometimes, 18.7% reported usually and 75.7% reported always. In same-sex households, 2.5% reported never, 10.7% sometimes, 31.6% reported usually and 55.3% reported always. There appear to be higher rates of difficulty getting needed medical care for same-sex households. Same-sex and heterosexual households report similar rates of high satisfaction of healthcare. In the heterosexual household, 10.3% of the responses are between 0 and 5 and 89.7% of the responses provided a higher rating (between 6 and 10) of healthcare. In the same-sex family households, 2.8% of the responses provided a rating between 0 and 5 while 97.1% of the responses provided a higher rating of 6–10. Thus, the same-sex family sample reported a higher percentage of satisfaction compared to the heterosexual family sample. This is interesting since prior research has documented negative and poor medical experience among sexual minority adults. This also seems to contradict the lower rates of ease of getting medical care. Additional research should examine how the medical experiences of children in same-sex households vary from the experiences of their parents.

Healthcare Utilization

There were large differences in the frequency of dental visits between the same-sex and heterosexual households. In the heterosexual households, 39.5% of the responses reported a frequency of two times a year or more, 27.1% of the responses reported a frequency of one time a year or more, 17.2% of the responses reported a frequency of less than one time a year and 16.2% of the responses reported never having a dental visit. In same-sex households, 16.9% of the responses reported a frequency of two times a year or more, 27.1% of the responses reported a frequency of one time a year or more, 26.1% reported a frequency of less than one time a year and 29.9% of the responses reported never having a dental visit. Thus, almost twice the percentage of same-sex parents reported that their child never had a dental visit in 2011 compared to parents in heterosexual households.

Reliability and Validity

The 2011 MEPS survey is designed in several panels which make it possible to determine how changes in respondents' income, employment, eligibility for public and private insurance coverage, use of services, and payment for care are related (meps.ahrq.gov). The 2011 MEPS HC survey was chosen for this study and a more updated survey may provide different results.

There are some additional limitations in this study. Although the 2011 MEPS HC contains data about the healthcare of children in same-sex families, the parents are the respondents of the survey. Thus, information about the household, including rating of healthcare is obtained from the responses of the parents.

Additionally, like many national health surveys, the 2011 MEPS does not collect information about sexual orientation. This makes identifying same-sex families very difficult. Therefore various demographic variables where utilized to identify same-sex households for the purpose of this study. This can be problematic since self-identified information about sexual orientation is not used and the researcher is categorizing same-sex households. This also results in very small numbers in the analytic sample, making analysis difficult. Thus, various same-sex families may not be captured in the analytic sample. National data samples that collect information on sexual orientation would address this issue. In terms of racial identification, the race variable utilized in this survey categorizes Hispanic individuals as white. As a result, the white racial category includes individuals who would also categorize themselves as Hispanic, making it difficult to make comparisons by racial/ethnic identity.

Discussion

The percentages for the healthcare satisfaction and utilization variables from the 2011 MEPS HC survey were compared between same-sex and heterosexual households. Although the analysis for this paper are simplistic, differences in the reported ease of obtaining medical care support previous research that has documented difficulty in obtaining adequate healthcare for this population (Black et al. 2000; Buchmueller and Carpenter 2010). The lower rates of ease of getting medical care may indicate that the difficulty to obtaining adequate healthcare of sexual minorities may extend to their children. However, the similar and higher rates of satisfaction between same-sex and heterosexual households align with previous finding from Rawsthorne (2009) and Shields et al. (2012), which suggest that same-sex families may not differ in the satisfaction of the healthcare of their children. Thus, there seems to be discrepancy in the rating of the healthcare they provide for their children versus the ease of obtaining these services. It may be that even though it may be more difficult to obtain necessary healthcare, their experiences with their children are more positive. More research with larger numbers of same sex families is needed to make more concrete conclusions.

Even though there were minimal differences among some of the satisfaction variables, there appeared a notable difference in the frequency of dental visits among children in same-sex and heterosexual families. More same-sex households reported that their children had never visited the dentist in 2011 than heterosexual households. Although same-sex parents were not reporting a difficulty in receiving medical care or a more negative healthcare experience, the lower rates of dental care visits point to fewer opportunities for children in same-sex families to receive necessary preventative oral health services. Among the same-sex households, the highest percentage of response for "frequency of dental visits" pertained to the "never" category and the lowest percentage of response pertained to the "two times a year or more" category. On the other hand, the heterosexual family sample displayed the opposite with the highest response category pertaining to the "two times a year or more" category and the lowest percentage to the "never." Additionally, same-sex households displayed a higher percentage of response to the "less than one time a year" category compared to the heterosexual family sample. Thus, the low rates of ease of obtaining necessary medical care and the low rates of dental visits suggest disparities in utilization and access of services between same-sex and heterosexual households. However, the more positive perception of healthcare services from same-sex households should be further investigated.

Conclusion

Minimal research exists on the healthcare of children in same-sex families. Many national probabilistic surveys that gather data on healthcare of children, fail to identify whether the child has same-sex parents. This results in data that groups children in heterosexual and same sex families together, even though prior research shows that sexual minorities experience negative and unequal healthcare experiences. This study compared healthcare satisfaction and utilization of same-sex and heterosexual households since this is lacking in the literature. Although slight differences in regards to satisfaction of healthcare arose between the same-sex and heterosexual households, there were large differences in the ease of getting medical care and frequency of child dental visits within the past year. Millbank (2003) argues that in the absence of good quality information, decision makers and policy makers may either ignore the existence of same-sex families or proceed on the basis of inaccurate or inappropriate assumptions. The limited studies on same-sex families and a lack of sexual orientation information in health surveys contribute to the neglect of the medical experiences of the children of sexual minorities. Thus, additional research is needed to confirm and identify other areas of unequal healthcare utilization among children in same-sex households.

References

Aaron, D. J., Chang, Y.-F., Markovic, N., & LaPorte, R. E. (2003). Estimating the lesbian population: A capture-recapture approach. *Journal of Epidemiology and Community Health, 57*(3), 207–209.

Ash, M., Lee Badgett, M. V., NacnyFolbre, L. S., & Albelda, R. (2004). *Same-sex couples and their children in massachusetts: A view from census 2000*. Massachusetts: The Institute for Gay And Lesbian Studies.

Badgett, M. V., Durso L. E., & Schneebaum, A. (2012). New patterns of poverty in the lesbian, gay, and bisexual community. The Williams Institute.

Biblarz, T. J., & Savci, E. (2010). Lesbian, gay and transgender families. *Journal of Marriage and Family, 72*, 480–497.

Black, D., Gates, G., Sanders, S., & Taylor, L. (2000). Demographics of the gay and lesbian population in the united states: Evidence from available systematic data sources. *Demography, 37*(2), 139–154.

Buchmueller, T., & Carpenter, C. S. (2010). Disparities in health insurance coverage, access, and outcomes for individuals in same-sex versus different sex relationships, 200-2007. *American Journal of Public Health, 100*(3), 489–495.

Buffie, W. C. (2011). Public health implications of same-sex marriage. *American Journal of Public Health, 101*(6), 986–990.

Gates, G. J. (2013). LGBT Parenting in the United States. The Williams Institute.

Hayman, B., Wilkes, L., Halcomb, E. J., & Jackson, D. (2013). Marginalized mothers: Lesbian women negotiating heteronormative healthcare services. *Contemporary Nurse, 44*(1), 120–127.

Hughes, C., & Evans, A. (2003). Health needs of women who have sex with women: Healthcare workers need to be aware of their specific needs. *British Medical Journal, 327*(7421), 939–940.

Litaker, D., Koroukian, S. M., & Love, T. E. (2005). Context and healthcare access: looking beyond the individual. *Medical Care, 3*(6), 531–540.

LGBT Families: Facts at a Glance. (2011). Movement Advancement Project.

Lynch, J. M. (2000). Considerations of family structure and gender composition: The lesbian and gay step-family. *Journal of Homosexuality, 40*(2), 81–95.

McCormick, M. C., Barbara, K., Anne, E., Joe, T., & Lisa, S. (2000). Annual report on access to and utilization of health care for children and youth in the united states-1999. *Annual Review of Child Health Care Access and Utilization*

Millbank, J. (2003). From here to maternity: A review of the research on lesbian and gay families. *Australian Journal of Social Issues Australian Journal of Social Issues*

Perrin, E. C., & Siegel, B. S. (2011). *Matter: How legal and social inequalities hurt lgbt families. Center for american progress*. Family Equality Council and Movement Advancement Project: Washington D.C.

Prokos, A. H. & Jennifer, R. K. (2010). Poverty among cohabiting gay and lesbian, and married and cohabiting

Scherzer, T. (2000). Negotiating health care: The experiences of young lesbian and bisexual women. *Culture, Health and Sexuality, 2*(1), 87–102.

Shields, L., Tess, Z., Diana B., Dip L., Rochelle W., Joan W., & Rose, C. (2012). Lesbian, gay, bisexual, and transgender parents seeking health care for their children: A systematic review of the literature. *Worldviews on Evidence-Based Nursing* 200–209.

Rawsthorne, M. (2009). Same-sex couples in the 2006 census: Countering symbolic exclusion. *Advances in Social Work and Welfare Education, 11*(1), 71-88.

Part II
Mortality and Morbidity in Developing Countries

Chapter 15
Implications of Age Structural Transition and Longevity Improvement on Healthcare Spending in India

Preeti Dhillon and Laishram Ladusingh

Introduction

Healthcare cost is age dependent. After the high cost in the first year of life, it is lowest for children, rises slowly throughout adult life and increases exponentially after the age of 50 years (Meerding et al. 1998). Bradford and Max (1996) found that annual costs for healthcare for elderly are approximately four to five times than in their younger ages. A number of studies viz. Colombier and Weber (2011), Ruggeri (2002), OECD (2006), Pammolli et al. (2008), Ogawa et al. (2009) and Johnston and Teasdale (1999) identify proportion of population as a key driver of healthcare costs. However, others like Newhouse (1992), Cutler (1995), Zweifel et al. (1999), Felder et al. (2000) and Seshamani and Gray (2004) hold a contrary view that longevity improvements rather reduce the healthcare expenditures by shifting the bulk of healthcare costs to higher ages due to the higher death related expenditure (proximity to death). However, in Indian context, there is limited literature to either support or negate the two schools of thoughts. A study by Arokiasamy and Yadav (2013) on Indian data provides evidence of expansion of morbidity among the elderly over time rejecting the hypothesis that total healthcare cost would decline with the longevity improvement.

India is experiencing gradual ageing. The proportion of its population aged 60 years and above is expected to increase from 7.7% in 2010 to 18.3% in 2050 (United Nations World Population Prospects, the 2012 revision). Visaria (2004) revealed that India will face a 'double burden of disease', that is an increase in chronic degenerative ailments, while major infectious diseases remain serious health problems. India's share in burden of non-communicable disease shall also increase with the ongoing epidemiological transition. Table 15.1 provides a

P. Dhillon (✉) · L. Ladusingh
Department of Mathematical Demography & Statistics, International Institute for Population Sciences, Deonar, Mumbai 400088, India
e-mail: pdhillon_maths@yahoo.co.in

Table 15.1 A comparative scenario of population ageing and health in India and World

Indicators	2015	2030	2015	2030	2015	2030
	India		**World**		**India's share (%)**	
Population (60+) (%)[a]	8.8	12.3	12.2	16.3	12.5	13.2
Life expectancy at birth[a]	66.3	69.5	70.0	72.8	–	–
Life expectancy at age 60[a]	17.0	17.7	20.0	21.1	–	–
Old age dependency ratio (%)[a]	13.9	19.2	19.8	27.1	–	–
	South Asia		**World**		**South Asia's share (%)**	
Share of age 60 and over in DALYs (%)[b]	15.3	22.0	18.5	25.3	23	24
Burden of Non communicable disease in 60+ aged						
DALYs (billion)[b]	50	72	235	315	21	23
DALY (%)[#]	86	89	90	91	–	–

Note Old age dependency ratio is measured as ratio of elderly aged 60+ years to working age (15–59) population; period for life expectancy is 2010–15 and 2025–30

DALYs Disability adjusted life years (the DALY combines in one measure the time lived with disability and the time lost due to premature mortality)

[#]Contribution of DALYs due to non-communicable disease in total DALYs

Sources [a]Authors compilation from United Nations World Population Prospects (the 2012 revision)

[b]Authors compilation from projection of mortality and global burden of disease, 2004–2030, World Health Organisation (2004 update)

projection of burden of disease for the South Asian region, the closest approximation of what the Indian situation could be by 2030.

It is predicted that the proportion of disability adjusted life years (DALYs) contributed by the elderly in South Asia will increase both within the region and as their share in the DALYS of the World population; going up from 15 to 22% and 23 to 24% respectively between 2015 and 2030. Other evidence indicates that extended years of life gained by the increase in life expectancy are translating into poor health resulting in an expansion of morbidity during the epidemiological transition (Crimmins et al. 1994, 1996, 1997; Andrews 2001; Arokiasamy and Yadav 2013) particularly in developing countries.

There is a lack of scholarly literature examining Indian data on overall healthcare expenditure across all age groups, by sources (public and private) and over time. There is little empirical evidence throwing light on the possible implications of population ageing in the future. Identifying the role of population age structure in prospects of healthcare spending may help to serve as a wakeup call for stakeholders about the extent of preparedness required and may point to the need to consider healthcare budgetary allocation according to the age composition of the population. This paper is an attempt to fill the gaps and strengthen empirical evidence on the implication of ageing on healthcare cost at the macro level. This is examined by linking information on expenditure for different healthcare components (such as antenatal checkups (ANC), delivery-care, immunisation, in-patient, outpatient care etc.) with sources of financing care while disaggregating healthcare expenditure by age groups at the national and state levels for the year 2004–05. Further, it presents an overview of healthcare expenditure as a share of GDP over the post-economic reform period by both public and private sources of spending finally deliberating over the possible role of age structural transition on future healthcare spending. It specifically discusses the expected implications of health transition and longevity improvement on healthcare expenditure across ages, over time.

Methodology

Data Sources The study utilises the following listed data sources:

Population Age Structure The age-sex population structure for the period of 1990–2050, by five-year age groups is taken from the United Nations World Population Prospects (The 2012 revision). In addition, we gather state-wide age-population data from the report of the Office of the Registrar General & Census Commissioner, Government of India (ORGI 2006).

Healthcare Expenditure (HCE) at Aggregate Level Data on private healthcare expenditure at the aggregate level have been collected from the reports on National Accounts Statistics (Ministry of Statistics & Programme Implementation (MoSPI 2011b)) for the period 1993–94 to 2004–05 and from National Health Accounts (MoHFW and WHO 2009) 2004–05 onwards. Further, aggregate level healthcare expenditure from a public source is taken from www.indiastat.com for the period 1993–94 to 2004–05 and from 2004–05 onwards it is from the National Health Accounts (MoHFW and WHO 2009). Wholesale price indexes were used to estimate public health spending for the period 1993–94 to 2004–05 at the price of 2004–05. These reports compile *public sector* data from various sources from the state budget documents and Central Ministries/Departments. The *private sector healthcare expenditure* includes out-of pocket (OOP) expenditure incurred by households for availing healthcare services, healthcare expenditure through the insurance mechanism and expenditure by corporate bodies on their employees and families.

Age-Specific Per Capita Healthcare Expenditure We estimate HCE per capita for five-year age groups by summing up age-specific per capita expenditure for different components of healthcare namely, inpatient, outpatient, maternal and child health (antenatal, institutional delivery, postnatal and immunisation), family planning as given in the framework of National Health Account of the Ministry of Health & Family Welfare (MoHFW and WHO 2009). For this purpose, individual level data from the 60th round of the National Sample Survey (NSSO 2006) has been used. This survey covered 73,868 households spread across all the states and union territories of India. Information on the utilisation of healthcare services by households for both hospitalised and non-hospitalised treatments by type of service provider, nature of ailment and a number of related characteristics have been collected through this survey.

The reference period for data collection was 15 days for non-hospitalised cases and 365 days for hospitalised cases and all other components. State-level analysis excludes all Union territories and small states namely Delhi and Goa to have sufficient sample size. We also combine the north-eastern states (Arunachal Pradesh, Nagaland, Sikkim, Tripura, Meghalaya and Manipur) together to achieve sufficient sample size in each cell.

Gross Domestic Product (GDP) GDP at factor cost at year 2004–05 prices is taken from the Macro Economic Aggregate and population from National Account Statistics Back Series 2011 (MoSPI 2011a).

Methods

First, we analyse the trends of healthcare expenditure per capita and HCE as share of GDP for the post-economic reform period (1993 onwards), disaggregated by public-and private sources. The age-specific HCE per capita for India and states is estimated for the year 2004–05. For this, first we estimate expenditure per person reporting ailment and per person hospitalised by five-year age groups followed by, calculation of HCE for the year 2004 by multiplying the average in-patient and outpatient expenditures with the estimated number of in-patients and outpatients. Further, we follow a similar procedure for estimating each component (ANC, PNC, Delivery, and Immunisation) of OOP except expenditure on family planning. For per capita health expenditure on family planning, we use aggregate level expenditure given in the National Health Accounts Report for 2004–05 (MoHFW and WHO 2009) and then allocate it by age-specific contraception prevalence rates taken from the National Family Health Survey-3 (IIPS 2007). This assumes that the expenditure on contraceptives among the couple from a particular age group is proportionate to their contraceptive prevalence rate. One of the limitations of doing this could be that the age pattern of contraceptive use and the costs therein differ by method (spacing and limiting). As the MoHFW and WHO (2009) does not provide aggregate expenditure by type of method, we were not been able to consider it.

The aggregate per capita healthcare expenditure out-of pocket for the year 2004 is 826 Indian rupees (INR) and its summation 930.92 billion for the total population. This has been normalised to 955.60 and 263.13 billion from private and public sources respectively in 2004–05 (MoHFW and WHO 2009). Finally, per capita household expenditure from private and public sources is estimated 848 and 233 INR in the year 2004–05. The detail of age-specific HCE per capita is given in Appendix 3. Similarly, we estimate age-specific HCE per capita for the states of India, and apply cubic spline method to smoothen the estimates.

To measure the implications of age structural transition on future healthcare expenditure, we calculate the Age Composition Index (ACI) for HCE using the following formula over the specific period

$$\text{ACI}_{\text{HCE},t} = \frac{\sum_i \text{Pop}_{it} \times \text{HCE}_{it}}{P_t} \qquad (15.1)$$

where, HCE_{it} is per capita health spending in ith age group at time t.

The age-compositional index can be used to project future healthcare cost using the following formula (Johnston and Teasdale 1999) and CBO (2007):

$$\text{HCE}_t = \text{HCE}_{t-1} \times \frac{\text{ACI}_t}{\text{ACI}_{t-1}} \times (1 + x_t)$$

where

$$x_t = \frac{\text{HCE}_t}{\text{HCE}_{t-1}} \times \frac{\text{ACI}_t}{\text{ACI}_{t-1}} - 1 \qquad (15.2)$$

is the excess growth of healthcare spending per-capita, in other words, the growth of HCE per-capita due to other factors excluding age-compositional effects.

Similarly, age-composition index for GDP can be defined as

$$\text{ACI}_{\text{GDP},t} = \frac{\sum_i \text{Pop}_{it} \times \text{WPR}_{it}}{P_t} \qquad (15.3)$$

where, WPR_{it} is work participation rate in ith age group at time t.

The excess growth of GDP per capita x_t can be defined as in Eq. 15.2 by taking GDP in place of HCE. The ACI in Eq. 15.3 is based on the questionable assumption that the productivity of workers from different ages is the same. A comprehensive literature review on age and individual productivity by Skirbekk (2004) reveals that, an individual's performance tends to increase in the first few years of his or her entry into the labour market and decreases towards the end of his or her career even though the earnings generally continue increasing until relatively late in his/her working life. Due to a lack of information on productivity by age in India, we consider age-specific work participation rates a viable indicator and assume that age specific productivity is in proportion to their work participation rates (as considered by Johnston and Teasdale 1999; CBO 2007).

In the present study, the ACI for HCE and GDP are calculated over the period of 1990–2050 by keeping the age profile of HCE per capita and GDP per capita constant at 2004–05. In addition, age profile of public HCE is assumed to be same as that of the private as the expenditure from public sources is available only at the aggregate level. However, we discuss the possible violation of assumptions with other literature.

Findings and Discussion

India's Changing Population Age Structure According to UN World Population long-term projections (The 2012 revision), the population of India will continue to grow, and is expected to reach 1.62 billion by 2050. The elderly as a proportion of the total population will increase from 7.7 in 2010 to 18.3 in 2050. This age structural transition varies by gender with the population of the female elderly growing more than the males. This is reflected in the growth in sex ratio in this age group which is predicted to increase from 1066 to 1130 females per thousand males during 2000–2050.

There is a huge diversity in population age structure across states of India (Appendix 1). Kerala had the highest proportions of the elderly (10.6%) in 2001, followed by Tamil Nadu (9%), Himachal Pradesh (8.8%), Punjab (8.7%), Maharashtra (8.3%) and Orissa (7.8%). By 2026, it is projected that Kerala will maintain its position at 18.3% followed by, Tamil Nadu (17.1%), Himachal Pradesh (14.7%), Karnataka, Punjab (14.5%), Andhra Pradesh and West Bengal (14.2%). The population between 15 and 59 years will increase with Bihar experiencing the highest pace, followed by Rajasthan, Haryana and Uttar Pradesh. The state wise variation in population age structure is indicative of the need to consider age composition as a key factor when planning state specific programmes. Further, it signals that a disaggregated state-level analysis of the associations between age structure, HCE and longevity be conducted.

Overview of Healthcare Spending (1993–2009) Financing of healthcare is one of the critical determinants of health outcomes in a country. In India, healthcare expenditure from all sources comprised 4.25% (0.84% from public, 3.32% from private, and 0.1% from external flow) of the Gross Domestic Product (MoHFW and WHO 2009) in 2004–05.

Trends of healthcare spending in the post-economic reform period in India (Table 15.2) suggest that though the ratio of healthcare spending to GDP is low on the whole, it is showing a gradual increase since 1993. This is a positive sign. Taking 2004-05 prices as the index one sees that healthcare expenditure per capita has increased from Indian rupees 538 (175 from public and 363 from private) to INR 1879 (510 from public and 1369 from private) during 1993–2008. Healthcare spending as a share of GDP has risen from 3.1 to 5.2% (1.0–1.4% for public and 2.1–3.8% for private) during the same period. The average annual growth of HCE per capita and GDP per capita in the period 1993–94 to 2008–09 is 8.2 and 5.1% respectively.

There is a significant gap between household and public healthcare spending throughout the period. Of the total health expenditure in 2004–05, the share of the private sector was the 78.1% while the public sector expenditure was a mere 19.7% (MoHFW and WHO 2009). However, in recent years public expenditure has shown an increase owing to measures such as the Central Government's National Rural Health Mission (NRHM) started in 2005 (Berman and Ahuja 2008) and the recently launched *Rashtriya Swasthya Bima Yojana* (RSBY) (2008). While the NRHM

Table 15.2 Trends of healthcare expenditure in India, 1993–2009

Year (base year, 2004)	Population (Cr)[a]	Public[b] HCE (Cr)	HCE per capita	Private[c] HCE (Cr)	HCE per capita	GDP[d] (Cr)	GDP per capita	HCE as % GDP Public	HCE as % GDP Private	HCE as % GDP Total
1993–94	89	15,597	175	32,278	363	1,522,343	17,105	1.02	2.12	3.14
1994–95	91	16,522	182	35,956	395	1,619,694	17,799	1.02	2.22	3.24
1995–96	93	16,017	172	40,023	430	1,737,740	18,685	0.92	2.30	3.22
1996–97	95	16,639	175	44,393	467	1,876,319	19,751	0.89	2.37	3.25
1997–98	96	18,275	190	49,240	513	1,957,031	20,386	0.93	2.52	3.45
1998–99	98	20,394	208	54,635	558	2,087,827	21,304	0.98	2.62	3.59
1999–00	100	22,542	225	61,246	612	2,254,942	22,549	1.00	2.72	3.72
2000–01	102	22,755	223	68,366	670	2,348,481	23,024	0.97	2.91	3.88
2001–02	104	21,891	210	78,049	750	2,474,962	23,798	0.88	3.15	4.04
2002–03	106	23,954	226	82,174	775	2,570,935	24,254	0.93	3.20	4.13
2003–04	107	24,550	229	84,924	794	2,775,749	25,942	0.88	3.06	3.94
2004–05	109	26,313	241	95,560	877	2,971,464	27,261	0.89	3.22	4.10
2005–06	111	34,446	310	115,000	1036	3,253,073	29,307	1.06	3.54	4.59
2006–07	112	40,679	363	127,840	1141	3,564,364	31,825	1.14	3.59	4.73
2007–08	114	48,685	427	142,690	1252	3,896,636	34,181	1.25	3.66	4.91
2008–09	115	58,681	510	157,393	1369	4,158,676	36,162	1.41	3.78	5.20

Note Cr. is one Crore = 10,000,000, figures are in Indian rupees. All figures are at 2004–05 price, population relates to mid-financial year
Sources [a]Macro Economic Aggregates and Population: Statement 1: (MoSPI 2011a)
[b]For years 1993–94 to 2004–05: nominal figures are taken from www.indiastat.com and then estimated at 2004–05 prices using wholesale price index; for 2005–06 year onwards: National Health Accounts (MoHFW and WHO 2009)
[c]For years 1993–94 to 2004–05: Statement 9: private consumption expenditure by objects (MoSPI 2011b); for 2005–06 year onwards: National Health Accounts (MoHFW and WHO 2009)
[d]Macro Economic Aggregates: Table 2 (Central Statistical Office, Accessed from www.rbi.org.in, 2013)

has helped in the reduction of out-of-pocket expenditures on delivery care (Mohanty and Srivastava 2012) the RSBY covering unorganised workers from below poverty line (BPL) households aims to shield them and their families from the financial burden of hospitalisation expenses.

Age Pattern of Per Capita Healthcare Expenditure Figure 15.1 shows the age profile of per capita and real healthcare expenditure in India. Per capita healthcare spending is the highest for the age group 0–4 years (INR 931) and reduces to INR 338 for the age group 10–14 years. It then rises steadily peaking for those between 70 and 74 years (INR 4823). On the other hand, overall healthcare expenditure is higher for the younger ages and declines with age advancement from 15 to 74. Post 74 it declines rapidly. Overall health spending is at the highest level for those in the age group of 0–4 years, followed by populations in the 25–29 and 45–49 years age groups. The higher per capita health expenditure in older ages suggests the positive association of age and poor health status and the consequent higher healthcare expenditures. An increase in the population of the elderly coupled with the higher prevalence of morbidity among them may thus entail a simultaneous increase in healthcare spending provided the assumption that differentials in treatment seeking behaviour among older and younger cohort will be at par with that of the younger populations holds true.

Figure 15.2 reveals that labour income is the highest in the age group of 35–39 years (INR 47784), which declines afterwards. However, the age group 25–29 years has the highest contribution (INR 4085.02 billion) to the overall GDP.

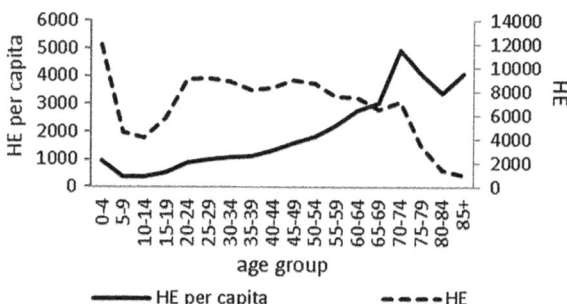

Fig. 15.1 Age pattern of healthcare expenditure, 2004–05

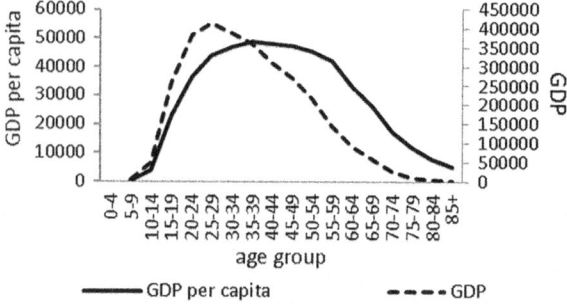

Fig. 15.2 Age profile of labour income, 2004–05

Healthcare Expenditure by States The age-specific HCE per-capita is shown in the Appendix 2. Almost all states reveal the positive relationship between HCE per-capita and age. Interestingly, most of the states are expected to show increasing age-compositional effects on health spending during 2005–25 (see Appendix 2). Assam and Punjab have shown the highest increase in ACI over the said period. On the other hand, the states of Uttar Pradesh, Rajasthan, Odisha and Jharkhand have shown lower age-compositional effects on healthcare spending.

During 2004–05, HCE per-capita among the elderly in Punjab is more than INR 4000, followed by, Kerala, Jammu and Kashmir, Karnataka, Maharashtra, Himachal Pradesh, and Gujarat where it is higher than INR 3000 (Fig. 15.3). On the other hand, the lowest per capita health spending among the 60+ age group is observed in Chhattisgarh (INR 600), followed by Uttarakhand and Odisha. For the population below age 60 years, spending was the highest in Himachal Pradesh, followed by Kerala and Punjab and the lowest was in Jharkhand, Assam and Bihar.

Although, the overall HCE per capita is higher in Punjab, Kerala and Himachal Pradesh, when we distribute HCE per-capita by age (Fig. 15.4), the proportion of HCE on the elderly is higher (30%) in Karnataka and Assam, while it is lowest in (10%) Uttarakhand and Chhattisgarh.

Implications of Age Structural Transition on Future Healthcare Spending The projected growth of age composition index adjustment to HCE per capita and GDP per capita is shown in Fig. 15.5. From this it appears that the growth of ageing effects on HCE shall increase from 0.5% in 2005 to 0.8% in 2025 and afterwards it shall be stable. It is the growing young population that has in the recent past contributed to GDP growth. However, the rate of population growth of the elderly is higher than that of the former in the projection years. Therefore, age compositional effects on GDP are showing a steady decline from 0.6% in 2005 to 0.4% in 2025 and 0.01% in 2050. In relative terms, ACI has encouraged the ratio of HCE to GDP over the projection period (Fig. 15.6). In other words, if we keep other factors constant, age compositional changes are going to expand HCE as share of GDP in coming years.

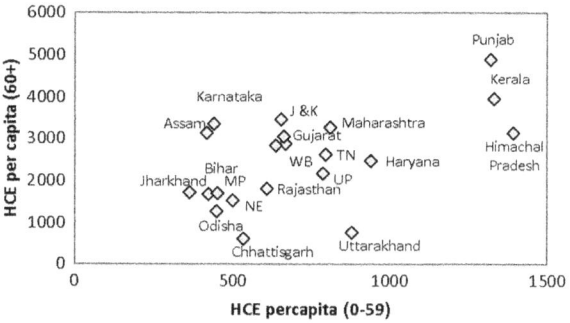

Fig. 15.3 State-wide healthcare expenditure by broad age groups

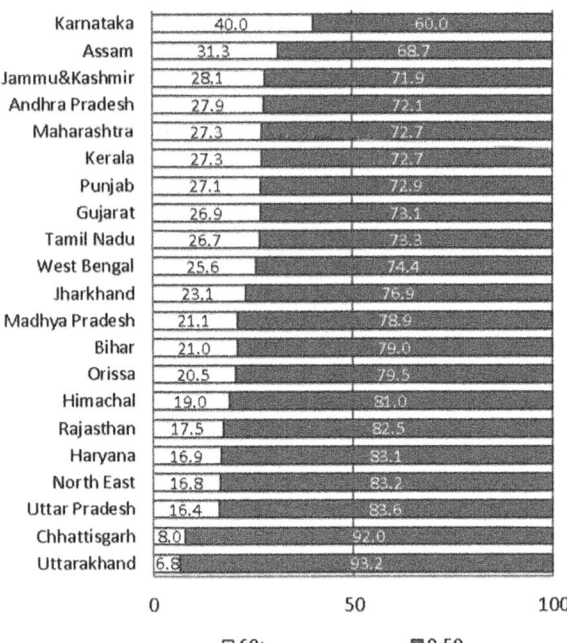

Fig. 15.4 Percent contribution of age 0–59 and 60+ in total HCE, 2004–05

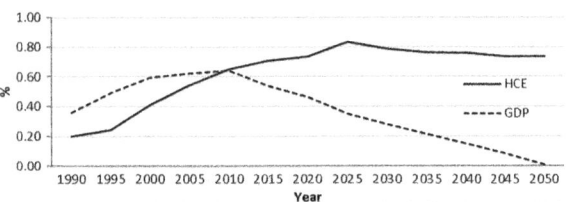

Fig. 15.5 Annual growth of age composition index of HE per capita and GDP per capita

Over the 15 years since 1992/93 to 2008–09, per capita health spending and GDP grew by the average of 8.2 and 5.1% respectively. Out of these growth rates, nearly 0.4 and 0.5% per year respectively is attributed to population change. In other words, the annual growth of HCE to GDP ratio between 1992/93 to 2008–09 is 2.9% out of that nearly negative growth of 0.13% attributed to population change and growth due to other factors than age compositional effect is 3% (1.08/1.05) in 1992–2008. In another study done for the U.S. Congress (CBO 2007), this excess growth was observed at 2.6% during 1975–1990 and 1.5% during 1990–2005.

The projections of ACI are based on the assumptions that hold age effects of HCE and GDP per capita in the projection period the same as observed in 2004–05. However, we discuss the possible implications under the following sections on

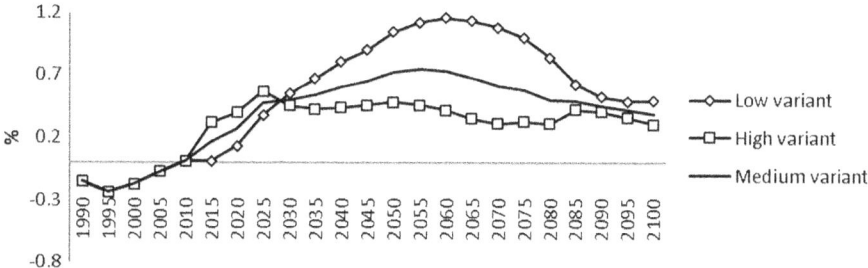

Fig. 15.6 Annual growth of ACI for HCE to GDP ratio using variable population projections

sensitivity to change in (i) per capita HCE by age, (ii) age-specific work participation rates and (iii) population age structure.

Sensitivity to Change in Per Capita Health Cost by Age The longevity hypothesis that has been discussed in several studies (Lubitz et al. 2003; Zweifel et al. 1999; Johnston and Teasdale 1999; Miller 2001; Wouterse 2013) reveals that a good current health status of the elderly tends to postpone the HCE to later ages and consequently reduces the per capita costs. Therefore, if health conditions of the elderly improve with the advancement of medical technology, environmental conditions and nutritional levels in the future, they may live healthier lives that may lead to shifting healthcare costs to much older ages and consequently lower the total healthcare spending.

The literature available on India however suggests that longevity improvements have been accompanied by worsening health conditions of the aged (Andrews 2001; Arokiasamy and Yadav 2013; WHO 2004). Hence, if these trends follow in future, India's HCE will be at a higher level. We also test the longevity hypothesis with state level data and find that the state wise healthcare expenditure correlates positively with life expectancy at age 60. States with higher longevities are showing higher proportions of healthcare expenditure with Punjab and Kerala registering the highest growth in healthcare spending.

Healthcare seeking behaviour across ages is also likely to change over time. The elderly are usually underprivileged when it comes to the question of seeking treatment as compared to the young population, particularly in economically poorer settings. With increasing awareness, income, savings and health insurance coverage elderly could tend to seek more care for their health problems and this will result in higher healthcare expenditure for them.

Sensitivity to Change in Work Participation Rates In the base line projection (Fig. 15.5), the age profile of income as observed in 2004–05 is held constant over the projection period. However, work participation rates for both entry and exit ends tend to shrink with the increase in educational attainment and organised sector jobs. The projections of age specific work participation rates in India have been carried out in Dhillon and Ladusingh (2013) which do not predict significant changes in age-specific work participation rates among males, while maintaining that work participation rates among elderly women will increase in coming years. Therefore, our projections of ACI for GDP per capita will not be affected due to the minimal changes in age-specific work participation rates.

Sensitivity to Changes in Population Projections The projections of ACI are based on medium variant population projections. However, we test the sensitivity to change in the projected population by taking 'low' and 'high' variant UN projected populations. The annual growth of ACI for HCE to GDP ratio under three scenarios is shown in Fig. 15.6. It reveals under the high variant assumption (high fertility and mortality assumption or relatively younger projected population) there will be relatively higher growth of HCE to GDP ratio until 2025. The growth of the ratio in the low variant scenario (low fertility and mortality assumptions, relatively old projected population) far exceeds this. The annual growth of ACI for HCE to GDP ratio is going to increase from 0.2% (0.01%, low variant; 0.32%, high variant) in 2010–15 to 0.7% (1.04%, low variant; 0.48%, high variant) in 2045–50.

Conclusions

Healthcare spending as percentage of GDP is quite low in India, however, it has been on the rise since the post-reform period (since 1993); an encouraging trend in the direction of achieving the goal of better health status at the population level. There is an improvement in per capita HCE from both public and private sources between 1993 and 2008 viz. from INR 175 to INR 510 and INR 363 to INR 1369 respectively. As the percentage of GDP, HCE has risen from 3.1 in 1993–94 to 5.2% in 2008–09.

The paper clearly reveals relatively higher per capita HCE in older ages reiterating the positive association between age and poor health status. Since India has a large young population, the total healthcare expenditure is higher in young ages and declines with the age advancement. The findings suggest with the transition of population age structure and total health spending will increase. The annual growth of ACI for HCE was 0.5% in 2005 that is projected to increase to 0.8% in 2025 after which it will be stagnant. It is noteworthy that the growth of ACI for HCE to GDP is increasing steadily over the projection period under the all population scenarios. Moreover, it was negative in the past years (1990–2010) and the study also recorded very high growth of HCE to GDP ratio due to factors other than age compositional effect with 3% in 1992–2008. There are other various factors playing roles in increasing HCE. That is why in the present study projections of HCE to GDP ratio could not be attempted with this limited information.

Moreover, the paper could identified the role of age structural change on health care spending by keeping other factors constant, it also has discussed the possible scenarios and the effects of other factors. Scientific evidence in India suggests that increasing longevity has not been translating into good health in the recent past. It predicts the possibility of increasing future healthcare costs due to changing patterns of morbidity, treatment seeking, rising income and health insurance. The present study recommends to increase the share of public sources in healthcare spending (which is currently quite low) to address the health care needs of a significant and growing population of the elderly. Finally, it is suggests that allocations for health budgets should be made based on demographic composition of the states.

Appendix 1

Percentage of population in different age groups in India and states, 2001 and 2026

India/State	2001			2026		
	0–14	15–59	60+	0–14	15–59	60+
Uttar Pradesh	41.1	52.9	6.1	28.8	61.3	9.8
Delhi	32.5	62.5	5.0	22.3	67.7	10.0
Madhya Pradesh	38.6	55.1	6.2	25.8	63.8	10.4
Rajasthan	40.1	53.9	6.0	24.5	64.6	10.8
Bihar	42.1	52.4	5.5	24.9	64.1	11.0
Assam	37.4	57.4	5.2	24.0	64.9	11.0
Jharkhand	39.8	55.2	5.0	24.5	64.2	11.3
Haryana	36.0	57.1	7.0	21.6	67.0	11.4
Chhattisgarh	37.0	56.6	6.5	24.9	63.5	11.6
Uttarakhand	36.4	56.3	7.3	24.3	64.0	11.7
Jammu & Kashmir	35.8	58.0	6.2	21.8	65.9	12.4
India	**35.4**	**57.7**	**6.9**	**23.4**	**64.3**	**12.4**
North-East States	36.4	58.2	5.3	21.4	66.2	12.4
Maharashtra	32.1	59.6	8.3	21.3	65.7	12.9
Gujarat	32.8	60.5	6.7	21.0	65.4	13.7
Orissa	33.2	59.0	7.8	21.0	65.1	13.8
West Bengal	33.3	60.1	6.6	20.4	65.4	14.2
Andhra Pradesh	32.1	60.8	7.2	20.2	65.5	14.2
Karnataka	31.9	60.8	7.3	20.4	65.1	14.5
Punjab	31.4	59.9	8.7	19.5	66.0	14.5
Himachal Pradesh	31.1	60.2	8.8	19.8	65.5	14.7
Tamil Nadu	27.0	64.0	9.0	18.7	64.2	17.1
Kerala	26.1	63.4	10.6	18.8	63.0	18.3

Source Authors compilation from ORGI (2006)

Appendix 2

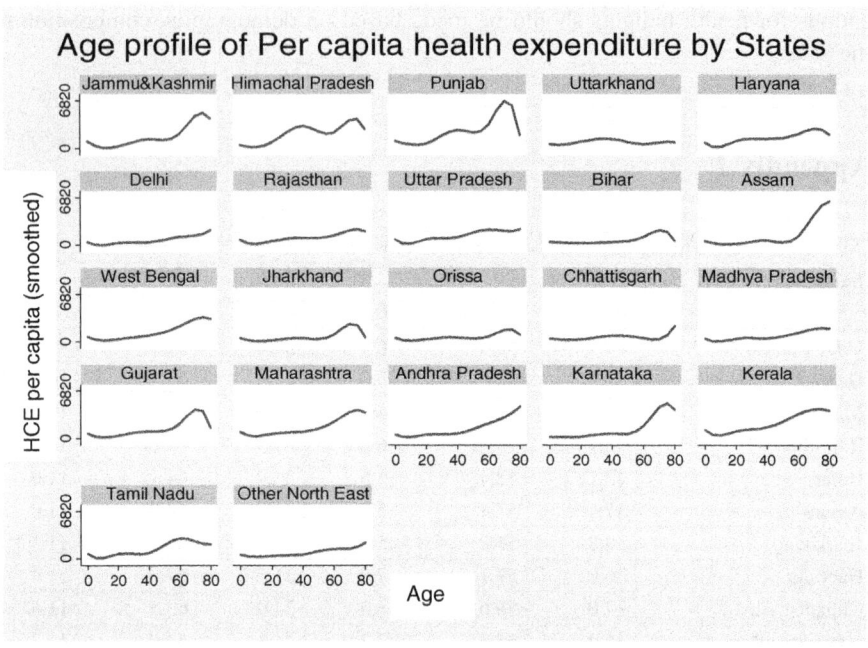

Note: Other North East combined data from North-Eastern states (excluding Assam)

Appendix 3

Per capita healthcare expenditure by age and components of healthcare

Per capita out-of-pocket healthcare expenditure, 2004–05

Age group	In-patient	Out-patient	Insurance/Premium	Abortion	Immunisation	Delivery	Anti-natal	Post-natal	Family planning	Medical attendant at death	Total	Public	Private
0–4	71	592	3		39						705	201	730
5–9	33	244	2								279	78	284
10–14	41	205	2								249	73	265
15–19	78	250	3			62.5	50.5	21.0	6.5		472	107	387
20–24	138	290	4			71.4	69.9	21.5	25.8		620	183	665
25–29	141	362	6			42.9	38.0	12.4	44.2		647	205	744
30–34	144	499	11			17.8	21.9	5.9	58.0		757	226	819
35–39	202	539	11			5.8	5.4	1.7	66.5		832	234	850
40–44	236	638	15			2.5	2.1	0.9	75.2		970	273	991
45–49	288	742	13			1.0	1.1	0.4	84.3		1131	333	1210
50–54	350	902	23								1275	386	1403
55–59	344	1270	15								1629	469	1705
60–64	420	1555	12								1988	580	2106
65–70	474	1749	8								2231	641	2326
70–74	876	2559	6								3441	1041	3782
75–79	582	2333	6								2922	862	3130
80–84	625	1787	5								2417	716	2599
85+	512	2580	14								3106	864	3138
Total expenditure												233	848
Calculated	188,819,804	628188112	7,987,267		4,919,407	20,822,444	19,115,186	6,508,963	27,004,694		903,365,877		
Reported (MoHFW and WHO 2009)	218,333,032	614774538		40,220	4,851,318	31,925,528	12,543,534	5,808,715	26,279,373	15,446,918	930,003,176		

References

Andrews, G. R. (2001). Promotion health and function in ageing population. *British Medical Journal, 322,* 728–729.

Arokiasamy, P., & Yadav, S. (2013). Changing age patterns of morbidity vis-a-vis mortality in India. *Journal of Biosocial Science.* doi:10.1017/S002193201300062X

Berman, P., & Ahuja, R. (2008). Government health spending in India. *Economic & Political Weekly,* 209–216, Special Article June 28, 2008.

Bradford, D. F., & Max, D. A. (1996). Implicit budget deficit: The case of a mandated shift to continuity-related health insurance. NBER Working Paper no. 5514. Cambridge, MA: National Bureau of Economic Research.

Central Statistical Office. (2013). Table 2: Macro economic aggregates (at constant price). Accessed from Reserve Bank of India, rbi.org.in/Scripts/PublicationsView.aspx?Id=15122. Accessed on September 16, 2013.

Colombier, C., & Weber, W. (2011). Projecting health-care expenditure for Switzerland: Further evidence against the 'red-herring' hypothesis. *The International Journal of Health Planning and Management,* July–September 2011, *26*(3), 246–263. doi:10.1002/hpm.1068. Epub October 10, 2010.

Congressional Budget Office (CBO) & Congress of the United States. (2007). The long-term outlook for health care spending. www.cbo.gov. Accessed on June 12, 2014.

Crimmins E. M., Hayward, M. D., & Saito, Y. (1994), Changing mortality and morbidity rates and health status and active life expectancy of the older population. *Demography, 31*(1), 159–175.

Crimmins E. M., Hayward, M. D., & Saito, Y. (1996). Differentials in active life expectancy in the older population of the United States, *Journal of Gerontology B-Psychology Sciences and Social Sciences, 51,* S111–S120.

Crimmins E. M., Saito, Y., & Ingegneri, D. (1997). Trends in disability-free life expectancy in the United States. *Population and Development Review, 23*(3), 555–572.

Cutler, D. M. (1995). The cost and financing of health care. *The American Economic Review, 85*(2), 32–37.

Dhillon, P., & Ladusingh, L. (2013). Working life gain from gain in old age life expectancy in India. *Demographic Research, 28*(26), 733–762. doi:10.4054/DemRes.2013.28.26

Felder, S., Meier, M., & Schmith, H. (2000). Health care expenditure in the last month of life. *Journal of Health Economics, 19,* 679–695.

International Institute for Population Sciences (IIPS) and Macro International. (2007). *National Family Health Survey (NFHS-3), 2005–06: India* (Vol. II). Mumbai: IIPS.

Johnston, G., & Teasdale, A. (1999). Population ageing and health spending 50-years projections, Ministry of Health Wellington, New Zealand Occational Paper no 2. ISBN 0-478-23902-5 (Booklet).

Lubitz, J., Cai, L., Kramarow, E., & Lentzner, H. (2003). Health, life expectancy, and health care spending among the elderly. *New England Journal of Medicine, 349,* 1048–1055.

Meerding, W. J., Bonneux, L., Polder, J. J., Koomanschap, M. A., & Van der Maas, P. J. (1998). Demographic and epidemiological determinants of healthcare costs in Netherlands: Cost of illness study. *British Medical Journal, 317*(7151), 111–115.

Miller, T. (2001). Increasing longevity and medicare expenditures. *Demography, 38,* 215–226.

Ministry of Health and Family Welfare (MoHFW) & World Health Organisation Country Office For India. (2009). National health accounts India 2004–05.

Ministry of Statistics and Programme Implementation (MoSPI). (2011a). National accounts statistics back series 2011 (1950–51 to 2004–05), S 1, 2, 3.

Ministry of Statistics and Programme Implementation (MoSPI). (2011b). National accounts statistics back series 2011 (1950–51 to 2004–05), Private, S 8–9.

Mohanty, S. K, & Srivastava, A. (2012). Out-of-pocket expenditure on institutional delivery in India. *Health Policy and Planning,* HEAPOL-czs057.

National Sample Survey Organization (NSSO). (2006). Morbidity health care and the condition of the aged: Jan-June, 2004, NSS 60th round Report 507. Ministry of Statistics and Programme Implementation, Government of India.

Newhouse, J. P. (1992). Medical care costs: How much welfare loss? *The Journal of Economic Perspectives, 6*(3), 3–21.

Office of the Registrar General and Census Commissioner (ORGI). (2006). Population projections for India and States 2001–2026, report of the technical group on population projections by the National Commission on Population, May 2006. http://nrhm-mis.nic.in/UI/Public%20Periodic/Population_Projection_Report_2006.pdf

Ogawa, N., Chawla, A., & Matsukura, R. (2009). Some new insights into the demographic transition and changing age structures in the ESCAP region. *Asia-Pacific Population Journal (Bangkok), 24*(1), 87–116.

Pammolli, F., Riccaboni, M., & Magazzini, L. (2008). The sustainability of European health care systems: Beyond income and ageing (p. 52). Università Degli Studi Di Verona, Working paper, October 2008.

Rashtriya Swasthya Bima Yojana (RSBY). (2008). http://www.rsby.gov.in/about_rsby.aspx. Accessed on October 14, 2015.

Ruggeri, J. (2002). Population ageing, health care spending and sustainability: Do we really have a crisis? *Caledon Institute for Social Policy*. ISBN: 1-55382-027-4

Seshamani, M., & Gray, A. (2004). Ageing and health-care expenditure: The red herring argument revisited. *Health Economics, 13*, 303–314.

The Organisation for Economic Co-operation (OECD). (2006). Projecting OECD health and long-term care expenditures: What are the main drivers? *OECD Economics Department Working Papers*, No. 477. OECD Publishing.

Skirbekk, V. (2004). Age and individual productivity: A literature survey. *Vienna Yearbook of Population Research, 2*, 133–153.

United Nations World Population Prospects: The 2012 Revision. United Nations Department of Economic and Social Affairs, Population Division, Population Estimates and Projection Section. http://esa.un.org/unpd/wpp/

Visaria, L. (2004). Mortality trends and the health transition. In T. Dyson, R. Cassen, & L. Visaria (Eds.), *Twenty-first century India—Population, economy, human development, and the environment* (pp. 32–56). New Delhi: Oxford University Press.

World Health Organization (WHO). (2013). Projection of mortality and global burden of disease, 2004–2030 (2004 update). Health Statistics and Informatics Department, WHO, Geneva, Switzerland. http://www.who.int/evidence/bod. Accessed on April 12, 2013.

Wouterse, B. (2013). *Economic consequences of healthy ageing*. Netherlands: Offsetdrukkerij Haveka bv. http://www.smo.nl/files/smo_items_files/Economic.pdf

Zweifel, P., Felder, S., & Meiers, M. (1999). Ageing of population and health care expenditure: A red herring? *Health Economics, 8*, 485–496.

Chapter 16
Impact of Scale-up of Maternal and Delivery Care on Reductions in Neonatal Mortality in USAID MCH Priority Countries, 2000–2010

Rebecca Winter, Thomas Pullum, Lia Florey and Steve Hodgins

Background

Millennium Development Goal 4 (MDG 4) established the target of a two-thirds reduction in under-five mortality between 1990 and 2015. Global estimates from 2012 show that approximately 44% of all deaths in children under age 5 occur during the neonatal period (UNICEF 2013). While many countries have made progress in reducing under-five mortality, these gains have been predominantly among children age 1–4 (UNICEF 2013). Far less progress has been made in reducing the mortality risk for children under age 12 months, and especially in the first month of life. As a result, as total under-five morality has decreased, the proportion of those deaths that occur during the neonatal period has increased (Lawn et al. 2005). In order to continue making improvements in under-five survival, a better understanding of the unique, complex causes of neonatal death is needed.

The vast majority of neonatal deaths occur in low and middle income countries, with the highest numbers occurring in South Asia and sub-Saharan Africa. In fact, more than 40% of all neonatal deaths worldwide occur in just three countries: India, Nigeria, and Pakistan (UNICEF 2013). Based on the distribution of the global burden of maternal and child death, the United States Agency for International

---

R. Winter (✉) · T. Pullum · L. Florey
The DHS Program, ICF International, Rockville, MD, USA
e-mail: Rebecca.Winter@icfi.com

T. Pullum
e-mail: Tom.Pullum@icfi.com

L. Florey
e-mail: Lia.Florey@icfi.com

S. Hodgins
Save the Children, Arlington, VA, USA
e-mail: SHodgins@savechildren.org

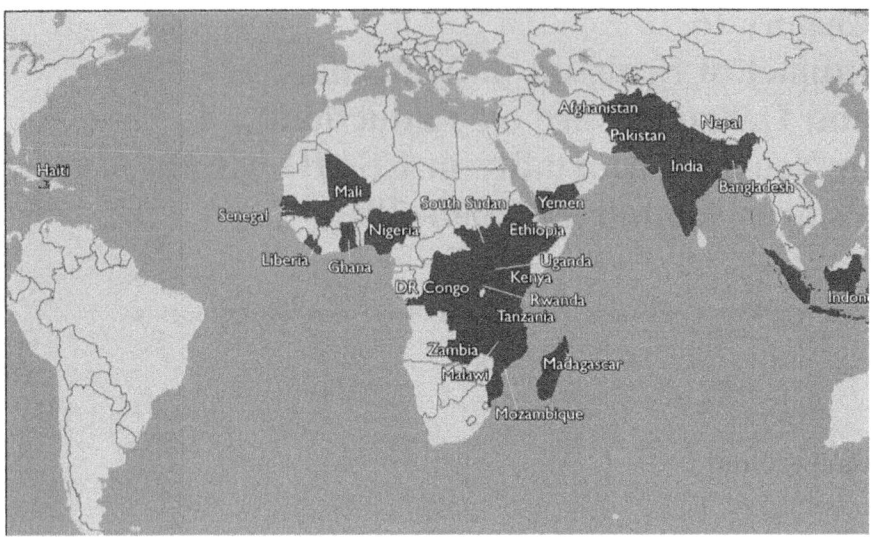

Fig. 16.1 USAID priority countries for maternal and child health

Development (USAID) selected 24 maternal and child health (MCH) priority countries—displayed in Fig. 16.1—to be the focus of programmatic efforts to scale-up high-impact interventions and strengthen health systems. These 24 priority countries, which account for more than 70% of global maternal deaths (USAID 2013), are the focus of the current study.

The primary causes of neonatal death globally are preterm birth complications (35%), intrapartum-related complications (24%), and sepsis, meningitis, or pneumonia (20%). An additional 9% of neonatal deaths are caused by congenital conditions, 2% by tetanus, and 1% by diarrhea (WHO 2014). Low birthweight, which encompasses both preterm birth and intrauterine growth retardation, is a major indirect cause of neonatal death. In many countries in sub-Saharan Africa, malaria during pregnancy is an important cause of low birthweight and is thus a major cause of neonatal morbidity and mortality (Guyatt and Snow 2001).

Most causes of neonatal death are treatable with simple interventions (UNICEF 2013). Recent efforts to promote newborn survival have focused on packages of interventions directed at women and infants along the continuum of care from preconception to infancy (Darmstadt et al. 2005; Liu et al. 2012; The Partnership for Maternal Newborn & Child Health 2011). These include reproductive health services, health promotion, and education for girls and women before they become pregnant; focused antenatal care; skilled attendance at birth, including emergency obstetric and newborn care; postnatal care for early identification and referral of illness and provision of preventive care; and emergency newborn care and kangaroo mother care for infants with low birth weight. In addition to these packages, several cross-cutting programs have been emphasized for their impact on maternal and child health: nutrition and breastfeeding promotion, prevention of mother-to-child transmission of HIV, malaria prevention, and immunization.

The recommended interventions to address malaria in pregnancy are sleeping under insecticide treated nets (ITN) and—in high and medium transmission countries in sub-Saharan Africa—intermittent presumptive treatment (IPTp) with sulfadoxine-pyrimethamine (SP). Both ITNs and IPTp have been found to be very effective in reducing malaria-attributable neonatal deaths (Eisele et al. 2012; Menéndez et al. 2010). Pregnant women are particularly susceptible to malaria and thus the use of ITNs is particularly important for women of reproductive age. Current recommendations for IPTp are for pregnant women in high and medium transmission settings in malaria endemic countries of Africa to receive a dose of SP at each antenatal care (ANC) visit, at least one month apart, starting in the second trimester of pregnancy (WHO 2012). However, during the study period the recommendation was for all pregnant women in areas of stable (high) malaria transmission to receive at least two doses of IPTp after the first noted movement of the fetus (WHO 2007).

To continue making gains in child survival, it has become increasingly important to understand and address the unique determinants of neonatal mortality, and to identify which interventions are effective in promoting neonatal survival. This study identifies USAID MCH priority countries with a statistically significant reduction in neonatal mortality between about 2000–2010, and examines the extent to which the scale-up of coverage of measurable components of maternal and delivery care is associated with the observed reductions. This chapter is based on a recent report published by The Demographic and Health Surveys (DHS) Program, which may be consulted for additional detail (Winter et al. 2014).

Methods

Data and Variables

The study uses data from DHS surveys conducted in the USAID MCH priority countries. These are nationally representative, population-based household surveys that monitor demographic trends, reproductive health behaviors, attitudes, and outcomes, and socio-demographic characteristics of women and men of reproductive age. All surveys include full histories of the live births of the interviewed women. The data are collected in face-to-face household interviews. A standard core questionnaire is included in each survey, enabling comparisons across countries and over time.

USAID MCH priority countries were eligible for inclusion in this study if two appropriately-timed surveys were available and a significant reduction in the neonatal mortality rate (NMR) was observed in the study population between the two surveys. For 18 of the 24 priority countries—Bangladesh, Ethiopia, Ghana,

Haiti, India, Indonesia, Kenya, Madagascar, Malawi, Mozambique, Nepal, Nigeria, Pakistan, Rwanda, Senegal, mainland Tanzania, Uganda, and Zambia—two DHS surveys were available around the years 2000 and 2010, with approximately 10 years between surveys. Baseline surveys conducted between 1997 and 2003 were eligible for inclusion, and endline surveys conducted between 2007 and 2013 were eligible. Of the 18 countries nine showed statistically significant reductions in neonatal mortality among all children born in the five years preceding the survey. In six of the nine countries—Bangladesh, India, Madagascar, Malawi, Rwanda and mainland Tanzania—the reductions remained significant after restricting the sample to the study population of women's most recent live birth in the five years preceding each survey (1–59 months preceding the month of interview). The study investigates the impact of maternal and delivery care in those six countries.

The restriction to women's most recent birth was made because several of the maternal and delivery care indicators are available only for this subsample of births. This restriction tends to bias the sample toward women who had only one birth in the five-year interval, and such women tend to be better educated, have longer birth intervals, etc. As a result, the NMR is lower for the most recent birth than for all births. Under the restriction to the most recent birth, interest should focus on changes and differences and not on the level of the NMR, because the estimates of the NMR are not representative of all children.

The key outcome examined in this study, neonatal death, is defined as a death that occurred in the first month of life (days 0–29). The study examines the impact of seven indicators of maternal and delivery care on improvements in neonatal survival. Indicator variables were constructed to identify children whose mothers made at least four ANC visits (yes/no), children whose mothers received tetanus injections during the pregnancy (2 or more/one/none), children whose mothers reported taking at least 90 days of iron and folic acid tablets/syrup during the pregnancy (yes/no), and children whose births were attended by a skilled birth attendant (SBA) (yes/no). The definition of skilled attendance varies across surveys in order to align with country-specific skilled care options and country-specific recommendations for delivery care; definitions used in in the study agree with those in the DHS final country reports. We also examine the community-level coverage of skilled birth attendance, measured as the proportion of women in each DHS cluster whose most recent birth was attended by an SBA. This indicator is an attempt to circumvent selection biases introduced by the fact that mothers with complicated pregnancies are more likely to seek out an SBA—especially in contexts where use of an SBA is uncommon—and the risk of neonatal death is higher in these cases. We interpret the community-level measure as a proxy for women's access to skilled assistance during delivery. The measure ranges from 0 to 1 and is included as a continuous variable in regression models predicting neonatal death.

For the study countries in sub-Saharan Africa, the analysis also includes indicators of two key malaria interventions: household ownership of a mosquito net and, where available and relevant, the mother's use of IPTp. The indicator of household mosquito net ownership identifies households that own at least one mosquito net of any type at the time of interview. Although long-lasting insecticide-treated nets

(LLINs) are now the standard mosquito net commodity purchased and distributed by National Malaria Control Programs, this was not the case in 2000. For comparability across surveys the analyses are restricted to looking at the potential protective effects of any nets, whether treated with insecticides or not. Furthermore, while we are interested in the mother's mosquito net use during pregnancy—when it would be helpful to prevent malaria-associated neonatal death—this information is not available; instead, we use ownership of a mosquito net at the time of interview as a proxy for ownership and use during the pregnancy. For Malawi, Madagascar, and mainland Tanzania, the mother's exposure to IPTp is defined as her use of two doses of SP during the pregnancy. Information about IPTp is not available in the baseline Tanzania or Madagascar surveys. Rwanda discontinued its IPTp policy in 2008 and the information was not collected in the 2010 survey, so we do not examine this indicator in Rwanda.

The study examines the scale-up of maternal and delivery care interventions within the broader context of known socio-demographic determinants of neonatal mortality. At the level of the household, variables were created for place of residence (rural/urban) and comparative household wealth (bottom third/top two thirds). Similar to the original DHS wealth index, the comparative wealth index (CWI) is based on household-level data on assets, services, and amenities, and ranks households according to their level of wealth. However, the CWI uses a fixed reference point, enabling comparisons over time and across countries (Rutstein and Staveteig 2014). The study population was classified by CWI tercile (thirds) using standard cut points derived from the distribution of wealth scores in the 2002 Vietnam DHS. The upper two-thirds were combined for the regression analysis, due to a small number of deaths in the wealthiest third. Furthermore, for the regression analysis we include the interaction between place of residence and comparative household wealth, since the effect of urban residence may depend on the household's wealth, and vice versa (urban upper two-thirds CWI/urban bottom-third CWI/rural upper two-thirds CWI/ rural bottom-third CWI). For Madagascar, Malawi, and mainland Tanzania, we also linked spatial data on the level of malaria risk with DHS data using cluster-level GPS locations (low/intermediate/high risk). In low-risk areas, the estimated proportion of children age 2–10 in the general population who are infected with *P. falciparum* at any one time ($PfPR_{2-10}$) is likely to be lower than 5%. In intermediate-risk areas, $PfPR_{2-10}$ is likely to be between 5 and 40%. In high-risk areas, $PfPR_{2-10}$ is likely to exceed 40%. Including this indicator of malaria risk in the analysis is important, due to potential variations in levels of use of malaria interventions by transmission as well as potential variations in the protective efficacy of the interventions based on level of transmission.

Indicator variables were created to identify the following characteristics of the mother: mother's age at child's birth (under age 18/18–34 years/35 years or older), marital status (currently married or in union/not currently married or in union), and educational attainment (none/primary/secondary or higher). To adjust for any maternal and household characteristics that cannot be measured, including genetic risk, an indicator was created to identify mothers who have lost another child under age five (yes/no). For India, where the scheduled castes and scheduled tribes are historically disadvantaged groups, the multivariate analyses also adjust for the mother's self-reported caste (scheduled caste/scheduled tribe/other backward caste/and none of these). Indicator variables were also constructed to identify several characteristics of the child: sex (male/female), preceding birth interval (less than 24 months/24–35 months/36 months or greater/first births), birth order (first or second/third/fourth or higher), and whether the child was a multiple birth (yes/no).

Several other indicators of maternal and delivery care were considered for inclusion but are not shown in final models. These include caesarian versus vaginal delivery, early initiation of breastfeeding, delivery in a health facility, and a postnatal care visit for the child within two days of birth. Since we cannot determine whether the caesarian section was medically necessary and are unable to identify pregnancy and/or delivery complications, the indicator is not included. Despite a strong association with neonatal mortality, early initiation of breastfeeding is not included because of issues with reverse causality. Since newborns with life threatening conditions may not be put to the breast or may be unable to breastfeed, the observed association is difficult to interpret. Because of its high association with place of delivery, delivery by a health professional is not included in the analysis. Finally, despite its relevance for neonatal survival, postnatal care is not included in the analysis because information about whether the child had a postnatal visit is not available for both surveys in any country.

Several additional socio-demographic controls were also considered but ultimately excluded from analyses. The analysis did not adjust for child's size at birth because low birth weight is a key pathway through which we would expect several of the components of maternal care (particularly mother's protection against malaria, tetanus vaccination, and other components of antenatal care) to result in lower levels of neonatal mortality. Mother's nutritional status (BMI and short stature) was not included because anthropometry was collected only in a subsample of respondents in several surveys, and not at all in the Tanzania 1999 DHS.

Analysis

First, overall trends in neonatal mortality were calculated among the study population of most recent children born in the five years preceding the survey. Log probability models were used to estimate the probability of dying in the first month of life, and a two-tailed z-test was used to test the significance of the reduction in neonatal mortality observed between the two surveys in each country. Second, multivariate log probability models were used to identify which components of maternal and delivery care are independently associated with neonatal mortality cross-sectionally within individual surveys. Third, decomposition of the observed reductions in the NMR was used to identify components of maternal and delivery care that are significantly associated with the observed reductions.

Multivariate decomposition is a technique to analyze differences in an outcome between two groups or, as in this case, between two points of time. In Eq. 16.1, this difference is represented by $Y_A - Y_B$. The study used the mvdcmp procedure in Stata, which is comparable to the Oaxaca-Binder Method but with the flexibility to use non-linear models. The decomposition procedure divides the total decline in neonatal mortality into two portions: the *endowments* portion that can be attributed to the change in the prevalence of a set of indicators (represented by X_A and X_B in Eq. 16.1), and the *coefficients* portion that can be attributed to the change in the effect of these indicators on the outcomes (represented by β_A and β_B in Eq. 16.1) (Powers et al. 2011).

$$Y_A - Y_B = F(X_A \beta_A) - F(X_B \beta_B)$$
$$= F \underbrace{(X_A \beta_A) - F(X_B \beta_A)}_{\text{Endowments}} + F \underbrace{(X_B \beta_A) - F(X_B \beta_B)}_{\text{Coefficients}} \qquad (16.1)$$

The decomposition procedure relies on two key pieces of information: the prevalence of the selected indicators at both points in time (presented in Table 16.2 in the results section), and the coefficients derived from multivariate regression models predicting neonatal death run separately at each time point (presented in Table 16.3 of the results section). The mvdcmp procedure assumes additivity of the components for composition and effect (Powers et al. 2011). Six decompositions were performed, to examine the decline in neonatal mortality between the two surveys separately in each country. Stata 12 was used to make all calculations.

Results

Reductions in Neonatal Mortality

The six study countries are those which had a statistically significant reduction in neonatal mortality between the baseline and endline surveys (see Table 16.1). In

Table 16.1 Trend in neonatal mortality rate among most recent children born in the five years preceding the survey, USAID MCH priority countries with significant reductions in NMR

Country (survey years)	Baseline			Endline			Difference
	NMR	LB	UB	NMR	LB	UB	
Bangladesh (1999/2000, 2011)	24.7	20.2	30.4	16.5	13.6	20.2	8.2**
India (1998/9, 2005/6)	28.5	26.6	30.6	24.9	22.9	27.1	3.6*
Madagascar (1997, 2008/9)	31.7	25.5	39.3	17.3	13.9	21.5	14.3***
Malawi (2000, 2010)	25.9	22.2	30.3	20.0	16.9	23.7	5.9*
Rwanda (2000, 2010)	29.4	24.7	35.1	14.1	11.4	17.5	15.3***
Tanzania (1999, 2010)	31.5	23.3	42.5	17.7	14.0	22.3	13.8**

Note * indicates $p < 0.05$; ** indicates $p < 0.01$; *** indicates $p < 0.001$. LB and UB refer to the lower and upper bounds of the 95 % confidence interval. Rates presented for all births may not match rates presented in DHS final reports, as the study uses children born in months 1–59 preceding the interview rather than months 1–60 preceding the interview

Bangladesh, the NMR among most recent children born in the five years preceding the survey fell from 25 deaths per 1000 live births at baseline to 17 deaths per 1000 live births at endline. In India, the NMR fell from 29 deaths per 1000 live births to 25 deaths per 1000 live births; in Madagascar, the NMR fell from 32 to 17 deaths per 1000 live births, in Malawi, from 26 to 20 deaths per 1000 live births, in Rwanda, from 29 to 14 deaths per 1000 live births, and in mainland Tanzania, from 32 to 17 deaths per 1000 live births.

Trends in Coverage of Maternal and Delivery Care

Table 16.2 presents trends in coverage of maternal and delivery care interventions, as well as trends in socio-demographic characteristics. The percentage of women who had at least four ANC visits from any provider for the most recent birth (which tells us only that contacts occurred, not what happened during them) increased between the two surveys in four of the six countries. In Bangladesh the percentage doubled from 11% at baseline to 24% at endline, and in Rwanda the percentage tripled from 10 to 36%. By contrast, in two countries there was a decline in the percentage of women with at least four ANC visits, from 57 to 46% in Malawi, and from 71 to 43% in mainland Tanzania.

We also examined two indicators of the content of care women received during pregnancy. Coverage of two or more doses of tetanus toxoid during pregnancy increased between the two surveys in three countries, from 68 to 77% in India, from 35 to 48% in Madagascar, and from 62 to 69% in Malawi. Coverage remained essentially unchanged in Rwanda, at 34% in the endline survey, and declined in both Bangladesh and mainland Tanzania from over 60% to under 50%. Coverage with the recommended 90+ days of iron and folic acid supplementation during pregnancy remains low, at under 10% in the endline surveys in Madagascar, Rwanda, and mainland Tanzania. Coverage in Malawi increased nearly threefold between the two surveys, reaching 32% at endline, while in India coverage fell from 40 to 23% between the two surveys.

Five of the six countries have made impressive gains in "skilled birth attendance" between surveys. We use quotation marks since our measure of SBA is based entirely on the occupation of the provider, and does not directly measure actual skills. In Rwanda, the percentage of children delivered by a skilled birth attendant increased most dramatically, from 26 to 72% between baseline and endline. In India, Malawi, and mainland Tanzania, the percentage of children delivered by a skilled birth attendant increased from 43 to 50%, from 55 to 74%, and from 47 to 55%, respectively, between baseline and endline. Use of skilled birth attendants is lowest in Bangladesh. Nonetheless, use more than doubled between surveys, from 13 to 29%. The percentage of children delivered by a skilled birth attendant remained unchanged at 47% in Madagascar.

In three of the four sub-Saharan African study countries, we were able to incorporate cluster-level spatial data on the level of malaria risk. The distribution of

Table 16.2 Trend in socio-demographic characteristics of the household, mother, and child, and in coverage of recommended maternal and delivery care, among women's most recent children born in the five years preceding the survey. USAID MCH priority countries with significant reductions in NMR

	Bangladesh		India		Madagascar		Malawi		Rwanda		Tanzania (Mainland)	
	Base-line	End-line	Base-line	End-line	Base-line	End-line	Base-line	End-line	Base-line	End-line	Base-line	End-line
	%	%	%	%	%	%	%	%	%	%	%	%
Characteristics of the household												
Place of residence												
Urban	17.4	23.4	22.2	26.8	20.4	12.4	13.4	15.4	14.7	12.8	22.9	22.8
Rural	82.6	76.6	77.8	73.2	79.6	87.6	86.6	84.6	85.3	87.2	77.1	77.2
Comparative wealth index[a]												
Poorest third	78.6	67.8	44.6	58.2	82.7	78.8	93.9	80.1	91.3	79.9	82.6	72.9
Middle third	11.2	12.3	24.8	13.8	11.6	9.0	4.2	11.4	4.3	13.3	11.0	13.9
Richest third	10.1	19.9	30.6	28.1	5.7	12.2	2.0	8.5	4.5	6.8	6.4	13.2
Place of residence and comparative wealth index												
Urban upper two-thirds CWI	10.1	16.7	20.3	21.4	10.8	10.1	5.2	10.3	7.9	9.0	13.9	18.3
Urban bottom-third CWI	7.3	6.8	1.8	5.4	9.6	2.3	8.2	5.2	6.8	3.8	8.9	4.5
Rural bottom-third CWI	71.3	61.0	42.8	52.8	73.1	76.5	85.7	74.9	84.5	76.1	73.7	68.4
Rural upper two-thirds CWI	11.3	15.5	35.1	20.4	6.5	11.1	0.9	9.6	0.8	11.2	3.5	8.8
Malaria risk[b]												
Low (<5% risk)	n/a	n/a	n/a	n/a	7.7	0.8	0.0	0.0	n/a	n/a	25.2	20.8
Intermediate (5–40% risk)					52.2	58.1	56.1	56.8			65.5	68.2
High (>40% risk)					40.1	41.1	43.9	43.2			9.3	11.0
Characteristics of the mother												
Mother's age at child's birth												
<18 years	17.2	14.8	8.9	5.7	9.8	9.7	6.7	6.0	1.6	1.3	6.7	5.6

(continued)

Table 16.2 (continued)

	Bangladesh		India		Madagascar		Malawi		Rwanda		Tanzania (Mainland)	
	Base-line	End-line	Base-line	End-line	Base-line	End-line	Base-line	End-line	Base-line	End-line	Base-line	End-line
	%	%	%	%	%	%	%	%	%	%	%	%
18–34 years	74.6	78.9	85.4	87.8	73.0	70.1	75.5	77.8	68.7	74.7	75.8	73.4
35+ years	8.2	6.3	5.7	6.6	17.2	20.3	17.9	16.2	29.7	24.0	17.5	21.0
Mother's marital status												
Currently in union	n/a	n/a	n/a	n/a	79.5	84.7	87.0	85.5	78.5	82.8	83.5	81.9
Not currently in union					20.5	15.3	13.0	14.5	21.5	17.2	16.5	18.1
Mother's educational attainment												
None	45.6	19.3	54.4	47.3	23.4	23.2	30.7	16.6	34.7	18.9	26.6	23.7
Primary	29.0	30.1	15.4	14.0	55.2	54.6	61.7	67.0	55.2	71.4	70.0	69.7
Secondary or higher	25.4	50.7	30.2	38.7	21.3	22.2	7.6	16.4	10.2	9.7	3.4	6.6
Previous child to mother died under age five years												
No	75.4	86.0	80.1	82.2	63.8	78.8	60.7	70.8	62.3	73.8	66.7	75.6
Yes	24.6	14.0	19.9	17.8	36.2	21.2	39.3	29.2	37.7	26.2	33.3	24.4
Characteristics of the child												
Sex of child												
Female	48.4	48.3	47.4	46.1	49.9	49.6	50.3	50.1	49.4	48.4	50.0	49.7
Male	51.6	51.7	52.6	53.9	50.1	50.4	49.7	49.9	50.6	51.6	50.0	50.3
Preceding birth interval[c]												
<2 years	16.0	11.1	21.8	24.5	22.2	20.2	16.2	13.7	20.3	18.2	13.8	12.8
2 years	25.0	19.2	33.0	32.8	38.6	32.4	36.7	32.9	36.0	37.8	38.9	37.4
3+ years	59.0	69.7	45.2	42.7	39.2	47.4	47.1	53.5	43.6	44.0	47.3	49.8

(continued)

Table 16.2 (continued)

	Bangladesh		India		Madagascar		Malawi		Rwanda		Tanzania (Mainland)	
	Base-line %	End-line %	Base-line %	End-line %	Base-line %	End-line %	Base-line %	End-line %	Base-line %	End-line %	Base-line %	End-line %
Birth order												
First	27.2	33.5	27.4	26.3	21.3	21.4	21.2	18.3	17.1	22.4	22.9	19.2
Second	25.9	29.7	26.0	28.7	17.8	19.2	18.6	19.0	17.6	19.0	18.0	19.3
Third	17.7	18.0	18.2	17.3	14.1	15.7	15.8	17.3	15.5	15.1	15.1	16.6
Fourth or higher	29.3	18.8	28.4	27.7	46.8	43.6	44.4	45.4	49.8	43.4	44.0	45.0
Multiple birth												
Single birth	99.1	99.1	99.3	99.1	99.0	98.9	97.5	97.6	98.6	98.5	98.6	98.4
Multiple birth	0.9	0.9	0.7	0.9	1.0	1.1	2.5	2.4	1.4	1.5	1.4	1.6
Recommended maternal and delivery care												
Mother attended 4 or more ANC visits												
Yes	10.6	23.7	30.1	37.4	40.5	49.9	56.6	45.9	10.4	35.5	71.0	43.1
No	89.4	76.3	69.9	62.6	59.5	50.1	43.4	54.1	89.6	64.5	29.0	56.9
Number of tetanus injections during pregnancy												
2+	64.1	47.7	67.6	77.0	35.0	47.9	61.6	69.4	30.7	34.4	62.0	48.3
1	17.2	22.6	8.4	6.7	14.7	15.0	20.4	18.5	34.7	42.6	21.4	24.7
0	18.7	29.7	24.0	16.3	50.2	37.1	18.0	12.2	34.6	23.0	16.7	27.0
Mother had 90+ days of iron and folic acid supplementation												
Yes	n/a	n/a	39.6	23.3	n/a	7.7	11.4	32.3	0.3	1.4	n/a	3.2
No			60.4	76.7		92.3	88.6	67.7	99.7	98.6		96.8

(continued)

Table 16.2 (continued)

	Bangladesh				India				Madagascar				Malawi				Rwanda				Tanzania (Mainland)			
	Base-line		End-line		Base-line		End-line		Base-line		End-line		Base-line		End-line		Base-line		End-line		Base-line		End-line	
	%		%		%		%		%		%		%		%		%		%		%		%	
Delivered by a skilled birth attendant																								
Yes	13.1		29.2		42.7		49.8		47.7		47.4		54.8		74.1		25.8		72.1		46.5		54.6	
No	86.9		70.8		57.3		50.2		52.3		52.6		45.2		25.9		74.2		27.9		53.5		45.4	
Delivered in a health facility																								
Yes	9.0		26.3		34.1		41.6		34.3		37.8		56.1		76.2		25.8		71.8		45.7		54.3	
No	91.0		73.7		65.9		58.4		65.7		62.2		43.9		23.8		74.2		28.2		54.3		45.7	
Household owns a mosquito bednet																								
Yes	n/a		n/a		n/a		n/a		n/a		68.4		13.9		77.4		8.1		93.2		29.3		89.1	
No											31.6		86.1		22.6		91.9		6.8		70.7		10.9	
Mother received two doses of SP during pregnancy[d]																								
Yes	n/a		n/a		n/a		n/a		n/a		5.8		29.3		52.9		n/a		n/a		0.0		28.4	
No											94.2		70.7		47.1						100.0		71.6	
Total N	5177		7254		28,313		39,251		3249		8569		7943		13,497		5062		6355		2101		5316	

Note Baseline surveys were conducted in 1999/2000 in Bangladesh, 1998/9 in India, 1997 in Madagascar, 2000 in Malawi, 2000 in Rwanda, and 1999 in mainland Tanzania. Endline surveys were conducted in 2011 in Bangladesh, 2005/6 India, 2008/9 in Madagascar, 2010 in Malawi, 2010 in Rwanda, and 2010 in mainland Tanzania

[a]The DHS-constructed comparative wealth index uses a fixed baseline (the 2002 Vietnam DHS) enabling measurement of improvements in wealth over time and comparison of absolute wealth across country

[b]In low-risk areas, the annual averaged *Plasmodium falciparum* infection prevalence in 2–10 year olds is likely to be lower than 5%. In intermediate-risk areas, *Plasmodium falciparum* transmission is likely to be between 5 and 40%. In high-risk areas, transmission is likely to exceed 40% (Malaria Atlas Project 2014)

[c]First births are excluded from the percentages

[d]Coverage of women's use of two doses of SP is assumed to be 0% for the Madagascar and mainland Tanzania surveys, as the policy had not yet been implemented

children across levels of malaria risk did not change substantially in Malawi, mainland Tanzania, or Madagascar between the two surveys. According to the recent Madagascar and Malawi surveys, over half of most recent children were born in areas of intermediate risk (i.e. areas where $PfPR_{2-10}$ is likely to be between 5 and 40%), while over 40% of children were born in high-transmission areas (i.e. areas where $PfPR_{2-10}$ is likely to be >40%). In mainland Tanzania, 68% of children were born in areas of intermediate transmission, 11% in high-transmission areas, and the remaining 21% in areas with low risk of transmission.

Studies have shown coverage of either IPTp or ITN to be associated with an 18% reduction in neonatal mortality among women in their first or second pregnancies (Eisele et al. 2012). In Malawi, ITNs first became available nationwide commercially and at health facilities in 2003, in mainland Tanzania in 2004, and in Rwanda, in 2005. All three countries have experienced dramatic increases in mosquito bednet coverage between the baseline and endline surveys, from 14 to 77% in Malawi, from 8 to 93% in Rwanda, and from 29 to 89% in mainland Tanzania. Mosquito bednet campaigns began later in Madagascar; PMI supported the first mass ITN distribution campaign in 2009/2010 (President's Malaria Initiative 2014). We could not measure household ownership of a mosquito bednet at baseline, but coverage was as high as 68% in the endline survey.

Malawi was one of the first countries in sub-Saharan Africa to adopt the policy of giving all pregnant women IPTp with SP in 1993. Madagascar adopted IPTp as a national policy in late 2004 in districts with stable malaria transmission occurs, and Tanzania and Rwanda adopted the policy in 2001 and 2005, respectively (Eisele et al. 2012; President's Malaria Initiative 2014). However, in 2008 Rwanda discontinued the program due to increased resistance to SP (President's Malaria Initiative 2013). Both Malawi and Tanzania have achieved widespread implementation of the policy. In Malawi, the percentage of women who received at least two doses of SP during pregnancy increased from 29 to 53%. In Tanzania and Madagascar, we can assume that in the baseline survey no mothers had received two doses of preventative SP for their most recent birth; by endline this percentage was 28% in mainland Tanzania, and 6% in Madagascar.

Trends in Socio-demographic Characteristics

Urban residence and household-level socioeconomic status are expected to be positively associated with neonatal survival. Between baseline and endline surveys, the percentage of most recent children born into urban households did not change substantially in Malawi, Rwanda, or mainland Tanzania (see Table 16.2). In Bangladesh and India there was an increase in the percentage of most recent children born into urban households—from 17 to 23% in Bangladesh and from 22 to 27% in India—while in Madagascar the percentage decreased from 20 to 12%.

The comparative wealth index shows that in five of the six countries there was improvement in absolute wealth across the decade (see Table 16.2). The percentage of children born into the poorest third of households declined from 79 to 68% in Bangladesh, from 94 to 80% in Malawi, from 91 to 80% in Rwanda, and from 83 to 73% in mainland Tanzania between the baseline and endline surveys. Madagascar showed more modest improvements, from 83 to 79%, while in India—the wealthiest of the six study countries according to the comparative wealth index—the percentage of most recent children born into the poorest third of households actually increased from 45 to 58%.

As the interaction between place of residence and household wealth illustrates, the contexts of urbanization and poverty are distinct across the six countries. In Bangladesh, the decline in the percentage of children born into households in the poorest comparative wealth tercile occurred almost entirely in rural areas, while in Malawi, Rwanda, and mainland Tanzania, the decline in poverty was shared between urban and rural households. In Madagascar, the percentage of children born into urban poor households decreased from 10 to 2%, but the percentage of children born into rural poor households increased from 73 to 77%. In India, the percentage of children born into both urban and rural poor households increased.

Several characteristics of the mother, including her age at the child's birth, educational attainment, and marital status, are believed to be associated with neonatal survival. Overall, changes in the composition of maternal age and marital status were minimal between the baseline and endline surveys. The percentage of children born to mothers in the lowest-risk age range, age 18–34, increased the most in Rwanda, from 69 to 75% between baseline and endline. There have been noteworthy improvements in mothers' educational attainment in Bangladesh, India, Malawi, and Rwanda. In Bangladesh and Malawi, for example, the percentage of mothers with secondary education or higher doubled between the two surveys, from 25 to 51% and from 8 to 16%, respectively. In contrast, in Madagascar and mainland Tanzania the educational attainment of mothers remained unchanged between the two surveys.

The prevalence of child-level risk factors also changed little across the two surveys in each country. However, in Bangladesh, Madagascar, and Malawi there were modest declines in the percentage of children born after an optimal interval, and in Bangladesh and Rwanda, the percentage of children who were first births increased between surveys, with corresponding declines in the percentage of children of fourth or higher order.

In order to control for potential unidentified genetic or household-level risk factors, a measure of whether the child's mother lost another child under age 5 is included in the analysis. In all countries except India (where the time period between surveys is shorter), there was a 5–10% point reduction in the percentage of children whose mothers lost another child under age 5. This reduction reflects the gains in child survival during the decade.

Results of Multivariate Analysis

The factors with improved coverage between the two surveys, summarized in Table 16.2, could have contributed to the observed declines in neonatal mortality only if they are associated with the probability of neonatal death. To examine the association between maternal and delivery care and neonatal mortality, log probability models were used to calculate the probability of dying during the first month of life, separately for each survey. The multivariate model includes the full set of maternal and delivery care indicators together with socio-demographic characteristics (see Table 16.3).

Recommended Maternal and Delivery Care

After adjusting for socio-demographic characteristics and for the mother's use of other components of care, the number of antenatal care visits that a mother had made remained significantly associated with neonatal survival in four of the 12 surveys (see Table 16.3). According to the baseline survey in three of the six countries, and according to the endline survey in Malawi, children whose mothers had made fewer than four ANC visits were between 1.7 and 2.9 times more likely to die in the first month of life compared with children whose mothers had made at least four visits; these effects can be interpreted as the benefit of ANC visits above and beyond the benefit of tetanus vaccinations, iron and folic acid supplementation, and provision of SP during those visits.

In Bangladesh and India, the number of tetanus injections the mother received during pregnancy remained independently associated with the child's risk of dying in the first month of life. According to the endline surveys in Bangladesh and India, children whose mothers received no injections during the pregnancy were 1.8 and 1.5 times more likely to die during the neonatal period, respectively, compared with children whose mothers received two injections, independent of the mother's use of other components of maternal and delivery care and after controlling for socio-demographic characteristics. Not having received the recommended two tetanus injections during the pregnancy also remained significantly associated with neonatal mortality in the baseline Malawi survey. We found no evidence that receipt of at least 90 days of iron and folic acid supplementation during pregnancy was associated with the risk of neonatal mortality, independent of the benefits of other components of maternal and delivery care.

Most surprisingly, we found no evidence that delivery by a skilled birth attendant was protective against neonatal mortality. To the contrary, according to the endline Bangladesh and India surveys, children whose birth was *not* attended by a skilled birth attendant were 52 and 22% less likely to die in the first month of life, respectively, compared with children whose birth was attended by an SBA. However, according to the endline India survey, there was a significant

Table 16.3 Adjusted relative risk of dying during the neonatal period, among women's most recent children born in the five years preceding the surveys, USAID MCH priority countries with significant reductions in NMR

	Bangladesh								India								Madagascar							
	Baseline				Endline				Baseline				Endline				Baseline				Endline			
	aRR	LB	UB	Sig.	aRR	LB	UB	Sig.	aRR	LB	UB	Sig.	aRR	LB	UB	Sig.	aRR	LB	UB	Sig.	aRR	LB	UB	Sig.
Characteristics of the household																								
Place of residence and comparative wealth index[a]																								
Urban upper two-thirds CWI	1.00				1.00				1.00				1.00				1.00				1.00			
Urban bottom-third CWI	1.12	0.52	2.41		1.23	0.56	2.69		0.64	0.31	1.36		0.97	0.66	1.42		0.58	0.17	2.02		1.19	0.41	3.44	
Rural bottom-third CWI	1.25	0.58	2.73		1.13	0.57	2.23		1.04	0.79	1.38		1.12	0.83	1.50		0.37	0.17	0.82	*	1.31	0.64	2.69	
Rural upper two-thirds CWI	1.06	0.44	2.58		0.83	0.38	1.78		1.13	0.88	1.47		1.15	0.85	1.55		0.63	0.21	1.91		0.97	0.35	2.66	
Malaria risk[b]																								
Low (<5% risk)	n/a				n/a				n/a				n/a				1.00				1.00			
Intermediate (5–40% risk)																								
High (>40% risk)																	0.98	0.59	1.64		1.31	0.81	2.11	
Characteristics of the mother																								
Mother's age at child's birth																								
<18 years	1.13	0.65	1.95		0.76	0.39	1.49		1.33	1.02	1.73	*	0.85	0.59	1.21		1.09	0.49	2.40		0.67	0.30	1.48	
18–34 years	1.00				1.00				1.00				1.00				1.00				1.00			
35+ years	0.89	0.39	2.05		2.52	1.10	5.76	*	1.60	1.14	2.25	**	1.35	0.97	1.89		1.15	0.59	2.23		1.82	0.86	3.87	
Mother's marital status																								
Currently in union	n/a				n/a				n/a				n/a				1.00				1.00			
Not currently in union																	1.66	0.94	2.93		0.93	0.57	1.53	
Mother's educational attainment																								
None	1.09	0.65	1.83		1.40	0.73	2.70		1.19	0.91	1.54		1.92	1.47	2.51	***	1.52	0.72	3.17		0.63	0.26	1.54	
Primary	0.84	0.47	1.50		1.87	1.15	3.06	*	1.03	0.77	1.39		2.10	1.58	2.79	***	1.35	0.66	2.79		1.16	0.57	2.34	
Secondary or higher	1.00				1.00				1.00				1.00				1.00				1.00			

(continued)

Table 16.3 (continued)

	Bangladesh								India								Madagascar							
	Baseline				Endline				Baseline				Endline				Baseline				Endline			
	aRR	LB	UB	Sig.	aRR	LB	UB	Sig.	aRR	LB	UB	Sig.	aRR	LB	UB	Sig.	aRR	LB	UB	Sig.	aRR	LB	UB	Sig.
Previous child to mother died under age five years																								
No	1.00				1.00				1.00				1.00				1.00				1.00			
Yes	1.58	0.94	2.66		1.64	0.87	3.07		1.92	1.53	2.42	***	1.80	1.41	2.30	***	1.46	0.82	2.61		2.57	1.54	4.27	***
Characteristics of the child																								
Sex of child																								
Female	1.00				1.00				1.00				1.00				1.00				1.00			
Male	1.26	0.90	1.77		1.42	0.94	2.14		0.99	0.83	1.17		1.10	0.93	1.32		1.40	0.93	2.12		1.45	0.90	2.35	
Preceding birth interval																								
2 years	1.00				1.00				1.00				1.00				1.00				1.00			
<2 years	2.37	1.22	4.60	*	3.20	1.29	7.92	*	1.18	0.92	1.52		1.53	1.18	1.98	**	1.65	0.89	3.07		1.34	0.73	2.46	
3 + years	0.70	0.35	1.39		1.87	0.82	4.29		0.76	0.60	0.96	*	0.75	0.57	0.99	*	0.88	0.46	1.69		1.13	0.65	1.96	
First birth	3.65	1.86	7.15	***	2.00	0.83	4.81		1.34	1.03	1.75	*	1.75	1.28	2.40	***	3.12	1.08	8.98	*	1.93	0.80	4.64	
Birth order																								
First and second	1.00				1.00				1.00				1.00				1.00				1.00			
Third	0.82	0.36	1.86		0.76	0.42	1.37		0.72	0.54	0.95	*	0.57	0.41	0.78	***	2.56	1.02	6.39	*	0.69	0.27	1.78	
Fourth or higher	0.96	0.46	2.00		0.34	0.14	0.86	*	0.64	0.48	0.86	**	0.70	0.51	0.96	*	1.85	0.78	4.40		0.50	0.20	1.28	
Multiple birth																								
Single	1.00				1.00				1.00				1.00				1.00				1.00			
Multiple	8.31	3.61	19.13	***	5.15	1.71	15.49	**	5.57	3.40	9.10	***	4.12	2.45	6.92	***	5.01	1.95	12.88	***	6.30	2.33	17.05	***

(continued)

Table 16.3 (continued)

	Bangladesh								India								Madagascar							
	Baseline				Endline				Baseline				Endline				Baseline				Endline			
	aRR	LB	UB	Sig.	aRR	LB	UB	Sig.	aRR	LB	UB	Sig.	aRR	LB	UB	Sig.	aRR	LB	UB	Sig.	aRR	LB	UB	Sig.
Recommended maternal and delivery care																								
Mother attended 4 or more ANC visits																								
Yes	1.00				1.00				1.00				1.00				1.00				1.00			
No	2.87	1.19	6.89	*	1.02	0.60	1.73		1.28	0.97	1.68		1.10	0.86	1.42		2.09	1.19	3.70	*	1.00	0.64	1.58	
Number of tetanus injections during pregnancy																								
2+	1.00				1.00				1.00				1.00				1.00				1.00			
1	2.09	1.29	3.39	**	1.18	0.68	2.03		1.59	1.19	2.13	**	1.07	0.76	1.50		1.39	0.63	3.04		0.60	0.29	1.25	
0	1.88	1.18	2.98	**	1.77	1.11	2.81	*	1.69	1.36	2.10	***	1.51	1.22	1.88	***	1.15	0.65	2.02		1.34	0.79	2.27	
Mother had 90+ days of iron and folic acid supplementation[c]																								
Yes	n/a				n/a				1.00				1.00				n/a				1.00			
No									1.13	0.91	1.41		0.97	0.75	1.25						1.54	0.61	3.88	
Delivered by a skilled birth attendant																								
Yes	1.00				1.00				1.00				1.00				1.00				1.00			
No	0.57	0.30	1.08		0.48	0.27	0.82	**	0.91	0.72	1.16		0.78	0.61	0.99	*	1.24	0.61	2.50		0.71	0.33	1.54	
Community coverage of SBA	0.66	0.13	3.40		1.40	0.44	4.42		1.01	0.68	1.52		1.61	1.06	2.46	*	1.58	0.42	6.03	*	0.82	0.25	2.69	
Household owns a mosquito bednet																								
Yes	n/a				n/a				n/a				n/a				n/a				1.00			
No																					1.47	0.89	2.42	
Mother received two doses of SP during pregnancy																								
Yes	n/a				n/a				n/a				n/a				n/a				1.00			
No																					0.81	0.39	1.70	

(continued)

Table 16.3 (continued)

	Malawi								Rwanda								Mainland Tanzania							
	Baseline				Endline				Baseline				Endline				Baseline				Endline			
	aRR	LB	UB	Sig.	aRR	LB	UB	Sig.	aRR	LB	UB	Sig.	aRR	LB	UB	Sig.	aRR	LB	UB	Sig.	aRR	LB	UB	Sig.
Characteristics of the household																								
Place of residence and comparative wealth index[a]																								
Urban upper two-thirds CWI	1.00				1.00				1.00				1.00				1.00				1.00			
Urban bottom-third CWI	2.07	0.64	6.65		0.76	0.27	2.17		0.52	0.12	2.36		3.25	0.98	10.86		1.42	0.31	6.49		0.75	0.27	2.09	
Rural bottom-third CWI	2.04	0.68	6.13		0.83	0.42	1.61		1.46	0.52	4.11		1.49	0.53	4.24		0.74	0.21	2.57		0.47	0.22	0.99	*
Rural upper two-thirds CWI	4.61	1.19	17.84	*	0.73	0.30	1.74		2.83	0.37	21.59		1.18	0.36	3.87		0.83	0.12	5.70		0.68	0.29	1.61	
Malaria risk[b]																								
Low (<5% risk)	1.00				1.00				n/a				n/a				1.00				1.00			
Intermediate (5–40% risk)	1.30	0.94	1.80		0.83	0.59	1.17										0.81	0.40	1.65		1.05	0.57	1.94	
High (>40% risk)																	1.33	0.41	4.30		2.12	0.89	5.04	
Characteristics of the mother																								
Mother's age at child's birth																								
<18 years	1.27	0.76	2.10		0.62	0.31	1.26		1.50	0.53	4.25		1.39	0.17	11.04		1.86	0.70	5.00		0.81	0.28	2.31	
18–34 years	1.00				1.00				1.00				1.00				1.00				1.00			
35+ years	1.44	0.87	2.38		2.23	1.44	3.46	***	1.36	0.86	2.14		2.04	1.16	3.60		6.11	1.62	23.01	**	1.97	0.94	4.12	
Mother's marital status																								
Currently in union	1.00				1.00				1.00				1.00				1.00				1.00			
Not currently in union	1.17	0.77	1.78		0.80	0.51	1.26		0.98	0.63	1.52		0.71	0.36	1.41		1.56	0.61	3.97		1.95	1.08	3.54	*
Mother's educational attainment																								

(continued)

Table 16.3 (continued)

	Malawi								Rwanda								Mainland Tanzania							
	Baseline				Endline				Baseline				Endline				Baseline				Endline			
	aRR	LB	UB	Sig.	aRR	LB	UB	Sig.	aRR	LB	UB	Sig.	aRR	LB	UB	Sig.	aRR	LB	UB	Sig.	aRR	LB	UB	Sig.
None	0.91	0.37	2.26		0.83	0.41	1.67		2.22	0.73	6.72		0.91	0.30	2.76		0.57	0.09	3.66		0.79	0.25	2.51	
Primary	1.24	0.56	2.77		1.16	0.64	2.08		1.50	0.53	4.23		1.04	0.39	2.74		0.75	0.14	3.93		1.27	0.49	3.30	
Secondary or higher	1.00				1.00				1.00				1.00				1.00				1.00			
Previous child to mother died under age five years																								
No	1.00				1.00				1.00				1.00				1.00				1.00			
Yes	1.89	1.22	2.93	**	1.66	1.16	2.39	**	1.09	0.74	1.62		1.48	0.92	2.37		2.51	0.91	6.92		0.93	0.47	1.87	
Characteristics of the child																								
Sex of child																								
Female	1.00				1.00				1.00				1.00				1.00				1.00			
Male	1.62	1.19	2.22	**	1.59	1.16	2.20	**	1.81	1.25	2.63	**	1.41	0.88	2.27		1.67	0.74	3.79		1.85	1.11	3.07	*
Preceding birth interval																								
2 years	1.00				1.00				1.00				1.00				1.00				1.00			
<2 years	1.62	0.97	2.71		2.84	1.62	4.98	***	1.62	0.96	2.74		3.91	2.02	7.57	***	0.43	0.10	1.83		1.61	0.61	4.24	
3+ years	0.97	0.61	1.54		2.21	1.36	3.57	**	0.97	0.63	1.50		1.32	0.68	2.57		1.11	0.36	3.44		1.33	0.68	2.61	
First birth	2.70	1.47	4.95	**	4.77	2.47	9.20	***	1.18	0.63	2.23		2.31	0.92	5.80		1.31	0.33	5.14		1.10	0.51	2.37	
Birth order																								
First and second	1.00				1.00				1.00				1.00				1.00				1.00			
Third	1.19	0.65	2.18		0.97	0.50	1.88		0.58	0.28	1.17		0.90	0.37	2.17		0.98	0.21	4.64		0.35	0.13	0.94	*
Fourth or higher	0.87	0.48	1.55		0.82	0.49	1.36		0.63	0.37	1.07		1.04	0.44	2.46		0.11	0.02	0.63	*	0.49	0.20	1.17	
Multiple birth																								

(continued)

Table 16.3 (continued)

	Malawi								Rwanda								Mainland Tanzania							
	Baseline				Endline				Baseline				Endline				Baseline				Endline			
	aRR	LB	UB	Sig.	aRR	LB	UB	Sig.	aRR	LB	UB	Sig.	aRR	LB	UB	Sig.	aRR	LB	UB	Sig.	aRR	LB	UB	Sig.
Single	n/a				n/a				1.00				1.00				n/a				n/a			
Multiple									10.55	6.02	18.50	***	3.77	1.32	10.80	*								
Recommended maternal and delivery care																								
Mother attended 4 or more ANC visits																								
Yes	1.00				1.00				1.00				1.00				1.00				1.00			
No	1.22	0.90	1.65		1.74	1.23	2.45	**	1.36	0.68	2.73		1.38	0.85	2.24		2.36	1.11	5.03	*	1.33	0.84	2.10	
Number of tetanus injections during pregnancy																								
2+	1.00				1.00				1.00				1.00				1.00				1.00			
1	1.34	0.89	2.03		1.23	0.83	1.81		1.24	0.81	1.89		0.81	0.43	1.52		0.98	0.31	3.03		1.01	0.52	1.96	
0	2.98	2.16	4.12	***	1.28	0.82	2.01		1.44	0.92	2.26		1.18	0.61	2.28		1.09	0.52	2.28		1.47	0.77	2.79	
Mother had 90+ days of iron and folic acid supplementation[c]																								
Yes	1.00				1.00				n/a				n/a				n/a				1.00			
No	1.07	0.60	1.91		1.23	0.86	1.77														0.83	0.24	2.85	
Delivered by a skilled birth attendant																								
Yes	1.00				1.00				1.00				1.00				1.00				1.00			
No	1.11	0.77	1.59		0.72	0.45	1.16		0.85	0.53	1.36		0.70	0.40	1.25		0.73	0.32	1.68		0.93	0.42	2.08	
Community coverage of SBA	0.77	0.35	1.70		1.50	0.43	5.24		0.77	0.31	1.89		1.71	0.48	6.11		1.05	0.24	4.61		0.60	0.17	2.12	
Household owns a mosquito bednet																								

(continued)

Table 16.3 (continued)

	Malawi								Rwanda								Mainland Tanzania							
	Baseline				Endline				Baseline				Endline				Baseline				Endline			
	aRR	LB	UB	Sig.	aRR	LB	UB	Sig.	aRR	LB	UB	Sig.	aRR	LB	UB	Sig.	aRR	LB	UB	Sig.	aRR	LB	UB	Sig.
Yes	1.00				1.00				1.00				1.00				1.00				1.00			
No	0.73	0.47	1.12		1.76	1.22	2.54	**	3.45	0.82	14.53		3.35	1.95	5.76	***	1.00	0.36	2.74		3.36	1.90	5.95	***
Mother received two doses of SP during pregnancy																								
Yes	1.00				1.00				n/a				n/a				n/a				1.00			
No	1.19	0.80	1.77		1.19	0.87	1.62														1.58	0.83	3.00	

Note * indicates $p < 0.05$; ** indicates $p < 0.01$; *** indicates $p < 0.001$. LB and UB refer to the lower and upper bounds of the 95% confidence interval. The table presents adjusted relative risk (aRR) estimates, which compare the probability of dying in one group relative to the probability of dying in the reference group, after adjusting for all other variables in the model. Note that for India, the regression model also adjusted for the mother's caste. Baseline surveys were conducted in 1999/2000 in Bangladesh, 1998/9 in India, 1997 in Madagascar, 2000 in Malawi, 2000 in Rwanda, and 1999 in mainland Tanzania. Endline surveys were conducted in 2011 in Bangladesh, 2005/6 in India, 2008/9 in Madagascar, 2010 in Malawi, 2010 in Rwanda, and 2010 in mainland Tanzania

[a]The DHS-constructed comparative wealth index uses a fixed baseline (the 2002 Vietnam DHS) enabling measurement of improvements in wealth over time and comparison of absolute wealth across country. This four-level indicator measures the effect of being in the bottom comparative wealth third separately in urban and rural households. Urban upper-two thirds is used as the reference

[b]This indicator has three levels: low, intermediate, and high risk. In low-risk areas, the annual averaged *Plasmodium falciparum* infection prevalence in 2–10 year olds is likely to be lower than 5%. In intermediate-risk areas, *Plasmodium falciparum* transmission is likely to be between 5 and 40%. In high-risk areas, transmission is likely to exceed 40%. Note that in Malawi, the population falls in just intermediate- and high-risk areas. In Madagascar, due to the small number of cases in the low-risk category in the 2008 survey, low-risk was collapsed with intermediate-risk

[c]While this indicator was calculated for Rwanda, due to the low prevalence of coverage of iron supplementation, the relative risk could not be calculated

community-level effect of SBA use in the expected direction, such that after adjusting for individual-level SBA use, children born in communities with no coverage of SBA were 1.6 times more likely to die during the first month of life compared with children born in clusters with full SBA coverage. This community-level indicator, though, was not significantly associated with neonatal mortality in any other survey.

In the four sub-Saharan African study countries, we were able to assess the benefit to the child of protection against malaria during pregnancy. Household ownership of a mosquito bednet remained significantly associated with neonatal mortality in the endline surveys in Malawi, Rwanda, and mainland Tanzania, even after adjusting for mother's use of ANC and other components of care, as well as socio-demographic controls. According to the endline Malawi survey, children born into a household without a mosquito bednet were 1.7 times more likely to die during the neonatal period than children born into a household with a mosquito bednet; according to the endline Rwanda and Tanzania surveys, children born into a household without a mosquito bednet were more than three times more likely to die during the neonatal period. Additional models were run to see whether the effect of mosquito bednet ownership on neonatal mortality depended on the malaria risk zone; the interaction was not statistically significant in any of the three countries for which malaria risk zone was available (data not shown).

We did not find evidence that women's use of two doses of SP during pregnancy was associated with lower risk of neonatal mortality, in Madagascar, Malawi, or mainland Tanzania.

Socio-demographic Characteristics

Several socio-demographic characteristics of the mother, child, and household were significantly associated with neonatal mortality in the final model. Children whose mothers were at least age 35 at the time of the birth had between 1.6 and 6.0 times the adjusted risk of dying in the neonatal period compared with children whose mothers were age 18–34, the lowest risk age range, according to at least one survey in Bangladesh, India, Malawi, and mainland Tanzania. The excess risk associated with the mother's young age at the child's birth was statistically significant only in one of 12 surveys, the baseline India survey, where children born to mothers under age 18 were 1.3 times more likely to die during the first month of life compared with children born to mothers age 18–34. In mainland Tanzania, children born to unmarried mothers were twice as likely to die during the neonatal period. Maternal education was associated with neonatal mortality in Bangladesh and India only; in the endline surveys in both countries, children whose mothers had primary education only were twice as likely to die in the first month of life compared with children whose mothers had secondary education or higher, and in India children whose mothers had no education were also twice as likely to die during the neonatal period. According to the endline surveys in India, Madagascar, and Malawi, children whose mothers had lost another child under age 5 were 1.6–2.6 times more likely to die during the first month than mothers who had not lost another child under age 5.

The length of the preceding birth interval was a significant predictor of neonatal mortality in four of the six countries, such that children born after a short interval had 1.5–3.9 times the adjusted risk of neonatal death compared with children born after a two-year interval. In four of the six countries, the child's birth order was also a significant determinant of neonatal mortality; according to the endline mainland Tanzania survey, third-order births had a 65% lower risk of neonatal death than first and second-order births. Boys had between 1.5 and 2.0 times the adjusted risk of dying in the neonatal period than girls, in one survey in Malawi, Rwanda, and mainland Tanzania. In all surveys, a multiple birth carried substantial excess risk.

We found little evidence that the child's place of residence or household wealth were associated with neonatal survival in the final models. Contrary to expectation, according to the baseline Madagascar survey and the endline Tanzania survey, children born in rural households in the lowest comparative wealth tercile were 63 and 53% less likely to die during the first month of life, respectively, compared with children born in urban households in the upper two comparative wealth terciles. These findings could be explained by greater assistance from extended family and the community in rural areas, or, alternatively, by differential underreporting of neonatal deaths, with more underreporting in poor and rural households in these surveys. In Madagascar, Malawi, and mainland Tanzania we found no evidence that the community-level risk of malaria was associated with the probability of neonatal death after adjusting for other socio-demographic characteristics and the mother's use of maternal and delivery services.

Multivariate Decomposition Results

Table 16.4 identifies factors associated with the reduction in the NMR between the baseline and endline surveys in the six focus countries. Within the population of most recent children born in the five years preceding each survey for which complete information on key indicators was available, the decline in the NMR was 8 points between the 1999/2000 and 2011 surveys in Bangladesh, 3 points between the 1998/9 and 2005/6 surveys in India, 12 points between the 1997 and 2008/9 surveys in Madagascar, 5 points between the 2000 and 2010 Malawi surveys, 16 points between the 2000 and 2010 Rwanda surveys, and 14 points between the 1999 and 2010 Tanzania surveys. The decomposition partitions these declines into a component due to "endowments" or coverage and a component due to "coefficients" or effects. The two components add up to the total decline. As will be seen, the two components may reinforce each other, with both having the same sign, or they may counteract each other, and have opposite signs.

Each decomposition tested whether the available maternal and delivery care interventions—use of four or more ANC visits, provision of at least 90 days of iron

Table 16.4 Multivariate decomposition of socio-demographic and maternal and delivery care related differences in the NMR between baseline and endline surveys, showing contributions to the NMR gap attributed to differences in endowments and to differences in coefficients. USAID MCH priority countries with significant reductions in NMR

	Bangladesh	India	Madagascar	Malawi	Rwanda	Mainland Tanzania
	Coef.	Coef.	Coef.	Coef.	Coef.	Coef.
Due to difference in characteristics (E)						
Household-level						
Place of residence and comparative wealth index[a]	−0.33	−0.24	−0.12	0.07	−1.49	0.58
Malaria risk[b]			0.02	0.03		0.23
Caste		0.15				
Mother-level						
Mother's age at child's birth	−0.18	0.19	0.35	−0.23*	−1.17*	0.57
Mother's marital status	1.64*	0.18***	0.04	−0.08	0.39	0.27*
Mother's educational attainment	−1.28	−1.30***	−0.01	0.83	0.51	0.03
Previous child to mother died under age five years	−0.77	−0.26***	−2.30**	−1.25**	−1.23	0.16
Child-level						
Preceding birth interval	0.22	0.16**	0.06	−0.20	0.05	0.22
Birth order	1.64*	0.18***	0.24	−0.06	−0.07	−0.57*
Sex of child	0.00	0.03	0.02	0.03**	0.10	0.00*
Multiple birth	−0.02*	0.08***	0.01***		−0.02*	
Recommended maternal and delivery care						
Mother attended 4 or more ANC visits	−0.04	−0.17	−0.03	1.32**	−2.19	1.83
Number of tetanus injections during pregnancy	1.05	−0.79**	−0.79	−0.39	−0.97	0.98
Mother had 90+ days of iron and folic acid supplementation		−0.13		−1.09		
Mother received two doses of SP during pregnancy				−0.92		
Delivered by a skilled birth attendant	1.86	0.43*	−0.02	1.53	4.23	0.12

(continued)

Table 16.4 (continued)

	Bangladesh	India	Madagascar	Malawi	Rwanda	Mainland Tanzania
	Coef.	Coef.	Coef.	Coef.	Coef.	Coef.
Community coverage of SBA	−0.85	−0.67*	−0.05	−1.72	−5.97	0.59
Household owns a mosquito net				−8.61**	−28.44*	−15.10**
Total	1.31	−2.35*	−2.57	−10.74**	−36.27*	−10.07
Percent	−16.04	75.04	20.86	206.76	228.10	70.39
Due to difference in coefficients (C)						
Household-level						
Place of residence and comparative wealth index[a]	−2.91	0.41	32.59	−24.49	5.72	19.33
Malaria risk[b]		0.70		−27.85		9.54
Caste			−1.61			
Mother-level						
Mother's age at child's birth	0.33	−0.53	0.65	0.79	5.22	12.43
Mother's marital status			−19.80	−11.66	−15.48	−13.04
Mother's educational attainment	3.36	−1.14	15.60	0.50	16.62	−5.35
Previous child to mother died under age five years	−0.69	0.54	−10.44	2.03	−7.08	−31.03
Child-level						
Preceding birth interval	9.25	1.17	−1.50	13.62	15.83	−5.57
Birth order	−9.27	−0.19	−22.42	−1.66	14.72	−24.25
Sex of child	1.98	0.62	0.35	−0.18	−5.52	−2.21
Multiple birth	−0.13	−0.01	0.03		−0.67	
Recommended maternal and delivery care						
Mother attended 4 or more ANC visits	−29.05	−1.08	−12.05	3.83	0.73	7.46
Number of tetanus injections during pregnancy	−3.20	−0.61	−0.51	−4.77	−9.86	−3.52
Mother had 90+ days of iron and folic acid supplementation		−1.01		3.76		

(continued)

Table 16.4 (continued)

	Bangladesh	India	Madagascar	Malawi	Rwanda	Mainland Tanzania
	Coef.	Coef.	Coef.	Coef.	Coef.	Coef.
Mother received two doses of SP during pregnancy				−0.18		
Delivered by a skilled birth attendant	−4.92	−2.86	−23.92	−16.50	−9.63	−16.21
Community coverage of SBA	19.66	2.81	−10.78	8.44	24.79	12.18
Household owns a mosquito bednet				42.93	−2.27	−97.39
Constant	6.07	0.39	44.05	16.94	−12.76	133.39
Total	−9.50**	−0.78	−9.76*	5.54	20.37	−4.24
Percent	116.04	24.96	79.14	−106.76	−128.10	29.61
NMR difference (per 1000)	−8.18**	−3.13*	−12.34**	−5.19*	−15.90***	−14.31*

Note * indicates $p < 0.05$; ** indicates $p < 0.01$; *** indicates $p < 0.001$. The total reductions in NMR may not exactly match those presented in Table 16.1, as the decomposition is restricted to children with complete data on all variables included in the model

[a]The DHS-constructed comparative wealth index uses a fixed baseline (the 2002 Vietnam DHS) enabling measurement of improvements in wealth over time and comparison of absolute wealth across country. This four-level indicator measures the effect of being in the bottom comparative wealth third separately in urban and rural households. Urban upper-two thirds is used as the reference

[b]This indicator has three levels: low, intermediate, and high risk. In low-risk areas, the annual averaged *Plasmodium falciparum* infection prevalence in 2–10 year olds is likely to be lower than 5%. In intermediate-risk areas, *Plasmodium falciparum* transmission is likely to be between 5 and 40%. In high-risk areas, transmission is likely to exceed 40%. Note that in Malawi, the population falls in just intermediate- and high-risk areas. In Madagascar, due to the small number of cases in the low-risk category in the 2008 survey, low risk was collapsed with intermediate risk

and folic acid supplementation during pregnancy, the number of tetanus injections during pregnancy, presence of a skilled birth attendant at delivery, community coverage of skilled attendance at delivery, and where available, household ownership of a mosquito bednet and mother's use of IPTp—are associated with the observed declines in neonatal mortality. Each model included the same set of socio-demographic characteristics that were included in the multivariate log probability models presented in Table 16.3.

In four of the six countries (India, Malawi, Rwanda, and mainland Tanzania), the total change in "endowments" or coverage in the covariates explained the majority of the observed reduction in NMR (statistically significant in three of the four countries, as shown in Table 16.4). In India and mainland Tanzania, the change in "endowments" explained 75 and 70% of the total observed change, respectively, and in Malawi and Rwanda, the change in "endowments" explained more than 100% of the change, because the effect of the change in "coefficients" was in the opposite direction and served to reduce or dampen the effect of changes in "endowments".

The results for Bangladesh and Madagascar followed a different pattern. Unlike in the other four countries, the endowments portion explained very little of the observed reductions in NMR and is non-significant in both countries. While the total change in coefficients was significantly associated with the observed reductions in NMR, no individual covariate's coefficient portion was statistically significant in either country, making the results difficult to interpret. In sum, in Bangladesh and Madagascar we found no evidence that either the scale-up of measurable maternal and delivery interventions or the change in distribution of socio-demographic characteristics contributed to the observed reductions in NMR.

Given that the decomposition did not identify any covariates—in any of the six countries—for which the change in coefficients between surveys was significantly associated with the observed reduction in NMR, we will focus on the endowments portion and examine the extent to which the scale-up of key maternal and delivery interventions is associated with the observed reductions in NMR.

Antenatal Care and Its Components

In four of the six study countries (Bangladesh, India, Madagascar, and Rwanda), there was an increase between the two surveys in coverage of women's use of four or more ANC visits during pregnancy, while in two countries (Malawi and mainland Tanzania) there was a decline in coverage. In Malawi, the reduction in coverage of women's having at least four ANC visits from 57 to 46% between surveys was associated with a 1.3 point increase in neonatal mortality. In mainland Tanzania the reduction in coverage from 71 to 43% between surveys was associated with a non-significant increase of 1.8 points in NMR. In India and Rwanda, the increase in coverage of women's use of four or more ANC visits corresponded with non-significant reductions in NMR.

In India, the increase in coverage of tetanus vaccination between baseline and endline was associated with a significant reduction in neonatal mortality of 0.8 deaths per 1000 live births. Apart from India, though, the relationship between change in vaccination coverage and change in neonatal mortality was not statistically significant.

In India and Malawi, we were also able to assess the independent contribution of taking at least 90 days' worth of iron/folate tablets or syrup during pregnancy to reductions in NMR. In India, coverage of iron/folate supplementation during pregnancy declined from 40 to 23% between surveys, while in Malawi coverage increased from 11 to 32%. In the decomposition, we found no evidence that these changes in coverage corresponded with changes in NMR.

Scale-up of Skilled Birth Attendance

In five of the six countries, coverage of skilled birth attendance at delivery increased between the two surveys. This increase was most dramatic in Rwanda, where skilled birth attendance during women's most recent birth increased from 26 to 72% between the baseline and endline surveys. The increase in individual use of an SBA was associated with an *increase* in NMR in five of the six countries (statistically significant in India only). However, after adjusting for individual-level use, the increase in cluster-level coverage of skilled birth attendance was associated with a *reduction* in NMR in the same five countries (again, statistically significant in India only). In India, the increase in coverage of individual SBA-use was associated with an increase in NMR of 0.4 deaths per 1,000 live births, while the increase in community-level coverage was associated with a decline in NMR of 0.7 deaths per 1000 live births. Again, however, apart from India, the increase in coverage is not significantly related to declines in neonatal mortality.

Scale-up of Interventions to Protect Women Against Malaria During Pregnancy

Of all the indicators included in the decomposition models for the three malarious countries with mosquito bednet data available, the dramatic increase in household ownership of a mosquito bednet was responsible for the greatest portion of the observed declines in NMR. On its own, the increase in mosquito bednet coverage was associated with an estimated reduction in the NMR of 9 deaths per 1000 live births in Malawi, a reduction of 28 deaths per 1000 live births in Rwanda, and a reduction of 15 deaths per 1000 live births in mainland Tanzania, after adjusting for socio-demographic characteristics, other indicators of maternal and delivery care, and the household's level of malaria risk. The association was statistically significant in all three countries.

In Malawi, where we were able to measure coverage of IPTp as well, we found no evidence to suggest that the increasing coverage of IPTp (i.e. the mother's being given two doses of SP during pregnancy) contributed to the reduction in the NMR.

Socio-demographic Changes

The changes in composition of several socio-demographic characteristics of the mother and child—including the mother's age at child's birth, marital status, educational attainment, and loss of another child under age 5, the child's sex, birth order, preceding birth interval, and multiple birth—were each associated with changes in neonatal mortality in at least one country. The change in composition of women's age at the child's birth, for example—and specifically, the increasing percentage of mothers in the lowest risk 18–34 age range—was significantly associated with a reduction in NMR of 1.2 points in Rwanda and 0.2 points in Malawi. In India, the increase in children born after a short birth interval from 22 to 25% was significantly associated with an increase in NMR of 0.2 points. In India, Madagascar, and Malawi, the reduction between surveys in the percentage of mothers who had lost another child under age 5 was significantly associated with reductions in NMR of between 0.3 and 2.3 points, suggesting that this indicator was able to capture and control for some of the unexplained residual household and maternal risk.

Surprisingly, we found no evidence to suggest that changes in the composition of births by urban-rural residence or increases in wealth during this period contributed to the decline in neonatal mortality. However, in India the increasing level of maternal education was associated with a significant reduction of 1.3 deaths per 1000 live births. There was a similar effect size in Bangladesh, although it did not reach statistical significance.

Discussion and Conclusions

Overall, of the 18 USAID MCH priority countries with two available DHS surveys around the years 2000 and 2010, only six showed significant reductions in neonatal mortality among most recent children born in the five years preceding each survey. In these six countries, the study investigated the extent to which scale-up of measured indicators of maternal and delivery care are associated with those reductions. In most settings, there was some improvement in the coverage of indicators of maternal and delivery care—e.g. four or more ANC visits made during the pregnancy, the provision of tetanus vaccination and iron/folic acid supplementation during pregnancy, the provision of two doses of SP during pregnancy in

SSA countries, delivery by a skilled birth attendant, and household ownership of mosquito bednets. Unexpectedly, there is little evidence that the scale-up of these interventions contributed to reductions in NMR. In Malawi, Rwanda, and mainland Tanzania, the rapid increase in mosquito bednet coverage stands out as a driver of improvements in neonatal mortality, but we did not find strong evidence that other interventions contributed to observed reductions. Detailed interpretations of these and other key findings are provided below.

Weak evidence that scale-up of skilled birth attendance contributed to reductions in neonatal mortality A scale-up of coverage of skilled clinical care in facilities (including skilled maternal and immediate newborn care, emergency obstetric care, and emergency neonatal care) has been hypothesized to have the potential to avert 21 to 44% of global neonatal deaths (Darmstadt et al. 2008). Over the past 15 years, international maternal and newborn health efforts have focused above all on increasing the coverage of institutional deliveries, with notable increases in five of the six study countries between 2000 and 2010. However, our analysis found only limited evidence that the scale-up of SBA coverage has in fact contributed to reductions in neonatal mortality. What conclusions can be drawn from these findings?

At the individual level, our null and inverse findings for the association between use of an SBA and neonatal mortality (in both the regression and decomposition analysis) are not surprising, as the results are likely to be driven in part by selection biases. In settings where use of SBAs is not the norm, women who seek out skilled birth assistance are more likely to have higher-risk pregnancies and birth complications, and the odds of survival are likely to be lower among these newborns. Lohela et al. (2012) report evidence of this pattern as part of a larger study examining distance to a health facility and early neonatal mortality in Zambia and Malawi. They report that in DHS clusters with a low frequency of facility delivery (less than 15% coverage), children born in a facility have greater odds of early neonatal death compared with children born at home, while in DHS clusters with a high frequency of facility delivery (more than 70% coverage), the odds of early neonatal deaths are lower among children born at a facility compared with children born at home (Lohela et al. 2012). While there are various possible interpretations for these associations, one such interpretation is that the pattern points to selection biases in care-seeking behavior.

More surprising, perhaps, are the weak results for the community-level indicator of women's access to skilled birth attendance. This community-level measure should not be subject to the selection biases mentioned earlier. In the decomposition analysis for India, we did find that the increase in community-level coverage of SBA is associated with a reduction in NMR, suggesting the importance of community-level access to emergency care in case of complications, rather than routine and universal use of those services. However, in the five other countries we found no evidence that the increase in community SBA coverage contributed to the observed reductions in NMR.

In fact, these findings fit into a growing body of evidence that the scale-up of institutional deliveries has not resulted in improved newborn (Lohela et al. 2012; Singh et al. 2012) or maternal survival outcomes (Scott and Ronsmans 2009). Ecological analyses find little correlation between facility delivery coverage and neonatal survival. At the national level, among 18 countries with SBA and NMR results available from at least two DHS surveys on STATcompiler, we find that the larger the increase in SBA coverage, the smaller the reduction in NMR (Pearson's $r = -0.33$, data not shown). These findings suggests that "skilled birth attendance" (or similarly, facility delivery) alone may not be protective against neonatal death. The indicators measure contact only; we do not know the content of care provided by the SBA, the level of training of the SBA, or the availability of emergency obstetric care during delivery. In other words, the scale-up in facility deliveries or "skilled birth attendance" may not correspond to an increase in the percentage of newborns delivered with comprehensive access to life-saving, high-quality obstetric care provided by genuinely skilled and well-equipped health workers.

In aggregate, the null findings may point to an issue of quality of care. If we take Rwanda, the country with the most impressive scale-up in coverage of skilled birth attendance, as an example, previous studies suggest that there may still be important deficiencies in the quality of maternal care services, despite the expansion of services. The 2007 Rwanda Service Provision Assessment found considerable deficits in availability of the basic supplies necessary for ANC, normal and complicated deliveries, and postpartum care (National Institute of Statistics of Rwanda (NISR) et al. 2008). While Rwanda MOH norms state that all health centers should provide basic emergency obstetric care and all district hospitals should provide comprehensive emergency obstetric care, findings from a recent quality of care assessment show that the actual availability of such standards of care is much lower (Ngabo et al. 2012). In rural India as well, where increases in coverage of hospital delivery were not found to be associated with declines in perinatal mortality, Singh et al. (2012) conclude that quality may not have improved along with the increased coverage. The authors cite the shortage of qualified service providers, equipment, and supplies in primary-level and secondary-level health facilities in India as a potential part of the explanation (Singh et al. 2012). Thus poor-quality services could in part explain the absence of any protective association between skilled birth attendance and neonatal survival.

Weak evidence that scale-up of ANC and its components contributed to reductions in NMR In the decomposition analysis, we found no evidence that scale-up of coverage of four or more ANC visits contributed to reductions in NMR. Like skilled birth attendance, this is a measure of contact rather than content, with similar limitations. We know neither what happened during the antenatal care visits nor the skill level of the provider.

The analysis did find limited evidence that the scale-up of one recommended component of antenatal care (tetanus vaccination) contributed to the observed reductions in NMR. In five of the 12 surveys, children whose mothers had received fewer than two doses of tetanus injections during the pregnancy were more likely to die during the neonatal period, even after controlling for socio-demographic characteristics and the use of other maternal and delivery services. However, only in India was there evidence that the scale-up of tetanus vaccination coverage contributed to the observed reduction in neonatal mortality. The tetanus immunization measure used here is crude; a more refined measurement identifying "full tetanus protection" might have produced stronger results. Furthermore, even though tetanus toxoid is known to be an efficacious treatment, the impact of increases in coverage may be small in settings where good umbilical cord hygiene practices are already the norm.

As for iron/folic acid supplementation, in the three countries where we were able to look at the scale-up of women's reported coverage of taking at least 90 days of iron and folic acid tablets/syrup during pregnancy, there was no evidence of an independent association with neonatal mortality after controlling for other components of maternal and delivery care and socio-demographic controls, and no evidence that scale-up of coverage contributed to the reductions in NMR in those countries. Two factors help explain the lack of contribution: first, coverage of full supplementation is relatively low in all three countries (<40%), which could make it difficult to detect an association. Second, only in one of the three countries (Malawi) was there an improvement in coverage. Furthermore, the responses to the survey question may not be a good reflection of the actual number of iron-folate tablets taken.

The importance of protecting the mother against malaria during pregnancy.
Study findings contribute to a growing body of evidence pointing to the importance of malaria interventions for neonatal survival (Eisele et al. 2012; Hill and van Eijk 2014; Winter et al. 2013). Of all the indicators included in the decomposition models for the three malarious countries with mosquito bednet data, the dramatic increase in household ownership of a mosquito bednet was responsible for the greatest portion of the observed declines in NMR.

Ownership of a mosquito bednet at the time of interview is an imprecise proxy for the mother's use of an ITN during pregnancy, but the observed association is plausible, given the well-documented association between malaria during pregnancy and elevated risk of neonatal death (Eisele et al. 2012; Guyatt and Snow 2001). In a multi-country study examining the impact of protection against malaria during pregnancy on neonatal mortality and the child's birth weight in 25 malarious countries in Africa, Eisele et al. (2012) found that exposure to malaria protection during pregnancy (either through mosquito bednet ownership or through IPTp) was associated with reduced odds of both neonatal mortality and reduced odds of low birth weight among first or second births.

In contrast to previous findings in malarious sub-Saharan African settings (Eisele et al. 2012; Menéndez et al. 2010), our study did not find a protective effect of IPTp on neonatal mortality in Malawi. The null finding could be driven by a lack of power, given the relatively low coverage of IPTp. Eisele and colleagues, for example, detected an effect of IPTp exposure in a pooled analysis combining data from 25 African countries (Eisele et al. 2012). Furthermore, in populations where there is a high level of ITN use, the marginal benefit of IPTp may be quite small.

The relevance of family planning to neonatal survival and the importance of identifying high-risk pregnancies. Several findings regarding the association between socio-demographic characteristics and neonatal mortality are worth noting. As expected, short preceding birth intervals are consistently associated with elevated risk of neonatal death. Initiatives should continue to emphasize optimal birth spacing (at least two to three years) to improve neonatal health outcomes. Multiple births are also associated with a substantially higher risk of dying during the first month after birth. Early identification of multiple pregnancies, referral for appropriate delivery care, and close monitoring during the neonatal period can prevent most of these deaths. Special initiatives should focus on identifying high-risk births with an emphasis on equity of care so that, regardless of household resources, precautions are available to all mothers with high-risk births.

As expected and in agreement with other recent findings (Dickson et al. 2014), in Bangladesh and India we found that higher levels of women's education were associated with lower risk of newborn death. In the decomposition analysis, the increase in women's educational attainment in India between the two surveys was associated with a reduction in neonatal mortality of 1.3 deaths per 1000 live births. Surprisingly, the study found no evidence of an association between household wealth and neonatal survival. It is possible that the bottom third of the comparative wealth index did not adequately identify the poorest households. Another possibility is that differential underreporting of neonatal deaths, with higher frequency of omission among poorer and less educated households, is masking a true association between wealth and neonatal mortality. Other recent studies have also found weak associations between wealth and child mortality (Bishai et al. 2014; Subramanian and Corsi 2014). In a study of 36 countries in sub-Saharan Africa using DHS data, Subramanian and Corsi (2014), for example, found that changes in country-level per capita GDP were not consistently associated with reductions in child mortality.

Despite major limitations in our ability to adequately measure the known, life-saving interventions for newborns using population-based survey data, the study has several strengths. First, the analysis was conducted at the individual level, thus providing a means for triangulation with other recent studies examining factors associated with reductions in child mortality at the country level (Bishai et al. 2014). Second, the study examines the contribution of interventions to actual observed reductions, rather than model-based approaches such as the LiST model, again, providing a source for triangulation and validation across methods. Multivariate decomposition provides a powerful tool for identifying factors that have contributed to major health outcomes. These methods will become even more useful as new, more precise measures of essential newborn interventions become available in survey data.

In conclusion, between roughly 2000 and 2010 only six of 18 USAID MCH priority countries showed significant improvements in neonatal survival within the study population of most recent children born, reinforcing the urgency of international commitment to the vision of "a world in which there are no preventable deaths of newborns or stillbirths" (WHO 2014). Study findings point to the importance of protecting the mother against malaria during pregnancy and reinforce the relevance of family planning to neonatal survival. However, the study found little evidence that the scale-up of other components of maternal and delivery care during this period contributed to observed reductions in neonatal mortality in six focus countries. Poor-quality services could in part explain the absence of any protective association between skilled birth attendance and neonatal survival, highlighting the need to ensure that there is an emphasis on strengthening health systems and improving quality of care alongside efforts to increase use of delivery health services. The weak findings also highlight the current lack of data on other practices that could impact neonatal mortality, such as immediate newborn care, care of the cord, resuscitation, and kangaroo mother care for low birth weight babies. Once indicators such as these become widely available in population-based survey data, it will be possible to more precisely evaluate the impact of scale-up of essential newborn care.

Acknowledgments The authors are grateful for input from Marge Koblinsky, Allisyn Moran, Anne Langston, Clara Burgert, Matt Pagan, and Bryant Robey. Funding for this research was provided by the United States Agency for International Development (USAID) through The Demographic and Health Surveys (DHS) Program. Views expressed are those of the authors and do not necessarily reflect the views of the USAID or the United States government.

References

Bishai, D., Cohen, R., Alfonso, Y. N., Adam, T., Kuruvilla, S., & Schweitzer, J. (2014). *Factors contributing to child mortality reductions in 142 low- and middle-income countries between 1990 and 2010.* Paper presented at the Population Association of America, Boston, MA.

Darmstadt, G. L., Bhutta, Z. A., Cousens, S., Adam, T., Walker, N., & de Bernis, L. (2005). Evidence-based, cost-effective interventions: how many newborn babies can we save? *The Lancet, 365*(9463), 977–988.

Darmstadt, G. L., Walker, N., Lawn, J. E., Bhutta, Z. A., Haws, R. A., & Cousens, S. (2008). Saving newborn lives in Asia and Africa: Cost and impact of phased scale-up of interventions within the continuum of care. *Health Policy and Planning, 23*(2), 101–117.

Dickson, K. E., Simen-Kapeu, A., Kinney, M. V., Huicho, L., Vesel, L., Lackritz, E., et al. (2014). Every Newborn: Health-systems bottlenecks and strategies to accelerate scale-up in countries. *The Lancet, 384*(9941), 438–454.

Eisele, T. P., Larsen, D. A., Anglewicz, P. A., Keating, J., Yukich, J., Bennett, A., et al. (2012). Malaria prevention in pregnancy, birthweight, and neonatal mortality: A meta-analysis of 32 national cross-sectional datasets in Africa. *The Lancet Infectious Diseases, 12*(12), 942–949.

Guyatt, H. L., & Snow, R. W. (2001). Malaria in pregnancy as an indirect cause of infant mortality in sub-Saharan Africa. *Transactions of the Royal Society of Tropical Medicine and Hygiene, 95*(6), 569–576.

Hill, J., & van Eijk, A. (2014). The contribution of malaria control to maternal and newborn health. *Vol. 10 of Progress & impact series.*

Lawn, J. E., Cousens, S., & Zupan, J. (2005). 4 million neonatal deaths: When? Where? Why? *The Lancet, 365*(9462), 891–900.

Liu, L., Johnson, H. L., Cousens, S., Perin, J., Scott, S., Lawn, J. E., et al. (2012). Global, regional, and national causes of child mortality: An updated systematic analysis for 2010 with time trends since 2000. *The Lancet, 379*(9832), 2151–2161.

Lohela, T. J., Campbell, O. M. R., & Gabrysch, S. (2012). Distance to care, facility delivery and early neonatal mortality in Malawi and Zambia. *PLoS ONE, 7*(12), e52110.

Malaria Atlas Project. (2014). The spatial distribution of *Plasmodium falciparum* malaria stratified by endemicity class map in 2010 globally. http://www.map.ox.ac.uk/browse-resources/endemicity/Pf_class/world/. Accessed July 20, 2014.

Menéndez, C., Bardají, A., Sigauque, B., Sanz, S., Aponte, J. J., Mabunda, S., et al. (2010). Malaria prevention with IPTp during pregnancy reduces neonatal mortality. *PLoS ONE, 5*(2), e9438.

National Institute of Statistics of Rwanda (NISR), Ministry of Health (MOH) [Rwanda], & ICF International. (2008). Rwanda service provision assessment survey 2007. Calverton, Maryland, U.S.A.: NISR, MOH, and Macro International Inc.

Ngabo, F., Zoungrana, J., Faye, O., Rawlins, B., Rosen, H., Levine, R., et al. (2012). Quality of care for prevention and management of common maternal and newborn complications—Findings from a National Health Facility Survey in Rwanda. http://www.mchip.net/sites/default/files/Rwanda_QoC.PDF. Accessed May 10, 2014.

Powers, D. A., Yoshioka, H., & Yun, M. (2011). mvdcmp: Multivariate decomposition for nonlinear response models. *The Stata Journal, 11*(4), 556–576.

President's Malaria Initiative. (2013). Malaria operational plan (MOP) Rwanda FY 2013 http://pmi.gov/countries/mops/fy13/rwanda_mop_fy13.pdf. Accessed April 9, 2014.

President's Malaria Initiative. (2014). Madagascar malaria operational plan FY 2014. http://www.pmi.gov/docs/default-source/default-document-library/malaria-operational-plans/fy14/madagascar_mop_fy14.pdf. Accessed April 9, 2014.

Rutstein, S., & Staveteig, S. (2014). Making the demographic and health surveys wealth index comparable. In *DHS Methodological Reports No. 9*. Rockville, Maryland, USA: ICF International.

Scott, S., & Ronsmans, C. (2009). The relationship between birth with a health professional and maternal mortality in observational studies: A review of the literature. *Tropical Medicine & International Health, 14*(12), 1523–1533.

Singh, S. K., Kaur, R., Gupta, M., & Kumar, R. (2012). Impact of National Rural Health Mission on perinatal mortality in rural India. *Indian Pediatrics, 49*(2), 136–138.

Subramanian, S. V., & Corsi, D. J. (2014). Association among economic growth, coverage of maternal and child health interventions, and under-five mortality: A repeated cross-sectional analysis of 36 Sub-Saharan African Countries. In *DHS Analytical Studies No. 38*. Rockville, Maryland, USA: ICF International.

The Partnership for Maternal Newborn & Child Health. (2011). A global review of the key interventions related to reproductive, maternal, newborn and child health (RMNCH), Geneva, Switzerland.

The World Bank. (2014). http://data.worldbank.org/indicator/SP.RUR.TOTL.ZS. Accessed April 10, 2014.

UNICEF. (2013). Committing to child survival: A promise renewed progress report 2013. http://www.unicef.org/lac/Committing_to_Child_Survival_APR_9_Sept_2013.pdf. Accessed April 10, 2014.

USAID. (2013). Global health programs progress report to congress FY 2012. http://pdf.usaid.gov/pdf_docs/pdacx520.pdf. Accessed April 10, 2014.

WHO. (2007). Malaria in pregnancy: Guidelines for measuring key monitoring and evaluation indicators. http://whqlibdoc.who.int/publications/2007/9789241595636_eng.pdf?ua=1. Accessed July 15, 2014.

WHO. (2012). *Intermittent preventive treatment of malaria in pregnancy using sulfadoxine-pyrimethamine (IPTp-SP). Updated WHO Policy Recommendation*. Geneva: World Health Organization.

WHO. (2014). Every newborn: An action plan to end preventable deaths. http://www.everynewborn.org/Documents/Full-action-plan-EN.pdf. Accessed July 15, 2014.

Winter, R., Pullum, T., Florey, L., & Hodgins, S. (2014). Impact of scale-up of maternal and delivery care on reductions in neonatal mortality in USAID MCH priority countries, 2000–2010. In *DHS Analytical Studies No. 46*. Rockville, Maryland, USA: ICF International.

Winter, R., Pullum, T., Langston, A., Mivumbi, N. V., Rutayisire, P. C., Muhoza, D. N., et al. (2013). Trends in Neonatal Mortality in Rwanda, 2000–2010. In *DHS Further Analysis Reports No. 88*. Calverton, Maryland, USA: ICF International.

Chapter 17
HIV/AIDS: A Survey of Beliefs, Attitudes, and Behavior in Post War Liberia

Komanduri S. Murty

Introduction and Purpose of the Study

Founded by liberated African-American slaves in 1822, Liberia, is Africa's oldest republic, spanning over a territorial area of 111,369 km^2 (equivalent to 43 thousand sq. miles), which is divided into 15 counties for self-governing purposes. Its borders include the North Atlantic Ocean, Côte d'Ivoire, Guinea and Sierra Leone (see Map 17.1). Liberia became popular for its long-lasting and bloody civil war that started in 1990, following the coup's overthrowing William Tolbert. Both the Liberian army and West African peacekeepers reached a peace agreement in 1995 and Charles Taylor was elected as president in subsequent elections. However, his leadership did not bring much relief to the nation. He was accused of supporting rebels in Sierra Leone in 1999, which resulted in anti-government protests that lead to Taylor's eventual stepping down and going into exile in Nigeria in 2003. A transitional government was then formed to govern the nation. Ellen Johnson Sirleaf was elected in 2005 presidential elections. It goes without saying that the civil war had an irreversible impact on the people's lives and the nation's economy. Over a quarter-million people were killed in the civil war and several thousands were injured; and, several hundreds of thousands fled to neighboring countries as refugees. The nation's economy was ruined and the country was overrun with weapons. The nation's capital, Monrovia, became a ghost town without electricity and running water. Corruption, unemployment, illiteracy, proliferation of risky behavior, morbidity, and mortality at all levels reached uncontrollable proportions (Barrbiero and Barh 2007; Central Intelligence Agency 2010; International Monetary Fund 2008; Ismail 2002). As a result the nation's population dwindled to 1.5 million in 1997 (Coleman 2014). After the end of civil war, the nation's

---

K.S. Murty (✉)
Department of Behavioral Sciences and Population Studies Center,
Fort Valley State University, Fort Valley, GA, USA
e-mail: murtyk@fvsu.edu

Map 17.1 Liberia

infrastructure and economic recovery efforts began gradually with the help of international partnerships and United Nations, which also gave rise to repatriation of the population. The 2014 World Bank estimates showed that Liberia's population surged to slightly over 4.3 million; its GDP was $2.03 billion; the GDP growth was still low at 0.5%; and, inflation was as high as 9.8% (The World Bank 2014). The rapid increase in population size also posed challenges for Liberians' health and welfare. For example, 46% of Liberia's population live in poverty, its death rate is 143.89/1,000 live births, overall life expectancy is 41 years, 70% do not have access to safe drinking water and HIV/AIDS prevalence rate is nearly 6% (Coleman 2014: 131–132; International Monetary Fund 2008: 13; Ismail 2002). The availability of essential health services in post-conflict Liberia was limited to those which were less complex to implement and to those which were supported by bilateral and multilateral health sector donors (Kruk et al. 2010).

It should not be surprising, given the historical relationships of African-Americans in the United States with African nations, that the United Negro College Fund Special Programs (UNCFSP) has been one of the first among international agencies to step forward to assist the post-war Liberia with rebuilding its infrastructure, restoring the economy, and more importantly, improving the quality of life of Liberians. The UNCFSP funded the partnership of Rust College of Holly Springs in Mississippi and Cuttington University College in Suakoko of Liberia to implement an intervention project based on three interconnected strategies of training; management and extension; and, community engagement. The overall goal of this project is to develop the capacity of health practitioners assigned to rural clinics and health centers to deliver better services to the most marginalized communities of women and children in an agrarian society recovering from nearly two decades of war. The first of the five phases, that were proposed to implement this project, was to *conduct a needs assessment* to identify and determine the magnitude of priorities of unmet needs. In an attempt to fulfill this objective, a survey was conducted among 170 Liberians. This paper presents the survey analysis.

HIV Prevalence in Liberia

The recent national survey conducted by the Liberia Institute of Statistics and Geo-Information Services (LISGIS 2014: 14) indicates that 1.9% of Liberians aged 15–49 years are HIV-positive; that it is higher among women (2.0%) than among men (1.7%); and, that it is higher in urban areas than in rural areas. Gender differences in prevalence rates are greater for young women (15–24 years) than young men (1.4 and 0.5%, respectively), indicating that young women are at a three times higher risk than young men. Moreover, the HIV prevalence rate is the highest among pregnant young women (5.3%) and women who are divorced/separated/widowed (4.6%). Income-wise, the wealthiest households are at a greater risk of the HIV infection (3.3%) including young men (1.3%) than those from lower economic strata, which indicates HIV prevalence increases with wealth. These prevalence rates are higher than those found in the 2007 survey, wherein the corresponding rates were 1.5% for all people in age 15–49; 1.8% for women; and, 1.2% for men (LISGIS 2008). Thus, men experienced a relative sharper increase of the infection in these six years than women, although women still maintain an overall higher risk level in both surveys. These risk levels may further increase if (1) the existing social and health conditions in Liberia continue; and/or, (2) the sexual networks are formed with peacekeeping personnel from countries with high HIV rates (Okigbo et al. 2014: 134) such as those in Southern and Eastern Africa (UNAIDS 2006). Additionally, the overall HIV prevalence rate is unavailable on most-at-risk populations; for example, sex workers and MSM—Men who have Sex with Men (National AIDS Commission 2010).

Review of Selective KAP Literature Related to HIV

The knowledge-attitudes-practice surveys (KAPs) are the basis for behavioral surveillance surveys (BSSs) that help track trends in HIV/AIDS knowledge, attitudes and risk behavior among populations (Spiegel and Le 2006). Mutha et al. (2014) conducted a cross-sectional survey among 500 college students in Mumbai, India, to determine their knowledge and awareness regarding sex and related matter along with the factors affecting the existing outlook and practices. They found that 84% of male and 72% of female respondents disagreed that virginity should be preserved until marriage; that 48% male and 18% of female respondents reportedly engaged in premarital sex. Of those individuals, 68% males and none of the females had more than one sex partner. Further, those who engaged in premarital sexual relations, 21% of males and 12% of females had used a contraceptive during sexual intercourse. Eighty-seven percent of males and 82% females disagreed that sex education in secondary schools contributes to an increase in premarital intercourse; that 40% of males and 13% of females viewed that birth control is primarily females responsibility; and, that 14% of males and 21% of females reportedly forced to have sex. Based on these findings the study concluded that these students, particularly females, lacked basic knowledge of sexuality and related matters; that males held a casual attitude towards having sex with multiple partners; and, that premarital sex appeared to be more common than prevailing belief. These factors reinforce the necessity of effective sexual education to youth for guidance toward healthy and appropriate sexual practices.

Gummerson (2013) examined the association between education and HIV risk behaviors among eight African countries (Ethiopia, Kenya, Lesotho, Malawi, Mali, Senegal, Tanzania, and Zambia) utilizing the demographic and health survey (DHS) data in 2001 and 2011. The analysis showed that education has a robust positive association with condom use and HIV testing; that educated men reduced their number of sexual partners to a greater extent than their less educated counterparts; that younger cohorts of educated women began entering marriage earlier than their predecessors did; and, that the education gradient did not change significantly over time for condom use. These findings suggest the desirability and necessity of disseminating HIV related information, such as information regarding safe sex, among marginalized and less educated population groups

Jedy-Agba and Adebmowo (2012) conducted focus group discussions and key informant interviews in four high volume tertiary care institutions that offer HIV care and treatment in Nigeria in order to examine their knowledge, attitudes and practices (KAPs) of AIDS associated malignancies. Their results showed that most participants had heard about cancer and considered it a fatal disease, but showed poor knowledge of AIDS associated cancers. People living with HIV expressed fear, denial and disbelief about their perceived cancer risk. Although some participants had heard about cancer screening, very few had ever been screened. These findings suggest the need for healthcare providers to intervene and develop primary cancer prevention strategies among HIV infected people in Nigeria.

Dahab et al. (2013) conducted a series of cross-sectional HIV behavioral surveillance surveys among refugees and surrounding community residents living in Kenya, Tanzania and Uganda in 2004–05 and again in 2010–11 for measuring changes in HIV-related behaviors, knowledge and testing. They found consistent decreases in reported multiple and casual sexual partnerships during the past 12 months due to increases in HIV testing levels and improvements in comprehensive HIV knowledge. However, the level of risky sexual partnerships remained high, especially casual sex among youths and multiple partnerships among adult males. Condom use was low during sex with a casual partner during last six months, and among youth condom use had actually decreased. Tanzanian males reported more frequently engaging in risky sexual behavior than their female counterparts, despite their reporting of higher levels of HIV knowledge, representing a large knowledge-practice gap. On the other hand, Kenya and Uganda refugees did not report significantly higher levels of risky sexual partnerships than surrounding community residents, indicating that refugees should not automatically be assumed to have higher levels of risky sexual behaviors than neighboring nationals.

Zhang et al. (2015) conducted a survey of knowledge, attitude, and practice (KAP) regarding reproductive health (RH) among 3933 men, aged 18–59 years in Yiling District, Yichang, China. They found that over one-half of respondents reportedly had knowledge and positive attitude about sexual physiology and safe sex, of whom 70% opted to visit a doctor when they experienced reproductive disorder. On the contrary, only 41.9% believed that HIV could be transmitted through breastfeeding, 64.6% were under the wrong impression that contracting STDs could be prevented by cleaning their genitals after intercourse. Forty-five percent discriminated against and were unwilling to be friends with infected persons. Approximately 45% of those with reproductive system disorder were unwilling to discuss their condition with friends or family members. These results show the importance of disseminating accurate knowledge of STD risk among these populations.

Yu (2012) reviewed 36 scholarly articles on teenage sexual attitudes and behavior in China, that were published between 2000 and 2010. The review revealed that young men were more likely to report having had sex than young women; and, that teens at vocational high schools were less likely to remain virgins than those at common/key high schools. The study suggested the need to develop more comprehensive programs in cooperation with youth, school systems, and health organizations; while increasing youth access to sexual and reproductive health services in China.

Wang et al. (2014) conducted a survey among 2753 rural migrants in Guangdong and Sichuan provinces of China to examine their HIV/AIDS knowledge, attitudes, and practices (KAPs) and use of healthcare services. They found that 58.6% of the respondents were aware of HIV/AIDS transmission; that 90% had a negative attitude towards AIDS patients; that 6.2% engaged in high-risk sex in the past 12 months; that only 3% of migrant workers received voluntary free HIV screening; and, that high-risk sex was associated with sex, marital status, income, migration and work experience. The study concluded that HIV/AIDS knowledge, attitudes, and practices among rural migrants in China was a problematic health issue, and called for an increased use of healthcare services.

Woodward et al. (2014) compared associations of HIV knowledge and perceived risk with reported HIV-avoidant behavior changes and sexual health choices from a community survey of 698 male and female Sierra Leonean refugees in Guinea. They found no significant association between HIV knowledge and reported HIV-avoidant changes, indicating that one may perceive high risk of HIV without making any significant behavioral changes in avoidance. Thus, programs emphasizing knowledge are inconsequential without behavioral change initiatives such as screening, male circumcision, etc. The study also found that certain contextual factors, such as desire for children, could play an important role for not using condoms or other contraception regardless of knowledge and risk perception.

Gledovic et al. (2015) conducted a cross-sectional study in the University Clinical Center of Montenegro in Podgorica to assess HIV-related knowledge, attitudes and practice (KAP) of healthcare workers (HCWs). They found that a high proportion of HCWs had an insufficient level of knowledge on HIV transmission and the risk after exposure; and inappropriate attitudes regarding the need for HIV testing of all hospitalized patients, as well as the obligation of an HIV+ patient to report his/her HIV status in order to practice universal precautions. Further, 6.2% of HCWs indicated that they would refuse to treat HIV+ patients. These findings suggest a need for continuous education of HCWs to increase their level of knowledge about the risk of infection at the workplace.

In sum, HIV-KAP studies are found to be vital to create baseline data among various segments of population, to assess the levels of risk behaviors, to examine behavioral changes through behavioral surveillance surveys, and to suggest policy implications.

Materials and Methods

A cross-sectional sample survey was conducted in early 2006 by local interviewers trained by Cuttington University College, Suakoko, Liberia. The survey utilized a structured questionnaire developed, pilot tested, and finalized by the two partnering institutions of higher education (Rust College in Mississippi, USA and Cuttington University, Liberia) under the supervision of UNCFSP consultants. The questionnaire was made up of questions in the following areas: respondents' socio-economic characteristics, alcohol use, and sex-life; respondents' awareness of HIV/AIDS; respondents' knowledge of HIV/AIDS; respondents' sources of information about HIV/AIDS; respondents' beliefs, attitudes and behavior;

respondents' opinions related to sexual practices; respondents' awareness of condom; and, respondents' access to media and acceptance of message on safe sex. Of the 170 interviews conducted, 109 were in Bong, 34 in Lofa, six in Nimba, and one was in Bassa counties. The remaining 20 did not report the county in which the interviews were conducted.

Results

Socio-economic Characteristics

Of the 150 respondents who reported their gender, 95% (n = 142) were female and the remaining 5% (n = 8) were male. Approximately 83% of those reported religion were Christian, followed by Traditional (8.9%) and Muslim (7.6%). Religiosity of these respondents was quite high as evidenced by the pattern of responses to a question *how important is religion to you?* Eighty-two percent said that religion was very important to them, and another 13.5% said it was somewhat important. Only seven respondents (4.1%) reported that religion was not important to them.

The age distribution of these respondents ranged from 15 to 50 years with a mean age of 28.2 years and standard deviation of 8.3 years. Of the 151 respondents, who reported their age, over one-half (51.6%) were in 20s, and another one-quarter (24.5%) were in their 30s. Of the remaining 24%, approximately 11% were teens and 13% were 40 years of age or older.

Nearly 72% (n = 123) claimed to have had some level of education. Of them, 29.3% reportedly completed primary school, 35.8% secondary school, and another 35% completed post-secondary education. Business (47.3%), self-employment (23.1%), and farming (18.9%) were the main categories of occupation for these respondents. Given the depressed post-war economy and high unemployment rate, it is not surprising that many of those interviewed were not engaged in traditional wage-earning occupations.

Many of these respondents reported stable living patterns in their villages/towns and communities, as evidenced from responses to two questions on duration of residence: (1) how long have you lived in this *village*? and (2) how long have you lived in this *community*? For comparative purposes their responses were classified in similar intervals for both questions. As shown in Table 17.1, the recent settlers (less than one year) constitute a small proportion in the community (12.3%) as well as in the village (7.7%). More than 4-in-10 respondents lived for five years or longer in the same village (47.7%) and in the same community (46.3%). This may be due to the fact that the majority of the sample is female.

Most of the respondents (75.2%) reportedly lived with a relative (39.1%) or a sex partner (36.1%). Only 12 respondents (7.1%) claimed to live with friends. A moderate percentage of 16.5% lived alone, and over 57% of these lonely dwellers (16 out of 28) were in the ages of 20–29 years.

Table 17.1 Distributions of respondents by socio-economic characteristics

Variable	Respondents (Pct.)
Gender, n = 150	
Male	8 (5.3)
Female	142 (94.7)
Religion, n = 168	
Christian	140 (83.3)
Muslim	13 (7.6)
Traditional	15 (8.9)
Religiosity, n = 170	
Religion is very important	140 (82.4)
Somewhat important	23 (13.5)
Not important	7 (4.1)
Age (years) mean ± standard deviation, n = 151	28.16 ± 8.269
15–19	17 (11.3)
20–24	39 (25.8)
25–29	39 (25.8)
30–34	20 (13.2)
35–39	17 (11.3)
40–44	9 (6.0)
45–50	10 (6.6)
Education, n = 123	
Primary	36 (29.3)
Secondary	44 (35.8)
Higher	43 (35.0)
Occupation, n = 169	
Business	80 (47.3)
Farming	32 (18.9)
Self employed	39 (23.1)
Other	18 (10.7)
Duration of residence in the village/town, n = 168	
Less than 1 year	13 (7.7)
1–2 years	36 (21.4)
3–5 years	39 (23.2)
6–10 years	30 (17.9)
More than 10 years	50 (29.8)
Duration of residence in the community, n = 106	
Less than 1 year	13 (12.3)
1–2 years	17 (16.0)
3–5 years	27 (25.5)
6–10 years	22 (20.8)
More than 10 years	27 (25.5)

(continued)

Table 17.1 (continued)

Variable	Respondents (Pct.)
Living status, n = 169	
Alone	28 (16.5)
With family relative	66 (39.1)
With sexual partner	61 (36.1)
With friends	12 (7.1)
No fixed place	2 (1.2)

Alcohol Use

The consumption of alcohol among the study respondents appeared to be moderate. About one-third (33.9%) reported to have had at least one alcoholic drink in the past four weeks; and, another 12.5% did not remember if they had any alcoholic drinks. The remaining 53.6% said that they did not have any alcoholic drinks in the past four weeks (Fig. 17.1).

Sex Life

About 97% of the respondents (165 out of 170) admittedly experienced sexual intercourse. Those who remembered their age at first sexual intercourse (n = 124) reported from 13 to 28 years with a mean age of 17.1 years and standard deviation of 2.7 years. Nearly 47% had their first intercourse between ages 15 and 18 years (the modal group). Most (98.8%) had first intercourse with an older sex partner, comprising of 41.7% with a sex partner of 1–5 years older and the other 57.1% with a partner 5–10 years older. Only two respondents (1.3%) reportedly had sex with persons of same age. Most of them (84.3%) did not use a condom during their first sexual intercourse; only 11.4% (n = 19) reportedly used condoms, and the remaining 4.2% did not remember. LISGIS (2008) survey also found that only 12%

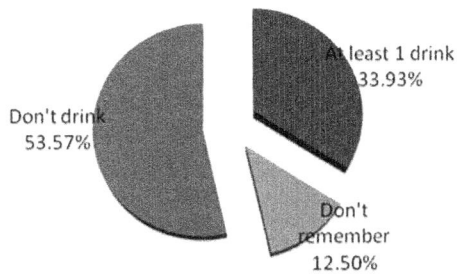

Fig. 17.1 During the past 4 weeks how many alcohol drinks did you have?

Table 17.2 Response patterns for sex life

Variable	Respondents (Pct.)
Have you ever had sexual intercourse? n = 170	
Yes	165 (97.1)
No	5 (2.9)
Age at first intercourse, n = 124 (Mean ± S.D., range)	17.1 ± 2.7, 13–28
Age-gap between sex partners at first intercourse, n = 156	
Same age	2 (1.3)
1–5 years	65 (41.7)
6–10 years	89 (57.1)
Condom used during the first intercourse, n = 166	
Yes	19 (11.4)
No	140 (84.3)
Don't remember	7 (4.2)
Number of sex partners in the last one month, n = 167	
None	3 (1.8)
One	119 (71.3)
Two	36 (21.6)
Three	6 (3.6)
Four or more	3 (1.8)

females and 15% of males reportedly used condoms. Many (71.3%) reportedly had one sex partner within the last one month and others had two or more sex partners. Only three respondents (1.8%) said that they did not have any sex partners in one month preceding the time of the survey (Table 17.2).

Awareness of HIV/AIDS and Source of Information

When respondents were asked how much they know about HIV/AIDS, 22% said *a great deal*; 25% a *moderate amount*; and, the remaining 53% said they knew *just a little*. Most (92.3%) of the respondents (n = 158) reportedly heard about HIV/AIDS, with three channels of communications reported for the source of information—personal/professional, institutional, and mass media. Among the *personal*/professional channels, information about HIV/AIDS was received in the following order: (1) doctor/nurse—49%; (2) Friends—47%; (3) health worker—47%; (4) parents—27%; and (5) teacher—25%. Thus, 25–50% of the respondents were reached through personal/professional channels; and, doctor/nurse is the most common professional channel. Two types of *institutional* channels; i.e., church and mosque, were reported by study respondents. As expected, church was more frequently mentioned (40%), since a majority of the respondents were Christians. Of the three *mass media* channels reported, radio was the most common source of information as specified by 73.5% of respondents, when compared to T.V. (18%) or

Table 17.3 Response patterns of source of HIV/AIDS information

Source of HIV/AIDS information	Respondents (Pct.)
I. Personal/Professional	
(a) Doctor/Nurse	86 (48.8)
(b) Health worker	79 (46.5)
(c) Friends	80 (57.1)
(d) Teacher	42 (24.7)
(e) Parents	45 (26.5)
II. Institutional	
(a) Church	68 (40.0)
(b) Mosque	8 (4.7)
III. Mass media	
(a) Radio	125 (73.5)
(b) T.V.	31 (18.2)
(c) Newspaper/Magazine	37 (21.5)

newspaper/magazines (22%). Three-in-four respondents (75.9%) owned a radio, but only 17.6% owned a television. Radio is not only the most effective mass media channel, it is also the most effective compared to other types of channels. Perhaps integrating the most effective of each type; for example, using doctors/nurses to announce HIV/AIDS information on radios, or announcing during the commercial breaks on radio during religious programs may prove to be beneficial (Tables 17.3 and 17.4).

Knowledge About HIV/AIDS

Sixty-six respondents (38.8%) said that they had seen or known someone who had HIV. Most of the respondents indicated that HIV infection occurs during sexual intercourse (81.4%); using injection needle/syringe that has been used on someone with HIV virus (84.1%), by receiving blood from someone who has HIV/AIDS (85.3%), or by using a razor blade that has been used by someone who has the HIV virus (82.4%); and, that a pregnant woman who had AIDS could give it to her unborn baby (78.2%). Only a small to moderate percentage had misconceptions, such as HIV/AIDS could be contracted by using public toilets (23.5%); bathing together (10.6%); hugging/touching (10.6%), shaking hands (5.9%), or "dry" kissing (23.5%)—all casual contacts (Madhok et al. 1986; Courville et al. 1998). Many thought that a person could be infected with HIV but might not show any symptoms (74.1%), who, nonetheless, could be a potential source of infection to others (88.8%). As for the cure of HIV/AIDS they were very pessimistic. Only a few thought that HIV/AIDS could be cured (8.8%), either by drugs (4.1%), or traditional healers (5.9%), or changing life-style (13.5%) (Tables 17.5 and 17.6).

Finally, they expressed little hope of survival for those who contracted HIV/AIDS. Close to one-half (47.6%) of the respondents thought *all* and another

Table 17.4 Respondents' knowledge about HIV/AIDS

Knowledge of infection of HIV/AIDS and cure	Respondents (Pct.)
I. Knowledge of infection	
(a) Sexual intercourse	152 (89.4)
(b) Using injection needle/syringe that has been used on someone with HIV virus	143 (84.1)
(c) Using public toilets	40 (23.5)
(d) Hugging and touching	18 (10.6)
(e) Shaking hands	10 (5.9)
(f) "Dry" kissing	40 (23.5)
(g) Bathing together	18 (10.6)
(h) A pregnant woman who has AIDS can give it to her unborn baby	133 (78.2)
(i) By receiving blood from someone who has HIV/AIDS	145 (85.3)
(j) By using razor blade that has been used by someone who has the virus	140 (82.4)
(k) A person can be infected with HIV but does not show any symptoms	126 (74.1)
(l) A person can catch HIV/AIDS from someone who has the disease	151 (88.8)
II. Knowledge of cure	
(a) HIV/AIDS can be cured	15 (8.8)
(b) By drugs	7 (4.1)
(c) By traditional healers	10 (5.9)
(d) By changing life-style	23 (13.5)
(e) By other means	8 (4.7)

Table 17.5 Respondents' beliefs, attitudes and behavior

Beliefs, attitudes and behavior	Respondents (Pct.)
HIV/AIDS is dangerous to our community	154 (90.8)
HIV/AIDS is going to be a serious health problem in this country	152 (89.4)
A person can avoid getting HIV/AIDS by changing his/her behavior	151 (88.8)
How many of your friends have changed their behavior or way of life as a result of hearing about HIV/AIDS? (n = 166)	
Very many	26 (15.7)
Not many	25 (15.1)
Very few	77 (46.4)
None	38 (22.9)
Have you made any change in your own behavior or way of life as a result of hearing about HIV/AIDS?	
Yes	136 (80.0)
No	28 (17.1)
Government should take steps to prevent the spread of AIDS in Liberia	155 (91.2)

(continued)

Table 17.5 (continued)

Beliefs, attitudes and behavior	Respondents (Pct.)
Do you think if people in your community will be willing to take the test? (n = 149)	
Yes	64 (37.6)
No	85 (50.0)
Are you willing to undergo the HIV/AIDS test? (n = 162)	
Yes	112 (65.9)
No	50 (29.4)
If you are willing to undergo the test, do you want to know the result? (n = 112)	
Yes	110 (98.2)
No	2 (1.8)

Table 17.6 Respondents' opinions related to sexual practices

Sexual practice	Respondents (Pct.)
Do married men have girlfriends outside of their marriage?	
Yes	155 (91.7)
No	14 (8.30)
Do married women have boyfriends outside of their marriage?	
Yes	147 (87.0)
No	22 (13.0)
Do you think it is good for a married man to have girlfriends outside of his marriage?	
Yes	5 (3.0)
No	164 (97.0)
Do you think it is good for a married woman to have boyfriends outside of her marriage?	
Yes	3 (1.8)
No	166 (98.2)
If a man has more than one wife, do you think he will want to sleep with other women? (n = 166)	
Yes	130 (78.3)
No	36 (21.7)
Do you think it is good for a single man to have many girlfriends?	
Yes	9 (5.3)
No	160 (94.7)
Do you think it is good for a single woman to have many boyfriends?	
Yes	5 (3.0)
No	164 (97.0)

(continued)

Table 17.6 (continued)

Sexual practice	Respondents (Pct.)
Is it good for many young girls to engage in sex for money?	
Yes	4 (2.4)
No	166 (97.6)
Is it good for many young boys to engage in sex for money?	
Yes	5 (3.0)
No	162 (97.0)

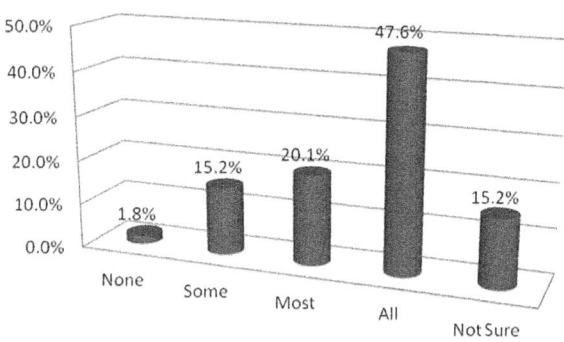

Fig. 17.2 How many of those with full blown AIDS would you think die of it?

20.1% thought *most* of those who had developed full blown AIDS would die of the disease. While 15.2% thought *some* would die of it, another 15.2% were ambivalent (i.e., not sure). Only three (1.8%) thought that no one would die of this disease. These observations are similar to those found in literature by Callen (1990), Herek (1999) and Rosenberg (1989) (Fig. 17.2).

Beliefs, Attitudes and Behavior

More than 90% of the respondents believed that HIV/AIDS is dangerous to their community and 89.4% said it could be a serious national health epidemic. Most (88.8%) thought that one could avoid contracting HIV/AIDS by changing one's behavior. A typical female response to what kind of change in behavior helps someone avoid contracting HIV/AIDS is as follows:

> These women should stop sleeping with different kinds of men. And they should know if the person they sleep with is good and do not give them any disease. For their own good, they should always tell the man to use condom. I always tell the man if you don't want to put it [condom] on don't come to me, go somewhere else.

Such a response indicates some sense of self-responsibility on their part. However, only 15.7% reported that *very many* of their friends have changed their behavior or way of life as a result of hearing about HIV/AIDS. On the contrary, 80% indicated that they changed their own behavior. Most (91.2%) thought that the Government should take necessary steps to prevent the spread of AIDS. Regarding the willingness to undergo screening for HIV/AIDS, 65.9% of the respondents expressed their willingness for it; and, 98% of them would want to know the result. On the other hand, only 37.6% thought that their community members would be willing for such screening. Thus, there is a clear subjective-objective paradox about themselves and others—a high approval rating for themselves versus a low rating for others (Tables 17.7 and 17.8).

Table 17.7 Respondents' awareness of condom

Awareness of condom	Respondents (Pct.)
Have you heard of some methods used to prevent pregnancy?	
Yes	140 (84.8)
No	25 (15.2)
Can use of condom prevent HIV/AIDS?	
Yes	128 (78.5)
No	35 (21.5)
Do you think, in general Liberians are using more condoms now to prevent HIV/AIDS?	
Yes	63 (37.3)
No	21 (12.4)
Don't know	85 (50.3)
Do you think women would accept the use of condoms by their partners?	
Yes	118 (73.3)
No	43 (26.7)
Where do you go to get condoms?	
My school/counselor	9 (5.3)
Clinic, hospital, VCT, doctors, health center	96 (56.5)
Drug stores and pharmacies	17 (10.0)
Family planning officials, CHO, HIV/AIDS workshops	26 (15.3)
Don't know	22 (12.9)
Can people here easily get condoms when they want them?	
Yes	73 (43.7)
No	44 (26.3)
Don't Know	50 (30.0)
Do you have to pay for the condoms?	
Yes	42 (25.0)
No	79 (47.0)
Don't know	47 (28.0)

(continued)

Table 17.7 (continued)

Awareness of condom	Respondents (Pct.)
What do you like about condoms? (n = 107)	
Prevent HIV/AIDS/STD	41 (38.3)
Prevent pregnancy	29 (27.1)
Safe life	16 (14.9)
Prevent infection	6 (5.6)
Protection for me and my partner	3 (2.8)
Easy to use	7 (6.5)
Don't like	5 (4.7)

Table 17.8 Respondents' access to media and acceptance of message

Access to media and acceptance of message	Respondents (Pct.)
Possess a radio	129 (75.9)
Possess a television	30 (17.6)
Visit a video house/cinema house	90 (52.9)
Frequency of visiting the video house/cinema house to watch tapes/cassette: (n = 90)	
Daily	11 (12.2)
Weekly	25 (27.8)
Monthly	6 (6.7)
Seldom	48 (53.3)
Read local news papers	66 (38.8)
Read magazines	65 (38.2)
Has access to materials such as leaflets, flyers, posters, and books on HIV/AIDS	72 (42.4)
Belong to a social group/youth group/peer group/health group in the community	72 (42.4)
Drama groups/theatre exist in the community	64 (37.6)
Attend drama theatre/folk theatre, or street plays	98 (57.6)
Frequency of watching plays/concerts: (n = 98)	
Weekly	13 (13.3)
Monthly	17 (17.3)
Seldom	68 (69.3)
Watched a play with HIV theme	90 (52.9)
Listen to sermon/speeches in church, Mosque or a place worship	134 (78.8)
Accept messages from sermons at the place(s) of worship (n = 134)	134 (100.0)
Listened to HIV related sermons	105 (61.8)

(continued)

Table 17.8 (continued)

Access to media and acceptance of message	Respondents (Pct.)
Frequency of listening to the sermons/speeches: (n = 105)	
Daily	9 (8.6)
Once a week	40 (38.1)
Monthly	48 (45.7)
Don't know	8 (7.6)

Opinions Related to Sexual Practices

Apparently, extramarital sexual relations occur frequently in these communities. Most (91.7%) of the respondents reported that married men had girlfriends outside their marriage; and, an overwhelming majority (87%) echoed that women too had boyfriends outside their marriage. However, they did think that that is not good either for a married man to have girlfriends (97%) or for a married woman to have boyfriends (98.2%) outside their marriage. A moderate percentage of 21.7% thought that if a man has more than one wife, then he would not want to sleep with other women, while other 78.3% disagreed with such an opinion. They were also opposed to the view that it is good for a single man to have many girlfriends (94.7%) or for a single woman to have many boyfriends (97%). They opined that neither young girls (97.6%) nor young boys (97%) should engage in sex for money. Thus, there is a tremendous gap between their moral ideal and practicality in terms of sexual practices. A similar gap was found in other studies (McCarraher et al. 2013).

Awareness of Condoms

Nearly 85% of the respondents reportedly heard of some methods of contraception, including condoms. A majority (78.5%) of the respondents were aware of condoms as a preventive deterrent to contracting HIV/AIDS. This level of awareness is consistent with the LISGIS 2013 Demographic and Health Survey data, which showed that 75% of men and women in age 15–49 know that the risk of HIV transmission could be reduced by use of condoms (Liberia Institute of Statistics and Geo-Information Services 2014: 13). However, only 37.3% thought that Liberians are using more condoms now to prevent HIV/AIDS, although 73.3% thought that women would accept the use of condoms by their partners. While nearly 13% did not know where to get condoms, 56.5% obtained them from clinics, hospitals, doctors or health centers; 15.3% from family planning officials, CHOs, or HIV/AIDS workshops; 10% from drug stores and pharmacies; and 5.3% from their schools and counselors. About 44% thought that people could get condoms easily when they were needed. While 47% reportedly did not have to pay for condoms, 25% indicated that they had to pay for them. Most (95.3%) were in favor of using condoms because it: prevents HIV/AID/STD (38.3%), prevents pregnancy (27.1%), provides safe life (14.1%), prevents infection (5.6%), protects sex partners (2.8%), and were easy to use (6.5%).

Access to Media and Acceptance of Message

As mentioned earlier, three-in-four respondents (75.9%) owned a radio, but only 17.6% owned a television. In addition, over one-half of the respondents (52.9%) had access to a video house/cinema house, of which a majority (53.3%) seldom visited; 6.7% visited once a month; 27.8% on a weekly basis; and only 12.2% visited daily for the purposes of watching tapes or listening to cassettes. Almost an equal percentage of respondents indicated that they read local newspapers (38.8%) or magazines (38.2%). About 42% reported to have had access to information on HIV/AIDS through leaflets, flyers, posters, and books; or through their membership in a local social group/youth group/peer group/health group. Only 37.6% acknowledged the existence of drama groups/theatre in their communities. However, more than one-half (57.6%) indicated that they would watch plays/concerts, if they had opportunity, ranging from weekly (13.3%) through monthly (17.3%) to seldom (69.3%). Nearly 53% admitted to have watched a play with an HIV theme. As for the role of religious institutions, 78.8% would listen to sermons/speeches in a Church, Mosque, or a place of worship; and all the listeners would accept the messages they get from such sermons/speeches. About 62% claimed to have listened to HIV related sermons either daily (8.6%), once a week (38.1%), or monthly (45.7%). A few (7.6%) listeners do not remember how often they listened to those sermons/speeches.

Conclusion and Recommendations

On the whole, the data revealed that most of the survey respondents were female in reproductive ages (with a mean age of 28.16 years) and Christians who believed that religion is very important. Many have attended school and over 80% attended secondary or post-secondary school. Most cited occupational categories were business and self-employment. Although no details regarding the nature of their business or self-employment were given, other studies found a high rate of transactional sex to obtain cash, food, clothing, western commodities, and school-fees (Atwood et al. 2011; Okigbo et al. 2014). Transactional sex is found to be associated with limited education, no earned income, longer duration of sexual activity, early sexual debut, history of sexual violence, and multiple sexual relationships (Okigbo et al. 2014). The Liberian Ministry of Health and Social Welfare also recognized transactional sex as an important risk factor in the spread of HIV (National AIDS Commission 2010: 7).

Most of the respondents had lived for a long time in their village/town as well as in their community. Thus, their mobility patterns are very limited. A majority (53%) of them claimed to not drink alcohol, but most of them were sexually active. They had their first intercourse in their teens (between 13 and 18 years) and had sex with older persons. About 70% reportedly had a single sex partner during the four weeks prior to the survey, but others had multiple partners during that period. Kennedy et al. (2012) also found from their study on HIV/AIDS risk behaviors among in-school adolescents in post-conflict Liberia that females were more likely to have older boyfriends, and that males were likely to have a greater number of sexual partners in the previous three months. Atwood et al. (2012a, b) found that even school-based HIV prevention programs had little impact on sexual initiation or multiple sex partnerships.

Regarding the awareness of HIV/AIDS and source of information, radio played a significant role in mass media, churches and mosques in institutional channels, and doctors among personal/professional channels. Perhaps integrating these three sources may prove to have a higher impact in reaching out to the target audience for better dissemination of HIV information. Many respondents appeared to have general knowledge about the risky behaviors and methods to avoid risks, which Kennedy et al. (2004) termed as *vague awareness*. However, they tend to believe that they were engaged in risk avoidance at a much larger level than others in the community. This self-denial syndrome must be addressed during the successive phases of this project implementation.

Most respondents were in theoretical agreement that sexual promiscuity would not be good either for them or for their community. However, there exists a wide gap between their ideal notions and practice of sexuality. Adulterous sexual relationships existed both among men and women. Most heard of condom use and agreed that men would use them if the women insist. Most believed that HIV/AIDS is an incurable disease—it is fatal at worst and chronic at best.

On the whole, the levels of awareness of HIV/AIDS, knowledge of its origins and knowledge of preventive behaviors appeared to be considerably higher than the level of protective behaviors for safe sex. These findings suggest that there is a critical need for capacity building and implementation of effective HIV/AIDS prevention strategies to overcome negative health related consequences, including dissemination, intervention and evaluation associated with the risk of contracting and spreading HIV/AIDS in Liberia. The Liberian National AIDS Commission's strategic framework is the first step in the right direction to address this important health problem; but it's success depends on effectively implementing and achieving sustainable behavioral changes in a sufficiently large number of individuals who are potentially at risk (see Coates et al. 2008). Future research may focus on evaluating the outcome of these strategic initiatives. Finally, any broad generalizations made from this study should take its limitations into account such as the study respondents were largely female living in Bong and Lofa counties.

References

Atwood, K. A., Kennedy, S. B., Barbu, E. M., Nagbe, W., Seekey, W., Sirleaf, P., et al. (2011). Transactional sex among youth in post-conflict Liberia. *Journal of Health, Population and Nutrition, 29*(2), 113–122.

Atwood, K. A., Kennedy, S. B., Shamblen, S., Tegli, J., Garber, S., Fahnbulleh, P. W., et al. (2012a). Impact of school-based HIV prevention in post-conflict Liberia. *AIDS Education and Prevention, 24*(1), 68–77.

Atwood, K. A., Kennedy, S. B., Shamblen, S., Taylor, C. H., Quaqua, M., Bee, E. M., et al. (2012b). Reducing sexual risk taking behaviors among adolescents who engage in transactional sex in post-conflict Liberia. *Vulnerable Children and Youth Studies, 7*(1), 55–65.

Barbiero, V. K., & Barh, S. B. (2007). *HIV situations and response assessment.* USAID/Monrovia. Report No. 07-001-49. Washington, D.C.: The Global Health Technical Assistance Project.

Central Intelligence Agency. (2010). *The world fact book: Unemployment rate.* Available online at: https://www.cia.gov/library/publications/the-world-factbook/rankorder/2129rank.html. Last accessed October 16, 2015.

Callen, M. (1990). *Surviving AIDS.* New York: Harper Collins.

Coates, T. J., Richter, L., & Caceres, C. (2008). Behavioral strategies to reduce HIV transmission: How to make them work better. *The Lancet, 372*(9639), 669–684.

Coleman, D. S. (2014). *Liberia: 2014 country review.* Houston, TX: Country Watch Inc.

Courville, T. M., Caldwell, B., & Brunell, P. A. (1998). Lack of evidence of transmission of HIV-1 to family contacts of HIV-1 infected children. *Clinical Pediatrics, 37*(3), 175–178.

Dahad, M., Spiegel, P. B., Njogu, P. M., & Schilperoord, M. (2013). Changes in HIV-related behaviors, knowledge and testing among refugees and surrounding national populations: A multicountry study. *AIDS Care, 25*(8), 998–1009.

Gledovic, Z., Rakocevic, B., Mugosa, B., & Grgurevic, A. (2015). *Collegium Antropologicum, 39* (1), 81–85.

Gummerson, E. (2013). Have the educated changed HIV risk behaviors more in Africa? *African Journal of AIDS Research, 12*(3), 161–172.

Herek, G. M. (1999). AIDS and stigma. *American Behavioral Scientist, 42*, 1106–1116.

International Monetary Fund. (2008). *Liberia: Poverty reduction strategy paper.* (IMF country report publication no. 08/219). Washington, D.C.: International Monetary Fund.

Ismail, O. (2002). Liberia's child combatants: Paying the price of neglect. *Conflict Security and Development, 2*(2), 125–134.

Jedy-Agba, W., & Adebmowo, C. (2012). Knowledge, attitudes and practices of AIDS associated malignancies among people living with HIV in Nigeria. *Infectious Agents and Cancer, 7*(28), 1–8. Available online at: http://www.infectagentscancer.com/content/7/1/28. Last accessed October 25, 2015.

Kennedy, S. B., Atwood, K. A., Harris, A. O., Taylor, C. H., Gobeh, M. E., Quaqua, M., et al. (2012). HIV/STD risk behaviors among in-school adolescents in post-conflict Liberia. *Journal of the Association of Nurses in AIDS Care, 23*(4), 350–360.

Kennedy, S. B., Johnson, K., Harris, A. O., Lincoln, A., Neace, W., & Collins, D. (2004). Evaluation of HIV/AIDS prevention resources in Liberia: Strategy and implications. *AIDS Patient Care and STDs, 18*(3), 169–180.

Kruk, M. E., Rockers, P. C., Williams, E. H., Varpilah, S. T., Macauley, R., Saydee, G., et al. (2010). Availability of essential health services in post-conflict Liberia. *Bulletin of the World Health Organization, 88*, 527–534.

Liberia Institute of Statistics and Geo-Information Services (LISGIS), Ministry of Health and Social Welfare [Liberia], National AIDS Control Program [Liberia], & Macro International, Inc. (2008). *Liberia demographic and health survey 2007.* Monrovia, Liberia: LISGIS and Macro International, Inc. Available online at: http://dhsprogram.com/pubs/pdf/FR201/FR201.pdf. Last accessed October 20, 2015.

Liberia Institute of Statistics and Geo-Information Services (LISGIS), Ministry of Health and Social Welfare [Liberia], National AIDS Control Program [Liberia] & ICF International (2014). *Liberia 2013 demographic and health survey key findings.* Rockville, Maryland, USA: LISGIS and ICF International. Available online at: http://dhsprogram.com/pubs/pdf/SR214/SR214.pdf. Last accessed October 16, 2015.

Madhok, R., Gracie, J. A., Lowe, G. D., & Forbes, C. D. (1986). Lack of HIV transmission by casual contact. *Lancet, 328*(8511), 863.

McCarraher, D. R., Chen, M., Wambugu, S., Sortijas, S., Succop, S., Aiyengba, B., et al. (2013). Informing HIV prevention efforts targeting Liberian youth: A study using the PLACE method in Liberia. *Reproductive Health, 10*(54), 1–17. Available online at: http://www.reproductive-health-journal.com/content/10/1/54. Last accessed October 20, 2015.

Mutha, A. S., Mutha, S. A., Baghel, P. J., Patil, R. J., Bhagat, S. B., & Watsa, M. C. (2014). A knowledge, attitudes and practices survey regarding sex, contraception and sexually transmitted diseases among commerce college students in Mumbai. *Journal of Clinical and Diagnostic Research, 8*(8), 14–18. Available online at: http://www.ncbi.nlm.nih.gov/pmc/articles/PMC4190736/. Last accessed October 24, 2015.

National AIDS Commission, Republic of Liberia (2010). *National HIV/AIDS strategic framework II, 2010–2014.* Available online at: http://www.ilo.org/wcmsp5/groups/public/---ed_protect/---protrav/---ilo_aids/documents/legaldocument/wcms_151222.pdf. Last accessed October 20, 2015.

Okigbo, C. C., McCarraher, D. R., Chen, M., & Pack, A. (2014). Risk factors for transactional sex among young females in post-conflict Liberia. *African Journal of Reproductive Health, 18*(3), 133–141.

Rosenberg, C. E. (1989). What is an epidemic: AIDS in historical perspective. *Daedalus, 118,* 1–17.

Spiegel, P. B., & Le, P. V. (2006). HIV behavioral surveillance surveys in conflict and post-conflict situations: A call for improvement. *Global Public Health, 1*(2), 147–156.

The World Bank. (2014). *Liberia: Country at a glance.* Available online at: http://www.worldbank.org/en/country/liberia. Last accessed October 17, 2015.

UNAIDS. (2006). *Expert think tank meeting on HIV prevention in high-prevalence countries in Southern Africa report.* Available online at: http://data.unaids.org/pub/report/2006/20060601_sadc_meeting_report_en.pdf. Last accessed October 20, 2015.

Wang, Y., Hao, M., Lu, F., Cochran, C., Shen, J. J., Xu, P., et al. (2014). Acquired immunodeficiency syndrome/human immunodeficiency virus knowledge, attitudes, and practices, and use of healthcare services among rural migrants: A cross-sectional study in China. *BMC Public Health, 14,* 158. Available online at: http://www.biomedcentral.com/1471-2458/14/158. Last accessed October 25, 2015.

Woodward, A., Howard, N., Kollie, S., Souare, Y., Roenne, A., & Borchert, M. (2014). HIV knowledge, risk perception and avoidant behavior change among Sierra Leonean refugees in Guinea. *International Journal of STD and AIDS, 25*(11), 817–826.

Yu, J. (2012). Teenage sexual attitudes and behavior in China: A literature review. *Health and Social Care in the Community, 20*(6), 561–582.

Zhang, L., Gong, R., Han, Q., Shi, Y., Jia, Q., Xu, S., et al. (2015). Survey of knowledge, attitude, and practice regarding reproductive health among urban men in China: A descriptive study. *Asian Journal of Anthropology, 17,* 309–314.

Chapter 18
Effects of Childhood and Current Socioeconomic Status on Health of Older Adults in India, China, Ghana, Mexico, Russia and South Africa: An Analysis of WHO-SAGE Data

Y. Selvamani, P. Arokiasamy and Uttamacharya

Introduction

During the last few decades, the socioeconomic status (SES) is recognized as one of the central markers in the field of Social Epidemiology (Adler et al. 1994; Blane 1995; Cutler et al. 2008). Socioeconomic status strongly predicts the health of the population; many researchers have documented the association of socioeconomic status with mortality, morbidity and poor health as mainly from high-income countries (Elo and Preston 1996; Herd et al. 2007; Kagamimori et al. 1983; Mackenbach et al. 1997, 2008; Marmot et al. 1998; Power et al. 1998; Ross and Wu 1995). Persisting association of socioeconomic status and health clearly highlight the causal pathways operating through different mechanism; people in higher socioeconomic status follow healthy behaviour, have better social circumstances, environmental exposures, improved cognitive development and better access to health care (Balia and Jones 2008; Becker and Newsom 2003; Currie and Goodman 2010; Evans and Kantrowitz 2002; Lynch et al. 1997; Vonneilich et al. 2011).

In recent years, a growing body of literature from developing countries recognizes the significance of socioeconomic status on health. However, the association across different health indicators appears to be inconsistent. Studies found a robust association of socioeconomic status with self-rated health and functional health (Arokiasamy et al. 2015a, b; Goli et al. 2014; Haseen et al. 2010; Hu and Hibel 2013; Lei et al. 2012; Smith and Goldman 2007; Zimmer and Amornsirisomboon

---

Y. Selvamani (✉) · Uttamacharya
International Institute for Population Sciences, Mumbai, India
e-mail: selvinsw@gmail.com

P. Arokiasamy
Department of Development Studies, International Institute
for Population Sciences, Mumbai, India

2001). Yet, studies also show higher socioeconomic status is positively associated with chronic diseases (Arokiasamy et al. 2015b; Subramanian et al. 2013). Additional studies show only a weak association between SES and chronic diseases (Zimmer and Amornsirisomboon 2001). These variations across Low and Middle Income Countries (LMIC) mainly occur as a result of inconsistency in reporting chronic conditions (Vellakkal et al. 2015).

At present, high and low-income countries are experiencing a rapid increase in aging population and its association with health emerged to be a global health challenge (Chatterji et al. 2015). Older population across countries face health and quality of life related challenges, the health burden of aging population living in low-income countries are increasing over time (Prince et al. 2015). Individual level socioeconomic status continues to impact old age too, however, the effect socioeconomic status on health across high and low income countries is not uniform; the evidence from developed countries reveals that socioeconomic differentials in health are converging at old age (Beckett 2000; Gjonça et al. 2009; Huisman et al. 2003; von dem Knesebeck et al. 2003, 2006). On the other hand, studies in developing countries argue that even in old age the socioeconomic status remains to be a strong factor influencing health (Beydoun and Popkin 2005; Lowry and Xie 2009). However, the mechanism by which the health differentials occur is still unclear, many researchers suspect the impact of early childhood conditions on health especially in later years (Crimmins 2005; Cutler et al. 2008). Also, studies testing the role of childhood socioeconomic status and health are limited in developing countries.

The growing body of evidence suggests that many diseases are likely to be rooted in childhood experiences; children living in a poor childhood socioeconomic status have more health problems during childhood and it biologically transmits to adulthood (Conroy et al. 2010). Moreover, the health of an individual accumulates over time; children growing in a low economic status tend to be poorer during adulthood and develop health problems faster than their counterparts (Case et al. 2002; Gupta et al. 2007). Further, the adverse childhood socioeconomic status leads to cumulative risk behaviour as a result of adopting a poor lifestyle such as tobacco use, alcohol consumption, poor diet largely through parental influence (Ben-Shlomo and Kuh 2002; Lawlor et al. 2004). Studies revealed that a poor childhood environment reflects in adult stature, on average, taller adults report better health than their shorter counterparts (Case and Paxson 2010; McGovern 2014). Poor childhood socioeconomic status has long-lasting effect on various health outcomes across the life course; people in low socioeconomic status during childhood have poor cardiovascular health (Beebe-Dimmer et al. 2004; Lipowicz et al. 2007; Poulton et al. 2002), increased the risk of diabetes (Lidfeldt et al. 2007; Pikhartova et al. 2014), report poor self-rated health and poor functional health (Haas 2008; Huang et al. 2011; Kestila et al. 2006; Lindström et al. 2012; Moody-Ayers et al. 2007).

Until recently, most of the existing studies on the association between childhood socioeconomic status and health were concentrated in high-income countries (Agahi et al. 2014; Haas 2007, 2008; Hudson et al. 2013; Hyde et al. 2006; Kestilä et al. 2006; Laaksonen et al. 2005; Luo and Waite 2005; Marmot et al. 2001; Moody-Ayers et al. 2007). Relatively limited studies have focussed on developing countries (Grimard et al. 2010; Guimaraes et al. 2014; Huang et al. 2011; Wen and Gu 2011).

Using pooled data from six LMIC countries, we examine the impact of childhood SES measured with parent education and childhood residence and indicators of current SES on subjective health. According to the World Bank (2011), the six countries included in the present study are categorized as low and middle-income countries based on GNI per capita in the country; India (lower–middle), China (lower–middle), Ghana (low income), Mexico (upper–middle), Russia (upper–middle) and South Africa (upper–middle). As the result of age structure transition, the proportion of aging population has increased in these countries. As estimated by the U S Census Bureau (2012), the proportion of 50+ population in the year 2010 in India (16.4), China (24.8), Ghana (10.9), Mexico (17.3), Russia (33.4) and South Africa (16.3). The growing proportion of older population has resulted in changes in the health profile of these countries (Prince et al. 2015). However, existing nationally representative data from six countries are limited, WHO-SAGE aimed to fill this gap by providing reliable and scientific estimates of health and wellbeing for adult population. The detailed country selection criteria and data collection procedure is provided elsewhere (Kowal et al. 2012; He et al. 2012).

Data Source

The present study used data from the first wave of WHO's Study on global AGEing and adult health (SAGE). SAGE provides data for six low and middle-income countries with nationally representative sample size aged 50 and above; India (6560), China (13,175), Ghana (4305), Mexico (2313), Russia (3938) and South Africa (3837), which was implemented during 2007–2010. SAGE in each country employed a stratified multi-stage cluster design for sampling. Household and individual weights were post-stratified according to country-specific population data (Naidoo 2012). Face-to-face interviews were carried out from the household selected based on one of two mutually exclusive categories: (a) all persons aged 50 and above were selected from "50+ households" (b) one person aged 18–49 selected from household classified as "18–49 households". Additionally in Mexico, supplementary and replacement sample were included for accounting loses in follow-up from wave 0. SAGE survey covers a total of 34 128 samples aged 50 and above and a comparative sample consisting of 8340 respondents aged 18–49. SAGE survey covers wide range of health and wellbeing indicators; specifically the survey collects data on socioeconomic characteristics, parental education and employment, health, health risk factors, subjective wellbeing, quality of life, health care utilisation and social networks. Apart from self-reported assessment, various biomarkers have been used to increase the accuracy of self-reported measures of health: Anthropometric (height and weight; waist and hip circumference), cognitive ability (verbal recall, forward and backward digit span and verbal fluency), chronic conditions (blood test from finger prick and blood pressure test), and physical function (vision tests, lung function, timed walk and grip strength) A more detailed description of study design and sampling methods is given in Kowal et al. (2012).

Methods

Self-rated Health (SRH)

In the present study, we use self-rated health as one of the outcome variables. Self-rated health is a common and widely used measure of health in epidemiology and public health. SRH is a strong predictor of mortality, subjective well-being and future health (Benyamini et al. 2003; Idler and Kasl 1995; Stenholm et al. 2014; Subramanian et al. 2005). In SAGE, self-rated overall general health was measured based on the question, "In general, how would you rate your health today?" with five possible response categories: (1) Very good, (2) Good, (3) Moderate, (4) Bad and (5) Very bad. For the analysis, we combined bad and very bad categories as 'bad health' and rest into other 'good health' to obtain a dichotomized health variable. 'Poor health' was the outcome of interest in the analysis.

Activities of Daily Living (1 + ADL)

The Functional health limitation is defined as the "*effect of specific impairments on the performance or performance capability of the person*" (Luckasson et al. 1992, p. 10). Functional health is a crucial indicator of health; it has implications on the ability of the individual in performing daily activities. In the SAGE survey, data were collected through self-reports of specific on Activities of Daily Living (ADL) during the last 30 days with a five-point scale ranging from none to extreme difficulty. The ADLs include sitting, walking, standing up, standing, climbing, crouching, picking up, eating, dressing, using the toilet, moving around home, transferring and concentrating for about 10 min. In the present study, severe and extreme difficulties were combined to represent the functional limitation. We have created dichotomous variable as no limitation and 1 + ADL limitations.

Measures of Socioeconomic Status (SES)

Current Socioeconomic Status
In this analysis, we identified years of schooling and household wealth quintile as a composite measure of adult socioeconomic status. In the literature on social determinants of health, education is recognized as a key measure of socioeconomic

status and a more plausible exogenous determinant of health than income and occupation (Elo and Preston 1996; Lynch and Kaplan 2000). Enhanced health knowledge, decision-making ability and greater access to use of resources and health are recognized as possible pathways in explaining the education health relationship (Cutler et al. 2008; Ross and Wu 1995). For analytical convenience, years of education have been grouped into four categories: no schooling, 1–5 years, 6–9 years and 10 and above years of schooling.

In addition to education, an asset-based index was constructed to generate household wealth quintiles. The wealth index has been generated using factor analysis on wealth indicators and the wealth index was grouped into 5 categories, namely first (lowest), second, third, fourth and fifth (highest) with cut-off points of 20% quintile each.

Control Variables

A group of individual and demographic characteristics such as age, sex, marital status and place of residence were included as control variables in the study. The age of the respondents was grouped as 50–59, 60–69, and 70+. Sex [male and female]. Marital status grouped into currently married [currently married and cohabiting] and, others [never married, separated/divorced and, widowed] and place of residence [urban and rural].

Childhood Socioeconomic Status

In the present study, we have used parental education as a proxy measure of childhood socioeconomic status. Parental education is a commonly used measure of childhood socioeconomic status; many studies have used parental education to represent the early life socioeconomic conditions (Hudson et al. 2013; Lynch et al. 1997; Laaksonen et al. 2005; Lipowicz et al. 2007; Marmot et al. 1998; McEniry 2013; Moody-Ayers et al. 2007). SAGE measures the level of parental education separately for mother and father. The answers were captured in seven categories from no formal education to post graduation. For the purpose of analysis, we have categorized the parental education into three categories: no formal education, up to primary school and secondary and above; this variable has been created separately for mother and father.

Statistical Analysis

Bivariate and multivariate techniques have been adopted. Bivariate technique is used to show the prevalence of poor health and functional limitation by country and socioeconomic status. All the outcomes were weighted using the sample weight.

Since, our outcome variable was coded dichotomous, we have used multivariate logistic regression model to assess the effect of adult and childhood socioeconomic conditions on self-rated poor health and 1 + ADL limitations. We fitted different logistic regression models to cover adult and childhood socioeconomic status. In model 1, we included only childhood socioeconomic status along with country dummy. In model 2, we incorporated individual characteristics with childhood SES and country dummy. In model 3, we included all the three; demographic, childhood and adult socioeconomic variables together. Separate logistic regression models were estimated for the two outcome variables: self-rated health and 1 + ADL limitations. STATA V.12 has been used to analyse the data.

Results

Table 18.1 shows the percent distribution of the sample in each category: age group, gender, residence, years of schooling, household wealth, childhood residence and parental education. In all of the countries, one in every six persons reported poor health. Among six countries, the prevalence of poor health was found to be higher in Russia (23.1%). The 1 + ADL limitation was found higher in India (52.1%), where more than half of the older adults reported having the functional limitation, in contrast to this, the prevalence was found to be lowest in China (12.9%).

The prevalence of self-rated poor health by demographic characteristics and by adult and childhood socioeconomic factors are shown in Table 18.2. The prevalence of poor self-rated health was higher among rural residents in all the countries except in Russia. A higher proportion women and oldest (70+) respondents reported poor health than the counterparts. A lower proportion of currently married older adults reported poor health than the counterpart [never married, separated/divorced and, widowed]. Years of schooling make a larger difference in self-rated poor health; a major proportion of respondents with no education reported poor health in Russia (78.2%), China (31.8%) India (26.5%); by comparison, older adults having 10+ years education have a much lower prevalence of poor self-rated health. In all countries, the percentage older adults reporting poor health reduces considerably from poorest to richest category. Residing in rural areas during childhood was positively associated with poor health in China (25.5%), South Africa (24.8%), India (22.9%) and, Russia (23.9%). An increase in mother's education is associated with less poor health among older adults. Similarly, higher father's education is associated with the reduction in poor self-rated health.

In almost all countries except in Ghana, residing in a rural area is associated with higher prevalence of 1 + ADL limitations (Table 18.3). Age is positively associated with 1 + ADL limitations, the prevalence much higher among older adults in the age group 60–69 and 70+ than those in 50–59. The proportion reported 1 + ADL is much lower among currently married older adults than their counterparts in all countries. The prevalence of 1 + ADL limitations was highest among older adults with no education in Russia (87.4%) and in India (60.8%). Higher

Table 18.1 Percent distribution of respondents by health outcomes, demographic variables, current and childhood SES characteristics across six LMICs WHO-SAGE (2007–2010)

	Characteristics	India	China	Ghana	Mexico	Russia	South Africa
Health indicators	*Self-rated health*						
	Not bad	77.59	78.82	82.88	83.02	76.89	82.5
	Bad	22.41	21.18	17.12	16.98	23.11	17.5
	1 + ADL						
	No Limitation	47.83	87.08	58.31	63.39	74.11	64.76
	At least 1 limitation	52.17	12.92	41.69	36.61	25.89	35.24
Demographic variables	*Age group*						
	50–59	48.61	44.93	39.74	48.05	45.19	49.88
	60–69	30.89	31.86	27.5	25.59	24.62	30.6
	70+	20.5	23.2	32.76	26.36	30.19	19.52
	Sex						
	Male	50.99	49.75	52.45	46.81	38.88	44.05
	Female	49.01	50.25	47.55	53.19	61.12	55.95
	Residence						
	Urban	28.91	47.34	41.09	78.79	72.74	64.86
	Rural	71.09	52.66	58.91	21.21	27.26	35.14
	Marital status						
	Currently married	76.93	85.04	59.32	73.0	58.34	55.9
	Others	23.07	14.96	40.68	27.0	41.66	44.1
Current SES	*Years of schooling*						
	No schooling	51.62	23.54	54.8	17.44	0.73	24.45
	1–5 years	19.09	25.18	8.42	38.14	5.83	21.53
	6–9 years	13.06	34.81	8.27	34.05	20.51	30.87
	10+ years	16.23	16.47	28.52	10.36	72.94	23.14
	Wealth quintile						
	First (Lowest)	18.18	16.27	18.24	15.3	16.21	20.71
	Second	19.5	18.13	19.09	24.71	19.58	19.89
	Third	18.79	20.49	20.46	16.79	19.12	18.23
	Fourth	19.64	23.36	20.66	16.61	20.54	19.83
	Fifth (Highest)	23.9	21.75	21.56	26.6	24.55	21.34
Childhood SES	*Childhood residence*						
	Urban	27.27	41.49	39.22	71.3	59.42	61.59
	Rural	72.73	58.51	60.78	28.7	40.58	38.41
	Mother's education						
	No formal education	90.19	87.39	94.97	61.84	17.91	62.49
	Less than primary	5.32	6.01	2.65	24.32	12.99	18.43
	Completed primary and secondary	3.9	5.11	1.21	12.03	39.53	14.06
	High school and above	0.59	1.5	1.17	1.82	29.56	5.02
	Father's education						
	No formal education	66.56	68.7	84.49	51.23	12.02	52.98
	Less than primary	13.28	12.85	4.63	28.0	11.85	19.07
	Completed primary and secondary	15.39	13.92	4.19	16.27	39.24	21.1
	High school and Above	4.77	4.52	6.69	4.5	36.88	6.85

All percentages are weighted

Table 18.2 Prevalence of self-rated poor health by demographic, adult and childhood socio-economic characteristics in six countries, WHO-SAGE (2007–2010)

Characteristics	India	China	Ghana	Mexico	Russia	South Africa	Pooled
Residence							
Urban	19.7	15.0	15.9	16.2	24.2	14.8	18.9
Rural	23.5	26.7	17.9	19.7	20.0	22.2	24.2
Sex							
Male	19.6	18.5	14.7	11.3	16.8	17.2	18.6
Female	25.2	23.8	19.7	21.9	27.0	17.7	24.7
Age group							
50–59	16.5	16.8	8.9	20.5	9.8	15.4	15.2
60–69	22.6	22.0	17.4	13.1	20.9	18.8	21.9
70+	36.0	28.5	26.8	14.0	44.6	20.6	34.6
Marital status							
Currently married	19.8	19.8	13.9	18.2	17.6	14.4	19.2
Others	31.1	29.1	21.7	13.6	30.7	21.3	29.6
Years of schooling							
No schooling	26.5	31.8	21.1	13.2	78.2	20.5	28.1
1–5 years	22.4	24.2	12.9	28.8	44.9	23.8	24.7
6–9 years	18.9	17.3	19.3	10.5	37.6	17.9	21.1
10+ years	11.6	9.98	10.0	1.6	16.4	5.7	13.5
Wealth quintile							
First (lowest)	31.0	33.4	22.5	16.6	35.1	27.4	32.3
Second	25.6	26.8	17.2	21.1	26.2	18.2	25.8
Third	25.0	22.0	18.9	29.8	25.1	18.6	23.5
Fourth	18.5	17.9	14.2	9.15	18.1	15.4	18.0
Fifth (highest)	14.1	10.0	13.2	10.2	15.1	8.1	12.6
Childhood SES							
Childhood residence							
Urban	20.9	14.8	17.1	17.1	22.5	12.0	18.4
Rural	22.9	25.5	16.9	16.5	23.9	24.8	24.0
Mother's education							
No formal education	23.0	22.2	17.3	19.0	35.5	19.2	23.0
Less than primary	18.7	17.5	13.4	8.1	28.4	10.3	21.0
Completed primary and secondary	13.0	11.1	5.62	10.0	22.3	12.9	18.9
High school and above	7.4	10.4	14.1	6.0	13.1	7.0	12.6
Father's education							
No formal education	22.0	23.8	17.8	21.7	35.5	20.6	23.3
Less than primary	22.7	17.3	14.7	7.5	32.9	14.0	22.0
Completed primary and secondary	21.9	13.8	11.4	8.8	23.2	10.3	19.8
High school and above	13.6	13.1	12.0	4.1	13.8	5.0	13.5

All percentages are weighted

Table 18.3 Prevalence of self-reported functional limitation (1 + ADL) by demographic, adult and childhood socioeconomic characteristics in six countries, WHO-SAGE (2007–2010)

Characteristics	India	China	Ghana	Mexico	Russia	South Africa	Pooled
Residence							
Urban	46.3	7.1	41.8	34.5	26.8	34.9	24.0
Rural	54.5	18.1	41.6	44.1	23.4	35.7	37.0
Sex							
Male	41.5	10.4	34.0	32.5	17.6	30.0	24.7
Female	63.1	15.3	50.0	40.1	31.1	39.3	36.8
Age group							
50–59	43.2	7.3	23.4	21.5	9.1	24.9	22.3
60–69	55.8	12.7	39.8	41.9	25.0	39.4	32.3
70+	67.6	24.2	65.4	60.4	51.4	54.7	46.7
Marital status							
Currently married	47.5	11.6	33.6	31.4	19.0	31.5	26.9
Others	67.5	20.3	53.5	50.5	35.4	40.3	43.8
Years of schooling							
No schooling	60.8	22.7	49.7	45.7	87.4	39.8	48.7
1–5 years	51.3	14.0	37.2	41.2	65.2	40.5	32.1
6–9 years	43.2	9.7	39.3	27.2	36.9	35.8	22.3
10+ years	32.8	4.6	28.3	34.2	18.9	23.9	18.8
Wealth quintile							
First (lowest)	61.1	20.1	47.2	55.2	37.5	34.1	40.3
Second	52.1	16.5	42.5	41.4	28.2	36.1	33.4
Third	54.9	13.9	42.7	27.4	33.1	36.8	33.3
Fourth	49.2	11.1	39.0	31.6	18.5	40.5	26.7
Fifth (Highest)	45.5	4.4	37.7	30.1	16.6	29.2	23.8
Childhood SES							
Childhood residence							
Urban	46.6	6.5	41.7	36.4	23.6	32.2	23.2
Rural	54.2	17.3	41.2	37.0	29.1	39.7	36.3
Mother's education							
No formal education	52.9	13.7	42.0	44.6	45.8	36.7	34.2
Less than primary	47.5	8.2	39.0	23.7	35.0	36.8	30.1
Completed primary and secondary	43.0	5.8	24.8	45.3	20.6	21.9	21.0
High school and above	31.4	5.1	35.2	45.6	14.6	21.4	14.5
Father's education							
No formal education	52.5	15.3	43.2	47.3	48.5	34.6	34.2
Less than primary	50.5	10.1	33.8	28.0	29.2	36.3	30.3
Completed primary and secondary	49.6	6.6	33.2	30.6	24.1	30.5	27.0
High school and above	47.3	3.0	30.9	59.9	17.7	24.9	20.4

All percentages are weighted

wealth status is negatively associated with 1 + ADL limitations in all the countries; with a drop found in Mexico among older adults in the highest wealth quintile category (30.1%) compared to lowest wealth category (55.2%). Older adults' childhood rural residence increases the prevalence of 1 + ADL limitation mainly in India, China, Russia and South Africa. Increases in parental education considerably reduces the 1 + ADL in all countries except in Mexico, where positive association is found with parental education.

Results from Logistic Regression Models

Self-rated Poor Health

Table 18.4 shows the impact of childhood and current SES on self-rated health. In Model I, older adults in Ghana, Mexico and South Africa are less likely to report poor health than older adults in India, and older adults in Russia are more likely to report poor health. Indicators of childhood SES strongly predict the health of older adults. Residing in rural areas during childhood increases the odds of reporting poor health [OR: 1.19; CI: 1.11–1.26; $P < 0.001$]. Mother's education inversely associated with health among older adults; older adults with mother's education high school and above are 57% less likely to report poor health. In Model 2, individual characteristics such as place of residence, age, sex and marital status are significantly associated with self-rated health. Age of the respondent is strongly correlated with poor health; older adults in 70+ age category are two times more likely to report poor health than individuals in the 50–59 age group. Older adults currently residing in rural areas, females and respondents in others category of marital status are more likely to report poor health. In the final model, the effect of childhood residence and father's education disappears; however, the mother's education strongly predicts the health of older adults, older adult's mothers with high school and above education are 36 percent less likely to report poor health than those with older adult mothers with no education. Further, years of education and wealth are strongly and inversely associated with self-rated health; moreover, household wealth emerged to be a stronger predictor of self-rated health. Older adults in wealthiest category [OR: 0.47; CI: 0.43–0.53; $P < 0.001$] are less likely to report poor health than the older adults with 10 years and above years of education [OR: 0.60; CI: 0.53–0.67; $P < 0.001$].

1 + ADL Limitations

Table 18.5 shows the impact of childhood and adult SES on 1 + ADL limitations for older adults in SAGE Countries. In model 1, Results of six countries reveal that older adults in China, Ghana, Mexico, Russia and South Africa are less likely to

Table 18.4 Results of logistic regression analysis of adult and childhood socioeconomic status on self-rated poor health, pooled analysis of six countries, WHO-SAGE (2007–2010)

Characteristics	Model I OR [95% CI]	Model II OR [95% CI]	Model III OR [95% CI]
Country			
India®			
China	1.05 [0.97–1.13]	1.07* [0.99–1.16]	1.03 [0.94–1.12]
Ghana	0.77*** [0.69–0.85]	0.70*** [0.63–0.78]	0.72*** [0.64–0.80]
Mexico	0.66*** [0.56–0.77]	0.53*** [0.45–0.63]	0.48*** [0.40–0.57]
Russia	2.64*** [2.33–2.99]	2.05*** [1.81–2.33]	2.10*** [1.83–2.42]
South Africa	0.88* [0.77–1.00]	0.80*** [0.70–0.91]	0.74*** [0.65–0.85]
Childhood SES			
Childhood residence			
Urban®			
Rural	1.19*** [1.11–1.26]	0.99 [0.89–1.09]	0.95 [0.86–1.05]
Mother's education			
No formal education®			
Less than primary	0.73*** [0.64–0.83]	0.78*** [0.68–0.88]	0.86** [0.75–0.99]
Completed primary and secondary	0.58*** [0.50–0.67]	0.67*** [0.58–0.78]	0.76*** [0.66–0.89]
High school and above	0.43*** [0.35–0.53]	0.55*** [0.44–0.68]	0.64*** [0.51–0.81]
Father's education			
No formal education®			
Less than primary	0.83*** [0.76–0.92]	0.91* [0.83–1.01]	1.01 [0.92–1.12]
Completed primary and secondary	0.79*** [0.71–0.87]	0.90* [0.81–1.00]	1.06 [0.96–1.19]
High school and above	0.76*** [0.65–0.89]	0.86* [0.74–1.00]	1.12 [0.95–1.32]
Residence			
Urban®			
Rural		1.38*** [1.25–1.52]	1.18*** [1.07–1.31]
Age			
50–59®			
60–69		1.56*** [1.45–1.68]	1.49*** [1.38–1.61]
70+		2.45*** [2.27–2.65]	2.24*** [2.07–2.43]
Sex			
Male®			
Female		1.25*** [1.17–1.33]	1.18*** [1.10–1.26]
Marital status			
Currently married®			
Others		1.29*** [1.20–1.39]	1.17*** [1.09–1.26]
Years of education			
No schooling®			
1–5 years			1.00 [0.92–1.09]
6–9 years			0.87*** [0.79–0.96]
10+ above			0.60*** [0.53–0.67]

(continued)

Table 18.4 (continued)

	Model I	Model II	Model III
Wealth			
First (lowest)®			
Second			0.83*** [0.76–0.90]
Third			0.74*** [0.68–0.81]
Fourth			0.61*** [0.56–0.68]
Fifth (highest)			0.47*** [0.43–0.53]

®Reference group, $*p < 0.1$, $**p < 0.05$, $***p < 0.01$

report functional health limitation than the older adults in India, especially older adults in China are at lower risk of reporting functional health limitation [OR: 0.13; CI: 0.12–0.14; $P < 0.001$]. Childhood SES indicators reveal that those residing in rural areas during childhood are more likely to report ADL limitations. Increase in parental education strongly and inversely associated with 1 + ADL especially mother with high school and above High School education are 58 percent less likely to report 1 + ADL limitations. Model 2, with indicators of individual characteristics reveals that older adults in advanced age (70+) are four times more likely to report functional health limitation. Further, rural residents, women and older adults in others marital category are more likely to report functional limitation. In the final model, the effect of father's education and childhood residence dissolve; nonetheless, the effect of mother's education remains a significant factor to influence the functional health after controlling for current SES and individual characteristics. The effect of current SES shows that older adults with 6 and above years of education are less likely report 1 + ADL than older adults with no education and 1–5 years of education. Increase in wealth at each level significantly reduces the odds of functional limitation.

Discussion and Conclusion

Using nationally representative data on older adults aged 50 and above from the six SAGE countries, this study examined the effects of childhood and adult SES on self-rated health and ADL limitations. The study makes an important contribution to the limited research in low and middle-income settings. First, we assessed the prevalence of poor health and 1 + ADL limitations by country and socioeconomic status. Secondly, we examined the effect of adult and childhood socioeconomic status on self-rated poor health and activities of daily living using regression analysis.

Our results show that the prevalence of poor health and functional limitation varied considerably by country and socioeconomic indicators. The highest prevalence of poor self-rated health was shown in Russia. The highest prevalence of

Table 18.5 Results of logistic regression analysis of adult and childhood socioeconomic status on 1 + ADL, pooled analysis of six countries, WHO-SAGE (2007–2010)

Characteristics	Model I OR [95% CI]	Model II OR [95% CI]	Model III OR [95% CI]
Country			
India®			
China	0.13*** [0.12–0.14]	0.10*** [0.10–0.11]	0.10*** [0.09–0.11]
Ghana	0.65*** [0.60–0.71]	0.55*** [0.51–0.61]	0.58*** [0.53–0.63]
Mexico	0.87** [0.78–0.97]	0.59*** [0.52–0.67]	0.56*** [0.50–0.64]
Russia	0.73*** [0.65–0.81]	0.43*** [0.38–0.49]	0.45*** [0.40–0.52]
South Africa	0.47*** [0.43–0.52]	0.38*** [0.34–0.42]	0.36*** [0.32–0.41]
Childhood SES			
Childhood residence			
Urban®			
Rural	1.22*** [1.15–1.29]	1.10** [1.00–1.21]	1.08 [0.98–1.18]
Mother's education			
No formal education®			
Less than primary	0.88** [0.79–0.98]	0.96 [0.86–1.08]	1.05 [0.93–1.18]
Completed primary and secondary	0.65*** [0.57–0.73]	0.77*** [0.67–0.88]	0.87** [0.76–0.99]
High school and above	0.42*** [0.35–0.52]	0.58*** [0.47–0.71]	0.67*** [0.54–0.83]
Father's education			
No formal education®			
Less than primary	0.80*** [0.73–0.87]	0.88** [0.80–0.97]	0.95 [0.87–1.05]
Completed primary and secondary	0.75*** [0.68–0.83]	0.87*** [0.79–0.96]	1.01 [0.91–1.12]
High school and above	0.77*** [0.68–0.88]	0.87* [0.76–1.01]	1.12 [0.97–1.30]
Residence			
Urban®			
Rural		1.27*** [1.15–1.39]	1.16*** [1.05–1.27]
Age			
50–59®			
60–69		1.82*** [1.70–1.95]	1.77*** [1.65–1.90]
70+		4.38*** [4.07–4.72]	4.14*** [3.83–4.46]
Sex			
Male®			
Female		1.82*** [1.71–1.93]	1.69*** [1.59–1.81]
Marital status			
Currently married®			
Others		1.18*** [1.11–1.26]	1.14*** [1.06–1.22]
Years of education			
No schooling®			
1–5 years			0.93 [0.86–1.02]
6–9 years			0.85*** [0.78–0.94]
10+ above			0.60*** [0.54–0.67]

(continued)

Table 18.5 (continued)

	Model I	Model II	Model III
Wealth			
First (Lowest)[®]			
Second			0.92* [0.84–1.00]
Third			0.91** [0.83–0.99]
Fourth			0.84*** [0.77–0.93]
Fifth (Highest)			0.73*** [0.66–0.81]

[®]Reference group, *p < 0.1, **p < 0.05, ***p < 0.01 1 + ADL is defined as at least one limitation include sitting, walking, standing-up, standing, climbing, crouching, picking up, eating, dressing, using toilet, moving around in home, transferring and concentrating for about 10 min

functional limitation was observed in India. The prevalence of functional limitation was lowest in China. The prevalence of poor self-rated health and 1 + ADL limitations was negatively associated with the socioeconomic status in all the countries. In India and Russia older adults are less healthy than those in other countries; the prevalence of both poor self-rated health and 1 + ADL limitations are much higher in Russia and India; this could be partly attributed to higher prevalence of multi-morbidity in India as shown in a recent study that multiple morbidities exert significant worsening effects on self-rated health and functional limitation (Arokiasamy et al. 2015a, b; Haseen et al. 2010).

The increase in wealth at each level minimizes the self-rated poor health as older adults of the wealthiest quintile enjoy better health. The association of wealth and self-rated health becomes stronger with additional years of education. Years of schooling are found to be a stronger predictor of functional health. Adjusted for the effects of age, residence, education and the wealth, the childhood SES measured by parental education is seen to be a significant predictor of self-rated health and functional limitation. Mother's education has especially long lasting implications on health measures. However, the effect of mother's education is more on self-rated health than the association of mother's education and functional limitation. Overall, Mother's education is an important and independent predictor of health status of older adults.

The association of wealth and health are stronger in this study as consistent with other studies (Aittomäki et al. 2010; Hajat et al. 2011). This is mainly due to the mediating effects of many factors, wealthier people chose a healthier lifestyle, such as having healthy diet, exercise, quit smoking, use moderate amounts of alcohol, higher levels of social network, and better use of health care (Read et al. 2015). Similarly, childhood socioeconomic status plays a significant role in predicting health. Our results reflected the findings from other studies mainly from high-income countries (Bowen and González 2010; Huang et al. 2011; Marmot et al. 1998; Moody-Ayers et al. 2007; Rahkonen et al. 1997). Also, older adults receive benefit from own education and mother's education as shown in other studies as well (Grimard et al. 2010; Luo and Waite 2005). In contrast to our findings, few existing studies show that there is no association between parental education and self-rated health (Guimarães et al. 2014; Laaksonen et al. 2005). However, in our study the parental education, especially mother's education shows an enduring effect on self-rated health and on functional health limitations.

Thus, this study reiterates the importance of parental education in determining the health of their children, especially mother's education is found to be more relevant in terms of their children's health in the life course. In addition, studies also have shown that mothers play a major role in the health and development of their children. Therefore, this study adds a strong empirical support to the association between mother's education and child health in support of existing literature (Case and Paxson 2001; Chen and Li 2009).

These findings should be viewed in the light of a few important limitations. First, this study is based on cross-sectional data, through which one cannot establish the causal pathways. Also, higher prevalence of chronic disease directly linked to poor subjective health; which, we have not included in our analysis. Further, to represent childhood SES, we have used parental education and childhood residence. The SAGE survey does not provide a wide range of childhood indicators to best understand the childhood socioeconomic status. Also, there is a chance of recall bias in reporting parental educational status.

To conclude, these results from low and middle-income countries call attention to the need to improve the health of the aging population, as the globe experiences the rise of aging population and morbidity, reducing the socioeconomic inequality will be necessary to converge health differentials. Moreover, both childhood and current socioeconomic circumstances were found to be strong predictors of the subjective health among older adults. Also, policies targeting aging population through financial support are not sufficient since developing countries face multiple disease burden and poor health conditions. This study calls for a life course intervention to curb the disease profile of the LMICs as a constructive measure of intervention. Policies, improving the women and girls' education have a central implication to the health of their children throughout life. Also, we recommend the need for longitudinal studies to incorporate more childhood indicators; thus strong evidence can be established to support the role of childhood socioeconomic status on health of low and middle-income countries.

Acknowledgments We are grateful to Ms. Kshipra Jain for her comments in the earlier version of this paper and we acknowledge WHO-SAGE team for facilitating the use of this data.

References

Adler, N. E., Boyce, T., Chesney, M. A., Cohen, S., Folkman, S., Kahn, R. L., et al. (1994). Socioeconomic status and health: The challenge of the gradient. *American Psychologist, 49*(1), 15.
Agahi, N., Shaw, B. A., & Fors, S. (2014). Social and economic conditions in childhood and the progression of functional health problems from midlife into old age. *Journal of Epidemiology and Community Health, 68*(8), 734–740.

Aittomaki, A., Martikainen, P., Laaksonen, M., Lahelma, E., & Rahkonen, O. (2010). The associations of household wealth and income with self-rated health–a study on economic advantage in middle-aged Finnish men and women. *Social Science and Medicine, 71*(5), 1018–1026.

Arokiasamy, P., Uttamacharya, U., & Jain, K. (2015a). *Multi-morbidity, functional limitations, and self-rated health among older adults in India* SAGE open (Vol. 5).

Arokiasamy, P., Uttamacharya, U., Jain, K., Biritwum, R. B., Yawson, A. E., Wu, F., et al. (2015b). The impact of multimorbidity on adult physical and mental health in low- and middle-income countries: what does the study on global ageing and adult health (SAGE) reveal? *BMC Medicine, 13*, 178.

Balia, S., & Jones, A. M. (2008). Mortality, lifestyle and socio-economic status. *J Health Econ, 27*(1), 1–26.

Becker, G., & Newsom, E. (2003). Socioeconomic status and dissatisfaction with health care among chronically Ill African Americans. *American Journal of Public Health, 93*(5), 742–748.

Beckett, M. (2000). Converging health inequalities in later life-an artifact of mortality selection? *Journal of Health and Social Behavior*, 106–119.

Beebe-Dimmer, J., Lynch, J. W., Turrell, G., Lustgarten, S., Raghunathan, T., & Kaplan, G. A. (2004). Childhood and adult socioeconomic conditions and 31-year mortality risk in women. *American Journal of Epidemiology, 159*(5), 481–490.

Ben-Shlomo, Y., & Kuh, D. (2002). A life course approach to chronic disease epidemiology: Conceptual models, empirical challenges and interdisciplinary perspectives. *International Journal of Epidemiology, 31*(2), 285–293.

Benyamini, Y., Blumstein, T., Lusky, A., & Modan, B. (2003). Gender differences in the self-rated health-mortality association: is it poor self-rated health that predicts mortality or excellent self-rated health that predicts survival? *Gerontologist, 43*(3), 396–405; discussion 372–395.

Beydoun, M. A., & Popkin, B. M. (2005). The impact of socio-economic factors on functional status decline among community-dwelling older adults in China. *Social Science and Medicine, 60*(9), 2045–2057.

Blane, D. (1995). Social determinants of health–socioeconomic status, social class, and ethnicity. *American Journal of Public Health, 85*(7), 903–905.

Bowen, M. E., & González, H. M. (2010). Childhood socioeconomic position and disability in later life: Results of the health and retirement study. *American Journal of Public Health, 100*(Suppl 1), S197–S203.

Case, A., Lubotsky, D., & Paxson, C. (2002). Economic status and health in childhood: The origins of the gradient. *The American Economic Review, 92*(5), 1308–1334.

Case, A., & Paxson, C. (2001). Mothers and others: who invests in children's health? *J Health Econ, 20*(3), 301–328.

Case, A., & Paxson, C. (2010). Causes and consequences of early-life health. *Demography, 47*, S65–S85.

Chatterji, S., Byles, J., Cutler, D., Seeman, T., & Verdes, E. (2015). Health, functioning, and disability in older adults-present status and future implications. *The Lancet, 385*(9967), 563–575.

Chen, Y., & Li, H. (2009). Mother's education and child health: is there a nurturing effect? *J Health Econ, 28*(2), 413–426.

Conroy, K., Sandel, M., & Zuckerman, B. (2010). Poverty grown up: how childhood socioeconomic status impacts adult health. *Journal of Developmental and Behavioral Pediatrics, 31*(2), 154–160.

Crimmins, E. M. (2005). Socioeconomic differentials in mortality and health at the older ages. *Genus, 61*(1), 163–176.

Currie, J., & Goodman, J. (2010). Parental socioeconomic status, child health, and human capital. *Int Encyclop Educ, 3*, 253–259.

Cutler, D. M., Lleras-Muney, A., & Vogl, T. (2008). Socioeconomic status and health: dimensions and mechanisms.

Elo, I. T., & Preston, S. H. (1996). Educational differentials in mortality: United States, 1979–1985. *Social Science & Medicine, 42*(1), 47–57.

Evans, G. W., & Kantrowitz, E. (2002). Socioeconomic status and health: The potential role of environmental risk exposure. *Annual Review of Public Health, 23*(1), 303–331.

Gjonca, E., Tabassum, F., & Breeze, E. (2009). Socioeconomic differences in physical disability at older age. *Journal of Epidemiology and Community Health, 63*(11), 928–935.

Goli, S., Singh, L., Jain, K., & Pou, L. M. (2014). Socioeconomic determinants of health inequalities among the older population in India: a decomposition analysis. *J Cross Cult Gerontol, 29*(4), 353–369.

Grimard, F., Laszlo, S., & Lim, W. (2010). Health, aging and childhood socio-economic conditions in Mexico. *J Health Econ, 29*(5), 630–640.

Guimaraes, J. M., Werneck, G. L., Faerstein, E., Lopes, C. S., & Chor, D. (2014). Early socioeconomic position and self-rated health among civil servants in Brazil: A cross-sectional analysis from the Pro-Saude cohort study. *BMJ Open, 4*(11), e005321.

Gupta, R. P. S., de Wit, M. L., & McKeown, D. (2007). The impact of poverty on the current and future health status of children. *Paediatrics & Child Health, 12*(8), 667–672.

Haas, S. A. (2007). The long-term effects of poor childhood health: An assessment and application of retrospective reports. *Demography, 44*(1), 113–135.

Haas, S. (2008). Trajectories of functional health: The 'long arm' of childhood health and socioeconomic factors. *Social Science and Medicine, 66*(4), 849–861.

Hajat, A., Kaufman, J. S., Rose, K. M., Siddiqi, A., & Thomas, J. C. (2011). Long-term effects of wealth on mortality and self-rated health status. *American Journal of Epidemiology, 173*(2), 192–200.

Haseen, F., Adhikari, R., & Soonthorndhada, K. (2010). Self-assessed health among Thai elderly. *BMC Geriatr, 10*, 30.

He, W., Muenchrath, M. N., & Kowal, P. R. (2012). *Shades of gray: A cross-country study of health and well-being of the older populations in SAGE countries, 2007-2010: US Department of Commerce*. US Census Bureau: Economics and Statistics Administration.

Herd, P., Goesling, B., & House, J. S. (2007). Socioeconomic position and health: The differential effects of education versus income on the onset versus progression of health problems. *Journal of Health and Social Behavior, 48*(3), 223–238.

Hu, A., & Hibel, J. (2013). Educational attainment and self-rated health in contemporary China: A survey-based study in 2010. *The Social Science Journal, 50*(4), 674–680.

Huang, C., Soldo, B. J., & Elo, I. T. (2011). Do early-life conditions predict functional health status in adulthood? The case of Mexico. *Social Science and Medicine, 72*(1), 100–107.

Hudson, D. L., Puterman, E., Bibbins-Domingo, K., Matthews, K. A., & Adler, N. E. (2013). Race, life course socioeconomic position, racial discrimination, depressive symptoms and self-rated health. *Social Science and Medicine, 97*, 7–14.

Huisman, M., Kunst, A. E., & Mackenbach, J. P. (2003). Socioeconomic inequalities in morbidity among the elderly; a European overview. *Social Science and Medicine, 57*(5), 861–873.

Hyde, M., Jakub, H., Melchior, M., Van Oort, F., & Weyers, S. (2006). Comparison of the effects of low childhood socioeconomic position and low adulthood socioeconomic position on self rated health in four European studies. *Journal of Epidemiology and Community Health, 60*(10), 882–886.

Idler, E. L., & Kasl, S. V. (1995). Self-ratings of health: do they also predict change in functional ability? *The Journals of Gerontology Series B: Psychological Science and Social Science, 50*(6), S344–S353.

Kagamimori, S., Iibuchi, Y., & Fox, J. (1983). A comparison of socioeconomic differences in mortality between Japan and England and Wales. *World Health Statistics Quarterly, 36*(2), 119–128.

Kestila, L., Koskinen, S., Martelin, T., Rahkonen, O., Pensola, T., Aro, H., & Aromaa, A. (2006). Determinants of health in early adulthood: What is the role of parental education, childhood adversities and own education? *The European Journal of Public Health, 16*(3), 306–315.

Kowal, P., Chatterji, S., Naidoo, N., Biritwum, R., Fan, W., Lopez Ridaura, R., et al. (2012). Data resource profile: The world health organization study on global AGEing and adult health (SAGE). *International Journal of Epidemiology, 41*(6), 1639–1649 (SAGE Collaborators).

Laaksonen, M., Rahkonen, O., Martikainen, P., & Lahelma, E. (2005). Socioeconomic position and self-rated health: the contribution of childhood socioeconomic circumstances, adult socioeconomic status, and material resources. *American Journal of Public Health, 95*(8), 1403.

Lawlor, D. A., Smith, G. D., & Ebrahim, S. (2004). Association between childhood socioeconomic status and coronary heart disease risk among postmenopausal women: Findings from the british women's heart and health study. *American Journal of Public Health, 94*(8), 1386–1392.

Lei, X., Yin, N., & Zhao, Y. (2012). Socioeconomic status and chronic diseases: The case of hypertension in China. Socioeconomic status and chronic diseases: The case of hypertension in China. *China Economic Review, 23*(1), 105–121.

Lidfeldt, J., Li, T. Y., Hu, F. B., Manson, J. E., & Kawachi, I. (2007). A prospective study of childhood and adult socioeconomic status and incidence of type 2 diabetes in women. *American Journal of Epidemiology, 165*(8), 882–889.

Lindstrom, M., Hansen, K., & Rosvall, M. (2012). Economic stress in childhood and adulthood, and self-rated health: A population based study concerning risk accumulation, critical period and social mobility. *BMC Public Health, 12*, 761.

Lipowicz, A., Kozieł, S., Hulanicka, B., & Kowalisko, A. (2007). Socioeconomic status during childhood and health status in adulthood: The Wrocław growth study. *Journal of Biosocial Science, 39*(04), 481–491.

Lowry, D., & Xie, Y. (2009). *Socioeconomic status and health differentials in China: Convergence or divergence at older ages?* Population Studies Center, University of Michigan.

Luckasson, R., Coulter, D. L., Polloway, E. A., Reiss, S., Schalock, R. L., Snell, M. E., et al. (1992). *Mental retardation: Definition, classification, and systems of supports* (9th ed.). Washington, DC: American Association on Mental Retardation.

Luo, Y., & Waite, L. J. (2005). The impact of childhood and adult SES on physical, mental, and cognitive well-being in later life. *Journals of Gerontology. Series B, Psychological Sciences and Social Sciences, 60*(2), S93–S101.

Lynch, J., & Kaplan, G. (2000). *Socioeconomic position: Social epidemiology*. New York: Oxford University Press.

Lynch, J. W., Kaplan, G. A., & Salonen, J. T. (1997). Why do poor people behave poorly? Variation in adult health behaviours and psychosocial characteristics by stages of the socioeconomic lifecourse. *Social Science and Medicine, 44*(6), 809–819.

Mackenbach, J. P, Kunst, A. E, Cavelaars, A. E. J. M., Groenhof, F., Geurts, J. J. M., and Health, EU Working Group on Socioeconomic Inequalities in. (1997). Socioeconomic inequalities in morbidity and mortality in Western Europe. *The lancet, 349*(9066), 1655–1659.

Mackenbach, J. P., Stirbu, I., Roskam, A. J., Schaap, M. M., Menvielle, G., Leinsalu, M., et al. (2008). Socioeconomic inequalities in health in 22 European countries. *New England Journal of Medicine, 358*(23), 2468–2481.

Marmot, M. G., Fuhrer, R., Ettner, S. L., Marks, N. F., Bumpass, L. L., & Ryff, C. D. (1998). Contribution of psychosocial factors to socioeconomic differences in health. *Milbank Q, 76*(3), 403–448, 305.

Marmot, M., Shipley, M., Brunner, E., & Hemingway, H. (2001). Relative contribution of early life and adult socioeconomic factors to adult morbidity in the Whitehall II study. *Journal of Epidemiology and Community Health, 55*(5), 301–307.

McEniry, M. (2013). Early-life conditions and older adult health in low-and middle-income countries: A review. *Journal of developmental origins of health and disease, 4*(01), 10–29.

McGovern, M. E. (2014). Comparing the relationship between stature and later life health in six low and middle income countries. *The Journal of the Economics of Ageing, 4*, 128–148.

Moody-Ayers, S., Lindquist, K., Sen, S., & Covinsky, K. E. (2007). Childhood social and economic well-being and health in older age. *American Journal of Epidemiology, 166*(9), 1059–1067.

Naidoo, N. (2012). SAGE Working Paper No. 5 WHO Study on global AGEing and adult health (SAGE) waves 0 and 1—sampling Information for China, Ghana, India, Mexico, Russia, and South Africa. Retrieved from the World Health Organization Study on global AGEing and adult health (SAGE). Available online: www.who.int/healthinfo/sage/SAGEWorkingPaper5_Wave1Sampling.pdf. Accessed on 14 July 2014.

Pikhartova, J., Blane, D., & Netuveli, G. (2014). The role of childhood social position in adult type 2 diabetes: Evidence from the English Longitudinal Study of Ageing. *BMC Public Health, 14*, 505.

Poulton, R., Caspi, A., Milne, B. J., Thomson, W. M., Taylor, Alan, Sears, Malcolm R., et al. (2002). Association between children's experience of socioeconomic disadvantage and adult health: A life-course study. *The Lancet, 360*(9346), 1640–1645.

Power, C., Matthews, S., & Manor, O. (1998). Inequalities in self-rated health: Explanations from different stages of life. *Lancet, 351*(9108), 1009–1014.

Prince, M. J, Wu, F., Guo, Y., Robledo, L. M. G., O'Donnell, M., Sullivan, R., et al. (2015). The burden of disease in older people and implications for health policy and practice. *The Lancet, 385*(9967), 549–562.

Rahkonen, O., Lahelma, E., & Huuhka, M. (1997). Past or present? Childhood living conditions and current socioeconomic status as determinants of adult health. *Social Science and Medicine, 44*(3), 327–336.

Read, S., Grundy, E., & Foverskov, E. (2015). Socio-economic position and subjective health and well-being among older people in Europe: a systematic narrative review. *Aging Ment Health*, 1–14.

Ross, C. E., & Wu, C-l. (1995). The Links between education and health. *American Sociological Review, 60*(5), 719–745.

Smith, K. V., & Goldman, N. (2007). Socioeconomic differences in health among older adults in Mexico. *Social Science and Medicine, 65*(7), 1372–1385.

Stenholm, S., Pentti, J., Kawachi, I., Westerlund, H., Kivimaki, M., & Vahtera, J. (2014). Self-rated health in the last 12 years of life compared to matched surviving controls: The health and retirement study. *PLoS One, 9*(9), e107879.

Subramanian, S. V., Corsi, D. J., Subramanyam, M. A., & Davey, S. G. (2013). Jumping the gun: The problematic discourse on socioeconomic status and cardiovascular health in India. *International Journal of Epidemiology*.

Subramanian, S. V., Kim, D., & Kawachi, I. (2005). Covariation in the socioeconomic determinants of self rated health and happiness: a multivariate multilevel analysis of individuals and communities in the USA. *Journal of Epidemiology and Community Health, 59*(8), 664–669.

U.S. Census Bureau. (2012). International data base. Accessed on February 17, 2016, at http://www.census.gov/population/international/data/idb/informationGateway.php

Vellakkal, S., Millett, C., Basu, S., Khan, Z., Aitsi-Selmi, A., Stuckler, D., et al. (2015). Are estimates of socioeconomic inequalities in chronic disease artefactually narrowed by self-reported measures of prevalence in low-income and middle-income countries? Findings from the WHO-SAGE survey. *Journal of Epidemiology and Community Health, 69*(3), 218–225.

von dem Knesebeck, O., Luschen, G., Cockerham, W. C., & Siegrist, J. (2003). Socioeconomic status and health among the aged in the United States and Germany: A comparative cross-sectional study. *Social Science and Medicine, 57*(9), 1643–1652.

von dem Knesebeck, O., Verde, P. E., & Dragano, Nico. (2006). Education and health in 22 European countries. *Social Science and Medicine, 63*(5), 1344–1351.

Vonneilich, N., Jöckel, K.-H., Erbel, R., Klein, J., Dragano, N., Simone, W., et al. (2011). Does socioeconomic status affect the association of social relationships and health? A moderator analysis. *Int J Equity Health, 10*, 43.

Wen, M., & Gu, D. (2011). The effects of childhood, adult, and community socioeconomic conditions on health and mortality among older adults in china. *Demography, 48*(1), 153–181.

World Bank. (2011). List of Economies (January 2011). Accessed on February 17, 2016, at http://librarians.acm.org/sites/default/files/Jan%202011%20World%20bank%20list%20of%20Economies.PDF

Zimmer, Z., & Amornsirisomboon, P. (2001). Socioeconomic status and health among older adults in Thailand: An examination using multiple indicators. *Social Science and Medicine, 52*(8), 1297–1311.

Chapter 19
Effects of Selected Socio-Demographic Variables on Fertility Among Diabetic Patients in Bangladesh

Md. Obaidur Rahman, Md. Rafiqul Islam, Clyde McNeil and M. Korban Ali

Introduction

Fertility is one of the three principal components of population dynamics that determine the size and structure of the population of a country (UN 1983). Uncontrolled fertility adversely influences the socio-economic, demographic and environmental development, especially sustainable development, of any country. Differentials in fertility behaviour and fertility levels in different areas and among population strata or characteristics have been among the most pervasive findings in demography (Cochrane 1979). Bongaarts (2008) has shown that steady decline in fertility occurred in most parts of Asia, North Africa and Latin America. Bangladesh, the eighth populous country in the world, remains an outlier among these regions, (PRB 2014). Bangladesh is widely regarded as a positive outlier among developing countries due to dramatic improvements in education, fertility, mortality, immunization, water and sanitation, rural roads and electrification, and microcredit (microcredit is a small amount of money loaned to very poor people for self-employment that generate income). However, the country still experiences challenges from low levels of per capita income, repeated natural disasters, weak governance, and the confrontational politics exist in Bangladesh.

Md. Obaidur Rahman · Md. Rafiqul Islam (✉)
Department of Population Science and Human Resource Development,
Rajshahi University, Rajshahi 6205, Bangladesh
e-mail: rafique_pops@yahoo.com

Md. Obaidur Rahman
e-mail: obaidur006@yahoo.com

C. McNeil
Hobby Center for Public Policy, University of Houston, Houston, TX, USA

M. Korban Ali
Manarat International University, Gulshan, Dhaka, Bangladesh

Bangladesh has been passing through a rapid phase of fertility transition. In the mid-seventies, the level of fertility started to decline. The decline occurred at a rapid rate during the period 1975 to 1993/94. The total fertility rate (TFR) was 6.3 in 1975 and decreased to 3.4 in 1993/94 (Mitra and Associates 1994). The TFR in 2014 is 2.4, and crude birth rate and rate of natural increase in Bangladesh are 22 per 1000 population and 1.5%, respectively (PRB 2014). In Mitra and Associates (2011), the general fertility rate (GFR) is 105 births per 1000 women of reproductive age and the mean number of children ever born (CEB) among currently married women is 2.8 births but allowing for mortality of children have an average of 2.3 living children in 2011. Moreover, the mean number of CEB among women aged 45–49 years is 5.04 of whom 4.1 survived in 2011 (Mitra and Associates 2011). In addition, in 1991, 45% of married women with two children wanted to have another child in the future, typically wanting to have two sons and a daughter (Mitra and Associates 2001). So, the average desired total fertility remains at three children.

Several factors are considered to be responsible for the fertility trend. There were significant associations between the urban/rural distinction and the mean number of children ever had, mean age at first marriage, mean number of living children lost, mean number of miscarriages and the mean age at first birth (Olalekan et al. 2011). It is a general convention that demand for a child decreases as the level of education increases (Sarkar 2004). In addition, women with formal education (the hierarchically structured, chronologically graded 'education system', running from primary school through the university and including, in addition to general academic studies, a variety of specialized programmes and institutions for full-time technical and professional training) (Coombs et al. 1973) had a fertility level about half of those with no formal education (Olalekan et al. 2011). Islam and Nesa (2009) reported that fertility declined considerably with women's education. They also found that place of residence, region, and household wealth status had significant effect on the CEB (Islam and Nesa 2009). Khuda and Hossain (1996) found significant effects of female education, female employment and access to mass media on fertility. Another study found that age at first marriage, literacy status, wealth status, religion, place of residence, use of any type family planning method, perceived ideal number of children and child death experienced by mothers had strongly significant effect on CEB (Adhikari 2010). Clearly, the effect of socio-demographic factors on fertility varies. However, these factors also have effects on diabetes, i.e.; diabetes mellitus was influenced by socio-demographic factors such as age, sex, body mass index (BMI), central obesity, residential area, physical activity, economic status and level of education (Islam and Rahman 2012; Rahman and Islam 2012a, b, c; Veghari et al. 2010). Maheshwari et al. (2007) stated that women with BMI = 25 kg/m^2 have a lower chance of pregnancy and have increased miscarriage rates, which are very harmful for health. So, it is clear that there are some common factors which influence both fertility and diabetes. This study is an attempt to investigate the fertility level among diabetic patients by these types of common factors. Since diabetes impacts older (60+ years) persons more severely (Islam and Rahman 2012; Rahman and Islam 2011, 2012b; Kasim et al.

2010; Porapakkham et al. 2008; Sanchez-Viveros et al. 2008; Hussain et al. 2007; Kim et al. 2006), many women with diabetes have almost completed their fertility period. The rationale of this study is to find out the level of fertility among diabetic patients based on different background factors. The picture of fertility level obtained from this study will be helpful for policy makers, program designers or planners to design or redesign program(s) for achieving replacement level of fertility. Thus, the specific objective of this study is to investigate the fertility levels by some socio-demographic variables and the intensity of their effects on fertility among diabetic women in Bangladesh.

Sources of Data

Data for this study came from the Rajshahi Diabetes Association of Bangladesh. Rajshahi Diabetes Association of Bangladesh collected data from a total of 160 diabetic patients during the months of August 13 to October 29, 2009. They used purposive sampling techniques to collect data from the female diabetic patients. The data were collected through standard questionnaires. Respondents provided responses to selected socio-economic, demographic, diabetic disease and health consciousness related questions to the interviewer. A Bengali version of the questionnaire was prepared for the convenience of accurate data collection. Responses were then converted to English for data entry and analysis with SPSS (Statistical Package for Social Sciences).

Methodology

The Multiple Classification Analysis (MCA)

The MCA provides estimates of each category of predictor variables and at the same time, provides the coefficients for explaining the strength of the relationship. In 1934, Yates invented MCA. It was later expanded and modified by Anderson and Bancraft (1952). The computerized MCA program was made by a group of researchers at the Survey Research Center of the University of Michigan in 1963. MCA requires one dependent variable and two or more independent variables. The dependent variable can be either a continuous or a categorical variable, but all of the independent variables must be categorical variables. MCA can equally handle the nominal and ordinal variables and can also deal with linear and non-linear relationships of predictor variables with the dependent variable. Mathematically, the model can be addressed by the following equation:

$$Y_{ijk} = \bar{y} + a_i + b_j + c_k + \text{---------------------}$$
$$\text{----} + e_{ijk}$$

Where: Y_{ijk} is the value or score of an individual who falls in the i-th category of the factor A, j-th category of the factor B and k-th category of the factor C. $\bar{y}$ is the grand mean of Y. a_i is the effect due to i-th category of the factor A, which is equal to the difference between $\bar{y}$ and the mean of its category of factor A. b_j is the effect due to j-th category of the factor B, which is equal to the difference between $\bar{y}$ and the mean of its category of factor B. c_k is the effect due to k-th category of the factor C, which is equal to the difference between $\bar{y}$ and the mean of its category of factor C. e_{ijk} is the error term related with Y_{ijk} score of the individuals.

The coefficients, which are estimated by solving the normal equation systems, are called the adjusted or net effect of the predictors. These effects measure those of the predictor alone after taking into account the effects of all other predictors. If there is no interrelation among the predictors, the adjusted and unadjusted effects of the predictors will be same. The unadjusted, eta-square (η^2) coefficient is a correlation ratio, which explains how well the predictor variable explains the variation in the dependent variable and is usually estimated by solving the normal equations with only one predictor. This unadjusted coefficient indicates the proportion of variance explained by a single predictor alone. Similarly, the beta-square (β^2) coefficient indicates the proportion of variation explained by the other predictor variables. The beta coefficient is compared to the partial correlation coefficient in multiple regressions.

The number of CEB by age of mother provides one measure of a population's fertility (Haupt and Kane 2004). In this model, number of CEB is taken as dependent variable. The number of CEB to a particular woman is an aggregate measure of her lifetime fertility experience up to the moment at which the data are collected (UN 1983), i.e., CEB to women in a particular age group is the mean number of children born alive to women in that age group, and socio-economic, demographic, diabetic disease and health consciousness related variables are treated as explanatory variables that are mentioned in the table. The analysis is made using the software SPSS and results are shown in Table 19.1.

Model Validation and Shrinkage Coefficient of the Model

To test out the validity of the model, the CVPP, ρ_{cv}^2, is applied. The mathematical formula for CVPP is

$$\rho_{cv}^2 = 1 - \frac{(n-1)(n-2)(n+1)}{n(n-k-1)(n-k-2)}(1-R^2);$$

where, n is the number of classes, k is the number of regressors in the fitted model and the cross-validated R is the correlation between observed and predicted values

Table 19.1 The mean value of CEB for diabetic patients with selected socio-economic, demographic, diabetic disease and health consciousness related variables by using MCA

Explanatory variables	N	Predicted mean		Correlation ratio	
		Unadjusted	Adjusted	η^2 (Unadjusted)	β^2 (Adjusted)
Age group				0.234	0.162
15–24 years	2	1	1.37		
25–34 years	13	2.77	4.91		
>34 years	145	4.31	4.11		
Educational group				0.456	0.428
0–5 years	66	5.17	5.19		
6–10 years	58	4.09	3.93		
>10 years	36	2.36	2.59		
Living house of respondents				0.217	0.158
Building	60	3.57	3.97		
Tin shed	69	4.70	4.54		
Mud made	31	4.03	3.59		
Current place of living				0.079	0.101
Urban	89	3.98	4.36		
Rural	71	4.35	3.88		
Age at first marriage				0.303	0.088
<18 years	141	4.40	4.21		
18–20 years	9	2.78	3.38		
>20 years	10	1.80	3.86		
Duration of marriage				0.419	0.216
≤5 years	3	0.33	1.31		
6–10 years	9	1.33	3.03		
11–20 years	18	3.17	3.84		
>20 years	130	4.56	4.33		
Body mass index (BMI)				0.041	0.020
Under Weight (<18.5)	2	4	4.48		
Normal Weight (18.5–24.9)	98	4.20	4.15		
Over Weight (25.0–29.9)	54	4.02	4.14		
Obesity (>29.9)	6	4.33	3.99		
Blood pressure				0.137	0.108
Normal	98	4.06	4.19		
More than normal	54	4.46	4.22		
Less than normal	8	3.00	3.04		
Duration of sleeping				0.166	0.147
Less than normal (<6 h)	50	4.16	4.32		
Normal (6 h)	39	4.77	4.59		
More than normal (>6 h)	71	3.79	3.77		

(continued)

Table 19.1 (continued)

Explanatory variables	N	Predicted mean		Correlation ratio	
		Unadjusted	Adjusted	η^2 (Unadjusted)	β^2 (Adjusted)
Duration of suffering from diabetes				0.204	0.073
<1 Year	51	3.55	3.99		
1–5 Years	61	4.20	4.13		
6–10 Years	37	4.57	4.21		
>10 Years	11	5.18	4.69		
Grand mean = 4.14 Multiple R^2 = 0.371 ρ_{cv}^2 = 0.2789 Shrinkage coefficient = 0.092					

of the dependent variables (Stevens 1996). The shrinkage coefficient of the model is defined by the positive value of ($\rho_{cv}^2 - R^2$); where ρ_{cv}^2 is CVPP and R^2 is the coefficient of determination of the model. The information of the validity of the model is presented at the bottom of Table 19.1. It is noted that this technique is also used as model validation technique (Islam, 2011, 2012a, b, 2013, 2014; Islam and Hossain 2013a, b, 2014a, b, 2015; Hossain and Islam 2013; Islam et al. 2013, 2014; Hossain et al. 2015; Islam and Hoque 2015).

Results

Different socio-demographic and health related factors may influence CEB. The MCA was used to investigate the differential mean values of CEB and the effects on fertility of diabetic patients. The results show that the proportion of variance explained by MCA is R^2 = 0.371 and grand mean is 4.14. Moreover, smaller shrinkage coefficient = 0.092 indicates the better fit of the model of CEB among some socio-demographic and health related characteristics for diabetic patients. Also, Table 19.1 shows the mean number of CEB both adjusted and unadjusted by various types of socio-demographic and health related characteristics for diabetic patients with the mean value of η^2 and β^2 produced from MCA.

Table 19.1, identifies education as the strongest influential factor for explaining the variation on CEB among all other variables. The proportion of variance explained for the educational group is η^2 = 0.456 and β^2 = 0.428 respectively. Those women with 0–5, 6–10 and >10 years of education have on average 5.19, 3.93 and 2.59 number of CEB respectively, demonstrating that the mean number of CEB for women who have 0–5 years of education is greater than those categories for high levels of education, with the number of CEB decreasing with higher educational levels. So, maternal education has a significant contribution on CEB. Moreover, education has a direct effect on CEB and has an indirect effect on employment, gender disparity, place of residence, age at first marriage etc.

Again, the adjusted average number of CEB for the respondents whose duration of marriage is ≤ 5, 6–10, 11–20 and >20 years are 1.31, 3.03, 3.84 and 4.33 respectively which indicates that the number of CEB increases with longer duration of marriage. Also, in case of Bangladesh, long duration marriages indicate early marriages. Early marriages facilitate early pregnancies and more frequent child birth. Women who pass long periods in their conjugal life have more time to conceive and are producing more children. Also, duration of marriage is found to be the second strongest influential factor for explaining the variation on CEB as well as the proportion of variance explained for duration of marriage is $\eta^2 = 0.419$ and $\beta^2 = 0.216$ respectively.

As observed from Table 19.1, respondent's age group was found to be the third strongest influential factor for explaining the variability of CEB and the proportion of variance explained for age group is $\eta^2 = 0.234$ and $\beta^2 = 0.162$ respectively. Also, it is revealed that the respondents who are 15–24 years, 25–34 years and >34 years of age have on average 1.37, 4.91 and 4.11 number of CEB respectively. It is clear that CEB is increasing with increasing age and women who are 25–34 years of age have produced more children. Again, the adjusted average number of CEB for the respondents whose living house is a building, tin shed or mud made is 3.97, 4.54 and 3.59 respectively, which is very high for all cases. That means, economic condition plays an important role for child bearing. Also, the proportion of variance explained for living house is $\eta^2 = 0.217$ and $\beta^2 = 0.158$ respectively and this factor was found to be the fourth strongest influential factor for explaining the variation on CEB.

The effect of duration of sleeping was found to be the fifth strongest influential factor for explaining the variation on CEB and the proportion of variance explained for duration of sleeping is $\eta^2 = 0.166$ and $\beta^2 = 0.147$ respectively. The adjusted mean number of CEB for the respondents who are sleeping less than normal (<6 h), normal (6 h) and more than normal (>6 h) is 4.32, 4.59 and 3.77 respectively. So, more sleeping has an effect on conceiving children. In addition, blood pressure was found to be the sixth strongest influential factor for explaining the variation on CEB; the proportion of variance explained for blood pressure is $\eta^2 = 0.137$ and $\beta^2 = 0.108$ respectively. The adjusted average number of CEB for the respondents who have normal, more than normal and less than normal blood pressure is 4.19, 4.22 and 3.04 respectively.

Also on Table 19.1, the proportion of variance explained for current living place is $\eta^2 = 0.079$ and $\beta^2 = 0.101$ respectively and it was found to be the seventh strongest influential factor for explaining the variation on CEB. The adjusted average number of CEB for the respondents whose current living place is in an urban versus rural area is 4.36 and 3.88 respectively. Moreover, the effect of age at first marriage was found to be the eighth strongest influential factor for explaining the variation on CEB and the proportion of variance explained for age at marriage is $\eta^2 = 0.303$ and $\beta^2 = 0.088$ respectively. The adjusted mean number of CEB for the respondents who are married at <18 years, 18–20 years and >20 years are 4.21, 3.38 and 3.86 respectively. It is clear that the greatest number of children are born to women who are married before 18 years of age and early marriage is one of the main variables in producing more children.

Duration of suffering from diabetes and BMI was found to be the ninth and tenth most influential factors for explaining the variation on CEB and the proportion of variance explained for duration of suffering from diabetes is $\eta^2 = 0.204$ and $\beta^2 = 0.073$, and for BMI is $\eta^2 = 0.041$ and $\beta^2 = 0.020$ respectively. The adjusted average number of CEB for the respondents who are suffering from diabetes for <1 years, 1–5 years, 6–10 years and >10 years are 3.99, 4.13, 4.21 and 4.69 respectively, and for the respondents who are under weight, normal weight, over weight and obese are 4.48, 4.15, 4.14 and 3.99 respectively. These clarify that CEB increases with increasing duration of suffering from diabetes but decreases with increasing BMI.

Discussion and Recommendation

Bangladesh is one of the most populous countries in the world which suffers from many direct and indirect population problems. Despite this, Bangladesh has undergone a remarkable demographic transition over the last two decades. Although the pace of fertility decline is comparable to the rapid transitions observed in East Asia (Casterline 2001), Bangladesh has not achieve the replacement level until now. This type of fertility behaviour influences population growth, which has consequences on resources, employment situations, health and other social facilities, and savings and investment. In turn, such influences have a great bearing on socio-economic variables that affect fertility and health behaviour. This study is an attempt to measure the fertility behaviour and the effects selected socio-demographic factors have on fertility for diabetic patients in Bangladesh. Among all diabetic patients, we found that the mean number of CEB is 4.14, which means the fertility level for diabetic patients is very high. Since diabetes affects more women in older ages (Islam and Rahman 2012; Rahman and Islam 2011, 2012b; Kasim et al. 2010), most of the diabetic patients have completed their most fertile years of life. As a result, they produced more children. These findings are supported by other findings because they also found that the mean number of live births among older women was 4 and above in developing countries (Alo 2011; Mitra and associates 2007). From this study, it is observed that CEB increases with increasing age, duration of marriage and duration of suffering from diabetes. CEB also decreases with increasing years of education, age at first marriage, BMI and duration of sleeping. The increasing of age, duration of marriage and duration of suffering from diabetes means that women pass long periods of time in their conjugal life and have more time to conceive and produce more children. Moreover, women are more fertile at 25–34 years of age, so, these are important determinants of fertility (Alo 2011; Pinborg et al. 2011). On the other hand, increasing years of education and age at first marriage means that women who achieve higher education levels marry at later ages than others i.e., higher educated women who marry later have a shorter period of reproductive opportunity, thus, they bear fewer children than others who marry at early ages. So, education may influence her child bearing choices. Sarkar et al. (2009) found that middle and upper class women have less desire for children than lower educated women. In many studies it is observed that education especially secondary or higher level is important for reducing fertility, infant and child mortality, improving the human capital of the population (Olalekan et al. 2011; Sarkar 2004). Now-a-days, higher educated persons are giving importance to the educated female for marriage, as a result, a balance is prevailing upon the families, which plays a negative role on child bearing (Ali 2003). In this study, most of the respondents are married before 18 years of age. Consequently, their fertility level is very high. Sayem and Nury (2011) found that most females (72.5%) experienced their first marital pregnancy during their teen years, with a mean age of 17.88 years. In Bangladesh, 100% of women aged 20–24 with at least five children had been married before they were 18 (UNICEF 2005). Palamuleni (2011) reported that early marriage and consequent early childbearing are related to high fertility, low status of women and adverse health risks for both the mother and child, and indicated that age, region and education were the most important determinants of age at first marriage. Again, Pinborg et al. (2011) found that the independent predictors of live birth were women's age, women's body mass index (BMI) and men's age. Also, they observed an inverse U-shaped relationship between BMI and the number of developed embryos. Maheshwari et al. (2007) stated that women with BMI = 25 kg/m^2 have a lower chance of pregnancy and have increased miscarriage rates which are harmful for health. Being overweight has a negative influence on the reproductive system (James et al. 2004; Maheshwari et al. 2007) which is similar to the findings of this study. Again, the respondents whose living house is a tin shed have more children and the mean number of CEB is similar for women who currently live in urban versus rural areas of Bangladesh. But various studies found that more rural women desired more children as compared with urban women (Olalekan et al. 2011; Nasra and Makhdoom 1998; Isiugo-abanibe 1997). Also place of residence, region, and household wealth status had a strongly significant effect on CEB (Adhikari 2010; Islam and Nesa 2009). However, this study has also identified that respondent's education, duration of marriage, age, living house, duration of sleeping, blood pressure, current living place, age at first marriage duration of suffering from diabetes and BMI has been found to be the first, second, third, fourth, fifth, sixth, seventh, eighth, ninth and tenth strongest influential factors for explaining the variation on CEB respectively, which is supported by Ginneken and Razzaque (2003). They also reported that women's education has the largest impact on the fertility decline while other socio-economic factors had only a small impact on the fertility.

In the light of above discussion, we may conclude that the fertility level is very high among diabetic patients in Bangladesh. The findings of the study strongly suggest the following to reduce the fertility rate, as follows:

(i) To increase the educational level of all people especially ever married women and increase their age at first marriage.
(ii) To provide better health care services/facilities including reproductive health care for all people, from which people could become more educated about family planning methods, and non-communicable disease etc.

References

Adhikari, R. (2010). Demographic, socio-economic, and cultural factors affecting fertility differentials in Nepal. *BMC Pregnancy & Childbirth, 10*, 19.
Ali, M. A. (2003) Fertility patterns and differentials in Bangladesh; M.Sc Thesis, Dept. of Statistics, University of Rajshahi; Bangladesh.
Alo, O. A. (2011). Fertility regimentation of the rural Yoruba women of South-west Nigeria: The case of Ido and Isinbode. *Journal of Social Science, 26*(1), 57–65.
Anderson, R. L., & Bancraft, T. A. (1952). *Statistical theory in research*. New York: Mcgraw Hill.
Bongaarts, J. (2008). Fertility transitions in developing countries: progress or stagnation? *Studies in Family Planning 39*, 105–110.
Casterline, J. B. (2001). The pace of fertility transition: National patterns in the second half of the twentieth century. *Population and Development Review, 27*(Suppl. Global Fertility Transition), 17–52.
Cochrane, S. H. (1979). *Fertility and education*. Baltimore: The John Hopkins University Press.
Coombs, P. H., Prosser, C., & Ahmed, M. (1973). New paths to learning for rural children and youth. New York.
Ginneken, J. V., & Razzaque, A. (2003). Supply and demand factors in the fertility decline in Matlab, Bangladesh in 1977–1999. *European Journal of Population, 19*, 29–45.
Haupt, A., & Kane, T. T. (2004). Population reference Bureau's population handbook (5th ed.). Eleventh printing, 2004.
Hossain, M. S., & Islam, M. R. (2013). Age specific participation rates of Curacao in 2011: Modeling approach. *American Open Computational and Applied Mathematics Journal, 1*(2), 08–21.
Hossain, M. K., Islam, M. R., Khan, M. N., & Ali, M. R. (2015). Contribution of socio-demographic factors on antenatal care in Bangladesh: Modeling approach. *Public Health Research, 5*(4), 95–102.
Hussain, A., Vaaler, S., Sayeed, M. A., Mahtab, H., Ali, S. M. K., & Khan, A. K. A. (2007). Type 2 diabetes and impaired fasting blood glucose in rural Bangladesh: A population-based study. *The European Journal of Public Health, 17*(3), 291–296.
Isiugo-abanibe, U. C. (1997). Fertility preferences and contraceptive practice in Nigeria. *Annals of the Social Science Council of Nigeria, 9*, 1–20.
Islam, M. R. (2011). Modeling of diabetic patients associated with age: Polynomial model approach. *International Journal of Statistics and Applications, 1*(1), 1–5.
Islam, M. R. (2012a). Mathematical modeling of age and of income distribution associated with female marriage migration in Rajshahi, Bangladesh. *Research Journal of Applied Sciences, Engineering and Technology, 4*(17), 3125–3129.
Islam, M. R. (2012b). Modeling and projecting population for Muslim of urban area in Bangladesh. *International Journal of Probability and Statistics, 1*(1), 04–10.
Islam, M. R. (2013). Modeling age structure and ASDRs for human population of both sexes in Bangladesh. *International Journal of Anthropology, 28*(1), 47–53.
Islam, M. R. (2014). Modeling of ASFRs and study the reproductivity of women of urban area in Bangladesh. *Advances in Life Sciences, 4*(5), 227–234.

Islam, M. R., Ali, M. K., & Islam, M. N. (2013). Construction of life table and some mathematical models for male population of Bangladesh. *American Journal of Computational and Applied Mathematics, 3*(6), 269–276.

Islam, M. R., & Hoque, M. N. (2015). Mathematical modeling and projecting population of Bangladesh by age and sex from 2002 to 2031. *Emerging Techniques in Applied Demography, Applied Demography Series, 4,* 53–60 (Chapter 5).

Islam, M. R., & Hossain, M. S. (2013a). Mathematical modeling of age specific adult literacy rates of rural area in Bangladesh. *American Open Demography Journal, 1*(1), 01–12.

Islam, M. R., & Hossain, M. S. (2013b). Mathematical modeling of age specific participation rates in bangladesh. *International Journal of Scientific and Innovative Mathematical Research, 1*(2), 150–159.

Islam, M. R., & Hossain, M. S. (2014a). Some models associated with age specific adult literacy rates of urban area in Bangladesh. *International Journal of Ecosystem, 4*(2), 66–74.

Islam, M. R., & Hossain, M. S. (2014b). Mathematical modeling of age specific adult literacy rates in Bangladesh. *Advances in Life Sciences, 4*(3), 106–113.

Islam, M. R., & Hossain, S. (2015). Some standard physical characteristics of students in Seoul: Modeling approach. *American Journal of Mathematics and Statistics, 5*(5), 230–237.

Islam, M. R., Hossain, M. S., & Faroque, O. (2014). U-Shaped pattern of employees' job satisfaction: Polynomial model approach. *International Journal of Ecosystem, 4*(4), 170–175.

Islam, S., & Nesa, M. K. (2009). Fertility transition in Bangladesh: The role of education. *Proceedings of Pakistan Academy Science, 46*(4), 195–201.

Islam, M. R., & Rahman, M. O. (2012). The risk factors of type 2 diabetic patients attending Rajshahi diabetes association, Rajshahi, Bangladesh and its primary prevention. *Food and Public Health, 2*(2), 5–11.

James, W. P., Jackson-Leach, R., & Mhurchu, C. N. (2004). Overweight and obesity. In E. A. D. Lopez, A. Rodgers, C. J. L. Murray, & M. Ezzati (Eds.), *Comparative quantification of health risks: Global and regional burden of disease attributable to selected major risk factors* (pp. 497–596). Geneva: WHO.

Kasim, K., Amar, M., El Sadek, A. A., & Gawad, S. A. (2010). Peripheral neuropathy in type 2 diabetic patients attending diabetic clinics in Al-Azhar University Hospitals, Egypt. *International Journal of Diabetes Mellitus, 2*(1), 20–23.

Khuda and Hossain. (1996). Fertility decline in Bangladesh: Toward an understanding of major causes. *Health Transition Review, 6,* 155–167.

Kim, S. M., Lee, J. S., Lee, J., Na, J. K., Han, J. H., Yoon, D. K., et al. (2006). Prevalence of diabetes and impaired fasting in Korea. *Diabetes Care, 29,* 226–232.

Maheshwari, A., Stofberg, L., & Bhattacharya, S. (2007). Effect of overweight and obesity on assisted reproductive technology—A systematic review. *Human Reproduction Update, 13,* 433–444.

Mitra, S. N., Ali, M. N., Islam, S., Cross, A. R., & Saha, T. (1994) Bangladesh demographic and health survey 1993 94, Calverton, Maryland. National Institute of Population Research & Training (NIPORT), Mitra and Associates, and Macro International Inc.

Mitra, S. N., & Associate. (2001). *Bangladesh demographic and health survey 1999–2000.* Dhaka, Bangladesh: Institute of Population Research and Training (NIPORT).

Mitra, S. N., & Associate. (2007). *Bangladesh demographic and health survey.* Dhaka, Bangladesh: Institute of Population Research and Training (NIPORT).

Mitra, S. N., & Associate. (2011). *Bangladesh demographic and health survey.* Dhaka, Bangladesh: Institute of Population Research and Training (NIPORT).

Nasra, M., & Makhdoom, A. (1998). Patterns of desired fertility and contraceptive use in Kuwait. *Social–Biology, 37*(2), 110–111.

Olalekan, W., Esther, A. O., Olusengun, J., & Olugbenga, A. (2011). A comparative study of socio-demographic determinants and fertility pattern among women in rural and urban communities in southwestern Nigeria. *Continental Journal Medical Research, 5*(1), 32–40.

Palamuleni, M. E. (2011). Socio-economic determinants of age at marriage in Malawi. *International Journal of Sociology and Anthropology, 3*(7), 224–235.

Pinborg, A., Gaarslev, C., Hougaard, C. O., Andersen, A. N., Andersen, P. K., Boivin, J., & Schmidt, L. (2011). Influence of female bodyweight on IVF outcome: A longitudinal multicentre cohort study of 487 infertile couples. *Reproductive Biomedicine Online*, doi:10.1016/j.rbmo.2011.06.010

Porapakkham, Y., Pattaraarchachai, J., & Aekplakorn, W. (2008). Prevalence, awareness, treatment and control of hypertension and diabetes mellitus among the elderly: The 2004 National Health Examination Survey III. *Thailand. Singapore Medical Journal, 49*(11), 868–873.

PRB. (2014). World population data sheet.

Rahman, M. O., & Islam, M. R. (2011). Association between fasting of ramadan and risk factors of diabetes: A study from Rajshahi City in Bangladesh. *Advance Journal of Food Science and Technology, 3*(5), 360–365.

Rahman, M. O., & Islam, M. R. (2012a). Influential determinants of blood glucose level of diabetic patients in Bangladesh. *International Journal of Current Biomedical and Pharmaceutical Research, 2*(1), 252–256.

Rahman, M. O., & Islam, M. R. (2012b). Socio demographic and health related determinants of over weighted diabetic patients in Bangladesh. *Current Research Journal of Biological Sciences, 4*(3), 337–344.

Rahman, M. O., & Islam, M. R. (2012c). Socio-demographic and health related determinants of abdominal obesity of male diabetic patients in Bangladesh. *Asian Profile, 40*(5), 409–420.

Sanchez-Viveros, S., Barquera, S., Medina-Solis, C. E., Velazquez-Alva, M. C., & Valdez, R. (2008). Association between diabetes mellitus and hypertension with anthropometric indicators in older adults: Results of the Mexican health survey, 2000. *The Journal of Nutrition, Health & Aging, 12*(5), 327–333.

Sarkar, S. K. (2004). Demand for a child in Bangladesh: A multivariate statistical analysis. Unpublished Ph. D. Thesis, Department of Statistics, University of Rajshahi, Bangladesh.

Sarkar, S. K., Midi, H., & Imon, A. H. M. R. (2009). Binary response model of desire for children in Bangladesh. *European Journal of Social Sciences, 10*(3), 364–373.

Sayem, A. M., & Nury, T. M. S. (2011). Factors associated with teenage marital pregnancy among Bangladeshi women. *Reproductive Health, 8*, 16.

Stevens, J. (1996). *Applied multivariate statistics for the social sciences* (3rd ed.). Publishers, New Jersey: Lawrence Erlbaum Associates Inc.

UN. (1983). Manual X: Indirect techniques for demographic estimation. Population studies, No. 81. New York.

UNICEF. (2005). *Early marriage: A harmful traditional practice*. New York: United Nations.

Veghari, G., Sedaghat, M., Joshaghani, H., Hoseini, S. A., Niknezad, F., Angizeh, A., et al. (2010). Association between socio-demographic factors and diabetes mellitus in the north of Iran: A population-based study. *International Journal of Diabetes Mellitus, 2*, 154–157.

Yates, F. (1934). The analysis of variance with unequal numbers in the different classes. *Journal of American Statistical Association, 29*, 51–66.

Chapter 20
Behavioral or Biological: Taking a Closer Look at the Relationship Between HIV and Fertility

Ayesha Mahmud

Introduction

The epidemic in Sub-Saharan Africa has undoubtedly had an effect on the demographic makeup of countries in that region. While the effect on mortality is unambiguous, there has been much debate over the impact of the epidemic on fertility. Understanding the relationship between HIV and fertility is important for several reasons. The relationship between HIV prevalence and fertility will affect population projections, and may also have economic consequences that affect the standard of living (Young 2005). A difference in fertility rates between infected and uninfected women also has important implications. First, the impact of programs aiming to reduce mother-to-child transmission will depend on the extent to which fertility rates differ between infected and uninfected women (Hunter et al. 2003). Second, there are implications for the estimates of HIV prevalence, since most estimates rely on studies of women who visit antenatal clinics. Unless the difference in fertility rates by HIV status are taken into account, antenatal surveillance may underestimate the actual prevalence of HIV in the population (Hunter et al. 2003; Zaba and Gregson 1998; Fabiani et al. 2006).

Evidence from several studies in Sub-Saharan Africa suggests that fertility is lower among HIV infected women (Hunter et al. 2003; Juhn et al. 2013; Terceira et al. 2003; Zaba and Gregson 1998). There is less conclusive evidence about the pathways through which HIV status affects fertility. Young (2005) found that the HIV infection rate had a strong negative effect on predicted fertility, after controlling for income, education, etc., in South Africa. In a follow up paper, Young (2007) finds evidence to suggest that the decline in fertility due to HIV "appears to reflect a fall in the demand for children, and not any adverse physiological consequences of the disease, as it is matched by changes in the expressed preference for

A. Mahmud (✉)
Office of Population Research, Princeton University, Princeton, NJ 08544, USA
e-mail: mahmud@princeton.edu

children and the use of contraception, and is not significantly correlated with biological markers of sub-fecundity." On the other hand, other studies have argued for both a behavioral and biological pathway linking HIV and fertility (Hunter et al. 2003; Sneeringer and Logan 2009; Juhn et al. 2013).

This chapter takes a closer look at the relationship between HIV status and fertility using both rounds of the Demographic and Health Surveys (DHS) that collected HIV test results. Specifically, the study used two survey waves of DHS data from eight countries in Africa—Cameroon, Cote d'Ivoire, Ethiopia, Kenya, Lesotho, Malawi, Zimbabwe, and Senegal—conducted between 2003 and 2011. Results confirm that HIV positive women had significantly lower fertility. The magnitude of the association between HIV status and fertility was consistent for women over the entire childbearing age and with different years of education. While HIV positive women desired fewer children compared to HIV negative women, the preference for smaller family sizes was not driving the relationship between HIV status and fertility. The relationship between HIV status and fertility held even after controlling for several indicators of risky sexual behavior, suggesting that changes in these indicators were not driving the observed relationship. HIV positive women had significantly lower fertility even after restricting the sample to respondents who had never been tested for HIV prior to the survey i.e. were presumed to be unaware of their HIV status and, thus, unlikely to be changing their behavior in response to their HIV infection. This provides evidence for a direct physiological effect of HIV infection on fertility.

Background

There is a long-standing debate on the impact of the HIV/AIDS epidemic on fertility. This is partially driven by the fact that the impact of the epidemic on fertility is ambiguous, as predicted by theories on fertility. In this study, fertility was defined as the number of children born to women in a three-year window. There are several pathways through which the HIV epidemic is hypothesized to affect fertility. First, HIV is believed to have a direct biological effect on the fertility of infected women. Evidence from clinical and cohort based studies suggests that HIV positive women may have significantly lower fecundity and odds of bearing children (Zaba and Gregson 1998). The lower fecundity among HIV positive women is a result of higher rates of stillbirths, fetal wastage, spontaneous abortions, greater risk of coinfection with other sexually transmitted infections, and reduced coital frequency as a result of the illness (Juhn et al. 2013; Gregson 1994; Lewis et al. 2004; Zaba and Gregson 1998). The reduction in fertility as a result of lower fecundity among HIV positive women is estimated to be around 30–40% (Carpenter et al. 1997; Hunter et al. 2003; Gray et al. 1998; Terceira et al. 2003). Furthermore, fertility has been shown to decrease significantly with disease progression and decreasing CD4 cell counts (Ross et al. 2004; Loko et al. 2005).

Second, behavioral responses of both infected and uninfected women may affect fertility, although the direction of the effect is ambiguous. Infected and uninfected women may change their sexual behavior in response to an epidemic to stop the disease from spreading or to protect themselves. The evidence for the impact of the epidemic on sexual behavior in Sub-Saharan Africa has been mixed. Several studies have documented little or no effect of the epidemic on sexual behavior (Bloom et al. 2000; Oster 2005). Other studies have suggested that there may be reductions in certain risky behaviors such as lack of condom use, having multiple sexual partners and early age at first sexual intercourse (Cheluget et al. 2006; Fylkesnes et al. 2001). HIV positive women, who are aware of their status, may also be worried about mother-to-child transmission, and desire fewer children as a result. Both of these behavioral responses would have the effect of depressing fertility.

On the other hand, traditional fertility models imply that a rise in youth and adult mortality causes an increase in fertility by creating a precautionary demand for children. This is a "hoarding effect" whereby parents bear more children than their desired total number of children, in order to insure against future deaths. In this case, the behavioral response would lead to a positive relationship between HIV status and fertility. If fertility decisions are made sequentially, then there may also be a "replacement effect" i.e. parents make decisions about having more children based on the survival of previously born children (Palloni and Rafalimanana 1999). For HIV negative women, this effect is likely to be small as HIV mostly affects youth and adults.

Finally, HIV and fertility may also be linked through other pathways. The HIV epidemic may affect fertility via its effect on parental wages. Most fertility models imply a negative correlation between parental income and fertility, a phenomenon that has been empirically observed. HIV positive women may find it harder to keep working or find work. As a consequence, HIV negative women may find it easier to find work in high prevalence regions if HIV positive women drop out of the workforce. Thus, the income effect may have differing effects on HIV positive and HIV negative women. There is also some evidence to suggest that HIV positive women are more likely to experience marital separation or divorce compared to HIV negative women (Porter et al. 2004). Thus, separation from the husband or partner may also be another reason for the observed lower fertility among HIV positive women.

A few studies have attempted to empirically clarify the ambiguity in the relationship between HIV and fertility suggested by theory. Using household data from South Africa, Young (2005) found that the historical HIV infection rate for each woman's age group, as recorded in maternity clinic seroprevalence surveys, had a strong negative effect on predicted fertility after controlling for income, education, etc. Young argues that "widespread community infection lowers fertility, both directly, through a reduction in the willingness to engage in unprotected sexual activity, and indirectly, by increasing the scarcity of labor and the value of a woman's time." In a follow up paper, Young (2007) found similar results using a larger sample of 27 countries. To examine whether lower fecundity among HIV positive women could explain the lower fertility, Young (2007) explored the relationship between positive HIV status and the probability of a recent menstrual period and the probability of a recent pregnancy resulting in a stillbirth, miscarriage or abortion. He found no evidence to suggest that the decline in fertility due to HIV is a result of lower fecundity among HIV positive women, and instead argues that it is due to a reduction in the desired number of children.

Juhn et al. (2013) utilized the first round of the DHS that collected HIV test results, and found that HIV positive women were significantly less likely (17–20% lower probability) to give birth in the year preceding the survey compared to uninfected women. Contrary to Young (2007), they argue that a large part of the relationship is driven by biological, as opposed to behavioral, factors. Sneeringer and Logan (2009) provides evidence for three countries—Uganda, Burkina Faso and Zimbabwe—and argues that in regions with high HIV prevalence, "women are attempting to avoid HIV while maintaining high fertility."

This study attempts to differentiate between the possible pathways linking HIV and fertility. First, the study looked at the extent to which changes in risky sexual behavior could explain the relationship between HIV status and fertility. Second, differences in the fertility preferences between HIV infected and uninfected women were examined. This may reflect either the "hoarding" or "re-placement" effect, or a desire to have fewer children due to fear of mother-to-child transmission. Finally, the study examined the relationship between HIV status and fertility for respondents who had never been tested for HIV i.e. were assumed to be unaware of their HIV status, to distinguish between a biological effect and a behavioral effect.

Data

Repeated cross-sections of the DHS for eight countries in Sub-Saharan Africa were used to examine the relationship between HIV and fertility. The DHS are nationally representative household surveys that collect data on a wide range of outcomes and indicators in the areas of population, health, and nutrition. The standard DHS are cross-sectional surveys of households with sample sizes that vary from 5000 to 30,000. They are conducted approximately every five years. The sample is usually based on a stratified two-stage cluster design. For this study, the sample was restricted to only countries that have two waves of DHS HIV data and have reasonably consistent region definitions over the two survey waves. This includes Cote d'Ivoire, Cameroon, Ethiopia, Kenya, Lesotho, Malawi, Zimbabwe, and Senegal. While it would have been ideal to include more countries in the study, this sample had good geographic variation and covered a range of HIV prevalence and fertility rates. Each country was divided into geographic locales that were defined by administrative divisions. The final sample had 64 regions, with two waves of data for each region. The survey waves were conducted in different years in different countries. The latest wave was conducted between 2008 and 2012, while the previous wave was conducted between 2003 and 2006. Table 20.1 shows the countries and survey years in the study sample. Figure 20.1 shows the geographic location, HIV prevalence and total fertility rates for the eight countries in the sample.

Table 20.1 Datasets

Cote d'Ivoire	2011	2005
Cameroon	2011	2004
Ethiopia	2011	2005
Kenya	2008	2003
Lesotho	2009	2004
Malawi	2010	2004
Senegal	2010	2005
Zimbabwe	2011	2006

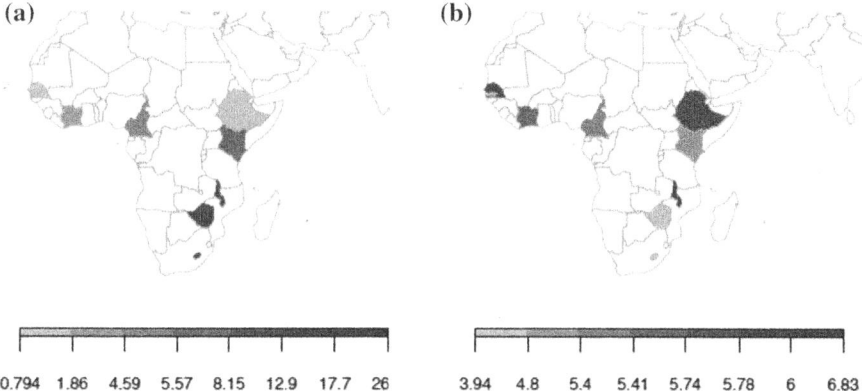

Fig. 20.1 HIV prevalence and total fertility rates (TFR) by Country. **a** HIV prevalence was measured in percentage points and calculated using test results for men and women between the ages of 15 and 49, and the HIV weights provided by DHS. **b** The period TFR, which is a sum of the period age-specific fertility rates, is defined as the average number of children a women would bear if she were to survive to the end of her childbearing period, and at each age experience the ASFR observed in that period. The period TFR was calculated using the number of children born to women in each age group in the three year interval preceding the survey

HIV Status and Prevalence

DHS started collecting HIV testing data in 2001. The study sample only included surveys where the HIV test results could be linked to the full DHS survey record. The HIV prevalence, expressed as percentage points, for each region within a country was calculated using the individual test results for men and women of reproductive age (between the ages of 15 and 49), and the HIV weights provided by DHS, which adjust for individual sampling probabilities and test non-response rates. The regional HIV prevalence varied from 0.068 percentage points in Senegal in 2005 to 30.940 percentage points in Lesotho in 2009.

Fertility

Each woman, in a DHS household survey, is asked about her complete birth history, including the sex, month and year of birth, age, and survival status for each of the births. In this study, fertility, $births_{i,r,t}$, was defined as the number of births to women i, living in region r, in the three years preceding the survey year t. DHS data does not allow identification of when an individual becomes HIV positive. The number of births in the last year, i.e. the year immediately preceding the survey may thus be most appropriate, but is likely to be a very noisy measure of individual level fertility. Using a large time window, such as a five year window, makes it a less accurate measure of period fertility and is more likely to be representative of an individual's lifetime or completed fertility. Therefore, in this chapter, the time window is set at three years.

Figure 20.2 shows the distribution of the number of children born to HIV positive and HIV negative women in the three years preceding the survey. HIV positive women were more likely to have had no births in the past three years, and were less likely to have more than one birth in the past three years compared to HIV negative women.

The DHS collects data on a wide range of demographic and socioeconomic variables. Table 20.2 shows the mean and standard deviation for the variables that were used in the analysis. HIV positive women were, on average, slightly older, more educated, and wealthier than HIV negative women, which confirms past research in this area. Furthermore, they were more likely to live in urban areas, less likely to be married, more likely to have used a condom during their last sexual encounter and had more partners on average compared to HIV negative women. To account for these observed differences, these variables were included as controls in the models.

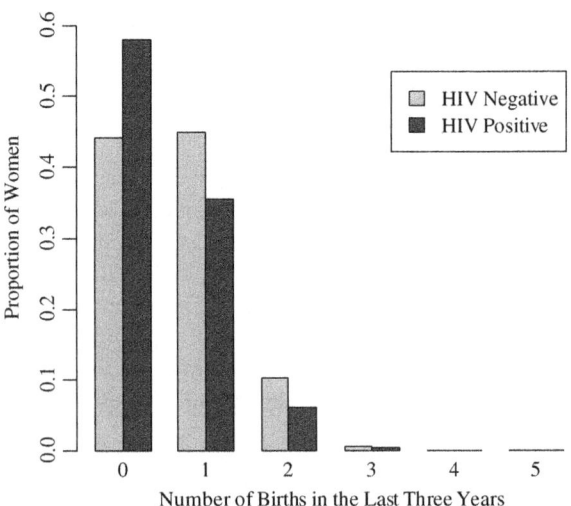

Fig. 20.2 Number of births by HIV status

Table 20.2 Mean and standard deviation of main variables by HIV status

	HIV positive	HIV negative
n	4807	27,952
Number of children born in past three years	0.49 (0.63)	0.67 (0.68)
Age	28.81 (7.21)	27.42 (8.09)
Education	7.48 (3.30)	6.45 (4.28)
No education (1 = Zero years of education)	0.06 (0.24)	0.19 (0.39)
Wealth quintile (1 = Poorest, G = Richest)	3.42 (1.36)	3.24 (1.41)
Never married (1 = Never been married)	0.10 (0.31)	0.12 (0.32)
Currently married (1 = Currently married)	0.69 (0.46)	0.82 (0.38)
Parity	2.06 (1.88)	2.18 (2.36)
Urban (1 = Urban residence status)	0.41 (0.49)	0.37 (0.48)
Number of partners	1.10 (0.96)	1.05 (0.42)
Used condoms during last intercourse (1 = Used condoms during last intercourse)	0.26 (0.44)	0.12 (0.33)
Age at first sexual intercourse	17.29 (2.82)	17.18 (2.93)
Wants more children (1 = Wants more children)	0.48 (0.50)	0.64 (0.48)
Ideal number of children	3.70 (1.8)	4.36 (2.16)

Two variables were used as indicators of risky sexual behavior—number of sexual partners (including husband) in the 12 months preceding the survey, and whether the respondent reported using a condom during her last sexual encounter in the 12 months preceding the survey. These variables were chosen as there is some evidence to suggest that the HIV epidemic in Sub-Saharan Africa is associated with changes in these indicators (Cheluget et al. 2006; Fylkesnes et al. 2001), and because these indicators are likely to capture any behavioral change in response to becoming HIV positive. The models also controlled for age at first sexual intercourse as it has been shown to be a significant predictor of HIV infection (Pettifor et al. 2004), and may affect fertility.

In addition, differences in the fertility preferences of infected and uninfected women were examined. Specifically, the study used two measures of fertility preference—the ideal number of children reported by the respondent, and whether or not the respondent wants more children. The information for the ideal number of children is collected via two possible questions. For women with living children, DHS asks questions such as "If you could go back to the time you did not have any children and could choose exactly the number of children to have in your whole life, how many would that be?" For women with no children, DHS asks questions such as "If you could choose exactly the number of children to have in your whole life, how many would that be?" (Integrated Demographic and Health Series 2015). It is unclear whether women would change their answer to these questions after becoming HIV positive and learning about their infection status. Whether or not a respondent reports wanting more children in the future may be more suited to capturing a change in fertility preferences as a result of becoming infected. Nonetheless, because it is impossible to know when a respondent became HIV positive, it is not possible to determine whether any association between HIV status and these measures of fertility preference is a behavioral response or simply a selection effect.

The final sample included 32,759 women from the full sample of 1,489,959 women. Only women with non-missing data on any of the variables of interest were included in the sample. It is important to note that there may be some selection bias both from the selection of women for testing as well as from the refusal of women to provide blood samples. DHS only collected blood samples from a subset of women interviewed for the main survey. In addition, the blood test was voluntary and respondents could refuse to provide a blood sample, which could introduce potential bias in the results. Table 20.3 shows the difference in means of the variables of interest by whether or not respondents were tested for HIV. Respondents whose blood samples were collected for an HIV test were on average younger, had more births in the three years preceding the survey, less educated, less wealthy, more likely to be at a higher parity, less likely to live in an urban area, more likely to want more children, had a lower age at first sexual intercourse, and had larger ideal family sizes. This suggests that generalizing the results to the entire population may be problematic due to potential selection bias. Future research will need to explore the extent to which differences between respondents who were and were not tested could be affecting HIV prevalence estimates.

Methods

The dependent variable, the number of births in the three years preceding the survey, was assumed to follow a poisson distribution. Linear models were also estimated, but the poisson count model was a better fit, based on the Akaike Information Criterion (AIC). The poisson distribution requires that the mean of the dependent variable be equal to its variance, conditional on observables. To deal with overdispersion, a negative binomial model was estimated, but the poisson count model had a lower AIC in all cases. Thus, the negative binomial regression results are not included here. All regressions were weighted by the HIV survey weights

Table 20.3 Difference in means of variables, by whether or not respondent was tested for HIV

	Not tested for HIV	Tested for HIV
n	1406	32,759
Number of children born in past three years	0.56	0.64[a]
Age	28.67	27.65[a]
Education	8.56	6.54[a]
No education (1 = Zero years of education)	0.08	0.17[a]
Wealth quintile (1 = Poorest, 5 = Richest)	3.79	3.18[a]
Never married (1 = Never been married)	0.11	0.12
Currently married (1 = Currently married)	0.82	0.80
Parity	1.95	2.19[a]
Urban (1 = Urban residence status)	0.55	0.35[a]
Number of partners	1.06	1.05
Used condoms during last intercourse (1 = Used condoms during last intercourse)	0.15	0.14
Age at first sexual intercourse	18.21	17.13[a]
Wants more children (1 = Wants more children)	0.55	0.62[a]
Ideal number of children	3.71	4.33[a]

[a] indicates whether the means are significantly different at the 95 % level

provided by DHS, and the standard errors were heteroscedasticity-consistent and clustered at the regional level. The full model specification took the form:

$$Log[E(births_{i,rc,t}|X)] = Log[exposure_{i,rc,t}] + \beta HIV\ Positive_i + \gamma X_i + D_{rc} + D_t \quad (20.1)$$

where $births_{i,rc,t}$ is the number of births to woman i, living in region rc, in the three years preceding the survey year t. $exposure_{i,rc,t}$ is the amount of exposure time (typically three years for most women, unless their fifteenth birthday occurred during the interval). $HIV\ Positive_i$ is a dichotomous variable that takes the value of one if the individual tested positive for HIV. X_i is a vector of covariates. Country-region dummies, D_{rc}, were included to capture differences across regions that are constant over time, and year dummies, D_t, to capture differences over time that are constant across countries. The covariates in the model included the regional HIV prevalence, which would capture any community level behavioral response to the HIV epidemic. The model controlled for age; an age-squared term was included to capture potential nonlinearities in the relationship between fertility and age. The model also controlled for parity, defined here as the number of births the woman already had prior to the births in the last three years. Controls were included for the number of years of education and the wealth quintile of the individual, since both have been shown to be related to fertility. In addition, a dummy indicator for having no education was included as there may have been additive effects of not having any education. Dummies for current marital status, urban/rural residence, and for never having been married were also included. To examine various pathways, this model was estimated both with and without controls for risky sexual behavior, and separately for respondents who had and did not have an HIV test prior to the survey.

It is possible that the observed negative relationship between HIV infection and fertility is due to selection effects. Unobserved, pre-existing differences between infected and uninfected women may be driving the observed differences in fertility. As a robustness check, the same model was estimated after one-to-one exact matching. One-to-one exact matching is the simplest way to obtain good matches for causal inference where the treatment was not randomized (Ho et al. 2007). Exact matching pairs each treated unit, i.e. an individual with positive HIV status, with a control unit, i.e. an uninfected individual with the same set of specified pre-treatment covariates. Individuals were matched on age, education, wealth quintile, urban/rural residence, age at first sexual intercourse, year of survey, and country-region. Since the data is cross-sectional it is impossible to determine whether any of these covariates are truly "pre-treatment". For instance, wealth and education may both change as a result of an individual getting infected i.e. due to the "treatment". Thus, while the results are presented as a robustness check, they should be interpreted with caution.

Finally, this study examined the effect of HIV status and regional HIV prevalence on fertility preferences of women. The relationship between ideal number of children reported by women and their HIV status was estimated using a poisson count model. The relationship between whether respondents desired more children and their HIV status was estimated using a logistic model. The model specifications were as follows:

$$Log[E(ideal_{i,rc,t}|X)] = \alpha + \beta\, HIV\, Positive_i + \gamma X_i + D_{rc} + D_t \quad (20.2)$$

$$Logit[E(want\, more_{i,rc,t}|X)] = \alpha + \beta\, HIV\, Positive_i + \gamma X_i + D_{rc} + D_t \quad (20.3)$$

where all variables are the same as Eq. 20.1; $ideal_{i,rc,t}$ is the respondent's ideal number of children, and $want\, more_{i,rc,t}$ is a dichotomous variable that is equal to one if the respondent indicated wanting more children.

Results and Discussion

Association Between HIV and Fertility

HIV positive women had significantly fewer births in the three years preceding the survey compared to HIV negative women. Figure 20.3 shows the estimated coefficients from the Poisson model described by Eq. 20.1 (full results are presented in

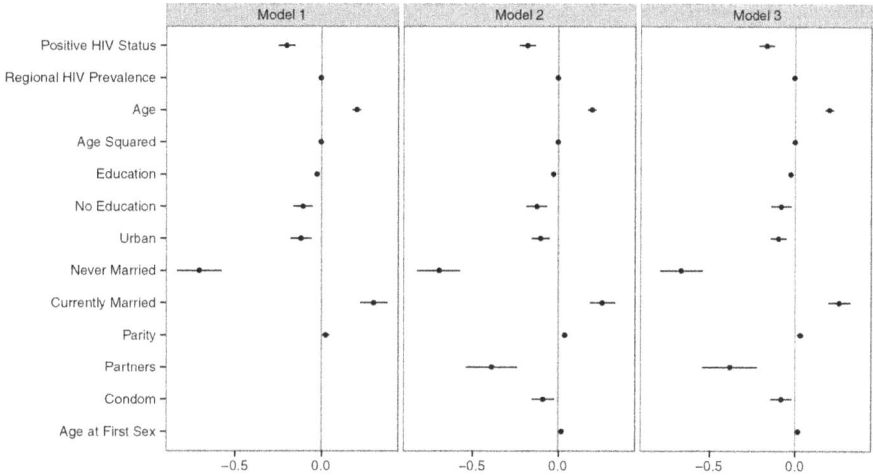

Fig. 20.3 Relationship between HIV status and the number of births in the last three years. (i) Estimated coefficients from a poisson regression are plotted along with the 95 % confidence intervals. Women with non-missing HIV status were used in the regressions. Education was measured in years. Regressions also included dummies for wealth quintiles. (ii) Models (2) and (3) controlled for number of partners, condom use, and age at first sexual intercourse. (iii) Model (3) included country by region dummies and year dummies

Table 1 in the Appendix). The estimated coefficient on HIV status was very similar in magnitude across all three model specifications, and remained significant at the 99% level.

The estimated coefficient on *HIV Positive$_i$* from the full specification (Model 3) was −0.172 (95% CI: −0.219 to −0.124) which translates to an incident rate ratio of 0.84. HIV positive women had 0.84 times the number of births that HIV negative women had in the three years preceding the survey (about 16% fewer births). The results hold after one-to-one exact matching on covariates (matching results are presented in Table 2 in the Appendix). These results are not driven by any particular country, as the estimated coefficients on HIV status and its standard errors were very similar when the analysis was conducted separately for each country (results not shown). Age, living in a rural area, being married at the time of the survey, parity, and age at first sexual intercourse were positively associated with the number of births in the last three years. Years of education, never having married, number of partners, wealth and condom use were negatively associated with the number of births in the last three years. These associations are consistent with findings from studies looking at the determinants of fertility in Sub-Saharan Africa.

Regional HIV prevalence was not significantly associated with fertility in the full model (Model 3). The coefficient on regional HIV prevalence may be biased due to endogeneity. For instance, it is possible that HIV prevalence in a region is higher because women in that region are having more births i.e. having unprotected sex. This would cause the coefficient to be positive. However, the model estimation

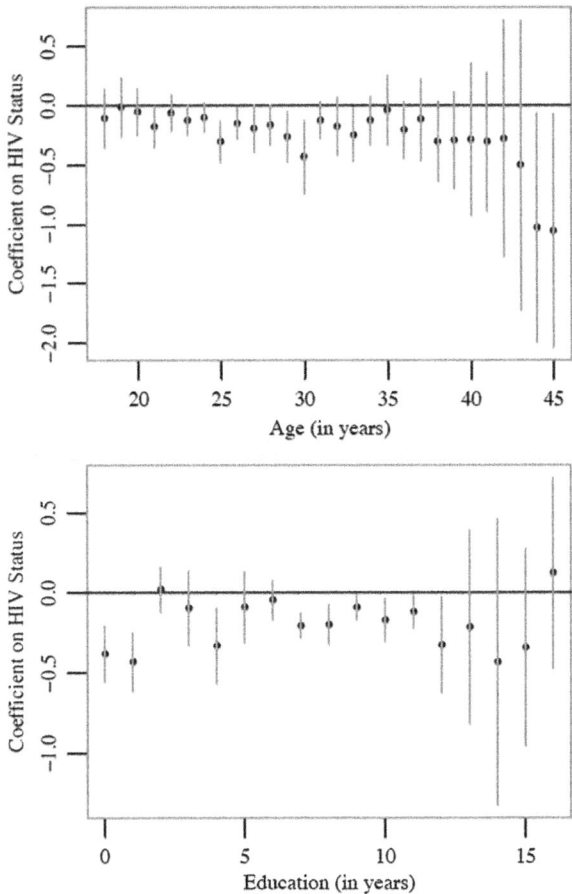

Fig. 20.4 Relationship between HIV status and fertility by age and education. Estimated coefficients on *HIV Positive$_i$* from estimating the analogue of Eq. 20.1 separately by single year of age and by single year of education are plotted along with the 95 % confidence intervals. Women with non-missing HIV status were used in the regressions

yielded a negative coefficient that was statistically insignificant in the full model. To test whether there was a behavioral response among uninfected women, the sample was restricted to uninfected women. If there were a behavioral response among uninfected women to the HIV epidemic, then we would expect the regional HIV prevalence to be a predictor of fertility. The estimated coefficient on regional HIV prevalence, when the sample was restricted to uninfected women, was small in magnitude and not statistically significant (results not shown). Thus, there is no evidence of a behavioral response to the HIV epidemic among uninfected women.

To further explore the relationship between HIV status and fertility, the analogue of Eq. 20.1 was estimated separately by single year of age and by single year of education, leaving out the age and education variables where appropriate. Figure 20.4 shows the estimated coefficient, and the 95% confidence interval, on positive HIV status by age and years of education.

Restricting the sample to specific ages or years of education increased the standard error for the estimates because of the greatly reduced sample sizes.

However, the interesting feature is that the estimated associations between HIV and fertility remained very similar and fairly constant over age and years of education. This suggests that the pathway through which HIV is influencing fertility is likely to be unaffected by age and years of education.

Behavioral Pathway: Risky Sexual Behavior

The estimated coefficient on HIV status barely changed when controls were included for indicators of risky sexual behavior (Model 3 in Fig. 20.3. When controls were added for number of partners in the last 12 months, whether or not the respondent reported using a condom during their most recent sexual encounter in the last 12 months, and age at first sexual intercourse, the estimated coefficient on *HIV Positive$_i$* changed from −0.182 to −0.172 (Models 2 and 3 in Fig. 20.3 and Table 1 in the Appendix). These results suggest that the relationship between HIV status and fertility is not operating primarily through changes in risky sexual behavior.

It is possible that these variables are poor indicators of risky sexual behavior, perhaps because of potential social desirability bias. It is also possible that HIV positive women are changing their sexual behavior in other ways, which in turn could be affecting their fertility. However, recent literature has provided little evidence for a shift in sexual behavior patterns in response to the HIV epidemic. For instance, Oster (2005) has shown that sexual behavior in a sample of African countries has changed very little over the course of the epidemic. Thus, the impact of any changes in sexual behavior on fertility is also likely to be small.

Behavioral Pathway: Fertility Preference

HIV positive women in the study sample had significantly smaller ideal family sizes. The results from estimating Eqs. 20.2 and 20.3 are presented in Figs. 20.5 and 20.6 (full results are presented in Tables 20.3 and 20.4 in the Appendix).

The estimated coefficient on *HIV Positive$_i$* from estimating Eq. 20.2 was −0.028 (95% CI: −0.050 to −0.005), which corresponds to an incident rate ratio of 0.97. In other words, the ideal number of births for HIV positive women is 0.97 times the ideal number of births for HIV negative women. This is a very small effect, but nonetheless suggests that there is some heterogeneity in fertility preferences between HIV positive and HIV negative women. Women living in regions with high HIV prevalence had significantly lower ideal number of children compared to women living in lower prevalence regions. The interaction between regional HIV prevalence and an individual's HIV status was small in magnitude and not significant (results not shown).

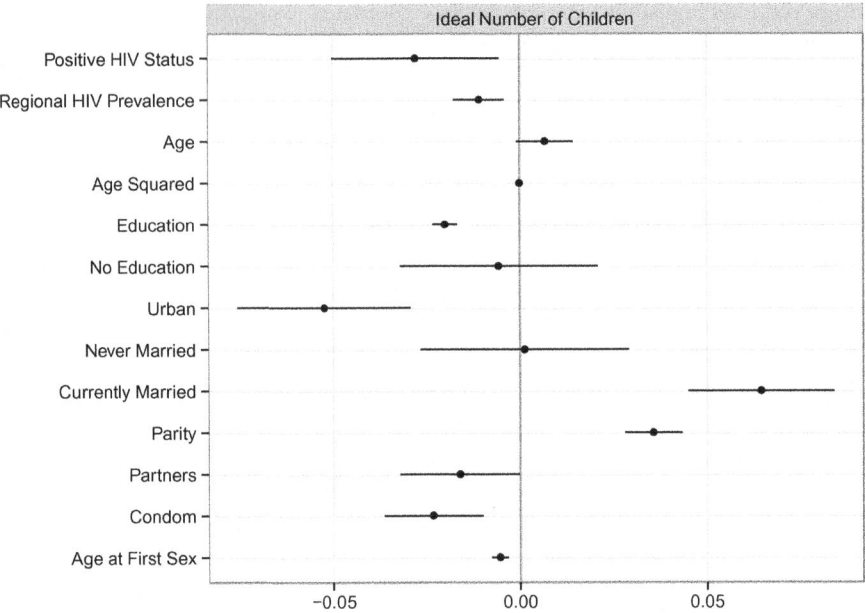

Fig. 20.5 Relationship between HIV status and the ideal number of children. Estimated coefficients from a Poisson regression are plotted along with the 95 % confidence intervals. Women with non-missing HIV status were used in the regressions. Education was measured in years. Regressions also included dummies for wealth quintiles, country by region dummies and year dummies

HIV positive women were also significantly less likely to want more children compared to women who are HIV negative. The coefficient on *HIV Positive$_i$* from estimating Eq. 20.3 was −0.244 (95% CI: −0.365 to −0.122) which translates to an odds ratio of 0.78. In other words, the odds for HIV positive women to want more children was 0.78 times the odds for HIV negative women, holding all else equal. When the sample was restricted to women who had never been tested for HIV, the association between HIV status and fertility preference was no longer significant at the 95% level (for both Eqs. 20.2 and 20.3). In other words, women who were HIV positive, but unaware of their HIV status, did not have significantly different fertility preferences from HIV negative women.

Given that HIV positive women have significantly smaller ideal family sizes, it is possible that the negative relationship between HIV status and number of children in the last three years is working primarily through HIV positive women wanting smaller families. In order to explore this possibility, it is important to examine how the ideal family size influences fertility and the extent to which this might differ for HIV positive versus HIV negative women. Table 20.4 shows the results of controlling for ideal family size in Eq. 20.1 (Model 2), and including an interaction term between HIV status and the ideal family size (Model 3).

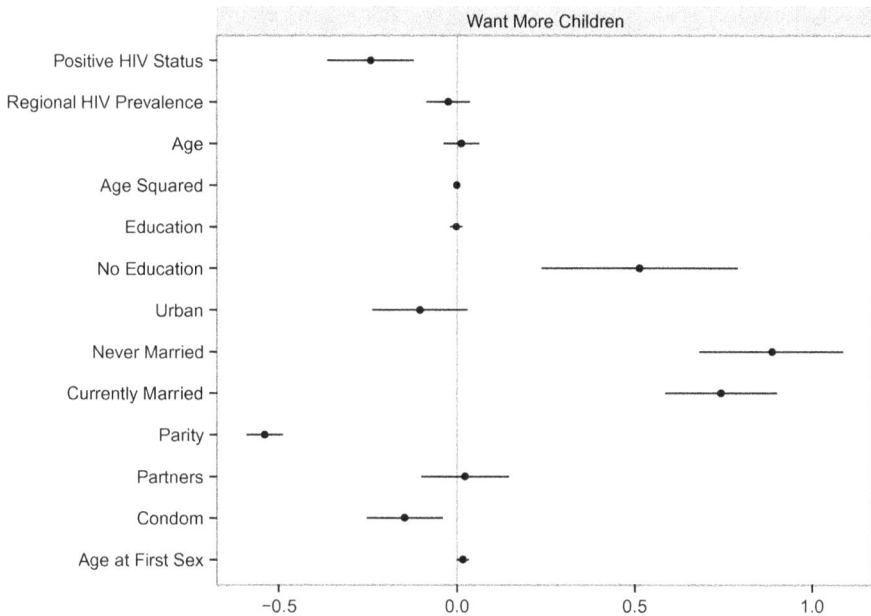

Fig. 20.6 Relationship between HIV status and the desire to have more children. Estimated coefficients from a logistic regression are plotted along with the 95 % confidence intervals. Women with non-missing HIV status were used in the regressions. Education was measured in years. Regressions also included dummies for wealth quintiles, country by region dummies and year dummies

Table 20.4 Relationship between number of births in the last three years and the ideal number of children

	Dependent variable		
	Number of births in the last three years		
	(1)	(2)	(3)
Positive HIV Status	−0.172***	−0.169***	−0.073
	(0.024)	(0.024)	(0.064)
Ideal number of children		0.019***	0.021***
		(0.007)	(0.006)
Ideal × positive HIV status			−0.025*
			(0.014)
Observations Akaike Inf. Crit.	32,759	32,759	32,759
	57,353.390	57,334.140	57,332.210

Estimates from a poisson regression. Women with non-missing HIV status were used in the regressions. All regressions controlled for age, age squared, years of education, no education, urban/rural status, marital status, never been married, parity, number of partners, condom use, age at first sexual intercourse, and included dummies for wealth quintiles, country by region dummies and year dummies

Note $^*p < 0.1$; $^{**}p < 0.05$; $^{***}p < 0.01$

Controlling for ideal family size barely changed the estimate for the coefficient on HIV status. The coefficient on the interaction term was small in magnitude and not significant at the 95% level. Thus, even though HIV positive women desire smaller family sizes, this result suggests that this alone cannot fully explain why HIV positive women are having fewer children.

Biological Pathway

To examine the relative importance of the biological pathway versus the behavioral pathway, the full model described by Eq. 20.1 was estimated for the sample of women who had never been tested for HIV prior to the survey. Here, it is assumed that women who reported never having been tested for HIV were unaware of their HIV status. Figure 20.7 shows the coefficients from estimating the full model for the sample of women who report having had at least one HIV test prior to the survey (Model 1), and the sample of women who report never having had an HIV test prior to the survey (Model 2). Full results are presented in Table 5 in the Appendix.

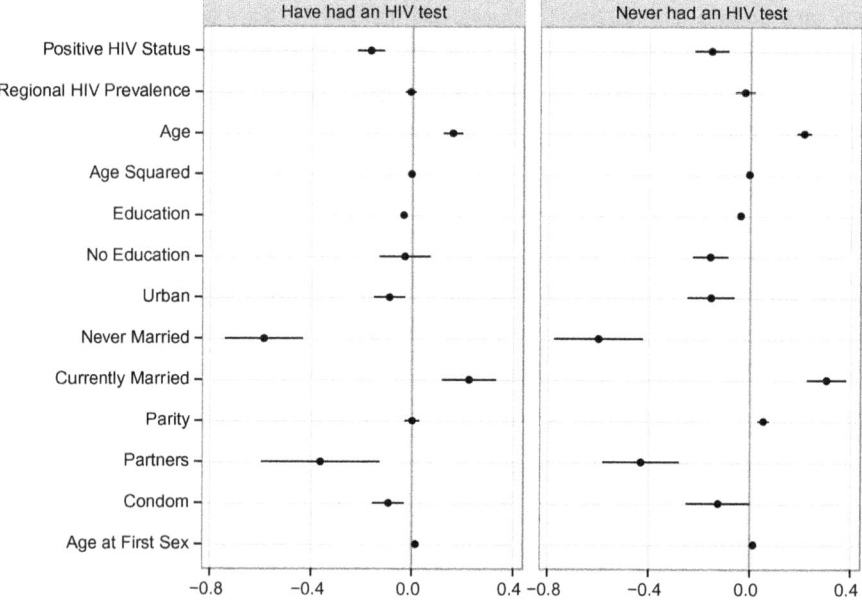

Fig. 20.7 Relationship between HIV status and the number of births by whether or not respondents were tested prior to the survey. Estimated coefficients from a poisson regression are plotted along with the 95 % confidence intervals. (i) Model 1 restricted the sample to women who had at least one HIV test in the past. (ii) Model 2 restricted the sample to women who had never had an HIV test. Education was measured in years. Regressions also included dummies for wealth quintiles, country by region dummies and year dummies

If there were no physiological effect of HIV on fertility and the sole pathway linking HIV and fertility was a behavioral response, then we would expect to see no association between HIV and fertility in the sample of women who have never been tested prior to the survey. On the other hand, if there is a physiological mechanism underlying the relationship, then we would expect to see an association between HIV status and fertility regardless of whether women are aware of their HIV status. Similarly, if a behavioral mechanism is present we would expect to see a larger effect of being HIV positive on fertility for women who have knowledge of their HIV status. The estimated coefficient on *HIV Positive$_i$* was statistically significant and similar in magnitude for the two samples (−0.167 in Model 1 vs. −0.155 in Model 2). In other words, being HIV positive was associated with lower fertility even among women who are likely to be unaware of their HIV status, although the magnitude of the association is slightly smaller. This provides evidence for a direct biological pathway linking HIV and fertility, and suggests that this pathway may dominate behavioral pathways.

It is possible that women who have never had an HIV test may still be aware of their HIV status, and may change their fertility preferences or sexual behavior as a response. Fertility may also be lower among these women because of the income effect or due to separation from a partner as discussed earlier.

Conclusion

This study confirms past findings of lower fertility among HIV positive women compared to uninfected women, and attempts to distinguish between the various hypothesized pathways underlying this empirical relationship. This relationship is consistent over all ages and for women with different years of education. Similar to Young (2007), this study attempts to distinguish between a direct biological link between HIV and fertility and an indirect behavioral response that could explain the relationship. Unlike Young (2007), which examines the relationship between community HIV prevalence and fertility, this study utilized the most recent rounds of the DHS, which links birth histories of women to their HIV test status.

Young (2007) argues that the relationship between the HIV epidemic and reduced fertility, "reflects broad communal responses, rather than the physiological or behavioral response of infected women alone." The results from this study provide no evidence for a community response to the epidemic. While HIV positive women desire fewer children and are less likely to want more children, this difference in fertility preferences is small in magnitude and cannot fully explain the observed relationship. Furthermore, when the sample is restricted to women who have never been tested for HIV prior to the survey, being HIV positive remains significantly associated with reduced fertility. Assuming that these women were unaware of their HIV status, this provides support for the biological pathway.

There are several limitations to this study. First, there may be selection bias due to the sampling of women for HIV testing and the refusal of women to give blood. Previous work has concluded that HIV prevalence estimates based on the DHS data are not biased by nonresponse (Mishra et al. 2006). Nonetheless, this is a concern that future work will need to address. Second, the cross-sectional nature of the DHS data makes it impossible to know when a woman who tested positive for HIV during the survey actually became HIV positive. Furthermore, it is also not possible to know for certain whether women are aware of their HIV status. Thus, this study used the number of births in the three years preceding the survey as the measure of fertility, and examined the relationship between HIV status and fertility for both women who had and did not have an HIV test prior to the survey. Third, the cross-sectional data also makes causal inference difficult. It is impossible to rule out reverse causality or omitted variables bias. As a robustness check, exact matching is used to pair infected and uninfected women based on several covariates. However, it is impossible to determine whether these covariates are truly "pre-treatment", a necessary condition for causal inference.

Furthermore, it is impossible to rule out other pathways that may be underlying the observed relationship between HIV status and fertility. While the study has addressed two potential behavioral pathways—risky sexual behavior and fertility preferences—and a physiological pathway, there are other independent pathways that could be at play. However, many other hypothesized pathways such as the income effect or the effect of separation from partner, are likely to be captured through their influence on sexual behavior and/or fertility preferences.

Finally, this analysis does not account for the widespread introduction of antiretroviral therapy (ART) in Africa in the 2000s. Kaida et al. (2006) propose several possible ways in which the use of ART could impact the fertility of infected women. They speculate that, "as antiretroviral therapy becomes increasingly accessible in Sub-Saharan Africa, the associated improvements in health, quality of life, and survival are anticipated to influence both the biological and behavioral fertility determinants of infected women." ART may increase the fecundity of HIV positive women. Drugs that reduce the probability of mother-to-child transmission may alter the fertility preferences of infected women. The availability of drugs that improve health and quality of life, while suppressing symptoms, may also encourage riskier sexual behavior (Juhn et al. 2013). However, there has been little empirical work to examine these hypotheses. The results presented here are similar across both survey waves, although this may be due to the fact that ART was already in use by the time the first survey round was conducted (between 2003 and 2006). Examining the role of ART in mediating the relationship between HIV and fertility is a potential direction for future research in this area.

Acknowledgments Support for this research was provided by grants from the Eunice Kennedy Shriver National Institute of Child Health and Human Development (grant #5R24HD047879) and from the National Institutes of Health (training grant #5T32HD007163).

References

Bloom, S., Banda, C., Songolo, G., Mulendema, S., Cunningham, A., & Boerma, T. (2000). Looking for change in response to the AIDS epidemic: Trends in AIDS knowledge and sexual behavior in Zambia, 1900 Through 1998. *Journal of Acquired Immune Deficiency Syndromes, 25*, 77–85.

Carpenter, L. M., Nakiyingi, J. S., Ruberantwari, A., Malamba, S. S., Kamali, A., & Whitworth, Ja G. (1997). Estimates of the impact of HIV infection on fertility in a rural Ugandan population cohort. *Health Transition Review, 7*(1997), 113–126.

Cheluget, B., Baltazar, G., Orege, P., Ibrahim, M., Marum, L. H., & Stover, J. (2006). Evidence for population level declines in adult HIV prevalence in Kenya. *Sexually transmitted infections, 82*(Suppl 1), i21–i26.

Fabiani, M., Nattabi, B., Ayella, E. O., Ogwang, M., & Declich, S. (2006). Differences in fertility by HIV serostatus and adjusted HIV prevalence data from an antenatal clinic in Northern Uganda. *Tropical medicine & international health: TM & IH, 11*(2), 182–187.

Fylkesnes, K., Musonda, R. M., Sichone, M., Ndhlovu, Z., Tembo, F., & Monze, M. (2001, February). Declining HIV prevalence and risk behaviours in Zambia: Evidence from surveillance and population-based surveys. *AIDS, 15*, 907–916.

Gray, R. H., Wawer, M. J., Serwadda, D., Sewankambo, N., Li, C., Wabwire-Mangen, F., et al. (1998). Population-based study of fertility in women with HIV-1 infection in Uganda. *Lancet, 351*, 98–103.

Gregson, S. (1994, November). Will HIV become a major determinant of fertility in sub-saharan Africa? *Journal of Development Studies, 30*, 650–679 (2014).

Ho, D. E., Imai, K., King, G., & Stuart, E. A. (2007). Matching as nonparametric preprocessing for reducing model dependence in parametric causal inference. *Political Analysis, 15*, 199–236.

Hunter, S. C., Isingo, R., Boerma, J. T., Urassa, M., Mwaluko, G., & Zaba, B. (2003). The association between HIV and fertility in a cohort study in rural Tanzania. *Journal of Biosocial Science, 35*, 189–199.

Integrated Demographic and Health Series. (2015). Demographic and health surveys 1988–2014. Data extract from DHS recode files. Integrated demographic and health series (IDHS), version 1.0, Minnesota Population Center and ICF International [Distributors]. Accessed from http://idhsdata.org

Juhn, C., Kalemli-Ozcan, S., & Turan, B. (2013). HIV and fertility in Africa: First evidence from population-based surveys. *Journal of Population Economics, 26*, 835–853.

Kaida, A., Andia, I., Maier, M., Strathdee, S. A., Bangsberg, D. R., Spiegel, J., et al. (2006). The potential impact of antiretroviral therapy on fertility in sub-saharan Africa. *Current HIV/AIDS Reports, 3*(4), 187–194.

Lewis, J., Ronsmans, C., Ezeh, A., & Gregson, S. (2004). The population impact of HIV on fertility in sub-saharan Africa. *AIDS (London, England), 18*(Suppl 2), S35–S43.

Loko, M. A., Toure, S., Dakoury-Dogbo, N., Gabillard, D., Leroy, V., & Anglaret, X. (2005). Decreasing incidence of pregnancy by decreasing CD4 cell count in HIV-infected women in cote d'Ivoire: A 7-year cohort study. *AIDS, 18*, 439–445.

Mishra, V., Vaessen, M., Boerma, J. T., Arnold, F., Way, A., Barrere, B., et al. (2006). HIV testing in national population-based surveys: Experience from the demographic and health surveys. *Bulletin of the World Health Organization, 84*(05), 537–545.

Oster, E. (2005). Sexually transmitted infections, sexual behavior, and the HIV/AIDS epidemic. *The Quarterly Journal of Economics, 120*(2).

Palloni, A., & Rafalimanana, H. (1999). the effects of infant mortality on fertility revisited: New evidence from Latin America. *Demography, 36*(106), 41–58.

Pettifor, A. E., van der Straten, A., Dunbar, M. S., Shiboski, S. C., & Padian, N. S. (2004). Early age of first sex: A risk factor for HIV infection among women in Zimbabwe. *AIDS, 18*, 1435–1442.

Porter, L., Hao, L., Bishai, D., Serwadda, D., Wawer, M., Lutalo, T., et al. (2004). HIV status and union dissolution in sub-saharan Africa: The case of rakai. *Uganda. Demography, 41*(03), 465–482.

Ross, A., Van der Paal, L., Lubega, R., Mayanja, B., Shafer, L. A., & Whitworth, J. (2004). HIV-1 disease progression and fertility: The Incidence of recognized pregnancy and pregnancy outcome in Uganda. *AIDS, 18*, 799–804.

Sneeringer, S. E., & Logan, T. (2009). A closer examination of the HIV/fertility linkage. Technical Report 63, MEASURE DHS.

Terceira, N., Gregson, S., Zaba, B., & Mason, P. (2003, November). The contribution of HIV to fertility decline in rural Zimbabwe, 1985–2000. *Population Studies, 57*, 149–164 (2014).

Young, A. (2005). The gift of the dying: The tragedy of aids and the welfare of future African generations. *Quarterly Journal of Economics, 120*(2).

Young, A. (2007). In sorrow to bring forth children: Fertility amidst the plague of HIV. *Journal of Economic Growth, 12*, 283–327.

Zaba, B., & Gregson, S. (1998). Measuring the impact of HIV on fertility in Africa. *AIDS, 12* (Suppl 1), S41–S50.

Chapter 21
Global Patterns of Multimorbidity: A Comparison of 28 Countries Using the World Health Surveys

Sara Afshar, Paul J. Roderick, Paul Kowal, Borislav D. Dimitrov and Allan G. Hill

Introduction

In the previous century, there was an observed shift of disease burden from communicable to non-communicable conditions (Omran 1971; Lim et al. 2012). Individuals are now surviving to older ages, and are being exposed to a number of risk factors throughout the life course, related to global patterns of consumption and behaviour, that give rise to non-communicable disease (NCD). While the debate about the role of population ageing in epidemiological transition continues, particularly in relation to the compression of mortality, this health transition is occurring globally, albeit with different patterns, determinants and rapidity (Fries 1980). Furthermore, the growth rate of the older population will remain signifi-

---

S. Afshar (✉) · P.J. Roderick · B.D. Dimitrov
Academic Unit of Primary Care and Population Sciences, Faculty of Medicine,
Southampton General Hospital, University of Southampton, Southampton SO16 6YD, UK
e-mail: sa2706@soton.ac.uk

P. Kowal
University of Newcastle Research Centre for Gender, Health and Ageing,
Newcastle, NSW, Australia

P. Kowal
World Health Organization's Study on Global AGEing and Adult Health (SAGE),
Geneva, Switzerland

A.G. Hill
Academic Unit of Social Statistics & Demography, Faculty of Social and Human Sciences,
University of Southampton, Southampton, UK

© Springer International Publishing Switzerland 2017
M.N. Hoque et al. (eds.), *Applied Demography and Public Health in the 21st Century*, Applied Demography Series 8,
DOI 10.1007/978-3-319-43688-3_21

cantly higher in low and middle income countries (LMICs) than in most high-income countries (HICs) for many decades to come (UN Population Division 2015).

Tackling multimorbidity remains one of the key challenges faced by the global community, particularly for LMICs, many of which are facing a rapidly ageing population (Kinsella and Velkoff 2001) and an onset of NCDs earlier in adulthood than in HICs (Caleyachetty et al. 2015). Multimorbidity, defined as the co-occurrence of two or more chronic conditions within an individual, is characteristic of an elderly population (Almirall and Fortin 2013). As populations continue to age, there is an expectant increase in the number of complex, multimorbid individuals. The implications of a study into the global patterns of multimorbidity are therefore wide-reaching, and consider evidence for better health planning, policy, and community interventions; particularly for LMICs facing a rising multimorbidity burden.

To date, global disease prevalence studies have largely been single-disease focused and undertaken in HICs. Population prevalence studies in Spain and Germany report very high multimorbidity prevalence, at approximately 60%, for people aged 65 years and above (Lim et al. 2012; Garin et al. 2014). The outcomes of multimorbidity have also been well documented in HICs, with multimorbidity being associated with reduced quality of life, decreased functional capacity, reduced survival; and high healthcare utilisation, cost and expenditure (Marengoni et al. 2009; Steiner and Friedman 2013). One study from six LMICs reported prevalence of multimorbidity in a pooled sample of 22% in adults aged 18 years and above, with increased ADL limitation, poor self-rated health, and depression and decreased quality of life with an increase in number of diseases (Arokiasamy et al. 2015).

Whilst inequalities in health, between and within countries, are considered 'avoidable' further work is needed to address gaps in knowledge on the social inequalities of multimorbidity. Current literature suggests that socioeconomic associations of multimorbidity may differ between HICs and LMICs. In HIC it is well recognised that there is an inverse gradient of multimorbidity and measures of socioeconomic status (SES) for example in Scotland and Canada (Barnett et al. 2012; St. John et al. 2014). This pattern was also found in South Africa (an upper-middle income country) (Alaba and Chola 2013). However in Bangladesh, a LIC, the wealthiest quintile of the population had an increased prevalence of multimorbidity (Khanam et al. 2011). The apparent difference between HICs and LMICs may be due to differential exposure to NCD risk factors, which may vary by socioeconomic group, as well as availability and access to health care services (Selmi et al. 2012).

This chapter describes global patterns of multimorbidity and compared prevalence across different countries including LMICs. It examined the World Health Survey data from 28 countries, and the variations in multimorbidity by age and education, using education level as a proxy for SES (Ullits et al. 2015).

Background

Definining Comorbidity/Multimorbidity

Definitions of multimorbidity are often discussed in relation to Feinstein's seminal work on comorbidity in the 1970s. Feinstein defined comorbidity as "any distinct additional clinical entity that has existed or may occur during the clinical course of a patient who has the index disease under study (Feinstein 1970)." The focus on an index disease is linked to the medical specialism that occurred during the 18th century and beyond. Nevertheless, within specialities such as psychiatry, there is an increasing recognition of comorbidity, described as the "rule" rather than the exception (Hall et al. 2009). Feinstein's definition assumes the central importance of a particular disease; and unless one disease is dominant in terms of the care and well-being of the individual, then this framework may not necessarily be advantageous when considering optimal care for patients with multimorbidity (Boyd and Fortin 2010) (Fig. 21.1).

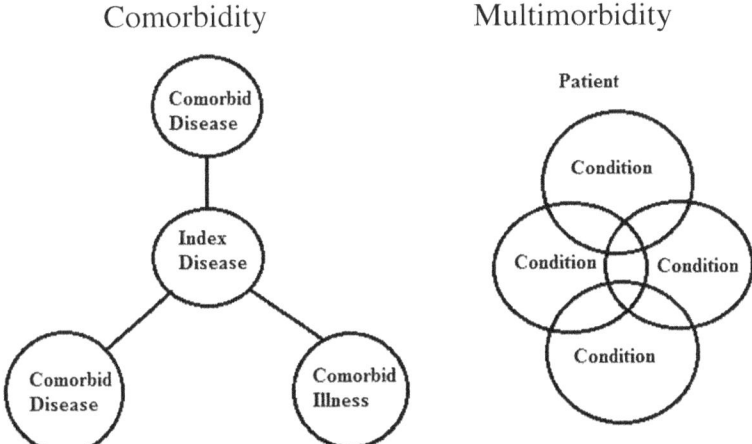

Fig. 21.1 "Comorbidity" versus "multimorbidity," a comparison of conceptual diagrams. Adapted from Boyd and Fortin 2010. The concept of an index disease in relation to other comorbid diseases has benefits for specialised care services, where often greater emphasis (in terms of diagnosis, treatment plan and prognosis) is given to the index disease, whilst consideration and often further opinion is sought from specialists particular to the individual's comorbid condition. In comparison, the "multimorbidity" concept places the patient at the centre, with an overall view of the multiple conditions, which may overlap. These overlaps may, for example, be due to common pathophysiology and psychological circumstances. This conceptualisation of multimorbidity is particularly useful for practitioners seeking a more holistic view of a patient's situation: in particular, their complexity of illness. Such concept of multimorbidity has advantages for the primary care setting, the public health and epidemiological perspective, as well as health economists and policy makers. Evidence suggests that health systems however are still orientated to manage single disease

Although there is no consensus on the definition of multimorbidity, studies agree that the term reflects the co-occurrence of at least two diseases. Some posit that the definition should not be confined with diseases that are chronic in nature, but include all diseases: both acute and chronic (Valderas et al. 2009). Furthermore, chronic diseases may be both communicable, such as HIV, and non-communicable. A recent online survey conducted by the International Research Community of Multimorbidity addressed the question of 'how to define multimorbidity;' there were 55 respondents, across 16 countries, all of whom had interests or were undertaking work in the subject of multimorbidity. Overall 69% of individuals considered multimorbidity to be defined as 'multiple co-occurring chronic or long term conditions, none considered as index disease.'

Previous studies have also used different operational definitions of multimorbidity. Methodological differences, such as the number of chronic conditions to include in a simple count, result in a wide variability in prevalence estimates (Fortin et al. 2010). To prevent further discordance on the definition of multimorbidity, the following study upholds that suggested by Fortin and colleagues that, multimorbidity is 'the co-existence of two or more chronic conditions, where one is not necessarily more central than others'.

Clustering of Disease

Multimorbidity forms groups, or clusters, sharing common risk factors (Prados-Torres et al. 2012). In the study by Prados-Torres et al., the cardiometabolic cluster was highest in prevalence amongst the elderly, age-dependent and overlapped with other clusters, such as neuropsychiatric conditions. The dominance of the cardiometabolic cluster is not surprising when one considers the shared pathways between distal and proximal risk factors that lead up to certain cardiac-related outcomes, such as coronary heart disease (CHD). Proximal factors are closer on the causal pathway to the disease and include diet, physical activity level, obesity, and smoking. These proximal factors directly affect physiological factors such as blood pressure and lipids, and the end result is the occurrence of vascular diseases such as CHD. Such proximal factors are in turn affected by distal factors, arising from the cultural and political context, which include socio-economic factors such as education and poverty for instance. The interactions of the risk factors of CHD have been well studied and documented (Murray et al. 2003).

Prado-Torres and colleagues identified five clustered patterns of multimorbidity: the cardio-metabolic, psychiatric-substance abuse, mechanical-obesity-thyroidal, psychogeriatric and depressive clusters. The cardiometabolic cluster was consistent with cardiovascular disease pathophysiology. These include diabetes, hypertension, obesity and dyslipidaemia occurring at younger age, with subsequent manifestations of CVD in older ages. The psychiatric cluster shared psychopathological processes, such as psychosis and neurosis, related to toxic substance abuse. In terms of the sex differences, the cardiometabolic cluster occurred in both sexes. The psychiatric cluster, on the other hand, appeared only in young men. Such patterns indicate that there are sex differences in multimorbidity. The connectivity between disease groups and clusters has also been explored using a method known as the phenotypic disease network (PDN). By analysing pairwise correlations of comorbidities, researchers were able to measure the strength of associations between within network of diseases; and understand the nature of the connectivity. They further highlighted some key gender and ethnic differences, which support the notion that the determinants of diseases differ between individuals (Hidalgo et al. 2009). This evidence suggests that common pathophysiological processes may be the primary explanatory factor in the clustering of diseases, so called concordant diseases. This does not provide the whole picture, however, since co-morbidities are commonly discordant: though even here common pathways can be postulated. The literature on disease clustering illuminates how different combinations of diseases arise through risk factor pathways, and how the socio-demographic profile varies by disease cluster. Given that the number of conditions in the survey questionnaire was limited to six conditions, it was beyond the scope of the study to examine clustering in detail. However, the literature on disease clustering has been referred to in the discussion, highlighting the need for further work at the global level.

Methods

Study Samples

We used data from the World Health Survey (WHS), which is publicly available from the World Health Organisation (www.who.int/healthinfo/survey/en/). The WHS is comprised of cross-sectional national studies, each of which follow a multi-stage clustering design to draw nationally representative samples of adults aged 18 years and older (Moussavi et al. 2007; Ustun et al. 2003). Seventy-one countries participated in the WHS between 2001 and 2004. The sample sizes varied between countries and depended upon feasibility and cost. Individual participants enrolled into the study were randomly selected for interview, and were aged 18 years or above. All surveys were implemented as face-to-face interviews; except for two countries, which used phone and mail-in interviews.

Of the seventy-one countries that participated in the WHS, eighteen countries were excluded from the analyses, mostly HIC countries from Western Europe, as they did not complete the long version of the questionnaire covering chronic condition status. Countries were also excluded if the response rate to the chronic health questions was less than 90% (eleven countries) or if they did not include post-stratification weights (six countries). A minimum of four countries were randomly selected from each region for further analysis, resulting in a total of twenty-eight of the remaining thirty-seven countries. Since the research questions aimed to address the differences between LMICs, 27 countries were LMICs. Due to low response rates in certain regions, such as Africa, countries from Eastern Europe and Central Asia were oversampled as they had higher response rates. We included one high income country for comparison. In total, six countries were selected from Africa; five from South-East Asia; four from South Asia; eight from Eastern Europe and Central Asia; four from Central and South America; and, one from Western Europe. Sampling weights were applied, as well as post-stratification weights to account for non-response.

Measures and Variables

In the WHS, chronic disease morbidity was defined by self-report, based on a set of six doctor-diagnosed conditions. The self-reported conditions were assessed based on responses to the question, "Have you ever been diagnosed with ...?" Using a simple count method, a binary variable for multimorbidity was created on the presence of two or more of the six conditions: arthritis, angina or angina pectoris (a heart disease), asthma, depression, diabetes, and schizophrenia or psychosis.

The individual level socio-demographic variables of interest were age, sex and highest level of education completed. The residence of the individual, defined as living in either an 'urban' or 'rural' area, was also used in the description of the country characteristics. Two different age groupings were generated for different analyses: first, three age groupings for those 18–49, 50–64 and 65+ years; and then by two groups for those younger than 55 (18–54 years) and those aged 55 years or older. The former was done to examine stratum specific differences, and the latter to examine generational differences. To examine generational differences, 55 years was taken as a cut point, representing a mid-way point within the WHS study population.

Level of education was used as a measure of country-level socioeconomic status (SES). 'Highest education level obtained' was collapsed from seven to four categories: (1) university or any higher education; (2) secondary school; (3) primary school; and, (4) less than primary school (including no formal education).

Inter-country socioeconomic differences were examined by using country estimates for GDP per capita. These were obtained from the United Nations Statistical Division records for 2003. Countries were then grouped according to the cut-offs for low- middle- and high-income based on the World Bank classification figures in 2003 (World Bank 2003).

Statistical Analysis

Survey estimates were used to calculate prevalence measures and extract nationally representative samples, accounting for non-response. To obtain valid comparisons across the countries, age-standardised multimorbidity prevalence rates were calculated using the direct method with the WHO Standard Population (2000–2025) (Ahmad et al. 2001). For the descriptive analyses, mean percentages were taken as an average across populations and normality of the distributions was tested using the Shapiro-Wilk test. We used non-parametric regression to produce a line of best fit, when comparing national estimates of multimorbidity with GDP. Individual countries were weighted by the survey size to produce regional estimates for comparisons of multimorbidity by age and education. Significance testing of the comparisons among independent samples was done by t-test or ANOVA while for those whose distributions deviated from the normal one—by the Wilcoxon rank-sum (for two variables) and Kruskal-Wallis (for more than two variables) tests. 'Prevalence ratios', defined as the relative number of individuals with multimorbidity by education, were calculated with the reference category being primary school education completion, and regression lines were fitted. Univariable models were fitted to analyse the association of both sex and age with multimorbidity. For the multivariable analyses, data were pooled at regional level. A random effects logistic regression model was fitted for the regional analysis, to account for the hierarchical nature of the data within countries and regions. Odds ratios (OR) and 95% confidence intervals (CI) are presented, with $p < 0.05$ taken as statistically significant, unless stated otherwise. All analyses were done using Stata version 12. Confidence intervals have been calculated based on recommendations for crude and age-specific rates (Department of Health, Washington 2012).

Results

Individual country characteristics are described in Table 21.1. Socio-demographic characteristics, including age and sex distributions are shown. Population age structures differed across the countries ($p < 0.05$), with a mean percentage of 9.0%

Table 21.1 Sample size, age, sex and urban/rural distributions for the selected World Health Survey Countries

WHS countries (n = 28)		N sample	Age category (%)			Sex (%)	Residence (%)	National income[a]
			18–49	50–64	65+	Female	Urban	
Africa	Burkina Faso	4948	82.8	12.7	4.5	52.8	17.8	LIC
	Ghana	4165	80.1	15.3	4.6	50.9	45.6	LIC
	Kenya	4640	87	9.6	3.4	51.2	39.9	LIC
	Morocco	5000	78.6	15.7	5.7	50.5	57.5	MIC
	Namibia	4379	78.5	13.4	8.1	53	33.2	MIC
	South Africa	2629	79.7	15	5.3	52	56.3	MIC

(continued)

Table 21.1 (continued)

WHS countries (n = 28)		N sample	Age category (%)			Sex (%)	Residence (%)	National income[a]
			18–49	50–64	65+	Female	Urban	
Central and South America	Brazil	5000	74.7	18.5	6.8	51.5	83	MIC
	Dominican Republic	5027	76.6	17	6.4	49.1	58.5	MIC
	Paraguay	5288	80	14.8	5.2	50.4	56.7	MIC
	Uruguay	2996	61.8	21.9	16.3	52.5	92.8	MIC
Central Asia and Eastern Europe	Bosnia and Herz	1031	66.4	21.6	12	51.1	44.6	MIC
	Czech Republic	949	57.8	27.4	14.8	52.1	73	MIC
	Estonia	1021	55.5	26.9	17.6	55.4	69.7	MIC
	Georgia	2950	60.9	23.8	15.3	53.3	51.5	MIC
	Hungary	1419	57.3	26.6	16.1	53.2	64.9	MIC
	Kazakhstan	4499	73.1	18.3	8.5	52.1	55.9	LIC
	Latvia	929	55.2	27.7	17.1	55.4	66.5	LIC
	Ukraine	2860	58.6	26.1	15.3	54.5	66.7	MIC
South Asia	Bangladesh	5942	81.1	14.7	4.2	48.5	24.3	LIC
	Mauritius	3968	73.6	18.7	7.7	50.8	43	LIC
	Pakistan	6502	76.4	19.2	4.4	49.6	33.9	MIC
	Sri Lanka	6805	71.5	20.6	7.9	47.9	20.6	MIC
South East Asia	Laos	4989	80	15	5	50.7	20.3	LIC
	Malaysia	6145	76.1	18.2	5.6	49.6	64.1	LIC
	Myanmar	6045	77	16.5	6.5	51.1	29.1	LIC
	Nepal	8822	78.1	16.8	5.1	49.5	15.2	MIC
	Philippines	10083	79.3	15.7	5.1	50.4	61.4	MIC
Western Europe	Spain	6373	59.2	22.1	18.7	51.5	76.8	HIC
	Mean	4478.7	72	18.9	9	51.5	50.8	

Notes [a]*MIC* middle income country; *LIC* low income country; *HIC* high income country. All income groupings based on 2003 World Bank estimate

(95% CI, 7.1–11.0) in those aged 65+ compared to 72.0% (95% CI, 68.4–75.7) in those aged 18–49. The mean percentage of those living in rural areas was 49.2% (95% CI, 41.3–57.1) compared to 50.8% in urban areas (95% CI, 42.9–58.7). Countries in Central Asia and Eastern Europe region had a higher proportion of individuals in the 65+ age category (mean = 14.6%; 95% CI, 12.5–16.7) compared to the African region (mean = 5.3%; 95% CI, 4.1–6.4; $p < 0.05$).

Individual morbidity estimates suggest that arthritis was the most common condition across the WHS countries, with mean prevalence of 12.0% (95% CI, 11.8–12.2) across the individual estimates. The mean prevalence for depression, angina, asthma, diabetes and schizophrenia, respectively, were 6.7, 7.5, 5.0, 4.0 and 0.9% [see

Table 21.2 Crude morbidity prevalence by country and region

		Crude morbidity prevalence (%)					
		Angina	Arthritis	Asthma	Diabetes	Depression	Schizo-phrenia
	Burkina Faso	11.8	12.7	2.4	0.5	2.6	1.1
	Ghana	4.6	7	4.2	0.9	1.5	0.7
	Kenya	2.5	4.1	2.9	1.3	5.5	0.7
	Namibia	7.7	10.1	3.6	2.1	7.7	3
	Morocco	5.1	17.2	3.4	3.9	3	0.7
	South Africa	4.7	10	6.3	8.6	9	1.2
Central and South America	Brazil	6.2	9.6	12.1	5.5	18.9	1.6
	Dominican Republic	3.8	11.3	9.6	4	8.5	0.9
	Paraguay	5.4	3.8	5.9	4.2	6.7	0.5
	Uruguay	5.7	9.5	8.7	5.1	10.5	0.7
Eastern Europe and Central Asia	Bosnia and Herz.	8	11.9	3.5	4.9	6.4	0.1
	Czech Republic	6.4	19.1	4.7	10.4	5.8	0.5
	Estonia	16	21	4.7	3.8	8.8	1.4
	Georgia	13.6	17.5	3.8	2.6	5.4	0.5
	Hungary	16.6	25.4	6.8	8.8	8.4	2.4
	Kazakhstan	11.8	15.2	1.8	1.9	1.6	0.5
	Latvia	18.9	13.2	4.2	5.5	5.9	0.7
	Ukraine	18.9	17.1	4.4	3.1	3.7	0.7
South Asia	Bangladesh	6.7	10.8	4.4	2.5	1.3	0.7
	Mauritius	4.2	7.3	4.6	9.1	6.3	0.6
	Pakistan	3.1	13.4	4.1	3.1	2.6	1.1
	Sri Lanka	2.9	6.3	3.8	2.7	1.1	0.7
South East Asia	Laos	4.7	8	3.4	0.5	1.9	0.4
	Malaysia	3.4	8.7	5.9	5	2.6	0.2
	Myanmar	2.7	4.3	2.9	0.5	0.5	0.3
	Nepal	5.5	14.1	3.9	2.7	33.6	2.6
	Philippines	5.6	12.7	8	2.1	3.7	0.4
Western Europe	Spain	3.8	13.8	7.2	6.7	13.8	0.5
	Mean (n = 28)	7.5	12	5	4	6.7	0.9

Table 21.3 Standardised multimorbidity prevalence by age category, with 2003 GDP per capita (in US$)

	Prevalence by age category (95 % CI)			Prevalence (95 % CI)[a]	GDP (US $)[b]
	18–49	50–64	65+		
Myanmar	1.30 (1.0–1.60)	1.9 (1.0–2.7)	3.1 (1.7–4.5)	1.7 (1.4–2.0)	200.0
Nepal	10.1 (9.3–10.9)	24.8 (22.2–27.5)	30.2 (26.2–34.1)	15.2 (14.3–16.0)	264.0
Burkina Faso	4.8 (4.1–5.5)	9.7 (7.2–12.2)	13.0 (9.0–16.9)	6.3 (5.6–7.0)	332.0
Laos	2.5 (2.0–3.0)	6.5 (4.6–8.4)	5.3 (2.7–7.8)	3.6 (3.1–4.1)	358.0
Bangladesh	2.9 (2.4–3.4)	10.9 (8.6–13.2)	12.6 (9.2–16.1)	6.8 (6.1–7.5)	419.0
Kenya	2.1 (1.6–2.5)	3.2 (1.8–4.6)	11.5 (8.1–14.9)	4.2 (3.6–4.8)	440.0
Pakistan	3.4 (2.9–3.9)	8.7 (6.8–10.6)	14.8 (11.1–18.5)	4.9 (4.3–5.4)	597.0
Ghana	2.0 (1.5–2.5)	4.4 (2.8–5.9)	6.6 (4.3–9.0)	3.6 (3.0–4.2)	603.0
Georgia	4.0 (3.0–5.1)	15.0 (11.8–18.1)	27.1 (23.3–30.9)	9.6 (8.4–10.8)	874.0
Sri Lanka	1.2 (0.9–1.5)	6.6 (5.2–8.1)	9.6 (7.1–12.0)	3.9 (3.4–4.3)	968.0
Philippines	3.8 (3.4–4.3)	12.0 (10.3–13.7)	17.2 (14.1–20.3)	7.1 (6.6–7.7)	1016.0
Ukraine	3.3 (2.4–4.2)	17.8 (14.6–20.9)	31.6 (27.1–36.1)	10.0 (8.8–11.1)	1049.0
Paraguay	3.2 (2.7–3.8)	9.4 (7.2–11.5)	12.0 (9.0–15.0)	5.7 (5.1–6.4)	1159.0
Morocco	3.0 (2.5–3.6)	13.6 (11.1–16.1)	17.5 (13.8–21.1)	6.4 (5.7–7.1)	1684.0
Kazakhstan	1.5 (1.1–1.9)	10.1 (7.9–12.3)	45.1 (37.4–52.8)	8.5 (7.6–9.4)	2109.0
Bosnia and Herz	2.3 (1.0–3.5)	11.7 (7.3–16.0)	30.2 (22.7–37.7)	7.6 (5.9–9.3)	2182.0
Dominican Republic	4.5 (3.7–5.2)	15.7 (13.0–18.5)	18.5 (14.9–22.1)	7.2 (6.4–8.0)	2210.0
Namibia	4.5 (3.7–5.2)	11.9 (8.9–14.9)	17.7 (13.4–21.9)	7.9 (7.0–8.8)	2489.0
Brazil	8.1 (7.1–9.0)	21.4 (18.4–24.4)	28.0 (23.7–32.3)	13.4 (12.4–14.5)	3039.0
South Africa	5.0 (3.9–6.0)	21.6 (16.6–26.6)	30.1 (20.6–39.7)	11.2 (9.8–12.5)	3589.0
Uruguay	4.1 (3.2–5.0)	12.4 (9.7–15.1)	17.0 (13.5–20.5)	7.3 (6.3–8.2)	3622.0
Malaysia	2.0 (1.6–2.5)	9.6 (7.8–11.4)	14.6 (11.2–17.9)	5.6 (5.0–6.2)	4607.0
Mauritius	3.3 (2.6–3.9)	15.8 (12.8–18.7)	19.3 (14.9–23.6)	7.8 (6.9–8.6)	4830.0
Latvia	2.7 (1.1–4.3)	16.0 (10.7–21.2)	35.6 (28.1–43.0)	9.6 (7.5–11.7)	4872.0
Estonia	6.2 (4.0–8.4)	14.4 (9.9–18.8)	34.4 (26.8–41.9)	11.5 (9.4–13.6)	7350.0
Hungary	7.8 (5.8–9.9)	27.9 (22.5–33.3)	32.3 (26.2–38.3)	15.0 (13.0–17.1)	8237.0
Czech Republic	3.5 (1.8–5.1)	11.6 (7.2–16.0)	39.4 (30.8–48.0)	9.4 (7.4–11.4)	9339.0
Spain	3.1 (2.5–3.8)	15.3 (13.3–17.3)	22.6 (20.5–24.6)	7.8 (7.1–8.5)	21035.0

World mean prevalence 7.8 (7.8–7.8)

[a]Multimorbidity prevalence (≥ 2 chronic conditions) standardised to the WHO standard population
[b]National GDP per capita from the UN Division Statistical Division, 2003

Table 21.2]. Multimorbidity prevalences by country and age are shown in Table 21.3. Both age-specific prevalences and age standardized prevalence are shown for each country. The mean world standardized prevalence for the 27 LMICs and 1 HIC was 7.8% (95% CI, 6.5–9.1) and the range was 1.7% (95% CI, 1.4–2.0) to 15.2% (14.3–16.0). The mean multimorbidity prevalence significantly increased with age in all countries ($p < 0.05$); 3.8% (95% CI, 3.0–4.6) for age 18–49, 12.8% (95% CI, 10.5–15.2) for 50–64; and 21.3% (95% CI, 17.1–25.5) for 65+.

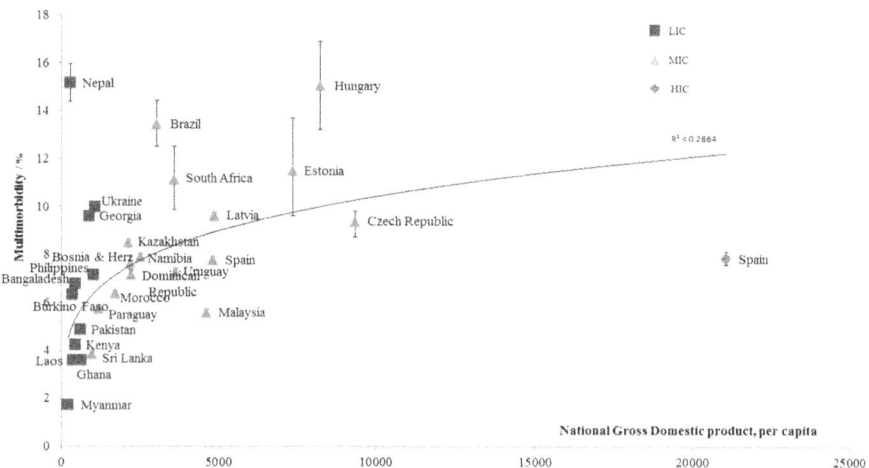

Fig. 21.2 World standardised multimorbidity prevalence for LMICs by GDP across World Health Survey countries (n = 28) in 2003 (with confidence intervals) HIC high income group; MIC middle income group; LIC low income group. Income groups are based on national estimates of 2001 GNI per capita, calculated using the World Bank Atlas method, and reported in the 'World Development Report 2003'

Figure 21.2 shows national levels of multimorbidity by country GDP per capita. There was a positive association between multimorbidity prevalence and GDP per capita (from GDP per capita of $200–$10,000). Above $10,000 the line flattens: Spain had a relatively low multimorbidity prevalence given its high GDP per capita.

Figures 21.3 shows the prevalence ratios of multimorbidity across socioeconomic groups, stratified into younger and older adults. Amongst younger adults, across all regions, there was a distinct negative socioeconomic gradient, with the highest burden on the least educated. In Western Europe (i.e. Spain) there appeared to be a wider variation between SES categories, whereas the gradient was smallest in South East Asia and Africa. Amongst older adults, there was less variation between SES categories compared to the younger adults, and South-East Asia had a positive gradient, with the highest burden on the most educated.

Univariate and multivariate analyses at the country level are shown in Table 21.4, showing correlates of multimorbidity with age, sex and education. Age was significantly associated with multimorbidity in all countries. The female sex was significantly associated with multimorbidity in all but seven countries.

The univariate pattern for SES was not significant when adjusted for both age and sex, except for certain countries where the pattern was consistent with an inverse gradient: as expected in HIC Spain and high MIC Hungary; but also in Bangladesh, Brazil, Mauritius, and Namibia. At higher GDP, multimorbidity was

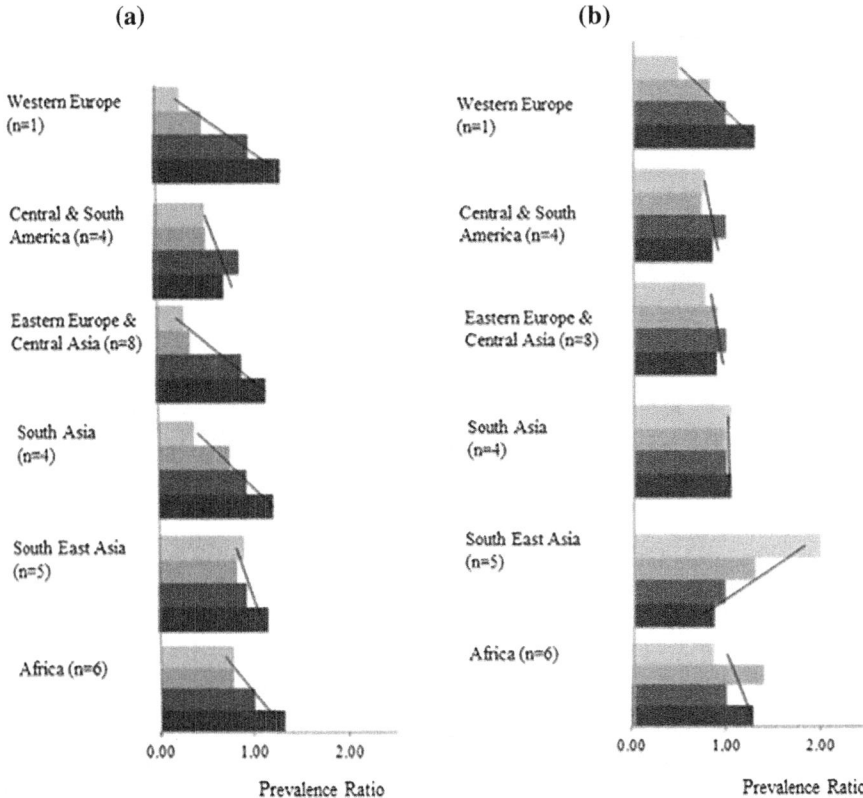

Fig. 21.3 a The socioeconomic gradient of multimorbidity by regions, for age category 1 (<55). **b** The socioeconomic gradient of multimorbidity by regions, for age category 2 (≥ 55). *The lightest shade* represents the first category (higher education achieved). The *darkest shade* represents final category (less than primary school education achieved). Multimorbidity prevalence ratios are based on the prevalence of multimorbidity in the third category, set at 1

statistically associated with the level of education after adjusting for age and sex. Contrarily, the poorest countries had a modest negative SES gradient, and some countries even had a positive SES gradient after adjusting for age and sex.

Similar to the country GDP per capita level, age and sex were both significantly associated with multimorbidity in all regions (Table 21.5). When adjusted for age and sex, the lowest education category was significantly associated with a higher risk of multimorbidity in Africa and Western Europe; and higher education categories were significantly associated with a decreased risk of multimorbidity in South Asia and Western Europe. Adjusted for age, sex, country and region, the 'all region' model suggests an overall negative gradient by education.

Table 21.4 Effect of age, sex and education on multimorbidity by GDP per capita: odds ratios in univariable, multivariable analysis

Country	Age (OR) 18–49 as reference		Sex (OR) Male as reference	Education (OR) Primary school as reference			Education (AOR)			GDP (USD$)
	50–64	65+		Less than primary	Secondary	Higher	Less than primary	Secondary	Higher	
Myanmar	1.4*	2.4*	0.5**	0.9	1.4	1.3	0.6	1.5	1.2	200
Nepal	2.9*	0.8*	1	1.3*	0.9	1.4	0.9	0.9	1.4	264
Brazil	3.1*	4.4*	0.5*	1.6*	0.6*	0.8	1.2	0.8***	0.8	332
Laos	2.7*	2.2*	0.9	1.5	0.5	0.2	1.3	0.5	0.3	358
Burkina Faso	2.2*	3.0*	0.7***	1.1	0.5	1.1	0.9	0.5	1.1	419
Kenya	1.6*	6.2*	1	2.3*	1.7	2.5	1.4	1.8	2.4	440
Pakistan	2.7*	4.9*	0.5**	1.4	0.6	1.1	0.9	0.6	1.1	597
Ghana	2.2*	3.5*	0.6**	1.2	3	1.2	0.9	0.3	1.2	603
Georgia	4.2*	8.8*	0.6**	1.9	0.7	0.8	2	2.3	2.9	874
Sri Lanka	5.9***	8.8****	0.7	1.2	0.5***	0.3	0.9	0.9	0.5	968
Philippines	3.4*	5.2*	0.6*	1.7*	0.8	1.1	1.3	1.1	1.3	1016
Ukraine	6.4***	13.7***	0.4***	0.7	0.5	0.3	0.6	1.4	1.3	1049
Paraguay	3.0*	4.1*	0.3*	1.2	1	1	0.8	1.1	1	1159
Morocco	5.0*	6.8*	0.6***	1.4	0.5	0.4	0.6	0.6	0.7	1684
Kazakhstan	7.4*	54.2*	0.5*	0.3	0.2*	0.1***	0.5	1.1	0.8	2109
Bangladesh	4.1*	4.9*	0.9	1.1	0.7	0.4***	0.8	0.7	0.4***	2182
Dominican Republic	4.0*	4.8*	0.3*	2.0**	0.7	0.9	1.3	0.6	0.8	2210
Namibia	2.7*	4.3*	0.6**	2.2*	0.7	1.2	1.7***	0.8	1.4	2489
Bosnia & Herz	5.7*	18.7*	0.4***	3.0**	0.6	$	1	1	$	3039

(continued)

Table 21.4 (continued)

Country	Age (OR) 18–49 as reference		Sex (OR) Male as reference	Education (OR) Primary school as reference			Education (AOR)			GDP (USD$)
	50–64	65+		Less than primary	Secondary	Higher	Less than primary	Secondary	Higher	
South Africa	5.3*	8.3*	0.6*	2.4*	0.8	0.5	1.6	1.1	0.7	3589
Uruguay	3.3***	4.8***	0.5***	2.0**	0.8	0.7	1.4	1	0.9	3622
Malaysia	5.2*	8.2*	0.8	1.8*	0.5*	0.5*	1.1	0.8	0.8	4607
Mauritius	5.6*	7.1*	0.6*	2.8*	0.4*	0.4***	1.3	0.5*	0.4	4830
Latvia	6.9*	20.0*	0.4**	1.6	0.9	1	0.7	1.7	1.3	4872
Estonia	2.6*	8.0*	0.6**	1.6	0.8	0.6	0.9	1.3	0.9	7350
Hungary	4.6*	5.6*	0.5*	2.9	0.4*	0.2***	3.4***	0.8	0.5***	8237
Czech Republic	3.7*	18.1	0.6	2.3	0.3***	0.4	1.3	0.7	0.7	9339
Spain	5.6*	9.1*	0.6*	1.8*	0.4*	0.2*	1.4***	0.8***	0.4**	21035

Notes p-value ***<0.05; **<0.01; *<0.001; OR unadjusted odds ratio; AOR adjusted odds ratios in multivariable analysis: all countries adjusted for age and sex. $Indicates no observations within the category. For Bosnia and Herzegovina the categories of secondary and higher education were combined for both univariable and multivariable analyses

Table 21.5 Effect of age, sex and socioeconomic status on multimorbidity: odds ratios in univariable, multivariable analysis using a random effects model

	Univariable					Multivariable		
	Age (OR) <55 years as reference	Sex (OR) male as reference	Education (OR) primary school as reference			Education (AOR)$		
	≥55		<Primary	Secondary	Higher	<Primary	Secondary	Higher
Africa	3.3*	0.6*	1.8*	0.8	0.7	1.2**	0.9	0.8
Central and South America	3.0*	0.4*	1.5*	0.7*	0.8***	1.1	0.8***	0.8
Eastern Europe and Central Asia	6.0*	0.6*	1.4***	0.5*	0.5*	1.0	1.0	0.9
South Asia	4.1*	0.7 *	1.7*	0.6*	0.6**	1.2	0.7*	0.6**
South East Asia	3.3*	0.8*	1.4*	0.8*	0.9	1.1	0.9	1
Western Europe	6.0*	0.5*	1.6*	0.4*	0.2*	1.3**	0.7*	0.4*
All regions (MV adjusted for region)	3.7*	0.6*	1.5*	0.7*	0.6*	1.2	0.9***	0.8*

Notes p-value ***<0.05; **<0.01; *<0.001; $Regional multivariable analyses adjusted for age, sex and country; *OR* unadjusted odds ratio; *AOR* adjusted odds ratios in multivariable analysis adjusted for age, sex and country

Discussion

This is the first study to describe global patterns of multimorbidity and to compare prevalence across different countries including LMICs. There are a few notable findings. Firstly, despite the variation in multimorbidity prevalence the mean world standard prevalence for LMICs was 7.8% (95% CI, 6.5–9.1), so even in LMICs the absolute multimorbidity prevalence was quite high. Secondly, multimorbidity age standardised prevalence was positively associated with country GDP per capita. There was however a non-linear relationship; our one HIC—Spain had low multimorbidity relative to GDP per capita. These results suggest an influence of other factors which may include, but are not limited to, more freedom to make better lifestyle choices and better social conditions and health systems for preventive care (Sen 2001). Such risk factors relate to the proximal causes of multimorbidity—as shown in work on clustering of multimorbidity. In comparison to Spain, the Eastern European countries had a relatively high multimorbidity prevalence. Historically, Eastern Europe has had poorer population health outcomes relative to their western counterparts exacerbated by the fall of communism in 1990. Such health outcomes were markedly influenced by exposure to risk factors, such as tobacco smoking and alcohol consumption (Leon et al. 1997; Gilmore and McKee 2004; Men et al. 2003). Thirdly, multimorbidity was significantly associated with age across all countries including LMICs. This finding has been found consistently across several studies (Barnett et al. 2012; Lochner and Cox 2013; Orueta et al. 2013; Rizza et al. 2012; Ward and Schiller 2013). Fourthly, multimorbidity as defined here, is also not limited to older adults, but affects younger adults in LMICs. This association of multimorbidity with age, however, might reflect the type of condition included in the disease count (e.g. asthma which has high prevalence in childhood and in younger adults) and their age of onset (Poblador-Plou et al. 2014). Fifthly, trend analyses of multimorbidity and education suggest a transgenerational difference: with a transition to a more negative SES gradient is observed for younger adults compared to older adults in LMICs. This transition may reflect a reversal in the social distribution of multimorbidity; as countries develop those from lower socioeconomic groups will have increased exposure to NCD risk factors through increased consumption and change in lifestyles. Our 'all region' model also suggests an inverse relationship between multimorbidity and education. These findings are consistent with what has been found in other studies of SES and multimorbidity in HICs (Barnett et al. 2012; Orueta et al. 2013). Finally, there are notable gender differences in multimorbidity: the female sex being associated with higher multimorbidity. This is a common observation in morbidity studies in LMICs, often attributed to greater ascertainment from greater use of health services and disease diagnosis (Fowkes et al. 2013; Mustard et al. 1998) though other studies also suggest the role of other factors, including behavioural and psychosocial (Green and Pope 1999; Chun et al. 2008). As previously discussed in the introduction, clustering patterns of multimorbidity differ for male and females; for example, the cardiometabolic cluster was reportedly more common in males. This occurrence could also be due to known differences in physiology, such as the protective effect of female hormones on CVD (Abad-Diez et al. 2014).

One of the study aims was to examine the variations of multimorbidity by SES here with education as a proxy. Our descriptive analyses of education and multimorbidity show that both regional differences and generational differences exist. In Western Europe and Eastern Europe and Central Asia, there was wider variation in prevalence ratios between SES categories, compared to other regions. For adults aged ≥ 55 years, the gradient was always negative; with one exception of older adults in South-East Asia. This suggests that in South-East Asia there might have been an inter-generational reversal in the socioeconomic gradient of multimorbidity. Such results have also been found in studies on obesity where transitional economies are experiencing a reversal in socioeconomic gradient thus resulting in a similar gradient to HICs (Selmi et al. 2012).

The global-level multivariable analyses show a negative association of multimorbidity with education. As expected, results from Western Europe (Spain) suggest a significantly negative education gradient of multimorbidity in HICs. In Africa, there is also a significantly negative education gradient in multimorbidity so that, despite most countries in this region being LMICs, the pattern is similar to the Western Europe region. These results are contrary to the Bangladesh study, which sampled 850 individuals (60 years and above) in a rural area and reported a positive association of multimorbidity with SES (Khanam et al. 2011). The SES index in their study, however, was based on household assets. Alternative measures of SES may show different relationships.

Strengths and Limitations

This study provides novel analysis on multimorbidity prevalence in nationally representative population samples using a consistent set of methods measures across multiple countries. One of its major strengths is the availability and comparability of the data across a wide range of countries using the World Health Surveys which were developed for this reason.

The study has some limitations. Firstly, prevalence estimates were based on a limited set of six conditions, one of which is rare (schizophrenia). The chronic conditions included in the WHS were chosen to reflect health system coverage (Ustun et al. 2003). The consequence is that the prevalence estimates of national multimorbidity prevalence were grossly underestimated. Using up to 40 morbidities, Barnett et al. reported a prevalence of 23% in a Scottish population, which reflects the dependence of prevalence estimates on the number of conditions included in the count (Fortin et al. 2010). Secondly, the study presents cross-sectional data from 2003. Further investigations should use more recent survey data, as well as longitudinal data, to ascertain changing patterns over time. For this, a follow-up study in six LMICs was undertaken by WHO (see, www.who.int/healthinfo/sage). Thirdly, only countries with a greater than 90% response rate to health status questions on chronic disease were sampled, which meant that a number of lower income countries, where response rates were low, were excluded from the analyses. Our resulting sample was 10 LICs, 17 MICs and 1 HIC. There was low representation from HICs, as these countries largely did not complete the chronic disease questions. As such the use of Spain only—to represent Western Europe—was a limitation. Fourthly, these results were based on self-reported measures of doctor diagnosis, which may result in disease underascertainment, underreporting and potential bias (Harlow and Linet 1989; Bush et al. 1989; Horwitz 1986). One study notes that self-reporting leads to differential underreporting amongst the poor, which would dampen SES gradients (Vellakkal et al. 2013). It may be that health literacy and health care access impact prevalence based on self-report of doctor diagnosis for countries at different levels of economic development. National GDP per capita is generally correlated with healthcare system investment and potentially healthcare access, which might affect the interpretation of the results. Spain, however, had low multimorbidity relative to national GDP despite having a good healthcare access. In order to understand the relationship between a country's development and multimorbidity as an appropriate health outcome, further studies are needed: with a fuller accounting of the effect of ascertainment.

Finally the use of education as a proxy for SES has been debated despite its wide use in population health research (Desai and Alva 1998; Basu 1994). There is evidence to suggest that after conditioning for the effect of socio-economic status, measured by household income or assets, education still has an independent and substantial effect on health outcomes (Baker et al. 2011). However, we were limited by the variables that were available in the survey questionnaire and therefore used education as a proxy measure.

Conclusion

Multimorbidity is common in LMICs and significantly increases with age in all countries. There is an inverse country association of multimorbidity with education a proxy for SES, which indicates an inequity of disease burden, and this gradient appears to be more marked in the younger generation. It may reflect the proliferation in younger generations of several key risk factors for these chronic conditions including unhealthy behaviours like tobacco use and poor diet and their inverse socio-economic gradient even in LMICs. The recent UN World Summit addressed the common risk factors of NCDs to be tackled with urgent priority; namely tobacco use, unhealthy diet, harmful use of alcohol and physical inactivity (United Nations 2011). There is an urgent need to introduce population measures to reduce the modifiable risk factors that will continue to drive multimorbidity prevalence in LMICs and to reduce the social inequity.

Moreover weak health systems and governance will not be able to support the care needs resulting from the complexities of a growing multimorbid population.

Better coordination and support through informed policy and planning of health care systems is needed to support the transition required for health systems to address future care needs.

Competing Interests

The authors declare that they do not have competing interests.

Funding

This work was supported by the World Health Organization and the US National Institutes of Health.

References

Abad-Diez, J. M., Calderón-Larrañaga, A., Poncel-Falco, A., Poblador-Plou, B., Calderon-Meza, J. M., Sicra-Mainar, A., et al. (2014). Age and gender differences in the prevalence and patterns of multimorbidity in the older population. *BMC Geriatrics, 14*, p. 75.

Ahmad, O. B., Boschi-Pinto, C., Lopez, A. D., Murray, C. J. L., Lozano, R., & Inoue, M. (2001). *Age standardisation of rates: A New WHO Standard.* GPE discussion paper series: No. 31.

Alaba, O., & Chola, L. (2013). The social determinants of multimorbidity in South Africa. *International Journal for Equity in Health, 12*, 63.

Almirall, J., & Fortin, M. (2013). The coexistence of terms to describe the presence of multiple concurrent diseases. *Journal of Comorbidity, 3*(1), 4–9, 498.

Arokiasamy, P., Uttamacharya, U., Jain, K., Biritwum, R. B., Yawson, A. E., Wu, F., et al. (2015). The impact of multimorbidity on adult physical and mental health in low- and middle-income countries: What does the study on global ageing and adult health (SAG) reveal? *BMC Medicine, 13*, 178.

Baker, D. P., Leon, J., Smith Greenaway, E. G., Collins, J., & Movit, M. (2011). The education effect on population health: A reassessment. *Population and Development Review, 37*(2), 307–332.

Barnett, K., Mercer, S. W., Norbury, M., Watt, G., Wyke, S., & Guthrie, B. (2012). Epidemiology of multimorbidity and implications for health care, research, and medical education: A cross-sectional study. *The Lancet, 380*(9836), 37–43.

Basu, A. M. (1994). Maternal education, fertility and child mortality: Disentangling verbal relationships. *Health Transition Review, 4*, 207–215.

Boyd, C. M., & Fortin, M. (2010). Future of multimorbidity research: How should understanding of multimorbidity inform health system design? *Public Health Reviews, 32*(2), 451–474.

Bush, T., Miller, S. R., Golden, A., & Hale, W. E. (1989). Self-report and medical record report agreement of selected medical conditions in the elderly. *American Journal of Public Health, 79* (11), 1554–1556.

Caleyachetty, R., Echouffo-Tcheugui, J. B., Tait, C. A., Schilsky, S., Forrester, T., & Kengne, A. P. (2015). Prevalence of behavioural risk factors for cardiovascular disease in adolescents in low-income and middle-income countries: an individual participant data meta-analysis. *The Lancet Diabetes and Endocrinology, 3*(7), 535–544.

Chun, H., Khang, Y. H., Kim, I. H., & Cho, S. I. (2008). Explaining gender differences in ill-health in South Korea: The roles of socio-structural, psychosocial, and behavioral factors. *Social Science and Medicine, 67*(6), 988–1001.

Department of Health, Washington. (2012). *Guidelines for using confidence intervals for public health assessment.* Washington: Washington State Department of Health. Accessed online at 24 September, 2014. www.doh.wa.gov/Portals/1/Documents/5500/ConfIntGuide.pdf

Desai, S., & Alva, S. (1998). Maternal education and child health: Is there a strong causal relationship? *Demography, 35*, 71–81.

Feinstein, A. R. (1970). The pre-therapeutic classification of co-morbidity in chronic disease. *Journal of Chronic Diseases., 23*(7), 455–468. doi:10.1016/0021-9681(70)90054-8.

Fortin, M., Hudon, C., Haggerty, J., van den Akker, M., & Almirall, J. (2010). Prevalence estimates of multimorbidity: A comparative study of two sources. *BMC Health Services Research, 10*(111), 511.

Fowkes, F. G. R., Rudan, D., Rudan, I., Aboyans, V., Denenberg, J. O., McDermott, M. M., et al. (2013). Comparison of global estimates of prevalence and risk factors for peripheral artery disease in 2000 and 2010: A Systematic review and analysis. *The Lancet, 382*(9901).

Fries, J. F. (1980). Aging, natural death, and the compression of morbidity. *New England Journal of Medicine, 303*(3), 130–135.

Garin, N., Olaya, B., Perales, J., Moneta, M. V., Miret, M., Ayuso-Mateos, J. L., et al. (2014). Multimorbidity patterns in a national representative sample of the Spanish adult population. *PLoS One.* doi:10.1371/journal.pone.0084794 (506).

Gilmore, A., & McKee, M. (2004). Moving east: How the transnational tobacco companies gained entry to the emerging markets of the former Soviet Union. Part I: Establishing cigarette imports. *Tobacco Control, 13*, 143–150.

Green, C. A., & Pope, C. R. (1999). Gender, psychosocial factors and the use of medical services: a longitudinal analysis. *Social Science and Medicine, 48*(10), 1363–1372.

Hall, W., Degenhardt, L., & Teesson, M. (2009). Understanding comorbidity between substance use, anxiety and affective disorders: Broadening the research base. *Addictive Behaviors, 34*(6–7), 526–530. doi:10.1016/j.addbeh.2009.03.010.

Harlow, S. D., & Linet, M. S. (1989). Agreement between questionnaire data and medical records. The evidence for accuracy of recall. *American Journal of Epidemiology, 129*(2), 233–248.

Hidalgo, C. A., Blumm, N., Barabási, A.-L., & Christakis, N. A. (2009). A dynamic network approach for the study of human phenotypes. *PLoS Computational Biology, 5*(4), e1000353. doi:10.1371/journal.pcbi.1000353.

Horwitz, R. I. (1986). Comparison of epidemiological data from multiple sources. *Journal of Chronic Diseases, 79*, 1554–1556.

Khanam, M. A., Streatfield, P. K., Kabir, Z. N., Qiu, C., Cornelius, C., & Wahlin, A. (2011). Prevalence and patterns of multimorbidity among elderly people in rural Bangladesh: A cross-sectional study. *Journal of Health, Population and Nutrition, 29*(4), 406–414.

Kinsella, K. G, & Velkoff, V. A. (2001). An aging world: 2001. U.S. Department of Commerce, Economics and Statistics Administration, U.S. Census Bureau. Accessed online at: https://www.census.gov/prod/2001pubs/p95-01-1.pdf

Leon, D. A., et al. (1997). Huge variation in Russian mortality rates 1984–94: Artefact, alcohol, or what? *Lancet, 350*, 383–388.

Lim, S. S., Vos, T., Flaxman, A. D., Danaei, G., Shibuya, K., Adair-Rohani, H., et al. (2012). A comparative risk assessment of burden of disease and injury attributable to 50 risk factors and risk factor clusters in 21 regions, 1990–2010: A Systematic analysis for the Global Burden of Disease Study 2010. *Lancet. 380*(9859), 2224-2260 (503).

Lochner, K. A., & Cox, C. S. (2013). Prevalence of multiple chronic conditions among medicare beneficiaries, United States, 2010. *Preventing Chronic Disease, 10*, 120137.

Marengoni, A., Von Strauss, E., Rizzuto, D., Winblad, B., & Fratiglioni, L. (2009). The impact of chronic multimorbidity and disability on functional decline and survival in elderly persons. A community-based, longitudinal study. *Journal of internal medicine, 265*(2), 288–295.

Men, T., Brennan, P., Boffetta, P., & Zaridze, D. (2003). Russian mortality trends for 1991–2001: Analysis by cause and region. *BMJ, 327*, 964.

Moussavi, S., Chatterji, S., Verdes, E., Tandon, A., Patel, V., & Ustun, B. (2007). Depression, chronic diseases, and decrements in health: Results from the world health surveys. *Lancet, 370* (9590), 851–858.

Murray, C. J. L., Ezzati, M., Lopez, A. D., Rodgers, A., & Hoorn, S. V. (2003). Comparative quantification of health risks: Conceptual framework and methodological issues. *Population Health Metrics, 1*, 1.

Mustard, C. A., Kaufert, P., Kozyrskyj, A., & Mayer, T. (1998). Sex differences in the use of health care services. *New England Journal of Medicine, 338*(23), 1678–1683.

Omran, A. (1971). The epidemiologic transition: a theory of the epidemiology of population change. *Milbank Quarterly, 83*(4), 731–757.

Orueta, J. F., Nuno-Solinis, R., Garcia-Alvarez, A., & Alonso-Moran, E. (2013). Prevalence of multimorbidity according to the deprivation level among the elderly in the Basque Country. *BMC Public Health, 13*, 918.

Poblador-Plou, B., van den Akker, M., Vos, R., Calderon-Larranaga, A., Metsemakers, J., & Prados-Torres, A. (2014). Similar multimorbidity patterns in primary care patients from two european regions: results of a factor analysis. *PLoS ONE,*. doi:10.1371/journal.pone.0100375.

Prados-Torres, A., Poblador-Plou, B., Calderón-Larrañaga, A., Gimeno-Feliu, L. A., González-Rubio, F., Sicras-Mainar, A., et al. (2012). Multimorbidity patterns in primary care: interactions among chronic diseases using factor analysis. *PLoS ONE, 7*(2), e32190. doi:10.1371/journal.pone.0032190.

Rizza, A., Kaplan, V., Senn, O., Rosemann, T., Bhend, H., & Tandjung, R. (2012). Age- and gender-related prevalence of multimorbidity in primary care: The swiss fire project. *BMC Family Practice, 13*, 113.

Selmi, A., Chandola, T., Friel, S., Nouraei, R., Shipley, M. J., & Marmot, M. G. (2012). Interaction between Education and household wealth on the risk of obesity in women in Egypt. *PLoS ONE,*. doi:10.1371/journal.pone.0039507.

Sen, A. (2001). *Development as freedom.* Oxford: OUP.

St. John, P. D., Tyas, S. L., Menec, V., & Tate, R. (2014). Multimorbidity, disability, and mortality incommunity-dwelling older adults. *Canadian Family Physician, 60*(5), e272–e280 (522).

Steiner, C. A., & Friedman, B. (2013). Hospital utilization, costs, and mortality for adults with multiple chronic conditions, nationwide inpatient sample, 2009. *Preventing Chronic Disease, 10*, 120292.

Ullits, L. R., Ejlskov, L., Mortensen, R. N., Hansen, S. M., Kramer, S. R. J., Vardinghus-Nielsen, H., et al. (2015). Soocioeconomic inequality and mortality—A regional Danish cohort study. *BMC Public Health, 15*, 490.

United Nations. (2011). *Political declaration of the high-level meeting of the General Assembly on the prevention and control of non-communicable diseases* (Document A/RES/66.2). In High Level Meeting on Prevention and Control of Non-communicable Diseases. New York: United Nations. Available from: http://www.un.org/en/ga/ncdmeeting2011

United Nations Population Division. (2015). *World population prospects: The 2015 revision.* New York: United Nations.

Ustun, T. B., Chatterji, S., Mechbal, A., & Murray, C. J. L. (2003). Chapter 58: The world health surveys. In C. J. L. Murray & B. E. David (Eds.), *Health systems performance assessment* (p. p761). World Health Organization: Geneva.

Valderas, J. M., Starfield, B., Sibbald, B., Salisbury, M. B., & Roland, M. (2009). Defining comorbidity: Implications for understanding health and health services. *The Annals of Family Medicine, 7*(4), 357–363. doi:10.1370/afm.983.

Vellakkal, S., Subramanian, S. V., Millet, C., Basu, S., Stuckler, D., & Ebrahim, S. (2013). Socioeconomic inequalities in non-communicable diseases prevalence in india: disparities between self-reported diagnoses and standardized measures. *PLoS ONE,*. doi:10.1371/journal.pone.0068219.

Ward, B. W., & Schiller, J. S. (2013). Prevalence of multiple chronic conditions among US adults: Estimates from the national health interview survey, 2010. *Preventing Chronic Disease, 10*, 120203. doi:10.5888/pcd10.120203.

Whitehead, M. (1990). The concepts and principles of equity and health. Copenhagen: World Health Organization. World Bank. *World Development Report 2003: Sustainable Development in a Dynamic World—Transforming Insitutions, Growth and Quality of Life*. World Bank; 2003.

World Bank. (2003). *World development report 2003: Sustainable development in a dynamic world—Transforming insitutions, growth and quality of life*. US: World Bank.

Chapter 22
Does Father's Education Make a Difference on Child Mortality? Result from Benin DHS Data Using Conditional Logit Discrete-Time Model

Fortuné Sossa, Mira Johri and Thomas LeGrand

Introduction

It is well known that parents' education is an important factor for reducing child mortality. However, despite a large number of studies emphasizing the effect of mother's education on child mortality over the past three decades in many developing countries, we still have limited knowledge about the effect of father's education, although parents' education are thought to contribute to their children's health and survival. This study investigates the relationship between father's education and child mortality using data from the 2006 Benin Demographic and Health Survey.

Mother's education has been often found to be the most critical determinant of child health outcomes (Bbaale and Buyinza 2012; Boyle et al. 2006; Buor 2003; Caldwell 1979; Fuchs et al. 2010; Hale et al. 2009; Hatt and Waters 2006; Hobcraft et al. 1984; Huq and Tasnim 2008; Nakamura et al. 2011; Smith Greenaway et al. 2012). Several of studies have also investigated the pathways through which mother's education contributes to the reduction of child mortality (see for example Cleland and Van Ginneken (1988), Caldwell (1979) and Schultz (1984)). According to these studies, it appears that mother's education is strongly associated with child health and child mortality more than father's education (for whom we recognize his "breadwinner" role in the household), since the mother is the most involved parent in child care (Grossman 2005). In addition to this, maternal behavior, particularly hygienic practices for a healthy and safe environment (use of

F. Sossa (✉) · T. LeGrand
Department of Demography, Université de Montréal, Pavillon Lionel-Groulx
C. P. 6128, Succursale Centre-Ville, Montréal, QC H3C 3J7, Canada
e-mail: fortune.sossa@umontreal.ca

M. Johri
Health Administration Department/ESPUM, Université de Montréal,
7101 Av du Parc, Montréal QC H3N 1X9, Canada

clean water, garbage disposal, careful about washing hands, etc.) and use of healthcare services (antenatal and postnatal visits, vaccination) are known to have a powerful impact on child's health and survival (Fuchs et al. 2010; LeVine and Rowe 2009). For the above mentioned reasons, fathers' education is less considered in child mortality reduction policies. Yet, there is a theoretical consideration of maternal and paternal education as a contributing factors in child's health and mortality (Mosley and Chen 1984). In addition to being a key factor of economic resources of the household, and hence to facilitate the procurement of the basic needs in the household and favorable conditions for the improvement of child survival, father's education may also affect child survival through its knowledge acquired by access to information, flexibility toward traditional rules which is reflected in better health outcomes of children, attitudes to the use of modern health services, and decision-making in the household which is likely to vary in the space and in time. Similarly, some authors (Fotso and Kuate-Defo 2005; Kuate-Defo and Diallo 2002) argue that in most African societies, the husband generally makes decisions regarding fertility, contraception and use of health care services, so that some behaviors and practices which may be more or less favorable for child health and survival depend on the father and specifically on his level of education.

For the few studies that have looked at the association of father's education with child mortality in developing countries, particularly in sub-Saharan Africa, the absence of effects that have been shown in the past is largely related to a lack of adequate control variables which may be unobserved or unmeasured, and the failure to apply appropriate statistical models.

In a comparative study of socioeconomic factors on child mortality, Hobcraft et al. (1984) found that father's socio-economic characteristics (woman's husband), especially his education was strongly associated with child mortality in Sub-Saharan Africa. The authors argue that in countries where the association was significant, fathers were often more educated than mothers, as shown in another study (Chen and Li 2009). They have also underscored the influence of the husband concerning children's health care practices (through health knowledge) and his actions against traditional practices (the same traditional medicine to treat any constipation, undernourishment in diarrhea, various taboos concerning the purification, etc.)[1] that can harm child health. Likewise, Baya (1998) has similarly reported lower child mortality risk among educated fathers in Bobo-Dioulasso (an urban area in Burkina Faso) in pointing out fathers attitude against harmful traditional practices that serve to prevent or treat children's diseases. This finding remains relevant in many African societies, where women have limited influence in decision-making about traditional practices regarding child health due to their low social status and low empowerment (Caldwell 1990). Controlling also for all other explanatory factors (at individual level) including father's education, Baya found also that mother's education in Bobo-Dioulasso did not have a significant effect on child's mortality risk, corroborating prior findings (LeGrand and Lalou 1996).

---

[1]For a more detailed description of traditional practices, see e.g. Barbieri (1991).

Another body of research has devoted more attention on community-level factors and has suggested that child mortality was influenced by the socio-economic resources of the community (Boyle et al. 2006; Montgomery and Hewett 2005; Pickett and Pearl 2001). For example, neighbourhood living standards might directly affect child health and survival, if living in a deprived neighbourhood is harmful to health, or indirectly through such mechanisms as the availability and accessibility of health care services, access to healthy foods, and to social networks. Such a community level contribution was also seen in recent researches of association between maternal education and child health, where it has been shown that when community-level factors are controlled, the impact of mother's education on child mortality was attenuated, suggesting that unmeasured community-level factors might be correlated with both education and child mortality. Specifically, education of other women of the community has been found to have a strong effect on children mortality (Kravdal 2004). Similarly, because educated mothers are more likely to engage in health-seeking behavior, it was found that the impact of environmental conditions (provision of health care and other public services) supersedes the impact of parental behavior in shaping child survival (Desai and Alva 1998). However, the question of whether the association of father's education with child mortality depends on community level factors were not investigated. As in the case for mother's education (Desai and Alva 1998; Fotso and Kuate-Defo 2005; Fuchs et al. 2010; Kravdal 2004), taking into account community-level factors such as human resources (including education) and material resources (socioeconomic infrastructures and availability of health-related services in the community) is likely to modify the relationship previously established with child survival. While controlling household-level and community-level factors, results from Zourkaléini (1997) on the data of Demographic and Health Survey of 1992 in Niger and that of Kravdal (2004) on the data of the National Family Health Survey of 1998–99 in India have shown that, father's education remains significantly associated with child survival, suggesting the independent effect that father's education can have on child mortality. With Indonesia data, Breierova and Duflo (2004) have found that the mother's and father's education seem equally important factors in reducing child mortality, suggesting that the differential impact of parent's education on child survival may be biased by failure to take into account assortative mating. [2]They argue that in the context of the functioning of the marriage market, educated women are more likely to marry educated men, not only for reasons related to living conditions (Behrman and Rosenzweig 2002; McIntyre and Lefgren 2006), but also because of the greater involvement of educated men in the care given to children. However, if these studies emphasize father's education effect on child survival, less is known if this influence varies according to maternal education, once the community-level factors are controlled. This distinction seems relevant to the extent where it allows us to know how parental education affects child survival.

---

[2]Assortative mating refers to the marriage market process by which women with higher levels of schooling tend to marry men who have the same level of schooling or more.

This paper attempts not only to fill this gap, but sheds light also on the growing literature that examines the relationship between education and child mortality in developing countries, particularly in Sub-Saharan Africa where effective strategies for reducing child mortality are constantly on going. Keeping in mind that characteristics of the community of residence might also be linked with both education and mortality, we hypothesize that controlling for community-level factors, children with both educated mother and father (i.e. compared to children of uneducated parents) experience lower child mortality risks. To verify this hypothesis, we stratify our analysis by mother's education and so, highlight effects of father's education for each category of mother education using models with and without controlling the community level variation. We expect to see whether there is an alteration in the relationship between father's education and the children's probability of death when community factors (observed or not) are controlled. Moreover, as we know that educated women are more likely to provide care to their offspring and have a high propensity to use health services, we assume that father's education may be more important in rural areas because of poor coverage in health infrastructure and less conducive environmental conditions for child's health and welfare than urban areas. If this hypothesis is verified, it supports the contention that in contexts with better health care supply (in cities), father's education will be less important as a determinant of child survival.

The remainder of the paper is organized as follows: In the next section we describe the methodology used (data and methods). Thereafter, we present the results of the analyses by starting with sample characteristics and descriptive statistics. The main findings are outlined and discussed in the latest section.

Methodology

Data

This study relies on the data from Demographic and Health Surveys (DHS) of Benin in 2006. This DHS is the third national survey conducted by the Institute of Statistic (INSAE) and Macro International Inc. Data were gathered with individual and community questionnaires using a stratified cluster-sampling design (750 clusters) covering 17,511 households (for details see INSAE and Macro International Inc 2007). The survey provides information on demographic and socio-economic characteristics of women, household members, and women's reproductive history (required for the analysis of child mortality).

Given the objective of this study, our analytical sample is based on data collected through an individual questionnaire administered for women aged 15–49 years. For the analysis, we restricted the sample to women ever married or in union (Kravdal 2004). Moreover, considering the fact that we have no information to control the community characteristics (except residence area), we take advantage of the cluster-sampling design to control for community characteristics that are not observed by using appropriate statistical methods.

Variables

The dependent variable is the risk of dying before age five, measured by the duration since the birth of the child until the age of his death (in months). Surviving children at the time of survey were censored at their age at the time of survey. We retained only the births of last five years preceding the survey for the simple reason that several characteristics on child health are not available outside this period.

The main explanatory variables are father's education[3] and mother's education (Educated = primary and more; Uneducated = no education). In addition, control variables relative to the child (sex, birth order and preceding birth interval), mother (age at child's birth, religion) and household characteristics (household wealth index, nature of toilet, nature of water, residence area) have been included in the estimation models. These control variables are consistent with many other studies that investigated relationships between parental education and child mortality.

Statistical Analysis

For the descriptive results, mortality rates were calculated using the indirect method proposed by Brass (1975). This method consists of applying coefficients to the proportions of dead children, classified by mothers age for determining the mortality rates according to education categories of parents. The indirect method was chosen (instead of the direct method often used in the DHS reports) because of problems related to the displacement of birth dates of surviving and dead children, and accurate information on ages at death. With DHS data of 2006, Rutstein et al. (2009) have indicated that the level of displacement is more important for children that died than for all children, indicating that this may lead to an underestimate of the true level of child mortality in Benin.

For multivariate analysis, we use two different models. First, we use the standard logit discrete-time model accounting for within-cluster correlation by using the Huber-White procedure (model 1). The second model is the conditional logit discrete-time model also called matched case–control designs (model 2). Because there is no information on community characteristics in the 2006 DHS data, we consider that they are unobserved in our data. For that, we take advantage of the cluster-sampling procedure of DHS data to control these unobserved community-level factors by estimating cluster-level fixed-effects models (model 2). In fact, model 2 has the same covariates as in model 1 in which we add the control of unobserved community-level factors.

---

[3]In the survey, we speak rather of the husband/partner of the child's mother than child's father. But because we examine child survival for the last five years preceding the survey, the husband/partner of the child's mother will be referred to as the child's father (Ducan et al. 1991).

To better understand the effects of father's education according to those of the mother's, we examine the coefficient of the father's education in each category of mother's education. This analytical strategy allows comparison, and supports the variability of results with (model 2) and without (model 1) adjusting the community-level factors. Moreover, because the community variables are not available, our second strategy is to compare the results for each area of residence (urban/rural), assuming that urban areas generally have more socioeconomic resources (e.g., modern health care system and other socioeconomic infrastructure) than in rural areas.

Results

Table 22.1 provides an overview of descriptive statistics for analysis variables according to the categories of mother's education. As can be seen, children of educated fathers are in higher proportion in the sample of educated mothers than uneducated mothers. These children reside mainly in rich households, live in better conditions as shown by variables related to the nature of toilets and drinking water, and live more in urban environments. The proportion of children who died during the last five years preceding the survey is very high in the sample of uneducated mothers compared to educated mothers. The proportion of children by sex is almost similar. Children of older mothers (35–49 years) are more numerous among

Table 22.1 Distribution (percentage[a]) of children (0–59 months) according to the selected variables for each category of mother's education, Benin DHS, 2006

Selected explanatory variables	Uneducated mother	Educated mother	Total
Child's sex			
Male	50.2	50.9	50.4
Female	49.8	49.1	49.6
Birth order and preceding birth interval			
First birth	15.5	28.5	18.7
2–3 and < 24 months	5.0	5.1	5.0
2–3 and ≥ 24 months	28.6	36.7	30.5
4+ and < 24 months	7.6	3.0	6.5
4+ and ≥ 24 months	43.4	26.8	39.3
Father's education			
Uneducated	62.9	18.4	6.5
Educated	31.1	73.8	41.5
Missing	6.1	7.8	6.5
Mother's age at child's birth			
<20 years	11.7	10.1	11.3
20–34 years	74.6	80.5	76.0
35–49 years	13.8	9.4	12.7

(continued)

Table 22.1 (continued)

Selected explanatory variables	Uneducated mother	Educated mother	Total
Religion			
Traditonal	22.6	9.6	19.5
Muslim	27.6	15.2	24.6
Christian	49.8	75.2	56.0
Household wealth index			
Poorest	27.1	7.3	22.3
Poor	24.2	9.5	20.6
Middle	22.8	15.0	20.9
Rich	18.2	25.9	20.1
Richest	7.7	42.3	16.1
Nature of water			
Tap water	17.5	49.0	25.1
Other	15.1	5.7	12.9
Fountain	12.3	8.6	11.4
Well/drilling/rain	55.1	36.7	50.6
Nature of toilet			
Toilet covered	12.4	32.1	17.2
Uncovered toilet	7.0	25.6	11.5
Nature/other	80.6	42.3	71.3
Residence			
Urban	25.5	58.7	33.6
Rural	74.5	41.3	66.4
Number of children	10,598	3,472	14,070
Number of deaths	1,033	266	1,299

[a]Weighted

uneducated mothers. According to the birth order, children of first birth are more numerous in proportion among educated mothers while those of higher-order are found mostly among uneducated mothers.

Table 22.2 describes the proportional distribution of mother's education and that of her husband in the 2006 survey. It shows a high concentration of educated women with men educated, and less in the group of educated men. This finding is not surprising given the tendency of educated women to stay in a relationship with educated men, as we see through the percentage (85%). Among uneducated women, more than half are in union with uneducated men.

Figure 22.1 shows child mortality rates according to mother's education and that of father's, using Brass (1975) approach. We found that child mortality rates vary by education of parents. Children with both parents uneducated have the highest mortality rate (158 ‰), followed by children whose mothers are uneducated and fathers educated (145 ‰). The mortality rate is less high in children with educated mothers and uneducated fathers (123 ‰). But for both educated parents, a sizeable decline in mortality rate was observed (89 ‰).

Table 22.2 Proportional distribution (%) of mother's education and that of her husband, Benin, 2006

Mother's education	Father's education			
	Uneducated	Missing	Educated	Total
Uneducated	56.9	5.1	38.0	11,334
Educated	10.3	4.6	85.2	6460
Total	7,108	877	9,809	17,794

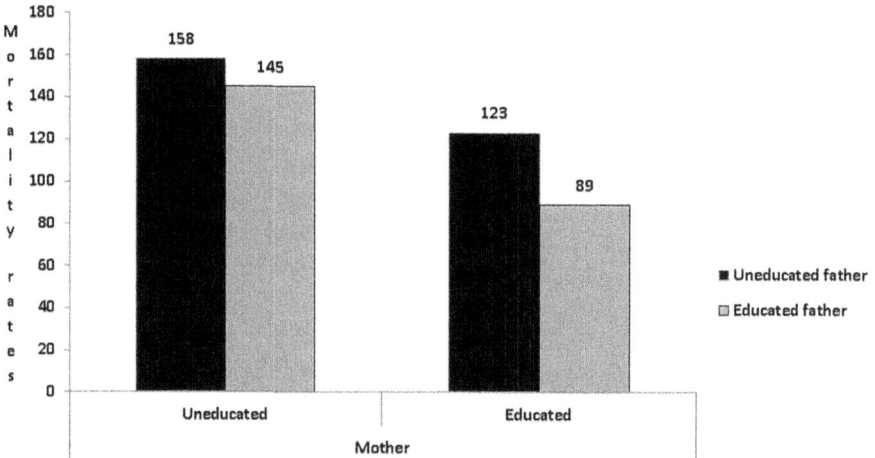

Fig. 22.1 Child mortality rates (‰) according to parents education, Benin DHS, 2006

Multivariate Analysis

Table 22.3 presents the results from two models (standard logit discrete-time model and conditional logit discrete-time model) assessing the association between father's education and child survival for each category of mother's education. As expected, the conditional logit discrete-time model controlling for unobserved community-level factors seems to produce a better estimation as shown by the AIC (smaller is AIC, greater is the adjustment). Further, as we see through the coefficients of covariates and the significant level, the pattern of associations between children's survival and parents education is not the same in the two models, corroborating prior findings (Desai and Alva 1998) which demonstrates the importance of attention to environmental and socioeconomic conditions in the community of residence.

As one would expect in the conditional logit discrete-time model, we found that in households where mothers are educated, children with educated fathers experience a lower probability of dying than children with uneducated fathers, suggesting that the father's education remains associated with child survival, even after controlling for community factors. These results have not been observed in the standard

Table 22.3 Odds ratios of standard logit discrete-time and Conditional logit discrete-time models for the influence of parents education on child mortality, Benin, 2006

Selected explanatory variables	Logit discrete-time model		Conditional logit discrete-time model	
	Uneducated mother	Educated mother	Uneducated mother	Educated mother
	Odds ratio	Odds ratio	Odds ratio	Odds ratio
Father's education (ref = uneducated)				
Missing	0.83	1.09	0.79	0.99
Educated	0.98	0.76	1.06	0.57**
Mother's age at child's birth (Ref = 20–34 years)				
<20 years	1.08	0.94	0.99	0.93
35–49 years	0.98	0.82	1.05	0.74
Religion (ref = traditional)				
Muslim	1.01	1.20	0.99	0.64
Christian	1.01	0.98	0.92*	0.59
Child's sex (ref = male)				
Female	0.96	0.80*	0.93	0.81
Birth order and preceding birth interval (Ref = first birth)				
2–3 and <24 months	1.53***	0.87	1.33*	0.50*
2–3 and ≥24 months	0.76**	0.57***	0.73**	0.58**
4+ and <24 months	1.47***	1.31	1.21	0.62
4+ and ≥24 months	0.88	0.78	0.79*	0.61**
Household wealth index (Ref = Poorest)				
Poor	1.08	0.65	1.10	0.48
Middle	1.18**	1.08	1.09	0.71
Rich	1.06	0.92	1.07	0.42*
Richest	0.84	0.55*	0.78	0.31**
Nature of water (ref = tap water)				
Other	1.10	0.95	1.07	1.17
Fountain	1.10	1.14	1.22	0.75
Well/drilling/rain	0.97	1.01	1.03	1.10
Nature of toilet (ref = toilet covered)				
Uncovered toilet	0.86	1.28	1.10	1.33
Nature/other	1.11	1.03	1.28	0.76
Residence (ref = urban)	1.14	1.02		
Constant	0.030***	0.064***		
AIC	9,030	2,444	6,983	1,406

Note $*p < 0.05$; $**p < 0.01$ and $***p < 0.001$

logit discrete-time model. Child's probability of dying is in the expected direction but not statistically significant.

Among uneducated mothers, father's education did not have any significant effect on a child's probability of dying as shown in the two models.

Furthermore, because the availability of health infrastructure is closely related to the development and urbanization levels of the community, we extend the analysis in both rural and urban areas in order to know if the environmental and socioeconomic conditions of the community have an effect in the relationship

Table 22.4 Odds ratios of Conditional logit discrete-time models for the influence of parents education on children mortality in each residence area, Benin, 2006

Selected explanatory variables	Urban area		Rural area	
	Uneducated mother	Educated mother	Uneducated mother	Educated mother
	Odds ratio	Odds ratio	Odds ratio	Odds ratio
Father's education (ref = uneducated)				
Missing	0.82	0.77	1.08	1.21
Educated	0.90	1.13	0.78	0.43***
Mother's age at child's birth (ref = 20–34 years)				
<20 years	1.23	0.91	0.97	0.91
35–49 years	0.76	1.14	0.98	0.52
Religion (ref = traditional)				
Muslim	0.84	1.00	0.67	0.48
Christian	0.68	0.94	0.67	0.56
Child's sex (ref = male)				
Female	1.00	0.92	1.15	0.50**
Birth order and preceding birth interval (ref = first birth)				
2–3 and <24 months	1.13	1.35	0.45*	0.49
2–3 and ≥24 months	0.74	0.72**	0.61	0.42*
4+ and < 24 months	1.01	1.22	0.52	0.59
4+ and ≥24 months	0.96	0.74**	0.80	0.41**
Household wealth index (ref = poorest)				
Poor	1.07	1.10	0.52	0.44
Middle	0.79	1.13	0.71	0.76
Rich	0.81	1.05	0.39	0.42
Richest	0.34**	1.40	0.36	0.16**
Nature of water (ref = tap water)				
Other	1.21	0.99	1.43	0.73
Fountain	1.51	1.12	0.56	0.74
Well/drilling/rain	1.61*	0.87	1.91	0.62
Nature of toilet (ref = toilet covered)				
Uncovered toilet	1.01	1.17	1.06	3.49***
Nature/other	1.04	1.36*	0.39**	1.42

Note $*p < 0.05$; $**p < 0.01$ and $***p < 0.001$

(Table 22.4). In the sample of uneducated mothers, there is no meaningful association between father's education and children's probabilities of dying, regardless the area of residence. For the sample of educated mothers, however, results indicate an increase of children's survival probability with educated fathers in urban areas but this is not statistically significant. In rural areas, we found a meaningful increase of children's survival probability with educated fathers.

Discussion

Given that mother's education is fundamental in reducing child mortality, the purpose of this study was to examine the effect of the father's education on child mortality by taking into account the mother's education, and exploring whether there is an alteration of this effect when community-level factors are controlled.

One of the major findings of this study is that the father's education has different effects according to mother's education. Corroborating a prior study (Zourkaléini 1997), we found that children with both educated fathers and mothers have a lower probability of dying compared with children of uneducated parents. These associations are robust to a set of factors at individual-level and community-level, as we saw through the standard logit discrete-time model and the conditional logit discrete-time model controlling for unobserved community-level factors. One could also expect that children with uneducated mothers would exhibit advantages in their survival if the father was educated (Mosley and Chen 1984). Curiously our results did not show a significant effect; we were rather in situation where both parents were educated. It becomes clear that comprehension of parent's education effects on child survival may be poorly estimated, mostly when we know that health facilities and others socioeconomic characteristics in the community can play an important role. Interestingly, the pattern of father's education effects on child mortality changed when we took the community-level factors into account. In urban areas we found that the meaningful effect of educated fathers previously highlighted in the sample of educated mothers has disappeared, while it remained significant in rural areas. These findings seem to clearly indicate that the impact of father's education on child mortality can depend on environmental conditions. Probably, the non significant effects observed in urban area might reflect the fact that in the context of a higher supply of maternal and child health services, a greater use of these services could supersede the impact of father's education in shaping child's survival. The evidence is that, in rural areas with low availability of health services, father's education has an independent effect on child survival.

However, with the data used, one limitation of this analysis is the lack of information at the community level to assess the real effects of community characteristics such as availability and the use of health facilities that are closely related to children mortality. Further research is needed to confirm our findings using measured variables at community level.

In conclusion to this study, our results that father's education makes a difference on child mortality may shed light on public policies in developing countries. This effect is particularly pointed out in households where both parents were educated. However, in more urbanized areas, father's education exhibited less effect on child survival than in rural areas. To reach a low child mortality, much attention should be given to father's education and not only to mother's education.

References

Barbieri, M. (1991). Les déterminants de la mortalité des enfants dans le tiers-monde. Dans CEPED (Dir.), (Vol. 18, pp. 47). Paris.

Baya, B. (1998). Instruction des parents et survie de l'enfant au Burkina Faso: Cas de Bobo Dioulasso. Dans CEPED (Dir.), (pp. 27). Paris.

Bbaale, E., & Buyinza, F. (2012). Micro-analysis of mother's education and child mortality: Evidence from Uganda. *Journal of International Development, 24,* S138–S158. doi:10.1002/jid.1762

Behrman, J. R., & Rosenzweig, M. R. (2002). Does increasing women's schooling raise the schooling of the next generation? *American Economic Association, 92*(1), 323–334.

Boyle, M. H., Racine, Y., Georgiades, K., Snelling, D., Hong, S., Omariba, W., et al. (2006). The influence of economic development level, household wealth and maternal education on child health in the developing world. *Social Science and Medicine, 63*(8), 2242–2254.

Brass, W. (1975). *Methods for estimating fertility and mortality from limited and Defective data.*

Breierova, L., & Duflo, E. (2004). The impact of education on fertility and child mortality: Do fathers really matter less than mothers? & N. B. E. Research (Éd.).

Buor, D. (2003). Mothers' education and childhood mortality in Ghana. *Health Policy, 64*(3), 297–309.

Caldwell, J. C. (1979). Education as a factor in mortality decline an examination of nigerian data. *Population Studies, 33*(3), 395–413.

Caldwell, J. C. (1990). Cultural and social factors influencing mortality levels in developing countries. *Annals of the American Academy of Political and Social Science, 510,* 44–59. doi:10.2307/1046793

Chen, Y., & Li, H. (2009). Mother's education and child health: Is there a nurturing effect? *Journal of Health Economics, 28*(2), 413–426. doi:10.1016/j.jhealeco.2008.10.005

Cleland, J. G., & van Ginneken, J. K. (1988). Maternal education and child survival in developing countries: The search for pathways of influence. *Social Science and Medicine, 27*(12), 1357–1368.

Desai, S., & Alva, S. (1998). Maternal education and child health: Is there a strong causal relationship? *Demography, 35*(1), 71–81.

Ducan, T., Strauss, J., & Henriques, M.-H. (1991). How does mother's education affect child height? *The Journal of Human Resources, 26*(2), 183–211.

Fotso, J.-C., & Kuate-Defo, B. (2005). Socioeconomic inequalities in early childhood malnutrition and morbidity: Modification of the household-level effects by the community SES. *Health & Place, 11*(3), 205–225. doi:10.1016/j.healthplace.2004.06.004

Fuchs, R., Pamuk, E. R., & Lutz, W. (2010). Education or wealth: Which matters more for reducing child mortality in developing countries? *Vienna Yearbook of Population Research, 8*(1), 175–199.

Grossman, M. (2005). Education and Nonmarket Outcomes. *Working Paper*(11582)

Hale, L., DaVanzo, J., Razzaque, A., & Rahman, M. (2009). Which factors explain the decline in infant and child mortality in Matlab, Bangladesh? *Journal of Population Research, 26*(1), 3–20. doi:10.1007/s12546-008-9003-0

Hatt, L. E., & Waters, H. R. (2006). Determinants of child morbidity in Latin America: A pooled analysis of interactions between parental education and economic status. *Social Science and Medicine, 62*(2), 375–386. doi:10.1016/j.socscimed.2005.06.007

Hobcraft, J. N., McDonald, J. W., & Rutstein, S. O. (1984). Socio-economic factors in infant and child mortality: A cross-national comparison. *Population Studies, 38*(2), 193–223.

Huq, M. N., & Tasnim, T. (2008). Maternal education and child healthcare in Bangladesh. *Maternal and Child Health Journal, 12*(1), 43–51. doi:10.1007/s10995-007-0303-3

INSAE, & Macro International Inc. (2007). Enquête démographique et de Santé (EDSB-III)-Bénin 2006 (pp. 492). USA: Institut national de la Statistique et de l'Analyse Economique (INSAE) [Bénin] et Macro Internatioanl Inc

Kravdal, Ø. (2004). Child mortality in india: The community-level effect of education. *Population Studies, 58*(2), 177–192.

Kuate-Defo, B., & Diallo, K. (2002). Geography of child mortality clustering within African families. *Health Place, 8*(2), 93–117.

LeGrand, T., & Lalou, R. (1996). *La mortalité des enfants du Sahel en ville et au village Population, 51*(2), 329–351.

LeVine, R. A., & Rowe, M. L. (2009). Maternal literacy and child health in less-developed countries: Evidence, Processes, and Limitations. *Journal of Developmental & Behavioral Pediatrics, 30*(4), 340–349. doi:10.1097/DBP.1090b1013e3181b1090eeff

McIntyre, F., & Lefgren, L. (2006). The relationship between women's education and marriage outcomes. *Journal of Labor Economics, 24*(4), 787–830.

Montgomery, M. R., & Hewett, P. C. (2005). Urban poverty and health in developing countries: Household and neighborhood effects. *Demography, 42*(3), 397–425. doi:10.2307/4147355

Mosley, W., & Chen, L. (1984). An analytical framework for the study of child survival in developing countries. *Population and development review, 10,* 25–45.

Nakamura, H., Ikeda, N., Stickley, A., Mori, R., & Shibuya, K. (2011). Achieving MDG 4 in sub-Saharan Africa: what has contributed to the accelerated child mortality decline in Ghana? *PLoS ONE [Electronic Resource], 6*(3), e17774.

Pickett, K. E., & Pearl, M. (2001). Multilevel analyses of neighbourhood socioeconomic context and health outcomes: A critical review. *Journal of Epidemiology and Community Health, 55* (2), 111–122. doi:10.1136/jech.55.2.111

Rutstein, S., Ayad, M., Ren, R., & Hong, R. (2009). Changements des conditions de santé et déclin de la mortalité infantile et juvénile. Dans I. Macro (Dir.).

Schultz, T. P. (1984). Studying the impact of household economic and community variables on child mortality. *Population and Development Review, 10* (ArticleType: research-article/Issue Title: Supplement: Child Survival: Strategies for Research/Full publication date: 1984/Copyright © 1984 Population Council), 215–235.

Smith Greenaway, E., Juan, I., & Baker, D. P. (2012). Understanding the association between maternal education and use of health services in ghana: exploring the role of health knowledge. *Journal of Biosocial Science, 44*(6), 733–747. doi:10.1017/S0021932012000041

Zourkaléini, Y. (1997). *Les déterminants socio-démographiques et contextuels de la mortalité des enfants au Niger* (Université de Montréal).

Index

A
Abortion, 37, 39, 42, 43, 45, 362
Activities of daily living (ADLs), 8, 72, 329, 332, 340
Activity limitations, 5, 183–187, 189, 196–199
Adolescent childbearing, 37
Adult health, 202, 331
Affordable Care Act (ACA), 2, 37, 40, 47
Africa, 8, 165, 269, 272, 281, 301, 302, 309, 331, 338, 349, 361, 363, 364, 367, 371, 378, 385, 404
Afshar, 9
Age-adjusted death rate, 13, 16, 26
Ageing, 3, 7, 70, 251, 259, 381, 382
Agreeableness, 3, 52, 60, 61
Ali, 357
American Community Survey (ACS), 184, 223
American Housing Survey, 222
Applied demography, 1
Arokiasamy, 8, 261
Asians, 4, 56, 95–97, 99, 102, 104, 108–110, 116
Averett, 201

B
Baird v. Eisenstadt, 39
Bangladesh, 8, 272, 276, 282, 283, 292, 296, 302, 349, 351, 356, 357, 397
Baseline, 3, 17, 56, 73, 75, 273, 276, 281, 283, 292
Benin, 9, 406, 407
Best, 3, 21, 26, 34, 82, 187, 343
Big five personality model, 3
Binns, 221
Birth rate, 26
Birth registration, 159
Birthweight, 4, 115, 117, 118, 126, 133–136, 270

Blood lead level, 6, 221, 222, 231
Borelli, 5
Burwell v. Hobby Lobby, 41

C
California Quality of Life Survey, 184
Capillary blood lead test, 223
Carey v. population services, 39
Census Bureau, 222, 224
Centenarians, 4, 81–83, 85, 87, 89
Chang, 56, 238
Childhood obesity, 6, 31, 201–203, 208, 210
Child mortality, 9, 82, 85, 86, 302, 357, 403–406, 409, 410
Children ever born, 8, 350
Child survival, 10, 271, 282, 404–406, 410
China, 5, 8, 163, 166, 171, 311, 331, 334, 338
Chinese Exclusion Act in 1882, 172
Chinese immigrants, 167, 172, 173, 176
Chronic diseases, 9, 16, 18, 24, 28, 73, 329, 384
Chronic health conditions, 31, 51, 208
Cohort, 4, 5, 26, 28, 30, 70, 77, 83, 84, 89, 116–119, 126, 133, 134, 135, 141, 142, 143, 148–159, 164, 168, 204, 258, 310, 362
Cohort mortality, 158
Collaborative Perinatal Project, 203
Communicable diseases, 15, 24
Community-level, 9, 272, 291, 292, 297, 299, 405, 407, 410
Comorbidity, 55, 56, 73, 76, 383
Comstock Act of 1873, 38
Concepts, 81, 96
Conditional logit, 9, 407, 410
Congenital, 270
Conscientiousness, 3, 51, 52, 57, 59, 61
Constructs, 51, 52, 54
Cox proportional hazards, 3, 73

Crossover, 5, 141–148, 153, 155, 156, 157, 158, 159
Crude mortality rate, 13
Current Population Survey, 149
Curtin, 4
Cuttington University College, 309, 312

D
Death rates, 13, 23, 26, 27, 99, 141, 145, 148, 152–158
Decennial census, 143
Defense of marriage act, 238
Deficient data hypothesis, 142
Demographic and Health Survey, 7, 9, 271, 310, 323, 362, 403, 405, 406
Demographic characteristics, 3, 37, 59, 61, 101, 104, 126, 271, 276, 281, 283, 292, 296–298, 333, 334, 387
Denominators, 99, 153
Dhillon, 7, 261
Differential frailty, 142, 146
Disability, 3, 19, 21, 29, 70, 73, 169, 183, 184, 186, 187, 252
Disability adjusted life years (DALYs), 252
Diseases of civilization, 17
Displacement, 407
Double burden of disease, 251

E
Elevated blood lead level, 228
Endogenous, 188, 215
English Longitudinal Study on Ageing (ELSA), 3, 69
Epidemiological transition, 17, 24, 29, 251, 381
Epidemiologic paradox, 117, 136
Estimates, 21, 86, 87, 110, 116, 141, 142, 143, 144, 155, 156, 158, 186, 193, 194, 196, 203, 213, 214, 222, 223, 224, 226, 240, 254, 269, 272, 290, 308, 331, 351, 361, 368, 372, 375, 378, 384, 386, 387, 388, 391, 397
Europe, 165, 166, 385, 388, 391, 392, 397, 398
Expenditures, 7, 201, 251, 254, 258

F
Father's education, 9, 334, 340, 403–405, 407, 408, 410, 413
Fertility, 8, 38, 204, 262, 349, 350, 352, 354, 356, 357, 361–364, 367, 369, 371, 373, 377
Fetal origins theory, 202
Fletcher, 6
Florey, 7
Fokum, 6

Foreign born, 120
Frailty, 3, 70, 71, 72, 73, 74, 75, 76, 77, 78, 142, 147
Fried frailty, 70, 77

G
Garcia, 4
Gaughan, 2
Gavrilov, 4, 81, 83, 85, 87, 90
Gavrilova, 4, 81, 83–85, 87, 89, 90
Gender, 2, 5, 6, 10, 56, 61, 83, 84, 91, 141, 148, 150, 152, 158, 159, 163, 164, 165, 166, 167, 180, 184, 185, 186, 188, 189, 190, 194, 195, 196, 197, 198, 199, 205, 227, 228, 256, 309, 313, 314, 334, 354, 385, 396
Genealogical records, 82, 89
Geriatric syndrome, 70
Gestational weight gain, 202
Griswold v. State of Connecticut, 39

H
Hazard ratios, 147
Health access, 2, 37, 38
Health and retirement study, 3, 53, 57
Healthcare, 5, 6, 16, 20, 24, 25, 42, 95, 101, 104, 163, 165, 166, 168, 169, 171, 173, 174, 178, 185, 222, 237–239, 241, 244, 245, 251–253, 255, 256, 258, 259, 261, 311, 382, 398
Health care expenditure, 7, 201
Healthcare utilization, 5, 166, 168, 169, 171, 173, 174, 178, 237, 239, 241, 244
Health inequalities, 9, 183, 186
Health insurance, 37, 40, 41, 45, 59, 165, 166, 173, 238, 240, 261
Health outcomes, 2, 3, 5, 28, 37, 51, 53, 55, 64, 69, 117, 135, 136, 163, 165, 168, 169, 172, 175, 183, 256, 302, 330, 396
Health selection, 165
Health status, 2, 8, 13, 15, 16–20, 23–27, 30, 31, 32, 33, 34, 117, 147, 169, 258, 261, 262, 342, 398
Health status indicators, 16, 24, 26
Health Survey for England (HSE), 70
Healthy migrant effect, 164
Heiland, 5
Heteronormative assumptions, 237
Heterosexual, 6, 183, 184, 186, 197, 237, 239–241, 244, 245
Heterosexual households, 7, 237, 240, 243–245
High Income country (HIC), 9, 386
Hill, 82, 84, 85, 88, 145, 301

Hispanic, 3, 4, 5, 51, 52, 54–56, 59, 60, 61, 62, 64, 96, 97, 98, 99, 101, 102, 104, 107, 108, 109, 110, 111, 115–122, 125, 126, 127, 128, 129, 130, 131, 132, 133, 134, 135, 136, 137, 141, 143, 150, 152, 163, 164, 165, 173, 188, 191, 206, 211, 212, 245
Hispanic immigrants, 163
Hispanic paradox, 109, 115, 163, 165
HIV/AIDS, 7, 20, 308, 310–312, 316, 317, 323, 362
Hodgins, 7
Homophobia, 237
Hoque, 354
Hoyert, 95
Hypertension, 3, 31, 51, 52, 54, 56–58, 61, 64, 95, 98, 101, 108, 169, 172, 173, 178, 384

I
ICD-10 codes, 96, 99, 119
ICU admission, 4, 97, 102, 104, 108
Illinois department of public health (IDPH), 6, 225, 226, 227, 228, 229, 231
Illinois Lead Poisoning Elimination Advisory Council, 232
Immigrants, 5, 18, 40, 117, 163–167, 171–174, 178
Independent variables, 171, 351
Indian immigrants, 167, 172, 178
Infant mortality rate, 27, 115, 116, 121
Institute of Medicine (IOM), 31, 183, 202
Integrated Public Use Microdata Series (IPUMS), 82
International Classification of Diseases (ICD), 20
International health, 299
Islam, 350, 354, 356

J
Japanese Americans, 164

K
Kamiya, 3, 70, 76
Kenny, 3
Kindergarten (KG), 201, 203, 222, 232
King v. Burwell, 41, 45
Knowledge-attitudes-practice surveys, 310
Kowal, 331

L
Ladusingh, 261
Lead-based paint, 221–223
Lead-exposed, 6, 221
Lead poisoning, 221, 223, 225, 231–233

Lead Program Surveillance Database, 223, 225, 226, 227, 228, 229, 231
LeGrand, 404
Lesbian/gay, 5, 183, 187, 189, 196, 198, 199
LGBT, 6, 237, 243
Liberia, 7, 307–309, 312, 325
Liberia Institute of Statistics and Geo-Information Services, 309, 323
Liberians, 7, 307, 308, 323
Life-course factors, 81
Life expectancy, 2, 13, 14, 16, 23, 24, 26–28, 32, 141, 142, 144, 153, 252, 261, 308
Life span, 82, 87
Life table, 141, 143, 144, 145, 146, 148, 149, 150, 152, 153, 155, 157, 158
Linked birth-death files, 4, 115
Logit discrete-time model, 9, 403, 407, 410
Longevity, 4, 14, 16, 81, 83, 85, 87, 88, 251, 253, 256, 261
Low and Middle Income Countries (LMICs), 8, 9, 330, 381

M
Mahmud, 9
Malaria, 7, 15, 29, 269–274, 276, 281, 291, 292, 297, 298, 301, 303
Malarious, 7, 269, 297, 301
Maternal and child health, 7, 253, 269–271, 413
Maternal morbidity, 4, 95–99, 100, 102, 103, 104, 108–111
Maternal mortality, 2, 4, 13, 14, 16, 24, 27, 33, 34, 95, 96, 97, 98, 99, 100, 101, 102, 103, 104, 108, 109, 110
Maternal obesity, 202, 208, 216
McGehee, 1
McNeil, 349
Mean blood level, 231
Medicaid, 38–41, 43, 45, 59, 109, 137, 171, 222, 228, 233, 239
Medical Expenditure Panel Survey Household Component (MEPS HC), 6, 237, 240
Mexico, 5, 8, 163, 166, 171, 329, 331, 338
Michlig, 2
Millennium Development Goal, 269
Morbidity, 2, 4, 10, 14, 15, 16, 17, 18, 19, 20, 21, 22, 23, 24, 25, 26, 28, 29, 31, 33, 34, 55, 56, 70, 72, 73, 75, 77, 95–99, 101–104, 107–109, 169, 180, 251, 252, 258, 263, 270, 307, 329, 342, 343, 386, 388, 389, 396
Mortality, 2, 4, 5, 7, 9, 404, 406
Mortality advantage, 141, 142, 143, 144, 148, 152, 155, 158, 159

Mortality crossovers, 141, 143, 144, 159
Mortality measures, 18
Mortality rates, 2, 4, 13, 14, 16, 18, 26, 27, 32, 34, 96, 97, 102, 109, 110, 111, 114, 116, 121, 125, 142, 144, 146, 147, 152, 153, 156, 158, 407, 409
Mosquito, 7, 269, 272, 281, 291, 296, 297, 299, 301
Multimorbidity, 9, 381–384, 386, 390, 396, 398
Multivariate analysis, 101, 283, 407, 410
Murty, 7

N

National Account Statistics, 7, 251, 254
National Center for Health Statistics (NCHS), 4, 18, 118, 119
National Death Index (NDI), 148
National Federation of Independent Business v. Sebelius, 41, 45
National Health Account of the Ministry of Health & Family Welfare, 253
National Health Interview Survey (NHIS), 19, 240
National Longitudinal Mortality Study (NLMS), 143
National Longitudinal Survey of Youth, 28, 31, 204
National Sample Survey, 7, 22, 251, 253
Neonatal death, 269, 271, 272, 275, 283, 292, 299, 300, 302
Neonatal mortality, 7, 269, 271_275, 283, 291, 296, 298, 299, 301–303
Neonatal survival, 7, 269, 271, 272, 274, 281, 283, 292, 300–303
Neurologic damage, 221
Neuroticism, 3, 51, 52, 55–57, 59, 61, 64
New Immigrant Survey (NIS), 5, 164, 168
Non-communicable disease, 251, 381
Notifiable diseases, 15, 20, 22, 29

O

Obesity, 6, 30, 31, 70, 95, 173, 186, 201–203, 205, 209, 210, 212, 214, 350, 384, 397
Office of Management and Budget (OMB), 96
Old-age mortality, 5, 143, 146, 148
Old-age survival, 5, 157
Older adults, 9, 29, 30, 168, 329, 334, 342, 391, 396, 397
OLS models, 6, 201, 203, 208, 209
Orientation, 188, 190, 199, 240, 241, 245, 246
Out-of-pocket expenditure, 258

P

Partnership for Maternal Newborn & Child Health, 270
Pecotte, 1
Personality, 3, 51–54, 56, 57, 59, 61
Personality constructs, 51, 52
Phenotype, 70
The pill, 39
Poor cognitive outcomes, 201
Population ageing, 7, 251, 252, 381
Population-based surveys, 7
Population health, 4, 91, 179, 396
Population policies, 37
Poverty, 41, 188, 224, 228, 238, 282, 308, 384
Pregnancy, 4, 6, 37, 43, 45, 95, 96, 98, 99, 101, 102, 104, 106, 107, 109, 110, 111, 120, 137, 202–210, 213, 214, 216, 270–274, 276, 281, 283, 286, 289, 290, 291, 293, 294, 295, 296–298, 300, 301, 303, 322, 324, 350, 357
Pre-pregnancy, 202, 205, 210
Pre-pregnancy BMI, 101, 104, 202–204, 208–210, 213, 215
Pre-pregnancy obesity, 6, 201, 202, 205, 208, 210, 213, 214
Preschool obesity, 6, 201, 208, 210, 212–214
Preterm birth, 116, 117, 126, 133, 135, 136, 270
Private insurance, 38, 39, 43, 59, 104, 188, 244
Psychological distress, 5, 54, 183, 184, 186, 188–190, 194–197
Psychosocial well-being, 3
Public health research, 10, 53, 240
Pullum, 7

Q

Quality of life, 29, 184, 198, 309, 330, 331, 378, 382
Quality of race, 234
Questionnaire, 22, 222, 271, 312, 351, 385, 406

R

Race differences, 54–56
Racial/ethnic disparity, 108
Racial/ethnic minorities, 238, 243
Rahman, 8, 350, 356
Rajshahi Diabetes Association, 8, 349, 351
Raymond Pearl's Lowell Institute, 143
Read, 1, 5, 163–166, 179, 180, 324, 342
Reczek, 5, 188, 196
Relationships, 24, 56, 61, 69, 70, 165, 172, 173, 190, 309, 324, 351, 397, 407

Reproductive health benefits, 38
Reproductive health outcomes, 2, 37, 38
Reproductive health policies, 2, 37
Roderick, 381
Rust college, 7, 309, 312

S
Safe sex, 7, 8, 307, 310, 313
Sahin, 5
Same-sex, 6, 184–186, 198, 237–239, 241, 243, 245
Same-sex households, 6, 239, 241, 244, 245
Same-sex partner, 198
Self-rated health (SRH), 5, 8, 51, 169, 172, 173, 175, 178, 329, 330
Self-rated Health, 332, 334, 382
Selvamani, 8
Sexual minorities, 5, 6, 183–186, 197, 245
Social engagement, 3, 69–71, 73, 75
Social epidemiology, 329
Social network, 69, 331, 342, 405
Socioeconomic status (SES), 8, 56, 137, 165, 221, 231, 281, 329, 330, 332, 333, 340, 342, 382, 386
Sossa, 9
Spiker, 5
Statistical methods, 406
Sub-Saharan Africa, 9, 269, 271, 272, 276, 281, 291, 301, 361, 363, 364, 367, 371, 404, 406
Survival advantage, 4, 5, 81, 115, 118, 126, 134

T
Thomas, 2
Title X, 39, 45
Title X of the Public Health Service Act, 39
Total fertility rate (TFR), 350, 364
Trait level, 3, 56
Trend, 2, 4, 13, 16, 17, 23, 25–31, 115, 117, 142, 147, 189, 196, 210, 254, 256, 261, 271, 274, 276, 281, 310, 350, 396
T-tests, 51, 59
Tuberculosis, 15, 20, 29
Tuthill, 6

U
U.S. Social Security Administration Death Master File (DMF), 84
U.S. Standard Certificate of Live Birth, 4, 95, 97
Uncertain, 110
Unintended pregnancy, 37
United Negro College Fund Special Programs, 7, 307, 309
United States, 2, 4, 28, 38, 39, 42, 51, 81, 83, 84, 87, 95, 97, 109, 110, 148, 165, 240, 269, 309
Universal health care, 37
University of Minnesota, 82
Unobserved community-level factors, 413
Uttamacharya, 8

V
Validated, 4, 77, 352
Variables, 5, 8, 58, 61, 72, 73, 77, 82, 85, 87, 88, 119, 150, 168, 169, 171, 187, 188, 190, 203, 204, 207, 208, 210, 215, 234, 240, 241, 245, 271, 273, 332–334, 351, 352, 356, 366, 368, 370, 372, 373, 378, 386, 387, 404, 407, 408
Venous blood lead test, 223
Vital statistics, 96, 110, 119, 141, 146

W
Williams Institute, 6, 237, 243
Winter, 271, 301
Woo, 4
World Health Organization (WHO), 95, 99, 205
World Health Survey, 382, 385, 397

Y
Yellow fever, 15
Younger Americans, 30
Youth, 31, 310, 311, 363

Y
Zelma, 237